Praise for *International Relations Theory*

"I was taught with an earlier version of this text, and I teach with the newest one today. It is simply the best introduction to IR theory, a one-stop shop that provides a strong foundation for more advanced study of the field. I cannot recommend it highly enough."

—Christopher J. Fettweis, Tulane University

"This is an excellent text for courses in international relations theory. With a great combination of historical context and modern approaches, no other text provides such an in-depth look at international relations theory that is so well written and easily accessible for undergraduate students."

—Andrew Miller, Wilkes University

"This book is vital to understanding the importance of international relations theories to our current times. Instead of focusing on just the main international relations theories, the authors link philosophy with modern approaches to understanding current events and interstate relationships. It is a must-read for people interested in studying international relations."

—Michael O. Slobodchikoff, Troy University

"The seventh edition of *International Relations Theory* offers an updated version of the comprehensive coverage of the wide arrays of perspectives within the field of international relations. From the intellectual origins of international relations theory to the contending voices within the discipline, this is a coherent, comprehensive, and well-organized book for students interested in the field."

—Bibek Chand, University of North Georgia

"The study of international relations has become increasingly complex as new approaches take their place in the field alongside traditional and historical perspectives. IR no longer is only about realism, liberalism, and constructivism. Now feminist and normative understandings and green theory have carved out niches in IR. For students, and even scholars, it can be difficult to stay abreast of the developments and debates ongoing within the field. Mark Kauppi and Paul Viotti offer an indispensable—and comprehensive—guide to the new and old intellectual trends that are shaping the study of international relations."

—Christopher Layne, Texas A&M University

"This is the most accessible and comprehensive textbook on IR theory I have ever come across. My students love how the theories are presented as living and evolving fields of inquiry rather than unchanging idols placed on pedestals. The authors' approach provides a solid foundation for student investigations into current events and incorporates fantastically into experiential learning opportunities."

—Patricia C. Rodda, Carroll University

"Kauppi and Viotti's seventh edition of *International Relations Theory* has succeeded in providing a comprehensive overview of the historical development and contemporary diversity of IR perspectives, including the axes between both empirical versus normative and traditional versus alternative approaches."

—Tami Amanda Jacoby, University of Manitoba, Canada

INTERNATIONAL RELATIONS THEORY

SEVENTH EDITION

MARK V. KAUPPI
GEORGETOWN UNIVERSITY

PAUL R. VIOTTI
UNIVERSITY OF DENVER

ROWMAN & LITTLEFIELD
Lanham • Boulder • New York • London

Executive Acquisitions Editor: Michael Kerns
Assistant Editor: Elizabeth Von Buhr
Sales and Marketing Inquiries: textbooks@rowman.com

Credits and acknowledgments for material borrowed from other sources, and reproduced with permission, appear on the appropriate pages within the text.

Published by Rowman & Littlefield
An imprint of The Rowman & Littlefield Publishing Group, Inc.
4501 Forbes Boulevard, Suite 200, Lanham, Maryland 20706
www.rowman.com

86-90 Paul Street, London EC2A 4NE

British Library Cataloguing in Publication Information Available

Library of Congress Cataloging-in-Publication Data

Names: Kauppi, Mark V., author. | Viotti, Paul R., author.
Title: International relations theory / Mark V. Kauppi, Paul R. Viotti.
Description: Seventh edition. | Lanham, Maryland : Rowman & Littlefield, 2023. |
  Includes bibliographical references and index.
Identifiers: LCCN 2023011655 (print) | LCCN 2023011656 (ebook) |
  ISBN 9781538171486 (cloth) | ISBN 9781538171493 (paperback) |
  ISBN 9781538171509 (epub)
Subjects: LCSH: International relations.
Classification: LCC JZ1305 .V56 2023 (print) | LCC JZ1305 (ebook) |
  DDC 327.101—dc23/eng/20230310
LC record available at https://lccn.loc.gov/2023011655
LC ebook record available at https://lccn.loc.gov/2023011656

Brief Contents

Contents

★ ★ ★

Preface

★ ★ ★

The genesis of this book dates to the 1980s when the coauthors were both living and working in Germany after graduate school. While strolling through the grounds of *Schloss Solitud* (a summer palace in Stuttgart), we discussed the diversity of thinking about international relations which, for some, was a frustration, and for others something to be celebrated. We aspired to bring some degree of order to the field, focusing on various images or perspectives and utilizing a common framework to make it easier for students to compare and contrast these alternative lenses. We began with what we termed realism, pluralism, and globalism that eventually evolved into realism (with its variants), liberalism, economic structuralism, and the English School. Normative theory remains central as does our treatment of intellectual precursors upon whose shoulders the corpus of IR theory rests.

Realism has traditionally dominated academic discourse, but by the 1980s the study of international organizations and transnational actors, both governmental and nongovernmental, became more prominent in the field—the basis for what has become known as the liberal image of world politics. At the same time, economic structuralist perspectives were developed by scholars interested in explaining the persistence of global inequality and the ongoing postcolonial domination of the capital-rich "north" over the economically least developed countries of the "Global South."

As the years passed, change and continuity remained hallmarks of both international politics and international relations theory that seeks to explain how the world works. With origins in the 1950s, the English School emerged as an effort to find a middle course in international society—a *via media*—between realism and idealism on the one hand and realism and a liberal, rule-based order on the other. Constructivist understandings in IR theory also became prominent as did the feminist, postmodern, critical, and green-theory understandings— alternative interpretive lenses for viewing issues in international relations and world politics. In every case, we strove to be as fair and even-handed in how we approached each image or perspective, albeit devoting what we considered an appropriate amount of text based on our assessment of the relative importance of each as reflected in the journals and books of the IR field.

When the Cold War ended in the early 1990s, there was hope in some quarters that great power conflict could be minimized in a new era of increasing globalization in a rule-based order. It was a time of developing or expanding cooperative international regimes whether dealing with global trade, investment for development, arms control, human rights, or other issues. Integration in Europe reached a high point in the establishment of a European Union (EU) by the new millennium in a step-by-step process that began in the 1950s. Some two decades plus into the twenty-first century, however, great power competition is back as evidenced by concerns over the rise of China and the ongoing implications of Russia's invasion of Ukraine in February 2022. Nonstate actors, however, continue to play an important international role. Global inequality is still with us. And over the past thirty-plus years, other critical issues have been added to the international agenda including the positive and negative effects of technology, global pandemics, concerns about the harm done to human beings in relation to gender, sexual orientation, human trafficking, labor exploitation, and other human rights challenges. Looming over everything is the issue of climate change.

What has not changed, however, is our rationale and objectives for this book. As noted in the preface to the first and subsequent editions, our goals are to discuss underlying assumptions, images, and interpretive understandings that influence scholarly work, reference representative samples of these works, discuss key concepts, and encourage the reader to scrutinize critically the analyses dealing with international or world politics.

What has also not changed is our mutual appreciation for political philosophy and history. We have found that over the years a deeper grounding in intellectual precursors of politics in general and international relations theory, in particular, has enriched our understanding of their contributions to more recent work. Indeed, most authors would probably agree with Sir Isaac Newton's sentiment from 1675 that "if I have seen further, it is by standing on the shoulders of giants." This emphasis on intellectual precursors, we would argue, sets our work apart from all other IR theory textbooks.

Furthermore, in this edition instead of referencing green or environmental thought in the images section of the book, we have made it a stand-alone chapter as a lens or interpretive understanding. This includes noting how realists and liberals tend to view the challenges posed by climate change. And while wishing to avoid dating ourselves by referencing a myriad of current (and hence soon-to-be out-of-date) international events, we felt it necessary to address how realist and liberal (or English School) theoretical perspectives have explained the cause, impact, and global reaction to the Russian invasion of Ukraine.

In sum, to understand the complexity of international relations or world politics, we need more than ever to comprehend the various images, interpretive and normative understandings, and intellectual roots of IR theory. We believe the person who has mastered this material will be well-equipped to engage intellectually—and perhaps professionally—with the world of international politics.

One stylistic and substantive note: A few current adopters of the previous edition suggested that we highlight key concepts in the text. These concepts also appear in the glossary. We have done so in the case of the introductory chapter and those dealing with more recent works on international relations theory that tend to be concept-heavy. We hope this enhances the learning experience as several concepts in the chapters are more fully explained in the glossary.

1

Thinking about IR Theory

★ ★ ★

International Relations Theory is designed for a wide range of readers. Our primary purpose is to bring together in one volume an overview of ancient, modern, and contemporary political thought on this topic. In part I, we identify what is sorely lacking in most books on IR theory: the intellectual and historical roots of the major ideas that underlie much of the present-day literature on international relations. In parts II and III, we discuss current approaches to international relations (IR) theory. In this introductory chapter, we set the stage by covering the following topics:

- How do we comprehend the world? What is epistemology, methodology, and ontology?
- What is theory?
- Make the case why a discussion of the intellectual roots of IR theory in part I is important to understanding twentieth- and twenty-first-century works.
- Summarize upcoming chapters in parts II and III on images, interpretive understandings, and normative considerations.

EPISTEMOLOGY, METHODOLOGY, AND ONTOLOGY

If a student of international relations wishes to analyze critically and understand contemporary approaches to IR theory, we believe one should first have a basic grasp of the roles of epistemology, methodology, and ontology in theory building. Theorists do not always make these roles explicit, yet they undergird and permeate the theory-building endeavor, often serving as unstated *assumptions*.

Epistemology involves the ways and means by which we come to know (or at least what we think we know) something about the world. For example, a popular epistemology is empiricism—the view that the only grounds for making truth claims is through direct observation of the world using our senses. Alternative epistemologies to empiricism exist as reflected in constructivist, critical theory, postmodernist, and feminist approaches to IR theory (all of which are discussed in subsequent chapters).

Positivism dominates IR theorizing and is reflected in the chapters on images (see the more extensive discussion in chapter 10). Depending on the scholar, it has been categorized variously as an epistemology, methodology, or combination of the two. Positivism consists of four underlying implicit assumptions or beliefs:

1. The unity of the natural and social sciences—we can study society as we study the natural world;
2. We can draw a distinction between facts and values;
3. Regularities exist in the social as well as the natural world and they can be identified; and
4. Empirical validation or falsification is the hallmark of "real" inquiry.

Positivism specifically endorses the use of formal hypothesis testing or causal modeling as *methodologies*—modes of research and analysis or a set of rules for the actual practice of investigating international relations. This may involve *quantitative* (use of statistics and mathematical equations) or nonquantitative—so-called *qualitative*—methods (such as employing in-depth case and comparative case studies) to test empirically the hypotheses we generate. Very often when one hears the term "scientific method," the reference is to positivism with the focus on what is observable, empirical, and measurable. This is a convention we adopt in this book.

Ontology refers to how each of us views the world—how we see or understand the essence of things around us. Are there, for example, actual structures out there that influence the behavior of actors? For example, the concept of an "international system" is prevalent in the literature. Is it an actual material, physical, tangible structure consisting of capabilities such as weapons, troops, and economic resources? Or can we also conceive of structure as consisting of internationally shared ideas, beliefs, and norms? Is what we observe caused, facilitated, or impeded by these material or ideational structures (e.g., distribution of power or cultures) external to the actors or within which they are immersed? On the other hand, are terms like system or structure merely abstract constructs that facilitate our understanding of the world around us?

What is my or your ontology or worldview? Do states or nonstate actors matter or, if both do, which matters more? How do we view these actors? If they are states, do we see them acting as if they are rational individuals? Do we assume these actors are more important in explaining international relations than the material or ideational structures? Do we see events or outcomes as effects having discoverable causes? Or are we prone, by contrast, to see events as largely random occurrences? Do we see (or come to see) human beings important as individuals, or do we instead look to larger groups or aggregations of people to find social meaning? Does the individual have a distinct identity, or is the concept of "self" a function of relationships with others and the environment within which one is immersed? Do human beings have the capacity to think and act freely, or are their actions and even their thoughts externally influenced or even determined? Do we see things in good and evil terms and thus have the propensity to draw moral distinctions? Or do we see what we observe, if not from a morally neutral position, then a more or less morally indifferent position?

The answers to such questions have profound consequences on one's scholarship and even the way we lead our lives. To clarify this admittedly difficult concept, let's turn to IR theory for examples. One of the more theoretically self-conscious IR theorists, Ernst B. Haas (1924–2003), describes how his work was influenced by an ontological orientation that "avoided fixed dogmas and unchanging universal values" and "highlighted human agency over other causal forces."

Another theorist, James N. Rosenau (1924–2011), sees some of us as ontologically more prone to engage in theorizing than others. Rosenau states that one's being "able to assume that human affairs are founded on an underlying order"—an ontological predisposition—is essential to thinking theoretically.[1] Beyond this ontological assumption, Rosenau adds eight more "preconditions for creative theorizing"—his answer to a student's question. As he puts it, "to think theoretically, one":

a. has to avoid treating the task as that of formulating an appropriate definition of theory;
b. has to be clear as to whether one aspires to empirical theory or value theory;
c. must be predisposed to ask about every event, every situation, or every observed phenomenon, "Of what is it an instance?";
d. must be ready to appreciate and accept the need to sacrifice detailed description for broad observations;
e. must be tolerant of ambiguity, concerned about probabilities, and distrustful of absolutes;
f. must be playful about international phenomena . . . [having] a creative imagination . . . the habit of . . . specifying unlikely conditions and analyzing them as *if* they prevailed;
g. must be genuinely puzzled by international phenomena; [and]
h. must be constantly ready to be proven wrong.

For their part, the ontologies Kenneth N. Waltz (1924–2013) and many other realists (chapter 5) bring to the IR field provide a darker view of the reality they are prone to see, a dimmer view of human beings and their potential than liberals typically hold. It is a tradition steeped in the thought of Thucydides, Niccolò Machiavelli, Thomas Hobbes, and even James Madison and Alexander

---

[1] Ernst B. Haas, *Nationalism, Liberalism and Progress*, vol. 2 (Ithaca, NY: Cornell University Press, 2000), 419. James N. Rosenau, *The Scientific Study of Foreign Policy*, rev. ed. (London: Frances Pinter, 1980), 19–31.

Hamilton—the latter two agreeing in the *Federalist Papers* on the term *depravity* to describe the human condition or the natural state in which human beings find themselves. Given such underlying ontologies, the realist image not surprisingly is of a world of competition among self-oriented states as principal actors with different interests and capabilities or power they bring to bear in the pursuit of these interests.

Waltz describes liberals (chapter 6), by contrast, as (mis)informed by taking the ontological position that harmony is the natural condition for human beings and dismissing dissension and strife as supposedly arising from "mistaken belief, inadequate knowledge, and defective governance."[2] Economic structuralists (chapter 7) share with realists a dim view of present reality, but one in which exploitation and victimization are the operative words to describe the human condition. Dialectical materialism is an example of a theoretical idea drawn from a Marxist, materialist ontology. Economic structuralists vary in their assessments of the future course and effects on the human condition of this historical mechanism. The future may be different from the present and the past. This guarded level of optimism is also evident in the English School (chapter 8) in which scholars who combine influences of both realist (Hobbes) and liberal (Grotius or Kant) to write of an international (or even world) society still under construction.

The ontologies we bring to the IR field influence the imagery we construct. Images are general perspectives on international relations and world politics that consist of certain assumptions about key actors and processes that influence our theorizing. There is a fine line between how we understand the essence of things (e.g., the condition or nature of human beings and the degree to which human beings as agents matter) and the images we have of international or world politics. To say ontologies and images are related, however, is not to say they are the same things.

WHAT IS THEORY?

The word theory also means different things to different people. It may even mean different things to the same person. In common parlance, for example, something may be true "in theory" but not in fact or in a particular case or set of circumstances. In this rather loose usage, "in theory" equates to "in principle" or "in the abstract."

Explanation and Prediction

Another meaning, more consistent with usage in this volume, is that theory is simply a way of making the world or some part of it more intelligible or better understood. Theories dealing with international relations aspire to achieve this goal. Making things more intelligible may, of course, amount to nothing more than better or more precise descriptions of the things we observe. Although accurate description is essential, theory is something more.

---

[2] Kenneth N. Waltz, *Realism and International Politics* (London: Routledge, 2008), 3.

For many people with a scientific or positivist bent, theory involves explanation. One goes beyond mere description of phenomena observed and engages in causal explanation based on certain prior occurrences or conditions. To assume this is possible is an ontological assumption about reality or "the world out there." Explanation from the positivist perspective involves establishing the phenomenon it explains as something that was to be expected in the circumstances in which it occurred. This is what Carl G. Hempel terms the "requirement of explanatory relevance." Information is explanatory only if it "affords good grounds for believing that the phenomenon to be explained does, or did, indeed occur. This condition must be met if we are to be entitled to say: 'That explains it—the phenomenon in question was indeed to be expected under the circumstances.'" This information will include one or more laws, as without a knowledge of regularities or patterns in international relations, we could not expect certain happenings at particular times.[3]

How do we identify these laws? The preferred positivist method is through the development of *hypotheses*—a proposition relating two or more variables. Thus, whenever *A* is present, then *B* can be expected to follow. "If *A*, then *B*" as hypothesis may be subject to an empirical test—that is, tested against real-world or factual data to determine its lawlike quality. "If states engage in arms races, then the likelihood of war increases" is an example of such a hypothesis. Alternatively, hypotheses can be stated in a "most likely" and "least likely" format. For example, "The stronger the leading sea power's relative capability position, the less likely it is that other great powers will balance against it."[4] Indeed, formal statements and testing of hypotheses through the use of a statistical methodology are seen by many positivists as central to the theory-building process. Resultant laws or lawlike statements, therefore, allow IR theorists to make at least tentative predictions about possible outcomes in international relations: "Given these circumstances as validated by our tested hypotheses, we can expect X, Y, or Z."

The primary research strategy that entails invoking laws in a scientific explanation can be called a generalizing or *covering-law* approach. Many realists and liberals are rooted in this tradition, seeking covering laws of such phenomena as war, deterrence, cooperation, and economic integration. The event to be explained is an instance of a certain type of event that follows regularly from the conditions specified.

---

[3] What is to be explained—the explanandum—is preceded by certain explanatory sentences—an explanans that "consists of general laws" and "other statements" concerning particular facts. Hempel applied this formalized deductive approach in the formulation of both universal and probabilistic lawlike statements. Carl G. Hempel, *Philosophy of Natural Science* (Englewood Cliffs, NJ: Prentice-Hall, 1966), 48, 51.

[4] Jack S. Levy and William R. Thompson, "Balancing on Land and Sea: Do States Ally against the Leading Global Power?" *International Security* 35, no. 1 (Summer 2010): 21. For examples of other hypotheses, see Michael P. Colaresi, Karen Rasler, and William R. Thompson, *Strategic Rivalries in World Politics: Position, Space and Conflict Escalation* (Cambridge, UK: Cambridge University Press, 2007), esp. chap. 6.

Jack Snyder, for example, has addressed the important question of why the Cold War ended peacefully. His explanation involved establishing the laws and initial conditions that would lead one to believe that, given these circumstances, the peaceful collapse of the Soviet empire was to be expected. He posits that expansionist myths coupled with, among other factors, the timing of industrialization provide a framework for understanding the type of collapse experienced by the Soviet Union.[5] Such factors could be applied to other cases.

Another example of positivist social science at work is the ambitious effort of Kenneth Waltz to offer a more formal theory of international politics to explain general tendencies and patterns of behavior among states. To Waltz, "Theories explain laws." Waltz identifies a power-based structure of the international system that purportedly explains the behavior of states as the system's principal actors. Having stated "the theory being tested," one proceeds to

> infer hypotheses from it; subject the hypotheses to experimental or observational tests; . . . use the definitions of terms found in the theory being tested; eliminate or control perturbing variables not included in the theory under test; devise a number of distinct and demanding tests; if a test is not passed, ask whether the theory flunks completely, needs repair and restatement, or requires a narrowing of the scope of its explanatory claims.[6]

The commitment to positivism is clear in the last comment that underscores the importance of falsifiability in the testing of theories.

While the covering-law strategy is the most popular for those operating within the positivist framework, there is also a reconstructive positivist strategy. In this case, no attempt is made to place the phenomenon under investigation into a larger class. Rather, the event is explained as the expected endpoint of a concrete historical sequence, not as an instance of category A, B, or C. Reconstructive explanations also rely on laws, but these are not covering laws but rather component laws—each pertains only to a part of the pathway that led to the event or phenomenon being explained.

For example, like Snyder, William Wohlforth attempts to explain the peaceful collapse of the Soviet empire. He does not, however, attempt to "cover" Soviet behavior by showing how we would expect it to be given the circumstances. Instead, he details the sequence of events leading up to the collapse of the Soviet empire. The behavior to be explained emerges from this analysis and historical reconstruction.[7]

In terms of methodology and methods, therefore, some IR scholars prefer a research strategy that relies on the formal construction of hypotheses and theories. These may be tested, for example, through the application of statistical

---

[5] Jack Snyder, "Myths, Modernization, and the Post-Gorbachev World," in *International Relations Theory and the End of the Cold War*, ed. Richard Ned Lebow and Thomas Risse-Kappen (New York: Columbia University Press, 1995), 109–26.

[6] Kenneth N. Waltz, *Theory of International Politics* (Reading, MA: Addison-Wesley, 1979), 6, 13.

[7] The Snyder and Wohlforth examples are from David Dessler, "Constructivism within a Positivist Social Science," *Review of International Studies* 25, no. 1 (January 1999): 129–30.

methods. Others prefer to rely on nonquantitative indicators or case and comparative case studies, historical methods, and reasoned argument—the so-called traditional or qualitative approaches to theory building.[8]

Whatever differences IR scholars might have among themselves, those with a positivist or scientific commitment all tend to agree on one thing: Theory is necessary and unavoidable when it comes to explaining and attempting to foresee or predict future outcomes. Because as human beings we are subjective creatures who see and make sense of the world around us from different points of view, even such scientifically oriented scholars approach their subject matter with diverse perspectives, paradigms, research programs,[9] theoretical constructs, or images. It is the theory and hypotheses or propositions we are holding (or challenging) that tell us what to focus on and what to ignore in making sense of the world around us. Without theory, we would be overwhelmed and immobilized by an avalanche of mere facts or occurrences around us. In short, the sense we make of what we observe is informed by both the perspectives and theories we hold.

In this admittedly positivist understanding, a theory is an intellectual construct composed of a set of interrelated propositions that help one to identify or select facts and interpret them, thus facilitating explanation and prediction concerning the regularities and recurrences or repetitions of observed phenomena. One certainly can think theoretically when it comes to explaining foreign policy processes in general or the foreign policy of a particular state. IR theorists, however, tend as well to be interested in patterns of behavior among diverse states and nonstate actors operating internationally or globally. In identifying patterns, the stage is set for making modest predictions about the possible nature and direction of change. To think theoretically, however, is not to engage in point predictions—"*A* will attack *B* the first week of the year"—regardless of how much foreign policy, national security, and intelligence analysts may aspire to such precision.

To think theoretically, therefore, is to be interested in central tendencies. The theorist views each event as an instance of a more encompassing class or pattern of phenomena. Fitting pieces into a larger whole makes theory-building analogous to puzzle-solving. In fact, for many theorists, the goal is not merely explanation of patterns of behavior, but explanations of patterns that at first glance seem counterintuitive or different from what one might expect.

War poses a most important puzzle for IR theorists. Why does the phenomenon persist even though wars are extremely costly in terms of lives and treasure lost? Quincy Wright's *A Study of War* and Lewis Richardson's *Statistics of Deadly Quarrels* were pioneering efforts at trying to solve this puzzle through the use of statistical methods or causal modeling. Bruce Bueno de Mesquita's

---

[8] For an overview of methods, see Stephen Van Evera, *Guide to Methods for Students of Political Science* (Ithaca, NY: Cornell University Press, 1997).

[9] Imre Lakatos observes that competitive "research programmes" exist in various fields of scholarly inquiry. See "Falsification and the Methodology of Scientific Research Programmes," in *The Methodology of Scientific Research Programmes: Philosophical Papers*, vol. 1, ed. John Worrall and Gregory Currie (Cambridge, UK: Cambridge University Press, 1978), 8–10, 47–52, 70–72, 85–93.

The War Trap and John Vasquez's *The War Puzzle* are also examples of work in this genre. Examples of continuing efforts to build better theory by using reasoned argument, historical and comparative cases, or other nonquantitative, qualitative methods include Kenneth Waltz's classic *Man, the State and War*, Michael Howard's *The Causes of Wars*, Stephen Walt's *Revolution and War*, Michael Doyle's *Ways of War and Peace*, and Stephen Van Evera's *Causes of War*.

Theory in a formal, positivist sense specifies relations among variables and ideally would weigh them with the precision one finds in an algebraic equation. Such fully developed theory is less common in the social sciences and certainly not in international relations; even positivists wedded to scientific modes of inquiry confess to be operating at a lesser level of theoretical development than the natural sciences.

General theories that strive to provide a complete account of the causes of war or other phenomena are less common than partial, or middle-range, theories that are more modest in the scope of what is to be explained or predicted. Part of the war puzzle addressed by such middle-range theorists, for example, involves crises and decision-making in crises. Are partial theories like building blocks that can eventually be assembled into a fully developed, general theory of war? Some theorists would say yes and that the most productive enterprise for the present is the development of better middle-range theories. Not everyone would agree. Partial or middle-range theories have tended to be essentially nonadditive: They are merely islands of theory without bridges to connect them into a coherent whole.[10]

Even if such connections might be made, the result would probably undercut the social science goal of developing theories that are parsimonious—explaining a great deal of behavior through the use of relatively few concepts. Theories that lack parsimony by definition contain too many factors or variables and quickly become as complex as, or more complex than, the reality they purport to explain. If practically everything is portrayed as a cause, then has anything really been found to explain or predict what we observe?

Abstraction and Application

The world of theory is an abstract one. Theories may actually exist apart from facts. Mathematical theorists, for example, deal entirely in the realm of abstraction, whether or not their work has direct relevance to problems of the world in which we live. Practical application for the work of mathematical theorists is sometimes found years later, if ever. From the positivist perspective, however, empirically based theories in the social or natural sciences, by contrast, relate to facts and provide explanation or prediction for observed phenomena. Hypotheses associated with these theories are subject to testing against real-world data. The theorist need not have any purpose in developing such empirical theories

---

[10] The nonadditivity of middle-range or partial theories was the challenge expressed by Ernst Haas in his lectures, but a preponderance of them might lead us to "creep up on the system."

other than satisfying his or her intellectual curiosity, although many will seek to make their work "policy relevant."

Policy-relevant theories may have explicit purposes that stem from the value preferences of the theorist, such as reducing the likelihood of war or curbing arms races. Acting on such theories, of course, is the domain of the policy maker, a task separate from that of the empirical theorist. Theorists who become policy makers may well make choices informed by what theories say will be the likely outcomes of implementing one or another alternative. Their choices may be informed by empirical theory or understandings of world events, but the decisions they make are still heavily based on value preferences.

As noted at the outset of this section, a common dismissive attitude toward theory is that while something may be true "in theory," it does not apply to the real world. For reasons discussed earlier, this is a very shortsighted view. Theory is actually a way to become engaged in an increasingly globalized world that goes beyond today's headlines. Theory can help us cut through the blizzard of information we are all faced with daily. Reflecting on his life's work theorizing in the IR field, Waltz speaks for many theorists with a positivist orientation to international relations, confidently telling us that "from theory all else follows." He adds that "theory explains and may at times anticipate or predict outcomes." In this regard, "a political theory, if it is any good, not only explains international outcomes, but also provides clues to situations and actions that may produce more of the desired and fewer of the undesired ones."[11] Put another way, there is nothing so practical as a good theory.

Levels of Analysis

Let us assume one is interested in theorizing about the causes of war. Where should one focus one's initial efforts? Does one deal with individual decision makers or small groups of individuals engaged in the policy process? How important, for example, are such factors as the correctness of individual perceptions or bargaining skills in determining the decision to go to war? On the other hand, if one looks outside the individual or small decision-making group to the entire state apparatus, society as a whole, or the international political system of states, one is acknowledging the importance of external or environmental factors as well.

The levels of analysis constitute a framework designed to organize and assist in systematic thinking about international relations. We differentiate the term *levels of analysis* (individual or group, state and society, and "system" as a whole) from *units of analysis*, the latter referring to states, organizations, individuals or groups, classes, and other entities. What one is trying to explain or study (such as the outbreak of war) is known as the dependent variable. Factors at different levels of analysis we suspect as being causally related to what we are trying to explain typically are termed independent variables. Thus, we can look both "inside" the state as a principal unit of analysis in a search for explanatory factors at individual or group and societal levels and "outside" the state to take

---

[11] Waltz, *Realism and International Politics*, vii.

account of factors that causally affect its actions and interactions with other states at an international "system" level.

Work by Waltz in the 1950s on the causes of war represented a path-breaking effort due to his identification of distinct levels of analysis and his attempt to specify the relations among these levels. Was the cause of war (the dependent variable) to be found in the nature of individuals? (Are humans innately aggressive?) Or in the nature of states and societies? (Are some types of states more aggressive than others?) Or in the nature of the international system of states? (Is anarchy a "permissive" cause of war, there being no obstacle to the use of force by sovereign states in a world without central governance?)

Each answer reflects a different level of analysis—individual (or group of individuals), state and society, or international (see figure 1.1). In 1961, the importance of the question of levels of analysis to the study of international relations was further discussed in detail in a then often-cited article by J. David Singer. Singer argues that one's choice of a particular level of analysis determines what one will and will not see. Different levels tend to emphasize different actors, structures, and processes.[12]

For example, it is quite common in international relations for the levels of analysis to include (1) the international system (distribution of power among states, geography, technology, and other factors), the capitalist world system (economic structuralists), or an international or world society composed of rules, norms, states, and nonstate actors (the English School); (2) the state (often treated as a unified actor) and domestic or national society (democratic, authoritarian, etc.); (3) groups as in bureaucratic politics and group dynamics—the domain of social psychology; and (4) individuals as in psychology, perception, and belief systems. It is also quite typical for these various levels to be used to explain the foreign policy behavior of states—the dependent variable. The state, in other words, is often the unit of analysis, and explaining its behavior could entail taking into account factors at all of these levels of analysis.

But which level of analysis, one may ask, is most important? To take a specific example, let us assume that the foreign policies of most states exhibit relative constancy, or slowness to change. How is this constancy to be explained? Some scholars point to external or exogenous factors such as the distribution or balance of power among states that is relatively slow to change in any major way. Still others instead look internally within the state to the interpretive understandings of decision makers that may exhibit constancy due to shared worldviews they hold or approaches they take with incremental or small changes being the rule.

Another example: How are arms races explained? Some scholars point to international factors such as the military expenditures and hostility of other states as well as competition between alliances that lead to an increase in the production of weapons. Other researchers emphasize the importance of domestic

---

[12] Kenneth N. Waltz, *Man, the State and War* (New York: Columbia University Press, 1959); J. David Singer, "The Level-of-Analysis Problem in International Relations," in *International Politics and Foreign Policy*, ed. James N. Rosenau (New York: Free Press, 1969), 20–29.

Individual Level (domain of psychology)
    Human nature and psychology
    Leaders and belief systems
    Personality of leaders
    Cognition and perception or misperception

Group Level (domain of social psychology)
    Government bureaucracy
    Policymaking groups
    Interest groups
    Other nongovernmental organizations

State and Societal (or National) Level
    Governmental
        Structure and nature of political system
        Policymaking process
    Societal (domain of sociology)
        Structure of economic system
        Public opinion
        Nationalism and ethnicity
        Political culture
        Ideology

International—World (or Global) Level
    Anarchic quality of international or world politics
    Number of major powers or poles
    Distribution of power/capabilities among states
    Economic patterns
    Level and diffusion of technology
    Patterns of military alliances
    Patterns of international trade and finance
    International organizations and regimes
    Transnational organizations and networks
    Global norms and international law

Figure 1.1   Levels of Analysis: A More Detailed Look

factors such as bureaucratic competition between branches of the military services and budgetary processes that encourage a steady increase in expenditures.

The easy answer to the question of which level of analysis should be emphasized is that all levels of analysis should be considered. Such a response is not particularly useful, however, because it suggests that we have to study everything under the sun. Few scholars would even attempt such a task, and the resulting theory, if any, would hardly be parsimonious. Hence, a great deal of the literature on international relations is constantly posing the questions of what should be examined within each level of analysis, and how actors, structures, and other factors or variables relate to one another across levels of analysis and over time.

As we will see in parts II and III, this issue of levels of analysis also subtly pervades the images and interpretive understandings we identify. Structuralists or neorealists, for example, note how the overall structure or distribution of power in the international system influences the behavior of states or the perceptions of decision makers. Hence, structural realist (neorealist) analysis emphasizes the systems level. Similarly, members of the English School look to international or world society as the principal level of analysis, even as they are quite comfortable crossing the different levels of analysis in seeking explanations. Moreover, certain economic structuralists examine how the historical development of the capitalist world economy generates states. Some constructivists argue that international structure can be conceived ideationally in shared meanings, rules, and norms that facilitate or constrain the actions decision makers consider.

Despite their differences, many of these scholars tend to start at the systems (or international, world, or global society) level of analysis. Those authors associated with the liberal image, however, who examine bureaucracies, interest groups, and individuals tend to emphasize the state-societal and individual levels of analysis. Some liberals and neoliberals, however, are also interested in how the development and spread of international norms influence state behavior—a global system- or world society-level focus.

There is a final important issue that should be mentioned in conjunction with the levels of analysis but that goes well beyond the latter as it raises ontological questions concerning the so-called *agent-structure* problem. As summarized by one author, the problem emerges from two uncontentious claims about social life: first, that human agency is the only moving force behind the actions, events, and outcomes of the social world; and second, that human agency can be realized only in concrete historical circumstances that condition the possibilities for action and influence its course. "People make history," observed Karl Marx in an often-quoted aphorism, "but not in conditions of their own choosing." These claims impose two demands on our scientific explanations: first, that they acknowledge and account for the power of agents; and second, that they recognize the causal relevance of exogenous or "structural factors"—that is, the conditions of action as decision makers understand them. The agent-structure problem refers to the difficulties of developing a theory that successfully meets both demands.[13]

---

[13] David Dessler, "What's at Stake in the Agent-Structure Debate?" *International Organization* 43, no. 3 (Summer 1989): 441–73.

This problem is usually viewed as a matter of ontology, the branch of metaphysics concerned, as noted earlier, with the nature of being. In this case, the ontological issue deals with the nature of both agents (very often viewed as the state or other organizational unit, but also including groups or individuals acting in their personal capacities) and structures (as in international politics) as well as relations between them. As we will see in the following chapters, a constant theme is how authors deal with the relative importance of human agents and structural factors, and the extent to which one influences the very nature of the other. Put another way, we ask not only how much voluntarism (or freedom of action agents have) or determinism (the extent to which they are constrained) there actually is in the world of which we are so integral a part, but also in the theories we construct that purport to explain or predict phenomena in that world. Very often unstated, one's position on this issue—the voluntarism inherent in agency and the determinism that comes from structures—heavily influences how one goes about explaining international politics as well as assessing the possibilities and means of peaceful change.

THE INTELLECTUAL ROOTS OF IR THEORY

Some might argue that if one wished to understand the basics of thinking about world politics, the study of Thucydides, Niccolò Machiavelli, Thomas Hobbes, Jean-Jacques Rousseau, Immanuel Kant, and perhaps Hugo Grotius is sufficient. This would be a mistake and is reflected in part I of this book—authors not affiliated with the Western intellectual tradition had some interesting and important things to say about world politics and are deserving of comment. Similarly, historians have argued that Asia has experienced developments quite relevant to the Western experience.[14] Other western writers directly influenced some of the more illustrious names in the field. Machiavelli, for example, owes an intellectual debt to such ancient writers as Polybius, Livy, and Plutarch. Indeed, in comparison to much of the current literature on international relations, it is striking the extent to which the authors surveyed were familiar with the arguments of their predecessors.[15]

This leads one to ask how much of the current work on international relations is really new in terms of its insights. We believe it is fair to say that there

---

[14] It is argued that Asia has been treated as a residual category and generally viewed only in terms of its encounters with Western colonialism. Studying the Mongol empire of the thirteenth and fourteenth centuries could teach us something about sovereignty and rethink how we look at the rise and decline of world orders. Ayse Zarakol, *Before the West* (Cambridge University Press, 2022).

[15] "We do not read Thucydides, Aristotle, or Rousseau as historical curiosities. We may and do add to them, and often criticize them, but we do not replace them. Long before the behavioral revolution, Aristotle claimed that generalizations about political life can be derived from the empirical data of common sense and historical experience, and that these generalizations can be treated in terms of cause and effect. Thucydides' hypothesis on the causes of preemptive war is as germane today as it was in 431 BCE. Rousseau's insights about the sources of war and the difficulties of cooperation in a condition of anarchy command our attention as much today as they did when first published." K. J. Holsti, "Mirror, Mirror on the Wall, Which Are the Fairest Theories of All?" *International Studies Quarterly* 33, no. 3 (September 1989): 257–58.

really is a lot less that is completely new in present-day IR theory than one might first suppose—a comment that no doubt applies equally well to political theory in general.

There is a certain hubris caused by lack of attention to intellectual antecedents. Political scientists sometimes cloak their ideas in present-day theories with a "newness," originality, or uniqueness that may not be warranted. In point of fact, international relations as a field of inquiry tends to suffer from the problem of fads. Research programs come and go and sometimes return under new titles. By studying classic and even somewhat obscure works, as historians tell us, one becomes more skeptical of passing fashions. Instead, we gain a greater appreciation for the continuity of thinking about international politics.

IMAGES

In part II of this volume we identify four broad alternative images or perspectives (we use the terms interchangeably) of international relations. To summarize:

1. *Realism* is a term that refers to both classical and neorealism (or structural realism). For the realist, states are the principal or most important actors on the international political stage and represent the key unit of analysis. States are viewed as unitary actors that behave in a generally rational or purposive manner. National security issues typically dominate the hierarchy of the international agenda. *Power* and *balance of power* are often key concepts in realist analyses.
2. *Liberalism* (and *neoliberal institutionalism*) presents a pluralist view of the world that is composed not just of states and their institutions, but also of multiple nonstate actors to include international and nongovernmental organizations, individuals, and groups. The state is disaggregated into its component parts and is continually subjected to outside influences. Political-economic issues are a primary research focus, and hence the hierarchy of world issues is not always dominated by matters of military security.
3. *Economic structuralism* identifies economic classes and other material structures as well as places a broader emphasis on multiple mechanisms of postcolonial dominance that maintain the so-called Global South in a subordinate status. For the economic structuralist, all actors must be viewed within the context of an overarching global structure. The defining characteristic of this structure is its capitalist nature; it must be viewed in a historical context. The more recent postcolonial literature provides greater understanding of the way capitalism operates now and in the past.
4. The *English School* tends to see politics occurring in an international society in which one finds operative not only realist, material understandings of power and balance of power, but also the impact of rules, norms, and institutions. These theorists, therefore, draw from both realist and liberal traditions and more recently from constructivism. The English School offers a *via media* or middle path, on the one hand, between realism and liberalism and, on the other, between realism and *idealism*.

We will examine these images and associated assumptions and concepts in greater detail in subsequent chapters. The image one has of international relations is of critical importance. Images are not theories, but they do inform substantially the way we see the world, thus influencing the formulation of the theories we construct to make better sense of the world around us. Thus, a balance-of-power theory may be informed by the assumptions or premises of a realist image of international relations, but the image itself does not have the standing of a theory.

These images, informed as they are by different ontologies or worldviews, lead one to ask certain questions, seek certain types of answers, and use certain methodological tools in the construction of theories and testing of hypotheses. The advantage is that such images bring order to the analytical effort and make it more manageable. We are among the first, however, to admit that this four-fold classification scheme also has its limitations. Accordingly, we offer several qualifications and clarifications.

First, we concede that the images of international relations we identify could be viewed as forms of (or bases for) interpretive understandings. Realism, liberalism, economic structuralism, and the English School are nothing more than constructs that have developed within the IR field, itself a construct that emerged within political science, yet another construct. We need to be humble about claims relating to constructs within constructs! These constructs that scholars have put together do not have an independent existence and, as such, are always subject to challenge. They are merely categories of inquiry or the bases of research programs, their value resting on the degree to which they make the world around us more intelligible, perhaps allowing us to explain or predict more accurately the phenomena we observe. Although the four images are heavily positivist in orientation, subsequent theories that are developed may evince, to varying degrees, aspects of interpretive understandings we discuss in the next section.

Second, the images should be viewed as *ideal or pure types* in that each emphasizes what several seemingly diverse theoretical approaches have in common. For example, there are substantial differences in the works of Hans J. Morgenthau, Kenneth Waltz, John Mearsheimer, and Stephen Walt, to mention just a few. But these and other scholars nevertheless draw from the same realist traditions. What unites them as IR theorists is more important for our purposes than what divides them.

Third, the overview of key assumptions of each of the four perspectives might give the erroneous impression that these images are mutually exclusive in all respects. This is not the case. Neorealists and neoliberal institutionalists, for example, both utilize rational actor assumptions and tend to treat the identity and interests of their constituent actors as givens.

Fourth, we acknowledge a certain amount of conceptual eclecticism by scholars in the study of international relations, perhaps reflecting the absence of a single, dominant perspective, much less a single paradigm or set of research programs. For some, conceptual diversity is to be applauded; for others, it is a source of despair. Be that as it may, our focus is primarily on ideas, trends, and both generalized images and interpretive understandings of international relations and only secondarily on the work of particular authors.

Fifth, the images tend to focus more on what is studied than on how to conduct such studies. Quantitative and nonquantitative methodologies transcend the images we have identified. Statistical methods, formal hypothesis testing, and *causal modeling* find their adherents within each of the perspectives, as do the more traditional, nonquantitative, historical, philosophical, legal, case study, and comparative case study methods. Our point remains that these are methods, not images of international relations or world politics. Images may influence the choice of methodology or methods employed, but they are not the same.

An image of international or world politics influences the selection of units or processes examined and variables identified and operationalized. Thus, for realists, states and state interactions are of key importance; for liberals, institutions, as well as transnational interactions to include communications flows across national borders, may well be the central focus; for the English School, the ways and means by which order is sustained and security provided in an anarchic international or world society are essential tasks; and for economic structuralists, patterns of class or North-South relations of dominance or dependence are perhaps most important.

Similarly, methods associated with the literature on *decision-making*, *game theory*, and public- or *rational-choice theory*—economic or rational models applied to political decision-making—transcend the four images we identify. Assumptions made about actors and processes are informed by realist, liberal, English School, and economic-structuralist images and color the use each method is given. Thus, collective goods theory, game theory, econometrics, and other approaches identified with the interdisciplinary field of political economy find their adherents among scholars holding diverse images or other interpretive understandings and thus are not the exclusive preserve of realists, liberals, the English School, or economic structuralists.

Finally, we wish to reiterate a point made earlier—that the four images we identify are not theories of international relations. Rather, they represent general perspectives on international relations out of which particular theories may develop. Assumptions of an image may become part of a theory (such as the realist assumptions of a unitary, rational, or purposive state-as-actor in some structural-realist works), but more often than not they simply help to orient a scholar's research by highlighting certain units of analysis for investigation in the construction of a theory as well as helping to determine what constitutes evidence in the testing of hypotheses.

INTERPRETIVE UNDERSTANDINGS

What we term interpretive understandings—constructivist, critical, postmodern, feminist, and green thought—share one thing in common: All have taken issue with one or more of the epistemological, methodological, and ontological assumptions that drive positivist theorizing in realism and liberalism in particular. What they offer is alternative lenses for interpreting what we observe.

Put another way, this approach to knowledge assumes that what we know is based on an interpretation of what we think we see, alerting us to the subjective character of all human beings, the institutions or units they construct, and the processes in which they engage. Try as we might to reduce bias, we remain subjective creatures. Pursuit of objectivity and value-free scholarship are at best elusive goals.

Although, as we will see, many scholars have contributed to the interpretive understanding approach to international relations, the German scholar Max Weber (1864–1920) deserves pride of place. Weber argues that "all knowledge of cultural reality is always knowledge from particular points of view." How research is conducted will be "determined by the evaluative ideas that dominate the investigator and his age."[16] In other words, each individual's work will be influenced by a particular doctrine, image of the world, ideology, paradigm, theory, understanding, or perspective. As a practical matter we try to identify as best we can how this subjective, human dimension affects our scholarship—an attempt to reduce substantially any bias that can adversely affect our theoretical work. Beyond that, the usual remedy is the scrutiny others give our work in what is inherently an intersubjective process. As he sought to establish the role of ideational factors in explanation by social scientific means, Weber was an important early influence on interpretive understandings, particularly the later development of constructivism.

In part III, we build upon this subjective, Weberian tradition of *Verstehen* or interpretive understanding. In chapter 9 we examine constructivism. The rise of constructivism in IR theory has been remarkably fast over the past twenty-plus years, passing economic structuralism, influencing the English School, and challenging realism and liberalism in terms of relative influence on the IR field. Constructivism is less than a theory of international relations and more than an image. It is best characterized as a theoretically informed, interpretive understanding related to the study of international relations. Although within this approach some could be characterized as positivists and embrace empirical methods, the type of explanation they seek is typically not that of the deductive covering law "out there" driving the behavior of states or nonstate actors, but rather causality that takes full account of subjective and intersubjective, human understandings.

Constructivists see states and nonstate actors not as mere products of world politics, the international system, or an international or world society, but rather as actually playing a decisive role in shaping it. These actors or agents influence (and are influenced by) the international norms and institutions they construct—activities that sustain or create new interests, values, and the ordering of foreign policy preferences. They take account of the relation between human beings and the organizations they construct as agents and the material and ideational structures that constitute actors and facilitate or constrain their actions. Most constructivists do not reject science or scientific methods associated with positivism, but caution greater humility and care in dealing with

---

[16] Max Weber, *Methodology of the Social Sciences*, trans. and ed. E. A. Shils and H. A. Finch (New York: Free Press, 1949), 90–93. See also, Max Weber, *Basic Concepts in Sociology*, trans. H. P. Secher (Westport, CT: Greenwood Press, 1962, 1969), 52–55.

concepts that, after all, are of human construction. They can be viewed as occupying the middle ground between positivists seeking causal explanatory theory and those postmodernists or others who reject any such possibility.

Chapter 10 takes up the ongoing debate between those committed to positivist science and their principal critics, the latter drawing heavily from *phenomenology*, which describes the phenomena we experience and the subjectivity that defines the essence of human beings. Although critical theorists tend not to reject positivism, they are prone to look under the cover stories that governments, organizations, leaders, policy makers, and even theorists use to justify their conduct—an effort to find the underlying power or other realities masked by these narratives.

For their part, postmodernists do not focus on some "objective" reality to be discovered "out there," but rather explore the ways human beings "in here" both construct or give meanings to objects, actions, or behaviors and employ narratives or stories that convey these meanings in what is essentially a subjective approach to understanding. Observers cannot be fully autonomous from the objects of their study, and relationships cannot be divided merely into the positivist categories of "causes" and "effects."

We take up feminism in chapter 11 as an interpretive understanding or lens that brings us to the often overlooked or understated importance and payoffs of applying the concept of gender to IR theorizing. Feminists highlight the dominance or exclusivity of masculinist understandings of the world around us that, they claim, profoundly influence much theoretical work in the IR field. Feminist understandings rest on a centuries-old body of literary and scholarly work that preceded and has been decidedly less influenced by phenomenology *per se*. Although critical theorists and postmodernists may be found among feminist scholars, some adopt positivist, scientific approaches albeit often informed by constructivist understandings of gender, sexual identity, and related concepts. Put another way, feminist scholarship is inherently interpretive as it challenges theories that either ignore (or marginalize) gender as a variable or, conversely, misuse gender to mask other purposes.

Chapter 12 examines green theory and how more mainstream IR theories approach (or fail to address) the myriad of challenges associated with global warming and environmental degradation. Green theory is also a lens—an umbrella term that includes strands of thought drawn from constructivism, critical theory, and feminism.

Chapter 13 addresses normative theory as a separate line of inquiry in international relations that brings us to moral or ethical values rooted in human understandings developed over more than two millennia. Normative IR theory has implications for both interpretive understandings and the images we use to capture the IR field, but it also remains a domain of inquiry in its own right that deals precisely with values and value preferences that inform human judgment. As with empirical theories, we can scrutinize normative theories on logical grounds, looking for flaws in reasoning used to sustain the argument. Unlike empirical theory, however, propositions in normative theory are not subject to empirical tests as a means of establishing their truth or falsehood.

Normative theory deals not so much with what is—the domain of empirical theory and the images and interpretive understandings associated with it—but rather with what should or ought to be. How should the world be ordered, and what value choices should decision makers take? Although the bulk of the effort in this volume is allocated to images, interpretive understandings, and the intellectual roots of IR theory, we consider normative theory to be an important and policy-relevant, if often neglected, enterprise. In dealing with normative theories relevant to international relations and foreign policy choices, we identify normative preferences typically associated with the four images and interpretive understandings of IR theory.

In sum, this initial chapter has provided some basic tools to help the reader engage with the vast academic literature on IR theory and provide a preview of coming attractions. Whether reading a book or journal article, there are some questions to keep in mind while sorting through, categorizing, and comparing various works. First, does the book or article reflect one of the underlying images or interpretive understandings? Does it fall within a positivist or post-positivist, interpretivist perspective? Can you discern, if it is not made explicit, the epistemology, methodology, and ontology of the authors? If a positivist approach, does it emphasize quantification, covering law, or a historical reconstructive strategy? What role may normative concerns play in the study? Such questions encourage critical thinking as opposed to simply memorizing which author is associated with which theory or approach.

PART I

THE INTELLECTUAL ROOTS OF INTERNATIONAL RELATIONS THEORY

2

The Ancients: Greek, Chinese, and Indian Thought

★ ★ ★

One finds the roots of realist thought in ancient Greek and Roman writers, given their obvious concern for the security of the city-state, republic, or empire. This is particularly true in the case of Homer, Herodotus, Thucydides, Plato, Aristotle, and Polybius in this chapter and Livy, Plutarch, Cicero, and others who are discussed in chapter 3. We also include commentary on Sun Tzu, the ancient Chinese philosopher writing during the sixth century BCE, and Kauti-lya, the Indian scholar who wrote around the fourth century BCE.

The impact these writers from ancient times have had on scholars over more than two millennia cannot be overstated. They provide present-day insights into the study of politics in general, and international relations in particular. For their part, Plato and Aristotle focused mainly on domestic politics. Plato sought a just society in an ideal republic. Both identified norms of right conduct by leaders and other citizens within a republic, polis, or city-state—the rule of law an ideal in itself. When realized, such domestic arrangements also contributed then, as now, to security in relation to other political units in the world outside their domains.

Writing in Italian in the late fifteenth and early sixteenth centuries, Niccolò Machiavelli saw the security of a city-state or republic in much the same way: dependent on good laws and good arms—the former the political and the latter the military components of security. Machiavelli's reading of the ancients thus led him to draw conclusions that he applied to domestic and international politics of his time, the former among city-states on the Italian peninsula and the latter in relations among these Italian states with France and Spain.

By his own admission, Machiavelli's ideas were drawn not just from observation of contemporary events, but also from the parallels he drew from extensive reading of such ancient writers as Polybius (c. 200–118 BCE, a late-Greek follower of Thucydides who wrote in Latin, the Roman language that Machiavelli could read), Livy (c. 60 BCE to 15 CE, a Roman historian), and Tacitus (c. 56–120 CE, a Roman senator and historian). What Machiavelli provided was a synthesis that later became a foundation or point of departure for realists who would identify with him and integrate his thinking in their theoretical and policy-oriented works.

The roots of liberal modes of thought, also present in ancient writings, received considerable attention from Greek writers, but the application of these ideas typically was contained within the bounds of a given city-state. The question of applying these ideas even in principle beyond the citizens of that unit did not seem to be on their minds. One of Aristotle's students, Alexander the Great, did spread Hellenic ideas as his army moved east from Macedonia across ancient lands to the Persian empire. It was the late-Greek and Roman Stoic writers, however, who developed notions of a community of humankind that transcended the boundaries of individual units, thus providing a conceptual basis for applying principles developed within a city-state or republic to the larger world.

Marxist and neo-Marxist understandings of social classes within society also have ancient roots. Plato and Aristotle wrote shortly after the time of Thucydides using class analysis, prescriptions for maintaining societal harmony and thus avoiding class conflict, a labor theory of value, and a defense of slavery—what Marx later would refer to as an ancient mode of production. Of particular relevance to this volume, Karl Marx applied these understandings to capitalism, seeing materially based classes as transcending state boundaries, not being confined by them. The economic structuralism we find in some IR theories reflects this Marxian class focus that resonates with classes in Plato's *Republic* and Aristotle's dismal defense of slavery as an economic necessity for the rulers and citizens of his time.

We are limited in our study of the ancients to the written records and artifacts left behind by these civilizations. That Greece and Rome figure so prominently in our view of the ancients is, in part, because we know more about them than we do of such other civilizations as the Sumerians in southern Mesopotamia (present-day Iraq) or Hittites in Anatolia (present-day Turkey). We cannot know of any great philosophical insights or other accomplishments if there is no record of them. This is not to say that civilizations leaving few records were somehow inferior to those that did. It is only to say that we do not know very much about them.

HOMER, HERODOTUS, SUN TZU, AND KAUTILYA

Our purpose here or elsewhere in this book is not to present a comprehensive history of the period under study. It is appropriate, however, to touch upon important historical events and sketch the nature of international politics—the context within which the authors lived. In this regard, we do identify historical highlights in table 2.1 to help frame the discussion in this chapter.

The Historical Context of Writings by Homer and Herodotus
The first period stretches from Homer (likely the eighth century BCE) to Thucydides (c. 472–400 BCE). It was a time of turmoil in which the security of Greek city-states was a central issue. We can hardly be surprised, then, that

Table 2.1   Timeline: Greco-Roman Historical Highlights (BCE)

3500 The Bronze Age: Sumerian civilization in Mesopotamia (present-day Iraq); Egyptians settle the Nile Valley

2800 Minoans settle the Mediterranean island of Crete

2300 Akkadians dominate Mesopotamia

2000 Amorites and Elamites invade Mesopotamia; Sumerian rule ends and Babylon Empire established; Hittites settle Anatolia (present-day Turkey)

1900 Greece settled by Achaens (Mycenians)

1800 Legal Code of Hammurabi established in Babylon (present-day Iraq); Hyksos invade Egypt

1300 Phoenician (Canaanite) trading posts established along the Mediterranean coast (present-day Lebanon, Syria, Israel, Palestine, and southwest Turkey); Trojan War (1250), Greeks defeating city of Troy on Turkish coast

1200 Iron Age; Dorian tribes invade Greece

1150 Dorians invade Minoans on Crete

750 Homer writes *Iliad* and *Odyssey* about defeat of Troy and aftermath

700 Assyrian imperial influence from Iraq to Egypt until imperial collapse around 612–609

500 Persian Wars: Cyrus the Great (d. 529) establishes Persian empire by conquest; Cambyses II (d. 521) conquers Egypt, extending empire from present-day Pakistan to Libya; Darius (d. 486) defeated at Marathon (490); Xerxes (d. 465) defeated at Salamis (480); Athens establishes Delian League, an alliance against Persia, the Greek Island of Delos its meeting place

484–430 Herodotus, "father of history" writes about Persian Wars

431–404 Peloponnesian War (Athens versus Sparta)

466–399 Socrates fights in Peloponnesian War and teaches Plato and others

472–400 Thucydides lives and writes about Peloponnesian War, an effort continued by Xenophon (434–354); Aristophanes (448–385) writes about war versus peace

427–347 Plato and Aristotle (384–322) deal mostly with domestic political arrangements, much less on relations among city-states or other political units

356–323 Alexander the Great, Aristotle's student, establishes the Macedonian Empire that extends eastward to present-day Pakistan and carries Hellenic ideas along his path of conquest

334–262 Zeno and other Greek Stoics lay the foundation for development of a more cosmopolitan worldview

264–146 Punic Wars between Rome and Carthage (Tunis), leading to defeat of Carthaginians (Phoenicians) and establishment of Roman Empire

200–120 Polybius, though Greek, writes in Latin about the Punic Wars and the rise of the Roman Empire

realist notions of power and balance-of-power politics prevailed among ancient writers. Security, if not an obsession, was at least a preoccupation for them.

One can distinguish between the world depicted by Homer and the world in which he lived. The *Iliad* and the *Odyssey*, epic poems attributed to Homer, were written around 750–700 BCE. Supposedly taking place in the twelfth century BCE, Homer's tales depict a world in which aristocratic warrior-chiefs rule over loosely united and defined territories, and only the earliest forms of government are evident. Towns exist, but life is essentially rural, with wealth a function of flocks and herds. Kingship is not so much an office with certain duties as it is a social position.

Extensive bureaucracies were not yet created, and what little peaceable contact existed was on the basis of guest or friendship among noble families, not formal diplomatic relations. Hence, when Paris of Troy (now Hisarlik by the Dardanelles Strait on the northwest Mediterranean coast of present-day Turkey) carries off Helen, wife of King Menelaus of Sparta, the Greek city-state, his act was as much an insult to private hospitality as it was a political outrage. Helen's was the beautiful face that launched a thousand ships—a famous line in Christopher Marlowe's *Dr. Faustus*, a 1604 play on evil forces in the world that, like Faustus, also tempt us.

Although the *Iliad* takes place in the later Mycenaean world of the Greek Bronze Age, we know from "Linear B" tablets (written in script predating the Greek alphabet) that the states depicted by Homer were in reality much more complicated and developed. In fact, his description is more characteristic of the period that fell between the Mycenaean Age (1600–1100 BCE) and the time of Homer.[1]

Thucydides also provides interesting evidence of this part of the world during the time of the Trojan War. He argues that "these various Hellenic states, weak in themselves and lacking communications with one another, took no kind of collective action before the time of the Trojan War [around 1250 BCE]. . . . Indeed, my [Thucydides's] view is that at this time the whole country was not even called 'Hellas' [i.e., Greece]." The shifting of populations regularly occurred, and pirates played a role almost as important as kings' armies. Thucydides notes how pirates would "descend upon cities that were unprotected by walls and indeed consisted only of scattered settlements." Aristotle similarly characterized this ancient period, describing the village as a union of families and a city as a union of villages.[2] In other words, we are a long way from the modern state and even from the more integrated Greek city-state or polis of future centuries.

As for the time in which Homer was actually writing, the self-sufficient and insular communities had given way to hundreds of separate city-states. These city-states typically consisted of an urban center and agricultural land within several miles. Populations were small, numbering only in the thousands. As some families acquired larger plots of land, the size of the nobility increased. Over time, hereditary monarchs often gave way to collective governments by the nobles from which an archon or chief magistrate was chosen. Nascent bureaucracies were formed, with councils of leading persons appointed to advise the rulers.

By the time of Homer's death, the domination of cities by families—so prevalent in the *Iliad*—was weakening. One reason was the introduction of a simple alphabet in the eighth century BCE that encouraged laws to be written down, hence strengthening the rights of citizens. For the Greeks, it was the

---

[1] P. J. Rhodes, *The Greek City States: A Source Book* (London: Croom Helm, 1986), 1; and W. Warde Fowler, *The City-State of the Greeks and Romans* (London: Macmillan, 1893), 66–67.
[2] Thucydides, *History of the Peloponnesian War*, trans. Rex Warner (Harmondsworth, UK: Penguin Books, 1954), I: 3, 5; and Aristotle, *The Politics of Aristotle*, trans. Ernest Barker (London: Oxford University Press, 1958, 1971), I: 2.

importance of law that distinguished them from the barbarians and was a defining characteristic of the city-state or polis.[3]

As the population of Greece grew, resources were stretched to the point where groups left to found colonies. As early as the eighth century BCE, Greek colonies were established in Italy and Sicily as well as on the coast of the Black Sea. The colonies were established according to the principles of the city-states in Greece with each colony supported by an existing polis. With increased contact with the wider world came increased trade, but also warfare. Inevitably, many strong states preyed on their weaker neighbors. This had an impact on the nature of Greek warfare, and toward the end of the eighth century BCE the hoplite phalanx—heavily armed, spear- and shield-carrying Greek infantrymen working closely together—became the basic form of military organization.

The appearance of the hoplites encouraged the development of the polis in two ways. First, it devalued the role of Homer's warrior-chieftain who heroically engages in single combat. Instead, steadfastness among the ranks was the key. Second, the creation of a phalanx required a communal effort and drew on the dedication and courage of all male citizens.[4] As we will see in the work of Herodotus (c. 484–425 BCE) on the Greek war with Persia (present-day Iran), such courage was enhanced if the soldier believed he was fighting for his liberty and the continuation of his way of life. Although power was widely dispersed among several city-states in this Greek "international" system, one in particular—Sparta—gained renown for its military prowess and martial spirit.

Homer's Epic Poems

Unfortunately, we know virtually nothing about Homer as a person. We are not even sure exactly when he lived; most accounts indicate sometime between the twelfth and eighth centuries BCE. The Greeks attributed the *Iliad* and the *Odyssey* to this single poet, with tradition suggesting he lived on the Greek island of Chios. In these two works, Homer creatively records the story of the Greek triumph over Troy and the fantastical adventures of Odysseus on his return home from the war. Historical accuracy was not Homer's purpose so much as it was to tell a good story. The importance of his works, then, is not so much for their contribution to history *per se* and certainly not any direct contribution to thinking about international relations.

Rather, Homer's influence on later Greek writers—all of whom were familiar with the *Iliad* and the *Odyssey*—stemmed from the fact that, for the Greeks, history and epic poetry were closely associated. Indeed, how Greek history was written and its depiction of many historical events as tragic drama can be directly traced to Homer and other Greek epic poets. Furthermore, many of the same questions Homer raised about the ability of individuals to control their fates and the nature of cause and effect in politics and international relations would be dealt with by Herodotus, Thucydides, Plato, Aristotle, Polybius, and

---

[3] Rhodes, *The Greek City States*, ix–x.
[4] Donald Kagan, *The Great Dialogue: History of Greek Political Thought from Homer to Polybius* (New York: Free Press, 1965), 17–18.

later Roman historians (even though their answers would be different and certainly less entertaining than Homer's rendering).

Determinism and Voluntarism

The *Iliad* presents a vivid and tragic view of the world, depicting the impact of events on both humans and the divine. The first line reflects this interaction between mortals and gods: "Sing, goddess, of the anger of Achilles, son of Peleus, the accursed anger which brought uncounted anguish on the Achaians and hurled down to Hades many mighty souls of heroes, making their bodies the prey to dogs and the birds' feasting: and this was the working of Zeus' will."[5]

Throughout the narrative, choices by individuals have dramatic consequences, such as the cause of the war between the Greeks and Trojans: Paris' seduction and abduction of Helen. Such individual actions as opposed to factors so familiar to the modern world—divergent ideologies, militaristic societies, or extreme nationalism—are critical. Even the depictions of battles very often come down to combat between individuals whose bravery and other virtues decide the outcome as opposed to the superiority of weaponry, so important in modern warfare.

Humans, however, do share center stage with the gods. As powerful as Agamemnon or Odysseus might be, the gods ultimately, and very often capriciously, determine matters of life and death. Their constant intervention places boundaries or limits on the ability of humans to control their fates. As Achilles says to Priam, who has come to plead for the body of his dead son: "This is the fate the gods have spun for poor mortal men, that we should live in misery."[6]

Notwithstanding these supernatural interventions, human will—agency in present-day theorizing—still can be decisive in Homer's epics. In the *Iliad*, for example, it is Achilles who takes the leading role in subduing the Trojans even though his own vulnerability subsequently will result in his death. The important point here, however, is not the death of Achilles, but what he can accomplish in life. To Homer, human beings are not merely or always the captive of fate, the gods, or even human nature. Individuals can have a decisive effect on the initiation, conduct, and outcome of wars because human agency—volition or free will—is possible.

Homer describes how the Greeks had constructed a huge wooden horse that they placed just outside the city gates of Troy. Thinking the Greeks had withdrawn their forces from the area, the Trojans pulled the horse inside the city only to be surprised that the Greeks had hidden soldiers within it. The stuff of legend, the tale does point to the decisive role human deception and surprise can play in warfare—whether it be in ancient times or the twenty-first century.

This belief that gods or other supernatural forces do play a role is an early example of the determinist mode of thought, emphasizing as well chance

---

[5] Homer, *The Iliad*, trans. Martin Hammond (Harmondsworth, UK: Penguin Books, 1987), I: 1–34.

[6] Homer, *Iliad*, XXIV: 491–537.

phenomena or the uncertainty that surrounds human events. Even biblical references in the Judeo-Christian tradition (as at Jericho where God gives Joshua the tactical guidance instrumental in producing a victory) are consistent with this *deus ex machina* way of thinking. Godly interventions matter.

Coping with uncertainty or fortune and the issue of volition, voluntarism, or free will are also recurrent themes in later writings on international politics. As part of the Greco-Roman revival in Western thought, for example, Machiavelli also raised this ancient theme in his discussion of how to deal boldly with *Fortuna* (chance phenomena feminized in effect as Lady Luck), a concern that would be echoed still later (1832) in Carl von Clausewitz's treatment of the uncertainties that obtain in the "fog of war" and "friction" (when put to the test, plans for combat are often at odds with realities that confront military commanders).

In the *Odyssey*, Homer underscores the importance of physical, moral, and intellectual strength that allows humans to prevail in their competition with external forces. Although he has the goddess Athena's backing and moral support, in adventure after adventure Odysseus, a veteran of the Trojan War, extricates himself and others from danger through application of human skill, particularly his mental agility and cleverness in dealing with often life-threatening situations.

While the *Iliad* is essentially a tragedy about war, the *Odyssey* is a romance. Taken together, these two great epic poems raise basic issues concerning the nature of human existence. As a result, they have had great effect not only on the subsequent course of Western literature but also on thinking about politics.[7]

Herodotus—The "Father of History"

Writing several hundred years after Homer and also known for his exaggerations, sometimes presenting supposition as fact, Herodotus (about 484 to 430 BCE) nevertheless is often referred to as the "father of history." Just as Homer had chronicled the Trojan wars, Herodotus details the Persian wars of Cyrus the Great (d. 529 BCE), Cambyses (d. 521 BCE), Darius (d. 486 BCE), and Xerxes (d. 465 BCE) and in the process takes many entertaining diversions that enlighten the reader on such matters as the Egyptian mummification process and the gruesome methods of sacrifice carried out by the Scythians in the eastern part of Persia or present-day Iran.[8]

The first half of his work concerns the rise of Persia, and the second half focuses on the great conflict between Persia and Greece. As he states, his purpose was to "set down to preserve the memory of the past by putting on record the astonishing achievements both of our own and of other peoples; and more particularly, to show how they came into conflict."

---

[7] Hammond, "Introduction" to *The Iliad*, 16.

[8] Herodotus, *The Histories*, trans. Aubrey de Selincourt and A. R. Burn (London: Penguin Books, 1954, 1972), II: 83–90; IV: 59–71. All quotes from Herodotus in subsequent pages are from this translation and are found in Books I, III, IV, V, VII, VIII, and IX.

Herodotus was particularly well suited for this role. Born in a town on the southern Aegean coast of Asia Minor, he was a subject of the Persian Empire. This is perhaps why he was able to travel so far and wide to Egypt, Babylon (in Mesopotamia or present-day Iraq), and up to the Black Sea. As a young man he apparently lived on the island of Samos, and came to exhibit respect and fondness for Periclean Athens, a city he obviously knew quite well. By the time of his death in an Athenian-founded state in southern Italy, the Peloponnesian War of 431 BCE had broken out. The deterioration in Athenian-Spartan relations was probably an impetus for Herodotus to remind the Greeks of their collective heroism in repelling Persian invaders at Marathon, Salamis, and Plataea.

Herodotus is of interest to those of us who study international relations for at least three reasons. First, conflict among different city-states, empires, and peoples is the pervasive theme throughout his work. Second, the primary interest of leaders has historically been the realist one of maintaining the security and autonomy of the state through the marshaling of a state's internal resources or by its participation in alliances, policies quite evident throughout *The Histories*. Finally, like Homer, Herodotus also was interested in how fate or the gods tended to frustrate the aspirations of statesmen and military leaders.

Herodotus on Conflict and War

Compared to Thucydides, Herodotus's *The Histories* places more emphasis on description than on causal or other analysis of events. He does not lay out a basic argument, for example, as to the underlying cause of war between Persia and its neighbors. Like Homer, Herodotus sees war as simply a fact of life, an occurrence as natural and inevitable as the changing of the seasons.

Familiarity with other cultures, states, or empires does not mean acceptance of them, much less any notion that there could be a community of mankind among them. For example, Herodotus notes: "Like the Egyptians, the Scythians are dead-set against foreign ways, especially against Greek ways." As a result, warring among the ancient peoples was the dominant mode of international relations, in which defeat very often meant the destruction of a city, the death of all male adults (or their enslavement), and the selling of women and children into slavery.

In describing the outbreak of various wars, Herodotus gives particular emphasis to what we today call the individual level of analysis. The desire of a ruler to secure power, glory, wealth, or revenge is very often all that is required to plunge a state or empire into war. Croesus (d. 547 BCE), king of Lydia, for example, had a "craving to extend his territories." Similarly, following the conquest of Egypt, Xerxes called a conference of the leading men of his country and addressed them as follows:

> Do not suppose, gentlemen, that I am departing from precedent in the course of action I intend to undertake. We Persians have a way of living, which I have inherited from my predecessors and propose to follow. I have learned from my elders that ever since Cyrus deposed Astyages and we took over from the

Medes the sovereign power we now possess, we have never yet remained inactive. This is God's guidance, and it is by following it that we have gained our great prosperity.

Of our past history you need no reminder; for you know well enough the famous deeds of Cyrus, Cambyses, and my father Darius, and their addition to our empire. Now I myself, ever since my accession, have been thinking how not to fall short of the kings who have sat upon this throne before me, and how to add as much power as they did to the Persian empire. And now at last I have found a way to win for Persia not glory only, but a country as large and as rich as our own—indeed richer than our own—and at the same time to get satisfaction and revenge.

His plan was to invade Greece and destroy Athens.

Herodotus on Security

Given the desire of such leaders to expand their power and the resultant conflicts, it is only natural that the key interest of all states is to maintain their respective security and autonomy. In a typical aside, Herodotus states that although "in most respects I do not admire" the Scythians, they "have managed one thing, and that the most important in human affairs, better than anyone else on the face of the earth—I mean their own preservation." Interest defined in terms of security is the criterion to be applied in any number of circumstances. Present-day realist works also emphasize survival or preservation—their security—as the core interest of states. Thus, in determining whether Athens would have command of a combined fleet from several Greek city-states, Herodotus notes that the proposal for Athenian command "had not been well received by the allied states." As a result, the "Athenians waived their claim in the interest of national survival" because they understood the danger attendant upon a lack of unity. The Athenians reasoned that "a quarrel about the command would certainly mean the destruction of Greece" at the hands of the Persians. Herodotus comments that in this the Athenians were perfectly right in trying to avoid internal strife.

This realism also admits to the use of deception as a means to survive and reap benefit in such a world. In a line of reasoning one finds in our own time, Herodotus quotes the Persian, Darius, who uses deception in an act of self-interest:

> If a lie is necessary, why not speak it? We are all after the same thing, whether we lie or speak the truth: our own advantage. Men lie when they think to profit by deception, and tell the truth for the same reason—to get something they want, and to be the better trusted for their honesty. It is only two different roads to the same goal. Were there no question of advantage, the honest man would be as likely to lie as the liar is, and the liar would tell the truth as readily as the honest man.

For Herodotus the security of the Greek polis is of special concern because the polis was a special political unit. Similar to the views of Plato and Aristotle,

Herodotus believes that the highest reward for an individual was to be honored and respected by citizens of the polis. Conversely, the worst possible fate was to be exiled. To fight bravely for one's city-state was particularly commendable, and death would bestow upon the individual a certain immortality.

This emphasis on the state as the object of one's loyalty and devotion is expressed in a mythical conversation between Croesus, the wealthy king of Lydia (located in present-day western Turkey), and Solon of Athens. Croesus asks Solon to name the happiest man he has ever met, assuming Solon will name the king. But Solon tells us it is Tellus of Athens because, besides living in a prosperous city and having fine sons and enough wealth to live comfortably, "he had a glorious death. In a battle . . . he fought for his countrymen, routed the enemy, and died like a soldier; and the Athenians paid him the high honor of a public funeral on the spot where he fell."

Herodotus's narrative repeatedly describes two basic approaches leaders can follow to maintain a state's security—by marshaling internal resources or through the creation of an alliance. More than two millennia later, Kenneth N. Waltz and other realists observe how states resort to internal or external means to enhance their security. If states cannot deter an aggressor through the existence or establishment of a balance of power, then sufficient internal resources have to be mustered to repel the invader.

Herodotus underscores the importance of a state controlling economic and military capabilities, key elements of power. Thus, he comments that the Persian king Darius, "having an immense revenue in money and an unlimited number of men to draw upon in his Asiatic dominions," felt strong enough to take on his enemies. Similarly, to conduct a war against the nearby Greek island of Aegina, Athens utilized "a large sum of money from the produce [silver] of the mines at Laurium" to construct two hundred ships. With the threat of the Persian invasion, Athens had to expand further this fleet by constructing new ships. Indeed, this emphasis on tangible or material capabilities is central to present-day realist understandings of how states provide for their security.

But superior economic and military capabilities are not enough to guarantee victory. In this regard, Herodotus also sees the nature of a social-political system (state-societal level of analysis) as a potentially important capability. Whether a function of unbiased historical analysis or his admiration for Periclean Athens, he presents one of his few explicit propositions when he observes that fighting capabilities were greater when Athens was in a democratic period with freedoms assured than "while they were oppressed under a despotic government."

Thus, they "had no better success in war than any of their neighbors," but once freed, "they proved the finest fighters in the world. This clearly shows that, so long as they were held down by authority, they deliberately shirked their duty . . . but when freedom was won, then every man amongst them was interested in his own cause." Some two millennia later, Machiavelli observed the fighting value of citizen armies. For their part, Oliver Cromwell in the English civil war, George Washington in the American revolution, and Napoleon Bonaparte in the French revolutionary war depended upon citizen soldiers to defeat armies made up of professionals and mercenaries.

Before the Persian invasion, Xerxes makes the same point to the Greek exile Demartus: "Will the Greeks dare to lift a hand against me?" Demartus observes how "poverty is my country's inheritance . . . but valor she won for herself by wisdom and the strength of the law." Speaking of the Spartans in particular: "They will not under any circumstances accept terms from you which would mean slavery for Greece."

Xerxes finds this hard to understand, believing that free men could not fight as well as those of his army who are made courageous due to a fear of their own generals and king. Demartus responds that "they [the Spartans] are free—yes—but not entirely free; for they have a master, and that Master is Law, which they fear much more than your subjects fear you. Whatever this master commands, they do." For Herodotus, it is this emphasis on the rule of law that sets the Greeks apart from the Persians and other "barbarians."

Herodotus thinks that the nature of a political-social system is a potential source of power that influences state behavior. In the debate among Persian leaders on the relative merits of democracy, oligarchy, and monarchy—the first time that this basic typology appears in Western literature—the advocate of democracy points to envy and pride as the "typical vices of a monarch" that "are the root cause of all wickedness: both lead to acts of savage and unnatural violence." By contrast, the argument is that when the people are in power they "do none of the things that monarchs do."

Or is it correct, as Darius argues, that "in a democracy, malpractices are bound to occur" and that oligarchies tend toward "violent personal feuds" and quarrels that "lead to open dissension, and then to bloodshed"? Whatever the truth in the matter, the important point is that, as Herodotus has constructed the debate, all agree on one thing—that the constitution or political structure and associated norms affect significantly the behavior exhibited by a state and its agents.

Does Herodotus suggest that democracies, oligarchies, or monarchies are more peaceful in terms of their foreign and military policies? No, he does not. Given the violent world of international relations at the time, Herodotus is simply making the narrower point that democracies are best able to ensure the security of the state as the citizens have something to lose—their liberty. As we will see, both Livy and Machiavelli address this theme at some length, arguing that republican regimes in which people have some degree of influence in the government are the most secure, but not necessarily peaceful.

As for the second means by which a state can meet a threat to its security—joining an alliance—Herodotus notes several instances where the threat was severe enough that various tribes or states joined together to repulse the invader. The Scythians realized "they were unequal to the task of coping with Darius in a straight fight," so they "sent off messengers to their neighbors whose chiefs had already met and were forming plans to deal with what was evidently a threat to their safety." The Scythian envoys asked for their support, pleading for a common plan of action. Failure to do so would affect them as much as the Scythians because "this invasion is aimed at you as much as at us, and, once we have gone under, the Persians will never be content to leave you unmolested."

There is, therefore, strength in unity. Lack of unity undercuts the capability to provide for defense. Herodotus observes how the Greeks had the "hope of uniting, if it were possible, the whole Greek world" against a Persian invasion led by Xerxes. After sending spies to observe the Persian forces and thus gather intelligence, diplomats were dispatched to conclude alliances with other Greek city-states to bring "all the various communities to undertake joint action in face of the common danger."

A common external threat, however, does not always lead to a countervailing alliance. As Xerxes's forces moved to conquer Greece, "various Greek communities . . . viewed the coming danger with very different eyes. Some had already made their submission and were consequently in good spirits." This bandwagoning effect was offset by the decision of Athens to commit its full military capabilities—particularly its navy—to an alliance with Sparta, its rival, in an attempt to defeat the Persians. Herodotus observes that "one is surely right in saying that Greece was saved by the Athenians. It was the Athenians who held the balance—whichever side they joined was sure to prevail." The Greek naval victory in 480 BCE at Salamis (near the Athenian port of Piraeus) led by Themistocles against Xerxes's Persian forces bore this out.

Unity against an external security threat is enhanced if the threatened states have developed some sense of common identity. Herodotus relates how Spartan envoys arrived in Athens, concerned lest the Athenians ally with the Persians against Spartan and other Greek interests. The envoys were assured by the Athenians that they would not betray the Greek cause, least of all to the Persians. Indeed, Athens would support "the Greek nation—the community of blood and language, temples and ritual; our common way of life."

But in the absence of an external threat, such common bonds may not be enough to unite people sharing a common identity. Herodotus tells us that "the population of Thrace [present-day northeastern Greece and Bulgaria] is greater than any country in the world except India." Thus, he comments that "if the Thracians could be united under a single ruler, or combine, they would be the most powerful nation on earth, and no one could cope with them."

At the time Darius was moving toward Greece, the Thracians were not unified and hence were conquered. Similarly, according to one Persian observer, in the absence of external threats, the Greeks tended to start fights among themselves "on the spur of the moment without sense or judgment to justify them." Somehow it was difficult for the Greeks even though "they all talk the same language . . . to be able to find a better way of settling their differences by negotiation, for instance, or an interchange of views—indeed by anything rather than fighting."

Fate—Determinism vs. Voluntarism

As for the issue of determinism versus voluntarism and the ability of leaders as agents to control and predict international events, Herodotus's account—like Homer's presentation—includes a great deal of the metaphysical. Oracles and prophecy do matter and hence heavily influence, if not determine, decisions and outcomes—the oracle taken as truth teller. Thus, Herodotus relates how the oracle warned the Euboeans (Euboea, the second largest Greek island after

Crete), but "this warning they ignored; and the result was great suffering." In yet another place, Herodotus asserts that "the prophecy of the oracle was fulfilled."

Cambyses, son of the Persian king, Cyrus, concedes "that it is not in human power to avert what is destined to be," but it is not clear that Herodotus himself always accepts such determinism. In some cases he merely is descriptive of these influences on decision-making. Thus, Xerxes was misled when his cousin only told him good news: "Any prophecy which implied a setback to the Persian cause he would be careful to omit."

At other times, advice from the oracles would be ignored. Concerning the Athenians, Herodotus tells us that "not even the terrifying warnings of the oracle at Delphi could persuade them to abandon Greece; they stood firm and had the courage to meet the invader." The oracle at Delphi was always a woman who spoke through intermediaries in riddles that needed to be interpreted. Sometimes fate seems to seal events, other times not to predestine them. In such circumstances, human agency—will or volition—may prevail.

SUN TZU

Far away from the world of the ancient Greeks, Sun Tzu (544–496 BCE), observed the conduct of political entities in ancient China, particularly on the ways and means of warfare. Sun Tzu's short treatise *The Art of War* is among the most quoted works today on leadership and strategy in the realms of warfare, sports, business, politics, and even marriage. It is also reflected in popular culture. In isolation, the pithy phrases from *The Art of War* can sound like clichés. But from the perspective of international relations, the work, taken as a whole, can be seen as providing a coherent argument and advice on how a leader can defend the state. As such, it reflects the realist perspective. As one of the foremost classic works of Eastern thought, it reflects Taoist philosophy and addresses the conduct of war and competition between states in an almost poetic fashion that one will simply not find in Western works on strategy and the conduct of international relations.

Over the years the work has enjoyed broad popularity. The text made its way to Japan via Korea around 516 CE. In 1772 it was translated into French by a Jesuit priest who came across the text in Beijing, China. In 1905 a British artillery captain studying in Japan made the first English translation.[9] An edition of the work was published during World War II under the assumption it would benefit the military planning of the British Royal Air Force. It was also supposedly utilized by both the Communist Chinese leader Mao Zedong and his nationalist rival, Chiang Kai-shek, during the Chinese civil war (1927–1949). In the West it has often been viewed as a means to discern the Chinese "mindset." With the current fascination and concern over the rise of China and its use of "asymmetric warfare," it can be expected that *The Art of War* will not lack for new and avid readers.[10]

---

[9] Sun Tzu, *The Art of War*, trans. Samuel Griffith (London: Oxford University Press, 1971), 169.
[10] See Ralph D. Sawyer and Mei-chün Sawyer, *The Tao of Deception: Unorthodox Warfare in Historic and Modern China* (New York: Basic Books, 2007).

Historical Context

The Zhou dynasty lasted longer than any other dynasty in Chinese history, approximately 1050–221 BCE. The eastern province was controlled until about 771 BCE when the weakening of centralized Zhou authority occurred. The royal court fled to the west where it maintained some degree of political influence for another five hundred years. Its flight was due to the rise of neighboring hegemonic kingdoms that vied for expanded power and territory, not unlike what would occur in Europe beginning in the fifteenth century. In the Chinese case, there were seven major competitors.

Fighting was initially seasonal and involved perhaps only a few thousand troops. But by the end of the sixth century BCE, as competition among rulers became fiercer, larger armies were created. In effect, an arms race occurred involving not only soldiers, but also supplies, weapons, and bureaucracies to administer them. A perpetual struggle for predominance required the mobilization of resources to engage in total war. This is also similar to what later occurred in Europe with the rise of centralized, expanded state power. In both China and Europe, Charles Tilly's observation seems to hold that war made the state and the state made war.[11]

This trend of competition continued over the next two hundred years so that by the third century larger states had created immense armies, in some cases up to 100,000 soldiers. This has been appropriately termed the Warring States period. It ended in 221 BCE with the victory of the Qin dynasty over its competitors.[12]

The Art of War

It was at the end of the sixth century BCE with the expansion of power and competition among warring rulers that *The Art of War* was likely written, though there has admittedly been much debate as to when the text was written and who was actually the author. A popular theory is that it was supposedly a general by the name of Sun Wu ("Wu" means "warrior") who desired an audience with the king of Wu, ruler of the eastern coastal state, to be able to impart practical martial wisdom. Little is known about Sun Wu. But what is known is that by the time of the Han dynasty (206 BCE–220 CE), his fame as a strategist and his treatise were well known in China. Given the life-and-death struggles among kings and warlords, any strategic advice that provided military advantage was welcome.

Sun Wu's advice is a series of aphorisms or maxims, some quite enigmatic, originally written on bamboo strips and tied together and rolled up into scrolls. This was typical of authors at the time who did not write "books" in the modern sense but rather wrote down sayings, verses, proverbs, short stories, and

---

[11] Charles Tilly, *Coercion, Capital, and European States, AD 990–1990* (Cambridge, MA: Blackwell, 1990).

[12] Discovered by farmers in 1974, it was around 210 BCE that the famous seven thousand terracotta warriors were created by artisans of the Emperor Qin.

essays.[13] In modern print the work is less than a hundred pages consisting of thirteen essays or chapters purportedly written by a "Master Sun Tzu." It is designed to be of practical worth, ranging from the strategic to the tactical, on how to manage these new mass armies in defense of the state and to deal with foreign threats.

If taken individually or out of context, the aphorisms can seem quite trite. But there is an interconnectedness to the entire work. It is the role of the commander or strategist to assess the relative importance of each component and, taken in combination, develop a strategy that can deceive an opponent. This emphasis on the role of rationality in planning for the defense of the state—the ultimate and most important responsibility of the ruler—is associated with Sun Tzu and others like Machiavelli in the sixteenth or Clausewitz in the nineteenth centuries who accepted what are essentially realist premises.[14]

The Art of War is an interesting contrast to much of the conventional wisdom of the time with its emphasis on martial virtues, valor, and the glory of war that was so much an aspect of the elite, aristocratic ethos. On the other hand, the work can also be seen as a refutation of the perspective of Confucius (561–479 BCE) who viewed war as evil and condemned the military obsessions of rulers. If war was to be fought, it should be done so in an ethical manner, meaning the cause must be a worthy one and have the support of the people. Hence *The Art of War* occupies a middle ground between these two other perspectives.

As a work of strategic theory with tactical insights applicable to the planning for battle, the thirteen chapters can be broken down in the following manner: chapter 1, making of plans; chapter 2, waging war; chapters 3 through 12, the required talents of a military commander; chapter 13, espionage.[15]

The initial chapter begins with an incontestable observation and justification for *The Art of War*: "War is a grave affair of state; it is a place of life and death, a road to survival and extinction, a matter to be pondered carefully." Such deliberations are framed by Five Fundamentals that allow one to compare and contrast the approach to war taken by different leaders and commanders. The first is "The Way," which requires military men to be of one mind with their rulers and be willing to die for them. Second, Heaven, is reflected in the yin and yang (the two positive and negative forces in the universe), cold and hot, and the cycle of the seasons. Third, Earth is viewed in terms of distance and proximity, open and confined ground, ease and danger, and life and death. Fourth,

---

[13] For many years there was skepticism concerning *The Art of War* regarding its authenticity with the suggestion it had been heavily rewritten over the years. There were also doubts that Master Sun had even existed. Then in the 1970s copies of the bamboo text were unearthed in two different places in China. When deciphered, the text essentially matched that of the accepted traditional text of thirteen. John Minford, "Introduction" to Sun Tzu, *The Art of War* (New York: Penguin Books), xxii.

[14] The role of emotion and passion is strikingly absent from *The Art of War*. This is quite different from the classic work by Carl von Clausewitz who emphasizes the role of passion (associated with the masses) as part of his analytical trinity. See Clausewitz, *On War*, ed. and trans. Michael Howard and Peter Paret (Princeton, NJ: Princeton University Press, 1984), 89.

[15] All subsequent direct quotes from *The Art of War* come from the Minford edition.

command consists of wisdom, integrity, compassion, courage, and severity. Finally, discipline is in terms of organization, chain of command, and control of expenditures.

Master Sun claims that "every commander is aware of these Five Fundamentals. He who grasps them wins; he who fails to grasp them loses." Such an assertion is to be found in the long history of political-military manuals and how-to works that claim to improve the chances of military victory for commanders.[16] Like Machiavelli, however, Sun Tzu also emphasizes the solidarity of the relationship between the commander and the ruler, of military strategy and tactics with political objectives. This is reflected in the fact that serious deliberation on war must start with this question: "Which ruler has the Way?" followed by "Which general has the ability?" All that follows—which army is more disciplined and stronger, which has the better-trained officers and system of rewards and punishment—is important, but of secondary concern to the qualities of the ruler and the commanding general.

Taken together, from the analysis of the Five Fundamentals "can be known victory and defeat." These "temple calculations" made before the battle is engaged are the keys to success. Poor calculation ahead of time leads to poor outcomes. Once a plan or strategy of military engagement is developed, the key to successful implementation is to "exploit the dynamic within" the plan to include opportunities that present themselves to the commander.

The emphasis on the use of deception at the strategic and tactical (battlefield) level is perhaps the best-known section of *The Art of War*—"The Way of War Is a Way of Deception." Pithy comments include "When able, feign inability"; "When near, appear far"; "Lure with bait; strike with chaos"; and "Attack where he is unprepared, appear where you are unexpected." Such advice is reflected in what has been termed the indirect approach to warfare as practiced by the Roman general Quintus Fabius against the Carthaginians in the second Punic War (218–202 BCE) and Nathaniel Greene in the Carolinas against the British during the American revolution.[17]

What could be termed an "effective force multiplier" to the Five Fundamentals and deception is the subject of the final chapter on espionage. The current world of cyber warfare refers to this as "information superiority." For Sun Tzu, the astute commander, collects and utilizes intelligence to his or her advantage. This involves not only its application in terms of deception operations against the enemy but also the use of spies.

Useful intelligence provided by espionage enhances the prospects of strategic and tactical success by not only helping to calculate where to strike the decisive blow against enemy forces but also to keep the enemy off-balance, thus

---

[16] For an overview of such historical works, see Beatrice Heuser, *The Evolution of Strategy: Thinking War from Antiquity to the Present* (Cambridge, UK: Cambridge University Press, 2010).

[17] In terms of strategic thinkers, the best-known exponent was the twentieth-century British writer B. H. Liddell Hart who emphasized the indirect approach in an age of mechanized warfare. Following Sun Tzu (whom he quotes extensively in the opening pages of his book *Strategy*), the dislocation of the enemy's psychological and physical balance is the prelude to victory. Surprise is a key component. See Hart, *Strategy* (New York: B.N. Publishing, 2009).

leaving his planning in a cloud of uncertainty. As he states: "Prior information enables wise rulers and worthy generals to move and conquer, brings them success beyond that of the multitude." It cannot be conjured up by spirits, but requires a substantial investment in time and money in individuals "who know the enemy's dispositions." In the context of the entire army, "none should be closer to the commander than his spies, none more highly rewarded." Enemy spies, if identified, might be bribed to become double agents and then used to spread disinformation. Sun Tzu ends his work with the observation that "spies are a key element in warfare. On them depends an army's every move."

The middle chapters, two through twelve, focus on specific strategic and tactical advice that any "skillful warrior" should consider in waging war. He begins the third chapter with perhaps the most famous and oft-quoted aphorism that is associated with Sun Tzu: "Ultimate excellence lies not in winning every battle, but in defeating the enemy without ever fighting." This is followed by his list of priorities that a commander should attack: the enemy's strategy, his alliances, his army, and finally the use of siege warfare against his cities. He is particularly scathing in his assessment of siege warfare and protracted warfare, which costs heavily in terms of time, men, and matériel. He repeats his adage that the skillful strategist ideally defeats the enemy without actually engaging in battle.

In terms of the relationship between the king and the commander—what today is termed the civil-military nexus—Sun Tzu sides with the commander. The general is "the prop of the nation" and "a ruler [who] can bring misfortune upon his troops" by "ignorant meddling in military decisions." Indeed, one of Sun Tzu's five essentials for victory is to "have a capable general, unhampered by his sovereign." Not surprisingly, such a perspective is understandably popular among uniformed military personnel who, once war is declared, would prefer their civilian overlords to avoid meddling in operational and tactical-level planning and operations.[18]

As *The Art of War* aspires to be a practical manual, it is understandable that the main focus is on the perspective of one side in a military contest. This might leave the impression that Sun Tzu does not adequately take into account the fact that the commander is not operating in a vacuum—the enemy, it is said, gets a vote as well. In other words, strategy and warfare, in the language of IR game theory, is at a minimum a two-person game. Each military decision that is carried out has to be recalibrated once the enemy has responded.

Sun Tzu, however, quotes an aphorism that must have been popular even in his day: "Know the enemy, know yourself, and victory is never in doubt, not in a hundred battles." In contemporary strategic thinking, this would be a call for "net assessment," the need to consider how the strategy and capabilities of both sides compare to one another. Sun Tzu, in other words, does indeed recognize the interactive nature of strategy and warfare. He goes on to note that

---

[18] For the argument that civilian leaders must be involved in all aspects of wartime military planning and even operations, see the case studies in Eliot Cohen, *Supreme Command: Soldiers, Statesmen, and Leadership in Wartime* (New York: Anchor Books, 2002).

if the commander knows only his side but not the enemy's, the result, at best, is one defeat for every victory. The worst possible situation is one in which the commander is ignorant of himself and the enemy, all but guaranteeing defeat in every battle.

The other middle chapters consist of specific military advice in such areas as the form and disposition of troops, indirect versus direct warfare, the chaos and energy of combat, the importance of the concentration of forces, the morale of the troops, and the impact of terrain. In these areas, one finds striking parallels to other works of war and strategy such as found in the works by Prussian Carl von Clausewitz and Swiss-born Antoine Jomini, which have influenced realist thinking.[19]

Kautilya

As best can be determined, Kautilya was the fourth-century BCE author of the ancient Indian political treatise, *The Arthashastra*.[20] He was supposedly the key adviser and mentor in assisting the rise to power of the first Mauryan emperor, Chandragupta, who ascended the throne in 321 BCE. As with many ancient works, there is debate among scholars as to whether Kautilya existed and, if he did, whether he was the sole composer of *The Arthashastra* or whether it is a compilation of various works. The manuscript was lost for many years but rediscovered in the twentieth century.

The focus is on the art of government in the widest sense. The purpose of the state is threefold: protect it from external aggression, maintain law and order within the state, and safeguard the welfare of the people. The advice is practical and presented in a rather didactic manner as one would expect from a handbook.

The section on foreign policy comprises less than one-fifth of *The Artha-shastra* but is the reason Kautilya has been deemed an important analyst of interstate relations. As with other writers, he is not concerned with a particular state at a particular point in time but wishes to generalize about international relations. The perspective he adopts is that of an individual king who, in modern parlance, is motivated by pursuing the national interest.

Kautilya, like Machiavelli, is especially concerned with the security and foreign policy of small states existing in a highly competitive international environment. Practical advice is derived from a focus on several considerations including relative power among states, the need to balance short-term advantages with potential future long-term advantages, and intangible and unpredictable factors that can affect foreign policy choices. By the use of hypothetical scenarios, he can explore various foreign policy options and avoid becoming bogged down in historical description.

---

[19] Clausewitz, *On War*; Antoine Henri de Jomini, *The Art of War* (London: Greenhill Books, 1996; First published in 1838).
[20] Kautilya, *The Arthashastra*, ed. and trans. L. N. Rangarajan (London: Penguin Books, 1992). All quotes are from this edition.

War is broadly defined to include four categories: war by diplomacy in which a king finds himself in a weaker military position and decides it is unwise to engage in battle; open warfare which involves specifying time and place for battle and devising an appropriate strategy; concealed warfare to include psychological warfare; and clandestine warfare designed to achieve the objective without actual battle, primarily by utilizing assassination as a tool. Defensive measures include the establishment of forts designed for different terrain—mountains, rivers, jungle, deserts. Kautilya goes so far as to list required ordnance for each fort to include weapons, armor, and siege engines. His obsession with practical advice leads him to specify the number of rations required for elephants, horses, and men. In terms of force structure, he follows the classic Indian approach of elephants, chariots, horses, and infantry and how they should be utilized in battle.

Covert operations and spying are important aspects of foreign policy. Covert operations require the creation of a secret service. Kautilya's detailed analysis delineates the various types of agents including assassins, poisoners, double agents, monks, and even "poor but intrepid widows, who need to work for their living." Useful disguises for the covert agents are, for example, traders, holy men, dwarfs, storytellers, and former thieves. As with Sun Tzu, the gathering of intelligence is critical: "A king shall have his agents in the courts of the enemy, the ally . . . to spy on the kings as well as their eighteen types of high officials." The secret service performs not only an external function but also a critical role in terms of domestic security by surveilling ministers as well as the general populace for signs of unrest or treason.

Although not rediscovered until 1904, Kautilya's work certainly deserves to be viewed as a pioneer in the analysis of statecraft. *The Arthashastra* shares interesting affinities with that of Sun Tzu, Machiavelli, and Clausewitz and hence is firmly in the genre of realist thinking.[21]

Overview of Early Greek, Chinese, and Indian Thinkers

Homer's influence on thinking about international relations stems from his framing epic poems in the context of determinism versus the voluntarism or free will of human agency. Individuals do matter, not only in terms of the onset of the Trojan war, but also concerning how it was fought—its outcome linked to physical, moral, and intellectual strength. Nevertheless, to Homer, gods and oracles still can dominate events if they choose to do so, making it difficult for mere humans to foresee the outcomes of their actions.

As for Herodotus, his history is also a tale of conflict, albeit with less emphasis on the intervention of gods in the affairs of human beings. A concern for the security and autonomy of tribes, cultures, and city-states is a dominant theme. Individuals and their thirst for power and glory, however, very often initiate conflicts. Concerning the ability of countries to withstand aggressors, Herodotus makes it quite clear that the success of the Greeks against Persia was

---

[21] See Michael I. Handel, *Masters of War: Classical Strategic Thought*, 3rd ed. (London: Frank Cass, 2001).

to a great extent a function of the nature of the Greek city-states and their ability to command the loyalty of citizens. Consistent with present-day works on national security, the marshaling of internal resources and joining an alliance are two basic ways to defend a state's autonomy.

Much of the writing in ancient Greece on war and peace contributed in one way or another to the realist tradition and its attendant preoccupation with security. An exception was the playwright Aristophanes (c. 448–385 BCE) who raises antiwar themes in his farcical comedy *Lysistrata* in which the women agree to deny their favors to their husbands until the latter finally renounce warfare and make peace.

Although the destruction and human pain of war are present throughout Greek literature, this "make love, not war" notion originated by Aristophanes is hardly a major theme in Greek thought. Martial values like heroism and glory displayed in the *Iliad* and *Odyssey* and Herodotus's focus on recurring armed conflicts are the more enduring themes. As we discuss in the next section of this chapter, this is evident in the work of Thucydides (c. 460 to 400 BCE) who is responsible for writing the centerpiece of ancient Greek thinking about international politics—*History of the Peloponnesian War*.

As noted, the aphorisms in Sun Tzu's *The Art of War* can seem quite banal if not viewed in a broader context that emphasizes the role of the commander in developing a strategy that can defeat, outwit, and deceive an opponent. As with Kautilya and, later, Machiavelli, the emphasis on rational planning is in pursuit of the most important responsibility of any ruler—the defense of the state. Although *The Art of War* and *The Arthashastra* were not widely disseminated and known in the West until the twentieth century, they justifiably should be considered part of the realist intellectual tradition.

THUCYDIDES AND THE PELOPONNESIAN WAR

Thucydides's *History of the Peloponnesian War* is an account of the first twenty years of the fifth-century struggle (431 to 404 BCE) between two alliances dominated by Athens and Sparta. An Athenian of what we would call today the upper-middle class, Thucydides (c. 472–400 BCE) was a naval officer who was stripped of his command and banished from Athens in the seventh year of the war for failing to arrive in time to prevent the fall to the Spartans of the northern Macedonia city of Amphipolis.

His alleged failure as a military leader was history's gain. Thucydides made the most of his circumstances by traveling throughout Greece, witnessing or faithfully recording accounts of events. In effect, his writings pick up where Herodotus left off. He diverged from his predecessor, however, in that his work has virtually no role for gods, oracles, and omens. The result of Thucydides's efforts was the foremost work of the ancient era on international relations. No matter the theoretical orientation of present-day IR scholars and students, all have been directly or indirectly influenced by his work.

As we will see, a major reason for such an accolade is that Thucydides exhibits an intellectual characteristic common to IR theorists—the use of actual events to illustrate underlying patterns of world politics. Shedding light on recurrent behavior and trends is a major goal of his work. Not only does this history of the war move beyond a simple recounting of campaign strategies and battle tactics to the illumination of trends, but also moral issues are intimately intertwined with his analysis of the war. Specifically, Thucydides is interested in highlighting the difficulties of what could be termed the morality of exercising power.

We begin by briefly reviewing events of the hundred years before this period to set the stage for the discussion of *History of the Peloponnesian War*.[22] Such a review is also useful because it allows us to describe the nature of international relations in that part of the world, providing a benchmark to which we can compare state-centric politics more than two millennia later.

Historical Context

As is discussed in the first part of this chapter, the Hellenic world of the fifth century BCE was composed of a variety of political entities that today we call city-states. Their small populations, limited control of territory beyond city walls, and their proximity to other city-states made them more akin to the Italian Renaissance city-state system than to modern states which, compared to the Hellenic world, often consist of large populations and vast territorial expanses.

The political forms of city-states, as discussed by Plato and Aristotle, included monarchies that often degenerated into despotisms. Both monarchy and despotism involved rule by powerful individuals. Other forms of rule ranged from enlightened aristocracies to exploitative oligarchies (rule by the few) and, in some cases, rule by the many—democracies, although the "many" was limited to males deemed worthy of the title "citizen."

These democratic polities, such as Athens at the time of Pericles, came closest to the idea of an integrated, organic relation between state and society—the polis. At the same time, however, slavery was an accepted institution throughout the Hellenic world. This was true even in the democratic city-states that excluded slaves from their citizenry. Within this Greek system of city-states, some city-states were naturally more powerful than others, dominating weaker city-states and, perhaps, extracting tribute in return for military protection. Diplomatic practices were rudimentary, generally consisting of delegations traveling to other city-states to present demands, resolve disputes, or negotiate trade agreements.[23]

In the middle of the sixth century BCE, the city-state of Sparta was ruled by an aristocracy—considered by the Spartans to be an excellent form of government compared to the many tyrannies and oligarchies that ruled elsewhere. Aristocracy depended upon participation of the upper classes, accountability on

---

[22] The title of the work comes from the fact that Sparta was located in the geographic area of Greece known to this day as the Peloponnesus (or Peloponnese).

[23] For an in-depth discussion of the elements of the Greek city-state system, see Martin Wight, *Systems of States* (Leicester, UK: Leicester University Press, 1977), chap. 2. See also Sir Frank Adcock and D. J. Mosley, *Diplomacy in Ancient Greece* (New York: St. Martin's Press, 1975).

the part of the individuals chosen to preside over the city-state, and a strong warrior caste. The latter was particularly important as the vast majority of the population consisted of an underclass known as the helots who were excluded from participation in government and politics.

The expansion of Spartan power was confined principally to the Greek peninsula south of Athens (known as the Peloponnese or Peloponnesian peninsula); the primary goal was to assure that neighboring states would not be in a position to stir up trouble among the helots. This concern for domestic security tended to limit the extent of Spartan ambitions beyond the Peloponnesian peninsula because the Spartan leadership did not wish to have its military forces off in foreign lands should a helot revolt break out. City-states allied with Sparta were allowed to conduct their own affairs and were assured of Spartan military protection, but were pledged to support Sparta in time of need.[24]

As a result of being generally content to be the dominant power in the Peloponnese, the Spartans played a minor role in repelling the Persian invasion of northern Greece in 490 BCE, which ended with the spectacular Greek victory at the battle of Marathon described by Herodotus. Ten years later, however, the Spartans reluctantly agreed to accept command of combined Greek forces to repel the second Persian invasion of King Xerxes in 480 BCE.

Spartan and allied forces were unable to hold back the Persians at Thermopylae (the so-called 300 Spartans of historical and popular culture fame). The Spartans proposed to make a final stand at the Isthmus of Corinth, the gateway to the Peloponnese and the Spartan heartland. Not surprisingly, this trading of space for time was not acceptable to city-states located in the path of the advancing Persian army. The city-state of Athens, known for its navy as well as its democratic form of government that placed a great deal of power in the hands of its citizens, argued for a naval confrontation. At the epic battle of Salamis, the Athenians took the lead in defeating the Persian fleet. The following year the Spartan army and allies routed the Persians at the battle of Plataea, and Xerxes's forces retreated.

With the repulse of the Persians, Sparta returned to its traditional concerns and more limited sphere of influence on the Peloponnese. At this point Athens came to the fore and championed the cause of keeping the Persians deterred from launching another invasion of Greece. The institutional expression of this policy was the creation of the Delian League, comprised principally of the city-states most vulnerable to Persian pressure to include those along the west coast of Asia Minor (present-day Turkey) and islands in the Aegean.

As a result of a need to protect these city-states and sweep the Persians out of northern Greece, Athens continued to expand the size of its navy and other military forces. In the process, it became a major military power. Aside from the military buildup, the Athenians also reconstructed what were known as the "long walls" running from Athens down to the port of Piraeus. The walls

---

[24] Given that Sparta seemed relatively unconcerned with imperial ambitions, Michael W. Doyle prefers to speak of Spartan "hegemony" as opposed to a Spartan "empire." See his *Empires* (Ithaca, NY: Cornell University Press, 1986), 59.

provided a defensive perimeter designed to protect Athens from invaders and allow Athenian access to its naval fleet.

After a series of further victories against Persian forces, the Delian League totaled some two hundred members. But as so often happened in alliances once the foreign threat is neutralized, problems among the member city-states soon began to appear. This was in part due to resentment and fear of Athenian domination. In many cases, those city-states controlled by democratic factions remained faithful to Athens while those ruled by aristocracies began to look to Sparta. Attempts at defection led to Athenian military and political intervention, resulting in the Delian League eventually looking more like part of an Athenian empire than an alliance of independent city-states. These states, although formally autonomous polities, were forced either to contribute ships and crews or pay tribute to Athens.

A deterioration in relations between Athens and Sparta led in 457 BCE to the outbreak of war. Athens dominated central Greece and was easily the supreme sea power while Sparta controlled the Peloponnesian peninsula and was the dominant land power. By 454 direct conflict died down and a truce finally came into effect in 451. As a result, the Athenians could turn their attention to keeping their erstwhile Delian League allies in line. Athens used League resources to extend its power in campaigns against Corinth—about halfway between Athens and Sparta on a narrow peninsula that connects the Peloponnese to the Greek mainland—and the island of Aegina, not far from Athens. These campaigns had little, if anything, to do with the League's avowed purpose of repelling the Persians.

Following a peace treaty between the Greeks and Persians in 449, the Athenian leader Pericles invited all Greek city-states to attend a conference in Athens to improve relations. The offer was rejected by the city-states in the Peloponnese and was viewed with suspicion by other city-states subject to Athenian rule.

The Athenians put down unrest supported by the Spartans in the region known as Boeotia in central Greece, an action that threatened to renew direct conflict between Athens and Sparta. Thereafter, Athens and Sparta negotiated another peace treaty that was supposed to last thirty years. In return for allowing several reluctant city-states to leave the Delian League, Athens received Spartan recognition of Athenian rule over its remaining allies. The treaty in effect recognized spheres of influence and the virtue of the two principal city-states being roughly balanced in terms of power—what present-day structural realists call a bipolar distribution of power (see chapter 5).

The ensuing peace allowed the two rivals to consolidate their control in their respective spheres. Thucydides takes up the story in detail in 435 BCE, discussing specific events that led to the outbreak of the second Peloponnesian War. While the Greek international system is generally viewed by most scholars to have been bipolar (two major powers) in the distribution of capabilities between Athens and Sparta, other city-states like Corcyra, Thebes, Argos, and Corinth also had significant capabilities that distinguished them from the vast majority of small, less powerful city-states.

History of the Peloponnesian War: The Work Itself

Thucydides's *History of the Peloponnesian War* is an easily accessible work that does not require the reader to have any background knowledge of Greek philosophy, Hellenic myths, or the artistic brilliance of Greek sculptors and poets. One can simply enjoy it as an extraordinarily gripping account of war in all its manifestations.

Thucydides presents us with vivid and timeless portraits of prudent statesmen and grasping politicians, heroic officers and short-sighted generals, and the moral dilemmas facing all states throughout history. While his prose is generally straightforward and without rhetorical flourishes, the cumulative effect of many of his descriptions at times can be overwhelming. This is evident, for example, in his moving account of the effect of a plague upon Athenian society, which almost led to the complete social disintegration of this renowned city-state.[25]

Similarly, his harrowing account of the civil war in Corcyra (now the Greek island of Corfu) that set brother against brother and father against son accurately captures the essence of this most devastating type of war. Nor is it possible to be unmoved by his detailed account of the destruction of the Athenian military expedition to Sicily, an account that creates in the mind of the reader the impression that he or she is actually on the scene as Athenian officers desperately attempt to rally their troops to avoid brutal death or slavery.

Aside from the enjoyment of a fascinating story, there are other reasons IR scholars might wish greater familiarity with *History of the Peloponnesian War*. First, the work provides numerous analytical insights on world politics that are useful to anyone interested in understanding even present-day dynamics in international relations.

Second, the work offers cautionary tales for statesmen engaged in the conduct of foreign policy; it is one of the best examples of "learning from history." While the particulars of the war were certainly of interest to Thucydides, he hoped to reveal larger truths about the human condition and to highlight certain situations he expected to recur throughout the ages. As he states: "My work is not a piece of writing designed to meet the taste of an immediate public, but was done to last forever."[26] Thucydides was writing for the ages and he succeeded admirably.

Finally, *History of the Peloponnesian War* is a prime example of what has come to be known as the realist perspective—an image of international relations that traditionally has dominated the halls of power as well as the halls of academe. We engage in a detailed discussion of realism in chapter 5. As is noted, however, realist claims to exclusivity in terms of Thucydides are subject to dispute. We now will examine each of these contributions: analytical insights, cautionary tales for policy makers, and the realist image of international politics held by many theorists.

---

[25] For a chronological overview of the war and its impact, see Jennifer T. Roberts, *The Plague of War: Athens, Sparta, and the Struggle for Ancient Greece* (New York: Oxford University Press, 2017).

[26] Thucydides, *History of the Peloponnesian War*, III: 22. All direct quotes are from the Rex Warner translation of *History of the Peloponnesian War* (Harmondsworth: Penguin Books, 1954).

Analytical Insights from Thucydides

We begin this section with a discussion of Thucydides's answer to the basic question of what caused the outbreak of the Peloponnesian War. Thucydides was not simply interested in describing what happened during the war. The purpose of his narrative was to draw larger lessons about the general phenomenon of war that would stand the test of time. In doing so he makes a crucial distinction that can be applied to any war—the difference between the underlying and the immediate causes of a given war. For Thucydides, the underlying cause involved factors that had developed over a long time. Immediate causes included specific events or more recent developments that made war more likely or accounted for the timing of its outbreak.

Underlying Cause of War

What was the underlying cause of the Peloponnesian War? Thucydides's answer is straightforward: "What made war inevitable was the growth of Athenian power and the fear this caused in Sparta." To put it another way, Sparta was afraid of its relative decline compared to Athens. The explanatory emphasis is on how the overall changing distribution or balance of power in the Greek system of city-states generated suspicion and distrust. Thucydides mentions, for example, that the fortification of Athens and the building of the protective long walls made the Peloponnesians uneasy, with the worst possible interpretation placed upon these actions.

Some present-day theorists hypothesize that a critical, underlying cause of war with applicability down through the ages is Thucydides's emphasis on the link between the outbreak of war and a changing distribution of power in an international system they characterize as anarchic (lacking any central authority with power over separate states). Graham Allison even calls it the "Thucydides's trap" and asks if it is inevitable that war will occur between China and the United States, given fear in the latter about the rising power of the former.[27] Allison's argument is consistent with present-day power transition theory, the contention being that when a rival begins to gain on the dominant or hegemonic state, the probability of war increases.[28]

As with a rear-end auto collision, the dynamics of the process may vary: State A (the challenger) may be increasing in power while State B (the hegemon) remains static; or State A may be increasing in power faster than State B; or State A is only gradually increasing in power while State B is losing power. Whatever the particular dynamics may be, power transition theory has been applied by modern scholars to analyze major wars. Despite differences among them, these scholars all owe an intellectual debt to Thucydides who deserves credit as the first to have articulated the basic elements of power transition theory.[29]

---

[27] See Allison's *Destined for War: Can America and China Escape Thucydides's Trap?* (Boston: Houghton Mifflin, 2017).

[28] The best example of this work is Robert Gilpin, *War and Change in World Politics* (Cambridge, UK: Cambridge University Press, 1981). Power transition theory is discussed more fully in chapter 5.

[29] For a critique of the power transition thesis in the context of Thucydides's work, see Mark V. Kauppi, "Contemporary International Relations Theory and the Peloponnesian War," in *Hegemonic Rivalry: From Thucydides to the Nuclear Age*, ed. Richard Ned Lebow and Barry Strauss (Boulder, CO: Westview Press, 1991), 101–24.

Would war have broken out if the situation had been the reverse, if it were the Athenians who feared the growth of Spartan power? Power transition theory suggests this would have been very likely. Feeling fear and being afraid of the consequences of a relative decline in power vis-à-vis another state is something all leaders can experience, no matter what the nature of the regime. If there is one theme that dominates Thucydides's narrative, it is how fear time and again is the basic reason a city-state takes a particular action in the hope of safeguarding its security and independence.

Thucydides provides numerous examples. Why did the Athenians claim they initially increased their power? Because their chief motive was fear of Persia. Why did the Thessalians and Magnetes prepare for war? Because they were afraid that the army of Sitalces, allied with Athens, might descend upon them. Why did the Athenians send a fleet of ships to Mytilene? Because they were afraid Mytilene would form an alliance with a neighboring state. Why did the Athenians tell the Melians they must side with Athens and cannot be neutral? Because the Athenians feared not only that they would look weak in the eyes of other city-states, but also that Sparta might force the Melians to ally with them.

If anarchy—the absence of any authority above the ancient Greek city-states—and the shift in the balance of power or capabilities are the critical factors in explaining the outbreak of the Peloponnesian War, what about other factors? Does it matter whether the city-states are more authoritarian or democratic? What about human nature or other factors related to individuals or the groups they form?

Thucydides emphasizes differences between the Spartan and Athenian societies when he reports a speech by the Corinthians and Pericles's famous funeral oration in which he praised the unique aspects of Athenian society that supposedly would aid Athens in winning the war.[30] While Thucydides would agree with Herodotus's general observation that the type of political system or society may influence a state's foreign policy behavior, Thucydides does not see such factors as underlying causes of the Peloponnesian War. In other words, he does not emphasize the internal makeup of Greek city-states. He does not say war was inevitable because Sparta was a society glorifying martial virtues or because Athens was a limited democracy.

As with many present-day scholars who identify with him, Thucydides is pessimistic about human nature. He tells us about the horrors of the Corcyraean civil war and argues that "love of power, operating through greed and through personal ambition, was the cause of all these evils." People engaged in "savage and pitiless actions" and were "swept away into an internecine struggle by their ungovernable passions. Then, with the ordinary conventions of civilized life thrown into confusion, human nature, always ready to offend even where laws exist, showed itself proudly in its true colors."

No one is deterred by the claims of justice nor by the interests of the state. But while human nature is generally portrayed in a negative light, Thucydides does not argue that human nature in and of itself accounted for these acts—it

---

[30] Thucydides, *History of the Peloponnesian War*, I: 68–71; II: 35–46.

was interstate war and the desire of aristocratic and democratic factions to enlist outside support that destroyed the constraints of law and "forced [people] into a situation where they have to do what they do not want to do."

Immediate Causes of War

Thucydides observes that two disputes were immediate causes of the war. First, there was the matter of the island of Corcyra, today known as Corfu. Corcyra had been founded as a colony of Corinth, but as it prospered Corcyra took an increasingly independent stance. These two city-states became involved in a struggle over the colony of Epidamnus and, after being defeated in a naval battle by Corcyra, the Corinthians planned a major military operation.

This alarmed the Corcyraeans who went to Athens and asked for an alliance. After a lengthy debate among its citizens, Athens agreed, stating it would be for defensive purposes only. There was a general feeling that war with the Peloponnesian states was bound to come sooner or later, and the Athenians did not want the Corcyraean navy to fall into the hands of the Corinthians. Subsequently thwarted in its desire to conquer Corcyra due to the intervention of an Athenian naval force, Corinth charged Athens with breaking the truce between the Spartan and Athenian leagues and began to plot its revenge.

The second incident involved the city of Potidaea in northern Greece whose citizens were colonists of Corinth, yet were also tribute-paying allies of Athens. The Athenians feared Potidaea would be induced by Corinth to revolt and hence demanded that the city fortifications be torn down and hostages sent to Athens. In response to a plea from Corinth and the Potidaeans, Sparta pledged to come to their aid if they were attacked. Potidaea and other cities then revolted against Athens. By this point, Thucydides notes both Athens and Sparta had grounds for complaints against each other.

Eventually, the Spartans voted that the Athenians had broken the peace treaty and hence war was declared. Almost a year went by, however, before full-scale fighting broke out. As Thucydides observes, Sparta and its allies spent their time preparing for the upcoming conflict and making various charges against the Athenians "so that there should be a good pretext for making war." Athens did the same. While the events involving Corcyra and Potidaea were the immediate causes of the war, Thucydides concludes his account of these incidents by once again arguing that Spartan fear of the further growth of Athenian power was the underlying cause of the conflict.

Similarly, historians have argued that the underlying cause of World War I was the rise to power of Germany and the fear this caused in Great Britain, France, Russia, and other major powers of the day. Others point to the decline in power of the Austro-Hungarian Empire while Russia increased in relative power after its 1905 defeat to Japan. Among the immediate causes of the war, the most important was the June 1914 assassination in Sarajevo of the Austro-Hungarian Archduke Franz Ferdinand. While his assassination lit the fuse, no one would claim that this was the major or underlying cause of World War I, any more than Thucydides would claim events in Corcyra or Potidaea in and of themselves were the reason for the second Peloponnesian War. Despite the emphasis Thucydides places on the underlying cause of the war, he is not saying that the more immediate factors are somehow less important; both underlying and immediate causes must be taken into account in explaining why the Peloponnesian War occurred and why it broke out when it did.

Differentiating between underlying and more proximate causes of war is central to Kenneth Waltz's account in his *Man, the State and War* (1959). For Waltz, the underlying cause of war is anarchy—the absence of central authority—in the international system of states. That there is nothing to stop states from going to war is the underlying or "permissive" cause of war. In addition to this underlying condition, more proximate or "efficient" causes are responsible for the outbreak of particular wars.

Thucydides emphasizes what many present-day realists like Waltz refer to as a system-level explanation—identifying the increase in Athenian power relative to Sparta and other city-states as the underlying cause of the war. By placing such explanatory weight on fears generated by changes in the distribution of power, Thucydides's narrative seems to have a rather deterministic cast—statesmen have little control over international events in the face of such basic trends as changes in the balance of power.

One of the reasons *History of the Peloponnesian War* is such a fascinating work, however, is that Thucydides's narrative seems to undercut the deterministic, "war was inevitable due to the rise of Athenian power" thesis. First, as some historians have noted, war broke out in 431 BCE, some twenty-five years after Athenian power had peaked. In 454 the Athenian military expedition to Egypt was destroyed at a cost of some 250 ships and 40,000–50,000 men. Revolts within the Athenian Empire in 452 and a military defeat at Coronea in central Greece in 446 further weakened Athens. Such setbacks encouraged Athens to seek peace with Persia in 449 and, in 446, it concluded a Thirty Years' Peace agreement with Sparta. This treaty cost Athens much of its continental empire and required it to withdraw from the Megarid, the strategic land route between Attica in southeastern Greece and the Peloponnese peninsula.[31]

Second, much of Thucydides's work contains extended debates among various participants concerning what policies a state should follow. The fact that a Corinthian delegation did a masterful job buttressing the Spartan war party's position did not mean the declaration of war with Athens was inevitable—the cautions of the Spartan King Archidamus were quite compelling. Conversely, participants in the Athenian debate on how to deal with the failed revolt by the city of Mytilene on the Aegean island of Lesbos did not necessarily have to conclude that it was in Athens' self-interest to avoid bloody retribution. Different decisions were possible, and hence different outcomes could have occurred.

---

[31] For the argument that the basic assumptions and arguments presented by Thucydides at the outset of his work are designed to create certain expectations in the mind of the reader and then later purposely subverted, see W. R. Connor, *Thucydides* (Princeton, NJ: Princeton University Press, 1984); Richard Ned Lebow, "Thucydides, Power Transition Theory, and the Causes of War," in *Hegemonic Rivalry*, 127–29; and Donald Kagan, *The Outbreak of the Peloponnesian War* (Ithaca, NY: Cornell University Press, 1969), 189, 373–74.

Finally, Thucydides obviously wished to warn future decision makers about reaching the sorts of strategic miscalculations committed by many of the participants he observed. If shifts in the balance of power make war inevitable, what would be the purpose of providing cautionary tales to policy makers? Nevertheless, this is undoubtedly one of Thucydides's goals.

Cautionary Tales: Lessons Drawn by Thucydides from the Peloponnesian War

Be Wary of Wars in Distant Lands

The launching of the Sicilian campaign by Athens is a classic example of how pride, prejudice, impatience, and ignorance can result in a disastrous foreign policy decision. The Athenians, their war against Sparta stalemated, decided the deadlock could be broken if Sicilian states allied with Sparta could be subdued. As Thucydides notes, the Athenians "were for the most part ignorant of the size of the island and of the number of its inhabitants," yet this did not dissuade them from declaring war on Syracuse, Sicily's principal city-state. Thucydides's own position is quite clear—be wary when deciding to engage in wars in distant lands.[32]

The Athenian desire to break the military stalemate parallels the German desire during World War II to break the stalemate by invading the Soviet Union in June 1941. Furthermore, in the public debate before the launching of the Athenian military expedition, some arguments were made that sounded eerily similar to those concerning American involvement in Vietnam as well as analyses of the Soviet invasion of Afghanistan in 1979. One is also reminded of General Douglas MacArthur's warning that the United States should be wary of engaging in a land war in Asia. Sending troops to Afghanistan following attacks by Al-Qaeda on September 11, 2001 (what would become a twenty-year war) and the US invasion of Iraq in March 2003 further destabilized an already unstable region are additional examples. Much of the discussion in Thucydides's work appears applicable to any power contemplating going to war far from home. There are very real risks.

A principal player in this ancient Greek drama was Nicias, one of the Athenians chosen to head the expedition to Sicily. Personally against the Sicilian campaign, he favored a policy of nonintervention. Specifically, Athens should not trust its supposed allies in Sicily who had their own reasons for seeing Athens "drawn into a war that does not concern us." This is "the wrong time for such adventures." Athens should not be dividing its forces, running risks, and "grasping at a new empire before we have secured the one we have already," nor should it underestimate the difficulties associated with governing rebellious foreigners living at the edge of the Hellenic world.

---

[32] Pericles's original strategy was "to abstain from attempts to extend Athenian domination and to avoid involvement in dangerous enterprises, to keep firm control of the allies . . . to maintain seapower and to avoid land conflicts with the main forces of the enemy." The Sicilian campaign and other Athenian military operations in Aetolia, Pylos, Megara, and Boeotia violated this Periclean strategy and reflected the views of Demosthenes and Cleon who came to power after the death of Pericles. A. J. Holladay, "Athenian Strategy in the Archidamian War," *Historia* 27, no. 3 (1978): 399 passim.

Sometimes the best foreign policy decision is to do nothing—putting one's reputation to the test against a distant power could have disastrous consequences if anything goes wrong. Athenians, per Nicias, should "spend our new gains at home and on ourselves" instead of on those "begging for assistance and whose interests it is to tell lies" and "leave all the dangers to others." Be wary of those who spew out patriotic platitudes but wish to go to war for their selfish reasons and run the risk of "endangering the state in order to live a brilliant life."

Alcibiades, also chosen by the citizenry to be one of the commanders, responded. He is certainly one of the more intriguing and colorful characters in history. The argument he made in favor of the expedition is clever, alternatively sarcastic, and cajoling. Alcibiades denigrated the Sicilians, disparagingly referring to their cities as having "swollen populations made out of all sorts of mixtures." They are supposedly not patriotic, lacking the feeling that they are fighting for their home and hence will most likely submit without much of a struggle once faced with Athenian power.

This optimism was tempered, however, by the warning that not intervening risks losing the entire existing empire. Alcibiades claimed Athens is virtually forced by the circumstances to plan new conquests otherwise "we ourselves may fall under the power of others." He goes on to make the case for expansionism, arguing that "the city, like everything else, will wear out of its own accord if it remains at rest." In this image, state and society become a virtual living organism that is impelled to expand or it will wither and die. The Athenians embraced the arguments of Alcibiades and, in a classic case of wishful thinking, dismissed the cautionary words of Nicias, hence committing Athens to a two-front war.

The expedition set forth, and very little went as planned. City-states they expected would aid them preferred to remain neutral: The Athenians "sailed down the Italian coast, finding that the cities would not provide them with a market or even allow them inside their walls." When the expedition reached the southern tip of Italy, the Athenians assumed that their ethnic ties to the people of Rhegium on the Italian coast across from Sicily would mean support for Athens. Instead, the leadership of Rhegium preferred to sit on the fence, stating that "they would not join either side, but would wait for a general decision from all the Greeks in Italy and would then act in accordance with it." At the same time, three Athenian ships that had gone to Egesta on Sicily seeking financial assistance for the expedition arrived at Rhegium and announced that "the promised sums of money did not exist and only thirty *talents* were available."[33]

Lamachus, one of the Athenian generals, argued that the fleet should sail straight to Syracuse and begin the war because "it is at the beginning . . . that every army inspires most fear; but if time is allowed to pass before it shows itself, men's spirits revive." He also claimed that if the Athenians attacked immediately with overwhelming force, "the rest of the Sicilians would at once be less inclined to ally themselves with Syracuse and would be more likely to come over to the Athenians without waiting to see which side was going to win."

---

[33] As a monetary measure, a Greek talent was equivalent to some twenty-six kilograms of a precious metal like gold.

The Athenians did, however, delay in mounting military operations, allowing the Syracusans to gain confidence. Even Athenian victories in battles did not seem to translate into concrete progress in terms of winning the war. Morale began to deteriorate, and Nicias sent a letter to Athens, stating "the time therefore has come for you to decide either to recall us, or else to send out another force, both naval and military, big as the first, with large sums of money."

Athens decided to send reinforcements as its Corinthian and Spartan rivals had escalated their commitment to the war effort in Sicily. This required total mobilization on the part of Athens and an increase in the draft, but further military setbacks "produced a feeling of bewilderment in the army and a decline in morale." The economic costs of the war began to be felt in Athens as taxes were raised. The Athenians, a proud naval power, were eventually faced with the imperative of winning the most important battle of the entire war in the Great Harbor of Syracuse. If they did not, the army would be cut off from a retreat by sea. It is worth quoting Thucydides's powerful description of the scene:

> For the Athenians everything depended upon their navy; their fears for their future were like nothing they had ever experienced; and, as the battle swung this way and that, so, inevitably, did their impressions alter as they watched it from the shore. As the fight went on and on with no decision reached, their bodies, swaying this way and that, showed the trepidation with which their minds were filled, and wretched indeed was their state, constantly on the verge of safety, constantly on the brink of destruction. So, while the result of the battle was still in doubt, one could hear sounds of all kinds coming at the same time from this one Athenian army—lamentations and cheering, cries of "We are winning" and of "We are losing," and all the other different exclamations bound to be made by a great army in its great danger.

The Athenians were utterly defeated. Forced to try to escape overland, the army was systematically cut to pieces. Those who survived as prisoners of war were held in stone quarries and suffered from disease, hunger, and thirst. The generals (including Nicias) were put to death, although by this time Alcibiades had defected to the Spartans. Thucydides concludes his account by stating that the Sicilian campaign was "the greatest action that we know of in Hellenic history—to the victors the most brilliant of successes, to the vanquished the most calamitous of defeats." On the home front, the public greeted this news with disbelief. Recriminations immediately began over who was to blame for this disaster.

Despite Thucydides's statement that the Sicilian campaign failed in part due to a loss of public support, his narrative also shows the Athenian public as enthusiastic about the war effort and quite willing to send reinforcements. Furthermore, tactical and strategic mistakes by Nicias in the field may well have cost Athens an early and relatively inexpensive victory.

Dangers of a Punitive Peace

A recurrent question raised by Thucydides is how should the victor deal with the vanquished—the powerful with the weak. Although it seems the phrase he uses most often in his narrative is "laid waste the land," neither side always engaged in completely ruthless actions. Such restraint is not a function of feeling sorry for the opposition but is generally the result of a pragmatic calculation that showing mercy is in the long-term interest of the state.

Ten years before the Sicilian campaign, for example, an Athenian force landed at a place known as Pylos, only forty-five miles from Sparta. The Athenians began to fortify the desolate headland, actions the Spartans viewed as a threat to their vital interests. A Spartan force soon took up positions on the mainland, on an island opposite Pylos, and in the harbor. An Athenian fleet arrived to relieve its men at Pylos and in the ensuing battles defeated the Spartan navy and cut off the Spartan troops on the island. During an armistice, Spartan representatives were sent to Athens where they suggested a treaty be signed to end the war. In making their case to the Athenians, two insightful observations were made that have since become conventional wisdom.

The first directly addresses the question, why is it so difficult to predict the course of international events? The Spartans argued that no matter how carefully one calculates, the course of war is impossible to predict. Today's winner may be tomorrow's loser with the fruits of victory quickly turning sour. True wisdom is recognizing that things will change. As the Spartans noted, intelligent leaders know that war is "governed by the total chances in operation and can never be restricted to the conditions that one or the other of the two sides would like to see permanently fixed."

Thucydides makes numerous references throughout the book to the uncertainty that Carl von Clausewitz later would call "friction" and the "fog of war," referring to either the conduct or outcome of specific battles. The best-laid plans too often go awry while, at other times, sheer luck can save the day. Hence, it is in one's own interest to imagine how one would wish to be treated in a similarly disadvantageous position.

Second, the Spartans warned Athens against pursuing the Athenian advantage at Pylos to the bitter end by destroying the Spartan troops besieged on the island. In another insight relevant throughout history, Thucydides states: "Where great hatreds exist, no lasting settlement can be made in a spirit of revenge." If an opponent is forced "to carry out the terms of an unequal treaty," a thirst for revenge will result. Hence the victor should make "peace on more moderate terms than his enemy expected," reducing the desire for revenge instead of placing the vanquished "under an obligation to pay back good for good."

The best modern example of this line of thinking concerns the handling of a defeated Germany after the two World Wars (1914–1918 and 1939–1945). The punitive Versailles Treaty of 1919 fueled a spirit of revenge in Germany and contributed to the rise of Adolf Hitler and the Nazis who capitalized on this public discontent. Conversely, the American, British, and French treatment following World War II of what came to be known as West Germany, particularly the provision of economic aid, did much to stabilize the country, undercut political extremism, and encourage the development of democracy. For Thucydides, the most effective leaders are those who recognize that the long-term interests of the state are often better served by not pursuing short-term advantages to the bitter end.

War Fever and a Fickle Public

Another catalyst to conflict noted by Thucydides is the initially strong public support for war that all too often quickly turns to dismay and a search for scapegoats. The Spartan king, Archidamus, noted that those in the older generation "are not likely to share in what may be a general enthusiasm for war." Pericles observed that the "enthusiastic state of mind in which people are persuaded to enter upon a war is not retained when it comes to action, and that people's minds are altered by the course of events."

As Thucydides comments: "At the beginning of an undertaking the enthusiasm is always greatest, and at the same time both in the Peloponnese and in Athens there were a number of young men who had never been in a war and were consequently far from unwilling to join in this one." Such attitudes not only provide an impetus to war, but they also foster overconfidence and a belief that the war will be of short duration. A classic case of war fever and jingoism involves the initial Athenian enthusiasm for the Sicilian expedition:

> There was a passion for the enterprise that affected everyone alike. The older men thought they would either conquer the places against which they were sailing or, in any case, with such a large force, could come to no harm; the young had a longing for the sights and experiences of distant places, and were confident that they would return safely; the general masses and the average soldier himself saw the prospect of getting pay for the time being and of adding to the empire so as to secure permanent paid employment in [the] future. The result of this excessive enthusiasm of the majority was that the few who actually were opposed to the expedition were afraid of being thought unpatriotic if they voted against it, and therefore kept quiet.

Initial public enthusiasm for war is a common phenomenon in international politics. World War I provides a classic example. Even the European social democratic parties and trade unions that had expressed pacifist tendencies got caught up in the war fever of 1914. It had been assumed that if the vast working classes of all the countries refused to fight, war would be impossible since the requisite "cannon fodder" would not be available. Instead, young men hurried to join the military, motivated by patriotism or merely afraid of missing out on the great adventure. Youthful enthusiasm for engaging in battle was buttressed then, as it is now, by the false assumption often made by young men that they are somehow indestructible. In sum, while Thucydides does not view public war fever to be an underlying cause of war, it is an important domestic contributor to an aggressive foreign policy, and such behavior is not restricted to any single type of political system.

Thucydides and IR Theory

Influenced by Homer and Herodotus, Thucydides went well beyond both in his attempt to generalize about international relations. As noted, his work has been viewed by many scholars as foundational to international relations as a field of study. If one is interested in war and conflict as many self-identified realists are, Thucydides is a major touchstone, although it is debatable as to exactly what type of realist he might be.[34] If one is interested in political and class conflict within states as are some economic structuralists (chapter 7), Thucydides's observations of the internal and international ramifications of the Corcyraean civil war are relevant—"practically the whole of Hellas was convulsed, with rival parties in every state—democratic leaders trying to bring in the Athenians and oligarchs trying to bring in the Spartans."

For someone interested in the role of justice, norms, and values in international relations (chapter 13) and why they do not play a more prominent role in international relations, Thucydides provides an excellent starting point.[35] A case has even been made that far from being a realist, Thucydides can be viewed as the first social constructivist (chapter 9) due to the critical use of dialogues that frame security issues and influence policies through words.[36] We turn now, however, to a closer look at several aspects of Thucydides's work that have influenced twentieth- and twenty-first-century IR theorists.

State as Principal Actor

The major actors in Thucydides's tale are Athens and Sparta along with their allies in much the same way as states have traditionally been the focus of IR theorists. Non-state actors such as mercenaries or the Oracle at Delphi are mentioned only occasionally, and they do not play a significant role when compared to the city-states that are at center stage. The importance of states is further reflected in the fact that, for Thucydides, it was the shift in relative power between the two most powerful states that accounted for the outbreak of the Peloponnesian War.

State as Unitary Actor

As we discussed in part I of this volume, many scholars of different theoretical and methodological orientations have found it useful for developing explanatory theory to view the state as a unified or unitary actor. Indeed, most of Thucydides's famous dialogues involve debates among representatives of various city-states. The arguments presented reflect the point of view of Athens, Corinth, Syracuse, and Thebes. Some of the more extraordinary debates, however, involve domestic arguments over what policy the state should follow. For example, the Athenians disagreed among themselves on how the rebellious city-state of Mytilene should be treated. Should a brutal example be made, making it clear that any revolt will be punished by death? Or would showing leniency and mercy better serve Athens' future interests?

But despite such lively domestic differences of opinion, the notion of the unified state is preserved since once the decision is taken on such issues, the

---

[34] Michael W. Doyle, "Thucydides: A Realist?" in *Hegemonic Rivalry*, 169–88.

[35] Clifford Owen, *The Humanity of Thucydides* (Princeton, NJ: Princeton University Press, 1994).

[36] Richard Ned Lebow, "Thucydides the Constructivist," *American Political Science Review* 95, no. 3 (September 2001): 547–60. Constructivists, as discussed in chapter 9, see what we take as facts in international politics as not being reflective of an objective or material reality, but rather being an intersubjective or socially constructed reality.

state speaks with one voice to the outside world. Moreover, Thucydides tells us that although Athens "was nominally a democracy" and thus allowed its citizenry to be free, in fact, "power was really in the hands of the first citizen," Pericles. In relation to the people, "it was he who led them, rather than they who led him." To Thucydides even democratic Athens was a unitary city-state, allowing one to speak of an "Athenian policy." Nevertheless, fractious domestic politics—particularly civil wars—had substantial impact on the Greek city-state system. Domestic and external politics are inextricably linked and Thucydides dramatically highlights this linkage in the course of his narrative.

Rational Reconstruction

Thucydides, like other educated Greeks, believed people were essentially rational beings. Hence much of his work consists of recounting arguments and debates, the assumption being that through this process a state can reach the decision that is in its best interests. This weighing of opposites is consistent, of course, with the Socratic method used by Plato in *The Republic*. (See the related discussion later in this chapter.) Thucydides was not present at all of the debates he records. He relies on other accounts and reconstructs the arguments, judging which words are appropriate for the situation. To put it another way, his reconstruction of the essence of an argument in the form of a dialogue is what a rational person, given certain policy preferences, would argue in such circumstances.

Thucydides also argues that political leaders must place themselves in the shoes (or sandals) of rival statesmen to anticipate what they might do—an empathetic analysis that one pursues in one's own interest. The question to ask is this: Given a certain situation with various constraints and opportunities, what would I do? As a Syracusan leader states: "When dealing with the enemy it is not only his actions but [also] his intentions that have to be watched." In a classic summation of the rational reconstruction perspective, the Syracusan notes how one should be wary of taking intelligence reports at face value and should not use them "as a basis for calculating probabilities, but instead will consider what a clever and a widely experienced people, as, in my view, the Athenians are, would be likely to do." This rationality assumption is central to the work of many IR theorists who otherwise might disagree on the best approach to developing theory.[37]

Limitations of the Rationality Assumption: Outcomes

Thucydides not only shows us the practical utility of the rationality assumption when one wishes to divine the intentions of a rival but also reconstructs debates that also illustrate foreign policy decision-making processes that generally attempt to consider the pros and cons of various suggested actions. As another Syracusan leader puts it concerning a state's decision to go to war: "The fact is that one side thinks that the profits to be won outweigh the risks to be incurred,

---

[37] Hans J. Morgenthau, *Politics among Nations*, 4th ed. (New York: Knopf, 1966), 5.

and the other side is ready to face danger rather than accept an immediate loss." This is the direct application of rational calculation seen as common sense.

An obvious question arises: Does such rational calculation guarantee a good outcome? Of course not. Thucydides presents us with several instances where sound calculation still leads to a poor outcome. A prime example involves the decision to revolt against Athens by Chios—an island city-state in the northeast Aegean. Thucydides notes that the Chians were sensible people, and their decision to revolt was not the result of overconfidence. Indeed, they first secured allies to share the risk and calculated that the time was ripe, given that the destruction of the Athenian expedition to Sicily had occurred, many states believing (erroneously) that Athens was near collapse. Chian calculations were incorrect, and they suffered the consequences.

Limitations of the Rationality Assumption: Perception

Thucydides makes a contribution to the IR field as a result of his emphasis on the rationality assumption. Indeed, he seems to have been granted paternity of this idea. But it would be more precise to state that Thucydides intended *The Peloponnesian War* to be an illustration of the limits of rationality, as opposed to a paradigmatic case study of rationality at work.

Thucydides presents us with numerous examples of not only the problem of translating intentions into desired outcomes but also the cognitive limitations of rational decision-making. There are, in other words, psychological pitfalls in attempts to achieve a rational decision-making process, and, even when the process works to virtual perfection, there is a disjuncture between the psychological milieu of statesmen and the operational milieu in which decisions are implemented.

Attempts by a state to enhance its security breed suspicion and can result in an unanticipated and unwelcome outcome: Other states may follow a similar logic, increasing the level of tension and suspicion throughout the international system. It is what twentieth-century scholar, John Herz, referred to as a *security dilemma*[38]—steps taken to enhance a state's security may result in countermeasures taken by opponents, the net effect reducing or undermining the security of the state that initiated the action. It is the stuff of arms races—what one state deploys militarily is countered by another state or states with new, or more, offensive or defensive weapons systems.

Within the psychological milieu, some possible misperceptions held by decision makers reinforce the adverse implications of international anarchy or a world with no common power to enforce order. There are three types of faulty perceptions discernable in the narrative of *History of the Peloponnesian War*:

1. Decision makers perceive the enemy to be more centralized and coordinated in its decision-making process than it actually is.

---

[38] John Herz, "Idealist Internationalism and the Security Dilemma," *World Politics* 2, no. 2 (January 1950): 157–80.

2. Those in authority experience "cognitive closure" as evidenced by a belief that few, if any, alternatives are open to them.
3. Leaders engage in "wishful thinking."

Social scientists interested in the cognitive processes of decision makers claim all three contribute to flawed assessments of rivals, undercut a rational decision-making process, and increase the possibility of war during a crisis. We will illustrate these three phenomena by referencing briefly Thucydides's text and selections from present-day literature.

Perception of Centralization

By adopting the logic of rational reconstruction, one attempts to place oneself in the mind of an opponent to discern what is the most likely course of action the rival may take. There is an obvious utility in this exercise as it provides some basis upon which one can plan a response. The trade-off, however, is that one may end up perceiving the opponent's decision-making process as being more centralized, coordinated, and integrated than it actually is. Potential divisions or bureaucratic politics might be downplayed, and an excessive amount of omniscience may be ascribed to the rival that comes to be viewed as clever, resourceful, and in complete control of its decision-making process.

Furthermore, coincidences, accidents, and unintended consequences are either viewed with suspicion or dismissed. Former US Secretary of State John Foster Dulles may indeed have been correct when he noted that "the Russians are great chess players and their moves in the world situation are . . . calculated as closely and carefully as though they were making moves in a chess game."[39] The question then becomes: How typical is such behavior? Contemporary research has provided an impressive array of examples illustrating the tendency of decision makers to assume a high degree of coherence and ascribe consistency to events that, in fact, lack these qualities. The greater the fear and suspicion one has of the adversary, the more likely this cognitive distortion will occur.

Perceptions of centralization in decision-making processes of an adversary, then, are the downside of attempts to discern an adversary's intentions through rational reconstruction. The corollary is that if one is divining the intentions of an ally, it is more likely that one will give that partner the benefit of the doubt, downplaying volition and instead emphasizing environmental factors beyond an ally's control to explain its behavior.

This psychological phenomenon is illustrated throughout Thucydides's narrative. The confidence with which various speakers assume to have divined the intentions of rival states is quite striking, attributing to these states some sort of strategic game plan that is being implemented. During the revolt of Mytilene, for example, ambassadors from that city-state went to Olympia to secure the support of Sparta and its allies. The Mytileneans argued that Athens all along

---

[39] As cited by Robert Jervis, *Perception and Misperception in International Politics* (Princeton, NJ: Princeton University Press, 1976), 320.

had a strategic plan for seizing control of all of Greece. They claimed that "the only reason why we were left with our independence was because the Athenians, in building up their empire, thought that they could seize power more easily by having some specious arguments to put forward and by using the methods of policy rather than of brute force."

Before the initial Spartan declaration of war, we also find the Corinthians claiming that Athens had been scheming to deprive states of their freedom and "[had] for a long time been preparing for the eventuality of war." Perhaps. Certainly a more benign interpretation could be placed upon Athenian actions concerning Corcyra, Potidaea, and Megara that emphasize a prudent concern for Athenian national security in the event war would break out with Sparta and an incremental decision-making process as opposed to slavish devotion to some sort of imperial game plan.

Cognitive Closure

Given Thucydides's belief that Athens and Sparta were compelled toward war, it is not surprising that he is pessimistic about the ability of humans to control their fates. Assuming he accurately recorded the gist of the debates, it is striking the number of times leaders made the basic assumption that there were few, if any, choices open to them. When Pericles told his countrymen, for example, why Athens must stand firm against Spartan demands, he concluded his argument by bluntly stating, "This war is being forced upon us."

Similarly, Sparta also believed the situation had reached a point that was no longer tolerable. This same thinking is also evident in the decision to launch the Sicilian expedition. At one point Alcibiades stated: "We have reached a stage where we are forced to plan new conquests and forced to hold on to what we have got." Choices and alternatives seemed to be lacking. The situations seemed to be characterized more by determinism than one in which human agency—free will or voluntarism—can be exercised effectively.

In certain circumstances this may indeed be the case, or choices may be severely circumscribed, such as when the Athenians delivered their ultimatum to the people living on the Greek island of Melos in the Aegean Sea just north of Crete: Capitulate or be destroyed. Other times, however, particularly in those cases involving the decision to go to war, one suspects Thucydides has recorded examples of premature cognitive closure—a failure to search seriously for alternative policies. In these circumstances, decision makers exhibit a certain air of resignation if not fatalism.

This psychological phenomenon is particularly dangerous during crises involving stress and time pressure. Several studies of the July 1914 crisis leading to the outbreak of World War I in August bear this out. As in the case of ancient Greece, there was a sense that war was inevitable. Once the armies of Russia, France, Germany, Austria-Hungary, and Britain began to mobilize, military leaders told the politicians it was impossible to stop the process. Events seemed to take on a terrible logic of their own, unable to be arrested by mere human beings. When German Chancellor Theobald von Bethmann-Hollweg stated "we have not willed war; it has been forced upon us," he was echoing the sentiments of Pericles and other statesmen before and after him.[40]

During the Corinthian speech designed to goad Sparta into war with Athens, Thucydides records a related psychological phenomenon—what we now refer to as the inherent bad faith model: No matter what a state may do, its actions are interpreted in the worst possible light because images, once developed, are highly resistant to change. Even conciliatory actions are viewed by a decision maker as a ruse to get him to drop his guard. Evidence that may undermine this hostile image is rejected.[41]

Hence, in claiming that Athens was preparing for war and bent on imperialist expansion, the Corinthians, with their own axe to grind, rhetorically asked the Spartans: "Why otherwise should she have forcibly taken over from us the control of Corcyra? Why is she besieging Potidaea? Potidaea is the best possible base for any campaign in Thrace, and Corcyra might have contributed a very large fleet to the Peloponnesian League."

Such actions were viewed as aggressive in intent as well as part of a carefully conceived strategic plan by which Athens would pursue its imperialistic objectives; everything Athens did was viewed in this light. The corollary to this phenomenon is the tendency of decision makers to assume that their own benign intentions are self-evident to an adversary. Hence, when the rival fails to respond favorably to a supposedly mutually beneficial initiative, the assumption of bad faith is reinforced. This is a recurrent event throughout Thucydides's narrative.

Wishful Thinking

Thucydides also makes it clear that wishful thinking and self-delusion may undercut attempts at achieving a rational decision-making process. After the Spartan capture of Amphipolis that cost Thucydides his job, other cities decided to revolt against Athenian rule. Such a decision is too often "based more on wishful thinking than on sound calculation . . . for the usual thing among men is that when they want something they will, without any reflection, leave that to hope, while they will employ the full force of reason in rejecting what they find unpalatable."

Thucydides records many instances in which leaders tended to reject unsettling information. For example, when Athens was suffering from the plague, the Athenians at first refused to believe that the island of Lesbos with its powerful navy had revolted, as this would have meant a dramatic increase in the military might of the opposition alliance at a most inconvenient time. Similarly, the Syracusans refused to believe initial reports that the Athenians were planning to launch an expedition against Sicily, although news of the expedition arrived from many quarters.

---

[40] Richard Ned Lebow, *Between Peace and War: The Nature of International Crisis* (Baltimore: Johns Hopkins University Press, 1981), chap. 5.
[41] Jervis, *Perception and Misperception*, 310–11.

The Athenians presented to the Melians the classic case of the dangers of wishful thinking:

> Hope, that comforter in danger! . . . Do not be like those people who, as so commonly happens, miss the chance of saving themselves in a human and practical way, and, when every clear and distinct hope has left them in their adversity, turn to what is blind and vague, to prophecies and oracles and such things that by encouraging hope lead men to ruin.

Despite the warning, the Melians put their faith in Sparta and, to say the least, were severely disappointed. When Melos refused to ally with Athens, the Athenians decimated the island.

Wishful thinking, however, is not reserved for those who are in fear or in deadly straits. Confident powers may also engage in wishful thinking by drawing on inappropriate historical analogies. Japan, for example, thought a limited war with the United States was possible in 1941 in part because the Japanese recalled how Russia had settled for a limited defeat earlier in the century rather than risk a long, drawn-out war. Similarly, Hitler assumed that France and Great Britain would not fight for Poland as they had not fought for Austria or Czechoslovakia.[42]

Perhaps the best example of wishful thinking based on arrogance involves Alcibiades's defense of the Sicilian expedition. He dismisses Nicias's concerns over enemies closer to home by stating that "our fathers left behind them these same enemies when they had the Persians on their hands." This questionable historical analogy helped to sway the Athenian citizens who eventually approved the expedition.

In sum, while Thucydides may have believed people were essentially rational and able to perceive alternative courses of action, he also recognized the limitations of rational discourse as well as the fallibility and foibles of human beings. Extreme emotional stress, cognitive blindness to realities, and faulty reasoning undercut presumably rational decision-making processes.

Security as the Most Important Interest

Given that his work deals with war, Thucydides is obviously preoccupied with security issues, the prime interest of all states. Hence, during the Athenian debate over how to deal with rebellious Mytilene, both Cleon and Diodotus stated that the Athenians should come to a decision based on "your interests."

While security is usually viewed by IR scholars in terms of military considerations (with the armed services playing the critical role), it also may include such factors as a productive economy and a society with a strong will to resist foreign subversion or another intrusion—the emphasis by Herodotus on why the Greeks defeated the Persian invaders.

---

[42] Jervis, *Perception and Misperception*, 278–79, 365–72. See also D. Clayton Jones, "American and Japanese Strategies in the Pacific War," in *Makers of Modern Strategy: From Machiavelli to the Nuclear Age*, ed. Peter Paret (Princeton, NJ: Princeton University Press, 1986), 703–8.

A state can enhance its security in one of two ways—by internal efforts to increase its capabilities and by external means as in joining an alliance. By pooling resources, it is assumed that the security of each state will be enhanced at a lower cost than if each state attempts to provide its own security on a unilateral basis. This latter option—the rationale for forming alliances—is a constant theme in Thucydides's work.[43] States taking internal or external measures to address potentially adverse changes in the balance of power was central to Kenneth Waltz's theorizing on how states try to maintain their relative position with other states.

Alliances

How are alliances formed and what is their relation to the onset of war? Thucydides notes that states may join one alliance or another due to compulsion, interest, moral principle, or cultural and racial affinity. Later scholars have not improved much upon this classification scheme. While Thucydides describes several instances in which decisions to join an alliance appear to be a function of complementary systems of government or society, the critical factor in alliance formation throughout Thucydides's narrative is the security interest of city-states.

Two alternative hypotheses in present-day IR literature address the choice of one's allies in attempting to maximize national security interests—balancing and bandwagoning.[44] According to the balancing hypothesis, states join an alliance to oppose other states that are perceived to be a threat. The greater the threat, the larger and stronger the alliance. The bandwagoning hypothesis suggests the opposite. Faced with an external threat, states will accommodate and ally with the threatening state either to avoid being attacked or to share in the spoils of victory.

Which of these hypotheses finds support in Thucydides's narrative? The evidence he presents suggests that fear of a rival made balancing the policy norm both before and during the Peloponnesian war, but concern with bandwagoning tendencies by some city-states preoccupied the leaders of the Athenian and Spartan alliances once the war began.

As for balancing as a policy to counteract a threat, a prime example involves Corcyra's seeking protection from Athens against Corinth: "They [Corcyreans] had no allies in Hellas, since they had not enrolled themselves either in the Spartan or in the Athenian League. They decided therefore to go to Athens, to join the Athenian alliance, and see whether they could get any support from that quarter." In pleading their case, the Corcyreans admitted: "We recognize that, if we have nothing but our own . . . resources, it is impossible for us to survive, and we can imagine what lies in store for us if they overpower us. We are therefore forced to ask for assistance."

---

[43] See, for example, the speech by the Syracusan leader Hemocrates, IV: 61.
[44] Stephen M. Walt, *The Origins of Alliances* (Ithaca, NY: Cornell University Press, 1987); Deborah Welch Larson, "Bandwagon Images in American Foreign Policy: Myth or Reality?" in *Dominos and Bandwagons: Strategic Belief and Superpower Competition in the Eurasian Rimland*, ed. Robert Jervis and Jack Snyder (New York: Oxford University Press, 1990), 85–111.

Even stronger states or empires may pursue a policy of balancing in attempting to prevent the rise of a major power. This is quite evident in the case of Persia, whose leader was advised by the omnipresent Alcibiades "not to be in too much of a hurry to end the war. . . . It was better to have the two parties [Athens and Sparta] each in possession of its own separate sphere of influence, so that if the King had trouble with one of them, he would always be able to call in the other against it." Such advice reinforced the Persian policy of "keeping the two Hellenic forces in balance against each other."

As for bandwagoning, there is some evidence of this occurring during the Peloponnesian War.[45] Thucydides's narrative provides evidence that in attempting to prevent alliance defections and the loss of neutrals to a rival's alliance, states may pursue counterproductive policies resulting in self-fulfilling policies. Athens was particularly preoccupied with possible defections from the Delian League.

It was not simply fear of losing the military capabilities of a league member that was of concern to Athens. Athens also worried about how such defections would be viewed by allies and enemies. The basic fear is that one defection might lead to others, and a stampede would begin as erstwhile allies attempted to get on board the rival's bandwagon. As with the Soviet Union and the Warsaw Pact during the Cold War, the alliance was not just directed against an external threat, but also was the organizational expression of an imperial or hegemonic power. As aptly stated by the Mytilenes, the Delian League was originally designed to liberate Hellas from Persia, not to be used to subjugate Hellas for Athens. One by one the allies became either subject states or, as in the case of Mytilene, nominally retained their independence.

Increasingly, compulsion instead of common interest held the alliance together. In the typically blunt words of Cleon to his fellow Athenians: "What you do not realize is that your empire is a tyranny exercised over subjects who do not like it." Compulsion, therefore, became the primary means for maintaining the alliance, not feelings of loyalty to allies or even fear of Persia. As a result, Athenian power was directed as much against subject states as it was directed against states outside the alliance, just as Soviet forces in the Cold War years not only confronted NATO, but also performed an internal policing function in its Eastern European sphere of influence, marked as it was by the Warsaw Pact alliance.

In the case of the Delian League, this made for a somewhat fragile alliance and the constant specter of defection. Mytilene, for example, had its own regional ambitions and revolted from Athens when the latter was suffering from the effects of the plague and war exhaustion. Mytilene joined the Peloponnesian League but soon returned to Athenian control. In the famous debate in Athens over what to do with Mytilene, Cleon argued that severe punishment was required. It is necessary to "make an example of them to your other allies," otherwise "they will all revolt upon the slightest pretext." Reputation is critical if one is to be taken seriously.

---

[45] Barry S. Strauss, "Of Balances, Bandwagons, and Ancient Greece," in *Hegemonic Rivalry*, 198–201.

Fear of defection is an understandable concern for leaders of alliances that are based more on compulsion than on common interest. On the other hand, an alliance leader's obsession with defection may result in counterproductive policies that have the unintended effect of actually encouraging an ally to defect. The dispute over Potidaea is a case in point. Thucydides notes how "Athens feared that . . . Potidaea might be induced [by Corinth] to revolt and might draw into the revolt the other allied cities in the Thracian area." To prevent this from occurring, the Athenians ordered the Potidaeans to pull down fortifications, provide hostages, and banish the Corinthian magistrates. If the goal was to keep Potidaea in the Athenian alliance and prevent its defection, the plan backfired.

The Potidaeans sent a delegation to Athens in hope of having the orders rescinded, but at the same time the Potidaeans hedged their bets by also sending representatives to Sparta to seek support. The Spartans pledged to invade Attica if Potidaea was attacked. What the Spartans failed to realize was that this pledge was an incentive for the Potidaeans to revolt. They did so, and Athens was compelled to go to war against them.

Fear of defection is a principal concern of states leading alliances based more on coercion than common interest. In the Melian Dialogue, Athens expressed a concern over alliance defections resulting from any perception of Athens being weak or indecisive. The Athenian decision involving Melos differed from its earlier decision on Mytilene's revolt. In the case of Mytilene, an Athenian ally, the Athenians eventually rejected Cleon's advice and did not punish the Mytileans. By contrast, Athens took harsh measures against Melos when it wanted to remain neutral—not allied with either Athens or Sparta.

Why the different decisions? Events in Melos took place during the seventeenth year of the war by which time Athens had suffered several setbacks. The events in Mytilene, by contrast, took place some eleven years earlier when Athens could afford to consider the possible payoffs of being seen as magnanimous. The same logic applies to the Spartan decision concerning the city of Plataea in central Greece. Spartan king Archidamus initially accepted the neutrality of Plataea as it was only the second year of the war and Spartan capabilities and confidence were still high.

Neutrals can affect alliances adversely, particularly when they gain leverage from threatening to ally with one's adversaries. In Thucydides's narrative, neutrals are particularly susceptible to bandwagoning once it is clear which way the wind is blowing. Thucydides records many instances in which neutral states join an alliance as soon as it is clear who is going to be the winner. Thus, following the destruction of the Athenian expedition, "the whole of Hellas, after the great disaster in Sicily, turned immediately against Athens. Those who had not been allied with either side thought that . . . they ought not to keep out of the war any longer."

While states may join alliances to enhance their security, the leader of the alliance (whether based on common interest, compulsion, societal identity, or ideological affinities) has to be wary of manipulation by smaller allies who may have a different security agenda. As so often seems to be the case throughout history, wars begin in small places. Sparta's ally, Corinth, sent troops to

Epidamnus (a colony of Corcyra in northwestern Greece). Corcyra retaliated with its naval forces, subsequently allying with Athens, thus bringing Sparta and Athens to the brink of the Peloponnesian war, which began in 431 BCE. Similarly, the assassination of Austrian Archduke Franz Ferdinand in June 1914 by an anarchist in Sarajevo was an event that precipitated the outbreak of World War I by bringing competing alliances into armed conflict.

In an attempt to settle a regional dispute, states call upon their alliance leaders for support. Corinth had its self-interest in mind when it goaded Sparta into declaring war on Athens. In the case of Sicily, the Silinuntines called for Syracusan support in their conflict with the Egestaeans over marriage rights and a piece of disputed territory. The Egestaeans, in turn, appealed to their long-time Athenian ally for aid and, in the process, presented the possibility of falling dominos if Athens did not favorably respond to their entreaties.

In sum, leaders of alliances are faced with two potential trade-offs. Fear of either bandwagoning or loss of an ally might lead to a policy of capitulation or confrontation with the ally. If the leader attempts to illustrate willingness to back an ally, the ally may be tempted to use this guarantee in pursuit of its regional ambitions. Conversely, a leader's worries about his state's reputation and subsequent attempts to coerce allies into remaining in the alliance could encourage the very result the leader seeks to avoid—alliance defections.

This discussion on the formation and dynamics of alliances is not to suggest that Thucydides believed the *only* concern for leaders should be security interests; throughout *History of the Peloponnesian War*, Thucydides quotes numerous leaders on the need to balance justice, honor, and state interests. In the revolt of Mytilene against Athens, ambassadors from Mytilene tried to convince the Spartans of the importance of justice and honesty and the importance of obligations among allies—"there can never be a firm friendship between man and man or a real community between different states unless there is a conviction of honesty on both sides and a certain like-mindedness in other respects."

The relation between justice and power is a major theme of the Melian Dialogue. This exchange between Athens and Melos, the small island city-state that wanted to be neutral in the conflict between Athens and Sparta, is a wellspring of normative IR theory. Do states have rights or is power ultimately always the decisive factor? Is the world little more than a jungle in which, as the Athenians argue, "the standard of justice depends on the equality of power to compel and that, in fact, the strong do what they have the power to do and the weak accept what they have to accept?"

Put another way, do the strong do what they will and the weak what they must? Does might make right? Is it in fact "a general and necessary law of nature to rule whatever one can"? Or were the Melians correct when they argued that the Athenians should not destroy a principle that was to the general good of all human beings—"namely, that in the case of all who fall into danger there should be such a thing as fair play and just dealing" if for no other reason than one day Athens may find itself in a similar predicament?

Like Melos, Belgium tried to be neutral in two twentieth-century world wars but suffered invasion by Germany in both. Caught geographically as it

was between the belligerents, Germany and France, it was in Germany's interest to invade as part of its effort to subjugate France. International law was on
Belgium's side. As a neutral it had a right to stay out of the conflict. That said,
German military might trampled Belgium's sovereign claim. One could hear a
realist echo of Thucydides's observation in the Melian dialogue that the strong
do what they will and the weak do what they must.

In any event, there is no doubt in Thucydides's mind that security should
be the primary interest of leaders. Yet, it is also apparent that for Thucydides
questions of morality and power should not be divorced from one another.
In reading his discussion of the Melian dialogue, for example, one can hear a
critical voice by Thucydides as he describes Athenian conduct that put military
power above moral principle. In the twentieth century, E. H. Carr, among others, came to a similar conclusion, brilliantly arguing for a balance or blend of
power and moral considerations in international relations.[46]

Reflections on Thucydides

History of the Peloponnesian War is of interest today to scholars of international relations because it provides analytical insights, offers several important
cautionary tales concerning matters of war and peace, and has contributed to
the later development of not only realist theories but also IR theory in general.

Thucydides certainly held a pessimistic view of human nature. But the
important point is not that human beings are innately evil, but rather that war
brings out the worst in people. As he astutely observes: "In times of peace and
prosperity cities and individuals alike follow higher standards because they are
not forced into a situation where they have to do what they do not want to do.
But war is a stern teacher; in depriving them of the power of easily satisfying
their daily wants, it brings most people's minds down to the level of their actual
circumstances." Hence even though one may be pessimistic about basic, underlying human nature, Thucydides reminds us that circumstances also matter.

Indeed, Thucydides's narrative seems to mute his "war is inevitable" thesis
by illustrating how options other than war or confrontation were seriously discussed and debated by leaders and citizens of both Athens and Sparta. Other
policies could have been pursued.

Thucydides makes allowance for voluntarism or free will on the part of
leaders. Who is leading a country can make a great deal of difference. In his
overview of Persian-Greek relations, Thucydides praises the Athenian Themistocles who "was particularly remarkable at looking into the future" and who
"through force of genius and by rapidity of action . . . was supreme at doing
precisely the right thing at precisely the right moment." Similarly, under Pericles
Athens "was wisely led and firmly guarded, and it was under him that Athens
was at her greatest."

As for the difficulty in predicting the course of international events, this is a
reality Thucydides commented upon rather than explained. Whether in politics
or war, it is extremely difficult to foresee how various factors may come together

---

[46] E. H. Carr, *The Twenty Years' Crisis, 1919–1939* (London: Macmillan, 1939, 1962).

to produce a certain outcome. The important point, however, is that whatever the outcome, it is the result of the actions taken by human beings—their agency, not destiny or the gods as occasionally invoked by Homer and Herodotus.

In terms of the relation between morality and power, Thucydides claims the Melians suggested that the two should not be divorced from one another. This should hold even during times of war, if for no other reason than a state may later be in a disadvantageous position and wish to be treated with compassion. One can read Thucydides as commentary that is critical, almost satiric in tone, of an Athens that advanced democratic values at home but did not necessarily practice them abroad. One sees this particularly in the Mytilenean debate and the Melian dialogue. Contradictions abound between what Athenians held as ideals and the way they conducted themselves in practice.

It is tempting to believe that everything written in the past 2,400 years or so on international relations is merely a footnote to Thucydides, his work a veritable Rosetta stone that can unlock the complexities of world politics. As one contemporary scholar has remarked: "In honesty, one must inquire whether or not twentieth-century students of international relations know anything that Thucydides and his fifth-century [BCE] compatriots did not know about the behavior of states."[47]

However, Thucydides was very much a person of his time. As one historian observes: "For classical Greeks, the fundamental metaphor of social relations was mastery. Life appeared to be a choice between dominating and being dominated, between ruling and being ruled. Politics was often treated as a zero-sum game in which one man's victory required another man's defeat."[48] Such a perspective would only be reinforced during times of war.

But suppose Thucydides had lived in more peaceful circumstances. Had he any desire to chronicle events, he might have described a very different world, one in which balances of power and war did not play such an overwhelming role. As a result, he might have drawn other lessons applicable to international relations. There is no doubt that some of the best writings on international relations we review in this volume have been done during times of crisis and war among states—Thucydides, Machiavelli, Thomas Hobbes, Carr. Much less, by comparison, has been written on the ways and means of peace.

AFTER THUCYDIDES: PLATO, ARISTOTLE, AND POLYBIUS

As with Herodotus and Thucydides, Plato, Aristotle, and Polybius carry forward what we now identify as realist understandings, but with important elements that set their works apart. Beyond conceiving of the politics of city-states and empires as contests among competing powers or coalitions of powers, they also discuss concepts consistent with present-day liberal or cosmopolitan images of international relations that would be advanced by later writers. Due to their influence on epistemology and the development of theory, of particular interest

---

[47] Robert Gilpin, *War and Change in World Politics*, 227.
[48] Strauss, "Of Balances," 202.

is the use of dialectical reasoning by Plato, the comparative method employed by Aristotle, and the discussion of the nature of causality in international relations by Polybius.

Historical Context

The Peloponnesian War that began in 431 BCE lasted until 404, around the time of the death of the war's principal historian, Thucydides. Xenophon (431–354 BCE)—a student along with Plato of Socrates—attempted to complete Thucydides's work on the Peloponnesian War. Unfortunately, Xenophon's exaggeration of fact and return to Herodotus's approach of incorporating supernatural explanation into his account, however enjoyable, clearly departed significantly from the approach used by Thucydides. As a result, over time Xenophon's work became less influential with scholars than it otherwise might have been.

The defeat of Athens and the subsequent peace treaty of 404 did not usher in a long period of stability in the Hellenic world. Sparta's domination was rather short-lived as it did not have the resources to maintain its hegemony. Athens soon began to plan its comeback. Sparta also had to deal with the ambition of Thebes, its erstwhile ally. Due to the destructive nature of the Peloponnesian War, the power of the Greek world as a whole to resist outside pressures weakened.

Throughout much of the fifth century BCE, Persia represented an imperial threat to the Greeks. By the fourth century, the security focus shifted to Philip, king of the growing Macedonian Empire that extended outward from northern Greece. As a tutor, Aristotle exposed Philip's son, Alexander the Great (356–323 BCE), to Hellenic thinking. At just twenty years of age, Alexander became king after his father's assassination in 336. In the decade that followed, Alexander commanded his army, defeating Greek city-states and moving eastward across Persia to present-day Pakistan and northwestern India. Greek culture and ideas learned from Aristotle and others spread to the foreign lands and peoples Alexander conquered.

Early in his campaigns when it was rumored that Alexander had died in battle, Thebes revolted from Macedonian control, supported by other city-states and urged on by Athens. Within two weeks Alexander's armies marched to Thebes. When the city refused to surrender, the city was destroyed, some six thousand citizens killed, and the survivors sold into slavery. This brutality understandably intimidated the rest of the Greek city-states, which allowed Alexander to leave modest garrisons to defend his territorial gains while turning his attention to the Persian empire to the east.

Alexander's personal life reflected the greater fluidity of sexual orientation and identity that had greater acceptance in the ancient world than over the millennia that followed. In addition to his having three wives and relationships with other women, he also connected most closely with his fellow warrior, Hephaestion. Aristotle described their relationship as "one soul in two bodies"[49]— a reference, perhaps, to the mythical metaphor in Plato's *Symposium* to the

---

[49] Quoted by Diogenes Laertius, biographer, third century CE.

bonding that takes place when one finds one's "other half." Alexander explicitly compared his relationship with Hephaestion to Achilles and his lover, Patroclus, who, as described in Homer's *Iliad*, fought together against the Trojans. We include this tale here precisely because it raises an issue of global concern on the present-day human rights agenda as advocates seek within and across national borders to advance the acceptance and equal treatment of persons regardless of their sexual orientation or identity.

In the *Symposium*, Aristophanes tells Socrates and his fellow followers that human beings in their original form were very powerful dual entities of three types: male-female, male-male, and female-female. Upset by the challenge all three were posing to the authority of the gods, Zeus sought to weaken them by cutting each in half. Thus, throughout life heterosexuals are persistently seeking their other halves in the opposite sex. In much the same way, homosexuals and lesbians are seeking their same-sex other halves. The story, though pure fantasy, nevertheless reflects a view prevalent at least among educated ancient Greeks that the sexual diversity one observes in society is part of human nature, not at odds with it.

Myths that captured diverse aspects of the human experience—often projected by the ancients onto the gods—were part of Alexander's understanding. Greatly grieved by Hephaestion's death (apparently due to typhoid fever), Alexander died within a year at just thirty-three years of age (precise cause of death disputed). Rivalries among his successors and rebellions within the sprawling empire led to a weakening of central control. Alexander had not lived long enough to consolidate his empire fully, but the influence of Greek thinking he carried remained a lasting legacy.

The same-sex relationship exhibited by Alexander and Hephaestion was in keeping with Greek military practice. For his part, Plato wrote approvingly in the *Symposium* that same-sex relationships contributed to military discipline and bravery on the battlefield:

> If there were only some way of contriving that . . . an army should be made up of lovers and their loves. . . . When fighting at each other's side, although a mere handful, they would overcome the world. For what lover would not choose rather to be seen by all mankind than by his beloved, either when abandoning his post or throwing away his arms? He would be ready to die a thousand deaths rather than endure this. Or who would desert his beloved or fail him in the hour of danger?

Although the practice was not followed by the armies of all Greek city-states, the elite three-hundred-man "Sacred Band" of Thebes composed of 150 couples was renowned for its bravery. It had significant victories on the battlefield against the Spartans in central Greece in both the Battle of Tegyra in 375 BCE and the Battle of Luectra in 371. Alexander's father, Philip II of Macedon, ultimately defeated the Sacred Band in 338 BCE at the Battle of Chaeronea (also in central Greece), but he was loud in his praise for its courage and fighting skill, allegedly weeping over their demise. The rest of the Theban army had fled, but the Sacred Band continued fighting to the last dying man.

Such same-sex pairing is anathema to the cultures and legal systems in most present-day militaries, particularly connecting older soldiers with younger.[50] On the other hand, most militaries do recognize the value of nonsexual bonding of soldiers, which does contribute to fighting capabilities and is commonplace in successful combat units. Bonding contributes to morale, and warriors in these units care for and look after each other's welfare, particularly in combat. Although bonding in present-day military units is essentially nonsexual, there is increasing acceptance, particularly in Western countries, of persons regardless of their sexual orientations or gender identities.

Notwithstanding the defeat of Athens in the Peloponnesian War and the eventual end of Hellenic independence, it was a golden age of Athenian scholarship in ancient Greece. More than just his contributions as a historian, Thucydides marked a watershed in the development of thinking about international relations. He had set a model for the study of international relations that others would emulate throughout history. His approach influenced three of the most famous Greek philosophers who wrote after him—Plato, Aristotle, and Polybius. We now turn to a discussion of these Greek scholars and their understandings that relate directly or indirectly to what we now call international relations.

Plato

Plato (c. 427–348 BCE) was born some four years after the beginning of the Peloponnesian war and a year or so after the death of Pericles (c. 495–429). He came from a distinguished family interested in politics, and during the war years, he witnessed the tendency of political leaders such as Cleon to pander to the public and undertake such actions as the Sicilian expedition that ended in disaster in 412. As a result of that ill-fated adventure, oligarchic control was established the following year and power invested in the Council of Four Hundred. A year later this was succeeded by the Government of Five Thousand, which subsequently succumbed to opposition forces that initiated six years of what could be termed "democratic terror."

In 404 when Plato was twenty-three, Athens was defeated by Sparta, leading once again to an oligarchic revolution that resulted in political and personal vendettas. This regime lasted only eight months. Democracy was restored, but in 399 the generally moderate leadership did something Plato would never forgive—they ordered the death of Socrates on the grounds of impiety and corruption of the young. Although friends and family had expected Plato to go into politics, his experiences as a youth helped to turn him to a life of philosophy and a belief that a new type of politician could be trained. This hope was translated into action in 386 with the establishment of the Academy.[51]

Plato had very little to say about international relations. He is a prime example, however, of a political philosopher whose indirect effect on thinking

---

[50] The older *erastês* or "lover" typically was in his twenties, the younger *erômenos* or "beloved" in his teens.

[51] Desmond Lee, Introduction to Plato's *The Republic* (London: Penguin Books, 1955, 1987), 11–17. All subsequent direct quotes from *The Republic* are from this edition.

about world politics has been profound. It is in some of Plato's dialogues, for example, that we find dialectical reasoning—dealing with opposites—as the key method used by his great teacher Socrates. Georg W. F. Hegel would find dialectics useful in the development of theory, as would Karl Marx. Beyond the more formal Hegelian and Marxian uses of dialectics to consider contrary possibilities, hypothetical opposites or conflicting analyses are at the core of the critical and creative thinking that is so essential to theorizing, whether in international relations or other fields of inquiry.

More generally, Plato and Aristotle deserve credit for beginning systematic thinking about politics and the function and nature of the state, hence influencing scholars who followed them. Indeed, to this day the state has remained the key unit of analysis in not only comparative politics but also most scholarly thinking about international relations. Although tangential to his primary focus on the domestic aspects of the state, the following questions that Plato touches on are of interest to present-day scholars of international relations—How does the state come into being, how can its security be enhanced, and what is the primary cause of war among states? Do different types of states exhibit different types of foreign policy behavior? What is the relation between power and justice? Each will be addressed in turn.

The State and Security

In the course of Plato's famous dialogue on the nature of justice in *The Republic*, Glaucon, one of his participants in the discussion, presents his view on the origins of the state that anticipates the social contract theories of the seventeenth and eighteenth centuries. He argues that conventional wisdom assumes that "according to nature," it is "a good thing to inflict wrong or injury, and a bad thing to suffer it." But after experiencing both, people decide that "as they can't evade the one and achieve the other, it will pay to make a compact with each other by which they forgo both. They accordingly proceed to make laws and mutual agreements, and what the law lays down they call lawful and right." Given the selfishness of human nature, people must be "forcibly restrained by the law and made to respect each other's claims."[52]

Later social contract theorists such as Thomas Hobbes use the myth of the social contract as a means by which to distinguish and justify the civil order found within states as compared to the anarchy of international politics. While Thomas Hobbes, John Locke, and Jean-Jacques Rousseau in the seventeenth and eighteenth centuries are interested in the problem of sovereignty (who should be the final authority and why the individual citizen should obey it?), Glaucon is concerned with establishing a morally justifiable as well as political basis of mutual obligation. He goes on to note that "no man is just of his own free will, but only under compulsion, and . . . he will always do wrong when he gets the chance."

But Socrates, more closely reflecting Plato's views, states that "society originates . . . because the individual is not self-sufficient, but has many needs that he can't supply himself." When Socrates proceeds to enumerate these needs in

---

[52] Plato, *The Republic*, I: 2.

order of importance—food, shelter, and clothing—personal security is not mentioned. This is one of the primary motivating factors social contract theorists such as Hobbes use to justify the state, but for Socrates, the security dimension comes to the fore only after the state begins to expand.[53]

In *The Laws*, however, Plato presents a different view of primitive man and his circumstances "after the flood," one which emphasizes man's innocence. Except for a few people at the early stages, there was enough food and clothing, and "they were not intolerably poor, nor driven by poverty to quarrel with each other. . . . These men were good [and] innocent of the techniques of warfare peculiar to city-life."

As Socrates and his compatriots proceed further to discuss the elements of this mythical state and its development and enlargement, Socrates suggests that eventually "the territory that was formerly enough to support us will now be too small." As a result, "we shall have to cut a slice off our neighbors' territory." He assumes, however, that if they, too, are growing in size they will also want a slice of our territory, and "that will lead to war."

At this point Socrates states that our concern is not with the effects of war, but rather to note that "we have found its origin to be the same as that of most evil, individual or social" acquisitiveness. To defend the property and possessions of the citizens, an army is required. Glaucon asks if a citizen army would be sufficient, but Socrates replies that "it is surely of the greatest importance that the business of war should be efficiently run." Hence those in the military require "complete freedom from other affairs and a correspondingly high degree of skill and practice."

This is the primary justification of the "auxiliaries" of Plato's Guardian class, which he compares to a watchdog of "utmost gentleness to those it is used to and knows, but to be savage to strangers [i.e., foreigners]." Aristotle disagrees with Plato on the treatment of foreigners: "Some say that to feel friendly at the sight of familiar faces and fierce at the approach of strangers is a requirement for the Guardians. . . . But what he [Plato] says about harshness to strangers is, I think, quite wrong; one ought not to behave thus to anyone, and fierceness is not a mark of natural greatness of mind except toward wrongdoers."[54] Nevertheless, as Plato observes in *The Laws*, "no better or more powerful or efficient weapon exists for ensuring safety and final victory in war" than the "combined and united action" of soldiers—the city-state's guardians.

Suspicion, if not hostility, to the world beyond the city-state, is typical of both Plato and Aristotle, who viewed the polis as the supreme form of organization because it was created by human beings acting in accordance with their own nature. It is in *The Laws* where an older Plato describes in great detail his utopian state that is to be insulated from the outside world as much as possible. In terms of foreign visitors, "good care" needs to be taken lest any "of this category of visitor introduces any novel custom."

---

[53] This image of what could be termed a state of nature is closer to Jean-Jacques Rousseau than to Hobbes. Plato, *The Laws*, trans. Trevor J. Sanders (London: Penguin Books, 1970, 1986), III: 4. Subsequent direct quotes from *The Laws* come from this edition.

[54] Aristotle, *The Politics*, trans. T. A. Sinclair (London: Penguin Books, 1962, 1981), VII: 7.

Contact with foreigners is to be kept "down to the unavoidable minimum." Consistent with this principle, "no young person under 40 is ever to be allowed to travel abroad under any circumstances; nor is anyone to be allowed to go for private reasons, but only on some public business, as a herald or ambassador or as an observer of one sort or another." Those who do go abroad for such purposes are obligated when they return to "tell the younger generation that the social and political customs of the rest of the world don't measure up to their own."

The State and Foreign Policy

In *The Republic* Plato's discussion of justice leads to the conclusion that in the "perfect state" people "should be governed by those of their number who are best at philosophy and war." In one of the major contributions to the study of comparative government and politics, Plato has Socrates describe four other "imperfect" types of states that are inferior to the one he is proposing—timarchy, oligarchy, democracy, and tyranny. Plato's discussion focuses on the nature of these types of states and how they degenerate or evolve one from the other. Very little is said about how the type of political system affects the foreign policy behavior of a state.

He does note that a timarchy—a military aristocracy similar to Sparta—prefers "simpler, hearty types" as rulers who prefer war to peace. Its citizens "will admire the tricks and stratagems that are needed in war, which will be its constant occupation." An oligarchy, on the other hand, exhibits an "inability to wage war" due to a fear of arming the people or a desire to avoid the heavy expenses associated with war. As for a democracy, Plato perhaps has the Corcyraean civil war in mind when he discusses the transition from oligarchy to democracy, defining the latter in terms of the individual being free to do what he likes: "It [democracy] will fall into sickness and dissension at the slightest external provocation, when one party or the other calls in help from a neighboring oligarchy or democracy."

Once democracy triumphs, individual liberty means "you needn't fight if there's a war, or you can wage a private war in peacetime if you don't like peace." Tyranny emerges from the chaos and excesses of democracy. A tyrant arises who leads a class war against the owners of property. Once in power and having defeated foreign enemies, "he will in the first place continue to stir up war in order that the people may continue to need a leader." In other words, real or imagined external threats can be used to enhance one's domestic political position.

Power and Justice

Analyzing the relation between power and justice is, of course, one of Plato's primary concerns. Furthermore, by arguing that justice consists of individuals each doing the job for which one is naturally suited, Plato begins the tradition of class analysis that informs much of the work of present-day scholars influenced by Marx and economic-structuralist understandings. But as for justice, it is not Plato's definition that is of greatest interest to scholars of international relations, but rather that of Thrasymachus who presents the "conventional wisdom" of the day in *The Republic*, very often propounded by the Sophists. He bluntly states: "I say that justice or right is simply what is in the interest of the stronger party."

The character Callicles in Plato's *Gorgias* reasserts this position. According to Callicles, nature "demonstrates that it is right that the better man should prevail over the worse and the stronger over the weaker. . . . Right consists in the superior ruling over the inferior and having the upper hand." He then gives the examples of Darius invading Scythia and Xerxes invading Greece, noting such actions "are in accordance with natural law."[55]

Such "might makes right" position is not Plato's. He merely represents it in effect as a straw man that can be knocked down in further discourse. As noted earlier, we see it as well in Thucydides's Melian dialogue in which Athenians argue that "it is a general and necessary law of nature to rule whatever one can." On the other hand, the Athenians divorce the question of "right" from that of power. They tell the Melians that they must submit to the power of Athens, not because "we have a right to our empire because we defeated the Persians," but rather, as stated by the Melians themselves, to "leave justice out of account and to confine ourselves to self-interest."[56]

Plato understandably has been characterized as an "idealist." His emphasis on the philosopher king in *The Republic* and the utopia depicted in *The Laws* reflect an optimistic, voluntarist predilection that assumes wise leadership can ensure the security of the city-state and, most importantly, a just and well-ordered society. But two cautions are in order. First, his teleological view of the development of the state is an obvious example of determinism in Plato's thought—that there are purposes or functions apart from (as well as greater than) the will of individual human beings that drive construction of the state. In other words, it is nature that wills a particular end, not the will of a man or woman.[57]

Second, and perhaps in contradiction, there is a strong undercurrent of pessimism in his work. While he hopes that a philosopher king can be nurtured through the right sort of education, he does not seem to have found many likely role models. In Plato's portrayal of the rather bitter debate between the advocates of political oratory and Socrates's defense of philosophy in the *Gorgias*, he denigrates the achievements of such noted Athenians as Pericles, Cimon, Miltiades, and Themistocles. In the words Plato attributes to Socrates, no one "has been a good statesman in this country." Hence while a ruler should strive to achieve perfection in conduct and policies, attaining the Platonic ideal of state and constitution appears to be highly unlikely. The works of Aristotle, however, seem to be not only of a more practical or pragmatic nature than Plato's but also more optimistic about what leaders can achieve.

---

[55] Plato, *Gorgias*, trans. Walter Hamilton (London: Penguin Books, 1960, 1988), 78–79.
[56] Thucydides, *History of the Peloponnesian War*, V: 89–90.
[57] Donald Kagan, *The Great Dialogue*, 201.

Aristotle

Aristotle (384–322 BCE) was born in Chalcidice, part of the dominions of Macedonia. At age seventeen he went to Athens and enrolled as a student in Plato's Academy. He remained there for some twenty years and, after Plato's death, traveled to Asia Minor (present-day Turkey) where he conducted scientific studies. In 343 he returned to his native land to teach King Philip's son, Alexander, for about two years, but eventually returned to Athens in 336. Two years before that, Philip had grouped most of the Greek states into a federation under Macedonian control. After ascending to the throne in 336, Alexander led his combined armies eastward across Asia to present-day Pakistan and northwest India. As Alexander was conquering the East, Aristotle established his famous school, the Lyceum. With the death of Alexander in 323, anti-Macedonian feeling intensified, and Aristotle—always a foreigner in Athens—felt it was prudent to move to nearby Euboea where he died at age sixty-two.

A recurrent theme of this work is how scholars stand on the shoulders of their predecessors. Greek and Roman scholars, including Polybius and Cicero, found Plato's *Republic* of greater interest than Aristotle's *Politics*. The real impact of Aristotle's *Ethics* and *Politics* is not apparent until the twelfth century when such religious scholars as Thomas Aquinas studied them closely. In the fourteenth century, Dante also was heavily influenced by Aristotle, his works also essential reading for Machiavelli, Jean Bodin, and Hobbes.

As an example of Aristotle's later influence, in a sentiment that would be repeated by Machiavelli, albeit in modified form, some two millennia later, the monarchical ruler needs to "give the impression of dignity, not of harshness, of being the kind of person who inspires not fear but respect in those who meet him." Of course, "this is not easy if he is readily despised." In such circumstances, when "he cannot manage to cultivate any of the other virtues, he should aim at least at valor in warfare, and establish for himself a military reputation."[58]

As with Plato's *Republic* and *The Laws*, Aristotle's *Politics* is domestically oriented—a search for the ideal constitution. This is rather interesting in that Aristotle lived at a time when militarily and politically the Greek city-states were progressively being overshadowed by the Macedonian Empire. Despite events unfolding around him, Aristotle had little to say about empires, or indeed international relations in general, which is a caution against assuming that a scholar's life work is overly determined by the times within which he or she lives. Nevertheless, Aristotle's work influenced later scholars interested in international relations in at least three ways—through his conceptual and empirical approach to political phenomena, his detailed examination of different types of state constitutions and the causes of instability, and his writings on economics. In the course of our discussion of states and stability, we will also discuss what little Aristotle had to say about security.

---

[58] T. A. Sinclair, "Introduction" to Aristotle, *The Politics* and Aristotle, V: vi.

Epistemology

While Aristotle, like Plato and other Greeks, is interested in determining the ideal state and constitution, his approach is more analytic. Plato believes all objects have a perfect form or ideal essence; such perfection could never be achieved but only approximated empirically in the world in which we live. Aristotle, while sharing Plato's teleological perspective, believes that things were continually moving toward their full completeness and, through this natural process, perfection could be achieved.

Hence, when Aristotle discusses the origins of the state, like Plato, he does not adopt a social contract perspective. As with the family and then the village, he notes in *The Politics* that the development of the city-state is a natural follow-on:

> While the state came about as a means of securing life itself, it continues in being to secure the *good* life. Therefore every state exists by nature, as the earlier associations too were natural. This association is the end of those others. . . . It follows that the state belongs to the class of objects that exist by nature, and that man is by nature a political animal.

Nevertheless, there is also a hint of the idea of the social contract when Aristotle states: "The point is that if a constitution is to have a good prospect of stability, it must be such that all sections of the state accept it and want it to go on in the same way as before."

Perfection is not some unattainable goal, floating among the clouds, but is a kernel residing in individuals or political communities that have the potential to achieve completeness. A desire to lend credibility to this perspective contributed to Aristotle's fascination with rigorous empirical observation, reflected in his studies in the natural sciences as well as those focusing on human institutions. Aided by his students at the Lyceum, he collected information on some 168 constitutions, classifying them based on conceptions of the just distribution of political power and assessing causes of their relative stability.[59] While not denying the normative and metaphysical appeal of Aristotle's works down through the ages, it is his interest in classifying, conceptualizing, and engaging in empirical research that has had the biggest effect on the social sciences, including international relations as a field of inquiry.

Constitutions, Stability, and Security

As noted previously, Aristotle is particularly interested in how states organize themselves internally, and hence he made a major effort to collect as many constitutions as possible. In *The Politics* he classifies constitutions in several ways. For example, he first classifies states based on the number and aim of the rulers—monarchy is rule by one, aristocracy rule by a few, and polity rule by

---

[59] While much of the data are found in *The Politics*, unfortunately only one such complete study survives. See *The Athenian Constitution* (London: Penguin Books, 1984, 1987).

many (the mass of the populace). What all have in common in these ideal forms is a concern for the common interest.

The "corresponding deviations" are tyranny (when monarchies become dictatorial), oligarchy (when the few use their position for self-aggrandizement), and democracy (when the many run rampant over the few). In this regard, the key criterion for classification is economic. What we now might identify as having present-day Marxist or economic-structuralist overtones is the emphasis Aristotle places on material factors. In this regard, he argues that "oligarchy occurs when the sovereign power of the constitution is in the hands of those with possessions, democracy when it is in the hands of those who have no stock of possessions and are without means." For his part, Marx was a voracious reader who incorporated such Greco-Roman insights to include his identification of slavery as an ancient mode of production one can find in Aristotle.

Finally, Aristotle suggests that another possible criterion that can be used to differentiate constitutions is the division of political power based on what is viewed by a particular society as being "just." What is of interest for our purposes, however, is that in Aristotle's detailed examination of various states and constitutions (which includes discussions of how to preserve these political systems), the reasons he offers for their downfall almost always stem from internal factors. External or international factors generally play little if any role at all. When they are mentioned, they tend to be of secondary importance. For example, in his discussion of the rise of factions within an aristocracy, five contributing factors are listed. Only one—the disparity of wealth between rich and poor—is related to the international environment.

Aristotle notes such disparity is "particularly likely to come about in time of war." Similarly, in democracies "the most potent causes of revolution is the unprincipled character of popular leaders," and in oligarchies it may result "when the oligarchs wrong the multitude" or arise "out of the oligarchs' own rivalry." This almost exclusive emphasis on internal factors as a means to understand domestic political stability is not unique to Aristotle. Indeed, it is only since World War II that political scientists have engaged seriously in systematic and comparative studies of the international determinants of domestic politics.

Discussing Plato's *The Laws*, Aristotle quotes his mentor's belief that "in framing the laws a legislator ought to have regard both to the territory and to the population." He also criticizes Plato by noting "but surely we should add that he ought to take note of the neighboring territories too" as a state "must provide itself with such arms for warfare as are serviceable not merely internally but also against the territories beyond its border."[60] Describing his ideal state in *The Politics*, Aristotle discusses basic security matters for essentially the first and only time. He obviously does not think much of those city-states or peoples who engage in war for reasons of aggrandizement—the Scythians, Persians, Thracians, and Celts. He notes "how completely unreasonable it would be if the work of a statesman were to be reduced to an ability to work out how to rule

---

[60] Similarly, Aristotle criticizes Phaleas's ideal constitution for "disregarding, as he ought not to do, relations with neighboring and other foreign states."

and be master over neighboring peoples." For him, war should only be a means to defend the good life.

Security, therefore, is essentially in the realm of defense, in which it is necessary to have "sufficient armed force to give the laws protection" and "to repel attempts at wrongdoing coming from outside." In one passage in *The Politics*, Aristotle goes into considerable detail describing appropriate defense preparations and emphasizing the need "to secure the greatest degree of protection that strong walls can afford." This is the best military measure when "the superiority of the attackers is too much for the valor" of the defenders, particularly in light of "all the modern improvements in the accuracy of missiles and artillery for attacking a besieged town."

Adversaries likely will be deterred from attacking well-defended city-states. In Aristotle's words: "An enemy will not even attempt an attack in the first place on those who are well prepared to meet it." This is one of the first statements of the military-strategic, realist view (in Latin): *si vis pacem, para bellum*—if you seek peace, prepare for war. It is also a basic element of present-day deterrence theory.

Consistent with the observations of nineteenth- and twentieth-century realist geopolitical strategists, Aristotle argues that a city-state's power or capabilities are affected directly by some other factors. For example, its location in relation to both sea and land is important, the objective being to make it "hard for a hostile force to invade, easy for an expeditionary force to depart from." Furthermore, "if it is to play an active role as a leading state, it will need naval as well as land forces large enough for such activities."[61]

It is apparent that, for Aristotle, good government, the theme of his book, is the critical source of security. He contends that "a state's purpose is also to provide something more than a military pact of protection against injustice, or to facilitate mutual acquaintance and the exchange of goods." It must "ensure government under good laws" and promote civic virtue among the citizenry. A good constitution—for Aristotle a mixed one or "polity" with a large middle class that blends elements of oligarchy and democracy—contributes to security and good living. Unity within the state under a system of good and effective laws is also important to the security of any city-state.

Economy

Finally, more so than the other ancient writers we have surveyed, Aristotle explicitly deals with the relation between economics and politics. His contributions to both domestic and international political economy provided a foundation upon which later writers would build. Like Plato, Aristotle in *The Politics* employs class analysis, an approach with both domestic and international (or transnational) applications in present-day scholarship. He asserts that "a division of the state into classes is necessary." Indeed, he provides a defense of slavery and the master-slave relationship as integral to the political economy of his times.

---

[61] See the discussion in this book on geopolitics in chapter 5.

Class formation, however, is not due solely to economic exigencies, but also to security threats stemming from possible slave revolts or foreign powers. Hence, just as Plato elevated warriors to an important class unto themselves, Aristotle claims the two critical parts of the state are the military and deliberative elements. Furthermore, in his extensive survey of constitutions, he notes that "the reason for the plurality of constitutions lies in the plurality of parts of every state." He initially defines this plurality in terms of economic classes: "Some must be wealthy, others poor, others in the middle." But he also notes that "in addition to wealth there are other *differentiae* of family, virtue, and any other similar feature described as 'part' of a state."

Such writings certainly influence the domestic views and worldviews of such classical economists as Adam Smith, David Ricardo, Karl Marx, and the others who found in Aristotle the basis for what would become their labor theory of value. In particular, Marx combines the class analysis and political economy of the ancients, transposing their view through history to the nineteenth-century circumstances he observed.

Marx's classic phrase in the *Communist Manifesto* that all history is the history of class struggles beginning with the master-slave relationship seems really to be a distant echo of Aristotle's notion of the rule of "master over slave." Indeed, Marx characterizes the dominant mode of production of the ancients as slavery, differentiating it from the successive historical and global modes of feudal and capitalist production that could not have been known to Plato and Aristotle.

On property rights, Aristotle argues that "while property should up to a point be held in common, the general principle should be that of private ownership." It is the same Aristotle, however, who expresses hostility toward the practice of charging interest for the loan of money, a sentiment also central to the thinking of the Middle Ages when all interest charges, however small, were regarded as sinful practice—usury. Aristotle's reasoning, similar to that of the medieval church that followed his lead, is that interest earnings are not the outcome of productive labor, but instead "the gain arises out of currency itself." This idea had a long shelf life through the Middle Ages and after, inhibiting financial transactions of the marketplace that we now view as essential to a capitalist mode of production.

Trade derives, according to Aristotle, from "men having too much of this and not enough of that," an observation that would be repeated by eighteenth- and nineteenth-century classical economists. Aristotle argues that "exchange" effectively is "carried on far enough to satisfy the needs of the parties." Moreover, Aristotle extends this logic to international trade and finance when he observes how "the import of necessities and the export of surplus goods began to facilitate the satisfaction of needs beyond national frontiers" and, consequently, that traders "resorted to the use of coined money."

While commerce may bring one into contact with foreigners, such awareness does not mean acceptance of diversity. Ethnocentric rejection of foreign ways was the more common response among most Greek writers, who contrasted themselves with the "barbarians" who lived outside of their city-states.

Aristotle seems to have shared these prejudices, perhaps in part because he was no fan of foreign trade and coined money that encouraged such contacts. He was concerned that foreigners and their ideas would undermine the unity of the state.

Hence Aristotle suggests that one should deal differently with foreigners when their disputes involved one's citizens. He argues, for example, that there should be two judicial courts—"one for foreigners disputing with foreigners" and "the other for foreigners disputing with citizens." The suggestion that human beings constitute a human family that extends beyond the borders of any given tribe, city-state, or set of city-states was not the dominant image in ancient Greece. Such thinking found later among the Stoics was quite foreign to Plato, Aristotle, and their contemporaries.

Aristotle's student, Alexander the Great, did spread his mentor's—and, more broadly, Greek—political ideas well beyond Athens and the other Greek city-states. A new cosmopolitanism that departed significantly from the ethnocentrism of Plato, Aristotle, and other Greeks was reflected in Alexander's policy of encouraging soldiers to marry within the local populations conquered by force of arms. In a larger sense, it was Alexander's conquests that effectively spread Hellenic ideas throughout the world of his time. As noted previously, the development of the idea of the unity of humankind would have to await Greek Stoicism, which developed in the century after Alexander and subsequently spread to Rome and elsewhere.

Polybius

The work of the Greek historian Polybius (c. 200–120 BCE) is not often read or even cited by most present-day political theorists. This omission is a mistake. Such obscurity is unwarranted. Indeed, the influence Polybius had on political philosophers as diverse as Machiavelli, Montesquieu, and the writers of the constitution of the United States is striking. Polybius takes a very rational approach to his study of politics by relating observations to theory. When possible, he uses primary sources and takes a critical view of the data he collected. Following the example set by Thucydides and relevant to the development of IR theory, he seeks causal explanations for the phenomena he observed.

More than other historians of his time, Polybius was a theorist in the modern sense of the term. His work is more than just a history of the Punic Wars between Rome and Carthage. Polybius focuses on the transformation of world politics—the rise of the Roman Empire—and seeks explanatory variables for the phenomenon at what today would be termed the international, domestic, and individual levels of analysis.

Polybius was born in Greece in the city of Megalopolis on the Peloponnese. The son of a wealthy landowner, he was attracted to history and political theory, but his talents and family connections led him to be elected a cavalry leader in the Achaean League to which Megalopolis belonged. During his life the Greeks were caught between the rival ambitions of the Macedonians and the Romans. With the defeat of the former at Pydna in 168 BCE, however, Rome moved to purge any Greek notables whom they suspected they could not trust.

Polybius was one of a thousand Greeks sent to Italy for cross-examination, and he remained there for sixteen years without ever being tried or even accused of any crime. He was, however, fortunate to be housed in Rome where he became close friends with Publius Scipio, son of the Roman general who had defeated the Macedonians at Pydna. Polybius became acquainted with many of Rome's leading families. He accompanied Scipio to Spain and also visited North Africa where he queried the aged King of Numidia about Hannibal. On his return to Italy, he detoured through the Alps to see where Hannibal's famous crossing had occurred nearly seventy years earlier.

Eventually those Achaean detainees who were still alive were allowed to return to Greece. Polybius, however, went to Carthage at Scipio's request to witness, if not advise, the Romans in their siege of the city. Following the capture and burning of Carthage, he traveled beyond Gibraltar and down the coast of Africa. He then returned to Greece and spent two years (146–144 BCE) acting as an intermediary between the Romans and the Achaeans. When the Achaean League was disbanded and Roman troops removed, Polybius began an ongoing effort to resolve disputes among the cities.

During the last part of his life Polybius visited Alexandria, Egypt, and probably traveled to Spain for a time with Scipio. He died at age eighty-two as a result of a fall from a horse. His work influenced, among others, Livy, Plutarch, and Cicero during the Roman era, and found a receptive audience at Constantinople in present-day Turkey. It was not until the fifteenth century, however, that his writings reappeared in Italy, his discussion of the Roman constitution clearly influencing Machiavelli and, in the eighteenth century, particularly Montesquieu.[62]

Polybius tells us at the very outset why he wrote *The Rise of the Roman Empire*:

> There can surely be nobody so petty or so apathetic in his outlook that he has no desire to discover by what means and under what system of government the Romans succeeded in less than fifty-three years in bringing under their rule almost the whole of the inhabited world, an achievement which is without parallel in human history.

He was particularly interested in enlightening his fellow Greeks as to why and how the vaunted city-state system had come under Roman domination.

This work is of interest to us for at least four reasons. First, Polybius's epistemology or approach to knowing about the world sounds quite modern to contemporary scholars. Second, his explanation of the rise of Rome takes into account the relative importance of different causes including both external and internal factors; it is, in the language of contemporary IR theory, a multilevel approach. Third, more so than any other writer discussed in this book, Polybius addresses the role of fate or chance in aiding or frustrating the political and

---

[62] F. W. Walbank, "Introduction" to Polybius, *The Rise of the Roman Empire*, trans. Ian Scott-Kilvert (London: Penguin Books, 1979), 12–15, 35–37. The quotes in the text of Polybius are from this source.

military designs of leaders. Finally, present-day realist and liberal images of international relations rest on foundation stones put in place by Polybius.

Epistemology

Thucydides provided Polybius with a model for historical research. This is clear from the criticism Polybius directs toward Timaeus and other historians who wrote after the time of Thucydides. Consistent with Thucydides, Polybius states that his purpose is "to write a history of actual events"—"not so much to give pleasure to my readers as to benefit those who devote their attention to history." To Polybius the best education for dealing with the vicissitudes of life comes from the serious study of history. In the opening statement of the work, Polybius emphasizes that his efforts are intended also to be policy relevant: "Humankind possesses no better guide to conduct than the knowledge of the past."

Epistemology—how we know what we think we know—is an issue of concern to present-day theorists. It is not a new question. Polybius lays out in some detail his views on the appropriate epistemological assumptions historians should adopt and the scholarly norms to which they should adhere. For him, history is much more than a collection of facts—explanation is the goal. He asserts that "the mere statement of a fact, though it may excite our interest, is of no benefit to us." It is only when "knowledge of the cause is added" that "the study of history becomes fruitful." A theorist in the present-day sense of the term, Polybius contends "that by far the most important part of historical writing lies in the consideration of the consequences of events, their accompanying circumstances, and above all their causes."

Aside from explanation for its own sake, a better prediction may also result: When we can "draw analogies between parallel circumstances of the past and of our own times," then we may be able "to make forecasts as to what is to happen." At the very least, "comparing and evaluating" these "parallel occurrences" provides "a far more reliable general picture than is possible if everything is judged in isolation." Such thoughts on how we understand or know about politics in general—or international relations in particular—seem rather commonplace today. In this regard, we owe a debt to such writers as Polybius and Thucydides who made causal explanation and prediction their principal tasks, their example followed by others.

Polybius also addresses the empirical research enterprise itself, favoring original or what we might call field research. Confining oneself to documentary or library sources is not enough. Although it "demands much greater exertion and expense," he favors "personal investigation" and the use of original and what we now refer to as primary sources. According to Polybius, it is "the business of making first-hand inquiries that is the historian's most important duty." Moreover, as much as is humanly possible one must be an impartial observer:

> Now in other spheres of human life we should perhaps not rule out such partiality. A good man ought to love his friends and his country, and should share both their hatreds and their loyalties. But once a man takes up the role of the historian he must discard all considerations of this kind.

While Polybius is addressing historians directly, in a broader sense he is addressing all theorists who attempt to explain what they observe, urging them to test their propositions or hypotheses with evidence or empirical data.

Not surprisingly, it follows that Polybius considers accuracy and honesty as imperatives in the scholarly enterprise. More specifically, he condemns plagiarists who "commit the disreputable act of claiming as one's own what is really the work of others." Beyond giving credit where it is due, telling the truth about what one observes is essential. In this regard, he notes that there are two kinds of falsehood, the one being the result of ignorance and the other intentional. Although we may "pardon those who depart from the truth through ignorance," we must "unreservedly condemn those who lie deliberately." Unintentional error "deserves kindly correction" whereas deception warrants "outright condemnation!" Indeed, as a general caveat, Polybius advises readers of history to be critical, cautioning them "not to be misled by the authority of the author's name, but to pay attention to the facts."

These concerns articulated by Polybius resonate with present-day challenges posed by mass communications and social networks that facilitate efforts by some to manipulate or distort facts or propagate lies that serve particular interests. Many people tend to accept distortions or outright falsehoods when they are repeated over and over again. Truthful counternarratives become essential to knowledge in the public sphere.

Explanation

In developing explanations, Polybius argues that one should differentiate causes from beginnings and pretexts, distinctions reminiscent of Thucydides's underlying versus immediate causes of war. Polybius is principally interested in causes, which he defines as "those events which influence in advance our purposes and decisions, that is to say our conceptions of things, our state of mind, our calculations about them and the whole process of reasoning whereby we arrive at decisions and undertakings." The examples he gives of these three terms come from the war between Greek King Antiochus (241–187 BCE) and the Romans. The cause of the war was "the anger felt by the Aetolians," the people in the mountainous coastal area by the Gulf of Corinth. The pretext for the war was "the so-called liberation of Greece," the beginning of the war "Antiochus' descent upon Demetrius."

Of interest to us here, of course, is not so much the correctness of the particular analysis as how Polybius framed the question—differentiating causes from beginnings and pretexts. To do this effectively, one must take a longer view of history that contains antecedent causes. To focus only on particular episodes at the expense of the longer view runs the risk of being driven "by sheer lack of subject matter to exaggerate the importance of trivial incidents and to write at length on matters that are scarcely worth mentioning at all."

Polybius is also sensitive to what present-day IR theorists call the levels of analysis problem. What unit should one study? Does one focus on the whole or on the parts that make up the whole? How does one relate the general to the specific? In a particularly insightful passage, he notes how a "grasp of the whole is of great service in enabling us to master the details while, at the same time, some previous acquaintance with the details helps us toward the comprehension of the whole." This is a very clear expression of the dynamic relation between theory building and data gathering. Even more to the point, Polybius treats the occurrences he observes as part of "an organic whole: the affairs of Italy and of Africa are connected with those of Asia and Greece" and are all part of a larger causal explanation. If one overlooks these relations and interrelations, explanation cannot be complete.

Following from previous statements, it is apparent that Polybius recognizes the importance of factors in the external environment that surround an empire, city-state, or other political unit. But domestic factors are also central to his explanation. He contends that "in all political situations we must understand that the principal factor that makes for success or failure is the form of a state's constitution." Thus, for Polybius, Rome's success in the wars with Carthage is related to "the perfection and strength of the Roman constitution," a position also taken by Livy, the Roman historian. Rome's "constitution contributed very largely not only to the restoration of Roman rule over the Italians and the Sicilians, but also to the acquisition of Spain, to the recovery of Cisalpine Gaul (northern Italy), and finally to the victorious conclusion of the war with Carthage and to the idea of attaining dominion of the whole world."[63]

The cohesiveness of a political unit—also emphasized by Herodotus and Thucydides—can be particularly enhanced if the constitution correctly allocates political power. In the case of Rome, "the result is a union that is strong enough to withstand all emergencies. . . . For whenever some common external threat compels the three [senate, consuls, and the people] to unite and work together, the strength that the state then develops becomes quite extraordinary." For Polybius, lack of unity is a particular problem for the Greeks, given numerous threats from foreign forces.

Machiavelli's writings reflect Polybius on the contribution of unity to security as well as when Polybius argues that "every state relies for its preservation on two fundamental qualities, namely bravery in the face of the enemy, and harmony among its citizens." When the customs, laws, and constitution are good, security is enhanced both internally and externally. Two other points emphasized by Polybius—the danger of placing the security of the state in the hands of mercenary troops and the role of religion as a means of keeping a political unit together—were to be further developed by Machiavelli. The idea of an integrating myth, if that is the way Polybius and Machiavelli both see religion, is also to be found in Plato's *Republic*.[64]

As for the role of the individual, in his causal explanation Polybius leans toward the voluntarism that allows human will to be decisive. As he argues: "The action of intelligent and far-sighted" persons can make a difference. He approvingly quotes the poet Euripides as saying that "one wise head can

---

[63] The northern Italian region was invaded by Celts in the late in 391 BCE. Celtic military forces finally were defeated by the Romans in 225 BCE.
[64] Plato, *The Republic*, III: 1.

outmatch a score of hands." More than 1,600 years later, Machiavelli adopts essentially the same perspective. Human agency matters.

The importance Polybius attributes to human volition or choice in determining outcomes is underscored by his remark that it is "the choice of the right moment that controls all human action, and above all the operations of war." Thus, Hannibal's strength as a commander stemmed from the fact that he "accurately plotted from experience the course he should steer." Polybius relates that Hannibal, who had anticipated how the Romans "would probably act, gave them neither the time nor respite to concert their plans." By contrast, Polybius criticizes the changes in the character and behavior of King Philip of Macedon that resulted in his loss of goodwill among his allies and the confidence of all Greeks.

Fate

Polybius does not assume that everything is predetermined or the result of fortune or fate. He cautions us lest we view outcomes merely as acts of divine beings. We should engage in causal analysis of "those events whose causes we can discover and give an explanation as to why they happen." Polybius comments how he has "criticized those writers who attribute public events" merely "to the workings of fate and chance" because they have taken the easy way out. It may appear reasonable when dealing with phenomena that are seemingly impossible or difficult for a mortal person to understand for one "to escape from the dilemma by attributing them to the work of a god or of chance." Scholars may confront problems that baffle our intelligence and confound our efforts to discover any rational cause. In short, the "answer must remain in doubt" only "where it is impossible or difficult to establish a cause."

At the same time, Polybius admits that some events do seem to be affected by chance, if not fate. He starts his manuscript by referring to "the vicissitudes of Fortune" and "the element of the unexpected" in human events. Much as Machiavelli observes centuries later, Polybius relates how some choose "to leave it to Fortune to decide whom she would honor." One particular turn of events may well "have been expressly designed by Fortune to demonstrate her power to humankind in general," underscoring the fact that "we are no more than mortal human beings, and we should at all times make due allowance for the unexpected, and especially in time of war."

Fortune is "like a good umpire" who can bring about an unexpected change in the contest. For example, Polybius observes how the first war that was fought between Rome and Carthage for the possession of Sicily was profoundly influenced by "decisive changes of Fortune." One can see clearly the influence of Polybius on Machiavelli's development of *fortuna*—chance phenomena—as a key concept in his work.

In identifying causes for the events or outcomes he observes, therefore, Polybius tries to strike a balance between voluntarist explanations that depend on human agency or choice and determinist formulations by which events or outcomes are produced by external factors seemingly beyond the capability of individuals to control or affect significantly. Polybius adds a normative element by suggesting that as individuals we ought to control what can be controlled and accept what cannot:

> Human nature is always fallible, and to meet with some unpredictable mishap is not the fault of the victim, but rather of ill-fortune, or of those who have inflicted it on him. But when we err with our eyes open and involve ourselves in great tribulations through sheer lack of judgment, then everyone agrees that we have nobody to blame but ourselves. It follows therefore that if a people's failures are due to ill-fortune, they will be granted pity, pardon and assistance, but if to their own folly, then all men of sense will blame and reproach them.

Notwithstanding the presence of fortune as a confounding factor, Polybius does not abandon his effort to explain the rise of the Roman Empire in just half a century, the wars between Rome and Carthage, or lesser events such as the successes of King Philip of Macedon and the Achaean League over the Aetolian League. The important point is not whether his cause-effect analyses are correct or not but rather that Polybius rejects as an inadequate explanation any approach that relegates cause merely to the work of chance. He argues forcefully that "we must rather seek a cause, since no chain of events, whether expected or unexpected, can reach its conclusion without a cause."

Putting aside David Hume's eighteenth-century empiricist critique of causality as purely abstract or metaphysical (after all, who has ever seen a cause?), it would be difficult to find in the ancients any clearer statement of the starting assumption for those engaged in international relations or other social science theorizing. As we will see in chapter 10, in the positivist tradition we assume there are causes for what we observe and then seek to find them.

Realism and Liberalism

There is little doubt that the work of Polybius is well within the tradition in which present-day realists reside. In his critique of the Athenian constitution, Polybius uses a ship as a metaphor for the state, emphasizing the importance of unitary and effective leadership to avoid instability and to keep the ship on course. In international relations, states "always reckon friendship or hostility in terms of advantage." Although one may enhance security by seeking allies, security is established most reliably when city-states do "not look to others for their safety, but [choose] to defend their cities and their territory with their own hands." It is what in our own time has been termed a self-help system—one way or another states provide for their own defense.[65]

As discussed earlier, Polybius places considerable emphasis on how a favorable constitution enhances the capabilities of a city-state or empire in relation to other political units. His concern for political stability strikes a responsive chord in readers with a realist persuasion. Though it is a secondary or subordinate theme, elements consistent with liberal thought also can be found in Polybius.

---

[65] Comments Polybius makes on spies, traitors, and treachery in international relations clearly influenced Machiavelli a millennium later. Deception—when a leader is "obliged to act and speak in public in a way that was quite inconsistent with his real intention"—is another familiar theme of Machiavelli.

The portrayal of Rome's constitution as a balance among the executive (consul), legislature (senate), and the people may not be entirely accurate because Polybius tends to idealize things Roman. Polybius, however, is similar to Aristotle and other Greek writers in his advocacy of a mixed constitution that blends elements of kingship, aristocracy, and democracy. His discussion of the adverse forms of one-man rule (tyranny), minority rule (oligarchy), and mob rule as well as the idea that there are cyclical shifts in constitutional type is consistent with mainstream ancient Greek thought.

What was new and what would be adopted by Montesquieu and others who followed is the idea of checks and balances among the branches of government. One hears Montesquieu (or James Madison and Alexander Hamilton in *The Federalist Papers*) in these words of Polybius:

> Whenever one of the three elements swells in importance, becomes overambitious and tends to encroach upon the others, it becomes apparent for the reasons given above that none of the three is completely independent, but that the designs of any one can be blocked or impeded by the rest, with the result that none will unduly dominate the others or treat them with contempt. Thus, the whole situation remains in equilibrium since any aggressive impulse is checked, and each estate is apprehensive from the outset of censure from the others.

Beyond its domestic application, one also finds here an exposition of the logic of balance of power which later IR scholars would apply to relations among states.

Although Polybius's idea of checks and balances is framed in a purely domestic context, his discussion of democratic ideas is an important part of the corpus of ancient Greek political thought that would provide a foundation for liberal formulations of both domestic and world politics during the Enlightenment of the seventeenth and eighteenth centuries. Consistent with Aristotle, Polybius sees human beings as social by nature. In particular, his version of the state of nature anticipates later use of the same metaphor (however different their interpretations) by such social contract theorists as Hobbes, Locke, and Rousseau to explain politics within a state or among states internationally. In looking for "the origins of a political society," he turns first to a state of nature composed of primitive human beings "herding together like animals and following the strongest and the bravest as their leaders."

At a later stage of societal development (and because humans "differ from the other animals in that they are the only creatures to possess the faculty of reasoning"), the choice of rulers is not due anymore to physical strength so much as to "the merits of their judgment and the power of their reasoning." The important point for democratic theory and the liberal perspective is that the choice of leaders is made by the people and the legitimacy of rulers stems from that process. Unless the people become dissatisfied, they are the ones who "ensure that the supreme power remains in the hands not only of the original leaders but also of their descendants." To Polybius, although he is vague on precisely how they perform the role, the people are the ultimate check—a rather modern idea to which Madison and Hamilton allude in *Federalist* 51.

Market-oriented values—a normative economic orientation usually associated with liberal thought on domestic and international political economy—are mentioned as characteristic of the inhabitants of the Mediterranean island of Crete:

> Their laws permit the citizen to acquire land without any restriction—the sky is the limit, as the saying goes—and money is held in such high regard among them that the possession of it is regarded as not merely necessary, but also as most honorable. And indeed, avarice and greed are so much ingrained in the Cretan character that they are the only people in the world who consider no form of gain to be shameful.

Because Polybius singles out the Cretans, it is clear that such notions, if not unique, are by no means universal—or even widespread. Nevertheless, commerce was extensive among the ancient civilizations throughout the Mediterranean area. Indeed, an important provision in the Rome-Carthage treaty that followed the first Punic War was an agreement to establish normal trade relations. Not until more recent centuries would work and commercial values—what Max Weber referred to as the "Protestant" work ethic (an important basis for accumulation of capital)—become universalized. The writings of Adam Smith on capitalism and David Ricardo on international trade added to the corpus of political-economic theorizing from which Karl Marx also would draw.

Commerce contributes in the long run to the development of broader conceptions of society beyond the borders of a given city-state or empire. Polybius comes close to developing such a concept when he refers to such democratic values as "equality and freedom of speech" within the Achaean League and their successful transfer to various Greek city-states. He observes that these values spread because of a common sense of humanity and of equality that is "the foundation and the prime cause of the harmony that prevails in the Peloponnese, and hence of its prosperity." Though only a glimmer in the writings of Polybius, this is an important theme that others developed over the centuries. With the expansion of the Roman empire, writers began to speculate on what we now call transnational phenomena and the necessity to develop a set of universal values—a rules-based order—that can unite disparate peoples.

Reflections on the Thought of Plato, Aristotle, and Polybius
The contributions made by Plato and Aristotle to thinking about international relations at best have been indirect. Their major impact is derived from four aspects: (1) their interest in thinking systematically about politics, (2) Plato's analysis of the relation between power and justice, (3) Aristotle's discussion of economics, and (4) their inspiration to later theorists who have investigated the relation between the nature of a state and its foreign policy behavior. Even in their own time, however, they had an uphill struggle against prevailing attitudes as exemplified by the Sophists who separated politics from morality and viewed the state as a mere convention, not in accordance with nature.

As for Polybius, it is apparent that his discussion of constitutions owes much to the classification devised by Plato, and he shares with Aristotle an interest in empirical observation and understanding causation. But he differs significantly from both Plato and Aristotle in his view of the purpose of the state. While his two predecessors argue that the ultimate purpose of the city-state is to make individuals virtuous and fulfill their potential as human beings, Polybius has a much more modest goal—political stability.

By the time in which he lived, the polis was in demonstrative decline due to the debilitating effects of the Peloponnesian war, followed by the military and political hegemony first imposed by Macedonia and then by Rome. Polybius does not see the purpose of the state as one of molding good persons and helping them lead a virtuous life. His dispassionate study of power, balanced appraisal of fate and human volition, and interest in the relative importance of internal and external factors to explain a state's power and status in the world mean Polybius has more in common with Thucydides and such later theorists as Machiavelli than he does with either Plato or Aristotle.[66]

REFERENCES

Classic Works (various editions)
Aristotle. *The Politics.*
Clausewitz, Carl von. *On War.*
Herodotus. *The Histories.*
Homer. *The Iliad* and *The Odyssey.*
Jomini, Antoine Henri de. *The Art of War.*
Kautilya. *The Arthashastra.*
Plato. *The Republic, The Laws,* and *Gorgias.*
Sun Tzu. *The Art of War.*
Thucydides. *History of the Peloponnesian War.*

Commentaries
Adcock, F. E. *The Greek and Macedonian Art of War.* Berkeley: University of California Press, 1962.
Adcock, Sir Frank, and D. J. Mosley. *Diplomacy in Ancient Greece.* New York: St. Martin's Press, 1975.
Allison, Graham. *Destined for War: Can America and China Escape Thucydides's Trap?* Boston: Houghton Mifflin, 2017.
Doyle, Michael W. *Empires.* Ithaca, NY: Cornell University Press, 1986.
Handel, Michael I. *Masters of War: Classical Strategic Thought.* London: Frank Cass, 2001.
Hart, B. H. Liddell. *Strategy.* New York: B.N. Publishing, 2009.
Heuser, Beatrice. *The Evolution of Strategy: Thinking War from Antiquity to the Present.* Cambridge, UK: Cambridge University Press, 2010.
Kagan, Donald. *The Great Dialogue: History of Greek Political Thought from Homer to Polybius.* New York: Free Press, 1965.

---

[66] Kagan, *The Great Dialogue,* 266–67.

————. *The Outbreak of the Peloponnesian War*. Ithaca, NY: Cornell University Press, 1969.

Lebow, Richard Ned, and Barry Strauss, eds. *Hegemonic Rivalry: From Thucydides to the Nuclear Age*. Boulder, CO: Westview Press, 1991.

Owen, Clifford. *The Humanity of Thucydides*. Princeton, NJ: Princeton University Press, 1994.

Pritchett, W. Kendrick. *The Greek State at War*. Berkeley: University of California Press, 1976.

Rhodes, P. J. *The Greek City States: A Source Book*. London: Croom Helm, 1986.

Roberts, Jennifer T. *The Plague of War: Athens, Sparta, and the Struggle for Ancient Greece*. Oxford, UK: Oxford University Press, 2017.

Tilly, Charles. *Coercion, Capital, and European States, AD 990–1990*. Cambridge, MA: Blackwell, 1990.

Wight, Martin. *Systems of States*. Leicester, UK: Leicester University Press, 1977.

3

Greco-Roman Thought and the Middle Ages

★ ★ ★

THE ROMAN EMPIRE AND THE DEVELOPMENT OF GRECO-ROMAN THOUGHT

Roman influence on the development of IR theory is profound. Writing in a tradition established by the Greeks, Livy's historical work was read closely some fifteen centuries later by Niccolò Machiavelli. However, a significant departure from realist premises is the universalism of Stoic thought, a perspective quite influential in the eighteenth and nineteenth centuries among such writers as Immanuel Kant.

Instead of a world fractured into mutually exclusive political communities, the Stoics offer an alternative vision of a unity in humanity that transcends the borders of any city-state or other political unit. To the Stoics, and to liberal writers centuries later, states and empires are not the only significant actors on the world stage. Individuals exercising their will also matter. Finally, the rule of law among nations, an idea directly traceable to Cicero, influenced the Dutch writer Hugo Grotius (1583–1645) and those who followed him as they looked to international law as a basis for order in international relations.

Historical Context

In his epic poem *Aeneid*, Virgil (70–19 BCE) tells us how the Romans "wandered as their destiny drove them on from one sea to the next: so hard and huge a task it was to found the Roman people." To him, it was the Roman destiny to rule Earth's peoples. Rome was "to pacify, to impose the rule of law, to spare the conquered, to battle down the proud."[1] The latter included Rome's major rival, the north African city of Carthage. With the power of Carthage broken by 201 BCE, the borders of the expanding Roman Empire suffered

---

[1] Virgil, *Aeneid*, trans. Robert Fitzgerald (New York: Random House, 1981, 1983), I: circa lines 17–40; VI: circa lines 846–48.

only occasional challenges. The Hellenistic monarchies to the east were weak, German and barbarian tribes to the north could threaten the frontiers, and the emergent Parthian Empire beyond the Euphrates was watched with suspicion. There was no organized state to the west in Spain, southern Gaul (France), and Liguria (in northwest Italy) that could pose an effective challenge to Rome. As a result, the major security preoccupation of Rome was to keep various tribes, states, and kingdoms within its sphere of influence under control and to guard the rather fluid borders of the empire. It is not surprising that Polybius, who died in 120 BCE, was so enamored of the rapid rise of Rome to imperial status (see table 3.1).

Domestically, despite Polybius's characterization of a balance of power among the consuls, senate, and people, the aristocrats in the senate had effective control of the government. In 133 BCE, however, a tribune named Gracchus challenged senatorial government when he proposed a bill that would distribute parcels of public land to the lower classes. The movement met some success, but also aristocratic resistance. Within a century populist leaders came to the fore, leading to the triumvirate of Crassus, Pompey, and Julius Caesar and eventually the civil war of 49 BCE. It was during this period that Cicero (106–43 BCE)

Table 3.1 Writing about Empire, Imperial and Civil Wars, and World Citizenship: Roman Thinking about International Relations

Date	Historical Developments	Writers and Commentators
(BCE) 753	Legendary date for the founding of Rome by Romulus	
500	Roman republic established	
300	Alexander the Great (356–323) establishes Macedonian Empire	
200	Punic Wars (264–146) between Rome and Carthage (Tunis), leading to the defeat of Carthaginians (Phoenicians) and rise of Rome as empire	Polybius (200–120), a Greek, writes about the Punic wars and the rise of Rome as empire
100	Crassus, Pompey, and Caesar form triumvirate to rule empire (60); Caesar conducts Gallic Wars, defeats Pompey in civil war, and emerges as singular leader (48), but is assassinated (44); Augustus is victor over opponents (31) and becomes emperor (27 BCE–14 CE)	Cicero (106–43) writes with the universalism of the Stoics; Julius Caesar (100–44) writes of Gallic and civil wars; Virgil (70–19) writes in epic style of Homer on Rome and its new empire; Livy (59 BCE–17 CE) writes Roman history
(CE)		Seneca (4 BCE–65 CE) promotes Stoic cosmopolitanism; Paul of Tarsus (Turkey, d. 67 CE) advances Stoic universal view in Christianity; Plutarch (45–120) writes political-military biographies; Tacitus (55–117) writes about Roman imperial decline
100	Period of Emperors Hadrian (117–138) and Marcus Aurelius (161–180)	Marcus Aurelius (121–180), a late Stoic, promotes brotherhood of mankind as concept
300	Emperor Constantine (324–337) becomes Christian	St. Augustine (354–430) combines Greco-Roman ideas and Christian theology

made his mark as politician and historian, and the events he witnessed played a major role in his analyses.

Despite the assassination of Caesar by his opponents in the senate in 44 BCE, Rome continued to enjoy military and political successes. After a period of turmoil and civil war, Augustus, the new "Caesar," assumed power in 27 BCE. By the time of his death in 14 CE, he had managed to consolidate much of the empire and avoid a recurrence of civil war—no small achievement!

It was during the reign of Augustus that Titus Livy wrote much of his history of the Roman Empire. In addition to less well-known Roman emperors who succeeded Augustus, all of the other authors under consideration in this section—Seneca (4 BCE–65 CE), Plutarch (45–120 CE), and Marcus Aurelius (121–180 CE)—lived during the reign of one or more of such diverse imperial personalities as Tiberius (14–37 CE), Caligula (37–41 CE), Claudius (41–54 CE), Nero (54–68 CE), Trajan (98–117 CE), and Hadrian (117–138 CE). Marcus Aurelius, of course, was emperor from 161 to 180. All, to varying degrees, expanded the empire, strengthened its frontiers, or put down revolts.

The term empire is derived from the Latin word *imperium* and, indeed, the greatest empire of the ancient world was certainly that of Rome. Roman administration of the empire varied, with some provinces under the direct control of the emperor through proconsuls, others designated as senatorial provinces, and still others treated as client states. For two centuries beginning with Augustus, the Roman Empire provided internal stability, used two common languages (Latin and Greek), and aided in the dissemination of Greek and eastern culture to western Europe. It was within such an international system that the authors under consideration in this chapter lived and worked.

The teachings of Plato and Aristotle were an inadequate guide to this new age of territorially expansive bureaucratic empires. A new philosophy was required. It needed to be one that could provide a basis not only for individual action now that the spiritual sustenance and intimate ties of the city-state were no longer available, but also a conceptual foundation that would relate the individual to the empire and the world at large. Under the Macedonian and Roman empires, a wide variety of peoples were brought into direct contact with different ethnic, religious, and political traditions. A more cosmopolitan outlook emerged.

Before turning to the Middle Ages, we examine the thinking of Greek and Roman Stoics and their philosophical conception of the world. This is followed by a discussion of Livy's historical works on the Roman Empire and Plutarch's analysis of noble Greek and Roman lives. Despite their differences, all these authors shared an interest in political communities that transcended the small city-state and ancient Greek politics among city-states and their alliances. This interest produced works that contributed, however indirectly, to the development of thinking about international relations.

The Greek Stoics

Although militarily and politically in decline by the fourth century BCE, the Greek world continued to exert its cultural influence. A process of Hellenization of the "barbarians" continued for several centuries, transmitting Greek values to a wider audience. At the same time, the rise of bureaucratic empires increased individual mobility and allowed people of different regions and backgrounds to settle in Greece and infuse aspects of their own cultures into the Hellenic world.

The best example of this involved the philosophical school of thought known as Stoicism, founded around 300 BCE by Zeno, a Cypriot of Phoenician background.[2] Although acceptance of one's circumstances and self-reliance are dominant elements in Stoic philosophy as it relates to individuals, it is the cosmopolitan notion that we are all part of a larger community of humanity that is of particular relevance to IR theory. Stoic ideas were very influential in Rome, and they anticipated the worldviews of the seventeenth-century Dutch legal writer, Hugo Grotius, and the eighteenth-century German scholar, Immanuel Kant. Stoic philosophy is at the core of contemporary liberal thought, which sees the world as made up not only of states, but also of individuals, groups, and other nonstate actors who can influence events.

Stoicism did not develop a theory of the state or theory of state action. Rather, the emphasis was on the individual, not as a member of an organized political unit as was the case with Plato and Aristotle, but as an independent actor. Stoicism requires the individual not to focus only on the laws or customs of one's political community, but rather to attempt to live in accordance with nature. The Stoic conception of nature is not that of Greek mythology involving the antics of the gods. To the Stoics, nature involves certain goals and principles and processes by which these goals and principles are to be attained with the supreme good being to lead a life of "virtue." It should be the duty of each individual to live according to nature and achieve in one's own life the harmony found in nature itself. To secure this good life, an individual attempts to reduce elements of chance and circumstance.

According to the Stoics, the ability to reason is a quality shared by all humans. Early Christians incorporated Stoic understandings into their religion. Reason is viewed as a divine spark, reflecting the God within us. Indeed, God is viewed as the author of these laws of nature and of the universe. This universal ability to reason, plus the fact that laws of nature are of universal applicability, results in a Stoic emphasis on the equality of people and on what unites as opposed to what divides them, whether those divisions be geographic, cultural, or political.

This emphasis on equality and the unity of humanity differs dramatically from Aristotle's view of the laws of nature. He does not see equality inherent in the laws of nature, as evidenced by his observations on the subordination of women to men in the city-states, slaves to citizens, and barbarians to the Hellenes as a whole. Although Thucydides does not discuss laws of nature, the Stoic emphasis on equality and unity of humankind is starkly at odds with the political world Thucydides depicts in *History of the Peloponnesian War*. His narrative illustrates that even the common cultural heritage of the Greeks could

---

[2] This discussion of Stoicism draws in part on William Ebenstein, *Great Political Thinkers: Plato to the Present*, 4th ed. (New York: Holt, Rinehart and Winston, 1969), 139–48.

not prevent personal ambition, love of power, and the dynamics of city-state competition from leading to war.

The Stoics, however, believed human beings could discern through reason the laws of nature and live in accordance with them. To a certain extent nature determines the course of an individual's life, but an individual has a certain amount of free will as well. Hence the Stoic philosophical tradition, as with other philosophies and religions, balances aspects of determinism and voluntarism. This is in contrast with Plato's notion in *The Republic* that what an individual does in life is almost wholly to be determined by heredity and environment with the state or city-state playing a critical role in the socialization process.

The Stoic emphasis on the unity and equality of humanity had obvious political implications if one accepted the philosophical notion that the world is held together by laws of nature that transcend the laws of any particular king or emperor. At best, laws made by kings and communities are derived from the laws of nature. Furthermore, the Stoics raised an issue debated to the present day: if everyone is part of humanity, to what extent do we have obligations to humanity as a whole as opposed to the more narrowly defined political community in which we live?

We also can credit the Stoics with one of the earliest secular justifications for a world state. Zeno of Citium (c. third century BCE) wrote a tract that attacks Plato's *Republic* and the idea that an individual state should strive for the attainment of Plato's ideal community. Rather, the ideal state is a world state with universal citizenship and one system of law based on reason as opposed to custom and convention. Again, the Stoic emphasis is on what united humanity, not what divided it. Laws of nature bind the world together, transcending the laws of any particular state or empire. Through reason these laws can be known, providing a basis for the harmonious conduct of relations among disparate political communities until reason leads political leaders to create a world state.

The Roman Stoics

Roman authors continued writing in the Greek tradition. Although Stoicism has its roots in the thought of Zeno and other late Greek writers of lesser renown, the Romans are the ones who developed these ideas and put them into practice within the empire. The writings of Cicero and the Stoics—Seneca and the emperor Marcus Aurelius—reflect central ideas in Roman thought. The organizing principle by which Rome managed imperial affairs was a universal image of humanity that transcended the boundaries of city-states and other small political units.

Thus, Seneca, though born in Spain, could be a prominent Roman citizen. The same, of course, was true for Paul of Tarsus in Asia Minor (St. Paul), an early Jewish convert to Christianity. The catholicism of the new religion—open to all human beings regardless of origin—conformed to the universalism present in Roman thought even as it was a departure from the Judaic and other traditions that tended to support more exclusive communities. Because of his missionary work among non-Jewish peoples, Paul is often credited with assuring this "Romanization" of early Christianity.

Beyond the idea of common citizenship within the empire, considerable autonomy was given to local rulers for practical reasons in a time when transportation and communications within so far-flung a realm were difficult at best. At the same time, Stoic ideas provided legitimacy for such an approach. As the Roman Empire expanded its territorial scope, so did ideas central to Greco-Roman thought. Indeed, Roman legal precepts went well beyond laws binding only on residents of particular political communities. The ideas of natural law (*jus naturale*) and a law commonly binding on all peoples (*jus gentium*) are important Roman contributions that have had profound influence on Western political thought in succeeding centuries, particularly on the development of international law.

Cicero

The orator and writer Marcus Tullius Cicero or, more commonly, Cicero (106–43 BCE), is one of the few philosophers to have attained high political rank—in his case, as consul of the Roman Republic. Son of a knight and educated in Rome and Greece, he served in the military and then made a reputation for himself as a lawyer. The age in which he lived was one of domestic turmoil, intrigue, and upheaval. Economic devastation was wrought in 91–89 BCE by the struggle between Rome and its neighboring allies that demanded citizenship and its attendant privileges.

Once this struggle ended, civil war broke out and in 84 BCE Sulla, the Roman military commander, marched on Rome and seized power. Domestic unrest, including the slave revolt led by Spartacus, occupied the senate and various rulers, including Cicero who was elected consul in 63 BCE. By then, Julius Caesar, a young senator, had gained a reputation as a popular leader, and in 60 BCE he formed a triumvirate with Pompey and Crassus. Cicero declined to join this political alliance and initially went into exile. Returning a year later, he agreed to align himself with the triumvirate but turned to scholarship. The power-sharing formula did not last, and in 49 BCE Caesar crossed the river Rubicon with his veteran soldiers from the Gallic Wars. This second civil war consumed the entire empire, and after Caesar's assassination in 44 BCE, Cicero hoped to make political use of Octavian, Caesar's adopted son. In doing so, he took a position against Octavian's rival, Mark Antony. When Octavian and Antony reconciled and formed a triumvirate with Lepidus, Cicero was arrested and killed, his head and hands placed on public display in Rome.

Although rarely read today, Cicero greatly influenced the works of later writers, particularly up until the end of the eighteenth century. Machiavelli closely studied Cicero due to the Florentine's interest in republicanism, ancient Rome, and civic virtue. Cicero was revered by Jean Bodin and studied by Hugo Grotius, the "father" of international law. While Thomas Hobbes rejected Cicero's republicanism and support of mixed constitutions, the Englishman acknowledged his debt to Cicero in the introduction to his translation in 1629 of *History of the Peloponnesian War*. John Locke considered Cicero among the "truly great men." Such praise peaked during the eighteenth-century Enlightenment. Voltaire, Montesquieu, and Denis Diderot were all admirers, as were David Hume, Adam Smith, Edmund Burke, and Thomas Jefferson.[3]

The ancient Greek writers profoundly influenced Cicero. His major political works, *De Re Publica* (*The Republic*) and *De Legibus* (*The Laws*), can be viewed as attempts to interpret Roman history in terms of Greek political theory. He even follows Plato's sequence of first writing about the ideal state and then turning to an ideal set of laws. Cicero also takes from Polybius directly (and Aristotle before him) the idea of a mixed constitution for the state, favoring "a balanced combination of the three forms"—kingship, aristocracy, and democracy.[4] The US Constitution follows this pattern, adapting to changed circumstances: a president, a senate or upper house, and a House of Representatives, often referred to as the people's house.

On international relations, Cicero's observations on three topics have had a lasting impact: identifying laws of nature that allowed him to conceive of a community of humankind, expressing his views on the state and statecraft, and addressing moral considerations on war (when it is right to go to war and what constitutes moral conduct in war)—the bases for a just war doctrine that Augustine, Thomas Aquinas, Grotius, and others would develop over two millennia.

Laws of Nature

The influence of Stoic ideas led Cicero to conceive of one world ordered by laws of nature that were discoverable through the application of human reason. Perhaps because of the breadth of his thought, Cicero is not usually categorized as a member of the Stoic school of philosophy, given the more focused scope of its philosophical concern. Nevertheless, the influence of earlier Greek Stoics on Cicero and, in turn, his influence on later Roman Stoics are unmistakable.

Cicero's inspiration is the notion that "as one and the same Nature holds together and supports the universe, all of whose parts are in harmony with one another," so people ought also to be united. Thus, one can speak beyond the civil law of a given commonwealth to a law among nations applicable to humanity as a whole (*jus gentium*) and to people individually. Cicero proposes that we "conceive of this whole universe as one commonwealth." He refers to humanity's fellowship and calls for citizenship in a larger community of humankind. There can, therefore, be a law of nations. Indeed, this concept of law common to the community of humankind was a powerful idea that proved central in the development of international law in the late Middle Ages.

---

[3] Neal Wood, *Cicero's Social and Political Thought* (Berkeley: University of California Press, 1988), 2–4.

[4] Unless otherwise noted, all direct quotes from Cicero are from either *The Republic* or *The Laws*. Convenient Penguin editions include *Selected Works*, *Selected Political Speeches*, and *On the Good Life*. The Loeb Classical Library edition of Cicero's *De Re Publica* (The Republic) and *De Legibus* (The Laws), trans. Clinton Walker Keyes (Cambridge, MA: Harvard University Press, 1928, 1988) is referenced (volume XVI in the collected works of Cicero). The Loeb editions contain both the original Latin and the English translation on facing pages.

Cicero sees law as "the bond that unites the civic association, the justice enforced by law" is the same for all. Justice is associated with fairness, but "the origin of Justice is to be found in Law, for Law is a natural force; it is the mind and reason of the intelligent man, the standard by which Justice and Injustice are measured." As with law, one will find the root of justice in nature: "True law is right reason in agreement with nature." As a part of our lives, law "summons to duty by its commands and averts from wrongdoing by its prohibitions."

Moreover, true law is of universal application, unchanging and everlasting. The universality of law assures that there ought "not be different laws at Rome and at Athens, or different laws now and in the future." Instead, Cicero argues that one eternal and unchangeable law should be valid for all nations and all times. Although some laws may be based on local customs, the law of nations and the laws of particular communities are to conform with what nature dictates uniformly.

As noted, Cicero believed law is based on rational principles and that human reason exercised rightly is how one discovers the law in nature. Importantly, however, law should not be understood merely as a product of human thought. It is instead "something eternal that rules the whole universe by its wisdom in command and prohibition." It has a divine quality: This power of law to compel nations "is not merely older than the existence of nations and States; it is coeval with that God who guards and rules heaven and earth."

Thus, as in Stoicism in general, there is in Cicero a liberal worldview—individuals as well as states matter and law should play an important role in regulating relations among peoples and states. In economics he also takes an individually oriented position. Cicero advocates moderation, saving money, and increasing one's wealth—a perspective, when accompanied by hard work, would come to be known in Max Weber's twentieth-century book, *The Protestant Ethic and the Spirit of Capitalism*.[5]

Following Plato, Aristotle, and Polybius, who all addressed economic issues, Cicero makes economics—private property in particular—an important component of his political works. He follows the Stoic tradition of viewing the acquisition of wealth and material possessions as a natural activity. Cicero's economic individualism is not without its influence centuries later on Adam Smith and on the social contract theorists, John Locke in particular.[6]

State and Statecraft

Cicero also contributes to the realist perspective on international politics. His realism is reflected in two ways: how he conceptualizes the state and his advice to political leaders. As we see in chapter 4, initial theorizing about the modern state is generally credited to such writers as Machiavelli, Bodin, Grotius, and Hobbes. Their views on the creation and nature of the state, however, are an expansion of the strain of ancient Greco-Roman thought that used social contract theory to explain and justify the creation of the state.

---

[5] Cicero, "On Duties," in *On the Good Life*, trans. Michael Grant (London: Penguin Books, 1971), 152, 169–70.

[6] See the discussion in Wood, *Cicero's Social and Political Thought*, 105–19.

Cicero sounds very modern in that, for him, the social contract is a result of individuals' natural quest for security: "nature has implanted in the human race . . . a desire to defend the common safety." To attain this safety, a commonwealth comes into existence by mutual agreement. In Cicero's terms, a commonwealth is "an assemblage of people in large numbers associated in an agreement with respect to justice and a partnership for the common good." A multitude becomes "a body of citizens by mutual agreement."

"To make human life safer and richer by our thought and effort," following our natural impulse, we increase the resources of humankind. As political leaders, we are urged "to increase our resources, to multiply our wealth, to extend our boundaries." Such sentiments, however, are tempered with the observation that justice requires us "to consider the interests of the whole human race."

In a theme developed more than 1,500 years later by Sir Thomas More (1478–1535), Cicero argues that the affairs of state are so important that the "wise person" who might like to engage in loftier pursuits than statecraft still can "not decline the duty if conditions force him to assume it." To Cicero, the noblest use of virtue, defined as reason completely developed, is service to the government of the state. Accordingly, one needs to study "this science of politics" if one is to be prepared to serve in such roles whenever called. Even the best-prepared person, of course, is still confronted by "the uncertainty of future events" and the vagaries of fortune or chance.

Maintaining domestic order or stability is part of the overall responsibility political leaders have for security of the state. Like Polybius before him and Machiavelli to follow, Cicero sees law and a legal system as central to security. He observes that "laws were invented for the safety of citizens, the preservation of States, and the tranquility and happiness of human life." According to Cicero, "the two elements that most conspicuously contribute to the stability of a State" are religion and the "spirit of tranquility." With regard to the latter, Cicero relates how it was possible in Rome's earlier history to quench "the people's ardor for the warlike life to which they had been accustomed." Fighting enemies abroad is thus not a necessary means for domestic unity to prevail. Popular passions can be turned toward "markets, games, and all sorts of occasions for the gathering of large numbers." The net effect of these measures in the earlier Roman experience was to turn "toward benevolence and kindliness the thought of those who had become savage and brutish through their passion for war."

Notwithstanding Cicero's intellectual orientation toward humanity as a whole, he acknowledges that for a particular state external influences may not be altogether salutary. It is a matter of fact to Cicero that a "certain corruption and degradation of morals" may stem from foreign influences. Maritime cities are particularly vulnerable in this regard for they receive an odd "mixture of strange languages and customs and import foreign ways as well as foreign merchandise, so that none of their ancestral institutions can possibly remain unchanged." Beyond crossing "the seas merely to gain knowledge and to visit other countries"—a cosmopolitan view—political leaders look abroad with the "more important task of defending our native land" from external danger.

Justice and War

Just as law is critical to the maintenance of domestic stability, war itself should be subordinate to law. Cicero is the initiator of this important idea in Western political thought. Laying foundations upon which both Augustine and Aquinas would build centuries later, Cicero addresses the relation between justice and war. Cicero's discussion of what would become the just war doctrine is the first known systematic treatment of this subject. Most present-day references to just war theory that acknowledge its intellectual roots cite Augustine, Aquinas, and Grotius—overlooking Cicero entirely. By contrast, Augustine himself gives Cicero the credit he is due, citing Cicero as a source.

Referring to the "law of war," Cicero claims that "in undertaking, carrying on, and ending a war, justice and good faith shall be supreme." In other words, law and concern for justice through law apply not only to the decision to go to war (what would become known as *jus ad bellum*), but also to the conduct of the war itself (*jus in bello*) and to the restoration of peace. Moreover, war is to be waged for legitimate objectives: "A war is never undertaken by the ideal State, except in defense of its honor or its safety." Unjust wars are those undertaken without provocation because only a war waged for revenge (redress for having been wronged) or defense can actually be just.

Moreover, just wars are waged by legitimate authorities: "The State shall have its official interpreters" of the law of war to guide its conduct and "no war is considered just unless it has been proclaimed and declared" by State authorities. Once declaring war, the authorities shall wage just wars justly. Accordingly, because their orders are presumed to be just, commanders may expect absolute obedience from their troops on the battlefield. Finally, there are legal provisions for the diplomacy of both war and peace.[7]

Seneca and Marcus Aurelius

Like Cicero, both Seneca (4–65 CE) and Marcus Aurelius (121–180) were statesmen and philosophers. Born in Cordoba, Spain, at about the same time as Christ, Seneca's father was an imperial procurator or commissioner for Rome. As a young man Seneca spent several years in Egypt where he gained experience in administration and finance. After studying law he entered the political scene in Rome and, when Caligula succeeded Tiberius in 37 CE, Seneca was a leading figure in the senate and hence viewed with suspicion by the new emperor. Caligula apparently ordered Seneca to be killed, but one version of the story says a woman close to the throne managed to have the order rescinded by claiming that Seneca, an asthmatic, was close to death from tuberculosis.

In 41 CE, in the first year of the reign of Claudius, Seneca (for unknown reasons) again received a sentence of death, which was commuted to banishment on the island of Corsica. This lasted eight trying years, whereupon the emperor's new wife, Agrippina, prevailed on him to return to Rome. Seneca received a high office and was made tutor to her son, who became the emperor Nero upon Claudius's death by poisoning.

---

[7] On diplomacy, see *The Laws*, II: ix; III: viii, xviii; and *The Republic*, III: xxix.

In conjunction with an army officer, Seneca achieved supreme influence in Nero's court. Not surprisingly, he made enemies who, perhaps justifiably, accused him of hypocrisy due to the large gap between his professed Stoic philosophy and his extravagant lifestyle. After he fell out of favor with Nero, Seneca retired from public life and devoted his last three years to philosophy and writing. In 65 CE a conspiracy against the emperor was foiled. Although it is not known for certain if Seneca was one of the plotters, he was ordered to commit suicide, the standard method of imperial execution.

Marcus Aurelius was born in 121 CE during the reign of Hadrian. After the death of his parents, he was adopted first by a grandfather and then, at age seventeen, by his uncle by marriage, Marcus Antoninus, who had recently become emperor. Upon the death of Antoninus in 161, Marcus and another son adopted by the emperor ruled jointly. A difficult time for the empire ensued with famine, plague, floods, and invasions by barbarians. Two years before his brother's death, Marcus joined the Roman legions on the Danube. Most of the rest of this emperor's life was spent in the field and, during this period, he wrote a series of reflections now known as *Meditations*. Marcus died of disease in a military camp in 180. Due to his varying moods and bouts of melancholy, Marcus did not always meet the standard of the true Stoic, which emphasizes pride and self-sufficiency. Instead, his remarkable modesty seemed more an anticipation of the Christian virtue of humility.[8]

We turn now to the works of these two writers in the context of three basic topics: the Stoic conceptions of humanity and reason, the state of nature, and the issue of causation and fortune.

Humanity and Reason

Seneca acknowledges the contributions of Zeno as the third-century BCE founder of the Stoic school, which he describes as "a school with an unequalled record for courageous and saintly living." Seneca is far removed from the realist perspective when he tells us that "the first thing philosophy promises us is the feeling of fellowship, of belonging to humankind and being members of a community" in which we live in conformity with nature. Philosophy is a beacon; it "does not set about constructing arms or walls or anything of use in war. On the contrary, her voice is for peace, calling all humankind to live in harmony." The Stoic concept of humanity, however, goes beyond individual human beings and their relationships. Indeed, "though human beings may perish, humanity in itself—the pattern on which every human being is molded—lasts."

Values, therefore, transcend particular communities, embracing all of humanity. That universals do exist and that they are discoverable by the exercise of human reason is a powerful idea that differentiated the Greek and Roman Stoics from the city-state-centric focus of Plato, Aristotle, and other Greeks who wrote more about particular political communities. The broader Stoic

---

[8] Seneca, "Introduction" to *Letters from a Stoic*, ed. Robin Campbell (London: Penguin Books, 1969); Marcus Aurelius, "Introduction" to *Meditations*, trans. Maxwell Staniforth (London: Penguin Books, 1964). All subsequent quotations are from these editions.

perspective, by contrast, influenced later scholars during the Middle Ages who accepted the idea of universalism so central to classical liberalism and strategies for universal peace.

One can see striking similarities, for example, between the second-century comments of Marcus Aurelius and the thinking of Immanuel Kant some sixteen centuries later. Marcus states:

> If the power of thought is universal among humankind, so likewise is the possession of reason, making us rational creatures. It follows, therefore, that this reason speaks no less universally to us all with its "thou shalt" or "thou shalt not." So then there is a world-law; which in turn means that we are all fellow citizens and share a common citizenship, and that the world is a single city. Is there any other common citizenship that can be claimed for all humanity? And it is from this world polity that mind, reason, and law themselves derive.

Marcus argues in favor of a community based on equality and freedom of speech for all. He sees individuals naturally as part of a social or human community and deplores the possibility of estrangement from it or allowing oneself to be cut off from society. We are always to remember our close bond with the rest of humanity: "All of us were born for one another."

The liberalism of his worldview, which sees unity despite the wide diversity of individuals, is at odds with Platonic and Aristotelian thinking, which sees society as highly stratified and views people outside of Greece as barbarians. Despite what may appear to be a chaotic universe, order and harmony can exist "when oneness of feeling exists between all parts of nature in spite of their divergence and dispersion."

As human beings we enjoy citizenship in a "great world-city." Speaking more personally Marcus observes that "the interest of every creature lies in conformity with its own constitution and nature. My own nature is a rational and civic one; I have a city, and I have a country; as Marcus I have Rome and, as a human being, I have the universe; and consequently, what is beneficial to these communities is the sole good for me."

Hence, while Marcus may start with the Platonic assumption that each person should conform to his or her own nature, identity is not defined in class terms. Nor does it end at the gates of one's city or the borders of one's country—we are all citizens of the world.

State of Nature

How do Seneca and Marcus Aurelius reach such conclusions? As with other writers before and later, Seneca develops an image of the state of nature as the foundation for his political theory. He argues that fellowship has always been natural among human beings: "The first men on this earth . . . and their immediate descendants followed nature unspoiled. . . . It was an age in which the bounties of nature were freely available for the use of all without discrimination." The operative rule in this state of primitive communism is share and share-alike as human beings enjoy nature and there is "undisturbed possession of resources

owned by the community." One can see Seneca's influence on such social contract theorists as John Locke and Jean-Jacques Rousseau, who also understand
the state of nature as a metaphor with implications for both domestic politics
and international relations.

Seneca does not argue that human beings in the state of nature are virtuous
but rather claims that their innocence is a result of ignorance. Because "they
lacked the cardinal virtues of justice, moral insight, self-control and courage,"
they were vulnerable to having their happy world upset. According to Seneca,
"Virtue only comes to a character that has been thoroughly schooled and
trained and brought to a pitch of perfection by unremitting practice. We are
born for it, but not with it. And even in the best of people, until you cultivate it
there is only the material for virtue, not virtue itself."

For his part, Marcus Aurelius sees human beings as motivated to serve the
common good and the community. He exhorts us to "love humankind." There
is a glimmer of Rousseau's eighteenth-century concept of the general will and
the realist concept of the unitary state in the argument that one ought to act
consistently with the "general accord" in one's community. Marcus contends,

> As a unit yourself, you help to complete the social whole; and similarly, there-
> fore, your every action should help to complete the social life. Any action that is
> not related directly or remotely to this social end disjoints that life and destroys
> its unity. It is as much the act of a schismatic as when some citizen in a com-
> munity does his utmost to dissociate himself from the general accord.

But particular communities also remain only parts of a larger whole. One
needs to understand "the world as a city and himself its citizen." In this cosmopolitan worldview, the common good or common interest goes beyond the
confines of any given community. We need to "think often of the bond that
unites all things in the universe, and their dependence upon one another. All are,
as it were, interwoven, and in consequence linked." Indeed, to Marcus "mutual
integration" is a universal principle.

His own extensive personal wealth notwithstanding, Seneca adopts in the
Aristotelian tradition what could be called an anti-market bias when he asserts
that he has "no respect for any study whatsoever if its end is the making of
money." To Seneca "there is really only one liberal study that deserves the
name—because it makes a person free—and that is the pursuit of wisdom." As
with Rousseau, Seneca believes it is the privatization of property that upsets the
harmony of interest in the state of nature: "Into this ideal state of things burst
avarice, avarice that in seeking to put aside some article or other and appropriate it to its own use, only succeeded in making everything somebody else's property and reducing its possessions to a fraction of its previous unlimited wealth.
Avarice brought in poverty."

As a result, human beings now live with a feeling of insecurity that contrasts
sharply with the earlier happy state of life in conformity with nature when to
govern is to serve, not to rule.

Wise leaders "kept the peace, protected the weak from the stronger, urged
and dissuaded, pointed out what was advantageous and what was not." They

are devoted to bringing well-being and prosperity to their subjects. According to Seneca: "That fellowship lasted for a long time intact, before men's greed broke society up." Unfortunately, with time "avarice and luxury split human beings up and got them to abandon partnership for plunder." He laments "that we can clothe ourselves without importing silks" and "we can have the things we need for our ordinary purposes if we will only be content with what the earth has made available on its surface."

Although "we were born into a world in which things were made ready to our hands, it is we who have made everything difficult to come by through our disdain for what is easily come by." One needs to speak out against the love of money and extravagance, and the proper limit to a person's wealth should be restricted to what is essential. Although not a very precise formulation, it is nevertheless one that addresses the distribution of wealth in human society, a theme that would echo in the writings of social contract and classical economic theorists centuries later.

On another question concerning political economy and social justice, Seneca departs sharply from Aristotle's defense of slavery. He condemns slavery and its harsh and inhuman behavior, specifically the abuse of slaves "as if they were beasts of burden instead of human beings." They are too important to be subordinate to narrow constructions of economic practicality. In the nineteenth century, Karl Marx identifies slavery as a historically distinct mode of production found in Egyptian, Greek, Roman, and other ancient societies. Slavery was accepted as a fact of life and thus had legitimacy among the ancients, Aristotle included. By contrast, Seneca diverged from the conventional wisdom of his day. Even if enslaving foreigners and others was a profitable form of ancient political economy, to Seneca doing so was wrong.

Causation and Fortune

Seneca also contributes to epistemology (the study of how one knows or how one gains knowledge), helping lay the intellectual foundation for the development of the theoretical enterprise. Following Polybius, he argues that causation can be understood as "everything in the absence of which a thing cannot be brought into being"—in other words, those elements necessary for its existence or occurrence. Central to discovery is the exercise of human reason. Marcus Aurelius adds that "what follows is ever closely linked to what precedes; it is not a procession of isolated events, merely obeying the laws of sequence, but [also] a rational continuity." Human beings have the capacity to reason and thus discover these causal relations.

At the same time, to be human is to live with uncertainty and considerable skepticism about reality. In this regard, Seneca states: "I should find it difficult to say which of these people annoy me most, those who would have us know nothing or the ones who refuse even to leave us the small satisfaction of knowing that we know nothing." Thus, chance is part of the causal equation. One should "always take full note of fortune's habit of behaving just as she pleases, treating her as if she were actually going to do everything it is in her power to do."

Seneca further observes how "misfortune has a way of choosing some unprecedented means or other of impressing its power on those who might be said to have forgotten it." Life is fragile and we are all vulnerable to the unexpected. In a striking statement on how misfortune can lead to unanticipated outcomes, he argues:

> Nothing is durable, whether for an individual or for a society. . . . Terror strikes amid the most tranquil surroundings and, without any disturbance, in the background to give rise to them, calamities spring from the least expected quarter. States that stood firm through civil war as well as wars external collapse without a hand being raised against them. How few nations have made of their prosperity a lasting thing!
>
> This is why we need to envisage every possibility and to strengthen the spirit to deal with the things that may conceivably come about. Rehearse them in your mind: exile, torture, war, shipwreck. Fortune needs envisaging in a thoroughly comprehensive way.

Aside from anticipating what could happen and preparing for it, Seneca is exhorting individuals to keep on course in the pursuit of ideals even when confronted with setbacks.

Similar sentiments pervade the writings of Marcus Aurelius, but he is more of an optimist. He notes how human beings can observe the world of space and the world of time. We can expect changes over time in "everything naturally comprehended in the universe." Reason allows us to find patterns. We can "look back over the past, with its changing empires that rose and fell" and, turning to prediction, we "can foresee the future too."

Moreover, our rational faculty gives human beings the capacity to control our conduct. Although we are confronted with uncertainties and the vagaries of chance, human beings retain free will. Not everything is determined for us. It is still a world in which individuals matter and what they do matters. Citing Epictetus, Marcus asserts, true to his voluntarist approach, that "the robber of your free will does not exist."

We find in Seneca and Marcus Aurelius, therefore, arguments in favor of the dignity of all individuals. This reflects a cosmopolitanism alien to classical Greek thinking and even many enthusiastic supporters of the Roman Empire who viewed most peoples beyond the borders as barbarians. It is somewhat ironic that such views were held by worldly persons who were intimately involved with the day-to-day machinations of imperial politics. Furthermore, despite their fates, their writings exhibit a high degree of voluntarism with respect to counteracting the vagaries of fate and fortune. They clearly are intellectual precursors of liberalism.

Titus Livy

Titus Livy, the most famous of the Roman historians and a major influence on Machiavelli, was born in Padua, Italy, around 59 BCE. We know very little about him, but he made quite a mark on the literary circles of Rome. The emperor Augustus apparently expressed an interest in his work, despite

Livy's praise of Pompey, a rival of Augustus. Livy was influenced generally by Polybius, but particularly by Cicero's emphasis on writing in pure Latin and avoiding the debasement of the language that very often occurred in the hands of lesser-known writers.

Furthermore, Cicero's works provided guidance on the theory and practice of historical writing, and both Cicero and Livy believed that history should serve as a guide to life. Livy's mammoth *History of Rome* consisted of 142 books, ending with the death of Drusus, brother of the emperor Tiberius, in 9 BCE. Unfortunately, only thirty-five of these books survived.[9]

His work is often overlooked, although Livy's first ten books were the subject of Machiavelli's *The Discourses*. Livy also was an influence on both Montesquieu and Rousseau. In a comment similar to an observation Machiavelli makes on the value of reading history, Livy explains his own commitment to such study: "In history you have a record of the infinite variety of human experience plainly set out for all to see; and in that record you can find for yourself and your country both examples and warnings; fine things to take as models, base things, rotten through and through, to avoid."

At the same time, Livy admits to factual problems in his enterprise, particularly concerning earlier Roman history. His account of the founding of Rome by Romulus and Remus, for example, is no more than myth duly recorded by a historian. Indeed, by his admission, authenticating facts and differentiating these from legends or myths was difficult and, as a result, much of Livy's treatment (particularly of earlier Roman history) is problematic. Livy defends his approach by arguing he "would have spared no effort if there were any way of research arriving at the truth, but, as it is, one must stick to tradition where the antiquity of events makes certainty impossible."

Anticipating Edward Gibbon's *The Decline and Fall of the Roman Empire*, Livy sees moral decay as undermining Rome's power position. One needs, he argues, to be concerned with any "general relaxation of the nation's moral fiber." He writes scornfully about how "wealth has made us greedy, and self-indulgence has brought us, through every form of sensual excess, to be, if I may so put it, in love with death both individual and collective." He condemns, for example, a Bacchic cult in which "rites were held promiscuously" and "no sort of crime, no kind of immorality was left unattempted." This moral concern pervades the entire work. He deplores the prevalence of sexual promiscuity, murder, plunder, and the like. Livy also makes clear how concerned he is when "might" proves to be "stronger than right." Although in other respects Machiavelli's writings parallel the views of Livy, the two tend to diverge on these normative grounds.

We now take up four of the themes present in Livy's work that are of interest to IR scholars: security and war, fortune and volition, class, and

---

[9] Penguin editions are convenient for Livy's *History of Rome*: Books I–V are contained in *The Early History of Rome*, Books VI–X are in *Rome and Italy*, Books XXI–XXX are in *The War with Hannibal*, and Books XXXI–XLV are in *Rome and the Mediterranean*. All subsequent quotes are from these editions.

republicanism. His discussion of the virtues of republican forms of government in terms of security is a major theme of Machiavelli's work.

Security and War

Livy's key concerns are of understandable interest to IR scholars. He tells us that survival—the safety of the state—has always been the primary goal of Roman leaders. The consul, for example, should "see to it that the state takes no harm" and should protect the frontier. Threats may obviously emanate from enemies outside the state as occurred in 389 BCE when the Volscians from the central-western part of the Italian peninsula attempted to conquer Rome. Similarly, Livy describes Rome at around 349–348 BCE as being "caught between two foreign wars at the same time, and worried too by the defection of their allies." In these circumstances, "the Senate realized that those who had not been bound by loyalty must be held down by fear." The consuls had "to exert all their powers of authority to recruit troops; for they must rely on a citizen army when their allies were leaving them." This emphasis on the use of citizens as opposed to mercenaries is also the advice Machiavelli gives in *The Prince* and *The Discourses*.

What are the causes of war? To Livy, war seems to be the product of rational choice. Councils evaluate the pros and cons of going to war and reach a decision. Wars are not so much accidental as they are calculated to achieve certain objectives—a basic realist assumption. Territorial expansion may be the aim. Livy certainly celebrates the grandeur of the Roman Empire, which extended its territory while, at the same time, admitting defeated enemies as citizens. War was how this empire was built. Livy asserts that "so great is the glory won by the Roman people in their wars" that they are entitled to the claim "that Mars [the god of war] himself was their first parent."

Wars between two parties are watched closely by other parties likely to be affected by the outcome. Whether to remain neutral or to take one side or the other thus was of concern to Philip, the King of Macedon, as he observed the progress of war between the two wealthiest peoples in the world—Rome and Carthage. In some instances, however, war between two parties may be due to relations with third parties. For example, Livy tells us that the cause of the war between Rome and Samnium "came from without and did not arise directly between them." The two went to war as the result of a complex set of entangling alliance commitments, circumstances similar to those before the outbreak of the Peloponnesian war as described by Thucydides. Although the factors leading to a decision to go to war may not be subject to control by the separate parties, it nevertheless remains, as realists argue, a deliberative process in which alternatives can be evaluated rationally by the personalities involved.

More than most other ancient writers but consistent with present-day IR scholarship, Livy identifies the important economic underpinnings of military capability that contribute to the power of the state. He refers in one passage, for example, to the mobilization of economic capacity by Carthage: "The city itself, with the smiths and artisans of all trades shut up in the state workshops, rang continuously with the sound of warlike preparations."

The ability to raise money to finance wars is also important. Resource limitations do indeed constrain military options. In deciding what to do about Hannibal and Carthage, the Romans calculated that "public funds cannot support two separate armies, one in Italy, one in Africa," particularly since "no resources are left for maintaining fleets and furnishing supplies." Stocks of weapons, provisions, and money thus are essential to successful war efforts. So is the availability of personnel, a Roman advantage over Carthage. Livy observes how "the Romans had their own populace and that of Latium in the central-west part of the Italian peninsula to supply a greater and more numerous body of young soldiers continually growing to take the place of their losses, however great." By contrast, "both the city and rural population of Carthage were utterly unwarlike—they were forced to hire mercenaries from the Africans."

For Livy, military service for the public good takes precedence over private or personal concerns. To be effective, military units need to exhibit "the soldierly qualities of courage, discipline, and endurance." Fairness and consistency are also essential elements in maintaining military discipline. Certainly one should not act as the general Scipio was accused, perhaps unfairly, of alternately treating "his soldiers with absurd indulgence and extreme brutality." The result, if this allegation was true, would have been that "almost more men had been lost through mutiny than had been killed in battle."

Favorable geography is also important. In addition to its possession of a considerably larger body of men of military age than other places, the city of Oaeneum on the western part of the Balkan peninsula, for example, was said to be "girdled with natural defenses, having on the one side a river, called Artatus, and on the other a very high mountain, a difficult ascent." Population and favorable geography gave the inhabitants hope for successful resistance against forces under the command of the warrior Perseus.

Finally, as is also argued by present-day realists, Livy observes how forming alliances can increase one's power, reduce external threats, and enhance security. While he sees the pitfall of being drawn into war by alliance commitments, he argues that such arrangements might be required to compensate for a state's relative lack of independent economic or military capability. Seeking support from the Romans, for example, the Campians expressed what they saw as the reciprocal security benefits to both: "Every time the Aequi [in the mountains of central Italy] and Volscians, your City's perpetual enemies, bestir themselves, we shall be on their backs, and what you have done first for our preservation, we shall always do for your empire and glory." Indeed, alliances allow for coordination of strategy and pooling of resources.

One occasionally gets the impression that Livy believes war is not necessarily all bad. He attributes to Hannibal, for example, the idea "that a country wasting away and moldering in idleness would be aroused from its torpor by the clashing of arms." Military values are exalted as when Livy praises the general Cato for living under the same discipline as his men "in frugal living, in endurance of sleepless nights and other hardships." Although he had the status and prerogatives of a senior commander, Livy assures us that Cato "enjoyed no privileges to distinguish him from the rest of his army."

Having said that, Livy does not gloss over the horrors of war. Included in Scipio's "war prayer," for example, is a request for "the power of vengeance upon those whom we hate and our country's enemies, and give to me and to the Roman people means to inflict upon the Carthaginian state the sufferings that the Carthaginians have labored to inflict on ours." In another passage he refers to indiscriminate slaughter with "Roman troops butchering armed and unarmed, Carthaginians or Tarentines [Taranto a Greek colony] alike."

There is, however, the sense in Livy that such effects of war should be moderated. Reference is made to the Romans having "anciently established the custom of sparing the conquered." There is even a suggestion, consistent with Cicero, that resort to war ought to be justified—*jus ad bellum*—as in Rome's war with Philip of Macedon who had conspired with the Carthaginians against Rome: "Your wrongs gave us adequate justification for war."

Fortune and Volition

To Livy the most important elements in war are "the numbers and courage of the soldiers, the talent of the commanders, and luck, which is a powerful influence on all the affairs of men and particularly in warfare." He identifies Alexander the Great as a model commander who, in addition to his other qualities, enjoyed good fortune that never failed him in a single battle. In his allusion to fortune and the uncertainties of warfare, we have the essential elements of an argument developed before him by Thucydides and Polybius and later by Machiavelli and Carl von Clausewitz—the latter using such metaphors as "fog of war" and "friction" to capture the idea that unaccounted-for variables might affect the military equation either positively or adversely.

Fortune is an extremely important factor that pervades Livy's entire body of work. We see it in the battle at Cannae, which the Romans lost to the Carthaginians under Hannibal. Was the Roman defeat "due to some fault and not to the anger of the gods, or to Fate, by whose law event is linked unalterably to event in human affairs"? Fortunes may change. The mark of a good commander is one able "to seize his good fortune when it offers and turn to good use any unexpected stroke of luck."

Hannibal recognized the demand on the battlefield commander's intellect: "Many problems naturally difficult are solved by a little brainwork." Caution and patience are virtues. One does not rush into battle; one should avoid precipitate action that is often associated with the impatience of youth. At the same time, when one is prepared, there is value in taking the offensive—devastating your enemy's country instead of seeing your own ravaged. One engages in "removing the threat from oneself" and "bringing the other man into peril." In sum, human beings are not powerless and can make efforts to effect desirable outcomes.

Class Analysis

Livy is often associated with realist thought, but one also finds throughout his work analyses of class and interclass conflict between patricians and plebeians in Roman society, important ideas in our own time among Marxist and other economic-structuralist scholars. Livy writes of "bitter class conflict both at home and abroad." Members of the Roman Senate opposed legalizing intermarriage between the nobility and the commons because "patrician blood would thereby be contaminated" and "hereditary rights and privileges of the *gentes*, or families, would be lost." There was concern among patricians lest "the highest office of state have to be shared with the dregs of society" or might even be "lost to the nobility and transferred to the commons." Plebeians would likely elect "men of their own class, and the most turbulent demagogues at that."

To Livy, rulers who favor their own patrician class and alienate the lower classes forget that their power rests ultimately on popular support. Such leaders may be confronted with revolutionary activity against their regimes. As an example, Livy relates how at around 371 BCE the opportunity for a revolution seemed to have come as a result of the crushing load of debt incurred by state authorities. In this situation "the people could hope for no relief except through placing their representatives in the highest office."

As Livy describes them, circumstances were also particularly bad in 210 BCE:

> It was the Roman people, it seemed, that the consuls had set about ruining and tearing to pieces. For years the people had been drained dry by taxation; they had nothing left but the land, and that was stripped bare. The enemy had burnt their houses, the state had stolen the slave labor from their farms, either impressing the slaves as oarsmen for the fleet, or buying them cheap for military service; any silver or copper money a man might have had been taken from him either for the oarsmen's pay or for the annual tax. They could not be compelled by any force or any authority to give what they have not got.

Livy also notes how at other times "the nobles were grabbing possession of public land, and there would be no room left there for the common people unless it was shared out before they seized it all." Patricians were preoccupied with "all the objects for which men's desire knows no bounds—land, money and advancement." Exploitation of the plebeians resulted in their enslavement for debt.

Class conflict such as this does not advance society and can be a catalyst for revolutionary activity. In Livy's view, divisiveness of any kind may weaken the state, exposing it to the threat of foreign invasion. By contrast, Livy claims that authority in the able hands of an effective ruler—whatever his background— "was enough to make the enemy withdraw from Roman territory." Livy notes how in history so long as nobody who had conspicuous ability was despised, Rome's power grew. In short, to Livy it was an individual's abilities, not his or her class origin, that should be the decisive factor.

Republicanism

As evidenced by Livy's comments on class, he agrees with all of his predecessors that domestic factors affect the security of the state. The strength or power of the state depends in part upon the legitimacy and cohesiveness of the political regime. In this regard, Livy's preferred political regime, like Machiavelli's in *The Discourses*, is a representative government or republic. Livy idealizes republican Rome "governed by annually elected officers of state and subject not to the caprice of individual men, but to the overriding authority of law." He relates how in 507 BCE the consul Valerius called a mass meeting of the people and, before mounting the platform, "ordered his lictors [officers who accompanied magistrates in public appearances], as a gesture of sympathy with popular feeling, to lower their rods." He explains that the gesture was well received because "the lowering of the *fasces*—the emblem of authority—in the people's presence was taken as an admission that the majesty of power was vested in themselves rather than in the consul."

To Livy the ultimate power in the state rests with the people rather than with an individual ruler who is merely exercising authority gained from this popular support. One of the clearest statements of this view is his reference in Book VIII to "the people, who held supreme power over everything." Patriotism, an identification with the political community that "is founded upon respect for the family and love of the soil," contributes to cohesiveness of the state and keeps it from being "torn to pieces by petty squabbles."

Finally, promulgation of laws makes possible the creation of a unified body politic. The ruler's own legitimacy is enhanced when measures are taken "to increase the dignity and impressiveness of his position." Livy argues that while Rome had originally been founded by force of arms, a new and solid basis of law and religious observance was later substituted for brute force as the foundation of the political community. Changes in the international environment also have their effects on domestic law: "Laws passed in peacetime are frequently cancelled by war; and peace often repeals the legislation of wartime: just as, in the handling of a ship some methods are of service in fair weather, other methods in time of storm."

Aside from domestic law, the Roman idea of international law that extends beyond a particular political community appears in several places in Livy. Treaties are binding (in international law the principle of *pacta sunt servanda*) and Livy criticizes those who "had broken faith in respect of their treaty obligations." On the other hand, circumstances at the time the treaty was signed may have changed (the international legal concept of *rebus sic stantibus*), resulting in an alteration of the original treaty commitments—"that everybody's interest would be better served if the old treaty were brought up to date." Finally, although Livy does not dwell on the notion, there is a fleeting reference to "matters of divine and human law"—a distinction developed later in the political theory of the Middle Ages.

While Livy's observations on international law and war were read by later scholars such as Grotius, of greater interest to students of international relations is Livy's belief, following Polybius, that the nature of republican Rome—particularly its balancing and integration of different political, economic, and social forces into a unified whole—accounts for its ascendancy in such a short period. Not only does republicanism enhance the domestic security and stability of the state, but also it aids in dealing with foreign threats and the expansion of the empire. Machiavelli also analyzed and praised the benefits to the domestic and international security of republics. As we will see, Immanuel Kant viewed the relation between the nature of republics and international relations in a quite different manner. Unlike Livy and Machiavelli, Kant believed an international system composed of republics was the best hope for international peace, not a source of imperialist expansionism.

Plutarch

Plutarch (46–120 CE) was one of the last classical Greek historians. Born in Chaeronea (some fifty miles east of Delphi), he studied philosophy in Athens and was heavily influenced by the works of Plato and the idea that knowledge is virtue. He became well known as a scholar and diplomat to Rome, where he made many influential friends. His *Lives of the Noble Greeks and Romans* consists of a series of paired portraits of various leaders such as Solon, Pericles, Lysander, Alexander, Caesar, Pompey, Cicero, and Cato. As a lover of tradition, he agrees with Livy that a better understanding of the past encourages contemporary leaders to emulate the more virtuous of their predecessors. Another purpose of his work was to show both Greeks and Romans that they could draw benefit from each other's traditions.[10]

More so than any other scholar surveyed in this work, Plutarch views momentous events in personal terms, and for this reason alone he is worthy of discussion. Unlike Thucydides, for example, he is not interested in uncovering underlying historical processes, nor does he claim, as does Polybius, that there is a natural and historical sequence in the life of a state. In present-day parlance, the individual level of analysis was supreme, with statesmen's policies essentially a function of their personalities, not the nature of the state or international system. These latter environments only provide the dramatic backdrop within which Plutarch's subjects operate.

For Plutarch, service to the state rather than the Stoic emphasis on humanity as a whole is a virtue. Hence, he describes Aristides of Athens as a man who "cared nothing for personal popularity or reputation. His efforts were always aimed at securing the utmost advantage for the state that was consistent with safety and justice." Similarly, he praises Pericles for his prudence that restrained the Athenian spirit of conquest, consolidated Athens' military gains, and kept Sparta in check. Pericles and Fabius Maximus are described as two men who through their "moderation, their uprightness, and their ability to endure the follies of their peoples and their colleagues in office, they rendered the very greatest service to their countries."

Whatever weaknesses an individual may exhibit in his private life, however, for Plutarch the critical criterion of greatness is whether or not a soldier or politician is willing and able to overcome personal vices in aid of the security of the state. While he depicts Aristides's political rival, Themistocles, as obsessed

---

[10] Plutarch, "Introduction" to *Fall of Athens: Nine Greek Lives*, trans. Ian Scott-Kilvert (London: Penguin Books, 1960). All subsequent direct quotes are from this edition.

with fame, ambition, money, and a grand style of living, Plutarch's respect for patriotic men of action is nevertheless quite evident.

Themistocles was able, for example, to put an "end to the fighting within Greece, to reconcile the various cities with one another and persuade them to lay aside their differences because of the war with Persia." Furthermore, Themistocles is praised for having the foresight to end the banishment of his longtime rival, Aristides, so the two could work together to defeat Xerxes's Persian forces at Salamis (near Athens) and Plataea (in central Greece). A similar willingness to subordinate pride to the safety of the state occurred when Pericles recalled from exile his rival, Cimon.

Although Plutarch reserves his deepest respect for those individuals who lead a virtuous private life, when a state's interests are at stake, another standard of behavior is acceptable. Hence, in foreign policy matters the much-praised Aristides "followed whatever policy his country had adopted, recognizing that this must involve a great deal of injustice on occasion." Similarly, it is perfectly understandable and acceptable that the Greek leader, Cimon, carried war into enemy countries, ravaged the land, and at times created new colonies.

One might have the impression that, given the emphasis Plutarch places on the ability of individuals to influence events and outcomes, he falls on the voluntarist extreme of the determinism-voluntarism spectrum. But he recognizes the limits to effective action. In the first place, one commendable leader may be up against a strong rival—witness Plutarch's (or Thucydides's) discussion of how Alcibiades outmaneuvered Nicias over the Athenian decision to launch the expedition to Sicily. Second, although not relied upon to the extent of other authors such as Polybius and Machiavelli, Plutarch occasionally admits to the role of fate in determining outcomes: "How intricate are the workings of fortune and how unfathomable to human reason." Nevertheless, of all the writers associated with the realist tradition who are discussed in this work, Plutarch emphasizes volition or free will the most.

Reflections on Thought in the Roman Empire

This chapter thus far has examined writers associated with the philosophy of Stoicism and writers known for their analyses of both republican and imperial Rome. The two intersect because the spiritual character of Stoicism made it the preferred and professed philosophy of Rome's educated elite. Conversion of Constantine (his reign, 306–337 CE) to Christianity—the new religion of the Roman Empire—further embedded the Stoic idea of universality. Nevertheless, there was an obvious disjuncture between the basic precepts of Stoicism and the actual development of the Roman Empire.

Incorporated within Christianity, Stoic universalism may even have provided a convenient pretext to justify imperial control from the center. Whether as philosophy or in Christian religious form, Stoicism was in effect the ideology that legitimated the actions of imperial Rome. The *Pax Romana* [Roman peace] was established by conquest with all the violence and brutality of war. Subjugated peoples were summarily incorporated into the empire, but they also were given considerable autonomy—the key to maintaining the empire over time.

Rome also promoted notions of unity and the universality of citizenship, and this often became a reality, at least for many of what we would call the elites in conquered territories. Notwithstanding the use of violent means contrary to Stoic principles, Rome as an empire moved Stoic universalism from the plane of philosophical abstraction to one of political reality.

Even when the Roman Empire went into decline, Stoic ideas survived through the Middle Ages and the rise of the state system down to the present day. Stoic universalism is reflected in the argument that the concept of "political community" need not be restricted to the territorial dimensions of the small and intimate city-state preferred by Plato and Aristotle, the modern bureaucratic state, or even an empire. In rejecting the almost exclusive realist emphasis on the territorial state, the Stoics substituted a universalistic doctrine that transcended not only territorial divisions and the diversity or plurality of humanity but also time as well—its laws assumed to be perpetually valid.

As Grotius and others advanced international law, they drew from the Stoic well-spring. Scholars who subscribe to the present-day English School image of IR theory focus on an international society in which states serve their interests but also follow agreed rules—some within the school even taking matters to the level of a global society driven by universally accepted norms.

Furthermore, the Stoic tradition emphasizes the individual level of analysis all too often forgotten, particularly by a realist tradition that focuses on states and elite decision makers and an economic-structuralist tradition concerned with sweeping economic and social forces. By linking natural laws to the individual, the way was opened for future generations of scholars and political activists to argue for the existence of universal human rights that no state should be able to abrogate. Furthermore, Stoicism's emphasis on virtue, humanity, and natural law is an easy fit with Christianity, which combines divine (and revealed) law with the laws of nature, a topic discussed in the next part of this chapter on political thought in the Middle Ages. Like Christianity, Islam is open to peoples of all races and ethnicities, thus continuing Stoic universality to Muslims from Africa eastward across the Middle East, South and East Asia to western China, Malaysia, Indonesia, Brunei, and the Philippines.

THE MIDDLE AGES

The decline and fall of the Roman Empire and the resulting decentralization of authority produced a high degree of pluralism in western Europe. Travel was not just a privilege of the elites, but also was at least possible for the faithful of more modest means, who were known to undertake religious pilgrimages far from home. The crusades even brought many to the Holy Land and elsewhere in the Near East. Trade grew by sea and over land but would until later centuries remain a marginal activity in relation to the localized concentration of economic activity that was characteristic of feudalism. Armed conflicts were frequent, though in principle, if not in fact, subject to the restraints of the developing just war doctrine.

Still, there was in the medieval mind a sense of unity in Christendom. This idea is central to understanding St. Augustine (354–430), St. Thomas Aquinas

(1225–1274), and other medieval writers. Even Dante Alighieri (1265–1321) and other critics who challenged the temporal authority of the church tended to see the universe as a unified whole. The Stoicism of the Roman Empire thus not only survived but rather was strengthened by early Christian writers who had quickly adopted its premises. Seneca, though of course never canonized, even came to be revered by many Christians *de facto* as a pre-Christian "saint." The rise of states, the emergence of market economies, and both the Renaissance and Protestant Reformation ultimately marked the end of this medieval era. It is useful to reflect upon the Middle Ages to reiterate the point that the state system and global capitalism we know today have not been the only forms of international organization.

Historical Context

As we have seen, whatever unity was provided by the Roman Empire was a function of Roman law, Roman legions, and Stoic philosophy that had become in effect the ideology of the empire. This unity was reinforced when the empire was Christianized by Emperor Constantine (272–337 CE). With the final collapse of Rome in the fifth century CE, the next thousand years came to be known by later scholars as the Middle Ages or Medieval period. Its endpoint is generally marked by the Renaissance and the Protestant Reformation of the fifteenth and sixteenth centuries.

This period is of particular interest to IR scholars as it encompasses the period immediately before the onset of the current state system. As we will see, the organization of the world into territorially based states claiming sovereignty was not an inevitable outcome of the Middle Ages. Other possibilities existed. Writers in the period also addressed the morality of war and warfighting and other issues that were the foundation for later development of the law of war.

During the Middle Ages the major purveyor of the notion of the unity of humanity was the Christian church, whose teachings had been sanctioned as Rome's official state religion in 393 CE. But as Rome's empire collapsed, Christians were understandably concerned that if an empire such as this could not even protect itself from barbarian invaders, how could it provide the necessary worldly power to help the church in its crusade to spread the teachings of Christianity?[11]

Principally due to the conversion to Christianity of the emperor Constantine, the church became an increasingly wealthy and privileged organization and therefore had much to lose from invasions and general chaos. Even later, as more and more "barbarians" came under the influence of Christianity, the church in self-defense continued to strengthen its organization and centralized authority in the papacy. Despite the often corrupt and hypocritical behavior of many members of the church hierarchy, Christianity was the framework within which medieval life, private as well as public, was conducted.[12] As we will see,

---

[11] William Ebenstein, *Great Political Thinkers*, 4th ed. (New York: Holt, Rinehart, and Winston, 1969), 172.

[12] "It [the church] governed birth, marriage, and death, sex, and eating, made the rules for law and medicine, gave philosophy and scholarship their subject matter." Barbara W. Tuchman, *A Distant Mirror:*

scholars associated with the Christian church were responsible for justifying the desired creation of a unified international system dominated by theocratic principles.

While the church in western Europe proclaimed the universality of its message in the sacred realm, political power in the secular realm was greatly fragmented with a wide variety of different types of actors claiming legitimacy. Charlemagne's early ninth-century Holy Roman Empire, centered in Germany, was, as Voltaire wryly noted, not very holy, Roman, or much of an empire compared to that of the Caesars or even that of Byzantium to the east.

Yet Charlemagne's successors provided a limited secular counterweight to the growing power of the church. Indeed, Christian doctrine initially allowed for two separate but essentially equal papal and imperial powers. The passing of Charlemagne (742–814) was followed by turmoil and the breakdown of the unity of his empire.[13] Smaller political units came to the fore due to internal weaknesses as well as invasions by the Saracens (Arabs or Turks), Magyars (Hungarians), and Norsemen (Scandinavians).

Kingdoms still existed, but administratively they lacked efficient bureaucracies and permanent military forces. As a result, kings generally had little power over local barons. The contradiction between the actual pluralism and diversity of medieval institutions and the religious and philosophical desire for greater unity, whether provided by imperial or papal authorities, was readily apparent.[14]

Feudalism, the preeminent form of authority that emerged earlier but became particularly evident by the tenth century, was a political, social, and economic response to the disorder and confusion resulting from the collapse of the Roman Empire. A defining characteristic of feudalism is public authority placed in private hands.[15] Barons enjoyed legitimacy stemming from their ownership of property and the security they provided for their domains.

It was during the chaos of late ninth-century Europe—a time in which the stability provided by Roman law and legions was fast fading from memory— that public authority came to be treated as the private possession of local lords who controlled territory known as fiefs. This authority was devolved to them by often weak and distant kings. Even courts of justice were administered privately by individual lords who conducted business as they saw fit. Similarly, a vassal's loyalty and obligation to a lord was personal; it was not owed to some distant and possibly abstract entity called "the state." Oaths of fealty or allegiance in exchange for the protection a lord could offer were, in effect, personal contracts.

The Calamitous 14th Century (New York: Alfred A. Knopf, 1978), 32.

[13] The Holy Roman Empire would have a long shelf life, its capital eventually shifting to Vienna in 1440 under the Habsburg dynasty. It came to an end in 1806 after Napoleon was victorious in the Battle of Austerlitz in 1805.

[14] Ebenstein, *Great Political Thinkers*, 212.

[15] Marc Bloch, *Feudalism*, trans. L. Manyon (Chicago: University of Chicago Press), chap. 29; J. R. Strayer, "Feudalism in Western Europe," in *Lordship and Community*, ed. Frederic L. Cheyette (New York: Holt, Rinehart, and Winston, 1968), 14.

Authority rested with the ruler who had the right to administer the inhabitants of his fiefdom.

Ownership of property by a vassal within a fiefdom was conditional on the owner accepting explicit obligations. For example, if a lord needed to defend his territory, he did not call upon all free men to bear arms in his service but rather summoned his vassals. Conversely, a lord promised to provide the vassal protection from an often hostile and uncertain world. This privatization of public authority in the hands of local nobles was a cause and consequence of the predominance of local government over the claims of kings, and the general fragmentation of political authority throughout Europe comprised what we identify as "feudalism."[16]

Political authority during feudal times was claimed by a heterogeneous collection of institutions and individuals, including local barons, bishops, kings, and popes. It was also a time in which middle-class merchants—the bourgeoisie of the towns—began to become a political force, often lending their support to religious or secular leaders in return for charters allowing them to establish free "communes" and, over time, commercial leagues.

Depending on their status, any one of these entities could be granted or denied the right of embassy—to conduct diplomatic relations. This medieval system, which seems so alien to the modern mind, in fact was "a patchwork of overlapping and incomplete rights of government" that was "inextricably superimposed and tangled." It was a world in which "different juridical instances were geographically interwoven and stratified, and plural allegiances, asymmetrical suzerainties and anomalous enclaves abounded."[17]

Besides such factors as poor communications and sparse populations, three sets of social, economic, and political institutions worked to retard the development of strong, centralized governments. First, as long as feudal institutions were strong and a great deal of authority fragmented and decentralized, it was difficult for the modern state to develop.[18] Second, while feudalism worked to restrict the development of the state "from below," the universal claims of authority by the church had a similar effect "from above." Finally, the claims of the Holy Roman Empire had an impact analogous to (although lesser than) the church through its sweeping claims of authority over Europe in the secular realm. Given this situation, there was very little political space during the Middle Ages within which the modern state could develop.

Can we speak of this polyglot collection of forms of political authority during the latter half of the Middle Ages as an international or "world" political system? Definitely so, even though it does not have the elegant simplicity of an international system composed of sovereign states. If any time in history

---

[16] Joseph R. Strayer and D. C. Munro, *The Middle Ages, 395–1500,* 5th ed. (New York: Appleton-Century-Crofts, 1970), 114–16.

[17] John Gerard Ruggie, "Continuity and Transformation in the World Polity," in *Neorealism and Its Critics,* ed. Robert O. Keohane (New York: Columbia University Press, 1986), 142.

[18] As one author argues: "A perfectly feudal condition of society would be not merely a weak state, but the negation of the state altogether." J. L. Brierly, *The Law of Nations: An Introduction to the International Law of Peace,* 6th ed. (New York: Oxford University Press, 1963), 3.

corresponded to the more fragmented or pluralist liberal image of multiple non-state actors playing substantial roles, it was the Middle Ages. The distinction between internal and external political realms with rigid territorial demarcations, a centralized bureaucratic structure (the state) claiming to exercise public authority, and a claim to act independently in the world—hallmarks of the current international state system—would have seemed odd to the medieval mind.[19] Religious or moral philosophy viewed the universe as if it were a single whole and humanity as an organic, interdependent society.

But during the Middle Ages, diplomacy still existed. The papacy adopted certain Roman principles and established new ones that have become part of international law: the safe conduct of ambassadors, secrecy in diplomatic negotiations, and condemnation of treaty violations.[20] In terms of secular contributions, just as the vassalic contract was based on a personal relationship between lord and vassal, so, too, were personal relationships a key to diplomacy. Marriages were particularly important.[21]

Territorial borders were fluid, and relations between kingdoms were a function of dynastic connections. One did not speak of the "national interest" but rather the interest of particular rulers or dynasties. The high Middle Ages was a much more cosmopolitan era for the elites of the time than anything we have seen since—political courtships and marriages could result in a prince of Hungary becoming heir to the throne in Naples, or an English prince legitimately claiming the Spanish throne in Castile. This web of dynastic interdependencies characterized by royal mobility was paralleled by the rising merchant classes whose interest in commerce also made for a more cosmopolitan view of the world.[22]

Nevertheless, despite the philosophical conception of Europe as an organic entity, in reality it was a period historians have characterized as one of "feudal anarchy." It was a time when "the system of rule relied, both for order-keeping and for the enforcement of rights and the redress of wrongs, on self-activated coercion exercised by a small, privileged class of warriors and rentiers [earning income from the lands they owned]."[23] When describing the Middle Ages of Europe as an international system, the key phrase is "system of rule." As one historian has argued: "Europeans lived in a society whose organization may

---

[19] Ruggie, "Continuity and Transformation," 142–43.

[20] Walter Ullman, *The Growth of Papal Government in the Middle Ages* (1952), 450 as cited by Martin Wight, "De Systematibus Civitatum," in *Systems of States* (Leicester, UK: Leicester University Press, 1977), 28–29.

[21] "Marriages were the fabric of international as well as inter-noble relations, the primary source of territory, sovereignty, and alliance and the major business of medieval diplomacy." Tuchman, *A Distant Mirror*, 47. As we shall see in chapter 4, however, the term "sovereignty" has distinctly modern connotations that render it an inappropriate term to use to describe medieval political units.

[22] On the other hand, the life of the commoner was marked by extreme insularity and parochialism. See, for example, Frances and Joseph Gies, *Life in a Medieval Village* (New York: Harper & Row, 1990). On relations between the few and the many, see the comparative study by Reinhard Bendix, *Kings of People: Power and the Mandate to Rule* (Berkeley: University of California Press, 1978).

[23] Gianfranco Poggi, *The Development of the Modern State: A Sociological Introduction* (Stanford, CA: Stanford University Press, 1978), 31.

seem excessively simple compared with ours, but it was organized. They shared certain mores, certain patterns of accepted behavior, certain ideals, and a store of acquired techniques."[24]

By the twelfth century, however, some headway had been made in the reconcentration of political power in the hands of kings because of changes in the nature of feudalism. Three trends were particularly important: monetarization, systematization, and bureaucratization of feudalism. Each is worthy of a brief discussion.[25]

First, the feudal relationship began to change from one based on personal service to one based on monetary payment. As vassals desired more time to develop their fiefs and pass them on to their heirs, they became less interested in spending their time engaged in personal service on behalf of the lord. Most lords acquiesced, coming to accept monetary payment from those running fiefs. This trend, however, benefited the rulers of provinces and kingdoms more than the local lords, since these greater lords (who, after all, claimed some control or suzerainty over lesser nobles) either attempted to monopolize the payments from the fiefs or to take from the local lord most of what the latter collected. This increase in revenues greatly aided in the strengthening of kingdoms and increasing centralized governments.

Second, feudal systems became more systematized and universalized, meaning that in such states as England and Normandy (in France) feudalism increasingly tended to resemble a pyramid with distinct lines of authority. This reflected a trend in which kings made great strides toward pulling together the scattered pieces of their kingdoms and began to reinforce half-forgotten claims of suzerainty or control. In France, for example, the king explicitly demanded a reaffirmation of homage from the lords of the realm. Although in the twelfth century the practical effect of this policy was not particularly significant, it established a precedent for the king's legal superiority.

Another example of the systematization of feudalism occurred in England and involved the development of a "franchise theory of justice." This meant that when a king granted a lord the right to dispense justice, the king reserved the right to intervene in the judicial process as well as define the original terms of the grant. This became the basis upon which appeals could be made from local courts. In the process, the links were further weakened between local lords and vassals as the latter increasingly looked to higher authorities for military and legal protection.

Finally, the twelfth century witnessed the bureaucratization of feudalism. This principally entailed not only the development of judicial courts but also the establishment of administrative and financial offices. The monetarization and systematization of feudalism required educated persons to oversee the expanding responsibilities and authorities of the greater lords and kings. While clerks

---

[24] Frederic L. Cheyette, "The Invention of the State," in *Essays on Medieval Civilization*, ed. Bede Karl Lackner and Kenneth Roy Philip (Austin: University of Texas Press, 1978), 149.
[25] The following three trends are developed from Joseph R. Strayer, *Medieval Statecraft and the Perspectives of History* (Princeton, NJ: Princeton University Press, 1971), 80–89.

were indispensable in running the centralized administrations, enforcement powers were granted to laymen who acted as local representatives of the king, staffed courts, and collected revenues. These positions were unusual in that they introduced into Europe a new source of income independent from that derived from the ownership of a fief. But this also meant that officials had to remain loyal to the king lest they be removed from their positions of authority and livelihood. This increase in bureaucracy was perhaps the critical factor in the trend toward the development of the modern state.

This gradual process of concentrating power was aided by larger trends evident by the twelfth century. The cessation of invasions from Europe's periphery allowed kings and nobles to devote more attention and resources to internal affairs and also helped to account for the dramatic increase in the size of the European population. A larger population helped to revive towns, increase the size of the artisan class, and encourage greater trade. With expanded economic activity, taxation reappeared and was levied against churches, towns, and nobles. This required the establishment of a salaried officialdom. Greater royal income encouraged the payment of troops as opposed to relying on the vassalic contract based on mutual obligation. Kings, therefore, began to acquire two of the key elements associated with effective rule—financial resources and coercive power.

The twelfth and thirteenth centuries were also an era in which major strides were made in education. It is impossible to underestimate the importance of the growth of literacy to the rise of the state. Up until the end of the eleventh century, Europe was a nonliterate or oral society in which education was restricted to a small group of clergymen. Even in the case of the clergy, writing was seen more as an art form involving manuscript illumination than a means of written communication.

As literacy expanded, the idea of written contracts gained currency, and ideals, norms of behavior, and laws were more easily passed from one generation to another.[26] Universities were established (Bologna, Paris, Padua, Naples, Oxford, Cambridge), Roger Bacon engaged in experimental science, Dante wrote in the language of the common person, Aquinas drew inspiration from the ancient Greek writers, and Giotto raised art to a higher level. With the rise of educated bureaucrats, states formed archives that were essential to the continuity of government.[27]

This was also an era in which major clashes ensued between the sacred and secular realms in three areas—learning, commerce, and politics. In terms of learning, in the thirteenth century, France was the center of Western culture and scholarship. The charter of the University of Paris is dated from 1200 and the institution was exempted from civil control. Members of the university were even haughty toward ecclesiastical authority and came into continual conflict

---

[26] One historian argues: "The invention of the state is the story of how this small minority of literate men slowly imposed upon the non-literate their special ways of thinking about politics and law." Cheyette, "The Invention of the State," 150.

[27] Marc Bloch, *Feudal Society*, vol. 2 (Chicago: University of Chicago Press, 1964), 421–22.

with bishops and popes. The future Pope Boniface VIII aptly illustrates the tension when he writes to scholars at the University of Paris: "You Paris Masters at your desks seem to think the world should be ruled by your reasoning. It is to us that the world is entrusted, not to you."[28] This clash between reason (or scholarship) and church authority has continued through the ages.

In the realm of commerce, the growth of market-oriented economic transactions led to a clash between the church's emphasis on religion and the emerging capitalist view on economics. The Christian attitude toward commerce was that those engaged in business should expect only a fair return for their efforts; earning interest on the loan of money (usury) and taking in large profits were considered particularly sinful. There was also a move away from the feudal notion that the ownership of property was conditional on explicit social obligations that must be carried out. Instead, there was the increasingly important, modern, liberal notion that property is private and possession and disposal of it is up to the individual.

Politically, the clash between the sacred and secular was epitomized by a breakdown in the balance of power between pope and emperor. This clash between church and empire contributed to the breakup of the unity of Christendom, hence assisting the rise of national states. In 1076 Pope Gregory VII and the German Emperor Henry IV were engaged in a power struggle. The emperor initially deposed the pope who, in turn, excommunicated and then deposed the emperor. Their struggle ended with the emperor's unconditional surrender to the pope. Clothed in penitential garb, the emperor stood barefoot in the winter cold outside the gate of one of the pope's palaces. He was forced to wait three days before being granted an audience, whereupon he pledged complete submission to the pope and was pardoned. This was, perhaps, the high point of religious power over the temporal realm.[29]

Two hundred years later, however, the situation dramatically changed. The center of secular power moved from the weakened empire to the emerging nation-state. This shift was evident when King Philip of France had Pope Boniface VIII arrested. Philip levied taxes on clerical income without the pope's blessing. Boniface responded by forbidding the clergy to pay any tax to secular rulers.

In 1302 Boniface went even further, declaring papal supremacy: "It is necessary to salvation that every human creature be subject to the Roman pontiff." Philip's response was to form a council to judge the pope on charges that included heresy, blasphemy, murder, sodomy, and sorcery. When the pope moved to excommunicate Philip, agents of the king arrested him in 1303. The aged pope died within a month.

The medieval hope of a universal church was dealt another blow when, under Philip's influence, a Frenchman was elected pope. Fearful of Italian reprisals for the treatment of Boniface, the new pope settled in Avignon in southern France. Although a fief of the kingdom of Naples and Sicily, Avignon soon fell

---

[28] Tuchman, *A Distant Mirror*, 22.
[29] Ebenstein, *Great Political Thinkers*, 263.

under the French sphere of influence.[30] These incidents were a consequence of the struggle between church and empire that weakened both and worked to the advantage of the rising nation-state.

This overview may leave the reader with the impression that the victory of what we now call the modern state was somehow assured. This clearly was not the case. As late as the thirteenth century, four other outcomes were still possible. First, a political federation or empire with loose centralized control could have reemerged. We have seen that empires had already been created in Europe under the Romans. Even the loosely connected Holy Roman Empire provided a certain degree or sense of unity that lasted (formally at least) for a thousand years from Charlemagne's coronation in 800 to the abdication of the Hapsburg emperor Francis II in 1806. By the thirteenth century, Europe culturally and economically was an even more homogeneous region than in earlier years because of the many changes we have cataloged, hence a better candidate for unification than at any time since the halcyon days of the Roman Empire.

Second, a theocratic federation unified by the church conceivably could have emerged. While the papacy's claim to universal jurisdiction was officially in spiritual matters, the claim "was made effective, through a massive international bureaucracy, that was the chief limitation on the rudimentary sovereignty" of smaller and separate political communities, some that eventually would evolve into modern states.[31] This bureaucracy was not dismantled until after the Council of Constance (1414–1418), which marked the development of national churches aligned with the emerging national states.

The conflict between church and empire was particularly intense from the tenth to the thirteenth centuries. The victory of secular over sacred power was by no means assured even in the thirteenth century, and religious notables held a great deal of political power for centuries to come. The papal states survived into the nineteenth century, and outside Europe (e.g., the Near East) large-scale, although decentralized, clergy-dominated empires persisted.

Third, an intensive trading network without a centralized political organization developed as a result of the spread of market capitalism. Trading cities in Germany and northern Italy long resisted being swallowed by large territorial states and conceivably could have lasted much longer and increased in power. With northern German origins in the twelfth century, the Hanseatic League became a successful commercial federation of trading cities or towns on the Baltic and North Atlantic coasts. In 1397, the Medici family of Florence opened its first branch bank in Rome and later in other European cities.[32]

---

[30] Tuchman, *A Distant Mirror*, 25–26. As one scholar has summarized the end of the Middle Ages, "The elaborate medieval theory that had been built up concerning their respective powers [Pope and Emperor] ceased to be effective during the fifteenth century. The unity of Christendom, which it maintained, was destroyed by the power of the French, Spanish, and English monarchies in the secular sphere, and by the Reformation in the sphere of religion." Bertrand Russell, *The History of Western Philosophy* (New York: Simon & Schuster, 1945), 392–93.

[31] Wight, "De Systematibus Civitatum," 28.

[32] See Tim Parks, *Medici Money* (London: Profile Books, 2005).

Finally, there is no reason to exclude the logical possibility that feudalism could have persisted for a much longer period.[33] The question of why the state by 1500 had won out over these possible alternatives has preoccupied many historians who have suggested a multiplicity of preconditions and facilitating factors. Some of these have been mentioned earlier. Further possible explanations are discussed in the next chapter.

Medieval Writers

With the sacking of Rome in 410, what had seemed to be a permanent fixture of the western European system of rule and a source of stability—the Italian-based Roman Empire—was swept away. The secular support base for Christianity was now to be found in the Byzantine Empire to the east under such rulers as Constantine (324–337) and Justinian (527–565). In the west, however, contemplation of the world fell basically to writers associated with religious orders as education was only available to a handful, in particular those associated with the church. Early writers desired to help hold together the Christian community at a time when it was under attack by providing a moral compass for individuals and assuring that the gains achieved by the church during the later years of the Roman Empire were not lost.[34] As the power of the church increased over the centuries, later writers were particularly concerned with delineating what they believed to be proper relations between religious and civil powers.

Given their focus on ideals, the three writers selected for consideration here—Augustine, Thomas Aquinas, and Dante—have all been labeled "utopians." The term utopian now has pejorative connotations, particularly among present-day realists who tend to question these figures' relevance to the "real world" of twenty-first-century international politics. There are three points, however, to keep in mind. First, at the time they were writing, the establishment of a religious or secular-based empire was not beyond the realm of possibility. It is only because we today view the past through the lenses of the modern state system that the views of Augustine, Aquinas, and Dante seem quaint, if not fantastical. Second, all three scholars were influenced by the Greek tradition of natural law that suggests there is a source of authority beyond those of temporal powers. In trying to bring some sort of order to a world composed of diverse actors with conflicting and overlapping claims of authority, they reflect one strain of modern liberal thought that seeks to find a basis for unity in diversity. Finally, realist thinking resonates with all three authors: They hold a sobering view of human nature, and hence understand all too well the obstacles to world peace.

---

[33] Charles Tilly, ed., *The Formation of National States in Western Europe* (Princeton, NJ: Princeton University Press, 1975), 26–27.

[34] "The rise of the Christian church, as a distinct institution entitled to govern the spiritual concerns of mankind in independence of the state, may not unreasonably be described as the most revolutionary event in the history of western Europe, in respect both to politics and political philosophy." George H. Sabine, *A History of Political Theory*, rev. ed. (New York: Holt, 1950), 180.

Augustine and Aquinas

Augustine was born in 354 and grew up in the north African realm of the Roman Empire. At age sixteen, the son of a pagan father and Christian mother went to Carthage (present-day Tunis) to complete his education. His interest in philosophy was stimulated by reading Cicero, and, in 383, he went to Rome to teach rhetoric. Augustine moved to Milan in 386 and there converted to Christianity. Very much attracted to women, in his *Confessions* the saint admits to having lived what he considers a life of sinful debauchery.

Returning to North Africa, Augustine founded a religious community where he was ordained a priest, and five years later he was selected as the bishop of Hippo in present-day Algeria. During his thirty-four years in the community, he produced a vast outpouring of written works, the two most important being *Confessions* and *City of God*. The latter work differentiates between the city of man and how human beings live in contrast to the goodness to be found in the heavenly city of God. This work was written in part to refute Cicero's conception of providence, particularly his argument in favor of free will.

Thomas Aquinas was born in 1225 in southern Italy, attended the University of Naples, and joined the Dominicans, who sent him to Cologne in present-day Germany for further studies. After four years there he went to Paris in 1252 where he began his career as a teacher at the Dominican college of the Jacobins. In 1259 he was appointed theological adviser and lecturer to the papal curia. It was at this time that he assiduously studied Aristotle's works. After ten years in Rome, he went back to Paris to help defend his former colleagues against political and religious attacks, and then proceeded to Naples, where he became director of Dominican studies at the university. He died in 1274 while on his way to attend the second Council of Lyons in France.

Augustine and Aquinas provide an interesting contrast, as their works reflect the changing position and power of the Christian church over the millennium that spanned the Middle Ages. Augustine wrote at a time when the church was in a tenuous position. He was particularly influenced by the works of Plato and, following in the Platonic tradition, also extensively read Cicero. Martin Luther (1483–1546), an Augustinian monk, draws heavily from Augustine in fashioning the theology of his reformation movement among German states, thus earning Augustine among present-day political theorists the label the "protestant saint."

While Roman Catholic thought was influenced by Augustine, Aquinas's thirteenth-century achievement was to provide a synthesis of theological doctrine drawn from the writings of the Greeks, particularly Aristotle, and Romans at a time when the church was at the height of its power and in need of a universal and systematic philosophical grounding.[35] The Aristotelian focus in Aquinas later earned him the label "Catholic saint."

Taken together, the work of Augustine and Aquinas includes four areas of inquiry with political import: (1) Aquinas's view of natural law, (2) the respective nature and relation between the sacred and secular realms, (3) Augustine's realism, and (4) the just war doctrine.

---

[35] Ebenstein, *Great Political Thinkers*, 215.

Natural Law

Both Augustine and Aquinas believed that the ancient Greeks were onto something important with the concept of a natural law that sets limits on earthly political authority. But just as law made by humans was subordinate to natural law, it was divine law or the laws of God that ultimately should dominate. In Aquinas's *Treatise of the Laws*, we learn that "the whole community of the universe" is governed by "Divine reason." Aquinas observes that "the very Idea of the government of things in God, the Ruler of the universe, has the nature of law." This law necessarily is eternal because "the Divine Reason's conception of things is not subject to time." Aquinas asserts "that no one can know the eternal law as it is in itself, except God himself."[36]

There are, therefore, severe limits to human reason that differentiate humans from God. Although one cannot know the eternal law directly, as a rational creature an individual does have a share of the "Eternal Reason" that he or she, through the exercise of this reasoning faculty, comes to know as the "natural law." It is these precepts of the natural law, discoverable through reason, that one applies to the domain of human laws. Human laws are to be in accord with natural law. Beyond natural law, there also is revealed law given by God. This divine law fills an important gap in human understanding of what one ought to do or what one ought to avoid. In any event, "all laws, insofar as they partake of right reason, are derived from the eternal law." What if certain human laws are not in accordance with natural and eternal law? For Aquinas, laws that are not just are not laws at all. Indeed, if a human law "differs from the law of nature, it is no longer a law but a corruption of law."

Beyond the civil or human law of a given political unit, there is a law of nations (international law) that is also derived from natural law. Reflecting both Aristotelian and Stoic influences, Aquinas argues that a law of nations exists because it conforms with humanity's nature as social animals who engage in commerce: "To the law of nations belong those things that are derived from the law of nature as conclusions from premises, just [or morally right] buyings and sellings, and the like, without which human beings cannot live together, which is a point of the law of nature, since humans are by nature social animals, as is proved in the *Politics* of Aristotle."

To say that international law is derived from general principles of the natural law is not to deny customary bases. Concerning human law in general, Aquinas notes how customs can have the force of law because "by repeated external actions the inward movement of the will, and concepts of reason are most effectually declared." In short, "when a thing is done again and again, it seems to proceed from a deliberate judgment of reason." Of course, to have legal effect, customary practice must be in accordance not just with natural law, but also with the divine law as revealed to human beings.

---

[36] Direct quotes are from St. Thomas Aquinas, "Treatise on Law," in *Summa Theologica*, part I of second part.

Sacred and Secular Realms

This hierarchical conception of divine, revealed, natural, international, and human law had two implications for the church's preferred organization of the medieval world. First, the unity of the physical and metaphysical worlds is reinforced by conceiving these realms in terms of parallel and mutually reinforcing hierarchies that reflect revealed and natural laws. In the medieval view, the metaphysical reflects the same structure as the more familiar physical world. The heavens have a hierarchy of saints who can intercede on behalf of the faithful in supplications to the Lord of Lords—much as in the physical world where a vassal might seek the favor of his lord to intercede for him to a higher authority. Even a writer such as Dante, whose work the church condemned,[37] adopted this perspective.

Unfortunately, the world is beset by human imperfection or sin, as reflected in Augustine's "city of man" (figuratively, Babylon), yet there are also the seeds of a perfect world, the "city of God" (the heavenly city, figuratively Jerusalem). The two cities or communities are not empirically distinct or separable, as individuals representing both are interspersed. They are "outwardly mingled together, yet separated in heart."[38] Human imperfection stems from the error of Adam, which has been perpetuated in the city of man—-commitment to self-oriented, earthly values.

The second politically explosive implication, however, is the relation between the sacred and secular realms. On the one hand, Augustine is primarily concerned with individual faith and salvation. He does not view the world as a struggle between church and state, but rather between two opposing ways of life—the love of self versus the love of God. Nowhere does one find Augustine calling for a theocracy. Aquinas, however, quite clearly comes down on the side of the church, arguing that secular kingdoms are ultimately subject to the church as the latter is concerned with the most important end of all—the salvation of souls.[39]

Augustine's Realism

The preceding observations on human imperfection speak to what can be termed the Augustinian tradition of political realism and his view that evil is to be found at the individual level of analysis. While the classical Greeks placed

---

[37] In the *Divine Comedy*, Dante identifies enemies (to include the pope) during his mythical journey through hell in the *Inferno* led by Virgil. In *De Monarchia*, Dante places the monarch as subordinate directly to God, thus cutting out the papacy. The poet was also falsely accused of corruption (financial wrongdoing), which also put him at odds with the church.

[38] Henry Paolucci, ed., *The Political Writings of St. Augustine* (Washington, DC: Regnery Gateway, 1962, 1990), 317. Subsequent quotations from *City of God* are from the 1984 Penguin edition.

[39] Ebenstein, *Great Political Thinkers*, 173, 220. Hence, for Aquinas the two key areas whereby the church could intervene in secular affairs were (1) situations where the state exceeded its jurisdiction, such as in matters of justice whereby manmade law should be subordinated to natural law as derived from divine law, and (2) violations of faith such as heresy. Charles N. R. McCoy, "St. Thomas Aquinas," in *History of Political Philosophy*, ed. Leo Strauss and Joseph Cropsey (Chicago: Rand McNally, 1963), 206–7.

a great deal of emphasis on the ability of the mind to control human passions, impulses, and lusts, Augustine is not so sanguine. He does not simply argue that the "rule of the flesh" dominates "the rule of the spirit"—it is unfortunately much more difficult than that. As he states: "The corruption of the body, which weighs down the soul, is not the cause of the first sin, but its punishment. And it was not the corruptible flesh that made the soul sinful; it was the sinful soul that made the flesh corruptible." Given this pessimism, it is not so easy, as the Stoics would have one believe, for an individual to obtain happiness through right conduct. Similarly, given the corrupted nature of human beings, Augustine would probably be more "realistic" about the slim possibility of achieving Plato's ideal republic than would Plato himself.

Moving from the level of human nature to the state-societal level, Augustine's realism is also evident. Aside from sobering assessments and descriptions of the problem of individuals living together in communities, he is fully aware of how secular authorities and state power could benefit the church and its missions. Despite Augustine's criticisms of the decadence and depravity of the Romans (Part I of *City of God*), he recognizes the fact that the empire served as a vehicle for the spread of Christianity. Hence, he praises Constantine and expects that Christian rulers should "put their power at the service of God's majesty, to extend his worship far and wide." Conversely, good Christians make for better citizens, which is to the benefit of the state. As with other authors we have surveyed, the unity of the state is an important source of domestic stability and international security. On this point there is even a suggestion of what Rousseau later would call the general will. The interests of a state as republic or commonwealth are common to all, given that the state amounts to "a multitude of human beings bound together by some bond of accord."

Finally, at the level of the international system (what he terms the "third level of human society" following the household and city), Augustine is also quite aware of the obstacles to a sense of world community. He states that "the world, being like a confluence of waters, is obviously more full of danger than the other communities by reason of its greater size." Cooperation is difficult as the diversity of languages separates people.

Even the attempt of the Roman Empire to create unity was at a high cost: "Consider the scale of those wars, with all that slaughter of human beings, all the human blood that was shed." And although those wars eventually ended, the "misery of those evils is not yet ended." Not only is there "no lack of enemies among foreign nations," but also "the very extent of the Empire has given rise to wars of a worse kind, namely, social and civil wars." Such pessimism is rooted in Augustine's conception of human beings whose self-love is the source of evil. His realism is the recognition of the power of egotism at the individual and collective level, and he hopes to attain, given the circumstances, the most achievable form of peace and justice.

Augustine's optimism and voluntarist inclinations captured by his understanding of human free will, however, are also evident in his work. Despite his view of human imperfection, it should be noted that Augustine holds out hope for individuals being able to enter the City of God because human behavior is not fixed or predetermined—"enmity to God arises not from nature but from choice, in violation of a nature essentially good."

According to Reinhold Niebuhr, for Augustine:

> Good and evil are not determined by some fixed structure of human existence. Man, according to the biblical view, may use his freedom to make himself falsely the center of existence; but this does not change the fact that love rather than self-love is the law of his existence in the sense that man can only be healthy and his communities at peace if man is drawn out of himself and saved from the self-defeating consequences of self-love.[40]

Human behavior is hence not permanently fixed. Individuals can make choices, and it is the role of the church to help guide people to the City of God. This city is not Plato's territorially defined and restrictive city-state, nor Cicero's empire, but rather is a spiritual bond that aspires to include the entire human race.

As Augustine states, the City of God or Heavenly City "is on pilgrimage in this world," calling out "citizens from all nations and so collects a society of aliens, speaking all languages. She takes no account of any difference in customs, laws, and institutions." All these differences will continue to exist; what is important is for more and more individuals to enter the spiritual heavenly city, for in so doing peace on earth will be enhanced.

Justice and War

Neither Augustine nor Aquinas, however, expected war to be abolished anytime soon. Recognizing this, both scholars feel compelled to address the issue of just war. Augustine modifies the Roman doctrine of Cicero by infusing it with a Christian spirit. He takes into account criticisms of the Roman doctrine by Tertullian and other early Christian pacifist writers who essentially argue against Christian participation in war. Augustine disagrees, stating that such participation in war is acceptable or just under certain circumstances, noting that Jesus accepted soldiers as performing a legitimate function; he does not tell them "to cast away their arms." Reconciling Christianity and the state, Augustine opposes "those who say that the doctrine of Christ is incompatible with the State's well-being." More to the point, it is entirely possible to please God while engaged in active military service." Augustine gives due credit to Cicero for having discussed the question of justice in war, an account from which Augustine draws heavily. The objectives of war must be just: "A state should engage in war for the safety that preserves the state permanently in existence." Moreover, just wars are waged for legitimate purposes or objectives not by individuals as such, but by legitimate authorities: "A great deal depends on the causes for which human beings undertake wars, and on the authority they have for doing so."

Although Augustine thus departs from the absolute pacifism of early Christians, he does not offer a bellicose doctrine in its place. It is instead a doctrine of

---

[40] Reinhold Niebuhr, "Augustine's Political Realism," in *Christian Realism and Political Problems* (New York: Charles Scribner's Sons, 1953), 130.

war avoidance and restraint in war. Indeed, he argues that it is "with the desire for peace that wars are waged" and "that peace is the end sought for by war." In general, one refrains from the passion of revenge and seeks instead "when one has suffered wrong, to pardon rather than punish the offender." War is thus not the first resort, but even the good may need to engage in war "for it is the wrong-doing of the opposing party that compels the wise man to wage just wars."

At the same time, because war is waged so that peace may be obtained, one must "even in waging war, cherish the spirit of peacemaker." He adds that "mercy is due to the vanquished or the captive." The means one uses in war thus are important if wars are to be just: "The real evils in war are love of violence, revengeful cruelty, fierce and implacable enmity, wild resistance, and the lust of power." By contrast, the use of force in just wars is restrained such that "after the resisting nations have been conquered, provision may be more easily made for enjoying in peace the mutual bond of piety and justice."

The practical effect of Augustine's writings on just war was to provide the doctrinal basis for the church in its struggle to contain or end violent feuds that were pervasive in the centuries following the collapse of the Roman Empire.[41] Perhaps of even more importance are the writings of Aquinas on just war doctrine. Aquinas uses a very precise, ordered form of logical exposition in his works—the so-called scholastic method—in which he takes a proposition and in reaching his own conclusion considers both the set of objections that can be raised against the proposition and the set of replies to these objections.

Citing Augustine's biblical reference to Jesus having accepted soldiering as a legitimate function, Aquinas in his *Summa Theologica* rejects the proposition that it is always sinful to wage war. At the same time, consistent with Augustine, Aquinas specifies three conditions for a war to be considered just:

> First, the *authority of the sovereign* by whose command the war is to be waged. . . . And as the care of the common weal is committed to those who are in authority, it is their business to watch over the common weal of the city, kingdom or province subject to them. And just as it is lawful for them to have recourse to the material sword in defending that common weal against internal disturbances . . . so too, it is their business to have recourse to the sword of war in defending the common weal against external enemies. . . .
>
> Secondly, a *just cause* is required, namely that those who are attacked should be attacked because they deserve it on account of some fault. . . .
>
> Thirdly, it is necessary that the belligerents should have a *right intention*, so that they intend the advancement of good, or the avoidance of evil.[42]

The second stipulation is the critical prerequisite for going to war and, when combined with the other two, represents the essence of the Thomist doctrine.

---

[41] Arthur Nussbaum, *A Concise History of the Law of Nations* (New York: Macmillan, 1947), 40–41.
[42] St. Thomas Aquinas, "Treatise on Faith, Hope and Charity," in *Summa Theologica*, part II of the second part, question 40 ("Of War"). Emphasis added.

As all three prerequisites are, according to Aquinas, norms of moral theology, the issue of just war falls within the jurisdiction of the church. Although Aquinas's views are not all that different from those of Augustine (or Cicero before him), it is his elaboration of the problem that became the basis for the Christian doctrine on war.[43]

Throughout the Middle Ages, writers argued for the existence of a universal moral community based on a Christian brotherhood among individuals—the modern territorial state associated with the idea of "national interest" did not exist. Hence, Augustine was essentially concerned with bloody and destructive feuds between individual princes. It was not until the sixteenth century that such religious scholars as the Spanish Dominican Francisco de Vitoria (1480–1546) break with the idea of universal empire, view the world in terms of independent states, and interpret just war doctrine as part of *jus gentium*, which concerns "what natural reason has established among all *nations*" as opposed to among *individuals* [emphasis added]. This line of thinking was later followed by the Spanish Jesuit Francisco Suarez (1548–1617).[44]

Dante

In the work of Dante Alighieri of Florence (1265–1321), we find an interesting amalgam of medieval and modern views. *The Divine Comedy* reflects one of the clearest expressions of the medieval worldview. There is an essential unity of the physical and metaphysical worlds, depicted as concentric circles, all being parts of a larger whole. Dante does differentiate between temporal and spiritual realms, but he also sees heaven, earth, and hell as interconnected places with what amount to passageways between these places—a unified worldview.

On the other hand, Dante's works also express several ideas that later are associated with the fifteenth-century Renaissance view of politics—the separation of philosophy from theology and church from empire. In the case of both Augustine and Aquinas, philosophy is part of, but necessarily subordinate to, the revealed wisdom of God contained within religious understandings. Similarly, while both claim to accept the notion of parallel secular and sacred kingdoms, they argue for the preferred ranking of the latter over the former.

As with Machiavelli two hundred years later, Dante's active participation in Florentine politics illustrated his voluntarist inclination that "all that concerns polity is subject to our power."[45] He came under attack for criticizing the pope for summoning a foreign army to help repress Florence's pro-republican, anti-church party to which Dante belonged. Dante's opponents won, however, and in 1302 presented trumped-up charges of graft against him. Ordered to pay a fine and banished for two years, he refused to pay the fine and the banishment was declared for life with orders given to burn him alive should he ever again

---

[43] Nussbaum, *A Concise History*, 42.

[44] For an elaboration of Francisco Vitoria's and Francisco Suarez's views on just war, see Nussbaum, *A Concise History*, 58–72.

[45] Dante Aligheiri, "De Monarchia," *The Portable Dante*, ed. Paolo Milano (New York: Penguin Books, 1977, 1988), 640. All subsequent direct quotes are from this edition.

set foot on the territory of the Florentine republic. Dante claimed he was now a citizen of Italy, if not the wider world, and joined those "to whom the world is [their] native country, just as the sea is to the fish." In the twenty years of exile until his death at age fifty-six, he never returned to Florence. As with other banned intellectuals who followed him, Dante put his time to good use by producing such works as *The Divine Comedy* and *De Monarchia.*

More so than either Augustine or Aquinas, Dante directly addresses topics of interest to students of international relations. In *De Monarchia* he lays out his solution to the problem of war, unrest, and the anarchic structure of the late Middle Ages—a world government run by a monarch. In the process he hoped "to set forth truths unattempted by others. . . . Amongst other unexplored and important truths the knowledge of the temporal monarchy is most important and least explored."

Dante states that universal peace is the most important blessing that can be bestowed upon humanity. To achieve it, the world needs to be organized properly. Taking his cue from Aristotle, Dante makes, in effect, a levels-of-analysis argument, noting that in the case of the individual household, village, city, and kingdom, each unit must be rightly ordered to achieve one particular end. In the case of the kingdom, the ultimate goal is tranquility or peace, and to achieve it, "there must be one king to rule and govern, else not only do they in the kingdom fail to reach the goal, but the kingdom itself lapses into ruin. . . . Thus it appears that for the well-being of the world there must be a monarchy or empire."

One aspect of his argument for world government has a distinctly modern ring—his call for the peaceful settlement of disputes where "between any two princes, one of whom is in no way subject to the other, contention may arise." What is needed is some power with "wider jurisdiction who, within the compass of his right, has princedom over both. . . . And he will be monarch or emperor." Dante then approvingly quotes Aristotle: "Things love not to be ill-disposed; but a multiplicity of princedoms is ill; therefore, one prince." Note that this ultimate power to keep principalities in line should be in the hands of a secular ruler with the church playing no role. This in part reflects Dante's admiration of the Roman Empire and the peace it enforced for so many years.

For Dante, the power of the monarch to intervene is to be derived directly from God, not via a religious intermediary such as the pope. Each, in effect, is directly subordinate to God. Dante is quite explicit about this: "The authority of the Empire by no means depends on the Church." This was truly a revolutionary idea at the time as it called for the strict separation of the church from the world state and a refusal to subordinate secular political life to that of religion. Church and universal empire are to be coordinate powers, each autonomous and supreme in their respective realms. The empire is to be guided by reason and philosophy; the church by faith and theology. Just as the empire is not to be subordinate to the church, so, too, should philosophy not be subordinate to theology, a distinctly nonmedieval view. Not surprisingly, *De Monarchia* was placed on the church's list of banned books, and it was not removed until the twentieth century.

Reflections on Thought in the Middle Ages

All too often any work that does not view politics through realist lenses is labeled idealist. The inappropriateness of this tendency to lump together what are essentially disparate views is evident when one compares the Stoics to the works of Augustine and Aquinas. While the Stoic emphasis on the community of humanity parallels, if not anticipates, Augustine's understanding of the City of God, there are basic differences.

Despite the professed Stoic emphasis on humanity as a whole, it is primarily an individualistic philosophy emphasizing an ability to accept calmly adversity. Even its profession of a belief in universal brotherhood does not tell us what practical steps can be taken to transform society to create a wider sense of humanity—it is a philosophy of acceptance of the world, not transformation of it. For Augustine and Aquinas, however, acceptance of the status quo is wrong. This is not to suggest that they are extreme voluntarists—far from it. Augustine, for example, in refuting complete free will strikes a balance between God's foreknowledge of one's acts and an individual's free will. The point is that the two religious scholars realize the road to the City of God will not be an easy one.

This is directly a result of their pessimistic view of human nature. It is not easy for individuals to triumph over self-love and the corruption of the soul—Augustine's own life is a witness to how difficult this is. As with Immanuel Kant, Augustine and Aquinas are "realistic" to the extent that they take seriously the difficulty of achieving a peaceful world community, given the nature of human beings (Augustine and Aquinas) or the nature of nonrepublican forms of government (Kant). The two religious scholars are also "liberals" to the extent that they recognize non-state forms of international authority that transcend borders (the church) and universal norms derived from divine law.

As for Dante, like Augustine and Aquinas, he also desired to see a universal community and an end to the anarchy of the Middle Ages. The two religious philosophers view this universal community strictly in terms of faith and the church. Dante's argument, by contrast, represents the beginning of a trend that would increasingly come to dominate the world—the political triumph of the secular over the sacred in temporal matters. Writers such as Marsiglio of Padua (1275–1343) and William of Ockham (c. 1290–1348), extending the ideas of Dante concerning separate religious and temporal realms, call for a much stricter separation of the state from ecclesiastical authority. By the Renaissance, the widespread reemergence of Greek classical thought provided further support for philosophy over theology as how to interpret and bring order to the world. This secularization of political thought is particularly apparent in commentaries on what would come to be known as the modern state.

REFERENCES

Classic Works (various editions)
Aquinas, Thomas. *Summa Theologica.*
Augustine. *The Confessions, The City of God,* and *On Christian Doctrine.*
Cicero. *The Republic* and *The Laws.*

Dante. *The Divine Comedy* and *De Monarchia*.
Livy. *The History of Rome*.

Anthologies

Paolucci, Henry, ed. *The Political Writings of St. Augustine*. Washington, DC: Regnery Gateway, 1962, 1990.

Seneca. *Letters from a Stoic*. Edited by Robin Campbell. London: Penguin Books, 1969.

Wood, Neal. *Cicero's Social and Political Thought*. Berkeley: University of California Press, 1988.

Commentaries

Bendix, Reinhard. *Kings of People: Power and the Mandate to Rule*. Berkeley: University of California Press, 1978.

Bloch, Marc. *Feudalism*. Translated by L. Manyon. London: Routledge, 1971, 2014.

Ebenstein, William. *Great Political Thinkers: From Plato to the Present*, 6th ed. Boston: Cengage Learning, 1999.

Niebuhr, Reinhold. *Christian Realism and Political Problems*. New York: Charles Scribner's Sons, 1953.

Russell, Bertrand. *The History of Western Philosophy*. New York: Simon & Schuster, 1945, 1967.

Sabine, George H. *A History of Political Theory*. New York: Dryden Press, 1951, 1973.

Strauss, Leo, and Joseph Cropsey, eds. *History of Political Philosophy*. Chicago: University of Chicago Press, 1963, 1987.

Tilly, Charles, ed. *The Formation of National States in Western Europe*. Princeton, NJ: Princeton University Press, 1975.

Tuchman, Barbara W. *A Distant Mirror: The Calamitous 14th Century*. New York: Alfred A. Knopf, 1978.

4

The Rise of the State and Modern Political Thought

★ ★ ★

The rise of states and a state system that replaced the sense (if not the reality) of unity in medieval Christendom and the bases of modern political thought are the subject of this chapter.

THE RENAISSANCE, REFORMATION, AND THE RISE OF THE STATE

Observers of these matters included such luminaries as Niccolò Machiavelli (1469–1527), Jean Bodin (1530–1596), Hugo Grotius (1583–1645), and Thomas Hobbes (1588–1679). Their writings begin conceptually with the international order, drawing on the writings of those who preceded them and developing in contemporary context ideas associated with power and the balance of power, sovereignty and sovereign authority, and international law. These concepts are closely tied to the development of the state and system of states, contributing both to understanding the transformation and legitimation of this newly emerging international order.

Historical Context

The movement from feudalism to the modern state system represents the most recent Western historical example of system transformation. As noted in chapter 3, however, the development of this European state system was not preordained. During the latter part of the thirteenth century, for example, representative assemblies were created throughout Europe that enhanced the power of the commercial or middle classes at the expense of kings bent on the centralization of power—Castile and León in 1250, Catalonia in 1285, the summons of Rhenish towns to the German diet in 1255, and the addition of lower classes into parliament in 1265 that would eventually become England's House of Commons. In 1302 in France the first representative assembly appeared: The Third Estate was composed predominantly of those who over time became identifiable as a new, non-aristocratic middle class or *bourgeoisie*—merchants or those with business interests and others.[1] While a critical function of these parliaments was to appropriate revenue that the kings hoped would enhance their centralization of power, in some cases these institutions instead became rivals to the power of kings.[2]

The fourteenth century, however, was a particularly difficult time due to the Black Death that swept through Europe from 1348 to 1352.[3] It was also a time of popular insurrections and the first concrete evidence of the rise of national consciousness. By the following century, Henry V could count on the passionate support of the English in wars against France—the Hundred Years' War, just as Joan of Arc appealed to the patriotism of the French. The fifteenth century was also a time of decay in parliamentary institutions. Over time, the power of the king and his councils increased—Louis XI in France, Edward IV and Henry VII in England, and Ferdinand in Aragon and Isabella in Castile (present-day Spain): "Parliaments, *cortes*, and estates-general were the bridge over which the medieval monarchs passed to the control of the centralized, popularly supported, governments of their respective countries."[4] England was the primary exception.

During the sixteenth century, there was much conflict and resistance to monarchical state-building on the part of ordinary people coerced into surrendering crops, labor, money, and sometimes land to the emerging states. In England, for example, rebellions were put down in 1497, 1536, 1547, 1549, and 1553. Not surprisingly, lesser nobles and other authorities, often members of local assemblies, also resisted. The religious wars in France in the sixteenth century were a contest between royal prerogatives and regional liberties. A common thread running through all types of resistance to the emerging state was the issue of taxes. Increased taxation provided monarchs with revenues that supported larger armies that, in turn, were then used to defend and expand frontiers and to overcome internal resistance to the centralizing states.[5]

The Renaissance and Protestant Reformation were two immensely important developments that began in the mid-fifteenth century and continued for more than one hundred years. Taken together, they were the twin cradle of modernity.[6] The Renaissance, generally associated with western Europe's cultural rebirth, contained ethical and humanistic overtones and tended to glorify the individual. The Reformation, closely associated with the German religious leader Martin Luther (1483–1546) and his personal struggle for a

---

[1] Aristocrats constituted the first estate, the clergy the second. As a commercial "middle" or capitalist class, the bourgeoisie ranked between the aristocracy and the peasantry or the emergent working class.

[2] Edward P. Cheyney, *The Dawn of a New Era, 1250–1453* (New York: Harper & Row, 1936, 1962), 331.

[3] This period is the subject of Barbara Tuchman's *A Distant Mirror: The Calamitous 14th Century* (New York: Alfred A. Knopf, 1978).

[4] Cheyney, *The Dawn of a New Era*, 332.

[5] Charles Tilly, "Reflections on the History of European State-Making," in *The Formation of National States in Western Europe*, ed. Charles Tilly (Princeton, NJ: Princeton University Press, 1975), 22–23.

[6] Lewis W. Spitz, *The Protestant Reformation, 1517–1559* (New York: Harper & Row, 1985), 5.

right relationship with God, was particularly important in undercutting not only papal authority in German states, but also the hope for the idea of unity of Christendom. This process was further aided by Luther's belief, shared by the French-born, Geneva Protestant John Calvin (1509–1564), that state or secular authority should be separate from religious authority. With the growth of religious pluralism, national monarchies grew in strength as religious differences among the ruling houses exacerbated political problems.

Conflict over religion and the power of the emperor of the Holy Roman Empire touched off civil war in 1618 in Bohemia (part of the present-day Czech Republic), eventually expanding throughout Europe into what has come to be known as the Thirty Years' War. The Thirty Years' War was three wars—first, the imperial civil war that ended with the Peace of Prague in 1635; second, the western war that pitted Spain against the Netherlands and France; and finally, the Baltic war that was fought mainly on German soil and at various times involving Denmark and Sweden against the emperor and his allies. Although religion was an important factor, the underlying cause of war arguably was the shifting balance of power among the major states, theoretically harkening back to Thucydides' discussion of the origins of the Peloponnesian war.

There were several important outcomes of the Thirty Years' War. First, the Peace of Prague in 1635 settled the religious problem in the empire, making it unlikely that religion would be the primary cause of war. As a result, secular leaders of Catholic countries could ignore the papacy's call for a militant counter-reformation policy. Second, with the growing power of some German princes, it became more appropriate to speak of the dominions of the Hapsburgs as opposed to the Holy Roman Empire.

The Hapsburg dynasty in Vienna became increasingly interested in lands to the east as their weaknesses elsewhere within the official boundaries of the empire were now evident. The chance, therefore, of a secularly based empire and a united Europe was now as distant as the pope's hope for the unity of Christendom under papal guidance. Finally, a new balance of power emerged that witnessed the rise of Brandenburg-Prussia, Sweden, and France as the most powerful states in Europe.[7] Their involvement in military struggles directly affected the character and organization of these states.[8]

All three consequences have one thing in common—the emergence of the territorial state as the primary political unit in Europe by 1660. Even just half a century earlier, "older institutional patterns like the empire, papacy, estates and free cities were still alive and active rivals."[9] The peace agreement at Westphalia in 1648 helped to solidify the trend of increasing power to the modern state at the expense of the other types of small political units headed by minor princes, dukes, and lords prominent in the earlier feudal period.

---

[7] Myron P. Guttman, "The Origins of the Thirty Years' War, in *The Origin and Prevention of Major Wars*, ed. Robert I. Rotberg and Theodore K. Rabb (Cambridge: Cambridge University Press, 1989), 181.

[8] This impact of war is an important theme in the works of Otto Hintze. See, for example, Felix Gilbert, ed., *The Historical Essays of Otto Hintze* (New York: Oxford University Press, 1975).

[9] Carl J. Friedrich, *The Age of the Baroque, 1610–1660* (New York: Harper & Row, 1952), xiii.

With the realignment of territorial borders, the concept of "sovereignty" of the state emerged, increasingly becoming the latest principle of the newly developing, state-based political order. Indeed, the Peace of Westphalia initiated a new diplomatic practice whereby at the end of a war ambassadors gathered to negotiate a peace settlement based on the sovereign equality of both victor and vanquished.[10]

Under the new dispensation agreed upon at Westphalia, the king, duke, or other princes could establish the state religion—choosing between Protestant and Catholic. Although there were some provisions for minority religious preferences, if the prince had so much authority over religion that in the present-day mindset is a personal matter, there seemingly was no practical limit to the authority of the sovereign. Thus, the Peace of Westphalia provided a practical basis for establishing the idea of sovereignty that had been part of intellectual discourse in the previous century. We take up the development of these philosophical ideas about authority, power, and the state, but it was the Westphalia agreement that gave them a more concrete basis. Put another way, ideas preceded facts in the social construction of sovereignty and the sovereign state.[11]

The rise of the state not only was seen in the political, diplomatic, and military spheres but also in the economic realm. Indeed, economic developments were critical in the ultimate victory of the state system over other contenders. For example, the seventeenth century was the heyday of large trading companies. In earlier years these companies were associated with particular families, but now monarchs chartered the companies in the name of the state—for example, the East India Company (1600), the Dutch East India Company (1602), and the Hamburg Company (1611). As these state or monarchy-backed firms increased in power, private city-based firms and trading associations declined. By 1629, for example, only the north German cities of Lübeck, Hamburg, and Bremen (members of the earlier Baltic commercial association or Hanseatic League) maintained their importance as separate urban centers. Similarly, leaders of large territorial states such as England and France worked to free themselves from their dependence on foreign interests, notably Florentine and German banking houses. In part this was because family-based and other small firms were unable to provide the amount of capital monarchs required to carry out their wars. Commercial and industrial firms also preferred more secure, domestic capital sources, which led to the rise of national banks.[12]

The development of state trading companies and banks was part of mercantilism, the dominant economic doctrine of the seventeenth century. Mercantilists held that the state should play a major role in the economy, seeking to accumulate domestic capital or treasure by running continual trade surpluses in relation to other states. This was not in pursuit of some lofty moral aim or

---

[10] Friedrich, *The Age of the Baroque*, 193. For an overview of the specific political and territorial provisions of the treaty, see also page 192.

[11] On social constructivism as an interpretive lens in IR theory, see chapter 9.

[12] Friedrich, *The Age of the Baroque*, 6–8.

simply for the benefit of private entrepreneurs; the ultimate objective was to provide resources that could be used for war, conquest or other purposes. As the French statesman and financier Jean-Baptiste Colbert puts it: "Trade is the source of public finance, and public finance is the vital nerve of war."[13] In the name of regulating and protecting commerce, authoritarian state bureaucracies emerged, contrasting dramatically with the primary economic units of the late Middle Ages, the autonomous and self-regulating guilds. These national bureaucracies viewed competition in zero-sum terms—whatever one state gained came at the expense of another.

In retrospect, all these developments may seem to have led inexorably to the rise of a system of autonomous, belligerent states. This certainly was the view of Florentine Niccolò Machiavelli and Englishman Thomas Hobbes—both intellectual precursors of present-day realist understandings. There also were developments working to counteract, or at least mitigate, this trend toward increasingly powerful states as core units in the newly emerging political order. Such developments of a transnational character that writers in the liberal tradition later would identify include the impetus to commerce resulting from the discovery of America and new routes to the Indies, a common intellectual background resulting from the flowering of the Renaissance, sympathy of co-religionists in different states that transcended national borders, and a common revulsion with armed conflicts due to the horrifying cost of religious wars. Such factors made "it certain that the separate state could never be accepted as the final and perfect form of human association, and that in the modern world, as in the medieval world, it would be necessary to recognize the existence of a wider unity."[14]

This universalism contributed to the development of international law and the concept of external sovereignty (the claimed right of all states to be independent or autonomous in their international relations with other states). Grotius and others abandon the medieval ideal of a world-state and accept the existence of the modern, secular, sovereign state. But they deny the absolute separateness of these states and the extreme version of international anarchy identified by Hobbes in his book, *Leviathan* (1651). However limited it might be, the idea of "community" or international society increasingly became associated in liberal thought with the modern state system.

That there is an international "society" of states with commonly accepted rules or laws to guide their conduct (the application of Grotius)—not just relations based on power and a balance of power (as in Machiavelli or Hobbes)—is core to present-day English School thinking that we address in chapter 8. Those within the school who see international politics moving toward acceptance of universal moral norms or principles of right conduct (as in Immanuel Kant) write of international society becoming a "world" society. As English School members readily admit, we are certainly not there yet.

---

[13] Friedrich, *The Age of the Baroque*, 12.
[14] J. L. Brierly, *The Law of Nations: An Introduction to the International Law of Peace*, 6th ed. (New York: Oxford University Press, 1963), 6–7.

Machiavelli

The importance of Niccolò Machiavelli (1469–1527) to political theory is well known—he is the first truly "modern" political theorist due to his emphasis on "what is" as opposed to "what should be." This supposed empirical, non-utopian orientation is captured quite nicely in his reference to much of the classical Greco-Roman and medieval philosophizing: "Many have dreamed up republics and principalities which have never in truth been known to exist; the gulf between how one should live and how one does live is so wide that one who neglects what is actually done for what should be done learns the way to self-destruction rather than self-preservation."[15]

The impact of Machiavelli's writings is, in the words of one historian, like "a sword that was thrust into the flank of the body politic of Western humanity, causing it to shriek and rear up."[16] The purpose of politics is not to make men virtuous; nor is the purpose of the state to pursue some ethical, religious, or metaphysical end as asserted by many ancient Greek and medieval writers. Rather, politics is the means to pursue and enhance the internal and external security of the state.

Despite being characterized as the first modern political theorist and the most important thinker in the realist tradition since Thucydides (whose work Machiavelli knew through his reading in Latin of Polybius, rather than from Thucydides's ancient Greek text he apparently could not read), he is also a transitional figure between the medieval and modern world. His affection for the Italian city-state and his admiration of the ancient Roman republic as forms of government are evident.

To grasp his contribution to the legitimation of the modern state, we begin by focusing on the context within which he was writing. Born in Florence into an old Florentine family, we know little of Machiavelli's youth. At age twenty-nine in 1498 following the execution of the Dominican priest, Savonarola, Machiavelli was appointed to a governmental administrative post in the Florentine republic. Engaged in diplomatic missions, Machiavelli also had the opportunity to observe domestic politics closely. In 1512 the Medici family was restored to power and the republic ended. The Medici briefly put Machiavelli in prison and tortured him to identify his republican connections. They saw him as an enemy of the newly restored principality.

Upon his release from imprisonment, the Medici allowed Machiavelli to live in exile in a small house belonging, perhaps, to his wife's family estate in Sant'Andrea in Percussina—a small hamlet south of Florence near the town of San Casciano. While in exile, he attempted to reenter the political arena. Just as with Thucydides after losing his naval command, Machiavelli had the leisure time to take up writing and analyze the world around him.

Political events during the last thirty years of Machiavelli's life had a tremendous influence on his work and view of politics. He witnessed the devastation

---

[15] Niccolò Machiavelli, *The Prince*, trans. George Bull (London: Penguin, 1981), XV.

[16] Frederich Meinecke, *Machiavellism: The Doctrine of Raison d'état and Its Place in History* (New York: Praeger Publishers, 1965), 49.

of Italy by invasions perpetrated by the French and Spanish. Governments collapsed, civil chaos spread, and more powerful city-states or alliances devoured smaller ones. Despite his republican credentials, Machiavelli acknowledged the reign of Lorenzo de Medici as a golden age of political stability. His writing in *The Prince* (1513), dedicated to two successive Medici princes, focuses on how the unification of the Italian city-states would restore civil order and security throughout Italy. Unity among Italian city-states not only would end conflict among them but also would keep foreign powers from intervening in Italian affairs. There is no evidence that the Medici prince to whom he dedicated his work even read it. In 1520 he was readmitted to the good graces of the Medici when he was commissioned by Cardinal Giulio de' Medici (later Pope Clement VII) to write *Florentine Histories*. He completed the work in 1525 and died within two years, never having regained the political position he so desperately coveted.

More generally, Machiavelli addresses the issue, as did Hobbes over a century later, of how to bring the state into existence and secure its independence. To answer these questions he turns to history. The humanist tradition of his age glorified the classical past, and so it was not surprising that Machiavelli turned to Roman history. To understand the dismal condition of sixteenth-century Italy, he was interested in learning what it was about republican Rome that had allowed it to succeed for as long as it did. His in-depth analysis and republican sentiments are found in *The Discourses* (1517). *The Discourses on the First Ten Books of Titus Livy* (the full title) directly reflects the influence not just of Livy, but also of Polybius, Plutarch, and Tacitus, among others.[17]

Republics and Security

Machiavelli begins by examining the development of Rome's constitution. Following the Aristotelian tradition, he contrasts principality, aristocracy, and democracy with the corresponding degenerate forms of tyranny, oligarchy, and anarchy. The three ideal forms are praiseworthy, but they are difficult to maintain and tend to slip into the degenerative forms. In adopting Polybius's cyclical theory of governmental change, he notes that as a result of domestic turmoil, the transition from one form of government to another may result in the state falling prey to a neighboring power. To avoid such dangers and the defects of each form of government, prudent legislators should choose a form of government that combines the best aspects of principality, aristocracy, and democracy.

As with Aristotle, Polybius, Cicero, and Livy, Machiavelli argues that a mixed form of government—a republic—is the most stable. The historical example he gives, probably based on Plutarch's account, is that of Lycurgus of Sparta who "assigned to the kings, to the aristocracy, and to the populace each its own function, and thus introduced a form of government that lasted for more than eight hundred years." Given his republican sentiments, Machiavelli believed that the importance of a free citizenry stems from its ability to restrain

---

[17] Niccolò Machiavelli, *The Discourses*, trans. Leslie J. Walker (London: Penguin, 1970, 1983). All subsequent direct quotations are from this edition.

the abuse of power by the governing class. The ability of rulers to mobilize popular support makes republics better at defending a state's security than any other form of government.

According to Machiavelli, the key virtue of a republic that aids stability is its flexibility. In a discourse with a title that would be appropriate for a contemporary study of comparative foreign policy ("The Need of Adaptation to Environment") Machiavelli argues that

> a republic has a fuller life and enjoys good fortune for a longer time than a principality, since it is better able to adapt itself to diverse circumstances owing to the diversity found among its citizens than a prince can do. For a man who is accustomed to act in one particular way, never changes. . . . Hence, when times change and no longer suit his ways, he is inevitably ruined.

A further advantage of republican flexibility is that in times of crisis, dictatorial powers can be temporarily granted to authorities. According to Machiavelli, during a crisis, the slow working of republican institutions poses a potential threat to the security of the state as it takes time to reconcile diverse views. Such powers, however, must be granted by the institutions of the republic, not unilaterally seized by a dictator.

For Machiavelli, it is possible even for dictators to work for the common good. He goes so far as to make it a general rule that a state—republic or kingdom—is "well-ordered at the outset" or able to be "radically transformed" only if it is done by one person. In organizing a kingdom or constituting a republic, when the outcome is a good one we can applaud the actions taken to achieve that purpose. While princes may be superior in creating kingdoms or republics, to Machiavelli the populace is "superior in sustaining what has been instituted." In other words, just as dictatorial powers may be required at certain times, so too the maintenance of the state requires an active and engaged citizenry. Whether kingdom or republic, it is essential that it be regulated by good laws, not the whim of the prince or the public.

Machiavelli's general preference for republics is also apparent in his discussion of confederations of states. Crises may require dictatorial powers as a temporary measure, at other times the fact that republics are slower to act is beneficial if the issue is whether or not to break a treaty or dissolve a confederation. In an argument with which Immanuel Kant probably would agree, Machiavelli claims that "republics abide by their agreements far better than do princes." The latter tend to break treaties for even small advantages, while republics tend to take a longer-term view of their security interests.

Machiavelli's emphasis on the virtues of domestic political stability (the state-societal level of analysis) seems to echo the importance given to political unity by Aristotle, Polybius, Cicero, Livy, and other writers. But his view of mixed government has a dynamism earlier theories lacked when he argues that discord among the elements of a republic actually can strengthen a state.

There are certain advantages at certain times to conflict among classes. For Machiavelli, the republican institutions of the Roman constitution and even liberty itself arose from such conflict. As he states near the beginning of *The Discourses*: "The quarrels between nobles and the plebs . . . were the primary cause of Rome's retaining her freedom." Machiavelli generalizes further that "in every republic there are two different dispositions, that of the populace and that of the upper class and that legislation favorable to liberty is brought about by the clash between them." Public tumult not only serves as a catharsis but also makes the citizenry see that it is an effective element of the political system.

Here, therefore, we have perhaps the most important theme in *The Discourses* that is of relevance to IR theory. According to Machiavelli, without the "affection of peoples for self-government. . . . cities have never increased either in dominion or wealth." It is not "the well-being of individuals that makes cities great, but the well-being of the community." Conversely, if tyranny replaces a republic, at a minimum the state ceases to grow in power and wealth, if not actually going into decline. What Machiavelli presents, in effect, is a theory of republican imperialism, using Rome as a case study. It is the dynamism of early Rome—exemplified by the creative tension between the people and the aristocracy—that is critical in accounting for Rome's territorial expansion and glory.

What other factors are important? First, he focuses on the importance of good laws and good arms. Machiavelli argues that aside from a good constitution, the political stability, power, and independence of the Roman state derived from its leadership, religion, a citizen army, and arms. These themes are also taken up in *The Prince*.

Machiavelli argues that the early Roman leaders in particular were successful because they had the talent to combine intelligence and will, thought and action. This ability to implement one's political ideas is essentially what Machiavelli means by the term *virtù*, sometimes translated as "prowess" or "prudence." It is an enlightened boldness.

If one weak prince follows another, the kingdom will probably not survive. By contrast, in early Rome where power was vested in elected consuls, an unending succession of competent and virtuous rulers was assured. The voluntarism in Machiavelli's thinking—that individual leaders can make a difference in the realm of politics—is clearly the message in *The Prince*, a practical handbook on politics dedicated to the ruler of Florence.

Second, Machiavelli also believed religion was a critical factor binding people together during the golden age of the republic. As he states in *The Discourses*: "All things considered, therefore, I conclude that the religion introduced by Numa [Romulus's successor] was among the primary causes of Rome's success, for this entailed good institutions; good institutions led to good fortune." Religion helps to unify the people, meaning a ruler does not have to rely on the self-defeating policy of coercion against his own citizens. Furthermore, pagan religions with their bloody sacrifices and rituals helped to incite warriors to be bold and fearless in war while Christianity "has glorified humble and contemplative men, rather than men of action." The decline of Rome's pre-Christian, pagan religion was associated with decay of the sense of community and the empire itself—an argument the Christian St. Augustine attempts to rebut in *The City of God*.

Machiavelli sees religion as a means to reinforce—not dominate—the secular order as well as being a force for unity. In the case of Italy at the time he was writing, Machiavelli believed the Church of Rome actually did more harm than good. Due to the "bad example set by the Court of Rome, Italy has lost all devotion and all religion." Worse yet, the church "has kept, and keeps, Italy divided."

On the one hand, "neither its power nor its virtue has been sufficiently great for it to be able to usurp power in Italy and become its leader" nor, on the other hand, "has it been so weak that it could not, when afraid of losing its dominion over things temporal, call upon one of the powers to defend it against an Italian state that had become too powerful. The Church, then, has neither been able to occupy the whole of Italy, nor has it allowed anyone else to occupy it." Machiavelli was not anti-religious or categorically anti-church. What he objected to were those religious authorities whose selfish or misguided policies resulted in undermining the possibilities of attaining Italian unity.[18]

Third, Machiavelli argues that one reason the ancient Roman republic was robust and strong is that it relied on a patriotic citizen army. The willingness of citizens to die for the republic was a sign of the essential unity and strength of the republic. Mercenary armies, typical of the Italian city-states of his day, could not be trusted. While rulers were afraid to arm poorer citizens, Machiavelli argues that it is even more dangerous to trust the fate of government to an army of mercenaries who are "disunited, thirsty for power, undisciplined, and disloyal."[19] Similarly, for a state to place its trust in the troops of an ally is equally misguided.

Finally, Machiavelli argues that is necessary for a state to be well armed to deter and defend itself from outside threats. While good laws aid domestic stability, well-armed states provide defense against enemies as well as expand the range of foreign policy choices for leaders.

Republics and Political Decay

Despite these virtues, however, the Roman polity and society eventually decayed. Why? It is here that Machiavelli introduces two topics—his view of human nature and a cyclical view of institutions. He accepts the part of the Christian tradition that views human beings as essentially fallen beings, sinful and corrupt if not evil, "wretched creatures who would not keep their word to you." He acknowledges that there is a slight possibility for moral improvement, but this can only be achieved by a combination of the aforementioned good constitution, good leadership, religion, citizen army, and arms. But due to the essential evilness of human beings, whatever institutions may be created and no matter how effective they may be at the outset, they seem destined eventually to decay.

---

[18] "Niccolò Machiavelli cannot be found to speak irreverently of God. The same cannot be said for his writings about the church and churchmen. Though divinity and morality are typically established in a church, church and religion are not the same." Sebastian de Grazia, *Machiavelli in Hell* (Princeton, NJ: Princeton University Press, 1989), 87.

[19] Machiavelli, *The Prince*, XII. All subsequent direct quotes are from *The Prince*.

This cyclical view of human institutions reflects the classical heritage, particularly the works of Polybius, which leads Machiavelli to argue that *fortuna* or chance plays a major role in determining how long constructive political institutions will last. This determinism in his work is offset by his counsel that the prince needs to exercise enlightened boldness when dealing with the uncertainties. This advocacy of human will to control as much as one can is also evidence of a voluntarism in Machiavelli's understanding of politics.[20] Individuals can and do matter even if they cannot control everything.

For Machiavelli, the social and political good is defined by the interests of the community or the common good. This means that in terms of the individual, one is pursuing the good if one acts for the interests of the community as a whole. This emphasis on serving the general interests of the community has a long tradition in Christian thought. But whereas Augustine and Thomas Aquinas emphasize a higher divine law, Machiavelli departs from this Christian tradition by restricting his argument to the level of a secular community. Christian thought, as exemplified by Augustine, puts forth two kingdoms, with the secular kingdom (City of Man) inferior to the City of God. Machiavelli rejects this idea, making earthly power and secular politics the centerpieces of his political thought.

Due to the cyclical nature of human institutions, there will be good as well as bad times for a political community. During bad times an effective leader needs to act in accordance with the prevailing morality. While Machiavelli's preference was for leaders to be able to act as did leaders of the early Roman republic, he lived during a time in which public order was lacking and war threatened the very existence of many Italian city-states. Hence, a leader "should not deviate from what is good, if that is possible, but he should know how to take actions that cause harm, if that is necessary."[21] In other words, the prince should focus on what is realistic and possible, not simply on what is desirable. Even during this difficult time, effective leadership could have contributed greatly to public order and the maintenance of a city-state's independence or even the unification of Italy.

It is this notion of using as one's standards the prevailing morality of an age that has given "Machiavellism" negative connotations. On the other hand, one ought not to overlook the last chapters of *The Prince* in which Machiavelli appeals to the national sentiment of all Italians, hoping that someone such as a Medici would unite Italy, end the civil chaos, and protect Italy from foreign invasions. This was the strategic purpose for which he wrote *The Prince*.

By emphasizing a strong leader who could use common identity as a means to strengthen the bonds of a political community, Machiavelli contributed to the literature that justifies the centralization of power in the modern state. On the other hand, his ideal community was the small Roman republic and he exhibited a sentimental attachment to the small Italian city-state. He realized, however,

---

[20] For Machiavelli's interpretation of Livy's view on fortune, see *The Discourses*, II: 29.
[21] Machiavelli, *The Prince*, xviii. The Italian word *male* is sometimes mistranslated as only meaning *evil*. We understand Machiavelli as meaning "harm" as when a prince puts troops in harm's way.

that the city-state system on the Italian peninsula was increasingly becoming a political anachronism during a time when decisive political power on the European stage was being wielded by France, Spain, and others that exercised the power of an increasingly modern state. To defend itself, Italy needed to be unified.

Realism

Machiavelli's contribution to the realist image of international politics can be summarized as follows. First, the primary concern of the leader should be the security and independence of the state. His definition of the state is found in the first line of *The Prince*: "All the states, all the dominions under whose authority men have lived in the past and live now, have been and are either republics or principalities." The three parts, therefore, are dominion (territory), the right or authority to command, and people located on the territory who obey and view the commands (laws, orders, decrees) as rightful.

In terms of security, the prince "must not flinch from being blamed for vices that are necessary for safeguarding the state." This requires him to be alert to two dangers: "internal subversion from his subjects and external aggression by foreign powers. Against the latter, his defense lies in being well armed" and, despite Machiavelli's reservations, having good allies. Internal turmoil can be avoided if the prince "keeps the people satisfied."[22] As for independence, "princes should do their utmost to escape being at the mercy of others."

Second, Machiavelli believed that a leader blessed with *virtù* or enlightened boldness can rationally plan and institute policies that enhance the security and independence of the state. This is the voluntarist strand found throughout *The Prince*. As we have noted, the other, more determinist part of the political equation, is *fortuna* or fortune. As he states: "So as not to rule out free will, I believe that it is probably true that fortune is the arbiter of half the things we do, leaving the other half or so controlled by ourselves." Indeed, these two concepts are constantly paired throughout his works.[23]

Finally, Machiavelli has a great deal to say about the conduct of relations among states. Much of his advice is located in his *Art of War* and in Book Two of *The Discourses*.[24] He examines such topics as the three methods of expansion (leagues, alliances, hegemonies), basic causes of war (provoked and unintended), the relative advantages and disadvantages of offensive and defensive strategies, and the dangers of following a policy of neutrality.[25]

---

[22] It is quite clear that Machiavelli sees the importance of a leader keeping the support of his subjects. As he states: "It is necessary for a prince to have the friendship of the people; otherwise he has no remedy in times of adversity."

[23] For examples of the relative importance of *fortuna* and *virtù* in the coming to power of two rulers, Francesco Sforza and Cesare Borgia, see Machiavelli, *The Prince*, VII. In the case of the rise of Rome, see his *The Discourses*, II: 1.

[24] Niccolò Machiavelli, *Art of War*, trans. Ellis Farneworth (New York: De Capo Press, 1990).

[25] Compare Machiavelli's analysis of neutrality with Thucydides's discussion of Athenian policy toward Mytilene and Melos. See *The Discourses*, II: 23; *History of the Peloponnesian War*, III: 36–50; V: 84–116.

As with many realists who followed him, Machiavelli believed that permanent or perpetual peace is a dangerous illusion. Any leader who operates under such assumption risks something worse than war—his country's loss of liberty, if not existence. He does not favor war for war's sake but rather speaks of "necessary" wars designed to keep what is worse than war at bay. In making his argument, Machiavelli uses the language of the just war doctrine. Toward the end of *The Prince* he approvingly quotes Livy: "Because a necessary war is a just war and where there is hope only in arms, those arms are holy." Arms can act as a deterrent, but they will also play a critical role in terms of defense.

In sum, Machiavelli was one of the foremost contributors to what became the realist image of international politics. He also became one of the foremost observers and analysts of the emerging modern state. But Machiavelli's thinking, as that of Thucydides, is not simply that of cynical power politics; such a depiction of his views borders on caricature. If one goes beyond *The Prince* and examines his other works, it is apparent that Machiavelli seriously wrestled with moral and ethical concerns. Furthermore, his recognition of the need for leaders to cope continually and creatively with political change and flux belies the stereotype of Machiavelli as a provider of little more than political platitudes devoid of historical context and nuance.

Thomas More

Thomas More (1478–1535) is a political theorist not often cited by scholars in the IR field. Writing at the same time as Machiavelli, he is generally viewed as an interesting contrast to the Italian. While Machiavelli is renowned for the political realism in his works, More is typically associated with the socialist idealism he depicts in his *Utopia* (1516). Such a dichotomy is overdrawn.

More and Machiavelli are strikingly similar in one important aspect—both agree on the need for kings of increasingly powerful modern national states to receive able advice from learned and experienced individuals to govern effectively and justly. Machiavelli, of course, initially served the republic of Florence and later hoped to return to public service. Two years after he finished *Utopia*, More was appointed privy councilor to Henry VIII, eventually rising to the important position of lord chancellor.

It is evident in Book One of *Utopia* that More was quite aware of problems in providing advice to princes. The central character, Raphael, has just returned to Europe after living five years in the distant land of Utopia. Far from being merely a professional sailor, Raphael is a man of rare qualities, "more like Ulysses, or even Plato,"[26] according to More's friend, Peter Gilles, who appears as himself in the book. Gilles tells Raphael: "I can't think why you don't enter the service of some king or other. I'm sure any king would jump at the chance of employing you. With your knowledge and experience, you'd be just the man to supply not only entertainment, but also instructive precedents and useful advice." More, also playing himself, asks Raphael to bring himself "even at the

---

[26] Thomas More, *Utopia*, trans. Paul Turner (London: Penguin Books, 1965), 38. All subsequent direct quotations are from this edition.

cost of some personal inconvenience," to apply his talents and energies to public affairs: "If you can't completely eradicate wrong ideas, or deal with inveterate vices as effectively as you could wish, that's no reason for turning your back on public life altogether."

Raphael, however, is skeptical, believing his unconventional views and straight talking would not be appreciated by kings and cause jealousy among the royal advisers. In a theme also of concern to Machiavelli, Raphael claims that royal advisers follow the maxim: "We'll never get human behavior in line with Christian ethics, so let's adapt Christian ethics to human behavior." Raphael cannot accept this cynical approach, arguing: "I can't see what good they've done. They've merely enabled people to sin with a clear conscience." The More character, however, argues that an adviser "must go to work indirectly. You must handle everything as tactfully as you can." It is undoubtedly in this dialogue between the characters of Raphael and More that the author explores his ambivalence toward public service addresses the pitfalls and problems of providing advice to the prince and raises the issue of the relation between politics and morality.

There are other interesting similarities to be found in the works of More and Machiavelli. Sharing an appreciation for classical works, both utilize contemporary events to illustrate major points. Even more importantly, both observe the national state emerging as the dominant political force in Europe—state power increasingly used arbitrarily, unchecked by moral understandings in philosophical or religious teachings. They also share the ideal of a smaller social, economic, and political unit. In Machiavelli's case, it was the early Roman republic. For his part, More was a critic of the enclosure movement that was destroying pastoral communities in England through the erection of fences to contain livestock. He was concerned that the growing power of the state was at the expense of the pluralism of medieval life. Favorably disposed toward the city-state called for by Plato and Aristotle, More was concerned that the growing power of the state was at the expense of the more localized lifestyle that had prevailed during the Middle Ages.[27]

More did not accept the Protestant Reformation and was sent to his death rather than accede to the absolutist claims to power by Henry VIII even in such religious matters. As for Machiavelli, though shunned by the rulers of Florence, his reluctant acceptance of the need for a strong national Italian state to repel foreign aggressors helped lay the intellectual groundwork for later justifications of the modern state system.

Botero and "Reason of State"

The development of a legitimating theory of statecraft that restrained dynastic exuberance and defined political interest in practical terms came to be known as

---

[27] Such a preference is also evident in the writings of Erasmus, who always signed his works "Erasmus of Rotterdam" and preferred to live in the small semi-independent communes of Switzerland and the Netherlands. Myron P. Gilmore, *The World of Humanism, 1453–1517* (New York: Harper & Row, 1952, 1962), 138.

raison d'état or reason of state—the justification states invoke for their conduct. The historian Friedrich Meinecke viewed the concept in the following manner:

> *Raison d'état* is the fundamental principle of national conduct, the State's first Law of Motion. It tells the statesman what he must do to preserve the health and strength of the State. . . . For each State at each particular moment there exists one ideal course of action, one ideal *raison d'état*. The statesman in power tries hard to discern this course, and so too does the historian surveying the past in retrospect.[28]

Here we have all the essential elements of the realist image of international politics—the state as the key actor with policy makers rationally calculating the best course of action for the state as a whole to preserve and strengthen the security of the state.

It was an Italian following in the footsteps of Machiavelli who popularizes the notion of reason of state or *ragione di stato*[29]—the justification, typically security, used by states to legitimate their actions. Giovanni Botero's (1540–1617) *Della Ragione di Stato* (1589) apparently was a must-read for those with an interest in policy. Botero was a counter-reformation Jesuit who tried to find a way to aid the papacy in pursuit of its goals. He felt that this required the church to seek secular support, just as it had following the collapse of the Roman Empire. He hoped to mobilize the resources of the state in pursuit of these papal goals.

Raison d'état could also be used to justify more secular pursuits and, over time, the power of the state became justified in such terms—the state a rational tool for the achievement of expressly political as opposed to political-religious or moral ends. Instead of being simply one political actor among various types of political units claiming autonomy, the centralized state acquires supreme authority and the power to defend the realm and carry out other duties. Indeed, it was under Cardinal Richelieu in France where what could be termed the cult of state reached its climax. To this day the term is capitalized in French as *État* as if to wrap the state in a cloak of mystery.[30]

Not surprisingly, there were also writers at the time who vigorously opposed such justification for increased state power. They endeavored to make the case for the maintenance of the powers of not simply the king, but also the nobility and clergy—the separate "estates" in the medieval order. The king was one estate among several—the sense of unity among them based on their adoption of a common Christian faith. In medieval times there was a greater fluidity of relations than after the rise of states—the separate estates carrying on negotiations with foreign princes or even other foreign estates.

---

[28] Meinecke, *Machiavellism*, 1.

[29] "'Reason of state' is a pragmatic rationality. . . . Its concern is purely with the question of how to conduct operations that lead to a successful conclusion." Carl J. Friedrich, *An Introduction to Political Theory* (New York: Harper & Row, 1967), 139.

[30] Friedrich, *The Age of the Baroque*, 15–17. For another brief overview of Botero, see Meinecke, *Machiavellism*, 66–70.

The Thirty Years' War (1618–1648) proved to be the turning point, decisively leading to the victory of the king's "state" over the estates that were a hindrance to the king who needed to marshal resources quickly to prosecute a war effectively. The degree of the king's power and authority certainly varied from state to state—less in England due to parliament's assertion of supremacy after the beheading of King Charles I in 1649, more in France as evidenced by the legislature (the Estates-General) not meeting between 1614 and 1789.

Hobbes

The writer in the seventeenth century who is most closely associated with *raison d'état* thinking and the elevation of the secular state to the status of the supreme and all-powerful political entity is the Englishman Thomas Hobbes (1588–1679). Along with Thucydides and Machiavelli, Hobbes is renowned for his brilliant contributions to political theory and what becomes the realist perspective on international relations. Aside from translating Thucydides's work into English, he attempted to do no less than place political philosophy on a scientific and secular basis and, in the process, became one of the foremost theorists on the state and the nature of power.

The son of a clergyman, Hobbes at age four could read and write, at six learned Greek and Latin, and at fourteen entered Oxford where he found the university to be an insufficient challenge to his talents. At twenty he became a companion and tutor to the eldest son of Lord Cavendish, one of the more prominent aristocratic families of the day. Hobbes's association with the Cavendish family lasted throughout his life. Through the family's connections, he met several noteworthy persons of his day including Francis Bacon, René Descartes, and Galileo Galilei. He also spent some twenty years on the continent, most of the time in Paris, which exposed him to a diverse array of philosophical and scientific developments.[31]

Given his association with the Cavendish family and his royalist leanings, Hobbes fled to Paris in 1640 when parliament asserted its authority and later beheaded King Charles I (1649) during the English civil war between the Stuart monarchy and the Puritan forces under the command of Oliver Cromwell. From 1646 to 1648 he served as a mathematics tutor to Crown Prince Charles, son of King Charles I—the young prince later becoming King Charles II. In 1651 Hobbes returned to England and pledged his allegiance to the newly established commonwealth that came about after the Puritans defeated the king's forces. Hobbes remained in England until his death in 1679.

Hobbes's most famous work, *Leviathan*, was published just before his return to England. Like Thucydides, who experienced the Peloponnesian wars, and Machiavelli, who witnessed the Italian wars, Hobbes also wrote during a period of conflict, the English civil war. It is an important work for several reasons, among them that it is the first modern work on political theory to be published in English.

---

[31] William Ebenstein, *Great Political Thinkers: Plato to the Present*, 4th ed. (New York: Holt, Rinehart and Winston, 1951, 1969), 363.

As with most political philosophers, Hobbes was principally concerned with issues associated with domestic rule such as the relationship between the ruler and the citizens. *Leviathan* is substantially devoted to this topic. But his impact on realist thinking about international relations has also been pervasive due to his discussion of two topics in particular—the "state of nature" and natural law.[32] Although subject to some dispute, scholars of international relations have come to see his arresting image of the state of nature as analogous to the anarchic international system—a world without central authority as if it were like the state of nature that Hobbes identifies as a state of war.

Hobbes's view of natural law breaks rank with the writers who preceded him in that his particular conception does not emphasize restraints placed upon rulers, but rather how natural law enables absolute power residing in the hands of the ruler. Taken together, the result is a view of international relations that sees sovereignty chiefly in terms of its internal aspects with much less attention paid to the sovereignty of a state in relation to other sovereign states. Thus, like Machiavelli, Hobbes believed that security and order in the state are of the highest importance. He leaves little hope either for international cooperation among states or for the mitigation of the effects of the international system's anarchic structure.

State of Nature

Hobbes does not claim that the state of nature he describes—a time before the creation of civil society—exists. Rather, the state of nature is his attempt to imagine what the world would be like without governmental authority or, for that matter, a society without any governmental structure. As with other political theorists, his critical starting point is the question of human nature. How one answers this question dramatically affects one's prescriptions concerning the most appropriate type of political system.

In the state of nature, human beings are ruled by their passions and though some may be physically stronger than others, "the weakest has strength enough to kill the strongest, either by secret machination, or by confederacy with others."[33] Out of this basic equality comes the hope of attaining desired ends, and, as two individuals cannot enjoy the same thing equally, conflict results: "During the time men live without a common power to keep them all in awe, they are in that condition which is called war; and such a war, as is of every man, against every man."[34] Hobbes is not suggesting that in such a state of nature there is constant fighting, but war still represents a constant "disposition" or "inclination," just as threatening weather may promise the possibility of rain.

---

[32] Thomas Hobbes never actually uses the term "state of nature" in *Leviathan.* Instead he refers to a condition "out of civil states" or one of "no common power." He uses the term "state of nature" in his *De Cive* (*The Citizen*). See Hobbes, *Man and Citizen,* ed. Bernard Gert (Gloucester, MA: Peter Smith, 1978), 114, 116.

[33] Thomas Hobbes, *Leviathan* (Harmondsworth: Penguin Books, 1968), I: 13. Unless otherwise noted, all subsequent direct quotations are from this edition of *Leviathan.*

[34] Or as he later states, "That the condition of mere nature, that is to say, of absolute liberty, such as is theirs, that neither are sovereigns, nor subjects, is anarchy, and the condition of war."

This condition has devastating consequences because in a state of nature such uncertainty over one's security means no industry, no culture, no trading, no cumulative knowledge, no arts, no letters, no society, and, worst of all, "continual fear, and danger of violent death; and the life of man, solitary, poor, nasty, brutish, and short." In such a situation there is no such thing as right or wrong because "where there is no common power, there is no law: where no law, no injustice. Force, and fraud, are in war the two cardinal virtues." In other words, it is only where civil society has been created with a supreme authority to regulate disputes and enforce contracts that we can speak of such things as "justice."

Hobbes's description of the state of nature has been viewed as analogous to the international system. Just as in the state of nature where human beings stand alone, so, too, in the international system do states strive to maintain their independence. Just as individuals in the state of nature have a predisposition toward war, so, too, is the international system marked by constant tension and the possibility of conflict. The single most important passage in which Hobbes makes the comparison is:

> But though there had never been any time, wherein particular men were in a condition of war one against another; yet in all times, kings, and persons of sovereign authority, because of their independency, are in continual jealousies, and in the state and posture of gladiators; having their weapons pointing, and their eyes fixed on one another; that is, their forts, garrisons, and guns upon the frontiers of their kingdoms; and continual spies upon their neighbors; which is a posture of war.

In the first line Hobbes acknowledges that he does not claim that a state of nature existed historically. To Hobbes the state of nature is a way of conceptualizing what life would be like if were there no social structure, much less culture. Thus, one removes in one's thinking notions of governmental or religious institutions, the family, and other human associations that we take for granted. In such circumstances we can more clearly see human nature no longer concealed by the structural and cultural layers that we have removed in this thought experiment.

The conclusion Hobbes reaches is a negative, "dog-eat-dog" perspective—a state of war of everyone against everyone else in which the life of any one person, as noted, is "solitary, poor, nasty, brutish, and short." The domestic remedy is to create a sovereign—either a monarch or parliament—that has the authority and capability to provide the security and order human beings require. Put another way, if governments do not exist, we have to create them.

As the passage indicates, no such remedy exists in international relations. The international system reflects a condition like his fabricated state of nature in which there is no common power or centralized authority to enforce order. In other words, it is a condition of *anarchy* that means, a system whose structure encourages suspicion and distrust among sovereigns. For Hobbes, such suspicion and distrust are due not just to the fact that no common power exists, but also because such attitudes and behavior reflect human nature unconstrained by any common power.

Natural Law

Is there any hope of escaping such a condition? What about natural law, which earlier writers claimed should encourage greater civility in relations among human beings and secular authorities by providing common and restricting standards of behavior? Hobbes believed in natural law but conceived of it in a new way. He breaks ranks with writers in the earlier tradition who argued that civil or manmade law is subordinate to higher natural or divine laws. Hobbes rejects this view, in part because he sees the revolutionary implications of such a view that would allow citizens to use natural law as a justification for the overthrow of a monarch, his preferred form of government, and in part because the crux of his analysis does not rely upon religious justification.

For Hobbes the key unit of analysis is the individual—laws of nature are rules of prudence designed to aid and guide individuals in their struggle for survival. They are not based on religious dictates. An individual's most basic right is that of self-preservation, resulting in the right of each person to do anything "in preserving his life against his enemies." According to Hobbes, since anyone can kill anyone else in the state of nature, the most basic of human passions is fear of death. This leads to the first law of nature, which inclines individuals to seek peace to avoid constantly being afraid of death. When combined with reason, this leads one to "lay down this right to all things and be contented with so much liberty against other men, as he would allow other men against himself." This second law of nature leads individuals to seek "convenient articles of peace, upon which men may be drawn to agreement" or covenant as a way to escape the state of nature.

Hobbes's other laws of nature, such as justice, cannot reach their full fruition outside an organized commonwealth that has transcended the state of nature. Their implementation requires a covenant, agreement, or "convenient articles of peace" among individuals. But what assurance is there that individuals will fulfill their obligations? Hobbes argues this requires the creation of what he termed a "leviathan" or supreme sovereign power. This leviathan (a scriptural reference to a fearsome, powerful entity of monstrous proportions) is charged with making sure the parties fulfill all aspects of the agreement.

The third law of nature, for example, defines justice in terms of individuals fulfilling their covenants. This is prudent because if each person does so, chances of escaping violent death are enhanced. But as Hobbes argues: "Therefore before the names of just, and unjust can have place, there must be some coercive power, to compel men equally to the performance of their covenants, by the terror of some punishment, greater than the benefit they expect by the breach of their covenant."

Hobbes offers a unitary conception of the state, whether republic or monarchy, when he asserts that all power may be conferred "upon one man, or upon one assembly of men, that may reduce all their wills, by plurality of voices, unto one will," but his preference for monarchy is evident. This leviathan "is called Sovereign, and said to have sovereign power; and every one besides, his subject."

Hobbes focuses on disorder and the lack of security one finds in the absence of a sovereign. It is the people (coming out of the state of nature) who covenant with a sovereign—whether a monarch or parliamentary assembly—to maintain order and provide security. This is a democratic remedy, in its time a revolutionary idea that the sovereign's authority is established by the people, not derived from God's will. Although Hobbes's preoccupation with the importance of maintaining order necessarily makes his text sound more authoritarian, he does advance a democratic basis for the legitimacy of sovereign authority.

It is not a divine right of kings that English kings had relied on as if they drew their authority from the will of God. No, it is the people who grant that authority to the monarch or parliamentary assembly. Accordingly, it is only they who have the right to remove the sovereign's right to rule, the one condition for doing so is the sovereign's failure to provide a secure order in which to live. After all, the people's covenant with the sovereign is based on the latter establishing and maintaining security. Failing to do so is a breach of that covenant and calls into question the legitimacy of a sovereign's authority.

Factions to Hobbes typically are as unjust as they are "contrary to the peace and safety of the people, and a taking of the sword out of the hand of the sovereign." Hobbes, therefore, turns the traditional conception of natural law on its head: Laws of nature do not result in restraints placed upon the ruler, but rather they devolve absolute power on him so that individuals who are party to a covenant can enjoy the benefits—particularly security—that accrue from escaping from the state of nature. As Hobbes states: "Covenants, without the sword, are but words."

We have thus come a long way from the medieval vision of community, and in the process see a major justification offered for centralizing power in the modern state. Aside from his image of the state of nature and his unusual conception of laws of nature, what else does Hobbes have to say about relations among commonwealths? Hobbes states that the leviathan is charged with providing citizens not only "peace at home," but also "mutual aid against their enemies abroad."

As with individuals in the state of nature, so, too, do commonwealths have the right to do anything to enhance their security: "So in states, and commonwealths not dependent on one another, every commonwealth . . . has an absolute liberty, to do what it shall judge . . . most conducing to their benefit. But withal, they live in the condition of a perpetual war, and upon the confines of battle, with their frontiers armed, and cannons planted against their neighbours round about."

Are there any circumstances under which commonwealths might band together? Hobbes states this is possible: "Therefore leagues [i.e., alliances] between commonwealths, over whom there is no human power established, to keep them all in awe, are not only lawful, but also profitable for the time they last." The overall tenor of his analysis, however, suggests that he did not have a great deal of faith in such alliances lasting a long time. Nor does one even find Hobbes suggesting that in conducting relations among kingdoms, ethical or moral considerations should play a role.

International law is never mentioned. Nor does Hobbes suggest that the essential anarchy of interstate relations can be overcome through the creation of a worldwide leviathan to provide peace and security. Put another way, he does not propose world government as a means to end international anarchy. As a result, Hobbes seems to be suggesting that the state of nature for individuals differs from the conditions faced by states; the former sees the logic in needing to transcend anarchy, the latter does not. For while Hobbes claims, as noted earlier, that kings "are in continual jealousies" and in "a posture of war," he continues "there does not follow from it [the posture of war] that misery, which accompanies the Liberty of particular men" in the state of nature. This suggests that one should be wary of making facile comparisons or analogies between Hobbes's depiction of the state of nature and international relations.

We see in Hobbes's work, therefore, the basic elements of the realist image, albeit presented in their most extreme form. The state is the supreme political organization. Unity is enforced by the leviathan who should not allow factions. It is also charged with dealing with the world beyond the kingdom's borders. While it is rational for the individual to escape the state of nature, it is also rational for individual leviathans (i.e., states) to guard against one another by "having their weapons pointing, and their eyes fixed on one another." It is a self-help system of states, not one in which a sovereign maintains international peace and security.

Sovereignty

Aside from *raison d'état*, another critical concept that helped to legitimize the idea of an international system of states is that of *sovereignty*. It is a social construction that developed philosophically over time in response to states needing to establish their authority and exercise power. The term is applicable both domestically—the right of the state to exercise exclusive jurisdiction over its territory—and internationally—the right for the state to be free or autonomous in the conduct of its foreign affairs. When sovereign states are coerced or invaded by others they may not be able to exercise these rights as a matter of fact (*de facto*), but that does not alter their right to do so as a matter of law (*de jure*), perhaps at a later point in time when invaders have withdrawn.

An example was the Soviet invasion of Estonia, Latvia, and Lithuania—the Baltic republics—in 1940. Governments representing the sovereignty of these states operated abroad in exile, waiting for a time when they could reassume political control of their homelands. *De facto* control rested with Soviet authorities in Moscow until the end of the Cold War some fifty-two years later when it returned to governments with a *de jure* right to rule.

The notion of sovereignty as the basis of state authority has been termed the constitutional justification for the state's exercise of power. The term appears in European history at a time when the issue of where supreme power should ultimately reside in the political community was in dispute. As argued by F. H. Hinsley, the concept of internal sovereignty is "an enforced compromise between those who claimed it lay with the ruler and those who claimed that it lay with the ruled. It is the justification of absolute authority that can arise and exist only when a final power is considered necessary in a body politic, and only when the body politic and its government are considered necessary to each other."[35]

These conditions are not met until the rise of the territorially based state in which one can differentiate between the ruler and the ruled, state and society, and there is a felt need to establish an appropriate relation between the two. The ancient Greeks did not need to develop the idea of sovereignty because the concept of *polis* did not distinguish between the community and the state.[36]

Conversely, while the Greek city-states were essentially communities without distinctive state forms, empires such as those of Macedonia were lords of many communities and varied peoples, as kings of kings, as rulers of a whole continent if not of the world. On the other hand, the impact of their forms of government upon the communities under their rule was negligible.[37]

In effect, the Romans and their Byzantine successors had developed the idea of internal sovereignty—though not called that—with final authority resting with the emperor. The impetus was a desire to overcome social and political chaos, and in the case of Rome the result was a despotic rule. With the decay of the empire and the decentralization and fragmentation of power, however, the Roman idea of a supreme central authority fades into the background.

Indeed, in medieval European communities there were many overlapping authorities claimed by many different actors or institutions. Although the notion of a final authority wielded by pope or emperor was not universally recognized, the pervasive influence of the medieval idea that Europe comprised a single community united as Christendom was one reason the idea of the internal sovereignty of states did not take hold until the sixteenth century. This idea of universal community, however powerful ritually, in reality was an inadequate basis for rule by a single sacred or secular authority that claimed dominion over all of Europe.

At the regional level, single rulership needed to be united with a true sense of community for the idea of internal sovereignty to take root, social disorder provided the needed impetus to move away from the excessive plurality of political authority in medieval Europe. These circumstances encouraged the concentration of power in the new regional, territorially based states.

Bodin

The critical formulation of this doctrine of internal sovereignty comes from Frenchman Jean Bodin's *Six Books on the State*, published in 1576. It is not surprising that it was in France that the concept of sovereignty came to the fore. The development of judicial, administrative, and legislative institutions

---

[35] F. H. Hinsley, "The Concept of Sovereignty and the Relations Between States," *Journal of International Affairs* 21, no. 2 (1967): 243–44.

[36] "The *polis*, while it had become a highly organized community, was still essentially a community where the outlook of its members had not yet freed itself from kinship and tribal limits, and where the structure of government had not yet sufficiently separated itself from the ways and institutions of the tribal society to produce the forms and procedures of the state." F. H. Hinsley, *Sovereignty* (London: C. A. Watts, 1966), 28.

[37] Hinsley, *Sovereignty*, 30–31.

occurred in a country where the sentiment of nationalism was evident even in the thirteenth-century struggle between King Philip IV and Pope Boniface VIII.

Jean Bodin (1530–1596) was born into the middle class, studied law in Toulouse, and lived at a time when Catholic-Protestant conflict threatened France's progress toward unity. As so often happens, fanaticism on both sides made reconciliation difficult. Bodin was associated with the *Politiques*, a group dedicated to halting fanaticism. Although Catholic, the *Politiques* placed the state and nation above the Church and recognized the political virtues of religious tolerance.[38]

In *Six Books on the State*, Bodin attempts to find a basis upon which harmony could be restored in the French political community. He agrees with Machiavelli and Hobbes that some centralized authority wielding unlimited power is needed to achieve this goal. Bodin rejects Machiavelli's argument that the solution entailed freeing the prince from all religious limitations and restraints based on custom. Bodin argues instead that the body politic should be viewed as comprising ruler and ruled (similar to Machiavelli's definition of the "state" in the first line of *The Prince*), but he declares that the ruler must respect moral and legal rules. The desire of the political community to escape chaos is not enough—the power has to be vested in a "sovereign"—that is, the state.[39]

Bodin defines sovereignty as "the absolute and perpetual power of the state, that is, the greatest power to command." Bodin makes an important distinction between "government" and "state." A particular government exercises sovereign functions for a period of time. Sovereignty itself, however, is unlimited and perpetual. Governments headed by diverse individuals come and go, just as different types of governments may come and go. But sovereignty continues as long as the state exists.

The "absolute" aspect of sovereignty refers to the assertion that there is no legal authority above the state. As Bodin claims: "Only he is absolutely sovereign who, after God, acknowledges no one greater than himself." The reference to God reflects the fact that Bodin still held the medieval sentiment that the sovereign king should not violate the divine laws of God and nature, which include the idea that a king must keep whatever agreements he has made with his subjects.[40]

Although his primary focus is on internal sovereignty, Bodin also deserves credit for beginning a discussion on the implications of external sovereignty. Two obvious external threats to the sovereignty of the state at the time were empire and the claims of the universal church. Bodin argues against their interference in the ecclesiastical and secular affairs of the state. As for relations with other states, Bodin views sovereignty as referring to the equal legal status of states. Political power, of course, varies, and some states *de facto* are politically and militarily dependent on others. But no state is *legally* subject to the *de jure* authority of any other state.

---

[38] Ebenstein, *Great Political Thinkers*, 349–50.
[39] Hinsley, *Sovereignty*, 121–22.
[40] Ebenstein, *Great Political Thinkers*, 350–51.

To summarize, the concept of internal sovereignty refers to final and absolute authority within the state and society, while the concept of sovereignty as applied to relations among states involves the principle that no supreme authority exists over and above a collection of states.[41] While internal sovereignty means that one supreme authority exists in the domestic realm, the external concept of sovereignty rejects the idea of one final, absolute international authority.

Each state *de jure* is equally sovereign with no other state having the right to tell it what to do internationally or how to handle its domestic affairs. While internal sovereignty works to aid domestic unity, sovereignty in its external manifestations reinforces state independence or autonomy vis-à-vis other states. These social constructions clearly undermined medieval and universalistic claims of the papacy and empire.

External Sovereignty

If it took hundreds of years for the idea of internal sovereignty to take root, the external application of sovereignty involved an even longer and more tortuous process. Indeed, constructivists (see chapter 9) view sovereignty as a concept or construct that emerged and evolved over centuries. Roman law was not much help because it reflected Rome's rapid transformation from tribal city and republic to empire with no stops along the way. The authority of the emperor in Rome was viewed in terms of its internal manifestations within the empire, not in terms of international or inter-empire relations.[42] Until the time of Bodin, kings might have claimed that they were *de jure* independent of the pope or emperor in terms of their right to govern their communities as they saw fit without external interference. But, this did not imply that they saw themselves and the kingdoms they governed as isolated from these universal authorities or even from other states. The reason for this goes back to the idea that, despite differences, these states and their leaders were still part of a single community united—in their minds at least—that they labeled Christendom.

It took perhaps another century after Bodin before the idea of applying sovereignty to interstate relations was worked out satisfactorily. The problem of developing an international version of sovereignty was similar to the earlier problem of developing the concept of internal sovereignty. Widespread acceptance of internal sovereignty required a balance between a ruler's desire to be superior to any manmade laws and his willingness to be subjected to ethical premises and political limits demanded by the ruled. In the case of the international application of the concept of sovereignty, it could not be applied "until the notion of the sovereign power of the individual state had been reconciled in some way with the ethical premises and the practical needs of an international community of states."[43]

By the end of the seventeenth century, there were four basic schools of thought on international relations, all but one failing to recognize the need for such a reconciliation.

---

[41] Hinsley, *Sovereignty*, 158.
[42] Hinsley, *Sovereignty*, 36–37.
[43] Hinsley, *Sovereignty*, 186.

First, some conservative writers were part of a pluralist-unity-despite-diversity school of thought. These were individuals who continued to cling to the medieval notion of the European international system as a single society in which divine and natural law, in the tradition of Aquinas and More, imposed common rights and duties on all states.

The best known of these scholars is the Spaniard Francisco de Vitoria (1480–1546), a Dominican professor of theology, who utilizes theological and natural law reasoning in his discussions of just war. Clerical writers naturally continued to argue for the power of the pope over the emperor and kings, or at least that the emperor should maintain power over local rulers in the name of the unity of Christendom. More secular-minded writers had other reasons to support the idea of a unified European order—fear of the growing anarchism of interstate relations and distrust of Machiavellism and *raison d'état* theories that appeared to encourage this anarchism.[44]

Second, legal positivists such as the Spanish Jesuit Francisco Suarez (1548–1617), and the Italian jurist or lawyer Alberico Gentili (1552–1608) emphasize the autonomy of the state and argue that international law could and should exist. The diplomatic practices of sovereign states that had evolved were a customary basis for international law. The extent to which a community of sovereign states existed was found in states being tied together by a mutually agreed upon body of law.

Third, so-called naturalists such as the German writer Samuel Pufendorf (1632–1694) argue that international political society cannot be created through the introduction of positivist—humanly constructed—international law. If there were to be any restraints involving relations among states, they would derive from laws of nature that predate the historical state. Pufendorf was optimistic that through experience and reason these laws of nature could be known and established as legally binding principles, but he had no illusions concerning the likelihood of a universal society. At best, a society of sovereign states could be established.[45]

Other naturalists exhibited even greater pessimism. The most extreme position was held by Benedict Spinoza (1632–1677), a Dutch Jew, who found it as a practical matter that might effectively make right: "the big fishes devour the little fishes by natural right." Thomas Hobbes, the most famous of those writers labeled as naturalists, argues that the international state of nature is really a state of war. Neither international law nor ethical restraints are mentioned in those few passages of his works that deal with international politics.[46]

The final school of thought that we could term the Bodin-Grotian perspective sees the need to reconcile the internal sovereignty of the autonomous state with the notion of an international community. In the process, these writers paved the way for the modern conception of external sovereignty.

---

[44] Hinsley, "The Concept of Sovereignty," 246.

[45] For a discussion of Samuel von Pufendorf's views, see Andrew Linklater, *Men and Citizens in the Theory of International Relations* (New York: St. Martin's Press, 1982), 62–79.

[46] Linklater, *Men and Citizens*, 246; Friedrich, *The Age of the Baroque*, 29. See the comments on Hobbes, Pufendorf, and Spinoza in Arthur Nussbaum, *A Concise History of the Laws of Nations* (New York: Macmillan, 1947), 112–18.

Grotius

The most important writer of this latter group is the Dutch legal theorist Hugo Grotius (1583–1645) who is credited with being the "father of international law." On the one hand, Grotius can be viewed as an intellectual precursor of realism in that he accepts the state as the key political unit and the fact that competition and war are inescapable aspects of international politics. On the other hand, he contributes to the liberal image by arguing that there is a basis upon which one can view the state system as a community that exhibits something less than a "war of all against all." As a Dutch person (from the town of Delft) and a Protestant, not surprisingly he rejected the direct or indirect authority of the Holy Roman Empire and the papacy.

Grotius combines two strands of thought, believing manmade and natural laws can both contribute to a tempering of conflict among states. Although he conceived of *jus gentium* (law of nations or "peoples") as manmade laws resulting from human volition—a positivist understanding—he follows the moral theology tradition of Aquinas and Vitoria by emphasizing laws derived from the laws of nature.[47]

According to natural law, human beings in the state of nature are equal and free with no superior authority above them. States, by the same natural law, are also free and equal. But just as individuals cannot live in isolation as they are not sufficient unto themselves and must associate with one another to survive, so, too, must states. This requires augmenting the basic laws of nature through the creation of the law of nations based on custom, consent, or contract.[48]

Hence, Grotius has no single term for "international law," but discusses *jus naturae et gentium*—the law of nature and of nations or peoples. He contributes greatly to the emancipation of international law from theology, however, by stating that the laws of nations still "have a degree of validity even if we should concede that which cannot be conceded without utmost wickedness, [that] there is no God, or that the affairs of men are of no concern to Him."[49]

This tentative yet obvious desire to liberate natural law from theology reflects the fact that although Grotius was apparently a committed Protestant, he was extremely tolerant compared to earlier Catholic and Protestant writers, who viewed those of differing religions as heretics. Perhaps because he was writing during the bitter religious wars of the first part of the seventeenth century, he realized that the growing corpus of international law had to be truly secular. Otherwise it would never be acceptable to both Catholics and Protestants.[50]

In his most famous work, *The Law of War and Peace* (1625), Grotius discusses all types of laws including laws among nations. His discussion of just war doctrine approvingly quotes such writers as Augustine, Aquinas, Cicero, Livy, and Thucydides. Grotius argues that there are three justifiable reasons for going

---

[47] Nussbaum, *A Concise History*, 104.

[48] James Brown Scott, "Introduction," in *The Law of War and Peace*, Hugo Grotius (New York: Bobbs-Merrill, 1925), xxx–xxxi.

[49] Hugo Grotius, "Prolegomena," in *The Laws of War and Peace*, 13. All subsequent direct quotations by Grotius are from this work.

[50] Nussbaum, *A Concise History*, 104–5.

to war: "defense, recovery of property, and punishment." But before war begins, the state that is accused of causing injury has the right to submit the matter to arbitration.

The realist in Grotius recognizes that in most cases this is unlikely, hence upholding the law of nations must be undertaken by the aggrieved party through the use of force. In other words, war is a means to enforce a state's legal rights, analogous to judicial remedies in a domestic polity. Aside from the fact that war should not be undertaken "except for the enforcement of rights; when once undertaken, it should be carried on only within the bounds of law and good faith."

It is in the third book that he deals with these rules of warfare. Grotius discusses such topics as the treatment of civilians, prisoners of war, pillaging, and the duty of the victor toward those who offer unconditional surrender. The key idea running through his discussion of the law of war is "moderation."[51]

The Law of War and Peace was an immediate success. The Latin original was published in almost fifty editions, and the book was translated into Dutch, English, French, German, Swedish, and Spanish. At Heidelberg University a chair for the "Law of Nature and Nations" was established, dedicated to the study and elaboration of Grotius's work. Other European universities followed suit.[52]

In sum, Grotius dramatically differs from Hobbes in that he believed states are subject to the law of nations, and that the observance of this international law is in the self-interest of states. Given the fact that he was writing during the Thirty Years' War, Grotius believed "such a work is all the more necessary because in our day, as in former times, there is no lack of men who view this branch of law with contempt as having no meaning outside of an empty name."

Grotius's work gained even greater importance after the Peace of Westphalia in 1648. The Thirty Years' War among Germanic states and its settlement completed the process of the *de facto* transformation of an international system based on the tenuous unity provided by the papacy and the Holy Roman Empire to a system of sovereign states. To regulate relations among these new entities, a system of law was required.

It was Grotius who provided the intellectual foundation for this evolving interstate system. He also served as an inspiration for later writers such as Emmerich de Vattel (1714–1767) who argued that a recognition of moral obligations among states could coexist with balance-of-power policies designed to assure the stability and independence of states.[53] Similarly, what Hedley Bull terms the "Grotian conception of international society" has directly influenced much of the literature on regional integration and international regimes.[54] Core to the

---

[51] See, for example, the headings to chapters 12 through 16 in Book 3, pp. 745–82.

[52] Nussbaum, *A Concise History*, 110.

[53] For an analysis of Emmerich de Vattel's work, see Linklater, *Men and Citizens*, 80–96.

[54] Hedley Bull, "The Grotian Conception of International Society," in *Diplomatic Investigations: Essays in the Theory of International Politics*, ed. Herbert Butterfield and Martin Wight (Cambridge, MA: Harvard University Press, 1966), 51–73. See also Hedley Bull, *The Anarchical Society: A Study of Order in World Politics* (New York: Columbia University Press, 1977), chap. 4.

present-day English School of international relations (see chapter 8) is the idea of an international society driven not just by power considerations, but also by international rules of conduct accepted by states as being in their enlightened self-interest—many of these rules legally binding, thus constituting a larger corpus of international law.

Reflections on the Thought of Writers Related to the Rise of States

All these authors grappled with the emerging international order in western Europe that followed the breakup of the sense of unity provided by Christendom and empire during the Middle Ages. Settlement of the Thirty Years' War (1648) carried with it explicit recognition of the authority of kings, dukes, and other princes over people living on territories under their jurisdiction.

Writing in the previous century, Niccolò Machiavelli—as noted earlier—drew upon the classical works of Greek and Roman scholars in his attempt to understand why Rome became such a world power in such a short period, hoping to find lessons and guidelines for rulers of emerging national states. For him, the key was to be found at the state-societal level of analysis—Rome's republican institutions. The dynamic nature of the republic allowed leaders to make the most of the opportunities provided by fate. In the course of his analysis, the usual moral justifications for state conduct were replaced by pragmatic considerations drawn from how states really act. His focus was more on how states do act than on how they ought to behave.

Practical concerns as to how a leader can get power and keep it came to the fore, paving the way for such writers as Giovanni Botero whose "reason of state" arguments were used to justify the further expansion of state power. If Machiavelli could still evince a certain nostalgia for the glory of the Roman empire, Thomas More exhibited a similar sentimental attachment to the small medieval community and city-state. Nevertheless, More was a realist to the extent that he recognized the increasing importance of the modern national state and the need for statesmen to be provided with sound advice on how to use their extraordinary power.

Thomas Hobbes placed political philosophy on a more scientific basis while using such traditional ideas as the state of nature and natural law. Such concepts were used to justify a powerful centralized state able to end domestic anarchy. In the process of making this argument, however, he elevated the concept of anarchy to that of the international system, noting the warlike posture of states in a world without a superordinate authority to enforce covenants. His concept of the all-powerful leviathan also contributed to the realist idea of the unitary, rational actor dedicated to maintaining the security and independence of the state.

The realist emphasis on the state as the principal actor in international relations—unified and calculating how best to preserve its physical integrity—was given a further boost by the emerging concept of sovereignty, which reinforced state autonomy and undermined the universal claims of papacy and empire. What Jean Bodin did for internal sovereignty, other scholars did for external sovereignty, gradually working out the implications for relations among states.

Various schools of thought held different views on the nature of the rights and duties among states, but it was Grotius who realized that it was necessary to develop some basis upon which states could relate to one another in an anarchic realm. In the process, he argued that to a certain extent an international community existed, thus contributing to the realist, liberal, and English School images of international politics. For all those writers who came after Hugo Grotius, interstate (or international) relations were a given in political life. Political thought therefore turned to analyzing the conduct of states in international politics.

EIGHTEENTH- AND NINETEENTH-CENTURY THINKING ON INTERNATIONAL RELATIONS

The formal emergence of the sovereign state and system of sovereign states in the 1648 Peace of Westphalia was reflected in the fifteenth-, sixteenth-, and seventeenth-century scholarly writings that preceded, accompanied, or soon followed this event. Steeped as they were in the corpus of Greco-Roman and medieval thought, these early modern writers established an important intellectual foundation that would be built upon in the eighteenth, nineteenth, and early twentieth centuries.

With the notable exception of Hugo Grotius, however, sixteenth- and seventeenth-century writers tended to focus primarily on the domestic aspects of the state and did not look very far beyond its borders. Thus, Niccolò Machiavelli was concerned largely with politics among city-states and the papacy on the Italian peninsula, although he certainly recognized the importance of such great powers of the day as Spain, France, and the Holy Roman Empire that consistently intervened and laid claim to Italian territory and royal titles. Similarly, Thomas Hobbes and Jean Bodin focused primarily on the domestic aspects of sovereignty. By contrast, Grotius and those writers on international law who followed him looked outside the confines of the state or the politics of a region to the world as a whole, going well beyond realism and contributing intellectually to the advancement of a liberal and English School conception of world order.

While speculation continued on the relation between human nature and conflict, the state-societal and international levels of analysis became increasingly important foci of attention. Whether or to what degree structure (or lack of it) in the international environment affects the nature and behavior of states is a question addressed by Montesquieu, Jean-Jacques Rousseau, and Immanuel Kant. Or is it the nature of the domestic regime or society that matters more? These questions as well as those on economic aspects of international politics as addressed by Adam Smith, Karl Marx, and nineteenth-century liberals are the central issues of this section. Despite differing interests, arguments, and conclusions, these writers share one characteristic: Their works are influenced, to varying degrees, by the basic assumptions and principles of the seventeenth- and eighteenth-century Enlightenment—an "Age of Reason" that embraced secular thinking independent of theological understandings (see table 4.1).

Table 4.1   Eighteenth- and Nineteenth-Century Thought

Date	Historical Developments	Writers and Commentators
1600	Colonialism in the Americas, Austrians defeat Ottomans outside Vienna (1683); William and Mary "Glorious Revolution" in England (1688)	Descartes (1596–1650)
1700	Treaty of Utrecht (1713) curbs French power for seventy-five years; publication of *The Federalist Papers* (1787–1788); French Revolution (1789)	Montesquieu (1689–1755), Hume (1711–1776), Rousseau (1712–1778), Smith (1723–1790), Kant (1724–1804), Hegel (1770–1831), Ricardo (1772–1823), Cobden (1804–1865)
1800	Napoleonic period of European conquest; defeat of Napoleon and Congress of Vienna (1815); Latin American independence movements; repeal of Corn Laws advances free-trade liberalism in England; 1848 revolutions sweep Europe; Crimean War curbs Russian power in southeastern Europe (1854–1856); Prussia defeats France in 1870–1871 war; Germany unites; Western imperialism in Africa, Middle East, Asia, and Pacific	Marx (1818–1883), Hobson (1858–1940), Weber (1864–1920), Lenin (1870–1924)
1900	World War I (1914–1918)	

Historical Context

The European state system in the years following 1648 was marked by rivalries and shifting alliances. The Turkish challenge to Austrian power was arrested by the defeat in 1683 of the Ottoman invaders just outside Vienna. English preoccupation with the domestic turmoil of the civil war was evident in King Charles I's execution on a charge of treason in 1649, the turmoil that followed, and the subsequent rise to power as "Lord Protector" the authoritarian Oliver Cromwell (1653–1658). This period came to an end in 1660 with the return by parliamentary consent of the Stuart dynasty under Charles II, son of Charles I—known in English history as the Restoration. James II, the Catholic brother of Charles II, acceded to the throne in 1685 but was displaced in 1688 as parliament invited William of Orange (Holland) and Mary Stuart (the daughter of English King James II)—both protestants—to take the throne. This accession is referred to in English history as the "Glorious (and Bloodless) Revolution." French ambitions on the continent were blocked militarily in a series of battles conducted by the British in association with the House of Savoy in northern Italy. The Treaty of Utrecht (1713) was part of a settlement that effectively curbed the French for seventy-five years before the revolution of 1789.

The French Revolution itself was a watershed, not just for France but for all of Europe. Competing ideas and emerging ideologies cast a long shadow over the nineteenth and twentieth centuries to our own time. In contrast to such liberal and democratic ideas as *liberté*, *egalité*, and *fraternité* was authoritarianism; whether Jacobin or Bonapartist, authoritarian models would find many emulators over the next two centuries. The Napoleonic period not only upset the Westphalia system by replacing it for a short time with an empire with France at its center, but also witnessed the spread of French language and culture, French-style central administration of state affairs, and the idea of universal, national military service by citizen-soldiers (*levée en masse*). All these elements remained in Europe long after Napoleon's final defeat and the subsequent restoration of the "Westphalia system" of sovereign, independent states at the Congress of Vienna in 1815.

Attention in Vienna was paid to restoring a balance among the great powers and providing a conflict-management system—the Concert of Europe. Thus, France was restored as a major power in what was seen as an overall balance on the continent and in Europe as a whole. Smaller wars were fought from time to time, but Europe remained free of general war until 1914.

The periodic conferences of the "concert" approach to managing conflict within an overall European balance proved reasonably successful in the immediate decades after the 1815 settlement but broke down as an effective instrument in the last half of the century. The breakdown of the concert was clearly marked by the Crimean War (1853–1856) in which Britain joined France and Turkey in a dispute against Russia that effectively curbed the latter's role in southeastern Europe. French defeat in the Franco-Prussian War (1870–1871) and the subsequent unification of Germany marked the beginnings of great power rivalry outside of any European concert, a development that ultimately reached its conclusion with the outbreak of World War I in 1914.

The heavy emphasis in this volume on European history stems from the fact that contemporary IR theory and practice are drawn primarily from this European experience. In the eighteenth and nineteenth centuries, we see the expansion of both the European system of sovereign states and European notions of a capitalist market economy to include the entire globe.

Colonialism that began in the late fifteenth century reached global scope in the eighteenth and nineteenth centuries. While some European states established colonies in Africa early, much of the rest of Africa and Asia was not colonized until the imperial era of the nineteenth century. Although most American states established independence from Europe early in the nineteenth century, large-scale decolonization in Africa and Asia did not occur until the twentieth century in the aftermath of two world wars.

The important point, however, is not the precise date when specific states came into existence. Rather, it is that all did so in accordance with a European pattern formally established in Westphalia. Ideas originating in Europe thus came to define international relations for the world as a whole. Moreover, the Europeans (and the Americans who were themselves a product of these European ideas) directly influenced approaches to world politics in present-day IR theory.

The Enlightenment

Despite the diversity of thought of such writers as Montesquieu, Rousseau, Kant, Hegel, Smith, and Marx, they have one characteristic in common—all are influenced, to greater or lesser extents, by the basic assumptions and principles of the seventeenth- and eighteenth-century Enlightenment. Despite a common starting point, however, their interests, analyses, and prescriptions vary widely.

The basic assumptions of the Enlightenment are perhaps best revealed in the works of the French rationalists of the eighteenth century who published the first volume of the *Encyclopédie* in 1751. Such individuals—Diderot, d'Alembert, Helvetius, d'Holbach, and later Condorcet—were influenced by the scientific method of the previous century that used mathematical reasoning as a means to establish truth by a method independent of God's revelation.

These writers contributed to the development of a systematic philosophy based on the classical Greek assumption that individuals are rational, reasoning beings and the assertion of René Descartes (1596–1650) that the mastery and possession of nature are possible.[55] They argue that through the application of reason, it is possible to overcome superstition, prejudice, and tradition in an effort to understand the laws that govern nature as well as, more importantly, human society. These laws were understood to be universal, particularly the law of reason, and hence applicable to all of humanity. This overpowering belief in the importance of acquiring knowledge and the development of a science of politics akin to what was occurring in the natural sciences resonates today in the social sciences, including much of the work on international relations. In this regard, the Enlightenment was to a great extent concerned with the issue of the appropriate methods required to understand human behavior.

But there is another important element of Enlightenment thought that moves one from the realm of analysis to the realm of action: Rational individuals can exercise reason to create eventually an environment reflecting the revealed laws of nature. For example, through reason the nature of justice can be discerned and, in turn, a just society can be created. Enlightenment thinkers had great faith in the progress of humanity, and a result is their political argument, following the Stoics: All people are linked by nature in universal brotherhood.

Some writers took the next step and argued that what divided humanity was the increasingly powerful sovereign state. As a result, writers who embraced unreservedly the values of the Enlightenment often called for world citizenship, with such diverse notables as Voltaire, Samuel Johnson, and Goethe deploring patriotic prejudice.[56]

The political implications, particularly in France, were revolutionary. By rejecting the idea of original sin and the assumption of innate aggressiveness, these writers argue that the failings attributed to human nature are not inborn, but rather the result of a corrupt environment. If the environment causes humanity to be less than reason and nature intended, a program of societal restructuring becomes a moral imperative. For these thinkers at the time, the perfectibility of humanity was possible. The embrace of this extreme form of voluntarism was exhibited during the French Revolution. Not only was it the duty of the revolutionaries to liberate the people of France from the *ancien régime* and the weight of the past, but they also believed it was their duty to engage in wars of liberation abroad.

---

[55] Leo Strauss and Joseph Cropsey, eds., *History of Political Philosophy* (Chicago: Rand McNally, 1963), 379. René Descartes is following the lead of Francis Bacon who was an enthusiast of the belief that through Machiavellian politics one could increase the possibility of mastering fortune or nature.

[56] "Enlightenment," *Encyclopedia Britannica*, vol. 8 (Chicago: William Benton, 1973), 601.

The excesses of the French Revolution not only destroyed the monarchy it also shocked the serene confidence in the perfectibility of man. The skepticism of David Hume (1711–1776), his thorough critique of human reason, and his claim that morality should be in accordance with passions contributed to the disintegration of this voluntarist movement. Our concern, however, is less with the historical political influence of the Enlightenment and more with its methodological implications as reflected in the authors under consideration.

In this chapter, as elsewhere in this volume, we have not attempted an exhaustive survey and summary of every writer whose commentaries have had a bearing on the development of IR theory. In our eighteenth- and nineteenth-century focus here, we necessarily have had to be very selective. We relate in this section the progression of thought on the state and system of states offered by Montesquieu, Rousseau, Kant, Hegel, Weber, and the authors of *The Federalist Papers* because of the profound effect their thought has had, directly or indirectly, on many present-day IR theorists. Given the importance of international political economy as a central part of international relations, we have selected the contributions of two classical political economists (Adam Smith and Karl Marx), the work of nineteenth-century liberals, and the analyses of imperialism by John A. Hobson and Vladimir Lenin as the subjects of the latter part of this chapter. Marx, Hobson, and Lenin are briefly discussed in chapter 7 in terms of their direct impact on modern-day economic structuralists.

Montesquieu

Charles Louis de Secondat, Baron de la Brede et de Montesquieu (1689–1755) was born to an old aristocratic French family, as his full name and titles suggest. After studying law at the University of Bordeaux, he moved to Paris but after the death of his father, he returned home to administer the family estate. His financial security allowed him to pursue his intellectual interests, which included further study of Roman law. It was, however, the publication of his satirical analysis of contemporary France, *The Persian Letters*, that brought him fame. Foreign travel, particularly his experiences in England, further stimulated his interest in politics and constitutions.

As a serious student of ancient Greek and Roman writings, Montesquieu was familiar with the mixed constitutions as they appeared in Plato's *The Laws* (Book 3) and Aristotle's *Politics* (Books 4 and 5). Like Machiavelli, he places great emphasis on statecraft and rejects the view of the Greek classics that the primary function of political theorizing was to encourage virtue. He is also more in tune with Machiavelli about the effect of both necessity and choice in the formation of laws, diverging from the Enlightenment's supreme confidence in voluntarism and the ability to transform societies. Indeed, in his *Spirit of the Laws* (1748), he describes how historical, geographical, and climatic circumstances create diverse human cultures and a diverse "general spirit" of each nation. All nations live more by passion and prejudice, and less by reason.[57]

---

[57] Montesquieu, *The Spirit of the Laws*, ed. David Wallace Carrithers (Berkeley: University of California Press, 1977), xxx. All subsequent direct quotations are from this edition.

Nevertheless, he argues that such diversity is intelligible only in the light of general causes. Montesquieu reflects Enlightenment thinking by defining laws in his famous opening formulation as being "necessary relations arising out of the nature of things," and this "necessity" is by definition universal. Following the Stoics, he claims these laws govern the actions of all things and provide the standard by which human law is to be judged. In contrast to Aquinas, nature— not God—is the ultimate source of law.

His view of natural law expresses hope of establishing a science of human affairs, parallel to Cartesian and Newtonian physics. Does this mean that only one particular form of government or set of laws is in accord with nature? No. "Law in general is human reason, inasmuch as it governs all the inhabitants of the earth; the political and civil laws of each nation ought to be only the particular cases in which this human reason is applied." Compared to the utopian French rationalists, this acceptance of diversity in part reflects Montesquieu's belief in the limits to purposive human action.

Polybius no doubt is responsible for Montesquieu's advocacy of separation of powers that would balance governmental powers among competing departments or branches—an idea adopted by American federalists concerned with avoiding too strong a central government. For Montesquieu, such an arrangement most effectively promotes liberty. While, like the ancients, he believed a stable polity is in and of itself a worthwhile goal, he ranks liberty as the top priority. One can read a similar concern for liberty in *The Federalist Papers* of Alexander Hamilton, James Madison, and John Jay.

On the relation between regime type for a given political system and the way that a country projects itself in its foreign affairs, Montesquieu's republican preference is clear. He states that "the spirit of monarchy is war and enlargement of dominion." By contrast, "peace and moderation [are] the spirit of a republic." This sentiment aligns him with such thinkers as Kant, as opposed to Machiavelli, who not only argues that republics are best able to defend themselves, but also are best at expansionism. What all three men have in common, however, was a belief that the domestic character of a state and its society does influence its behavior internationally.

There are intellectual links among Montesquieu, Rousseau, and Kant in their writings on politics in general and international relations in particular. Montesquieu influenced Rousseau, and we know that Kant incorporated insights drawn from his reading of Rousseau. In formulating their positions, all three reject a Hobbesian (or Machiavellian) negative view of the nature of man. There is in Montesquieu a profound critique of Hobbes. One can find it in his early work, *The Persian Letters*, as well as in his *Spirit of the Laws*. To Montesquieu it is not man's nature that is defective. The problem arises when human beings enter civil society from their natural state. Moreover, the formation of separate nations and the relations that occur among them compound the problem. Montesquieu's argument therefore links together three levels of analysis—the nature of the individual, society, and the international system.

Jean-Jacques Rousseau's argument on the formation of society upon departure from a state of nature has a familiar sound when one already has read

Montesquieu. The state of nature is not, as Hobbes would have it, a state of war. Indeed, Montesquieu tells us that "as soon as mankind enters into a state of society, they lose the sense of their weakness, the equality ceases, and then commences the state of war." The state of war thus occurs after the formation of society, not before. For Montesquieu (and for Rousseau who would follow this line of reasoning), war is an artifact of society, not characteristic of human nature as such.

How is such societal strife to be overcome? Part of the answer is to be found in what Rousseau would later term the "general will." Montesquieu observes that "the particular force of individuals cannot be united without a conjunction of all their wills." It is the conjunction of those wills that Montesquieu calls "the civil state." Laying a foundation upon which Rousseau would build in *Émile*, Montesquieu also places emphasis on the Enlightenment concern with education by which individuals are prepared for civil life.

Montesquieu recognizes divine and natural law but focuses on the different categories or "orders of laws" that apply to moral, religious, domestic, and international domains of human beings and their societies. Montesquieu refers to the law of nations as "the civil law of the universe, in which sense every nation is a citizen." From a juridical perspective, then, states are like persons and, as such, are understood as unitary actors. Rousseau's later development of the idea of a general will for a society clearly would be consistent with this unitary notion of state as singular actor representing the multitude of individuals comprising it. Indeed, in realist thought one of the clearest expressions of Rousseau's general will is the notion that the foreign policies of states are unitary and are formulated in service of the national interest.

In a world of many nations "each particular society begins to feel its strength" and, as a result, there "arises a state of war between different nations." To regulate their conduct, Montesquieu writes, nations "have laws relative to their natural intercourse, which is what we call the law of nations." He observes that the law of nations holds "that different nations ought in time of peace to do one another all the good they can, and in time of war as little harm as possible, without prejudicing their real interests." And a central interest for all nations is their preservation. Indeed, Montesquieu tells us that "the safety of the people is the supreme law."

States thus have a right to go to war in their own defense. Montesquieu comments that "among societies the right of national defense carries along with it sometimes the necessity of attacking" as "when one nation sees that a longer peace will enable another to destroy it, and that to attack that nation instantly is the only way to prevent its own destruction." Moreover, Montesquieu allows for a right of conquest, but he argues that it rests upon this same preservationist principle.

In sum, Montesquieu's work reflects an appreciation for republican or mixed forms of government, a tradition of thought dating back to ancient Greece. As with Immanuel Kant, but contrary to Niccolò Machiavelli, Montesquieu believed "peace and moderation [are] the spirit of the republic." His realism is evident in his acceptance of the diversity of states and a view of international law that conceives states as unitary actors pursuing their respective national interests. Statecraft is important, requiring leaders to make reasoned choices while operating under constraints. War is to be expected, and therefore states develop laws and norms to regulate their relations to the extent possible. His realism downplays the idea that individual leaders can control foreign policy outcomes or collectively work to transform the international system into a different type of order.

Rousseau

Jean-Jacques Rousseau (1712–1778), whose work reflects influences as diverse as Montesquieu, Locke, and Plato, provides an extraordinary intellectual legacy subject to numerous interpretations (and misinterpretations). The problem in understanding Rousseau stems from the complexity of his thought, which is compounded by changes made to his manuscripts by editors who did so without his approval. Born in Switzerland and the son of a watchmaker, his *Confessions* describes a difficult early life filled with varied experiences, including being the ward and then lover of Madame de Warens. Various trips to Paris to seek his fame and fortune in the arts met with little success.

His interest in social-political matters was stimulated by his association with Denis Diderot, editor of the *Encyclopédie*. At Diderot's encouragement, Rousseau competed in an essay contest on the relation between morality and the sciences and the arts. He won, and fame immediately followed. Two of his works, *Émile* and *On the Social Contract*, offended authorities, and the subsequent issuing of an order for his arrest caused him to flee France. Eventually he went to England under the encouragement of David Hume, but the two quarreled, and Rousseau returned to France where he lived out his days.[58]

The influence of Enlightenment thinking on Rousseau, as with other social contract theorists such as John Locke, is best expressed in his argument that individuals escape the state of nature by way of a mutually beneficial agreement or social contract; creation of society is an act of volition or will. One finds Rousseau's concept of the state of nature (a formulation that departs from the natural law concept so central to Locke's presentation of human rights) most clearly stated in his *Discourse on the Origin of Inequality*. Rousseau's state of nature is an egocentric world in which "man's first sentiment was that of his own existence; his first concern was that of his preservation." In this primitive state, individuals may collaborate "but only insofar as present and imperceptible interests could require it." They are concerned only with the short run "since foresight meant nothing to them, and far from concerning themselves about a distant future, they did not even give a thought to the next day."[59]

In a passage particularly noteworthy for IR theorists, Rousseau states: "Were it a matter of catching a deer, everyone was quite aware that he must

---

[58] "Rousseau," *Encyclopedia Britannica*, vol. 19 (Chicago: William Benton, 1973), 659–61.

[59] Jean-Jacques Rousseau, "Discourse on the Origin of Inequality," part II, in *Basic Political Writings*, trans. and ed. Donald A. Kress (Indianapolis, IN: Hackett, 1987). All subsequent direct quotes are Rousseau's "Discourse" or "On the Social Contract."

faithfully keep to his post in order to achieve this purpose; but if a hare happened to pass within reach of one of them, no doubt he would have pursued it without giving it a second thought, and that, having obtained his prey, he cared very little about causing his companions to miss theirs."

For many current theorists, the importance of this passage stems from its presenting a scenario that exhibits the same sorts of dilemmas and dynamics that result from the anarchical structure of the international system. Are states like these primitive hunters, serving their individual, short-run self-interests? Or do they recognize the advantages of fulfilling mutual commitments? In short, will states be willing to forgo short-term gratification for themselves and act for common interests that serve longer-term advantages for all—an enlightened self-interest?[60]

As should be apparent by now, the authors under consideration in this work overwhelmingly explain conflict and lack of cooperation among states in terms of human nature and the nature of states or societies. In Rousseau, we see a rare emphasis on how the decentralized structure of a system—the state of nature and, by analogy, the international system—also contributes to suspicion, distrust, and conflict. In other words, the difficulty of cooperation among egocentric actors (states or individuals) stems as much from the self-help nature of the system itself as it does from the nature of the actors themselves.

To Rousseau, therefore, the structure and values of the social setting (including the international environment) have a great deal to do with the behavior of individuals (and states) within it. Echoing Montesquieu, Rousseau tells us when individuals leave the relatively happier state of nature: "Emerging society gave way to the most horrible state of war since the human race, vilified and desolate, was no longer able to retrace its steps or give up the unfortunate acquisitions it had made." Rousseau laments:

> The first person who, having enclosed a plot of land, took it into his head to say *this is mine* and found people simple enough to believe him, was the true founder of civil society. What crimes, wars, murders, what miseries and horrors would the human race have been spared, had someone pulled up the stakes or filled in the ditch and cried out to his fellow men: "Do not listen to this impostor. You are lost if you forget that the fruits of the earth belong to all and the earth to no one."

Thus, property and the divisions that stem from the resulting inequality are, to Rousseau, at the root of human conflict whether among individuals or states. Rousseau observes how "more murders were committed in a single day of combat and more horrors in the capture of a single city than were committed in the state of nature during entire centuries over the entire face of the earth." These are the "effects one glimpses of the division of mankind into different societies." The anarchy of the state system is responsible for national wars, battles,

---

[60] For an argument that such collaboration is possible because hunters can "make informal rules regulating the separate or cooperative hunting of hares," see Ernst B. Haas, *Beyond the Nation-State* (Stanford, CA: Stanford University Press, 1964), 69–71.

murders, and reprisals. The numerous political units exist in a condition more deadly than previously had existed among the private individuals of whom they were composed.

At the state-societal level of analysis, Rousseau argues that in these political bodies governance is to be in accordance with the general will as if the political community were a single person or unit. The present-day realist view of the state as a unitary, rational actor is certainly consistent with this Rousseauan view of a political unit guided or driven by a singular, general will: "So long as several men together consider themselves to be a single body, they have but a single will, which is concerned with their common preservation and the general well-being." It is only the general will that can "direct the forces of the state according to the purpose for which it was instituted, which is the common good."

Sovereignty cannot be divided into parts; it "is indivisible for the same reason that it is inalienable. For either the will is general, or it is not. It is the will of either the people as a whole or only a part." Moreover, articulation of policy is with one voice: "Each of us places his person and all his power in common under the supreme direction of the general will; and as one we receive each member as an indivisible part of the whole."

Rousseau departs from Montesquieu in questioning whether war for conquest could be a right. Moreover, he is a strong advocate of *jus in bello*: "War does not grant a right that is unnecessary to its purpose." More specifically, the prince who wages war is under real constraints: "Since the purpose of war is the destruction of the enemy state, one has the right to kill the defenders of that state so long as they bear arms. But as soon as they lay down their arms and surrender, they cease to be enemies or instruments of the enemy. They return to being simply men; and one no longer has a right to their lives."

Rousseau had a diverse influence on other writers. Many have seen in Rousseau's general will a wellspring of democratic thought; however, others have seen the general will as justification for authoritarian rule—the more effective way to serve the common or societal interest. Karl Marx and Friedrich Engels pick up Rousseau's ideas on property and its relation to inequality. They answer Rousseau's famous claim that "man is born free, and everywhere he is in chains" with an equally famous assertion in *The Communist Manifesto* that by committing themselves to revolution, the working men have "nothing to lose but their chains."

Finally, Rousseau contributes to the ideology of nationalism, noting the important role of political indoctrination in creating a national identity: "It is the task of education to give to each human being a national form, and so direct his opinions and tastes that he should be a patriot by inclination, by passion, by necessity. On first opening his eyes a child must see his country, and until he dies, must see nothing else."[61]

Realists Kenneth N. Waltz and Stanley Hoffmann have made much of their differences in interpretation of Rousseau's view of international relations. They

---

[61] As quoted by Michael Howard, *The Lessons of History* (New Haven, CT: Yale University Press, 1991), 145.

agree on a number of points, such as the fact that "the international milieu" is one "in which the absence of any common superior over states is seen as the 'permissive' cause of war."[62] As Waltz would have it, "Rousseau's answer is really that war occurs because there is nothing to prevent it. Among states as among men there is no automatic adjustment of interests. In the absence of a supreme authority, there is the constant possibility that conflicts will be settled by force."[63] Hoffmann comments, however, that "the solution to the problem of war and peace in Rousseau's mind" is not at the international but at the state level: "Establish ideal states all over the world, and peace will follow."[64]

Where Waltz and Hoffmann differ substantially is on the degree to which they see Rousseau emphasizing federation (or confederation) of states as a solution to the security problem posed by the international anarchy of sovereign, independent states. In dispute are passages drawn from two of Rousseau's lesser-known essays *State of War* and his summary and critique of the Abbé de St. Pierre's *Perpetual Peace*. Waltz believes a federation is Rousseau's prescription to remedy the problem of international anarchy if it were, in fact, desirable to alter that condition. In Hoffmann's view, however, Rousseau put relatively more emphasis on improving states and their citizens than on making changes in the structure of the international environment. Hoffmann observes that Rousseau's preference was for smaller communities, which are more conducive to the effective realization of the general will than would be possible in a large federation. For advocacy of the latter, Hoffmann gives more credit to Kant.[65]

A close reading of Rousseau's critique of St. Pierre's proposal for a confederacy as a means to establish peace makes clear that Rousseau is not so hostile to the logic of St. Pierre's argument as he is to its impracticality, the very real obstacles Rousseau thinks will preclude putting such a mechanism into effect. While Rousseau is concerned with avoiding universal monarchy or too strong a central authority, he does not express this as his reason for opposing St. Pierre's scheme, which to Rousseau is as well intentioned as it is naive. The problem with St. Pierre's vision is not so much that it would fail to eliminate war or, in doing so, threaten the general will of the smaller communities or states within the federation. According to Rousseau, the problem lies in what he considers the utopian character of St. Pierre's vision.

Kant

The East Prussian scholar Immanuel Kant (1724–1804) attended the University of Königsberg. After serving as a tutor to several aristocratic families, he became an instructor at the university, lecturing on such diverse topics as physics, logic, and the natural sciences. In 1781 he published perhaps his most famous work, *Critique of Pure Reason*, and during the last twenty years of his life, he wrote

---

[62] Stanley Hoffmann, "Rousseau on War and Peace," *American Political Science Review* 57, no. 2 (June 1973): 326.
[63] Kenneth N. Waltz, *Man, the State and War* (New York: Columbia University Press, 1954, 1959), 188.
[64] Hoffmann, "Rousseau," 329.
[65] Hoffmann, "Rousseau," 330.

many remarkable books and papers. He does not ignore politics and shares Rousseau's interest in the problem of war and peace in international relations. An optimist, Kant believed the ultimate perfection of individuals and their countries is to be slow but steady; humanity is not condemned to an endless repetition of wars and civil strife.

Because he supported the American Revolution against England and his belief in the validity of the values of the French Revolution, it took courage to publish his *Idea for a Universal History* (1784) and *Perpetual Peace* (1795) during the reign of Prussian King Frederick William III. While influenced by Hume and Rousseau, the Stoic roots of Kant's thought on world politics are also clear in these works—his universalism, his concept of world citizenship, and his advocacy of a federation of (or compact among) states as a means to peace. Kant's vision is of a liberal world order in which human beings can live freely and without war. The achievement of such a vision would allow individuals to fulfill their duty to fellow citizens and the state as well as to humanity as a whole.[66]

Kant, however, is no naïve idealist. He rejects the idea that the transformation of world politics is either imminent or easy to achieve. For him, the sovereign state is a reality, and any plan to deal with international anarchy must take states into account. Even if it were possible, for example, to eliminate states and create an empire, this would not solve the problem of war, as the inevitable result would be the rise of warring groups and the ultimate dissolution of the empire.

Similarly, the idea of trying to overcome anarchy by creating a federation of states with a combined military force is not realistic; such a force, if effective, would put states out of business, something government leaders would not allow. As one scholar has noted, Kant parts company with such predecessors as Hugo Grotius, Samuel von Pufendorf, and Emmerich de Vattel in that he believed none of them pay "the Stoic-Christian ideal of the unity of mankind the supreme compliment of taking its political consequences seriously."[67] His task, therefore, is to come up with a proposal that balances aspiration with practicality.

Familiar as he is with Rousseau's thought, and holding to liberal principles, Kant proposes "a federation of states which has for its sole purpose the maintenance of peace" because it "is the only juridical condition compatible with the freedom of the several states."[68] This "league of nations" still leaves the separate sovereignties of league members intact: "This league does not tend to any dominion over the power of the state but only to the maintenance and security of the freedom of the state itself and of other states in league with it." International law presupposes the separate existence of many independent but neighboring states. Kant prefers a federative union because in his view it "is rationally preferable to the amalgamation of states under one superior power" or "universal monarchy."

---

[66] See Hannah Arendt, *Lectures on Kant's Political Philosophy*, ed. Ronald Beiner (Chicago: University of Chicago Press, 1982), 16, 28.

[67] W. B. Gallie, *Philosophers of Peace and War: Kant, Clausewitz, Marx, Engels and Tolstoy* (London: Cambridge University Press, 1978), 33.

[68] Immanuel Kant, *Perpetual Peace*, ed. Lewis White Beck (New York: Macmillan, 1957), 51. All subsequent direct quotations are from this edition.

How does Kant arrive at this conclusion? As with a number of writers, an important starting point is his view of human nature. He shares with Rousseau a vision of individuals in the state of nature as subsisting "in anarchic freedom by hunting, fishing, and shepherding." On one important point, however, Kant agrees with Hobbes (and thus differs from Rousseau) when he notes that "the natural state is one of war" or "at least an unceasing threat of war." Peace thus must be established as a result of human action. Similarly, just as Hobbes characterizes kingdoms as being in a "posture of war," Kant asserts that "peoples, as states, like individuals, may be judged to injure one another merely by their coexistence in the state of nature (i.e., while independent of external laws)." The negative effect of anarchy is further increased, as Kant notes, by "the perverseness of human nature which is nakedly revealed in the uncontrolled relations between nations."

Still, there is hope. Adversity and discord among human beings will lead them to learn ways in which to avoid future wars. It is part of nature's design: "Nature brings it to pass through selfish inclinations" of human beings who come into conflict with one another that they employ "reason as a means for its own end, the sovereignty of law, and, as concerns the state, for promoting and securing internal and external peace."

Furthermore, a development emphasized, in particular, by nineteenth-century liberal theorists—economic imperatives—aids this process of moving toward peace. As Kant argues: "The spirit of commerce, which is incompatible with war, sooner or later gains the upper hand in every state." Given the fact that money is a critical source of state power, "states see themselves forced, without any moral urge, to promote honorable peace."

Kant takes a strong position against conduct that leads statesmen to sow discord at home and abroad and to be bold and unapologetic in pursuing state interests aggressively. Such practice, he argues, amounts to "an immoral doctrine of prudence" or expediency. Again, he has the faith that ultimately the good in world politics will displace the evil, "though only through a slow progress." Kant notes in this regard that "moral evil" has the quality of "being opposed to and destructive of its own purposes."

Thus, Kant sees that morality and politics are inextricably linked: "True politics can never take a step without rendering homage to morality." If "politics says, 'Be ye wise as serpents' [then] morality adds, as a limiting condition, 'and guileless as doves.'" As a practical matter, then, there is continuing tension between power and principle in politics—a theme the twentieth-century writer E. H. Carr will raise in his discussion of international politics between the two world wars.[69] However descriptive of international politics this tension may be (or had been in Carr's or Kant's time), Kant's position is that with the progress of humanity over time, expediency ultimately must give way to moral principle: "Nature inexorably wills that the right should finally triumph."

---

[69] See E. H. Carr, *The Twenty Years' Crisis, 1919–1939* (New York: Harper & Row, 1939, 1964), 11–13.

Hannah Arendt comments on how Kant was deeply concerned toward the end of his life with the "problem of how to organize a people into a state, how to constitute the state, how to found a commonwealth, and all the legal problems connected with these questions."[70] In human discord the necessary element in nature's design by which progress is possible exists for Kant. War itself carries the seeds of later progress toward peace, as human beings gradually come to realize how awful it is. Arendt summarizes Kant's view: "It is by virtue of this idea of mankind, present in every single man, that men are human, and they can be called civilized or humane to the extent that this idea becomes the principle not only of their judgments but [also] of their actions." From a Kantian perspective, Arendt observes how "one is a member of a world community by the sheer fact of being human; this is one's 'cosmopolitan existence.'"[71]

How then is progress toward peace to be made? Echoing Montesquieu, Kant prefers constitutional arrangements that check or balance competing interests. A federation of such republics inclined toward peace and under the law of nations can be extended gradually to include additional members, a line of argument later associated with American President Woodrow Wilson. Harmonization comes from structuring the domestic and international environments within which we live. Although transformation of the human condition will not be achieved in a short time, it remains "our duty to work toward this end."[72]

The influence of Hugo Grotius on theories of regional integration and international regimes is noted earlier. Similarly, Kant's emphasis on the ability of leaders to learn and to realize that it is rational and in their individual and collective self-interest to cooperate, his belief in the possibility of change, and his recognition of the need to link aspiration and reality is also characteristic of much of this literature.

The Federalist Papers

The writers of *The Federalist Papers*—Alexander Hamilton, James Madison, and John Jay—were faced with the practical problem of helping to sway the American public to support the idea of replacing the current confederation of states with a republican form of government that would entail greater power at the national level. As part of this effort to persuade the states to ratify the proposed constitution, a series of articles attributed to the pseudonym Publius appeared in New York newspapers between 1787 and 1788.

The Federalist Papers makes interesting reading in that it reflects a point consistently made throughout this work—the tendency of the writers under consideration to be thoroughly conversant with the works of their predecessors. This is evidenced in the heavy reliance on Montesquieu; obvious familiarity with earlier works on republicanism; and references to Plato, Polybius, Plutarch, and Grotius. Similarly, the use of such phrases and terms as state of nature, human

---

[70] Arendt, *Lectures*, 16.

[71] Arendt, *Lectures*, 75.

[72] See also Arendt, *Lectures*, 75, where she constructs a categorical imperative implicit in Kant's writings on peace through federation: "Always act on the maxim through which this original compact can be actualized into a general law."

nature, love of power, perpetual peace, anarchy, passions, justice, interests, virtue, reason, and self-love evinces an impressive grasp of the concerns of political theory through the ages.

The Federalist Papers should be of interest to students of international relations for at least two reasons. First, it is often suggested that realism was essentially introduced into the realm of American foreign policy by European-born scholars following World War II. The writers of *The Federalist Papers*, however, exhibit a thorough realist perspective when discussing relations among states or factions. Second, Madison's important discussion on factions has influenced work on interest group theory by American political scientists that, in turn, has found its way into the IR literature dealing with bureaucratic politics and the domestic sources of foreign policy.

An early theme discussed by the authors is the nature of relations among the states if each claimed sovereignty and went their separate way, or even if they remained associated only in the loosest form of confederacy. The argument made by both Jay and Hamilton is that the result would be similar to relations among any state—conflict. According to Jay: "Like other bordering states, they would always be either involved in disputes and war, or live in the constant apprehension of them." In an argument that sounds remarkably similar to that of present-day power transition theorists, he argues that even if the states are initially of equal strength, this condition will soon change. Various circumstances will work to "increase power in one part and to impede its progress in another" so that the "relative equality in strength and consideration would be destroyed." Jay then advances a hypothesis that could have been written by Thucydides when Jay argues that if any state "should rise on the scale of political importance much above the degree of her neighbors, that moment would those neighbors behold her with envy and with fear."[73]

Hamilton takes up this theme in the next paper, arguing that "to look for a continuation of harmony between a number of independent, unconnected sovereignties situated in the same neighborhood would be to disregard the uniform course of human events, and to set at defiance the accumulated experience of ages." Compared to Jay, however, he presents a wide array of possible causes of conflict among states that ranges up and down the levels of analysis to include the observation that "safety from external danger is the most powerful director of national conduct." "Men are ambitious, vindictive, and rapacious" and exhibit a "love of power" and a "desire of pre-eminence and dominion" as well as "equality and safety."[74]

Hamilton then examines the state-societal level of analysis and refers to "visionary or designing men" who advocate a "perpetual peace" among states and claim that republics are pacific and that "the spirit of commerce" dampens the possibilities of war. Hamilton raises a historical and empirical question still of research concern today: "Have republics in practice been less addicted to war

---

[73] John Jay, *The Federalist Papers*, no. 5.
[74] Alexander Hamilton, *The Federalist Papers*, nos. 6, 54. The comment on "external danger" is from nos. 8 and 67.

than monarchies?" He observes that there have been almost as many popular wars as royal wars, and in many cases these are "contrary to the real interests of the state." As for commerce, he argues that commercial motives have indeed contributed to the onset of wars. By way of example, he cites the experiences of Sparta, Athens, Rome, and Carthage.[75]

Perhaps the most famous tracts are *Federalist* 10 by Madison and 51 by Madison and Hamilton. In the first, Madison outlines the problems of factions and the danger they present to the unity of the state—a traditional republican concern. Passions, divergent interests, and unequal distribution of property divide mankind and make it difficult to cooperate for the common good. One of the virtues of a republic, however, is that representative government tends to "refine and enlarge the public views by passing them through the medium of a chosen body of citizens, whose wisdom may best discern the true interest of their country."[76]

But in a brilliant line of reasoning, Madison and Hamilton go on to argue in *Federalist* 51 that far from requiring a leviathan to overcome domestic divisions, factions can actually be turned into a virtue. This is because in a republic "the society itself will be broken into so many parts, interests and classes of citizens, that the rights of individuals, or of the minority, will be in little danger."[77] This multiplicity, or what we could term plurality of interests, keeps a permanent majority from forming and encourages the creation of various coalitions depending on the issue at hand. This is similar to some versions of the balance-of-power theory that predict that it is natural for states to band together to prevent being dominated by a larger state or coalition of states. It is also a contribution to the liberal image of domestic and international politics that emphasizes the variety of actors or groups that makes up a state and the competition among them.[78]

This thesis concerning the virtues of republican forms of government is quite different from the argument made by Machiavelli. While Machiavelli says conflict among classes may ultimately serve to enhance the external power and prowess of the republic, Madison and Hamilton make the case that the salutary effects of checks and balances are designed to keep too much power from being concentrated in any one domestic institution or group. Foreign policy considerations are secondary.

Finally, a central theme found in the first nine *Federalist Papers* by Jay and Hamilton is that the security of a federal republic is to be found in unity. Unification avoids armed conflicts among states in the union as well as provides a bulwark against threats or attacks by other states. It is the same argument made by Machiavelli in *The Prince* where he advocates unification among Italian states for domestic security as well as for defense against outsiders.

---

[75] Hamilton, *The Federalist Papers*, no. 6.

[76] James Madison, *The Federalist Papers*, nos. 10 and 82.

[77] Madison, *The Federalist Papers*, no. 51.

[78] For two classic statements of American politics as group conflict, referenced in chapter 6, see Arthur F. Bentley, *The Process of Government* (Chicago: University of Chicago Press, 1908); and David Truman, *The Governmental Process* (New York: Alfred A. Knopf, 1951).

Hegel

The perspective that Georg W. F. Hegel (1770–1831) has on international relations is often overlooked, perhaps because of the complexity of his worldview, an aversion to his authoritarian orientation in relation to state power, or its later association with Marxism (notwithstanding his emphasis on the role of ideas in changing history in contrast to Marx's materialism). This is unfortunate. Indeed, certain writings of his have had a direct bearing on the development of methodology and realist thought.

For Hegel, history is not the random occurrence of unconnected events. The historical process is one in which humanity has continued to make spiritual and moral progress. This is in part due to the ability of individuals to reflect upon their circumstances and increase self-knowledge. Reason and history are inseparable, and the historical process is essentially a rational, dialectical process that unfolds the "Ideal of Reason," which is apparent in the historical development of the state. Hence, the function of philosophy is not to dream up some ideal state or to discern supposedly transhistorical natural laws, but rather to deal with the reality of the state in a particular historical epoch.[79]

Hegel's adoption of a historical perspective contributed greatly to the rise of a tradition of political theory that became increasingly important in the nineteenth century—historicism. Historicism is highly critical of the individualistic and universalistic components of the so-called rationalist thought associated with the Stoics and the Enlightenment. Historicists reject the "uniformity of human nature and the supposed timelessness of moral principles."[80]

First and foremost, historicists argue that moral beliefs and values vary from culture to culture and have done so throughout history as well. For example, the natural law teachings of the Stoics simply reflect a response to the historical dissolution of the Greek city-state. As there is no universal, suprahistorical, and transcendental set of values or natural laws, procedures to criticize beliefs and actions differ from society to society. In other words, reason is relative to culture; therefore, one should not utilize some universal standard of behavior to judge a state.

Furthermore, historicists are critical of social contract approaches to the origins of the state and the emphasis on the individual; they argue that values held by an individual are socially produced, not a reflection of universal laws of nature. Hence, the fundamental fact of humanity is cultural diversity, resulting in the division of the world into states.[81] As one of the foremost exponents of the historicist perspective, Heinrich von Treitschke, states: "The idea of one universal empire is odious—the ideal of a state co-extensive with humanity is no ideal at all."[82] A state has an absolute right to sovereignty, disputes among

---

[79] Pierre Hassner, "Georg W. F. Hegel," in *History of Political Philosophy*, ed. Leo Strauss and Joseph Cropsey (Chicago: Rand McNally, 1963, 1972, 1987), 628–29.

[80] Linklater, *Men and Citizens*, 122.

[81] Linklater, *Men and Citizens*, 122–24.

[82] Heinrich von Treitschke, "The State Idea," in *The Theory of International Relations: Selected Texts from Gentili to Treitschke*, ed. M. G. Forsyth, H. M. A. Keens-Soper, and P. Savigear (New York: Atherton Press, 1970), 326.

states are inevitable, and moral ties among individuals of various states as well as perpetual peace are illusory.

Such themes are found in Hegel's writings, particularly his preoccupation, if not obsession, with the state, his acceptance of the sovereignty of individual states, and consequently the international anarchy that exists among states. As Hegel asserts in *The Philosophy of History*: "The State is the Divine Idea as it exists on Earth," the "embodiment of rational freedom, realizing and recognizing itself in an objective form."[83] Furthermore, "the nation state is mind in its substantive rationality and immediate actuality and is therefore the absolute power on earth. It follows that every state is sovereign and autonomous against its neighbors."[84]

As duty is to one's state, Hegel rejects the long tradition of political thought that asserts a community of nations should, could, or does exist. In contrast to Rousseau and especially Kant, Hegel does not seek perpetual peace or anything approaching it. To him, war has a salutary effect on societies by keeping them from the decline associated with long-term peace. More important, history's progression is the result of wars. War is not entirely an accident in an anarchic system—a view also found in Rousseau and the work of some present-day realists.[85]

Clausewitz

Carl von Clausewitz (1780–1831), a Prussian military officer, is best known for the phrase that war is "a continuation of political activity by other means." Policy makers—not the military—must decide the overall strategic objectives of the state. The military then develops plans for the application of force, keeping the political objectives in mind. War is not fought for glory or is an end in itself but is utilized to enhance the security of the state. This formulation is reflected in realist conceptions of power and its use.

Much of Clausewitz's writing took place in the interwar period between the defeat of Napoleon in 1815 and Clausewitz's recall to duty in 1830 for service in East Prussia. Clausewitz died in 1831, never having completed his major work, *On War*. His legacy, nevertheless, remains a central contribution to realism thanks to the successful efforts by his wife Marie to publish the manuscript posthumously.

The use of force in battle aims to destroy or substantially weaken the war-making capability of an adversary, which undermines (or precludes) the will to continue fighting. Leadership is important, and the commander is crucial in this essentially rational enterprise, adapting to changing circumstances and employing such principles as surprise, mass, and concentration of forces. Attacks effectively

---

[83] Hegel, *Philosophy of History* (New York: P. F. Collier and Son, 1900), 87 and 96.

[84] Georg W. F. Hegel, *Hegel: The Essential Writings*, ed. Frederick G. Weiss (New York: Harper & Row, 1974), 298. For Hegel's discussion of sovereignty and related issues concerning international relations, see 284–306.

[85] The historicist emphasis on history and culture, challenges to Enlightenment conceptions of man and society, and an interest in works dealing with the linguistic construction of reality are reflected in much of the current "critical theory" work on international relations that questions positivist or empiricist approaches to knowledge. See chapter 10.

directed to an enemy's "center of gravity" (however this may be defined in operational terms) can cause an enemy's capability to collapse. Because one's military forces are necessarily finite, one is not wasteful in their use—an economy of force essential to sustaining military capabilities against an adversary.

Just as Machiavelli referred to *fortuna* and Thucydides to fate as blunting even the best-laid plans of the prince, Clausewitz identifies the uncertainty that attends decision-making in battlefield conditions—the "fog of war." He is also well aware that rationally made plans often run into obstacles or "friction" when actually implemented. He is cautionary when he warns that one ought to not take the first step into war without realizing where the last step may lead.

These are the kinds of observations one readily finds in present-day strategic literature in the realist genre that owes much to Clausewitz. As significant as his view that the military is properly a political means is his exposition of societal (including social and economic) dimensions of national capabilities. At the same time, his focus on national security problems places him in the mainstream of present-day realist thought.

Weber

Another German, Max Weber (1864–1930), is a prime example of a theorist and social scientist who is generally not associated with the IR discipline, but whose impact—however indirect—on realists and liberals has been profound. His influence is particularly pronounced in four areas: the sociology of knowledge, his conception of the state, the study of bureaucracies, and political leadership.

Weber is part of the scientific tradition—dating back at least to Aristotle—in which it is assumed that there are regularities in human behavior. Hence, through deductive and inductive reasoning, it is possible to generate hypotheses and subject them to empirical testing. This faith in the scientific method as a means to comprehend a complex reality was not unusual at the turn of the century. Indeed, the expansion of knowledge in the natural sciences during the previous one hundred years buttressed confidence—dating back to the seventeenth century—that similar advances could be made in understanding human behavior and, as a result, the functioning of societies.

In contrast to a number of noted academics of the nineteenth and early twentieth centuries, however, Weber rejects essentially mono-causal explanations in his attempts to explain the development and functioning of societies. Marx's insights on economic factors, for example, are noted by Weber, but balanced with a careful weighing of cultural, political, and military considerations. Understanding, according to Weber, requires interpretation.

The realist in Weber is best revealed in his belief that the modern state represents the ultimate form of sovereign political authority. This is because the modern state "has been successful in seeking to monopolize the legitimate use of physical force."[86] Like Hegel, Weber was a German nationalist, albeit of liberal

---

[86] Max Weber, *From Max Weber: Essays in Sociology*, trans. and ed. H. H. Gerth and C. Wright Mills (New York: Oxford University Press, 1946), 82–83. All subsequent direct quotations from Weber are from this edition.

persuasion and hence suspicious of state power interfering with the autonomy of the individual. Personal preferences aside, Weber's emphasis on the state is in part a result of his lifelong study of why empires and decentralized feudal authorities ceased to exist in the modern world.

For Weber, the critical factor is what he calls the process of "rationalization." Weber states, for example, that far from Marx's characterization of capitalism as "anarchy of production," capitalism is actually the very embodiment of rationality in terms of the productive use of resources. Similarly, Weber equates the rise of bureaucratic administration—within the public as well as private spheres—with rationality. Indeed, the principle of rationalization is the key component of Weber's view of history, although he sees the process interrupted by the occasional emergence of charismatic movements that abhor routine.

As noted, the process of rationalization is exemplified by how the modern state manages to monopolize the legitimate use of physical force. While during ancient times, the early medieval period, and feudalism the individuals who composed the armies were essentially self-equipped, the modern military state provides the equipment and provisions. As a result: "War in our time is a war of machines. . . . Only the bureaucratic army structure allowed for the development of professional standing armies that are necessary for the constant pacification of large states of the plains, as well as for warfare against far-distant enemies."

The realist in Weber is also quite evident in his observations on international relations. For him, "all political structures [i.e., states] use force," but "the attitude of political structures toward the outside may be more isolationist or more expansive." Switzerland, he notes, tends toward an isolationism and its independence is protected by a balance of power among the larger states. Furthermore, contrary to Marxist-inspired theories of imperialism, economic factors at best "codetermine the extent and manner of political expansion." The norm, however, tends to be for political leaders of states to be driven by a "desire for power-oriented prestige," which "means in practice the glory of power over other communities." As Weber argues, "Every political structure naturally prefers to have weak rather than strong neighbors. Furthermore, as every big political community is a potential aspirant to prestige and a potential threat to all its neighbors, the big political community, simply because it is big and strong, is latently and constantly endangered."

For Weber, therefore, political threats to peace often result in war due to the desire for prestige on the part of "those having vested interests in the political structure."

Weber's attitude toward the historical process of "rationalization" is ambivalent. While bureaucratic machines may be more efficient, the liberal in Weber obviously feels for "the individual bureaucrat [who] cannot squirm out of the apparatus in which he is harnessed. In contrast to the honorific or avocational 'notable,' the professional bureaucratic is chained to his activity by his entire material and ideal existence." Furthermore, Weber is fully aware that however efficient and effective bureaucratic organizations may generally be in the fulfillment of their assigned tasks, they also have limitations. In a footnote he comments: "Here we cannot discuss in detail how the bureaucratic apparatus may, and actually does, produce definite obstacles to the discharge of business."

The functioning of bureaucracies in general, and the possible dysfunctions they spawn, has been the focus of attention on the part of the public administration discipline, which is heavily indebted to the works of Weber.[87] In turn, the IR literature that examines the role of bureaucracies in foreign policy decision-making and crisis situations is also beholden to the Weber legacy.[88]

Finally, Weber has an affinity with Machiavelli in terms of sympathy and respect for the dilemmas and problems the professional politician faces.[89] Just as Machiavelli refuses to find comfort in the universal laws of nature, so too does Weber question the Enlightenment's faith in the power of reason to overcome the political problems of governing. For Weber, states pursue conflicting values, and hence the statesman's primary duty is to promote national values.[90]

Just as Machiavelli argues that political leaders have to deal with the unexpected as reflected in the concept of *fortuna*, so too does Weber realize how political actions result in unintended consequences: "The final result of political action often, no, even regularly, stands in completely inadequate and often paradoxical relation to its original meaning." The dilemmas faced by a politician are best expressed in Weber's famous speech "Politics as a Vocation" at Munich University in 1918 in which he addresses the issue of the relation between ethics and politics.

He argues that ethical conduct for those engaged in politics can be guided by two very different maxims: an ethic of ultimate ends (as an individual driven for religious or other purposes) or an ethic of responsibility (as when political leaders must anticipate the consequences of their decisions and actions). To follow the ethic of ultimate ends—which Weber associates with writers of the Enlightenment and nineteenth-century liberals—is to assume that the goal being pursued is of such importance that how one achieves the goal or the concomitant costs are of secondary importance; it is the view of the impassioned prophet. Hence, a true believer in revolution may undertake actions that precipitate a harsh government reaction that is to the immediate detriment of the working class because of the belief that such sacrifices are required in the name of the revolution.

The ethics of responsibility, however, require one to take into account the possible results of one's actions. Weber is very sympathetic to the individual who "is aware of a responsibility for the consequences of his conduct and really

---

[87] James G. March and Herbert A. Simon, *Organizations* (New York: Wiley, 1958), 36–37.

[88] For example, Graham Allison notes: "The classic study of bureaucracy is, of course, [by] Max Weber." *Essence of Decision: Explaining the Cuban Missile Crisis* (Boston: Little, Brown, 1971), 298–99, n. 2.

[89] Note even Weber's choice of words in the following observation: "Everywhere the development of the modern state is initiated through the action of a prince." Weber, *From Max Weber*, 82.

[90] According to Leo Strauss, Weber essentially agrees with many present-day social scientists that "natural right is then rejected today not only because all human thought is held to be historical but likewise because it is thought that there is a variety of unchangeable principles of right or of goodness which conflict with one another, and none of which can be proved to be superior to the others." Strauss, *Natural Right and History*, 36.

feels such responsibility with heart and soul." But for one to have a true call-ing for politics, an ethic of ultimate ends and an ethic of responsibility must be balanced, requiring both "passion and perspective." This sensitivity to the dilemmas faced by political leaders is part of a realist tradition dating back to Thucydides, and such thinking influences twentieth-century writers in the realist tradition such as Hans J. Morgenthau and Raymond Aron.[91]

International Political Economy

Beyond their domestic political concerns, the eighteenth- and nineteenth-century writers already discussed in this chapter—Montesquieu, Rousseau, Kant, Hegel, and Weber—devote varying degrees of attention to international politics. Similarly, the authors to be discussed subsequently also adopt a worldview. However different their theoretical perspectives, explanations, and predictions, they all share an interest in understanding the relation between economics and politics. Increased attention to political economy was understandable. The eighteenth- and nineteenth-century industrial revolution—the heart of the mod-ernization process—had what can only be described as revolutionary impact on people around the globe. For those living in the West, very few areas of life were left unaffected, and it was to be expected that some of the best minds turned their attention to analyzing the political, social, and economic implications.[92]

Adam Smith

Although Adam Smith (1723–1790) is often overlooked by contemporary IR theorists (or portrayed incorrectly by others as a one-sided ideologue), a read-ing of Smith's *The Wealth of Nations* and *Theory of Moral Sentiments* reveals important roots of many subsequent ideas and efforts, particularly in interna-tional political economy.

Product of the Scottish Enlightenment and a professor at Glasgow Univer-sity, Smith turns his sights on the workings of markets in a world economy. Read in one way, his approach to finding the ways and means of the wealth of nations is state-centric (and thus in accord with a realist worldview). At the same time, however, his notion that states in most instances ought not to place restrictions on the market—thereby allowing investors, producers, workers, and consumers the freedom to make economic choices—is consistent with a world-view grounded in liberal principles and opposed to mercantilism.[93]

Smith insists that freedom in the marketplace should apply to all "social orders," what Karl Marx and others later will identify more specifically as classes.[94] Indeed, Smith expresses anger toward owners of the means of produc-tion who are sometimes prone to abridge liberal principles in relation to other

---

[91] Stanley Hoffmann, "Raymond Aron and the Theory of International Relations," *International Studies Quarterly* 29, no. 1 (March 1985): 22.

[92] See Karl Polanyi, *The Great Transformation* (Boston: Beacon Press, 1944, 1957); and E. J. Hobsbawn, *The Age of Revolution, 1789–1848* (New York: New American Library, 1962).

[93] See Adam Smith's arguments against mercantilist restraints on trade in Book 4 of *The Wealth of Nations* (New York: Modern Library, 1937).

[94] Smith mentions these social orders at the end of Book 1 of *The Wealth of Nations*.

social orders—using state power, for example, to restrict the right of workers to bargain for their wages. Smith refers to those working for wages as not always comprehending their interests (what Marx will call a lack of class consciousness) in contrast to landowners receiving rents and owners of capital receiving profits—both of whom are well aware of their interests.

Smith stops short, however, of using such terms as class conflict and exploitation of one class by another, but the threads of such arguments are clearly present. Beyond providing a basis for alternative images of international relations that would be adopted by others, Smith's treatment of the international dimension of political economy is a salient contribution. He does not consider economic matters to be the stuff merely of low politics. Commerce is as much a part of international relations as the security concerns in statecraft dealt with by Machiavelli.

Finally, Smith's brief allusion in Book 4 of *The Wealth of Nations* to an "invisible hand" in a free market that allocates factors of production—land, labor, and capital—in ways unintended by those making individual economic decisions is a powerful idea that has found the application well beyond Smith's usage. In Smith's words, the individual:

> intends only his own gain, and he is in this, as in many other cases, led by an invisible hand to promote an end which was no part of his intention. Nor is it always the worse for society that it was no part of it. By pursuing his own interest he frequently promotes that of the society more effectually than when he really intends to promote it. I have never known much good done by those who affected to trade for the public good. It is an affectation, indeed, not very common among merchants, and very few words need be employed in dissuading them from it.[95]

From this passage we can draw the idea of a system as a different level of analysis from the individuals, firms, or other groups or units of which it is composed. At the individual level, each actor is expected to act rationally to maximize self-interest. In a market of freely competing individuals or firms, the efficiency produced by this competition results in greater aggregate output of goods and services, whatever may be the equity of its distribution across a given society. To Smith, the wealth of nations is enhanced precisely by allowing free-market principles to prevail not only domestically, but also internationally.

Smith's view of free markets composed of competitive, interacting units that result in equilibrium prices for quantities produced and supplied to markets will be adapted by some realists when talking about the equilibrium or balance of power that occurs among competing states. In this sense, the state competing with other states becomes the analog of the firm much as firms compete in the marketplace. The result in both cases is an equilibrium that may or may not have been intended by any of the actors acting individually.[96]

---

[95] Smith, *The Wealth of Nations*, Book 4, chap. 2, 423.
[96] According to Kenneth N. Waltz: "Balance-of-power theory is a theory about the results produced by the uncoordinated actions of states." *Theory of International Politics* (Reading, MA: Addison-Wesley, 1979), 122.

This particular systemic perspective contrasts with alternative realist formulations that emphasize balance of power as a prudent policy that should be followed by statesmen. David Hume, for example, makes such an argument, drawing on the historical analyses of Thucydides and Polybius, while at the same time making one of the earliest arguments for free trade.[97]

Despite Smith's praise of free trade, he expresses reservations about the impact on society in terms of the ability of a nation to defend itself. He states that the "bad effect of commerce is that it sinks the courage of humanity, and tends to extinguish the martial spirit." This is the result of the division of labor in advanced economies. Those engaged in commercial activities have no time or interest in performing military service, hence the protection of the country is assigned to military professionals. The result is that "among the bulk of the people military courage diminishes. By having their minds constantly employed on the arts of luxury, they grow effeminate and dastardly." While a commercial country may be formidable abroad due to its navy and standing armies, it tends to be easily overcome when invaded. As an example, he mentions the Carthaginians, who were successful in foreign wars, but not when defending their own territory.[98]

Setting such reservations aside, David Ricardo (1772–1823), another classical economist wedded to a labor theory of value, became the intellectual champion of free trade. Building on Smith's free-market capitalism, Ricardo develops a theory of comparative advantage in which free-market forces, unhampered by trade restrictions, will lead to international specialization based on relative efficiency, thus maximizing overall production. Ricardo is particularly critical of protectionist agricultural policies in Britain that favored landholding aristocratic interests at the expense of capital-owning and labor or working-class interests.

Marx

One can find in Smith and Ricardo a basis for arguments later developed by Karl Marx (1818–1883), another classical economist, although Marx and his followers take Smith's and Ricardo's ideas far from their liberal moorings. Indeed, an understanding of Marx is incomplete without a reading of both Adam Smith and David Ricardo. Seeing history in stages with progression from one form of political economy (or mode of production) to another is an idea with its roots in Smith, who also addresses the rise of towns and their relation to the countryside.[99]

This should not be surprising in that Marx, though born and educated in Germany, did much of his work in London at the British Museum library and was intimately familiar with the writings of Smith, Ricardo, and other classical economists whose work preceded his efforts. It is to these sources that Marx

---

[97] David Hume, "Of the Balance of Power," in *Essays: Moral, Political and Literary* (London: Oxford University Press, 1963), 339.

[98] Adam Smith, *Lectures on Jurisprudence*, ed. R. L. Meck, D. D. Raphael, and P. G. Stein (Oxford, UK: Clarendon Press, 1978), 540–41.

[99] One can find Smith's overview of the history of Europe since Rome in Book 3 and his discussion of primitive economy in Book 2 of *The Wealth of Nations*.

owes the labor theory of value that figures so centrally in his theoretical work.[100] In this regard, challenges to Marxian use of the labor theory of value have to be understood as critiques of all classical economic theorists, each of whom is wedded to this idea in one form or another. It will not be until the work of such neoclassical economists as Léon Walras (1834–1910) from France, Alfred Marshall (1842–1924) from the United Kingdom, and Thorstein Veblen (1857–1929)—an American of Norwegian heritage—that value (as the price of a good or service) becomes generally understood not by the hours of labor put into its production as classical economists had held, but rather as a function of its supply and the demand for it in free markets.

It is, of course, not our purpose here to argue that Marx was dependent intellectually on insights drawn exclusively from Smith or Ricardo. Our only point is that Smith's influences on Marx are usually overlooked, perhaps because their conclusions are so different. Due to his avid and wide reading, Marx was influenced by as diverse a group of writers as Plato, Aristotle, Rousseau, Hegel, and Kant. Thus, as we discussed earlier, class analysis as method and slavery as form of political economy (or mode of production in Marx's terms) are present in the works of Plato and Aristotle. As noted, the metaphor of the working man in "chains" seems to have been borrowed directly from Rousseau. Marx adapts Hegel's view of history as a dialectical clash of ideas to emphasize the economic underpinnings of ideas in what is usually referred to as dialectical materialism in history.[101]

Marx was not writing about the political economy of individual states as much as he was about capitalism as a global phenomenon. In describing the world economy, Smith and Marx recognize the different levels of development and associated wealth of individual countries. Both view countries not as isolated entities, but rather as part of a larger whole—a critical element of the economic-structuralist perspective on international relations (see chapter 7). Indeed, Smith's anti-mercantilist position rests on his view that the wealth of nations increases in a free-trade environment that allows for the accumulation of capital. To see Marx purely in terms of class and class conflict within a given state will also be a misreading. Marx's vision is an internationalist one, however much he differs from Smith in his political-economic descriptions or future preferences.

Marx sees the world as divided by materially based class conflict. These horizontal, transnational class divisions cut across state boundaries and are a prime source of conflict, an analysis in direct contrast to the realist emphasis on conflict arising from interstate competition.

Nevertheless, Marx is hopeful. According to him, the growing class consciousness of the proletariat or working class will reach its climax in a proletarian revolution. Then, over an unspecified period, the state (an instrument of

---

[100] On Marxian economics and political economy, also Karl Marx's *Capital*, especially volume 1 (1867) and portions of volume 3 (published posthumously); and the *Grundrisse* (1857–1858).
[101] For Marx's discussion of dialectical materialism in history, see the first part of *The German Ideology* and *The Communist Manifesto*.

control by the dominant capitalist class) will fade away and, consequently, so will international (or interstate) relations.

Marx's work is an interesting blend of determinist and voluntarist inclinations, of agent and structure, as reflected in the statement that "men make their own history, but they do not make it just as they please; they do not make it under circumstances chosen by themselves, but under circumstances directly found, given, and transmitted from the past."[102] In sum, he believed that human beings can understand the historical process, and that "reality is not merely objective datum, external to people, but is shaped by them through consciousness" and action that can enhance the possibility of achieving greater individual freedom and dignity.[103]

This epistemological—and not merely normative—perspective is quite different from the positivist epistemology that traditionally has informed much of the works in international relations. Such work often seeks to discern essentially ahistorical, universal laws or forces and very often assumes that empirical and normative concerns can—or at least should—be separated. Nevertheless, Marx's belief that people can shape their world is reflected in the literature, discussed in chapter 10, which attempts to develop a critical theory of international relations.[104]

Cobden and Liberalism

The assumption of the potential for harmony among states and peoples in conjunction with the faith that unrestricted economic activity will enhance the possibility of achieving that harmony comes together in the works of nineteenth-century liberals and utilitarians.[105] Richard Cobden (1804–1865) is perhaps the foremost exponent of this perspective. Entering the British House of Commons in 1841, he was the leader of the Anti-Corn Law League and managed to get this act repealed in 1846 against the wishes of the protectionist landed interests. It was also a victory for the free-trade thinking of David Ricardo. While his arguments for free trade emphasize that such a policy would enhance a nation's prosperity, Cobden also addresses the issues of the relation between free trade and war, the influence of military establishments on war, and the pernicious effects of balance-of-power policies.

He makes three rather ambitious claims concerning the impact of free trade on peace. First, he asserts that states fight most wars to achieve their mercantilist goals. Free trade would show leaders a much more effective—and peaceful—means to achieving national wealth. Second, even in the case of wars not arising from commercial rivalry, those domestic interests that would suffer

---

[102] Karl Marx, "The Eighteenth Brumaire of Louis Bonaparte," in *The Marx-Engels Reader*, ed. Robert C. Tucker (New York: W. W. Norton, 1972), 436.

[103] John Maclean, "Marxist Epistemology, Explanations of 'Change' and the Study of International Relations," in *Change and the Study of International Relations: The Evaded Dimension*, ed. Barry Buzan and R. J. Barry Jones (New York: St. Martin's Press, 1981), 55.

[104] Both positivism and critical theory are discussed in chapter 10.

[105] The argument is developed at length by Kenneth N. Waltz, *Man, the State and War* (New York: Columbia University Press, 1959), 80–123.

from the interruption of free trade due to war will restrain and oppose hostilities. Finally, Cobden hypothesizes that with an expansion of free trade, contact and communication among people would expand. This, in turn, would encourage international friendship and understanding: "Free Trade! What is it? Why, breaking down the barriers that separate nations; those barriers, behind which nestle the feelings of pride, revenge, hatred, and jealousy, which every now and then burst their bounds, and deluge whole countries with blood."[106]

This posited relation between international trade and international peace has been a recurrent proposition since Cobden's day. Indeed, it is found in some of the modern IR theory works on interdependence and arguments that international trade can have pacifying effects on the behavior of states.[107] While the expansion of free trade may contribute to the growth of coalitions favoring peace over war, Cobden argues that military organizations will be against such developments as they would, in effect, virtually render militaries obsolete.

But Cobden assumes, as do other liberals, that "the great masses of mankind are disposed for peace between nations," and hence he is optimistic that they would, through the power of public opinion, negate the power of those who have a vested interest in the maintenance of international conflict.[108] As the threat of war recedes, a peace dividend would become apparent to all as tax dollars would be diverted to domestic programs.

Finally, Cobden argues that an important obstacle to the reduction in spending on armaments is the policy of balance of power. Cobden's attack on the balance of power is as passionate as it is sweeping. He first notes—as have many modern theorists of international relations—that the balance of power suffers from vague and multiple definitions.[109] He then argues that as a policy for Britain, it is little more than a smokescreen for British interests, with the word balance designed "to please the public ear; it implied something of equity; whilst England, holding the balance of Europe in her hand, sounded like filling the office of Justice herself to one-half of the globe."[110] But, the balance of power has been the cause of wars and a "pretence for maintaining enormous standing armaments." In ringing prose, he claims, "The balance of power is a chimera! It is not a fallacy, a mistake, an imposture—it is an undescribed, indescribable, incomprehensible nothing."[111]

---

[106] "Richard Cobden," in *The Anglo-American Tradition in Foreign Affairs*, ed. Arnold Wolfers and Lawrence W. Martin (New Haven, CT: Yale University Press, 1956), 193.

[107] As Richard Rosecrance states: "A new 'trading world' of international relations offers the possibility of escaping such a vicious cycle [episodes of chaos and warfare] and finding new patterns of cooperation among nation-states. Indeed, it suggests that the benefit of trade and cooperation today greatly exceeds that of military competition and territorial aggrandizement." See *The Rise of the Trading State: Commerce and Conquest in the Modern World* (New York: Basic Books, 1986), ix.

[108] "Richard Cobden," *The Anglo-American Tradition*, 197.

[109] See, for example, Ernst B. Haas, "The Balance of Power: Prescription, Concept or Propaganda?" *World Politics* 5, no. 4 (July 1953): 442–77.

[110] "Richard Cobden," in *The Theory of International Relations: Selected Texts from Gentili to Treitschke*, ed. M. G. Forsyth et al. (New York: Atherton Press, 1970), 308.

[111] "Richard Cobden," *The Theory of International Relations*, 309.

In sum, Cobden's emphasis on free trade as a means to mitigate the aggressive tendencies of states, his faith in the ability of political leaders to learn alternative means to achieve national interests, and his analysis of the important role played by domestic constituencies in foreign affairs epitomize nineteenth-century liberal thought on international politics. These ideas have also contributed to the development of the liberal image of international relations. (See chapter 6.)

Hobson

While Richard Cobden's arguments concerning the link between capitalist free trade and international peace influenced a great number of people, a more pessimistic line of thinking developed by Karl Marx also has its advocates. This is most clearly exhibited in those works on imperialism that have contributed to the economic-structuralist image of international politics. (See chapter 7.) One of the most influential analyses is by a non-Marxist, the English economist John A. Hobson (1858–1940).

In his work *Imperialism: A Study* (1902), Hobson discusses what he terms the "economic taproot" of imperialism. He notes that capitalist societies suffer from three interrelated problems: overproduction of goods due to the efficiency of modern machinery; underconsumption of these products by the lower classes, whose meager wages do not give them sufficient purchasing power to buy the excess goods; and oversavings on the part of capitalists, aided by paying workers low wages.[112]

For capitalists, the supposed solution to the problem of excess goods and capital is to find new markets. Western capitalist markets, however, suffer from the same maladies, so they cannot be the outlet for another state's goods and capital. Capitalists therefore urge their governments to lay claim to the underdeveloped territories in parts of Asia and Africa that represent untapped markets. The result, according to Hobson, is imperialism, defined as "the endeavour of the great controllers of industry to broaden the channel for the flow of their surplus wealth by seeking foreign markets and foreign investments to take off the goods and capital they cannot sell or use at home." For Hobson, such factors as the "spirit of adventure" or a "mission of civilization" are "clearly subordinate to the driving force of the economic factor."[113]

For Hobson, imperialism does not benefit the home country as a whole. Instead, selected groups such as industrialists, financiers, and the individuals who staff the colonial empires profit. Furthermore, because the flag follows trade, large military expenditures are required to protect the imperialist system. The drive for capitalist profits by securing overseas territories leads to competition and rivalry among European powers. Hence, imperialism is to Hobson a major cause of war, and Hobson suggests that capitalists may indeed profit from such conflicts.

---

[112] John A. Hobson, *Imperialism: A Study* (Ann Arbor: University of Michigan Press, 1965). All subsequent direct quotes are from this work.

[113] Nor is imperialism an irrational "objectless disposition on the part of a state to unlimited forcible expansion," as argued by Joseph Schumpeter. See his *Imperialism and Social Classes*, trans. Heinz Norden, ed. Paul M. Sweezy (Oxford, UK: Basil Blackwell, 1951), 6.

According to some analysts, imperialism is inevitable as everywhere there are excessive powers of production, excessive capital in search of investment appears. Hobson disagrees. It is the maldistribution of consuming power that prevents the absorption of goods and capital within a particular country. The solution, therefore, is to divert from the capitalists "their excess of income and make it flow, either to the workers in higher wages, or to the community in taxes." Either policy will increase domestic consumption and, as a result, "there will be no need to fight for foreign markets or foreign areas of investment." As for the "possessing classes," social reform will not "inflict upon them the real injury they dread." To the contrary, it is actually in their best interest in that the current use of surplus capital and goods forces "on their country a wrecking policy of Imperialism."

Lenin

The impact of Hobson's analysis can be seen in perhaps the most famous work in this genre, Vladimir Ilyich Lenin's *Imperialism: The Highest Stage of Capitalism* (1916). Writing during World War I, Lenin was interested in not only explaining the capitalist exploitation of lesser-developed countries but also the causes of war among advanced capitalist states. More important, he had the expressly political purpose of trying to convince Marxists that the time was ripe for revolutionary action.[114]

The result of Lenin's efforts is a highly influential theory of international political change. From Hobson, Lenin accepts the critical importance of under-consumption and overproduction as stimuli for the search for foreign markets and hence colonialism. From the German Social Democrat Rudolph Hilferding (1877–1941), Lenin adopts the argument that the critical feature of imperialism is not so much industrial capital, but rather finance capital. As Lenin concludes:

> Imperialism is capitalism at that stage of development at which the dominance of monopolies and finance capital is established; in which the export of capital has acquired pronounced importance; in which the division of the world among the international trusts has begun, in which the division of all territories of the globe among the biggest capitalist powers has been completed.[115]

Marx argues that the internal contradictions of capitalism and its inherently exploitive nature will eventually lead to working-class or proletarian revolutions. When the predicted revolutions failed to occur, the disciples of Marx attempted to explain what had happened. For Lenin, imperialism was the answer. Imperialism provided the European working class a taste of the spoils, the result of the exploitation of colonies, thus dampening proletarian discontent.

---

[114] "Lenin's concern was not to construct an abstract historiography of the development of capitalism: it was rather to convince all those who called themselves Marxists that the time had now arrived when revolutionary action to overthrow capitalism had become imperative." Neil Harding, *Lenin's Political Thought*, vol. 2 (Atlantic Highlands, NJ: Humanities Press, 1983), 69.

[115] V. I. Lenin, "Imperialism, The Highest Stage of Capitalism," in *The Lenin Anthology*, ed. Robert C. Tucker (New York: W. W. Norton, 1975), 244. All subsequent direct quotes are from this work.

But such a breathing space was not to last. Once the "whole world had been divided up, there was inevitably ushered in the era of monopoly possession of colonies." Then, there followed a "particularly intense struggle for the division and the redivision of the world." This struggle among capitalist states was intensified due to the continual, yet uneven growth of capitalism, which saw the rise of some states and the relative decline of others:

> The only conceivable basis under capitalism for the division of spheres of influence, interests, colonies, etc., is a calculation of the *strength* of those participating, their general economic, financial, military strength, etc. And the strength of these participants in the division does not change to an equal degree, for the *even* development of different undertakings, trusts, branches of industry, or countries is impossible under capitalism. Half a century ago Germany was a miserable, insignificant country, if her capitalist strength is compared with that of Britain of that time; Japan compared with Russia in the same way. Is it "conceivable" that in ten or twenty years' time the relative strength of the imperialist powers will have remained *un*changed? It is out of the question.

What Lenin posits, therefore, is a version of power transition theory (see chapter 5), albeit one that relies almost exclusively upon economic determinants at the expense of political factors. His emphasis on the exploitive nature of capitalism and its universality has contributed to the economic-structuralist image of international politics.

Reflections on Modern Thought Related to States and Capitalism

The writers we have discussed throughout most of this chapter were observing the development of a new world order—one marked politically by the emergence of states and economically by capitalism. These developments required a fundamental change in mindset from medieval notions of the essential unity of the heavenly and earthly orders. New concepts and ideas were introduced. For those writers associated with the realist and liberal traditions, states are understood as sovereign entities with no authority above them.

Greater attention was paid to analyzing the nature of international politics as opposed to viewing international conflict as stemming only from the nature of humanity or the nature of states and societies. In this new world, statecraft is recognized as the most important enterprise. How much opportunity there is for statesmen to influence events effectively (or how much is determined by the environment external to the state) is an important question still facing theorists and policy makers. But writers such as Immanuel Kant and the nineteenth-century liberals actually favor constraints such as republicanism and public opinion and their being placed on decision makers whose excess "voluntarism" was often viewed as a major cause of war.

For realists, power and power politics are seen as resulting, whether intended or not, in balances of power among states. For liberals and economic structuralists, markets and commercial relations are to be viewed as transcending national borders with important political consequences. For liberals, such economic transnationalism can have an integrating and pacifying effect on relations among states. By contrast, economic structuralists see the spread of capitalism as a destructive and exploitative process. These are powerful ideas with a long shelf life. Just as scholars debated these ideas during the years between World Wars I and II, the insights and observations offered by these writers remain with us to the present day, underpinning much of contemporary thinking and theorizing about international relations.

REFERENCES

Classic Works (various editions)

Clausewitz, Carl von. *On War.*

Grotius, Hugo. *The Law of War and Peace.*

Hobbes, Thomas. *Leviathan, The Citizen,* and *The History of the Peloponnesian War.*

Hobson, John. *Imperialism.*

Kant, Immanuel. *Perpetual Peace.*

Machiavelli, Niccolò. *The Prince, Discourses, Art of War,* and *History of Florence.*

Madison, James, Alexander Hamilton, and John Jay. *The Federalist Papers.*

Montesquieu. *The Spirit of the Laws.*

More, Thomas. *Utopia.*

Smith, Adam. *The Wealth of Nations.*

Weber, Max. *Economy and Society* and *The Protestant Ethic and the Spirit of Capitalism.*

Anthologies

Rousseau, Jean-Jacques. *Basic Political Writings.* Translated and edited by Donald A. Kress. Indianapolis, IN: Hackett Publishing, 1987.

Tucker, Robert C., ed. *The Lenin Anthology.* New York: W. W. Norton, 1975.

———, ed. *The Marx-Engels Reader.* New York: W. W. Norton, 1972.

Weber, Max. *From Max Weber: Essays in Sociology.* Edited and translated by H. H. Gerth and C. Wright Mills. New York: Oxford University Press, 1946.

Commentaries

Arendt, Hannah. *Lectures on Kant's Political Philosophy.* Edited by Ronald Beiner. Chicago: University of Chicago Press, 1982.

Hinsley, F. H. *Sovereignty.* London: C. A. Watts, 1966.

Lebow, Richard Ned, ed. *Max Weber and International Relations.* Cambridge, UK: Cambridge University Press, 2017.

PART II

IMAGES OF INTERNATIONAL RELATIONS THEORY

5

Realism: The State and Balance of Power

★ ★ ★

MAJOR ACTORS AND ASSUMPTIONS

Realism is an image and approach to international relations based on four principal *assumptions*. Scholars or policy makers who identify themselves as realists, of course, do not all perfectly match the realism ideal type. We find, however, that the four assumptions identified with this perspective are useful as a general statement of the main lines of realist thought and the basis on which hypotheses and theories are developed.

First, states are the principal or most important actors in an anarchical world lacking central legitimate governance. States represent the key unit of analysis, whether one is dealing with ancient Greek city-states or modern nation-states. The study of international relations is the study of relations among these units, particularly major powers as they shape world politics and engage in war, armed interventions, and economic and other actions. Realists who use the concept of *system* usually refer to an *international system* of states.

What of nonstate actors? International organizations such as the United Nations may aspire to the status of independent actor, but from the realist perspective, this aspiration has not in fact been achieved to any significant degree. Realists tend to see international organizations as doing no more than their member states direct. Multinational corporations, terrorist groups, and other transnational and nongovernmental organizations are frequently acknowledged by realists, but the position of these nonstate actors is always one of lesser importance. Individuals also receive less acclaim outside of their governmental roles. For realists, states remain the dominant actors.

Second, the state is viewed as a unitary actor. For purposes of theory building and analysis, many realists view the state as being encapsulated by a metaphorical hard shell or opaque, black box. We need not look much inside this shell or black box that figuratively contains domestic actions and interactions among diverse state and nonstate actors. Realists portray the state as an integrated unit facing the outside world. Indeed, a common assumption associated with realist thought is that political differences within the state are ultimately resolved authoritatively such that the government of the state speaks with one voice for the state as a whole. The state is a unitary actor in that it is usually assumed by realists to have one policy at any given time on any particular issue. To be sure, exceptions occur, but to the realists these are exceptions that demonstrate the general rule and support the idea of the state as an integrated, unitary actor.

Even in those exceptional cases in which, for example, a foreign ministry expresses views different from positions taken by the same country's defense ministry, corrective action is taken in an attempt to bring these alternative views to a common and authoritative statement of policy. "End-running" of state authorities by bureaucratic and nongovernmental, domestic, and transnational actors is also possible, but it occurs unchecked by state authorities in only those issues in which the stakes are relatively low. From the realist perspective, if the issues are important enough, higher authorities will intervene to preclude bureaucratic end-running or action by nongovernmental actors that are contrary to centrally directed state policy. In this regard, governments are merely the agents of states.

Third, given this emphasis on the unitary state-as-actor, realists usually make the further assumption for theory-building that the state is essentially a *rational* (or purposive) actor. A rational foreign policy decision-making process would include a statement of objectives, consideration of all feasible alternatives in terms of existing capabilities available to the state, the relative likelihood of attaining these objectives by the various alternatives under consideration, and the benefits or costs associated with each alternative. Following this rational process, governmental decision makers select the alternative that maximizes utility (maximizing benefit or minimizing cost associated with attaining the objectives sought) or at least achieves an acceptable outcome. The result is a rank ordering of policy preferences among viable alternatives.

As a practical matter, the realist is aware of the difficulties in viewing the state as a rational actor. Governmental decision makers may not have all the factual information or knowledge of cause and effect they need to make value-maximizing decisions. The process may well be clouded by considerable uncertainty as decision makers grope for the best solution or approach to an issue. They also have to deal with the problem of human bias and misperception that may lead them astray. In any event, the choice made—if not always the best or value-maximizing choice in fact—is at least perceived to be a satisfactory one. It is a *satisficing* or suboptimal choice—less than a value-maximizing choice— but still good enough in terms of the objectives sought. The assumption of the unitary, rational actor is particularly important in the application of *game theory* and other rational-choice methods to deterrence, arms control, balance of power, the use of force, economic advantage, and other studies of interest to realists.

Fourth, realists assume that within the hierarchy of issues facing the state, national or international security usually tops the list. Military and related political issues dominate world politics. A realist focuses on actual or potential conflict between state actors and the use of force, examining how international stability is attained or maintained, how it breaks down, the utility of force as a means to resolve disputes, and the prevention of any violation of its territorial integrity. Economic matters are important to the extent that they contribute to the power or relative power of the state.

Given the state's objectives, goals, or purposes in terms of security, it seeks and uses *power* (commonly understood in material terms as capabilities relative to other states), which is a key concept to realists as is the *balance of power* among states. The *structural realist* (or neorealist) puts particular emphasis on the security implications of the distribution of power (or underlying structure) of the international system of states: unipolar (one great power), bipolar (two great powers), or multipolar (three or more great powers).

States use the power they have to serve their interests or achieve their objectives. To most realists, the struggle for (or use of) power among states is at the core of international relations. In the words of Hans J. Morgenthau: "International politics, like all politics, is a struggle for power. Whatever the ultimate aims of international politics, power is always the immediate aim or means to an end."[1]

Further comment is necessary concerning assumptions two and three. The important point is that from the standpoint of methodology, the image of a unified, rational state is truly an assumption, not a description of the actual world. Realists who embrace positivism use such assumptions to build theories, not describe reality. Assumptions should be viewed not in terms of descriptive accuracy, but rather in terms of how fruitful they are in generating insights and valid generalizations about international politics. From this point of view, assumptions are neither true nor false; they are more or less useful in helping the theorist derive testable propositions or hypotheses about international relations.

Once hypotheses are developed, they are tested against the real world. The image of the unified, rational state is, therefore, the starting point for realist analysis, not a concluding statement. This is true whether one is a *classical realist* emphasizing the impact of history, international law, and actions taken by political leaders or a more recent structural or neorealist who believes the basis for a theory of international relations has to have at its core an understanding of the distribution of capabilities among states, particularly great powers.

Morgenthau, a classical realist, explains the utility of the rational, unitary actor assumption as follows:

> We put ourselves in the position of a statesman who must meet a certain problem of foreign policy under certain circumstances, and we ask ourselves what the rational alternatives are from which a statesman may choose . . . and which of these rational alternatives this particular statesman, acting under these circumstances, is likely to choose. It is the testing of this rational hypothesis against the actual facts and their consequences that gives meaning to the facts of international politics and makes a theory of politics possible.[2]

---

[1] Hans J. Morgenthau, *Politics among Nations*, 4th ed. (New York: Knopf, 1966), 25.
[2] Morgenthau, *Politics among Nations*, 5. On these assumptions, see James D. Fearon, "Rationalist Explanations for War," *International Organization* 49, no. 3 (1995): 379–414.

The point is that neorealist theorizing that focuses primarily on material structure (the distribution of power or capabilities) as the principal explanatory variable depends on the same rationalist assumptions of classical realists. This occurs even though classical realists are more likely to accept such nonmaterial factors as ideas or norms as part of the theories they develop as well as the possible important role played by individual state leaders.

Game theory is a realist example of the use of such simplifying assumptions as an aid to developing hypotheses and theories about the causes of various international political phenomena. Many works on deterrence and *coercive diplomacy* (or compellence) also use the rational, unitary actor assumptions as do other explanations of international conflict. The rationality assumption is similarly central to *expected utility* models of international politics. These and similar formulations comprise rational-choice theorizing. Not confined to realism, rational choice is also part of theorizing associated with the liberal (particularly neoliberal institutionalist) image discussed in the next chapter.

As an image of politics, then, realism focuses on power and power politics among states. Neorealists such as Kenneth N. Waltz, John J. Mearsheimer, and Christopher Layne emphasize the overall distribution of power among states and are highly skeptical of the extent to which international norms and international institutions can ameliorate competition among states. Classical realists such as Morgenthau (1904–1980), E. H. Carr (1892–1982), and Arnold Wolfers (1892–1968) and their present-day followers—sometimes referred to as *neoclassical realists*—have had a more inclusive approach.[3]

While recognizing the importance of the balance of power, they also have argued for the serious consideration of how factors at the domestic or societal level of analysis influence international relations. Possible factors include the impact of leaders, whether a state is revisionist or status quo oriented as well as the role of *norms* and institutions. Hence, as with other images discussed in this book, adherence to basic realist assumptions can still result in different interpretations and theoretical applications based on these assumptions.

INTELLECTUAL PRECURSORS AND INFLUENCES

Where did these assumptions of current realist thought come from? They obviously did not appear out of thin air following World War II, the Cold War, or in recent decades. Rather, they represent the culmination of thinking about international relations over the millennia. We identify here some of the more notable intellectual precursors who have had a significant impact on the writings of contemporary realists. Much greater detail is provided in part I in the intellectual roots of IR theory. We then discuss several twentieth- and twenty-first-century writers in the realist tradition and how realism has informed their approach to theory-building.

---

[3] Gideon Rose introduced the term in his "Review: Neoclassical Realism and Theories of Foreign Policy," *World Politics* 51, no. 1 (October 1998): 144–72.

Thucydides (472–400 BCE) is usually credited with being the first writer in the realist tradition as well as the founding father of the IR discipline. Anyone who has taken a class in political philosophy would probably agree that the profound insights of many ancient Greek writers are not easily grasped on first reading. One might initially find this less a problem with Thucydides's *History of the Peloponnesian War* because this famous work chronicles twenty-one of the twenty-eight years of war between Athens and Sparta (and their respective allies) in the fifth century BCE. Taken simply as history, it is a masterful account of this era, filled with tales of heroism and brutality, victory and defeat, brilliance and stupidity, honor and deceit. These human traits are certainly exhibited not only in one particular war but also in wars throughout the ages. This is what makes the work such a classic.

The task Thucydides set for himself, however, was much more ambitious than simply describing what was occurring. Particular events are dealt with in great and vivid detail, but his goal is to say something significant not only about the events of his own time but also about the nature of war and why it continually recurs. For Thucydides, the past was the guide for the future. He is less interested in the immediate causes of the Peloponnesian War than he is in the underlying forces at work. Leaders might point to a particular event to justify a policy, but for Thucydides this simply obscures more profound factors that operate throughout history, such as his famous trinity of fear, honor, and interest, a typology that is hard to improve upon. At heart, for realists *History of the Peloponnesian War* is a study of the struggle for military and political power.

By his admission, the Italian political philosopher Niccolò Machiavelli (1469–1527) draws heavily from his study of ancient, especially Roman, writings. In some respects, the situation in fifteenth- and sixteenth-century Italy, divided as the peninsula was into separate city-states, was similar to the Hellenic world of Thucydides. Machiavelli worked as a civil servant and diplomat until the Republic of Florence fell in 1512. Thought to be a republican counterrevolutionary opposed to the aristocratic Medici family that had assumed power in Florence (as well as in Rome), he was tortured by their interrogators. During his subsequent enforced idleness at his family farm south of Florence, he put his time to good use by reflecting on the chaos and political instability among the Italian city-states.

Like Thucydides, Machiavelli writes of the importance of personality in politics, power, the balance of power, the formation of alliances, and the causes of conflict between different city-states. His primary focus, however, is on what present-day writers refer to as national security. For Machiavelli, survival of the state (identified with the ruling prince) is paramount. The prince can lose his state by not coping effectively with both internal and external threats to his rule. The German term *Realpolitik*, so central to realist thought, refers to power and power politics among states. Machiavelli's most famous work, *The Prince*, is a practical manual on how to gain, maintain, expand, and lose power.

The political philosophy of the Englishman Thomas Hobbes (1588–1679) was developed during the first fifty turbulent years of the seventeenth century. For three years, he tutored the son of Charles I, the latter eventually being executed in 1649 during the English civil war. After publishing his famous work *Leviathan*, Hobbes returned to England (from France where he had fled in 1640) in 1651, pledging loyalty to the newly established republican or parliamentary regime. Indeed, marking the end of divine right of kings, *Leviathan*—the first general theory of politics in English—provided that either a monarch or an assembly (i.e., parliament) could be tasked by the people to assure their security as the primary responsibility of government.

Like Machiavelli and Thucydides, Hobbes has a pessimistic view of human nature. His primary focus in *Leviathan* is domestic politics, and his goal is to make the strongest case possible for the necessity of a powerful, centralized political authority. To illustrate his philosophical points, Hobbes posits that before the creation of society, human beings lived in a "state of nature"—a condition of war of "every one against every one." There is in this state of war "a continual fear and danger of violent death; and the life of man, solitary, poor, nasty, brutish, and short."

Hobbes does not argue that such a state of nature had ever really existed. To him, the state of nature is the result of a thought experiment: imagining what the world would be like without governmental authority or any other social structure. Accordingly, he is interested in showing how people can escape from this hypothetical situation—a state of war of everyone against everyone else—by agreeing to place all power in the hands of a sovereign or leviathan (a supreme ruler, either a monarch or parliament) that would end the anarchy of the state of nature, using power to maintain order so essential to daily life.

Hobbes's impact on the realist view of international relations stems from an image of states as if they were individuals in a mythical state of nature. Although his focus in *Leviathan* is on domestic societies, his observations are also relevant to international politics and have had a major impact on realism, particularly his assessment of why conflict and violence between individuals or states are to be expected. In the absence of a sovereign or central, superordinate authority, the anarchic world described by Hobbes is a rather dismal one.

Although the impact of Hugo Grotius (1583–1645)—a Dutch contemporary of Hobbes—is part of the classical-realist literature, it is also related to both the liberal and English School images. Known as the father of international law, Grotius introduces the consideration of norms or rules that states follow in their enlightened self-interest—a perspective found in both classical and neoclassical realism. Liberal or neoliberal institutionalists and writers in the English School discussed in subsequent chapters also draw from Grotian understandings.

Carl von Clausewitz (1780–1831), a Prussian officer who rose to the rank of general and who served in the Napoleonic wars, thinks the military element of a state's power to be extremely important but subordinate always to the political. Consistent with the writings of Machiavelli on war, Clausewitz argues in an often-quoted phrase that war is "a continuation of political activity by other means." War or the use of force, implemented by the resourceful commander in the field, is thus a means that policy makers may choose rationally to accomplish their state objectives; it decidedly is not an end in itself. This formulation is reflected in realist conceptions of power and its use.

Writing in a Chinese cultural context and in an earlier historical period, Sun Tzu (about 544–496 BCE) addresses the ways and means of warfare. The experiences of militaries of states and empires in nineteenth-century Europe and those among ancient Chinese militaries leads Clausewitz and Sun Tzu to draw similar conclusions. Much as Clausewitz does, Sun Tzu puts a premium on the mental capacity of commanders—their cleverness and adaptability to changing circumstances, reliance on intelligence, knowing when to fight and when not to do so, how to think strategically as in maximizing advantage regardless of whether or not one's side has superior numbers, and similar calculations.

Particularly noteworthy is Sun Tzu's claim that the best approach to achieving objectives might not involve combat. Superiority in command is achieving objectives without fighting at all. It is Sun Tzu's understanding of the high costs of warfare in both lives and treasure that rationally informs his preference to avoid the use of force when objectives can be achieved by other means.

Geopolitical Writers

Geopolitics—that a state's (or empire's) geographic location or the territory it controls (or seeks to control) has significant political implications—is a branch of realism that fell into disfavor during World War II and in the post-war years, but variations of geopolitical understandings return from time to time in the minds of policy makers. Overthrowing the Saddam Hussein regime in Iraq in 2003 was seen by some geopolitical advocates as a strategic move to assure American dominance of the region, despite how poorly this policy unfolded. Indeed, from this geopolitical perspective, Iraq was at the top of the Persian (or Arab) Gulf oil-export lanes, flanked by Iran and Pakistan to the east and Saudi Arabia and Syria to the south and west, respectively. More recently, Russia's invasion of neighboring Ukraine in February 2022 was justified, in part, by Vladimir Putin based on geography and his claim that Ukraine was increasingly turning to the West.

The American naval strategist Alford Thayer Mahan (1840–1914) observes how command of the seas was central to British imperial power. He argues the United States could (and did) emulate the British in the twentieth century beginning with President Theodore Roosevelt's pledge to build an American fleet that could circle the globe. This is to be seen not as a challenge to the United Kingdom's Royal Navy, but rather as a basis for the extension of American power and influence, particularly to Asia and the Pacific. This perspective remains part of US Navy thinking and is reflected in such present-day realist writings as the "offshore balancing" grand strategy proposal.[4]

The British geographer Sir Halford Mackinder (1861–1947) takes a different approach, focusing on control of land areas. Mackinder declares in his 1904 paper ("The Geopolitical Pivot of History") that "who rules Eastern Europe

---

[4] See, for example, Christopher Layne, "From Preponderance to Offshore Balancing: America's Future Grand Strategy," *International Security* 22, no. 1 (Summer 1997): 86–124; Stephen M. Walt, *The Hell of Good Intentions: America's Foreign Policy Elite and the Decline of U.S. Primacy* (New York: Farrar, Straus and Giroux, 2018).

commands the heartland, who rules the heartland commands the world island [Eurasia], who rules the world island commands the world." Nicholas J. Spykman (1893–1943), a Yale political scientist, modifies Mackinder's argument, defining the "heartland" as the core within the Eurasian land mass, but not including the sea coast areas, which he calls the "rimland," that extended to south and southeast Asia and all of Araby in the Middle East. Put in political terms, controlling the rimland was key to preventing dominance by any heartland power. For Spykman, "Who controls the rimland rules Eurasia" and "who rules Eurasia controls the destinies of the world."

This understanding became a geopolitical basis for the Cold War containment doctrine advanced by George Kennan[5]—keeping the Soviet Union within its borders by pursuing a policy of balance-of-power alliances that surrounded and thus contained the USSR (and China after the communist revolution there in 1949). In geopolitical terms, both countries controlled the eastern rimland, but neither had control of the southern or western rimland of the Eurasian "world island."

Germany's failed effort to control the Eurasian "heartland" was an application of geopolitical thought influenced by the German Friedrich Ratzel (1844–1904) who racialized the concept by writing of *Lebensraum*—"living space"—later defined by National Socialists under Adolf Hitler as land in Eurasia required by the Aryan "master race" to thrive. Defeat of Germany in World War II not surprisingly was accompanied by the rejection of such thinking, which also discredited the geopolitical enterprise as a whole.

Mid-Twentieth-Century Writers

Many students of international relations consider Edward Hallett Carr's *The Twenty Years' Crisis, 1919–1939* a classic. Although Carr (1892–1982) can be viewed as an intellectual precursor for realists and a forerunner of the present-day English School, his work transcends narrow classification in that he has also been influential, as has Grotius, on the thinking of certain authors whom we would label liberals or neoliberal institutionalists discussed in the next chapter.

The writings of Thucydides, Machiavelli, Hobbes, Grotius, and Clausewitz illustrate how great works are often written during the most difficult times. *The Twenty Years' Crisis* is no exception in that it was completed in the summer of 1939 with the shadow of war looming over Europe. As with other authors we have discussed, Carr is less interested in apportioning blame to particular leaders for the imminent onset of World War II than he is in attempting "to analyse the underlying and significant, rather than the immediate and personal, causes

---

[5] Although US State Department official George Kennan (1904–2005), the generally recognized author of the US containment doctrine, does not explicitly use this geopolitical rationale in developing the doctrine, it was part of the thinking of many policy makers in the 1940s and 1950s. See "The Long Telegram" Kennan sent from Moscow in 1946 and his anonymous "X" article on "The Sources of Soviet Conduct," *Foreign Affairs* (July 1947). Kennan was a friend of Morgenthau who hosted Kennan's series of lectures at the University of Chicago, which were foundational to Kennan's *American Diplomacy: 1900–1950* (New York: New American Library, 1962). See William E. Scheuerman, *Hans Morgenthau: Realism and Beyond* (Cambridge, UK: Polity Press, 2009), 90.

of the disaster." Unless this were done, he argues, we will fail to understand how war could break out twenty short years after the signing of the Versailles Treaty in 1919. He dedicated his book "to the makers of the coming peace." In attempting to understand the more profound causes of the contemporary international crisis, echoes of Thucydides can be discerned. Carr, for example, places a great deal of emphasis on the role of fear in explaining World War I.

Throughout *The Twenty Years' Crisis*, Carr refers to the impact of Machiavelli and Hobbes on realist thinking. Although his work is best known as a critique of utopian or idealist thought, which dominated the fledgling discipline of international relations after World War I, Carr also challenges the more extreme versions of realism that posit the divorce of morality from politics in international relations. He argues that sound political thought must be based on elements of both utopia (i.e., values) and reality (i.e., power). Where utopianism has become a "hollow and intolerable sham," serving merely as a disguise for the privileged, the realist provides a service in exposing it. Pure realism, on the other hand, can offer nothing but "a naked struggle for power which makes any kind of international society impossible." Hence, for Carr, politics is made up of two elements, inextricably intertwined: utopia and reality—values and power.

Consistent with classical-realist understandings that go beyond just power and interest, more than a third of the book is devoted to such Grotian topics as the role of morality in international relations, the foundations of law, the sanctity of treaties, the judicial settlement of international disputes, peaceful change, and the prospects for a new international order. Because Carr critically assessed the strengths and weaknesses of utopianism as well as realism, he can be viewed as an important influence on many contemporary IR theorists. Particularly given his insightful critique of proposed liberal solutions to the problems of recreating international order following World War I, Carr remains relevant to the post–Cold War era given China's rise and Russia's reassertion of power.

Born in the same year as Carr, the American theologian Reinhold Niebuhr (1892–1971) is an example of the kind of utopian or idealist Carr describes. His Christianity, informed by the horrors of World War I, made Niebuhr a pacifist during the interwar period. Misgivings about his idealism as ineffectual for dealing with real-world problems led him to adopt a "Christian realist" perspective. The absence of an effective, power-based challenge to the rise of national socialism and fascism underscored Niebuhr's abandonment of his pacifist sentiments and his embrace of realism combined with moral understandings—precisely the same conclusion is drawn in Carr's secular argument on the essential relation between values and power.[6]

Hans J. Morgenthau (1904–1980) remains one of the most influential IR theorists. In many ways he exemplifies those classical realists who came before

---

[6] See his *Moral Man and Immoral Society: A Study of Ethics and Politics* (New York: Charles Scribner's Sons, 1932). See also Niebuhr's *The Nature and Destiny of Man: A Christian Perspective* (Louisville, KY: Westminster John Knox Press, 1943, 1996) and *The Irony of American History* (Chicago: University of Chicago Press, 1952, 2008). For an anthology drawn from his principal writings, see Elizabeth Sifton, ed., *Reinhold Niebuhr: Major Works on Religion and Politics* (New York: Library of America, 2015).

him due to his emphasis on a holistic approach to international relations that encompasses all the levels of analysis to include the impact of human nature, the blurring of the distinction between society and the international system, and a concern for justice.[7] Born in Germany to a Jewish family, Morgenthau fled to the United States when the Nazis came to power. While he was a professor at the University of Chicago, he published his 1948 book *Politics among Nations*, which has been viewed by some as a tutorial for post–World War II American policy makers who now lead a country of preeminent international power and that no longer could seriously contemplate isolationism from the rest of the world.

Morgenthau posits six principles of political realism: (1) "politics, like society in general, is governed by objective laws that have their roots in human nature"; (2) in international politics, "interest [is] defined in terms of power"; (3) interest defined as power is not endowed with a meaning that is fixed once and for all: "the kind of interest determining political action depends on the political and cultural context within which foreign policy is formulated"; (4) there is "tension between the moral command and the requirements of successful political action," but that, as a practical matter, "universal moral principles . . . must be filtered through the concrete circumstances of time and place"; (5) "political realism refuses to identify the moral aspirations of a particular nation [such as the United States] with the moral laws that govern the universe"; and (6) "interest defined as power" is an understanding that gives international politics a separate standing and thus emancipates it from other fields of study.[8] Following this perspective, some scholars give Morgenthau credit, among others, for helping establish the legitimacy of international relations as a separate discipline within political science—and not just a part of history, international law, or philosophy. Yet he also made the point that "the essence of international politics is identical with its domestic counterpart. Both domestic and international politics are a struggle for power. . . . The tendency to dominate, in particular, is an element of all human associations."[9]

Not unlike Thucydides and other ancient Greeks, Morgenthau had essentially a tragic view of international relations. While he may have developed the above precepts to help guide decision makers through the rocky shoals and dangers of international relations, he realized all too well that history is replete with examples where individuals and the states they represented made a grab for international domination—alliances and balances of power failed to keep the peace. The temptation to overturn existing power arrangements and norms of international conduct strongly pulled at leaders whether of ancient Athens, Rome, absolutist France in the Napoleonic period, Imperial Germany, or Hitler's Third Reich.

---

[7] For an intellectual biography that deals with his ideas on realism, morality and power, the national interest, nuclear weapons, and the Vietnam War, see Scheuerman, *Hans Morgenthau: Realism and Beyond*, op. cit.

[8] Morgenthau, *Politics among Nations*, 4–11.

[9] Morgenthau, *Politics among Nations*, 32.

Much as Carr had done, John H. Herz (1908–2005)—a Düsseldorf-born American professor—offers a more nuanced view on the way values, not just raw power, influence the conduct of international relations. The synthesis he posits between power and values—what he calls "realist liberalism"—earns him the label of being an idealist internationalist.[10] One still can achieve ideals in a world of power politics. Notwithstanding raw power calculations, compliance with international law also may be in the enlightened self-interest of states. It is the stuff of classical realism that incorporated both power and values or aspirations.

The *security dilemma* arises from military or other measures taken by states to compete that lead to countermeasures taken by adversaries. As a consequence of this action-reaction behavior, neither side advances its security. Actions taken by one side threaten the opponent and lead to a response in kind that undermines the security of one's side.

In a debate with his fellow realist and friend, Hans J. Morgenthau, at the 1980 International Studies Association meeting in Los Angeles, Herz articulates his universalist vision. In an article published subsequently, he clarifies how his perspective is consistent with realist understandings: "I have tried to keep my approach equidistant from a utopianism that would substitute world authority for the nation-state system from a superrealism that denies the feasibility of any internationalist policy altogether." In this regard, he argues that states could take on difficult global challenges that he identifies as including "population pressure, resources depletion, environmental destruction, and, last but not least, armament races and nuclear superarmament."[11]

This brief overview of some of the intellectual precursors of contemporary realism illustrates a distinct realist preoccupation with armed conflict or war. A concern with the causes and consequences of conflict helps to explain why the realist perspective is held widely by policy makers throughout the world: Over the centuries, leaders have engaged in the very battles and struggles described by authors from Thucydides to Morgenthau. Realism, from the statesman's point of view, is indeed realistic as it tends to correspond to historical understandings and personal experiences both in diplomacy and in war.

Among realists, two basic concepts traditionally have been the foci of analysis at the state and international levels: power and system in which states are the principal actors. In the following pages, we discuss how realists have attempted to define these terms. We then give examples of how theorists have used these concepts in generating insights and explanations of the causes of war. This is followed by a discussion of how realists deal with the concepts of globalization, interdependence, and change. We conclude with a critique of the realist image of international relations.

---

[10] See his classic *Political Realism and Political Idealism* (Chicago: University of Chicago Press, 1951). For an interesting "dialogue" constructed as if it were between Herz and a present-day political scientist, see Andrew Lawrence, "Interview with John Herz," *The Return of the Theorists*, ed. Richard Ned Lebow et al. (New York: Palgrave Macmillan, 2016), 254–62.

[11] "Political Realism Revisited," *International Studies Quarterly* 25, no. 2 (June 1981): 182–97. One of us (Viotti) had the good fortune to witness the Morgenthau-Herz debate.

POWER

Definitions

In our discussion of several of the more important intellectual precursors of realism, the concept of *power* was mentioned time and again. Any attempt to give the reader a more complete understanding of the realist image of international relations starts with a discussion of this crucial term. Power is *the* core concept for realists.

Having said this, it is rather ironic that even among realists, there is no clear consensus on how to define the term. Some realists understand power to be the sum of military, economic, technological, diplomatic, and other capabilities at the disposal of the state. Others see power not as some absolute value determined for each state as if it were in a vacuum but, rather, as capabilities relative to the capabilities of other states. Thus, the power of the United States is evaluated in terms of its capabilities compared to the capabilities of other states.

Both of these definitions—whether treating capabilities of a state in isolation or relative to the capabilities of other states—are termed a materialist view. Both also assume a static view of power: It is an attribute of the state that is the sum of its capabilities whether considered alone or relative to other states.

An alternative, dynamic definition of power focuses on the interactions of states. A state's influence (or capacity to influence or coerce) is not only determined by its capabilities (or relative capabilities) but also by (1) its willingness (and perceptions by other states of its willingness) to use these capabilities and (2) its control or influence over other states. Power can thus be inferred by observing the behavior of states as they interact. The relative power of states is most clearly revealed by the outcomes of their interactions.

Examples of diverse views of power are the following definitions drawn from the literature: power as the capacity of an individual, group, or nation "to influence the behavior of others in accordance with one's own ends"; power as "control over the minds and actions of others"; and power as "the ability to prevail in conflict and overcome obstacles." For his part, Joseph Nye differentiates between *hard power* as in economic or military capabilities, and the *soft power* that comes, for example, from cultural dimensions or the values that define the identity and practices of a state. This would include the diplomatic capacity to influence other states bilaterally or multilaterally in international organizational contexts.[12] Whether the power of states, like money, is *fungible* and can readily be transferred from one issue area to another is a point of some dispute among IR theorists.

Soft power involves attracting others to your agenda in world politics and not just relying on carrots and sticks, which entails getting others to want what you want. Combining hard and soft power assets effectively is essential to attaining national objectives and affecting the behavior of others. Soft power

---

[12] Joseph Nye's ideas on power occur in a number of his publications. See, for example, an early statement in "Hard and Soft Power in American Foreign Policy," *Paradox of American Power* (Oxford: Oxford University Press, 2002), 4–17.

becomes manifest in international institutions (listening to others) and in foreign policy (promoting peace and human rights).

An advocate of multilateralism, Nye sees sustaining American power as dependent upon strategic restraint, reassuring partners, and avoiding a unilateral and arrogant foreign policy. Consistent with classical realism as well as theorists working within the liberal image of international relations, Nye's argument addresses the ideational, not just the material dimensions of power. He also focuses on the limits of balance-of-power and hegemonic power theories as applied to the United States.

Seeing power as having different dimensions was how one of Nye's mentors at Harvard, Stanley Hoffmann (1928–2015) sees it. Hoffmann—himself a student of the French realist Raymond Aaron (1905–1983)—used the metaphor of economic, military, diplomatic, and other "chessboards" to capture these different dimensions affecting the way different states applied their power. Others, like Kenneth N. Waltz (1924–2013), prefer not to dissect power in this fashion, but rather to view it as an integral concept that states apply in different ways in the pursuit of their objectives in international relations.

Measurement

Given these definitional and conceptual disputes, it follows that attempts to measure power will also be divergent for those hoping to apply scientific standards to their work. First, if one understands power as being equivalent to capabilities, one looks for some way to measure military, economic, and other component elements. Even if one assumes that it is possible to measure these capabilities adequately through such indicators as defense expenditures or gross national product, the further problem remains of aggregating or adding up such diverse capabilities into a common measure of power. How can one combine different component capabilities that use different measures such as dollars spent on defense expenditures as opposed to overall gross national product? Even more challenging is how does one measure geographic, technological, or diplomatic factors with any degree of precision? What about the unity and strength of a society? The type of political regime? What is the metric? And, if capabilities are difficult to measure, are not relative capabilities between and among states even more difficult to specify?

The approach used by Waltz to bridge this gap was to use measures of economic size—gross national (or gross domestic) product as an indicator of a state's overall power. Indeed, military capabilities are dependent on the availability of economic resources, available technologies, and political decisions to allocate these resources to developing armed forces. Left out of these economic and military components are the soft power elements such as cultural, diplomatic, and other, less tangible, assets.

Second, some would say that the view of power as a unitary concept calculated by aggregating component capabilities or relative capabilities misses the key point, which is that the power of a state is dependent on the issue involved. Consider, for example, this argument: Some states, such as Japan, have substantial economic power but are militarily weak. Hence, in a particular area, the Japanese are powerful. Conceiving world politics in terms of separate issue areas—Hoffmann's alternative "chessboards" or Nye's soft and hard power—fits with the observation that use of power by states varies by issue area.[13]

Opponents of this disaggregation of power into its component capabilities note that persuasive as it may be on the surface, it is misleading because it overlooks the relations among the various power components. Thus, the economic capabilities of Japan as a global trader are said to be related to its military ties with the United States that assure Japan's freedom to engage in commerce. From this perspective, whether addressing the power of Japan, China, or European or other countries, one cannot understand economic, military, political, or other component capabilities of power as if they are factors independent of one another. Much as military ties and divisions among states may define the framework within which economic relations take place, military capabilities of states are bolstered (or weakened) by the strength or relative strength of their economies. Indeed, military capabilities depend upon underlying economic and technological capabilities.

SYSTEM

In the preceding section, we discussed the concept of power and attempts to measure state power. Using that discussion as a basis, we now move on to a discussion of the concept of system. Not all realists portray relations among states in systemic terms, but some (particularly neo- or structural realists) do. When applied to international relations, the term *system* has currency within each of the four images we have identified—realism, liberalism, economic structuralism, and the English School. As one might expect, however, there is considerable diversity among theorists on both the definition of the term and the uses to which it should be put in the construction of IR theory.

Scholars who understand system to be the set of interactions among states operate from a positivist behavioral methodology. This approach was dominant in the 1960s and 1970s as efforts were made to count, track, and code interactions among states in the hope of identifying patterns of conflict and cooperation. Journals such as *International Studies Quarterly* continue to publish research in this tradition, emphasizing studies that attempt to draw meaning from aggregate numbers and data sets that are amenable to probability and statistical analyses, causal modeling, and the development of mathematical equations that capture what we observe in the relations among states.

For more than forty years, however, realist scholars identified as structural or neorealists have argued that counting interactions has provided limited insights into international relations. A more useful starting point, they argue, is the various distributions of power or capabilities among states—unipolar, bipolar, multipolar. The polarity of the system is measured by the number of major powers, and different polarities will have different effects on international

---

[13] Stanley Hoffmann, "Weighing the Balance of Power," *Foreign Affairs* 50, no. 4 (July 1972): 618–43.

relations, including interactions among states (discussed in greater detail later in this chapter).

However system may be defined, the uses to which the concept is put vary considerably. Some theorists are content to use systems merely as taxonomies or frameworks for organizing knowledge about international relations. Hence, one can speak of the international political system, the international economic system, or the international social system. Systems are therefore mental images that may help to describe international phenomena. They are, in effect, super-imposed on the real world by a scholar to make the real world more intelligible or somewhat easier to understand.

Others are more ambitious and use the system concept to explain and predict outcomes of international relations. In the process of theory building, they may ascribe to systems such properties as *equilibrium*, or balance, of their component parts (e.g., among states). Critics, however, find little use in such notions as balancing or "equilibrating tendencies" allegedly to be found in a system of states. The approach of treating a system as if it were a concrete or tangible entity and ascribing properties to it is of questionable validity from this point of view. To do so, according to critics, is to be guilty of the methodological error of *reification*—treating abstractions as if they are real and have a life of their own.

A response by some system theorists to this line of criticism is that dealing in abstractions is useful in the generation of propositions or hypotheses about international relations. These, in turn, can be tested empirically to determine whether or not they have factual support. To the extent, then, that use of the systems concept enables the theorist to describe, explain, or predict international phenomena, the use of the concept is justified.

The reader may or may not wish to visualize international relations or world politics as a system that is defined in terms of patterns of interactions, polarity, equilibrating tendencies, or some other characteristics. Some may share the English School preference for seeing international or global politics as actually occurring in a societal (rather than in a seemingly more mechanical, systemic) context. We do note, however, that the systems concept as an approximation to the nature of world politics is present within the mainstream of contemporary realist thought, even if some (particularly classical) realists avoid its use.

Speaking of abstractions, we admit this discussion has been rather abstract. To lend substance to the concept of system, we next examine how the concept of system has been used by some realists: system as anarchy plus the distribution of capabilities. Scholars have intended to explain some aspect of international relations concerning such matters as instability, conflict, and war. In keeping with realist assumptions, the state and state power have been a key focus of analysis and investigation, so too has the analytical assumption of rationality.

Game Theory and Anarchy

Game theory is an approach to determining rational choice or optimum strategy in a competitive situation. Each actor tries to maximize gains or minimize losses under conditions of uncertainty and incomplete information, which require each actor to rank order preferences, estimate probabilities, and try to discern what the other actor is going to do. In a two-person zero-sum game, when one competitor wins, the other loses. In a two-person, non-zero-sum or variable-sum game, gains and losses are not necessarily equal; possibly, both sides may gain. This is sometimes referred to as a positive-sum game. In some games, both parties can lose, and by different amounts or to a different degree. So-called *n-person games* include more than two actors or sides. Game theory has contributed to the development of models of deterrence and arms race spirals, but it is also the basis for work concerning the question of how collaboration among competitive states can be achieved: The central problem is that the rational decision for an individual actor such as a state may be to "defect" and go it alone as opposed to taking a chance on collaboration with another state actor.

For many realist writers, game theory is highly relevant to understanding international relations due to the realist emphasis on the conditions of anarchy and the distribution of capabilities or power among states. These so-called system-level structural attributes are viewed as crucial because they act as constraints on decision makers. As we will see, the condition of international anarchy is seen by realists as contributing to the amount of distrust and conflict among states. Realists have also been concerned about whether particular distributions of capabilities involving various balances of power make war between states more or less likely. We will first take up the concept of anarchy and related terms.

The word *anarchy* brings forth images of violence, destruction, and chaos. For realists, however, anarchy simply refers to the absence of any legitimate authority above states. States are sovereign. They claim a right externally to be independent or autonomous from other states, and they claim a right internally or domestically to exercise complete authority over their territories. Although states differ in terms of the power they possess or can exercise, none may claim the right to dominate another sovereign state.

Realists distinguish between authority and power. When they use the term anarchy, they are referring to the absence of any hierarchy of legitimate authority in the international system. There *is* hierarchy of power in international politics, but there is not a hierarchy of authority. Some states are more powerful than others, but there is no recognized authority higher than that of any state.

Anarchy, so understood, is the defining characteristic of the environment within which sovereign states interact. Violence and war may be evident, but so too are periods of relative peace and stability. This absence of any superordinate or central authority over states (such as a world government with authority to enforce rules and to maintain order) is fundamentally different from domestic societies, where authority exists to maintain order and to act as an arbiter of disputes except in cases of total government collapse or in civil wars when legitimate authority may be unclear.

Realists argue that the absence of a central and overriding authority helps to explain why states come to rely on power, seeking to maintain or increase their power positions relative to other states. For one thing, the condition of anarchy is usually accompanied by a lack of trust among states in this environment. Each state faces a *self-help* situation in which it is dangerous to place the security of one's own country in the hands of another. What guarantee is there against betrayal, however solemn another state's promises may be to an ally? Consistent with the world described by Hobbes, there is really nothing to keep a supposed ally from reneging on a security agreement or any other international pact. There is no world governmental authority to enforce covenants or agreements among states. In such a world, it is logical, rational, and prudent to look out for number one—the security of one's own state. Indeed, this is the same counsel reported by Thucydides when he notes Athenian advice to the Melians not to place their hope for survival in the hands of the Spartans and their allies.

Given international anarchy and the lack of trust in such a situation, states find themselves in what has been called a *security dilemma*.[14] The more one state arms to protect itself from other states, the more threatened these states become and the more prone they are to resort to arming themselves to protect their national security interests. The dilemma is that even if a state is sincerely arming only for defensive purposes, it is rational in a self-help system to assume the worst in an adversary's intentions. How can one know for certain that a rival is arming strictly for defensive purposes? This is the stuff of arms races. Isn't it best to hedge one's bets by devoting more resources to match a potential adversary's arms buildup? Because a state may not have sufficient resources to be completely self-reliant, it may join an alliance in an attempt to deter aggression by any would-be adversaries.

Given an understanding of the anarchic condition of international politics, one can more easily grasp the game-theoretic dynamics of arms races. All sides involved may sincerely desire peace, but the anarchical nature of international politics leads states to be suspicious of one another and engage in worst-case analyses of one another's intentions. This realist insight, it is argued, is just as applicable to understanding the ancient competition between Sparta and Athens as it is to understanding contemporary international relations. It is a system-level explanation in that the emphasis is placed on the anarchic structure of international politics as a whole, not on the internal nature of a particular state. An example of an explanation that relies on internal factors is the claim that a given country keeps building more and more weapons because of demands from its military-industrial complex or because of the nature of a national mentality that reflects its regional or global ambitions. External factors such as the anarchic structure of the system or the actions and reactions of other states are ignored.

Finally, an anarchical, self-help system obviously makes cooperation among states difficult to achieve. How are states to act in such a world? Is it inevitable that they will be self-seeking, attempting to maximize their short-term individual or self-interests? Or is it possible that states can upgrade their common (perhaps enlightened) self-interests over both the short and long term? What is the rational thing to do? The informing image for some realists is provided by the allegory of the stag hunt, taken from the writings of the Geneva-born,

---

[14] John H. Herz, "Idealist Internationalism and the Security Dilemma," *World Politics* 5, no. 2 (January 1950): 157–80.

	Individual interests: pursue the hare	**Group/collective interests:** pursue the stag
Short run	Serve immediate self-interest	May provide basis for possible collaboration
Long run	No apparent basis for collaborative behavior	Serve long-term common interest

Figure 5.1   The Stag Hunt Fable: A Dilemma of Rational Choice

eighteenth-century philosopher Jean-Jacques Rousseau (1712–1778).[15] It is an excellent example of game theory at work.

Each of five individuals in the state of nature—a world without government or any other form of social structure—has to decide whether (1) to collaborate in the hunting of a stag necessary to meet the hunger needs of all five or (2) to defect from the group to capture a hare. To choose the latter course of action would be to serve one's self-interest at the expense of the group (see figure 5.1).

If the individual prefers to serve the common interest (go after the stag), can he or she trust the others to do so? And if one cannot trust the others, is it not rational to go for the hare and defect from the group before any of the others do? Or is it possible to develop the basis for collaboration by all five? Scholars who deal with game theory attempt to answer such questions.[16]

How one understands Rousseau's stag hunt fable has a great deal to do with how one sees states interacting in world politics. Some tend to see the state as serving only narrow self-interest. Pessimists point to the number, duration, and intensity of wars. They tend to see international politics as sets of competitive games in which decisions or choices may be zero-sum—one side's gains are losses for the other. Those of a more optimistic bent see great potential for collaboration among states, noting how in fact many states live in peace and harmony for decades and even centuries. In competitive settings, the players can find ways in which all parties can gain, albeit to different degrees—so-called positive- or variable-sum games. When losses have to be taken, optimists argue they can be distributed to minimize damage to each party. As such, the payoffs (gains or losses) typically are "asymmetric" or uneven, but still the best that can be achieved for all players.

---

[15] J. J. Rousseau, "A Discussion on the Origins of Inequality," in *The Social Contract and Discourses*, trans. G. D. H. Cole (New York: E. P. Dutton and Co., 1950), 235–38. Kenneth N. Waltz develops the stag hunt allegory in his *Man, the State and War* (New York: Columbia University Press, 1959), 165–71. For a critique of Waltz's interpretation of Rousseau, see Stanley Hoffmann, "Rousseau on War and Peace," *American Political Science Review* 57, no. 2 (June 1963): 317–33.

[16] For a discussion of games such as stag hunt, prisoner's dilemma, deadlock, and chicken, see Robert Axelrod and Robert O. Keohane, "Achieving Cooperation under Anarchy," *World Politics* 38, no. 1 (October 1985): 226–54.

For IR theorists, however, it is not simply a matter of having a pessimistic or optimistic nature. Aside from the assumptions that states are unitary and rational actors, structural realists also tend to make the analytical assumption that states are largely concerned with *relative* rather than just *absolute gains*. What is the difference? If a state is concerned with individual, absolute gains, it is indifferent to the gains of others—"As long as I'm doing better, I don't care if others are also increasing their wealth or military power." If, however, a state is concerned with relative gains, it is not satisfied with simply increasing its power or wealth but is concerned with how much those capabilities have kept pace with, increased, or decreased relative to other states.[17] This harkens back to the issue of how one defines and measures power.

Differing assumptions about a state's preferences lead to different expectations about the prospects for international conflict and cooperation. For structural realists, the relative gains assumption makes international cooperation in an anarchic world difficult to attain, particularly among great powers prone to improving their relative position or, at least, hold their own in this international competition. Structural realists do not have to rely, therefore, on such classical-realist assumptions that humanity is inherently aggressive as found in the works of Machiavelli and Hobbes. More optimistic about the prospects for international cooperation, English School scholars, neoliberal institutionalists, and social constructivists are much more likely to assume that states may well be satisfied with absolute gains due to the development of international norms, collaborative institutions, and the ability to redefine national interests.

Distribution of Capabilities and the Balance of Power

Realists see anarchy as continuing to be a defining characteristic of the international system unless one state or some kind of superior international authority were constructed to provide a new order to the world through its position of dominance. Within this anarchical environment, various distributions of capabilities or power among states emerge in dynamic, competitive relations among states. Indeed, anarchy plus the distribution of capabilities among states define for many realists the international system at any one time, described by them typically as unipolar, bipolar, or multipolar. Balances of power and alliances among states are the means realists conceive for sustaining international order.

As we have seen, many realists begin with the security dilemma in an anarchic world. Where does order come from under such conditions? What keeps states from continually attacking one another? One answer offered by realists is that states find it expedient to band together and pool their capabilities or power whenever one state or group of states appears to be gathering a disproportionate amount of power, thus threatening to dominate the world, or even a portion of it. On the other hand, influenced perhaps by the thought of Grotius, many classical realists (as well as constructivists and other scholars in the English School) observe some degree of order provided by the development and

---

[17] See Robert Powell, "Absolute and Relative Gains in International Relations Theory," *American Political Science Review* 85 (1991): 1303–20.

acceptance over time of international norms and practices, particularly those that come to be codified in international law.

This reasoning—the need to maintain a *balance of power* to avoid the triumph of a dominant power—is a realist concern dating back to the works of Thucydides. It is also found in a report of the British Foreign Office written before World War I:

> History shows that the danger threatening the independence of this or that nation has generally arisen, at least in part, out of the momentary predominance of a neighboring State at once militarily powerful, economically efficient, and ambitious to extend its frontiers or spread its influence. . . . The only check on the abuse of political predominance derived from such a position has always consisted in the opposition of an equally formidable rival, or a combination of several countries forming leagues of defense. The equilibrium established by such a grouping of forces is technically known as the balance of power, and it has become almost an historical truism to identify England's secular policy with the maintenance of this balance by throwing her weight now in this scale and now in that, but ever on the side opposed to the political dictatorship of the strongest single State or group at a given time.[18]

A *bipolar* balance of power (two states of comparable or relatively equal great power) or a *multipolar* balance of power (three or more states engaging in checks and balances) are two realist categorizations of particular distributions of capabilities. Such power configurations have occurred in the aftermath of major European wars—the Peace of Westphalia in 1648 following the Thirty Years' War, the Congress of Vienna in 1815 following the defeat of Napoleon, and the settlements following both twentieth-century world wars. Although the post–World War I arrangements bought only twenty years of peace, the Congress of Vienna was more successful in establishing a basis for maintaining a balance of power without general or major war for almost a century. Assessing the efforts of the diplomats at Vienna and subsequent meetings, Henry A. Kissinger concluded: "Their goal was stability, not perfection, and the balance of power is the classic expression of the lesson of history that no order is safe without physical safeguards against aggression." In short, according to Kissinger, a "new international order came to be created with a sufficient awareness of the connection between power and morality; between security and legitimacy."[19]

Four questions in this regard are subject to debate among realist scholars: (1) Do balances of power automatically occur, or are they created by diplomats or statesmen? (2) Which balance of power—bipolar or multipolar—is more likely to maintain international stability and is unipolarity a durable condition? (3) How much power should states seek in order to feel secure? (4) How can nonsystemic factors (those at individual and state-society levels of analysis) be integrated into structural or neorealist accounts to explain the onset of war?

---

[18] Reprinted in Fred A. Sondermann, David S. McClellan, and William C. Olson, eds., *The Theory and Practice of International Relations*, 5th ed. (Englewood Cliffs, NJ: Prentice Hall, 1979), 120.

[19] Henry A. Kissinger, *A World Restored: The Politics of Conservatism in a Revolutionary Age* (New York: Grosset & Dunlap, 1964), 317–18.

Balance of Power: Voluntarism and Determinism

The voluntarism-determinism debate is comparable in some ways to the theological dispute over determinism and free will. As we use the term, however, *voluntarism* does not refer only to freedom of choice, but rather to the ability of human beings to influence the course of events. How free are individuals to determine their own fates? How much effective choice do they have? How much are events determined by factors independent of humans will be exercised by statesmen? In the context of international relations, the question is whether states or their decision makers can affect their environment or whether their actions are severely constrained by other states interacting in a system of states. How much is free? How much is determined? Put another way, how much is the behavior of states and other units driven by the international system or its structure, and how much is socially constructed by human volition—statesmen and diplomats, institutions and groups, and other human actors? As noted in chapter 1, this is referred to in international relations as the *agent-structure* debate.

As to the first question, Henry Kissinger (a classical realist) emphasizes voluntarism—the balance of power is a foreign policy creation or construction by statesmen; it does not just occur automatically. Makers of foreign policy are not prisoners of the balance of power. Rather, they are its creators and those charged with maintaining it. They are free to exercise their judgment and their will as agents for their states in the conduct of foreign policy with the expectation that they can have some constructive effect on outcomes.

In contrast to this voluntarist conception is that of Kenneth Waltz, who sees the balance of power as an attribute of the system of states that will occur whether it is willed or not. He argues that "the balance of power is not so much imposed by statesmen on events as it is imposed by events on statesmen."[20] For Waltz, the statesman has much less freedom to maneuver and much less capability to affect the workings of international politics than Kissinger would allow.

How does Waltz reach this conclusion? Given the assumptions that the state is a rational and a unitary actor that will use its capabilities to accomplish its objectives, states inevitably interact and conflict in the competitive environment of international politics. States may be motivated to improve their positions to dominate others, but such attempts likely will be countered by other states similarly motivated. Waltz observes that in international relations, "the freedom of choice of any one state is limited by the actions of all the others."[21] Thus, a balance of power more often than not occurs as states tend to balance against a rising power as opposed to joining its bandwagon. The structure of the international system itself—anarchy plus the distribution of capabilities—affects the calculations and choices of decision makers. Balance-of-power theory so viewed can be used to account for arms races, alliances and counter-alliances, coalitions and countercoalitions, and other forms of competitive behavior among states that transcend any particular historical era.

---

[20] Waltz, *Man, the State and War*, 209. For a biography on his life and thought, see Paul R. Viotti, *Kenneth Waltz: An Intellectual Biography* (New York: Columbia University Press, 2024).
[21] Waltz, *Man, the State and War*, 204.

This image of the balance of power, therefore, refers to a recurrent phenomenon characteristic of international relations. It seems to matter little whether the states are democratic or authoritarian; the systemic tendency toward balance or equilibrium is always the same. It is as if states were billiard balls colliding with one another. The faster and larger balls (the major powers) knock the smaller balls (the lesser powers) out of the way, although their own paths may also be deflected slightly by these collisions. These interactions, it is argued, tend toward international equilibrium or stability just as billiard balls eventually come to rest, at least until the balance is upset once again. But then the same tendency toward equilibrium repeats itself, only to be upset again. And so forth. The actors involved in this timeless drama remain the same. As Ernst B. Haas (1924–2003)—a critic of the determinism he observed among structural realists and many other balance-of-power theorists—put it: "[They] see the components [of systems, that is, states] as relatively unchangeable and arrange them in an eternal preprogrammed dance. The rules of the dance may be unknown to the actors and are specified by the theorist. The recurrent patterns discovered by him constitute a super-logic which predicts the future state of the system."[22]

In his classes at Berkeley, Haas would refer to "billiard ball" theorists—realists enamored of the balance of power including his colleague and age contemporary, structural realist Kenneth N. Waltz. The metaphor is introduced by Arnold Wolfers (1892–1968), himself a classical realist critical of theorists focused only on states since doing so reduces the complexity of international relations to the actions and interactions of states as if they were merely interacting like balls on a pool table. To Wolfers, such formulations are problematic because they effectively overlook or minimize the role of nonstate actors:

> The "billiard ball" model of the multistate system that forms the basis for the states-as-actors theory leaves room for no corporate actors other than the nation-state. By definition, the stage is preempted by a set of states, each in full control of all territory and resources within its boundaries. Every state represents a closed, impermeable, and sovereign unit, completely separated from all other states. Since this obviously is not an accurate portrait of the real world of international politics, one can say that reality "deviates" in various ways from the model because corporate bodies other than nation-states play a role on the international stage as coactors with the nation-states. To the extent that these corporate bodies exert influence on the course of international politics, knowledge about them and about the deviations that permit them to operate becomes indispensable to the development of a well-rounded theory.[23]

Actor combinations involving two or more states can be observed throughout history as the mechanical workings of the balance of power: multipolar through much of the eighteenth and nineteenth centuries, before World War II (1939–1945), and bipolar (the United States and the Soviet Union) in the years

---

[22] Ernst B. Haas, "On Systems and International Regimes," *World Politics* 27, no. 2 (January 1975): 151.

[23] Arnold Wolfers, *Discord and Collaboration: Essays on International Politics* (Baltimore: Johns Hopkins University Press, 1962), 19.

following the war. The post–Cold War world has been described as a unipolar system due to the preponderant power of the United States, and this has caused problems for realist balance-of-power theorists, a subject we will subsequently discuss. For some, a rapidly rising China presages a return to a bipolar world while, at the same time, a militaristic Russia is desperately trying to hold its power position, effectively making the world multipolar with Russia remaining a great power alongside the United States and China.

In a sense, then, Kissinger and Waltz represent alternative ends of a spectrum of realists conversant with balance-of-power thinking. Realists, such as Waltz who emphasize a balance of power as a system tendency, have been labeled as "structural realists" or "neorealists" because they have departed from a realist tradition that granted the statesman or policy maker greater freedom from constraint and thus greater ability to affect international events. For Waltz, individuals (perhaps with the notable exception of figures like Otto von Bismarck and Franklin D. Roosevelt) are far less important theoretically than the international structure that influences the conduct of states.

Kissinger's position is closer to the voluntarist pole, but he definitely would not argue that foreign policy makers are totally free of external constraints. Indeed, their ability to maneuver within these constraints is at least partly a function of their diplomatic skills. Similarly, Waltz would reject the idea that he is in any way a system determinist—that the structure of the international system necessarily determines state behavior. Indeed, he acknowledges the possibility of a state or "unit-level cause negating a structural effect."[24] Nevertheless, his views are far removed from the purely voluntarist pole. The implication of his view of the balance of power is that individual decision makers and their states have much less freedom or capability to affect the course of events than others such as Kissinger would assert.

In some respects, the writings of Morgenthau are an earlier attempt to combine the two perspectives, thus inviting wrath by proponents of both. Morgenthau acknowledges the balance of power as a tendency within international politics while, at the same time, prescribing what statesmen should do to maintain the balance. He argues that "the balance of power and policies aiming at its preservation are not only inevitable but are an essential stabilizing factor in a society of sovereign nations." Quite apart from the apparent determinism in this statement, Morgenthau assigns to diplomats, not just the task of maintaining the balance of power but also charges them to "create the conditions under which it will not be impossible from the outset to establish a world state."[25]

In short, for Morgenthau, escape from the balance of power and the voluntarist creation of a new world order remained possibilities worthy of pursuit. At the same time, his detractors have noted that, on the one hand, to argue that the balance of power is an inevitable system tendency and, on the other hand, to prescribe what should be done to maintain a balance or transform the system

---

[24] This is a direct quote from Kenneth N. Waltz at a roundtable at the Annual Meeting, American Political Science Association, Washington, DC, August–September 2005.
[25] Morgenthau, *Politics among Nations*, 161, 519, respectively.

itself is to argue in contradictory terms. Be that as it may, Morgenthau's thinking represents a middle ground between realists who tend toward voluntarist or determinist poles. The theoretical debate between structural realists and social constructivists is a more recent manifestation of this continuing controversy—the latter far more voluntarist in its formulations, but also understanding that *both* ideational and material structures (or understandings of them) may facilitate or constrain state actions.

Polarity and System Structure

The second question is a long-standing realist debate: Is a bipolar or a multipolar balance of power more conducive to the stability of the international system? Stated another way, is war more likely to occur in a bipolar or a multipolar world?

The best-known statements on the stability of bipolar and multipolar distributions are by Waltz on the one hand and J. David Singer (1925–2009) and Karl Deutsch (1912–1992) on the other.[26] All three agreed that the amount of uncertainty about the consequences of a particular action taken by a state increases as the number of international actors increases. The logic of this assumption is that as the number increases, a state's policy makers have to deal with a greater quantity of information; more international actors mean more information is generated that has to be taken into account in the formulation of foreign policy. Therefore, all three authors concurred that as an international system moves from being bipolar to being multipolar, the amount of overall uncertainty in the system increases. So far, so good.

Where they part company is on the matter of whether an increase in the number of actors (and hence uncertainty) makes war more or less likely. Waltz argues that greater uncertainty makes it more likely that a policy maker will misjudge the intentions and actions of a potential foe. Hence, a multipolar system, given its association with higher levels of uncertainty, is less desirable than a bipolar system because multipolarity makes uncertainty and thus the probability of war greater. Singer and Deutsch, however, make the opposite argument, believing that a multipolar system is more conducive to stability because uncertainty breeds caution on the part of states. Caution means following tried and true policies of the past and avoiding deviations. Furthermore, they argue that "the increase in number of independent actors diminishes the share [of attention] that any nation can allocate to any other single actor." This, it is argued, also reduces the probability of war because a state's attention is allocated to a larger number of actors.

This theoretical debate on the effect of polarity on systemic stability was inconclusive at the time, but there is more of a consensus now on bipolarity (as in the Cold War between the United States and the Soviet Union) as having been more stable than either post–Cold War unipolarity (the United States)

---

[26] Kenneth N. Waltz, "The Stability of a Bipolar World," *Daedalus* 93 (Summer 1964): 881–909; Karl W. Deutsch and J. David Singer, "Multipolar Power Systems and International Stability," *World Politics* 16, no. 3 (April 1964): 390–406.

that invites new balancers or the emergence of a multipolar world that complicates relations and decisions by several great powers.[27] Other realist work has addressed two other dimensions of polarity at the systemic level of analysis—disparities in capabilities among poles (not simply the number) and the implications of whether the capability growth rates of states are static or dynamic.[28]

How Much Power? Defensive and Offensive Realists

Realists also disagree on the implications of anarchy and how much weight it should be accorded as a contributing factor to power-seeking behavior by states. So-called *defensive realists* such as Waltz start by assuming that states at a minimum merely aim to survive, above all else seeking security. Other objectives may be added to the list, and their capabilities or power applied to achieving them. This requires paying close attention to the balance of power. Anarchy in particular requires states to engage in competitive behavior as opposed to classical-realist Morgenthau's emphasis on human nature and the drive for power, causing security competition.

Waltz and other defensive realists, however, argue that while the international system provides incentives for expansion, this is only under certain circumstances. While under anarchy the security dilemma causes states to worry about relative power and the intentions of other states, efforts to increase power may inadvertently generate spirals of hostility. The pursuit of expansionist policies may be generated by this fear and the mistaken assumption that aggressive behavior and words are the best way to make a state more secure. States cannot escape the security dilemma they face. Under anarchy, war remains possible, but its outbreak is by no means inevitable.

Certain structural factors can have a significant impact on whether states go down the road of cooperation or conflict. One factor that has generated a great deal of study is the *offense-defense balance*. The argument is that at any point in time military power can favor the offense or the defense. If defense dominates over offense, then conquest is difficult and the major powers have little incentive to use force to gain power. Rather, the incentive is to hold on to what they have. If, however, offense has the advantage, then the temptation is for states to attempt to conquer one another, generating major wars. But as the offense-defense balance is usually in favor of the defense, conquest becomes more difficult and hence states are discouraged from pursuing aggressive policies.

---

[27] On structural considerations, see Kenneth N. Waltz, *Realism and International Politics* (London: Routledge, 2008), x, xiv. See also Waltz, "The Emerging Structure of International Politics," *International Security* 18, no. 2 (Fall 1994): 44–79, and John J. Mearsheimer, "Back to the Future: Instability in Europe after the Cold War," *International Security* 15, no. 1 (Summer 1990): 5–56. See also Christopher Layne, "The Unipolar Illusion: Why New Powers Will Arise," *International Security* 17, no. 4 (1993): 5–51, and Michael Mastanduno, "Preserving the Unipolar Moment: Realist Theory and US Grand Strategy after the Cold War," *International Security* 21, no. 4 (1997): 49–88.

[28] See, for example, Randall L. Schweller, *Deadly Imbalances: Tripolarity and Hitler's Strategy of World Conquest* (New York: Columbia University Press, 1997), and Dale C. Copeland, "Neorealism and the Myth of Bipolar Stability: Toward a New Dynamic Realist Theory of Major War," *Security Studies* 5, no. 3 (Spring 1996): 29–89.

The policy implication is that states should carefully consider the real possibility that moderate strategies may enhance their security, but with the full recognition that at times expansionist strategies will end up being the means to achieving this goal. Hence, while recognizing the importance of anarchy, defensive realists caution that analysts should not overstate its importance. They argue that security is readily available, particularly if states adopt prudent strategies. The assumption is made that the international system provides incentives for cautious and restrained behavior on the part of states and that reckless, expansionist behavior is more the result of domestic factors, as opposed to systemic conditions such as anarchy.[29] Hence, defensive realists have been charged as having a status quo bias.

This is certainly not a criticism leveled at *offensive realists* who hold a very different assumption on the question of how much power states want and the implications of anarchy, arguing that the latter actually provides strong incentives for the expansion of power capabilities relative to other states. States strive for maximum power relative to other states as this is the only way to guarantee survival. Offensive realists argue that status quo powers are rarely found in international politics as the structure of the international system creates strong incentives to gain power relative to one's rivals. Defensive realists, it is claimed, cannot explain at the systemic level state expansion because international incentives for such behavior are lacking in the defensive-realist formulation.

John J. Mearsheimer exemplifies this perspective. He emphasizes his structural realism on offensive or power-maximizing in contrast to the defensive, "status quo" realism he finds in Waltz and other realists. Offensive realism is both a descriptive theory about how states behave as well as a prescriptive one that states ought to follow as the best way to survive in a dangerous world. He is critical of the defensive-realist focus on states supposedly more interested in maintaining the existing balance of power as opposed to increasing their share of it. By contrast, he sees states as trying to maximize their power positions—a state's ultimate goal in principle is to be the hegemon in the system. For Mearsheimer, the "best way for a state to survive in anarchy is to take advantage of other states and gain power at their expense."[30]

The assumption is that anarchy and the distribution of capabilities matter most in explaining the big issues of international politics such as war and peace. Little attention is paid to the role of individuals, domestic politics, and ideology. He argues that from this theoretical perspective, it does not really matter whether Germany in 1905 was led by Bismarck, Kaiser Wilhelm, or Hitler, or whether Germany was democratic or autocratic. What matters from an offensive realism perspective is how much relative power Germany had. Mearsheimer readily acknowledges that in those cases where such domestic factors actually do play a major role, then offensive realism does not have a lot to say. Such is

---

[29] The theoretical foundation of defensive realism is found in Robert Jervis, "Cooperation under the Security Dilemma," *World Politics* 30, no. 2 (January 1978): 167–214.

[30] John J. Mearsheimer, *The Tragedy of Great Power Politics* (New York: W.W. Norton, 2001). See also his more recent *The Great Delusion: Liberal Dreams and International Realities* (New Haven, CT: Yale University Press, 2018).

the cost of simplifying reality and attempting to develop parsimonious theories that tell us a few things about important matters.

Echoes of Morgenthau's earlier conceptualization of power in international politics can be heard as Mearsheimer characterizes states as maximizing power, not just as "a means to an end (survival) but [also] an end in itself." But as a structural realist, Mearsheimer agrees with Waltz that this drive for power is a function of the structure of the international system, not human nature as Morgenthau argued. Great powers pursuing power as an end may still come to understand the limits of their power, constrained by other states pursuing the same ends. In the great game of international politics, "the trick for the sophisticated power maximizer is to figure out when to raise and when to fold."

Mearsheimer notes that the actual distribution of military might among great powers is critical in terms of war. If a great power has a marked power advantage over its rivals, it is more likely that it will behave aggressively as it has the capability and incentive to do so. If, however, it is facing powerful opponents, it is less likely to consider offensive action and more likely to focus on defending the existing balance of power. Mearsheimer thus reflects the basic realist assumptions outlined at the beginning of the chapter in terms of states carefully calculating the costs and benefits of offensive action, aware of its strengths but also its limitations.

Finally, is there no place for cooperation among states in the world of offensive realists? Great powers certainly do cooperate as exemplified when they form alliances and act against common enemies. But extensive cooperation is limited by two concerns—relative gains and the prospect of cheating. As noted earlier, if each side is pursuing absolute gains, then there is little concern with what others are gaining or losing. But in a world of balance of power, states have to be concerned with relative gains as those of a rival could upset that balance. Once again, the international system is structured in such a way that cooperation is difficult to achieve, and conflict is often more likely. Concerns over cheating in the military realm that hold out the prospect of defeat also work against cooperation.

Nonsystemic Factors

Classical realists have always blended various units and levels of analysis into their accounts of international relations. In his attempt to develop a parsimonious systemic theory of international politics, the preeminent structural realist Kenneth Waltz purposely downplayed domestic factors as has Mearsheimer. Waltz, however, has highlighted in other works the importance of the state-societal level of analysis.[31]

Other defensive realists influenced by Waltz, while agreeing that his work can explain some state behavior, have tried to overcome structural realism's limitations, in particular its inability to explain those cases where major powers

---

[31] Kenneth N. Waltz, *Foreign Policy and Democratic Politics: The American and British Experience* (Boston: Little, Brown, 1967) and his earlier *Man, the State and War* (New York: Columbia University Press, 1959).

act in nonstrategic ways. This has required delving into the realm of the individual and state-societal or unit levels of analysis and examining the role of such factors as human agency—for example, the roles human beings play in domestic politics and their cognitive understandings, perceptions or misperceptions, and elite belief systems.

Waltz's earliest work—his dissertation, written in 1954, which later became his first book, *Man, the State and War* (1959)—is more clearly in the classical-realist tradition he encountered as a doctoral student of William T. R. Fox (1912–1988), the Columbia University professor who coined the term "super-power." Earlier studies of war were conducted by Quincy Wright (1890–1970) in his *The Causes of War and the Conditions of Peace* (1935) and his two-volume *A Study of War* (1942), which led him to advocate strong international organization as a remedy for the war problem.

Focusing on how political theorists over the millennia have conceived of the causes of war, Waltz developed an early formulation of what came to be known as "images" or *levels of analysis*: Were the causes of war to be found at the individual, state-societal, or interstate system levels of analysis? Some argue that human nature is the basic cause of war. Others see the internal organization of states as the key to understanding war and peace, while still others focus on the impact of the structure of the interstate system.

It is international systemic anarchy—the absence of central or superordinate authority in the international system—that is the permissive cause of war as no power or authority can keep a state from using force against another. "Efficient" causes of particular wars can be found at any or all of the three levels of analysis. In *Man, the State and War* Waltz refers particularly to Jean-Jacques Rousseau in developing the "third image"—the systemic level of analysis.

Waltz draws from an obscure, critical piece by Rousseau on the proposed "Project for Perpetual Peace" by the Frenchman Abbé de Saint Pierre (1658–1743) and another essay by Rousseau on "The State of War." Although Rousseau is sympathetic to the Abbé de Saint Pierre's ideas on a European confederation as an antidote to war, he finds such thinking impractical (as does Waltz) and thus not likely to be achieved. One problem is that ministers likely have selfish reasons for encouraging princes to reject the plan—an individual level of analysis explanation.

Most importantly, however, for Rousseau it is the "condition of absolute independence that draws sovereigns away from the rule of law." In other words, war is a product of the social context within which the state finds itself—one in which there is no authority higher than the state itself. In this regard, Rousseau distinguishes a civil state where individuals are subject to laws, but "as nations each enjoys the liberty of nature." Like Hobbes, Rousseau thus recognizes the importance of what has come to be termed the anarchic structure of the international system, but he emphatically disagrees with Hobbes's negative view of the nature of human beings.

Following Rousseau, Waltz is not surprised that under anarchy states resort to the use of force. As they seek to enhance their power to accomplish their objectives, they are challenged by the power of other states and a balance of power emerges within the system. Alliances and counteralliances are observable. Even when changes in the distribution of capabilities or power occur, there is an inherent tendency within the system that tends toward equilibrium—a dynamic balance of power, an enduring characteristic in an anarchic international system.

Stephen Walt, one of Waltz's students and now a prominent professor in his own right, recasts balance-of-power theory (states align against the most powerful states), arguing that a balance-of-threat theory offers more historically correct explanations.[32] Hence, intentions need to be taken into account (states balance against states that are not only powerful but also threatening). Walt observes that states are attracted to strength and "a decline in a state's relative position will lead its allies to opt for neutrality at best or to defect to the other side at worst." Threats matter in Walt's analysis, not just power as such. Thus, one finds that "the greater the threat, the greater the probability that the vulnerable state will seek an alliance."

In this regard, Walt distinguishes balancing (allying with others against the prevailing threat that is the dominant tendency in international politics) and bandwagoning (the opportunistic option of aligning with the source of danger, particularly if it is a strong state). Balancing behavior is more common, tending to reflect restraint and, perhaps, an effort to "minimize the threat one poses to others." By contrast, bandwagoning, though less common, typically occurs in a much more competitive context.

Walt has also used this theoretical adjustment to balance-of-power theory to analyze how revolutionary domestic changes can increase the risk of international war by intensifying international security competition. Dangers posed by states matter, not just their power or relative power positions per se. So understood, it is imbalances of threat that cause alliances against the most threatening state. He concludes, then, that balance-of-threat theory provides a stronger explanatory handle than traditional balance-of-power theory offers.

Much as Walt deals with threats or perceptions of danger,[33] Stephen Van Evera, also a former student of Waltz, adds the ideational—ideas, perceptions, and misperceptions—to the material understandings of power and its distribution.[34] Going beyond gross distinctions captured by the terms *multipolar, bipolar,* and *unipolar,* Van Evera introduces what he labels a "fine-grained structural realism" that takes into account such considerations as the offense-defense balance, the advantage of taking the first move, the size and frequency of power fluctuations, and available resources. Perception and misperception matter, and war is more likely when states believe that conquest is easy (whether it is or is

---

[32] Stephen Walt, *The Origins of Alliances* (Ithaca, NY: Cornell University Press, 1987) and his *Revolutions and War* (Ithaca, NY: Cornell University Press, 1996). See also Thomas J. Christensen and Jack Snyder, "Chain Gangs and Passed Bucks: Predicting Alliance Patterns in Multipolarity," *International Organization* 44, no. 2 (Spring 1990): 137–68.

[33] Stephen Walt's focus on the perceptions and understandings of leadership elites is also found in his work on foreign policy. See his *The Hell of Good Intentions: America's Foreign Policy Elite and the Decline of U.S. Primacy* (New York: Farrar, Straus and Giroux, 2018).

[34] Stephen Van Evera, *Causes of War: Power and the Roots of Conflict* (Ithaca, NY: Cornell University Press, 1999).

not in reality). Other war-causing ideas include windows of vulnerability, the hostility of other states, threatening diplomatic tactics (as in coercive diplomacy), and when war is considered cheap or even beneficial.

Barry Posen—yet another of Waltz's former students—tests two theories (organization theory and balance-of-power theory) to see which does a better job explaining how military doctrine takes shape and influences the grand strategy decisions of French, British, and German officials during the years between World Wars I and II. Not surprisingly, Posen finds that the causes of state behavior are found at both the state and international levels of analysis with the latter a slightly more powerful tool for the study of military doctrine.[35]

Finally, one of the most ambitious efforts to understand the conditions under which large-scale war is likely to occur is Dale Copeland's *The Origins of Major War*. In the process he integrates several issues, concepts, and debates dear to the heart of many realists: Is a multipolar or bipolar system more likely to encourage war? How important are relative gains and losses to an explanation of war? How can the insights from two competing camps of structural realism (offensive and defensive) be reconciled? Are rising powers or declining powers more likely to initiate war and under what conditions? Copeland's bottom-line argument, based upon the application of what he calls his dynamic differentials theory to ten historical case studies, is that great powers that anticipate deep and inevitable relative decline are more likely to initiate major wars or pursue hardline policies that substantially increase the risk of major war through inadvertent escalation.

The dependent variable in the theory is the variation in the probability of major war over time within a bipolar or multipolar system. The key explanatory variable is the dynamic differential, defined as "the simultaneous interaction of the differentials or relative military power between great powers and the expected trend of those differentials, distinguishing between the effects of power changes in bipolarity versus multipolarity."[36]

In multipolar systems, a declining power must possess significant military superiority over each of the other great powers before initiating war or hardline policies that risk war. Lacking such superiority, the prospect of facing a balancing coalition or fighting several debilitating bilateral contests is likely to deter the state from taking on the rest of the system. In a bipolar system, however, the declining power need not be militarily superior. In fact, it could even be slightly militarily inferior—before initiating war or implementing such policies against its major rival. In facing only one major adversary, the chance of costly bilateral wars is minimal. The likelihood of major war therefore derives largely from the strategy adopted by the declining power.

---

[35] Barry R. Posen, *The Sources of Military Doctrine* (Ithaca, NY: Cornell University Press, 1984). See also his *Restraint: A New Foundation for U.S. Grand Strategy* (Ithaca, NY: Cornell University Press, 2015), and *Inadvertent Escalation: Conventional War and Nuclear Risks* (Ithaca, NY: Cornell University Press, 2013).

[36] Dale Copeland, *The Origins of Major War* (Ithaca, NY: Cornell University Press, 2001), 15. See also his *Economic Interdependence and War* (Princeton, NJ: Princeton University Press, 2014).

If leaders of the major power expect the trend to be one of rapid and inevitable decline in power (disaggregated into military, economic, and potential indices), the more likely they will be tempted to engage in preventive war. Dynamic differentials theory attempts to explain not only this likelihood but also associated diplomatic and military strategies that might be pursued by utilizing the rational actor assumption of leaders who are risk and cost-neutral. Copeland does not, therefore, fall back on subsystemic or unit auxiliary theories such as threat perception, individual pathologies, ideology, civilian-military relations, and military doctrine. But by utilizing the rational actor assumption, his work aspires to be a theory of international relations and also a theory of foreign policy.

Realists and the Russian Invasion of Ukraine

Major shocks in the international system occurred when the Soviet Union collapsed in 1991 and, in 2001, when terrorists attacked the United States—the 9/11 attacks on the World Trade Center in New York and the Pentagon in Washington, DC. Russia's invasion of Ukraine in February 2022 and subsequent events mark the latest watershed in international politics.

Realists soon claimed their perspective on the world was validated. In particular, it was noted that going back to the fall of the Soviet Union, realists had cautioned against expanding NATO eastward, incorporating former Soviet satellite states into the organization.[37] Such a development would inevitably be viewed by Russia as a threat to its security. The logic of anarchy, self-help, and the security dilemma require states to be concerned about their relative power. This meant the United States' unipolar moment would eventually end, balance of power politics reasserting itself. At the time, there was little Russia could do, given its weakened position, and there was some expressed optimism among political leaders, diplomats, analysts, and scholars of the liberal school of IR theory that Russia could evolve into a satisfied member of the western community—accepting the liberal rules-based order.

The realists claimed their perspective was validated by subsequent events. Russia was too weak in 2004 to keep the Baltic states out of NATO. At the 2008 NATO summit in Bucharest, however, a statement was issued that Ukraine and Georgia could eventually become part of NATO as well. It was also assumed that Ukraine would at some point become a member of the European Union. Russia clearly stated the expansion of NATO to the Russian-Ukrainian border was simply unacceptable and Putin declared such an event would be a "direct threat" to Russian security; as a great power would the United States accept a similar situation on its borders? This was soon followed four months later by Russia's invasion of the former Soviet republic of Georgia. The Russian takeover of Ukraine's Crimea occurred in 2014 and then the full-scale invasion of Ukraine in 2022.[38]

---

[37] See the quotes in https://twitter.com/RnaudBertrand/status/1498491107902062592.
[38] For an example of the offensive realist perspective, see John J. Mearsheimer, "Why the Ukraine Crisis Is the West's Fault: The Liberal Delusions That Provoked Putin," *Foreign Affairs* (September/October

Realists emphasize they are not justifying Russia's actions, and indeed heartily condemn them. But they would note that moral condemnation alone would not prevent such actions. Russia was acting in defense of perceived national security interests and was not deterred by its assessment of Ukrainian military power in 2014, nor (mistakenly) in 2022. As a realist would further expect, the United States and its allies—not only members of NATO—dramatically revised their assessment of the Russian threat and engaged in balancing behavior by responding with severe sanctions and massive shipment of arms and other aid to Ukraine.

CHANGE

Realists stress the continuity of international relations. Many of the insights of Thucydides are deemed to be as relevant today as they were more than two millennia ago. Looking at modern history, a balance of power involving states has existed at least since the fifteenth and sixteenth centuries—whether viewed as a policy they have pursued or as a recurrent, expected outcome from the interactions of states using power to pursue their own separate interests. Although continuity is the watchword for realists, this does not mean that they are uninterested in change. For many theorists of international relations, understanding the evolution of the international system and predicting its future should be preeminent research goals. The methods for discovering global patterns may vary. Some scholars have applied quantitative measures to historical data.[39] Others have approached the issue of international political change by attempting to discern cycles of national power and their relation to the outbreak of war.

Power Transition

As the title of his book suggests, Robert Gilpin (1930–2018) is interested in developing a framework for thinking about hegemonic or great power war in his *War and Change in World Politics*. He believed "it is possible to identify recurrent patterns, common elements, and general tendencies in the major turning points in international history." Reflecting his offensive realism perspective, Gilpin argues international political change is the result of efforts of political actors to change the international system to advance their own interests, however, these interests may be defined (security, economic gain, ideological goals, etc.).

Gilpin claims that "a state will attempt to change the international system if the expected benefits exceed the expected costs (i.e., if there is an expected net gain)." Various periods of history are marked by equilibrium (such as after the

---

2014): "No Russian leader would tolerate a military alliance [NATO] that was Moscow's mortal enemy until recently moving into Ukraine. Nor would any Russian leader stand idly by while the West helped install a government there that was determined to integrate Ukraine into the West."

[39] Classic examples of work in this genre are J. David Singer's *Explaining War: Correlates of War Project* (Thousand Oaks, CA: Sage, 1979), his *The Wages of War, 1816–1965: A Statistical Handbook* (Hoboken, NJ: Wiley, 1972), and Lewis F. Richardson's *The Statistics of Deadly Quarrels* (Chicago: Quadrangle Books, 1960).

Congress of Vienna in 1815) or disequilibrium. As long as the system can adjust to the demands of its constituent states, stability is maintained. What accounts for change and the undermining of the status quo? The key factor "is the tendency in an international system for the powers of member states to change at different rates because of political, economic, and technological developments. In time, the differential growth in power of the various states in the system causes a fundamental redistribution of power in the system."[40]

What has been the principal mechanism of change throughout history? War, because wars determine which states will govern the system. The peace settlement after the war codifies the new status quo. This equilibrium reflects the new distribution of power in the international system until eventually, the differential growth in the power of states leads to another attempt to change the system.

Like balance-of-power theory, therefore, *power transition* is a system-level theory. Realist adherents to both theories claim that the distribution of power among states is the key to understanding international relations. Power-transition theorists, however, are much more likely to call our attention to change in the international system as opposed to balance-of-power theorists with their emphasis on stability whether in a bipolar or multipolar world. Power-transition theorists see the international system as hierarchically ordered, with the most powerful state dominating the rest, which are classified as satisfied or dissatisfied with the ordering of the system. But while balance-of-power theorists argue that the equality of power leads to stability, if not peace, power-transition theorists claim that war may be more likely when states are relatively equal, particularly when the differential growth in two states' economies brings a challenger close to displacing the reigning hegemon's power.

Given the emphasis on the importance of war in changing the structure of the system, are we currently experiencing a lull before some sort of global cataclysm? In this regard, Graham Allison raises this possibility—that fear or deep concerns in the United States about the rise in power of China could lead to war, much as Thucydides argued that fear in ancient Sparta about the rise of Athens was the underlying cause of the Peloponnesian Wars.[41]

When one state is in the process of overtaking the power position of another, the likelihood of war increases markedly. War is least likely when we find the ways and means of satisfying (or, one might add, at least dampening or minimizing dissatisfaction among) the challengers and defenders of existing power positions. The converse—dissatisfied challengers and defenders—is the

---

[40] Robert Gilpin, *War and Change in World Politics* (New York: Cambridge University Press, 1981), 3, 10. For his part, George Modelski argues that the global political system goes through distinct and identifiable historical cycles or recurrent patterns of behavior. See his *Long Cycles in World Politics* (New York: Palgrave Macmillan, 1987).

[41] See Graham Allison's *Destined for War* (Boston: Houghton Mifflin Harcourt, 2017). Allison's argument is similar to the position taken earlier by Ronald L. Tammen, Jacek Kugler, and their associates. They warn us that periods in which the distribution of power is in transition are more prone to war: Ronald L. Tammen et al., *Power Transitions* (New York: Chatham House Publishers, 2000). Influential to their work on power-transition theory was A. F. K. Organski (1923–1998).

condition that makes the outbreak of war most likely. How power transitions take place is important, affecting the duration, severity, and consequences of war. Rather than adopting a laissez-faire approach, power-transition authors call for managing alliances, international organizations, the distribution of nuclear weapons, and crises wherever and whenever they emerge.

Power-transition work on war has been criticized on historical, empirical, and conceptual grounds. Yet this is true of all work that attempts to explain important issues of war and peace. Furthermore, given the ongoing shifts in the distribution of world power and interest in the implications of such rising powers as China, India, and a resurgent Russia, it can be expected that scholars will continue to mine such works for theoretical insights.

GLOBALIZATION AND INTERDEPENDENCE

There is no doubt that the term *globalization* has captured the imagination of journalists, policy makers, the general public, and writers of textbooks on international relations. Realists generally do not share this enthusiasm. First, there is the problem of definition. A generally accepted definition of globalization does not exist although it is common to emphasize—as liberals do—the continual increase in transnational and worldwide economic, social, and cultural interactions among societies that transcend the boundaries of states, aided by advances in technology. Second, the term is descriptive and lacking in theoretical content. Hence, it hardly qualifies as a "concept" suitable for use in theory building. Third, the term is trendy, which alone makes realists suspicious. It is rare for academic theoretical concepts to gain such widespread public currency. Fourth, and most importantly, the literature on globalization assumes the increase in transactions among societies has led to an erosion of sovereignty and the blurring of the boundaries between the state and the international system. For realists, anarchy is the distinguishing feature in international relations, and anything that questions the separation of domestic and international politics threatens the centrality of this key realist concept.

Finally, globalization has an affinity with another popular concept that came to the fore of the IR field in the 1970s: *interdependence*. As with the case of globalization today, some realist scholars were skeptical of the conceptual utility of the concept. For those realists who have utilized the concept, interdependence is viewed as being between or among states. This is not surprising given the underlying assumptions of realism. They make several related points. First, the balance of power can be understood as a kind of interdependence. To be sure, some realists of a more eclectic sort acknowledge interdependence involving nonstate actors such as multinational corporations and try to take them into account. But at the core of realist thought is the image of interactions among states.

Second, for any one state, interdependence among states is not necessarily such a good thing. Rather than being a symmetric relation between coequal parties (which is how many people view the term), interdependence is typically a dominance-dependence relation with the dependent party particularly vulnerable (a key realist concept) to the choices of the dominant party. Indeed, vulnerability interdependence is a source of power for one state over another. To reduce this vulnerability, realists have argued that the state should be independent or, at least, minimize its dependency on other states. For example, the state needing to import oil or natural gas is vulnerable to an embargo or price rise engineered by the state or states exporting the commodity. To reduce this vulnerability would require reducing oil and gas imports by, for example, finding alternative sources.

Third, and following from earlier, interdependence does not affect all states equally. This applies to the economic realm as much as the military realm. For example, although the economies of most oil-importing countries are affected by dramatic rises in oil prices, they are not all equally vulnerable. Vulnerability is in part a question of what alternatives are available. For example, as a matter of policy, the United States has increased domestic production, created a strategic oil reserve to be drawn from only in emergencies, found other foreign sources of oil, and substituted alternative forms of energy such as natural gas whenever feasible. By doing so, the United States has reduced its vulnerability to any new oil embargo or disruption of supply due to war or other regional instabilities in the Middle East or elsewhere. Similarly, Europe has worked hard to reduce its reliance on Russian energy following the invasion of Ukraine in 2022.

In any event, if a state wants to be more powerful, it avoids or minimizes economic dependency just as it avoids political or military dependency on other states if this were to amount to a reduction in its relative power position. Dependency on others is to be minimized, whereas dependency of others on one's state may be desirable to the extent that it increases one's leverage over those other states. In short, in any given issue area, not all states are equally vulnerable. Therefore, the realist is suspicious of such blanket statements as "given increasing globalization, the entire world is increasingly interdependent or interconnected"—as if this were a good thing—particularly when such claims are supposedly equally applicable to all states.

Finally, realists have made interesting arguments concerning interdependence and peace, and it can be inferred they might apply similar observations to the effects of globalization. Interdependence, according to realists, may or may not enhance prospects for peace. Conflict, not cooperation, could just as easily result. Just as in household, sectarian, and community conflicts, one way to establish peace is to eliminate or minimize contact among opponents or potential adversaries. Separation from other units, if that were possible, would mean less contact and thus less conflict. Hence, realists would be as unlikely to argue that the increase in globalization among societies has a pacifying effect any more than they would assume interdependence leads to peace.

REALISTS AND INTERNATIONAL COOPERATION

Classical realists perhaps have more faith than structural realists in the ability of international organizations to make a substantive contribution to international stability if not peace; after all, they draw from the same Grotian intellectual wellspring as do those in the English School. But other realists have made a theoretical contribution to our understanding of how under conditions of anarchy international cooperation may be enhanced. For some, this involves the application of game theory and its attendant assumptions of unified, rational state actors. For others, the starting point is the systemic distribution of power and the implications of hegemonic leadership.

According to the theory of *hegemonic stability*, the hegemon, or dominant power, assumes leadership, perhaps for the entire globe, in dealing with a particular issue. Thus, Britain was seen as offering leadership in international monetary matters in the nineteenth and early twentieth centuries. The gold standard associated with the international exchange of money was managed from London by the Bank of England. After World War II, the leadership role was assumed by the United States.

The absence of *hegemony*, or leadership, may result in chaos and instability, as happened in the 1930s when the United States was unwilling to assume leadership of the world economy and Britain, given its weakened position, was unable to do so.[42] Competitive depreciation of currencies, the erection of trade barriers, and a drastic reduction in the volume of trade were the outcomes.

Although not all realists would subscribe to the view, stability is therefore seen by some as enhanced by a concentration of power in international politics; there is virtue in inequality among states. The hegemonic state or states benefit, but so too do other, less powerful states that find a more stable world advantageous. By contrast, the decline of hegemony and the consequent fragmentation of power in international politics is said to produce disorder—a breakdown or unraveling of previously constructed international agreements. Leadership provided by hegemonic states is understood as facilitating achievement of collaboration among states.

Theoretical and empirical controversy in the 1980s, 1990s, and 2000s were mirrored by public debate as to whether or not the United States was a hegemon in decline. The debate was sparked primarily by the work of the historian Paul Kennedy, who examines the rise and fall of great powers over some five hundred years.[43] The debate influenced (and was influenced by) a discussion already underway mainly among structural realists on how the United States might be able to adapt to hegemonic decline and how stability in the international economic system could be sustained after hegemony.

REALISTS AND THEIR CRITICS

Realism: The Term Itself

What is perhaps most impressive about the realist image of international politics is its longevity. Although modifications, clarifications, additions, and methodological innovations have been made through the years, the core elements have remained basically intact.

---

[42] See Charles P. Kindleberger, *The World in Depression, 1929–1939* (Berkeley: University of California Press, 2013).

[43] Paul Kennedy, *The Rise and Fall of the Great Powers* (New York: Random House, 1987).

If realism represents a "realistic" image of international politics—one represented as close to the reality of how things are (not necessarily how things ought to be)—what does that say about competing images? Are they by definition unrealistic? In debate and discourse, labels are important. A good example of this involves the period between World War I and World War II during which realists were challenged by advocates of the League of Nations, world federalism, or peace through international law. Many of these individuals came to be known as *idealists* or utopians as E. H. Carr referred to them at the time.

The very labels attached to these competing images of world order put the so-called idealists at a disadvantage. Realists can claim that they are dealing with the world as it functions. The idealists, on the other hand, are supposedly more concerned with what ought to be. "Yes," a realist might say, "I too wish the world was a more harmonious place, but that unfortunately is not the case." Those persons who are placed in the idealist camp certainly do not choose this particular label for themselves. Who does? The realists. By so doing, the opposition is stripped of a certain amount of legitimacy. Idealism conjures images of impractical professors, unsophisticated peace advocates, and utopian schemes.

Realists would respond that realism should be taken at face value; it is an appropriate term precisely because its basic tenets in fact closely approximate the world as it is. This is nothing of which to be ashamed. The longevity of the realist tradition is not simply a function of the expropriation of a particular label but a result of realism's inherent descriptive, explanatory, and predictive strengths.

Another reason for the longevity of realism is that this particular image of the world most closely approximates the image held by practitioners of statecraft. Realism has always had strong policy-prescriptive components, as we have already noted. Machiavelli's *The Prince*, for example, is expressly presented as a guide for the ruler. Nor is it mere coincidence that some of the best-known American political scientists who have held national security advisor positions in the White House—Kissinger in the Nixon-Ford years, Brent Scowcroft in the Ford and H. W. Bush administrations, Zbigniew Brzezinski in the Jimmy Carter years, Condoleezza Rice in the George W. Bush administration, Thomas Donilon under Barack Obama, neoconservative John Bolton in the Trump White House, and Jake Sullivan in the Biden administration—are self-professed (or easily classified as) realists. Indeed, the realist as academic speaks much the same language as the realist in policy-making positions: power, force, national interest, and diplomacy.

Critics argue that some realist writers help to perpetuate the very world they analyze. By describing the world in terms of violence, duplicity, and war, and then providing advice to policy makers on how they should act, these realists are justifying one particular conception of international relations. Realism becomes a self-fulfilling prophecy. Even efforts to place realism on a stronger theoretical foundation (as in structural realism or *neorealism*) that favors explanation over policy prescription have the same effect. Critics contend that such realists suffer from a lack of imagination and an inability to consider seriously alternative conceptions of world politics and how these might be achieved.

The realist response is that there is nothing inherently wrong with being policy-relevant and helping leaders navigate through dangerous waters. Advice based on wishful thinking and questionable assessments of international forces and trends could lead to disastrous policies, particularly if one is the lone "idealist" leader in a world of realists. Moreover, most criticism is understood to be based on a selective reading of realists, ignoring their genuine concern not only with the causes of war but also with how peace and stability can be achieved or maintained. Indeed, many realists over the years have cautioned against what they consider to be ill-advised foreign policies. Kenneth Waltz was against US involvement in the Vietnam War. George Kennan argued the expansion of NATO eastward after the end of the Cold War would needlessly provoke Russia. Finally, not all realists would claim to be particularly interested in providing advice to statesmen. They would rather use realist assumptions and insights to develop better theories of international politics. Being policy-relevant or ingratiating oneself with political leaders is not the goal for these realists who merely entertain the scholarly goal of explaining how the world functions.

The System and Determinism

As we have seen, the concept of system is critical to many realist writers. Whether the rather simple notion of anarchy or the more elaborate formulations devised by contemporary realist authors, the system is deemed important for its impact on international actors. It is charged, however, that recent realist writers portray the system as having a life of its own. The system is seemingly independent of the wishes and actions of states, even though it is the result of the preferences and powers of the constituent states. Statesmen are granted too little autonomy and too little room to maneuver, and the decision-making process is seemingly devoid of human volition. Human agents are pawns of a bloodless system that looms over them, a structure whose functioning they do not understand and the mechanics of which they only dimly perceive. Statesmen are faced with an endless array of constraints and few opportunities. It is as if they are engaged in a global game, a game called power politics, and they are unable to change the rules even if they so desire. In sum, critics claim there is a fatalistic, deterministic, and pessimistic undercurrent to much of the realist work.

Realists differ among themselves as to how much explanatory emphasis is to be given to the international system. There is disagreement as to what extent the system functions as an independent variable in influencing state behavior. For *structural realists* or neorealists, the system is more than the aggregation of state interactions. Rather, it represents a material structure that does indeed influence the behavior of states that are part of the system. It is these scholars who have drawn the most criticism, but they reject the charge that they are structural determinists who ignore actors operating at the unit, or state, level of analysis. As noted earlier, some so-called defensive realists have explicitly introduced unit or nonsystem variables to explain instances where states do not seem to be acting with what a purely system-structure perspective would lead one to expect.

Consistent with Wolfers, Morgenthau, Kissinger, and others of more recent vintage, traditional or classical realists have often made the distinction between imperialist, revolutionary, or revisionist states on the one hand and status quo powers interested in maintaining their own position in a relatively constant regional or global order on the other. "Neoclassical realists" such as Randall Schweller, while appreciating the insights of neorealism, have attempted to incorporate international institutions and explanatory factors at the state-society level of analysis. Similarly, still other realists have examined relations among states that analytically fall between the level of system structure and the level of state and society—arms racing and arms control, and alliance behavior (balancing or bandwagoning). Such factors, it is argued, will affect the stability of either bipolar or multipolar systems and, consequently, the possibility of moving toward a more peaceful world.

Realists, therefore, differ on the extent to which policy makers impose themselves on events, or vice versa. No realist is completely determinist or voluntarist or exclusively emphasizes structure or agents—human actors. It is not a matter of either-or but varying assessments as to how strong are the constraints and how much room leaders have to maneuver.

Realists and the State

The state is the centerpiece of realist work. Few persons would disagree as to the importance of the state in international affairs. The criticism, however, is that realists are so obsessed with the state that they ignore other actors and other issues not directly related to the maintenance of state security. Other nonstate actors—multinational corporations, banks, terrorists, and international organizations—are either excluded, downplayed, or trivialized from the realist perspective. Furthermore, given the national security prism through which realists view the world, other concerns such as the global environment, the socioeconomic gap between rich and poor societies, and the implications of globalization rarely make the realist agenda. At best, such issues are dealt with in a derivative manner. A preoccupation with national security and the state by definition relegates other issues to secondary importance or bans them entirely from the realist agenda.

Realists counter that simply because nonstate actors are not dealt with in-depth does not mean that they are considered irrelevant. A theory concerned with explaining state behavior naturally focuses on states, not multinational corporations or terrorist groups. Theories are constructed to answer certain questions and to explain certain types of international behavior and outcomes. As a result, they purposely limit the types of actors analyzed. Second, realists would argue that, of course, the deteriorating global environment is an absolutely critical global concern with stark implications for the national security goals of all states. But solving such problems is going to have to be done by states taking the lead.

Finally, some realists argue that focusing on the state is justified on normative grounds. Many scholars are concerned with how unbridled arms races and military spending contribute to international tension, devastating regional wars, and socioeconomic deprivation. Because it is almost exclusively states that spend this money to buy or produce military hardware, it makes sense to focus on them as the unit of analysis. Hence, far from being enamored of states, many realists are critical of these political entities that are deemed too important to be ignored.

Realists and the Balance of Power

Given the emphasis on the state and the concern with national security issues, we have seen how the concept of balance of power has played a dominant role in realist thought and theory. Although balance of power has been a constant theme in realist writings down through the centuries, it has also come in for a great deal of abuse.

Balance of power has been criticized for creating definitional confusion. Morgenthau discerned at least four definitions: (1) a policy aimed at a certain state of affairs; (2) an objective or actual state of affairs; (3) an approximately equal distribution of power, as when a balance of power existed between the United States and the Soviet Union; and (4) any distribution of power including a preponderance of power, as when the balance of power shifts in favor of either superpower. Another critic—Ernst B. Haas—found at least seven meanings of the term then in use: (1) distribution of power; (2) equilibrium; (3) hegemony; (4) stability and peace; (5) instability and war; (6) power politics generally; and (7) a universal law of history.[44] Indeed, one is left with the question that if the balance of power means so many different things, can it mean anything?

Balance of power has also been criticized for leading to war as opposed to preventing it, serving as a poor guide for policy makers, and functioning as a propaganda tool to justify defense spending and foreign adventures. Despite these constant attacks and continual reformulations of the meaning of the term, balance of power remains a crucial concept in the realist vocabulary.

At times, it has appeared that the harshest critics of balance of power as a concept have been the realists themselves. All these criticisms have been acknowledged and some are deemed valid. Attempts have been made, however, to clear up misconceptions and misinterpretations of balance of power, placing it on a more solid conceptual footing. Waltz makes one such notable effort.[45] Even his formulation, however, is not without its critics, as Waltz soon replaced the late Morgenthau as the lightning rod drawing criticism to the realist and structural realist projects. In fact, the debate between Waltz and his critics lasted almost four decades and has included challenges from the neoliberal institutionalist, constructivist, critical theory, and postmodern perspectives.

Realism and Change

Given the realist view of the international system, the role of the state, and balance-of-power politics, critics suggest that very little possibility is left for the fundamental and peaceful transformation of international politics. Realists, claim the critics, at best offer analysis aimed at understanding how international stability is achieved, but nothing approaching true peace. Realist stability reflects a world bristling with weapons, forever on the verge of violent conflict and war. Alternative world futures—scenarios representing a real alternative to the dismal Hobbesian world—are rarely discussed or taken seriously. The

---

[44] Morgenthau, *Politics among Nations*, 161; Ernst B. Haas, "The Balance of Power: Prescription, Concept or Propaganda?" *World Politics* 5, no. 2 (July 1953): 442–77.

[45] Kenneth N. Waltz, *Theory of International Politics* (New York: McGraw-Hill, 1979).

timeless quality of international politics, its repetitious nature and cycles of war, and a world in which the strong do as they will and the weak do as they must dominate the realist image. We are given little information, let alone any hope, say the critics, as to how meaningful and peaceful change can occur and thus help us escape from the security dilemma.

Realists, it is further argued, simply assume state interests, but tell us little about how states come to define their interests, or the processes by which those interests are redefined. Interests are not simply "out there" waiting to be discovered, but are constructed through social interaction. Alexander Wendt and other constructivists claim that international anarchy is what states make of it—interests not being exogenous or given to states, but actually constructed by them.[46]

The issue of change, of course, is intimately connected to that of determinism and to what is referred to in chapter 1 as the agent-structure problem. Although power politics and the state are central to all realist analyses, this does not mean that fundamental change is impossible or that change is limited to war and the cyclical rise and fall of states. Realists claim that fundamental change *is* possible and is taken into consideration in their work. Once again, however, the strength of this view varies substantially depending on the author under consideration.

Realism: The Entire Enterprise

Critics of realism have always felt that they have been faced with a difficult task because the image comes close to approaching an impregnable edifice seemingly unscathed by years of criticism. Indeed, scholars who at one time in their careers struggled to devise alternative approaches based on alternative images of international politics have in some instances given up the quest, become converts, or resigned themselves to modifying existing realist explanatory frameworks.

Critics are faced with several problems. First, as noted earlier, given realism's affinity to the real world of policy-making, this particular image of the world is automatically imbued with a certain degree of attractiveness and legitimacy. It represents the world out there, not some ivory tower perspective on human events. Not only is the realist perspective the accepted wisdom of the Western foreign policy establishments, but even outside the northern hemisphere, leaders more often than not speak the language of realism as a result of concern over the survival of their regimes and states. Within the halls of academe, realism also has great attractiveness; "peace studies" programs sometimes find it advantageous to change the title to "security and conflict studies" to generate student interest. Realism can be as seductive to the academic professional as it can be to the student.

Second, realism is also seductive in that it has been given an increasingly scientific face. Earlier criticisms of the realist literature were very often based on the contention that such concepts as balance of power had less to do with theory building and more to do with ideology and self-justification of one particular

---

[46] Alexander Wendt, *Social Theory of International Politics* (London: Cambridge University Press, 1999).

approach to conducting international relations. Much of the classical-realist work is, therefore, considered "unscientific"—insight without evidence. But many defensive and offensive realists have cast their hunches and insights in the form of hypotheses, testable either quantitatively or with nonquantitative indicators. The work is better grounded scientifically and placed within the context of the *positivist* view of how we comprehend reality. The positivist approach to knowledge remains prominent in the social as in the natural sciences. Indeed, in some circles any image of international politics that can be presented in the cloak of positivism is immediately granted a certain stature above those that do not.

What realists see as a virtue—a positivist orientation—is viewed by postmodernists and others as erroneous. The heart of their perspective on realism goes to the question of what is this "knowable reality" of international relations that realists claim to be true. This involves serious consideration of the underlying issues of ontology—how theorists view the essence of politics—the nature of the actors (states) and how they are prone to act; epistemology—verification of knowledge claims (how we know what we think we know); and methodology (modes of research and analysis). Is reality simply "out there" waiting to be discovered? Or is reality constructed, for example, by discourse and hence realism is best viewed as simply another perspective or construction of how the world works?

A reminder concerning criticism of any image or interpretive understanding: It is not particularly difficult to find fault with the work of individual theorists and then blanket an entire approach for the supposed sins of an individual author. As this chapter illustrates, although realists may find common ground in terms of basic assumptions and key international actors, there are differences between classical (and neoclassical) realists and structural realists, and, in turn, offensive and defensive realists. Realists of any persuasion may differ in several important respects, such as methods they use, levels of analysis they choose, and what they assume about the ability of decision makers to influence international outcomes. That is why it is imperative to refer to the original sources.

REFERENCES

Copeland, Dale. *The Origins of Major War*. Ithaca, NY: Cornell University Press, 2001.

Gilpin, Robert. *War and Change in World Politics*. New York: Cambridge University Press, 1981.

Mearsheimer, John J. *The Great Delusion: Liberal Dreams and International Realities*. New Haven, CT: Yale University Press, 2018.

———. *The Tragedy of Great Power Politics*. New York: W.W. Norton, 2001.

Morgenthau, Hans J. *Politics among Nations*, 4th ed. New York: Knopf, 1966.

Posen, Barry R. *The Sources of Military Doctrine*. Ithaca, NY: Cornell University Press, 1984.

Van Evera, Stephen. *Causes of War: Power and the Roots of Conflict*. Ithaca, NY: Cornell University Press, 1999.

Walt, Stephen. *The Origins of Alliances*. Ithaca, NY: Cornell University Press, 1987.

Waltz, Kenneth N. *Man, the State and War*. New York: Columbia University Press, 1959.

———. *Theory of International Politics*. New York: McGraw-Hill, 1979.

6

Liberalism: Interdependence and Global Governance

MAJOR ACTORS AND ASSUMPTIONS

Realists are primarily interested in power and the balance of power—explanations of political and economic competition, war, and other conflicts that are so prevalent in IR. Liberals, by contrast, are primarily interested in explaining the conditions under which international cooperation, collaboration, or *multilateralism* becomes possible. For many realists, particularly structural realists, the international system is the starting point for analysis, and factors at the unit or state-societal level of analysis are of secondary importance. For many theorists in the liberal tradition, however, the opposite is the case, with such "second-" and "first-image" factors being critical to explaining international outcomes.[1] The liberal image of international relations is a large, seemingly all-inclusive tent—not just states, but also international and nongovernmental organizations and the often cross-cutting networks that connect them. With liberal lenses firmly in place, the focus may be on democratic peace theory, integration, interdependence, regime theory, neoliberal institutionalism, or the ways and means of *global governance*.

Underlying the liberal image of international relations are five key assumptions. First, states as well as nonstate *transnational* actors are important entities in world politics. International organizations, for example, may on certain issues be independent actors in their own right. Similarly, other nongovernmental, transnational organizations such as multinational corporations (MNCs) and human rights and environmental groups play important roles in world politics. On occasion, even individuals can have a significant impact. The liberal image is therefore a pluralist one in which multiple kinds of state and nonstate actors

---

[1] Following Kenneth N. Waltz's typology developed in his early volume *Man, the State and War*, the first image is an individual (or small group) level of analysis, the second a focus on state and society, and the third on the international system as a whole.

play substantial roles in world politics. Indeed, many liberals prefer *world* or *global* rather than *international* politics since the latter term tends to privilege the state over international and nongovernmental organizations, groups, and individuals. To these liberals, referring to international politics is really a euphemism for interstate politics—an understanding more suited to realists. The analytical challenge for liberals is to explain how, to what extent, and under what circumstances these diverse actors influence world politics.

Second, many liberals see economic or other forms of *interdependence* or interconnectedness among both state and nonstate actors as tending to have, if not a pacifying effect, then at least a moderating one on state behavior. As the world is ever more closely bound with a veritable cobweb not only of economic but also social, cultural, and political or transnational ties, the literature on interdependence naturally flows into the discussion of the process of *globalization*. In an increasingly globalized world, liberals see states, international organizations, nongovernmental organizations, MNCs, groups, and individuals operating in complex arrays of overlapping or cross-cutting coalitions and networks. The growth of transnational networks oriented around common strategies and goals epitomize the rapid expansion of "sovereignty-free" actors and the coining of the term *global civil society*. On the other hand, terrorist and criminal organizations could be viewed as the dark side of globalization, posing various degrees of threats to states and peoples.

Third, for liberals the agenda of international politics is extensive. The liberal rejects the notion that the agenda of international politics is dominated only by military-security issues. The distinction between *high and low politics* is falsely drawn. Economic, social, and environmental issues also matter. Sometimes they also can be understood as security issues, perhaps even more salient than other military-related security matters.

Fourth, as opposed to structural realists with their "top-down" view on how *anarchy* and the distribution of capabilities affect state behavior, many liberals take an "inside-out" view that examines how factors at the state-society and individual levels of analysis affect international relations and outcomes. For its part, *democratic peace theory* attempts to show how political culture, values, and domestic political structures influence the prospects for international peace. Other work examines the role of perception, small-group behavior, and decision-making processes. Particular policies may enhance the bureaucratic power, prestige, and standing of one organization or institution at the expense of others or of the state as a whole. Decision-making processes associated with coalition and countercoalition building, bargaining, and compromising may not yield the best or optimal decision for a particular state.

Fifth, the key analytical task is to discover under what conditions international collaboration, if not peace, might be achieved. The role of international organizations is a major focus, for example, in the work on regional integration and interdependence. The task is to go beyond mere description and achieve explanation. Toward that end, for example, *neoliberal institutionalists* (as do structural realists) utilize the *rational-actor* assumption to help generate testable hypotheses on how international organizations can affect states' calculations of interests. The staff of an international organization may play an important role in monitoring and adjudicating disputes arising from decisions made by constituent states. Or the organization may have a great deal of power in terms of agenda setting as well as in providing information that may influence how states define their interests. Other liberals note that calculations of interest or utility—gains and losses—can also be affected by misunderstanding or misperceptions on the part of state decision makers as a result of incomplete information, bias, or uncertainty about cause-and-effect relations related to policy options under consideration.

Even in the absence of a formal international organization, scholars of *regime theory* argue that collaboration is possible where principles, norms, and actors' expectations converge on a particular issue area. Liberalism therefore takes from game theory a positive-sum perspective—the size of the pie can be increased. Absolute gains (all can win) are opposed to the realist assumption of *relative gains* that supposedly drives interstate competition—when one gains or loses disproportionately more than others or when one's gain is another's loss, a zero-sum outcome. Despite their differences, integration, interdependence, regime, and neoliberal institutionalist theories all examine the possibilities of upgrading the common interest to include the impact of nonmaterial factors such as ideas and norms. Hence, some liberals incorporate social constructivist understandings within their work.

In sum, for liberals, human agents matter as we take into account how they relate to the material or ideational factors that may facilitate or constrain their conduct. Liberal theorists dealing with agency may refer to states and international and nongovernmental organizations as actors, but they also are prone to look within the state or other institutions to find agency at the human level of individuals and small groups. Although cognizant of the impact of *system-level* influences, these efforts challenge the realist assumption of a rational, unified decision maker, except as a methodological starting point to understand the role of international organizations and regimes in enhancing collaboration among states. The liberal approach to theory, then, can be characterized as building separate islands of theory (each explaining some things but not others), perhaps with the eventual goal of connecting them within a more general theory of international politics. Compared to structural realists and many economic structuralists, in particular, liberals tend to be voluntarists. While globalization is not without its costs, liberals tend to be cautiously optimistic that international collaboration or partial global governance is achievable. Explaining the logic and circumstances under which this can be achieved is their major theoretical and empirical challenge.

INTELLECTUAL PRECURSORS AND INFLUENCES

In part I we provided an in-depth discussion of the myriad of writers who have contributed to the liberal image—the Greek Stoics, the development of Greco-Roman thought, and certain eighteenth- and nineteenth-century thinkers such as Montesquieu, Jean-Jacques Rousseau, Immanuel Kant, Adam Smith, and

Richard Cobden. These writers have directly and indirectly informed work on transnationalism, interdependence, democratic peace theory, global governance, and decision-making.

In the case of liberalism, however, the impact of more recent theorists has tended to be overlooked if not ignored. Many of these writers have not been observers of international relations per se but have been economists, social scientists, theologians, or political scientists primarily interested in domestic politics. Their one common denominator, however, has been an interest in not simply the state, but also the individual or group. Agency—a focus on actors—is an important theme among these more recent intellectual precursors of the liberal image of international relations.

Interest Group Liberalism

Human agents at the individual and small-group levels of analysis particularly matter in liberal understandings. Indeed, the liberalism we find among many American and European IR scholars is not unrelated to the way they also see domestic politics.

It is a multi-actor pluralism of individuals in groups interacting and forming coalitions and countercoalitions in the domestic arenas of politics that many liberal scholars project as capturing the essence of politics across the entire globe. From this perspective, known as *interest group liberalism*, international political processes are not all that different from, and may even be considered an extension of, those conducted within the boundaries of a given state. As a result, many liberals reject the realist distinction between "international" and "domestic" politics. For the liberal, one is an extension of the other. This perspective is quite evident in much of the literature on decision-making and transnationalism that disaggregates the state-as-actor into its component parts, placing particular emphasis on agency—the decision makers themselves.

The American political scientist Theodore J. Lowi observes that interest group liberalism assumes the "role of government is one of assuring access to the most effectively organized, and of ratifying the agreements and adjustments worked out among competing leaders and their claims." Second, there is a "belief in a natural harmony of group competition." Finally, interest group liberalism defines both "the policy agenda and the public interest . . . in terms of the organized interests in society."[2] All three observations are consistent with the liberal notions of (1) the state as neutral arbiter, (2) the potential for a natural harmony of interest, in this case among groups of individuals, and (3) public concern for, and participation in, a policy process not restricted to elites.

In the image of politics held by adherents of interest group liberalism, conflict and competition, as well as cooperation and collaboration, among interest

---

[2] Theodore J. Lowi, *The End of Liberalism: Ideology, Policy, and the Crisis of Public Authority* (New York: Norton, 1969), 48, 71. Subsequent quotes are from David Truman, *The Governmental Process* (New York: Knopf, 1959), ix, 519–20; Robert A. Dahl, *A Preface to Democratic Theory* (Chicago: University of Chicago Press, 1963), 173; see also Harold D. Lasswell, *Politics: Who Gets What, When, How* (New York: McGraw-Hill, 1936).

groups thus play an important role. There is a proliferation of interest groups. Individuals form interest groups in attempts to outmaneuver, end-run, or over-whelm opposing groups or coalitions. Viewed in this way, politics is a game, but a game with very real stakes to be won or lost. Authoritative choices (or deci-sions) are made by government decision makers as the outcome of this process.

David Truman, whose writings are in the school of interest group liber-alism, acknowledges his intellectual debt to Arthur F. Bentley, whose 1908 volume *The Process of Government* served as the principal benchmark for his thinking. Truman observes that the outstanding characteristic of American politics is the "multiplicity of co-ordinate or nearly co-ordinate points of access to governmental decisions." He proceeds to describe the conflictual nature of American politics, but comments that "overlapping membership among orga-nized interest groups" provides "the principal balancing force in the politics of a multi-group society such as the United States."

The writings of Harold Lasswell and Robert Dahl are also illustrative of this image. Dahl describes American politics as a "system in which all the active and legitimate groups in the population can make themselves heard at some crucial stage in the process of decision." Noting that it is a decentralized system, he observes that "decisions are made by endless bargaining." Groups are central to the process. Rather than either majority rule or minority rule, Dahl argues that the term "minorities rule" is more accurate. Politically active groups—minori-ties—are the most influential.

Thus, the image of politics that interest group liberals holds—at least in terms of democratic representative polities—is of a fragmented political system, one in which multiple actors compete. Human agents matter to liberals at least as much as (and for many a good deal more than) societal factors, systems, or structures do. The image is shared by most American political scientists even though their views may differ greatly on other conceptual and normative mat-ters. The scholars mentioned are not, of course, creators of this image of Ameri-can politics. Certainly, *The Federalist Papers*, especially the writings of James Madison, and later the work of the Frenchman Alexis de Tocqueville expose one to a good dose of this pluralist view of American domestic politics.

In sum, what the group is to the interest group liberal, the individual is to the liberal philosopher. What they have in common is agreement on the fragmented nature of the state and society and the potential for harmony to develop within representative democracies out of competition and conflict. The state is not an independent, coherent, autonomous actor separated or aloof from society. Its primary function is as the arbiter of conflicting demands and claims, or as an arena for the expression of such interests. Furthermore, the focus of analysis is less on the state and more on both competition and cooperation among indi-viduals and groups as agents of both state and nonstate actors in world politics.

Let us now turn to an overview of theoretical efforts that reflect the influ-ence of the liberal tradition in an attempt to understand how international order and collaboration can be achieved to enhance the prospects for material welfare and peace. Our discussion presents these theorists in roughly the chronologi-cal order in which their works appeared. As will become evident, their efforts to a certain extent reflect the international problems confronted at the time of their research and writing, running from the end of World War II and the Cold War that followed to the current twenty-first-century challenges posed by globalization.

INTERNATIONAL ORGANIZATION

The League of Nations established in the aftermath of World War I as an effort to maintain peace drew upon European diplomatic experience—the post-Napoleonic peace found in a Concert of Europe—and reflected liberal ideas found in Immanuel Kant and others. Influenced by American President Woodrow Wilson's liberal thought, negotiators moved away from alliances (and secret agreements among them that were thought to have triggered World War I), power, and the balance of power. These were understood to be more the causes of war than mechanisms for maintaining peace. It was instead to be a *collective security* based on the rule of law. Aggression was prohibited and war was even later declared illegal. Law-abiding states in these collective security arrangements were to come together as collective law enforcers against any state committing aggression. Realist critics observed that such *idealism* posed no effective obstacles in the interwar years (1918–1939) to stop aggression by Germany, Italy, Japan, and other states that joined with them.

This failed experience with collective security through the rule of law was at the root of the realist-idealist debate in the interwar period that continued after World War II. On security matters, the new United Nations retained collective security (see chapter 7, particularly Article 42 of the UN Charter) but augmented it with collective defense—a euphemism for bringing alliances back into the mix (see Articles 51 and 52) as a supplement to a sovereign state's right to self-defense under international law. In practice, then, liberal and realist conceptions came together in the multilateral security mechanism constituted under the authority of the UN Security Council. In other respects, liberal ideas became embedded in a wide variety of UN-affiliated and other international organizations—the World Bank, International Monetary Fund (IMF), the General Agreement on Tariffs and Trade and later the World Trade Organization, the International Telecommunications Union, the International Civil Aviation and Maritime Organizations, the World Health Organization, the Food and Agricultural Organization, the International Labor Organization, and the UN High Commission on Human Rights, to mention just a few.

The present-day story of liberalism and IR theory, then, begins in Europe in the aftermath of World War II. Notwithstanding *embedded liberalism* in international organizations, with the advent of the Cold War, realism secured a preeminent place in the study of international relations. But while headlines focused on crises in Berlin and the rise in East-West tensions, Europe was also the test bed for theories in the liberal tradition. The economic rebuilding of Western Europe was not simply a humanitarian priority, but a political one as well. The fear was that a failure to rebuild Europe would make communist subversion and political unrest more likely, particularly in Germany. Furthermore, the hope was that a rebuilt Europe would eventually tie together states such as France and Germany into a web of interdependencies to reduce the likelihood of another devastating war. In keeping with liberal theory, increased economic ties would play a major role in regional integration.

INTEGRATION

The first scholar to explicate the hope and logic of *integration* was David Mitrany. In the process he broke away from the liberal tradition of merely describing international organizations and exhorting the expansion and application of international law. His goal was to develop a theory as to how collaborative behavior among states could be achieved. The result was his theory of *functionalism*. Mitrany argued that modern society faced a myriad of technical problems that can best be resolved by experts as opposed to politicians. This is true within states as well as among states in multilateral arrangements. Indeed, he saw the proliferation of common problems logically requiring collaborative responses from states. Hence, these essentially nonpolitical problems (economic, social, scientific) should be assigned to nonpolitical experts from the affected countries for resolution.

Mitrany reasoned that successful collaboration in one particular technical field would lead to further collaboration in other related fields. Governments would recognize the common benefits to be gained by such cooperative endeavors and so would encourage or allow for a further expansion of collaborative tasks. In effect, Mitrany saw a way to sneak up on the authority of the sovereign state. As states and societies became increasingly integrated due to the expansion of collaboration in technical areas in which all parties made absolute gains, the cost of breaking these functional ties would be great and hence give leaders reason to pause before doing so.

The interest in Mitrany's functionalist theory—and integration in general—was spurred by the successful creation of the European Coal and Steel Community (ECSC) in 1952 and the formation of the European Economic Community (EEC), or Common Market, in the 1956 Treaty of Rome. The EEC even seemed to hold out promise for the eventual political integration of Western Europe. Furthermore, the EEC's initial successes in the realm of economic integration increased interest in the more general question: Under which conditions is integration among states possible? Scholars noted that what was occurring in Western Europe did not match the Hobbesian image of states constantly prepared to go to war, an image that included little faith in the possibility of collaborative behavior among sovereign states.

Karl Deutsch pioneered the development of the concept of a security community in Europe. He argued that peace can be achieved through a shared sense of community resulting from the increase in communication and collaboration in economic and social activities. The pacifying effect of webs of interdependence and interconnectedness across an increasingly integrated Europe reflected the thought of Kant and influenced the logic of modern democratic peace theory.

The most prominent theorist of regional integration was Ernst Haas, whose work and that of his colleagues were referred to as neofunctionalism. Mitrany's functionalist logic of technical tasks driving the creation of international organizations had discounted the importance of politics. *Neofunctionalists* now put politics back in center stage. The prefix *neo* was added to the term "functionalism" precisely to acknowledge how integral politics is to integration processes. While acknowledging his intellectual debt to Mitrany, Haas and fellow neofunctionalists parted company with Mitrany by rejecting the notion that one somehow can separate technical tasks from politics. For integration to occur, Haas argued that it must be perceived by politically connected elites to be in their interest to pursue such aims—whether they be experts in economics and finance, agriculture, health, environment, telecommunications, education, or any other specialization.

An early constructivist (even before the term came into common usage), Haas saw ideas grounded in the interests of the actors as driving forces in politics. The assigning of tasks to an international organization—even if this involves a seemingly technical function such as supervising an international mail system—will be attained and sustained only if actors believe their interests are best served by making a political commitment to constructing and maintaining such institutions. Applying game theory to neofunctional understandings, politics can produce a variable- or positive-sum outcome for all actors. Stated another way, the perspective on Rousseau's stag hunt fable discussed in the chapter on realism is that collaborative behavior is possible and in the enlightened self-interest of states. Rather than just compete in ongoing zero-sum contests, optimizing short-term self-interest at the expense of others, they can upgrade service of their common and long-term interests through cooperative and collaborative efforts reflected in international institutions—the organizations they construct and the processes they establish.

The internal logic of neofunctionalism applied to the European case led theorists to anticipate how increased integration in particular economic sectors would "spill over" into other related sectors—a process carried by politically connected elites seeing positive gains to be found in increased collaboration as states became increasingly integrated economically. Six European states (Germany, France, Italy, Belgium, Netherlands, Luxembourg) agreed in 1958 to move beyond the coal and steel community (ECSC) established in 1953 to establish two additional communities—one for atomic energy (EURATOM) and the other the EEC—a full customs union that finally was achieved by 1967.

Achieved with much fanfare, the EEC countries renamed themselves the European Union (EU) in 1992 and set their sights on a full economic and monetary union by the dawn of the new century. Some members, guarding their national prerogatives, chose not to go all the way down to this deepest level of integration, but most did. Critics later observed that European integration had become à la carte, allowing members to pick and choose the level of integration that suited their fancy. The problem has grown with the expansion of the EU as it incorporated European states of great diversity in levels of economic development; critics of "widening" the membership have noted that doing so would make the "deepening" of integration ever more difficult. Be that as it may, the overall level of integration that has been achieved was thought decades earlier as highly unlikely, if not impossible to achieve in so short a period.

Integration as a robust research program has faded, no longer enjoying the luster it once had. Indeed, the focus now is on the resurgence of populist nationalism in Europe due to refugee crises and economic difficulties and whether the EU experiment can even survive. Haas himself concluded years before that regional integration theories should be subordinated to a broader theory of interdependence, which did not anticipate a transfer of state sovereignty to regional organizations. As we look back, however, we can find within the neofunctional and integration research program the seeds of the still unresolved agency-structure debates that remain prominent in the IR field, particularly among constructivists. How ideas relate to material considerations in the minds of agents and how material structures enable or constrain these same agents are not new topics. For his part, Haas held to the position that agency matters. Individuals need not be captives of system structure but can in fact influence the course of events. Changing knowledge, for example, can lead to redefining interests. Organizations composed of thinking people can adapt, learn, and innovate in changing circumstances.

Though not an integration theorist, much of James Rosenau's (1924–2011) work focused on the important roles played by both state and nonstate actors in world politics. Like Haas, Rosenau also identified turbulence as a substantial challenge.[3] In this regard, Rosenau revealed his ontology as one seeing two competing "worlds"—the first he described as state-centric and the other multicentric involving diverse state and nonstate actors. The agency-structure issue is reflected in the distinction he drew between parameters at micro-level (individual) and macro-level (system structure) and the "relational one" that tries to put the micro and macro together. Change is propelled by the dynamics of technology, the emergence of complex issues, the reduced capacity of states to deal effectively with many contemporary problems, and the emergence of "subgroupism" and individuals who are analytically ever more capable and diverse in orientation. Agents obviously mattered to Rosenau, as they also did to Haas.

TRANSNATIONALISM

By the early 1970s, just as neofunctional understandings of regional integration were losing conceptual steam, the concept of *transnationalism* entered the mainstream IR theory lexicon. Attention turned to the increasing role of MNCs abroad and the challenge they posed to the sovereign prerogatives of states as they transited across national boundaries in the daily conduct of their business transactions. Interest in international *political economy* increased substantially. The unilateral decision by the United States in 1971 to go off the gold-exchange standard of $35 an ounce (a rate the US Treasury had maintained since 1934)

---

[3] See the full argument in James N. Rosenau, *Turbulence in World Politics* (Princeton, NJ: Princeton University Press, 1990).

and allow the dollar's value to float caused turmoil in international currency markets. Similar disruption of the status quo occurred when major oil-producing countries in the Organization of Petroleum Exporting Countries (OPEC) cartel dramatically raised the cost of oil by regulating its supply to global markets. Economics now seemed to be "high politics" as opposed to merely "low politics."

Even on security matters things seemed to be changing. Zero-sum calculations and relative gains prominent in realist thought were augmented by positive-sum understandings more common among liberals. An initial thawing of US-Soviet relations in the late 1960s—still in the middle of the Cold War—had produced *détente*, or a relaxation of tensions between the two superpowers, a climate conducive to arms control. Explicitly intended as balance-of-power politics vis-à-vis the Soviet Union, Washington also played its "China card" and reached out to Beijing, setting in motion a process that would lead to normalization of relations between the two Cold War adversaries. At the same time, power-based realist ideas—that the strong do what they will and the weak do what they must—had difficulty accounting for why a superpower like the United States could get bogged down and eventually lose a war in Vietnam, where the former was forced to evacuate its remaining forces in 1975.

These events in the late 1960s and early 1970s contributed to ferment in the IR field, setting the stage for new developments in both realist and liberal theories in international relations. In 1971 and 1972, two works raised the question of the conceptual adequacy of the realist approach to international relations. John W. Burton argues in *World Society* that a "cobweb" model of multiple state and nonstate actors better captured the nature of current reality than did the realist "billiard ball" model merely of states interacting with one another. He also asserts that the idea of a "world society" is descriptively more accurate than the concept of international relations.

Also published at this time was the seminal work *Transnational Relations and World Politics* by Robert O. Keohane and Joseph Nye Jr.[4] This work brings attention to MNCs and other nongovernmental, transnational organizations as well as bureaucratic agencies, departments, or other components of governments that in their own right operate across state boundaries. Sometimes these entities even form transgovernmental coalitions and countercoalitions with their counterparts in other countries. Thus, diplomats and civil servants in the US State Department might find common ground with fellow professionals in Germany or the United Kingdom on an issue like arms control that might be at odds with views in their respective defense ministries.

Liberal theories in the 1970s moved to center stage within the IR field. The term *transnational* was used to describe either an actor (i.e., MNC) or a pattern of behavior (i.e., "MNCs act transnationally"). The new focus was on studying these actors, their interactions, and the coalitions they form across

---

[4] John W. Burton, *World Society* (Cambridge, UK: Cambridge University Press, 1972); Robert O. Keohane and Joseph S. Nye Jr., eds., *Transnational Relations and World Politics* (Cambridge, MA: Harvard University Press, 1971).

state boundaries that involved diverse nongovernmental actors such as MNCs, banks, churches, and eventually human rights, environmental, and terror or criminal networks. Transgovernmental links at the level of bureaucracies were also a new item on the liberal agenda, challenging realist claims of the state as unitary actor. Links or coalitions between nongovernmental organizations and transgovernmental actors also became a subject of some interest.

Was there in fact a chipping-away or leakage of state sovereignty? Just as the regional integration literature posited the possibility of going beyond the nation-state, so, too, did much of the transnational literature leave the impression that states, assuming they survived as actors over the long term, would become ensnared like Gulliver in Jonathan Swift's classic political novel *Gulliver's Travels*.

A problem with this new transnational literature, however, was that in most cases the work was highly descriptive, lacking in theoretical content. A realist response—reasserting the enduring importance of the state and capabilities or power among states—was soon heard from realists, such as Kenneth N. Waltz in his 1979 book *Theory of International Politics*.

INTERDEPENDENCE

In 1977 Keohane and Nye published their influential *Power and Interdependence: World Politics in Transition*. The title says it all: To develop the concept of *interdependence* and make it analytically useful, power must be taken into consideration. For Keohane and Nye, interdependence is simply defined as mutual dependence resulting from the types of international transactions cataloged by transnationalists—for example, flows of money, goods, services, people, communications. Interdependence exists when there are "reciprocal [though not necessarily symmetrical] effects among countries or among actors in different countries."[5] There is, in other words, sensitivity in Country *B* to what is going on in or emanating from Country *A*. Although there are costs associated with interdependence, as it by definition restricts autonomy, benefits to either party or both may outweigh these costs. Thus, interdependence is not necessarily only a matter of Country *B*'s vulnerability to Country *A*, which is the realist perspective. While Keohane and Nye fully recognize the importance of vulnerability interdependence such as when one country can manipulate the flow of oil to other countries, their interests lay elsewhere.

The centerpiece of their work was the concept of *complex interdependence*—an ideal type constructed to analyze situations involving transnational issues. In a situation of complex interdependence, where multiple channels connect societies, there is an absence of hierarchy among issues, and military force is not used by governments against other governments involved in the interdependent relation. While some enthusiasts greeted *Power and Interdependence* as a challenge to realist conceptions of international relations, Keohane and Nye

---

[5] Robert O. Keohane and Joseph S. Nye Jr., *Power and Interdependence: World Politics in Transition* (Boston: Little Brown, 1977), 8.

have always asserted that the work was designed to provide analytical insights and a research program in areas that the traditional realist's focus on matters of military-security and force tended to discount.

INTERNATIONAL REGIMES

Keohane and Nye's work on complex interdependence did not displace the state as principal focus of study. As noted, interdependence involves reciprocal effects among countries or other actors in different countries. Furthermore, even though most of the elements of the complex interdependence model involved states—the goals of which varied by issue area—states could use their power resources to manipulate interdependent relations, and it was states that would experience difficulties in linking issues together.

One important area that was highlighted, however, was that of international organizations. International organizations were not just institutions composed of state members, but also actors that could set agendas, encourage coalition formation, and act as arenas for political action even by small, relatively weaker states. Nongovernmental organizations were also quite capable of establishing their own ties with these intergovernmental organizations. Instead of viewing the policies of these international organizations simply as the dependent variable (decisions or actions to be explained), they and their agents (leaders and staffs) came to be understood as independent variables in their own right, sometimes with substantial influence on states.

This was a new "institutionalism" that found its way into the IR field even before such studies became prominent in other areas of political science during the 1980s. In liberal IR scholarship, the institutional turn took the form of a robust research program on the role of *international regimes*—rules agreed to by states (some with the binding character of international law) concerning their conduct in specific issue areas (trade, monetary exchange, navigation on the high seas or in the air, nonproliferation of weapons of mass destruction, etc.) and often associated with international and nongovernmental organizations linked to these regimes.

The regime literature has focused, then, on the ways and means of constructing and maintaining or managing interdependent relations found in these multilateral, institutionalized arrangements. The term *regime* was borrowed from domestic politics, where it refers typically to an existing governmental or constitutional order (democratic, authoritarian, or otherwise). In its international context, given the absence of a superordinate or overarching central authority, these rules are voluntarily established by states to provide some degree of order in international relations. Thus, there is a strong *Grotian* strain in liberal thought, particularly when talk turns to managing interdependence through the construction of regimes.

As sets of principles, norms, rules, and procedures, international regimes are not the same as international organizations (although they usually are associated with them) as they do not require a mailing address or possess the capacity to act. In IR theory they are merely analytical constructs defined by observers. Action remains with states and both international and nongovernmental organizations. Furthermore, an organization associated with a particular regime (e.g., the International Telecommunications Union that regulates the global distribution of frequencies) also may concern itself with other regimes covering diverse issue areas in a global context within what is referred to as the United Nations' "system" of international organizations.

The regime literature, then, is concerned with such basic questions as: How and why are international regimes formed? What accounts for rule-based cooperation? How do regimes affect state behavior and collective outcomes in particular issue areas? How and why do regimes evolve or dissolve? There are several schools of thought on such questions.

Power-based realist theories. These theories emphasize, not surprisingly, the role of anarchy and the impact of the relative distribution of capabilities. The best-known realist regime theory, *hegemonic stability*, was discussed in chapter 5. The basic argument is that regimes are established and maintained when a state holds a preponderance of power resources, as did the United States after World War II. Once this hegemonic power declines and power is spread more equally among states, if regimes do not adapt themselves to changed circumstances, they can be expected to decline. Although a few realists are completely dismissive of international regimes and organizations, most would accept Stephen Krasner's view that regimes help states avoid uncoordinated action and, in some cases, can be a source of power for weaker states.[6]

Knowledge-based cognitive regime theories. Scholars associated with these theories have been critical of both realist (hegemonic stability) and the neoliberal institutionalist perspective discussed below. *Cognition* theorists (some identified as constructivists whom we discuss in chapter 9) argue that state interests are not given, but rather created. This leads them to examine the role of normative and causative beliefs of decision makers in explaining preferences and interest formation. In other words, the focus is less on overt behavior and more on intersubjective understandings. Learning matters when a change in beliefs or understandings influence subsequent behavior. Cognition theorists attempt to demonstrate that states can redefine their interests without any shift in the overall systemic distribution of power and use regimes and institutions to "lock in" to their advantage the learning that has occurred.

One way knowledge might come to be shared by decision makers is through the influence of transnational, *epistemic communities*, defined as "network[s] of professionals with recognized expertise and competence in a particular domain and an authoritative claim to policy-relevant knowledge within that domain."[7] Epistemic communities (e.g., environmentalists, scientists, international economists, and other specialists), it is argued, can influence the creation and maintenance of international regimes in several ways.

---

[6] Stephen D. Krasner, "Global Communications and National Power: Life on the Pareto Frontier," *World Politics* 43 (1991): 363.

[7] Peter M. Haas, "Introduction: Epistemic Communities and International Policy Coordination," *International Organization* 46, no. 1 (1992): 3. Subsequent quote also from this article.

Pathbreaking work on epistemic communities by Peter Haas, Emanuel Adler, and others has had a substantial impact on liberal understandings of how ideas carried by transnational groups of specialists impact policy processes. These communities are composed of politically connected elites one also finds in the earlier work on integration by Ernst Haas. Common understandings and ideas held by these communities of professionals or experts have global impact on how policies are made in diverse institutional contexts. Peter Haas observes that "members of epistemic communities not only hold in common a set of principled and causal beliefs, but also have shared notions of validity and a shared policy enterprise." When called upon by policy makers, these specialists bring their socially constructed interpretations of facts or knowledge and causality to the questions at issue. Studying the roles played and influence on policy by epistemic communities was itself a major research program.

International regimes are embedded in the broader normative structures of *international civil society* and, as a result, states typically are not free to ignore institutional commitments without paying a price. A focus on self-interest alone will not explain regime maintenance. Regimes have more than a regulative function that requires states to behave in accordance with certain norms and rules. They also create a common social world that interprets the meaning of international behavior. In other words, regimes have what is called a *constitutive* dimension. They are socially constructed.[8]

This view of regimes can therefore be placed in the broader social constructivist approach to international relations. As discussed in chapter 9, the focus is on the social construction of world politics and identities in particular. It is argued that actors in international politics make decisions based on what the world appears to be and how they conceive their roles in it. These conceptions derive from systemic, intersubjective shared understandings and expectations. In terms of regimes, it logically follows that rule-governed cooperation can, over time, lead actors to change their beliefs about who they are and how they relate to the rest of the world. Cooperative and collaborative behaviors can become a matter of habit.

NEOLIBERAL INSTITUTIONALISM

Perhaps the most widely cited approach to regime theory was *neoliberal institutionalism* developed by Robert Keohane, his colleagues, and students in the 1980s. In fact, for Keohane, "regime theory" is too limiting a term to describe his approach to the conditions under which international cooperation can be achieved. He developed the broader concept of "institutions" that he defines as "persistent and connected sets of rules (formal and informal) that prescribe behavioral roles, constrain activity, and shape expectations."[9] Thus defined, international institutions can take one of three forms:

[8] Friedrich V. Kratochwil and John Gerard Ruggie, "International Organization: A State of the Art on an Art of the State," *International Organization* 40 (1986): 764, 766.

[9] Robert O. Keohane, "Neoliberal Institutionalism: A Perspective on World Politics," in *International Institutions and State Power: Essays in International Relations Theory*, ed. Robert O. Keohane (Boulder,

1. *Formal Intergovernmental or Cross-National, Nongovernmental Organizations*: These are purposive entities, bureaucratic organizations with explicit rules and missions. The United Nations is a prime example of the former, the International Committee of the Red Cross (ICRC) of the latter.

2. *International Regimes*: Institutionalized rules explicitly agreed upon by governments that deal with a particular set of issues. Examples would include the international monetary regime established in 1944 but adapted to changing circumstances since then, the Law of the Sea regime developed in the 1970s, and the various arms control agreements between the United States and the Soviet Union during the Cold War.

3. *Conventions*: Informal institutions (or customary norms and practices) with implicit rules and understandings. These implicit understandings allow actors to understand one another and coordinate their behavior. Not only do they facilitate coordination, but they also affect actors' incentives not to defect in those situations where at least in the short term it might be in their interest to do so. "Reciprocity" is an example of a convention; political leaders expect reciprocal treatment in international dealings, both positive and negative, and anticipate costs of one kind or another if they violate the convention. Diplomatic immunity is an example of a convention that existed for centuries before it was codified in formal agreements in the 1960s.

The point to keep in mind is that Keohane's neoliberal institutionalist formulation is not restricted to formal organizations and regimes. It is a counter within liberal thought to what some perceive as the intellectual hegemony of structural or neorealist writings within the IR field. Keohane's starting point is the proposition that "variations in the institutionalization of world politics exert significant impacts on the behavior of governments. In particular, patterns of cooperation and discord can be understood only in the context of the institutions that help define the meaning and importance of state action."[10]

His first stab at a theory of institutions was in *Power and Interdependence* in what he and Nye referred to as the international organization model of regime change. Subsequent work in the 1980s was done against the backdrop of rising challengers to the primacy of the United States in world politics. Much to the consternation of many scholars associated with regime theory and global civil society, Keohane's *After Hegemony* (1984) adopts several realist premises. They include a desire to explain behavioral regularities in a decentralized international system, yet epistemologically sensitive to the fact that while theories can and must be tested, it is naive to believe that reality can be objectively known. Furthermore, state power must be taken seriously, and it is assumed that leaders of states calculate the costs and benefits of contemplated courses

---

CO: Westview Press, 1989), 3. The rest of this section draws on this chapter of Keohane's collected essays as well as his *After Hegemony: Cooperation and Discord in the World Political Economy* (Princeton, NJ: Princeton University Press, 1984).

[10] Keohane, "Neoliberal Institutionalism," 2.

of action. Finally, he also shares with neorealists an interest in the applicability to international relations of economic theories of market behavior. With these premises as a starting point, he addresses the puzzle of why even self-interested, rational egoists—individuals seeking to maximize gains—would pursue multilateral, cooperative behavior.

Yet Keohane argues that despite these affinities with neorealism, neoliberal institutionalism is a distinct school of thought. First, neorealists and neoliberal institutionalists agree that international relations or world politics lack a stable hierarchy due to its anarchic or decentralized character. Neoliberals, however, are much more emphatic that there is no necessary logical link between the condition of anarchy and war. If any connection does exist between warfare and lack of harmony among states, it is conditional on the nature of prevailing expectations among actors to include those held by institutions.

Second, some realists, particularly neorealists, claim that in a condition of anarchy, *relative gains* are more important than *absolute gains*. States, therefore, are concerned with preventing others from achieving advances in their relative capabilities. So even though two states may both make material gains such as enhancing their military capabilities, the important question to most realists is who gained more. Is the power gap widening? This realist formulation seems to characterize US-Soviet relations during the Cold War and, perhaps, the security implications of a rising China and resurgent Russia.

Neoliberals counter that this realist understanding does not accurately describe US policy toward Europe or Japan in which the United States actively promoted economic recovery and development. At least in the case of Europe, the United States has pleaded (and continued to plead even after the Russian invasion of Ukraine in February 2022) for greater European defense spending on the part of its North Atlantic Treaty Organization (NATO) allies. Nor does the neorealist formulation explain the peaceful relations among members of the EU where, despite economic integration favoring some states more than others, members across the board for decades were willing to accept an asymmetric distribution of absolute gains—some clearly gaining more than others. Neoliberals concede, of course, that the absolute gains argument may be more applicable in conditions where substantial mutual gains can be achieved and when governments do not expect others to threaten to use force against them.

As with all propositions in IR theory, such statements are conditional. But conditionality for neoliberals is a function of prevailing rules and expectations. States use international institutions, which perform important tasks that enhance cooperation, for self-interested reasons. For example, the transaction costs—making, monitoring, and enforcing rules—are reduced when institutions provide information to all parties and facilitate the making of credible commitments. What, however, are the guarantors of compliance with the commitments made by states? Reputation is one. Reciprocity is another, which includes threats of retaliation as well as promises of reciprocal cooperation.

While Keohane's interest in trade, monetary, and energy issues deals with material self-interest in which reciprocity plays a key role, he argues that the same framework works with environmental issues that often include a normative dimension and the role of principled ideas. His work with Judith Goldstein underscores the importance of ideas as a significant independent variable in explanations of foreign policy.[11] Worldviews, principled beliefs, and causal beliefs are ideas that become embedded in institutions and impact the making of policy by acting as cognitive road maps. Ideas define the universe of possibilities for action. To Keohane "interests are incomprehensible without an awareness of the beliefs that lie behind them." These ideas shape agendas and, as a result, directly affect outcomes. When ideas become institutionalized, they assume a life of their own as socially embedded norms. Ideas linked to interests do influence the making of foreign policy choices.

Neoliberals like Keohane claim that institutions and regimes matter because they enable states to do things they otherwise could not do. With rising levels of interdependence and interconnectedness in world politics, it is hypothesized that states likely will rely more heavily on regimes for their own selfish reasons. Hence, while realists tend to view regimes as constraints on state behavior, neoliberals view regimes more positively as actually enabling states to achieve mutually beneficial outcomes.

Such thinking brings us back to Rousseau's stag hunt allegory discussed in chapter 5 and the possibilities of upgrading the common interest, despite the underlying condition of anarchy. In sum, the literature on international organizations, regimes, and institutions in the liberal tradition offers insight into how states may accommodate differences and upgrade the interests they share. Consistent with Rousseau's stag hunt fable, the actors may agree to collaborate in certain circumstances in hunting the stag rather than serve only narrowly defined, short-term self-interest. Absolute gains for all are possible as policy makers learn the benefits of cooperation in areas of interest to them.

GLOBAL GOVERNANCE

The increasing complexity of issues on the global agenda brings neoliberal institutionalists to the question of global *governance*. The concept is not new. Indeed, Kant's proposal of a decentralized, self-enforcing peace without world government is an example. Governance involves the processes and institutions, both formal and informal, that guide and restrain the collective activities of groups. Keohane describes a "partially globalized world" as one with "thick networks of interdependence in which boundaries and states nevertheless matter a great deal."[12] With increasing interdependence in this partially globalized world, Keohane sees greater institutionalization as the world becomes more like a polity with governance essential to trade, finance, environment, security, and other matters of global import.

Keohane decidedly does not see global governance as if it were the same as world government—a new, unitary superstate. It is merely a design that

---

[11] See Judith Goldstein and Robert O. Keohane, eds., *Ideas and Foreign Policy: Beliefs, Institutions, and Political Change* (Ithaca, NY: Cornell University Press, 1993).

[12] Robert O. Keohane, *Power and Governance in a Partially Globalized World* (New York: Routledge, 2002), 258. Subsequent direct quotes are from this book.

integrates "networks among agents and norms—standards of expected behavior—that are widely accepted among agents." Devising better, more effective global institutions to serve the needs of humankind is imperative. On this, Keohane boldly asserts that "the challenge for American political science resembles that of the founders of the United States: how to design institutions for a polity of unprecedented size and diversity."

He notes that "increased interdependence among human beings produces discord, since self-regarding actions affect the welfare of others." Moreover, he is concerned that institutional approaches to problems may not always be benign. Indeed, left to their own devices, they "can foster exploitation or even oppression." He observes that "the stakes in the mission" of establishing the ways and means of global governance are high, noting that "if global institutions are designed well, they will promote human welfare, but if we bungle the job, the results could be disastrous."

To avoid adverse outcomes, we need instead to draw insights "from a variety of perspectives, including game theory, the study of political culture, and work on the role that ideas play in politics" to learn "how important beliefs are in reaching equilibrium solutions and how institutionalized beliefs structure situations of political choice." It is indeed a large order for applied theory to fill! As Keohane puts it: "From traditional political theory we are reminded of the importance of normative beliefs for the practice of politics . . . from historical institutionalism and political sociology we understand how values and norms operate in society . . . [and] from democratic theory we discover the crucial roles of accountability, participation, and especially persuasion in creating legitimate political institutions."[13]

In sum, most issues on the global governance agenda cannot be managed unilaterally even if states wished to do so. Global economy, health, the environment, human rights, and human security are among the issues on global governance agendas of both governmental and nongovernmental organizations. Developing consensus on what is to be done is by no means an easy task, much less finding resources that can be allocated to these matters. Quite apart from opposition to proposed remedies by those whose economic or other interests would be adversely affected are genuine disagreements over outcomes to be sought as well as confusion about the science associated with particular problems—that is, understanding cause-effect relations associated with different options under consideration.

Those who continue to work in this realm express concern that over the past two decades, there has been a noticeable slowdown, if not a growing "governance deficit," in progress toward global governance in many issue areas. There has been a resultant shift from examining how interest alignment among states in multilateral settings can be aligned to reimaging global governance as a more explicit realm of disputes and confrontations.[14]

---

[13] For Keohane's assessment of the impact of populism on the liberal international order he has long advocated, see his essay (with Jeff Colgan), "The Liberal Order Is Rigged: Fix It Now or Watch It Wither," *Foreign Affairs* 96 (2017): 36–44.

[14] Tom Pegram and Michele Acuto, "Introduction: Global Governance in the Interregnum," *Millennium* 43, no. 2 (2015): 584–97.

ECONOMIC INTERDEPENDENCE AND PEACE

The eighteenth- and nineteenth-century argument associating increased trade among states with peace discussed in chapter 4 is reflected in Richard Rosecrance's *The Rise of the Trading State*.[15] Rosecrance contrasts the realist military-political world with the liberal trading world, utilizing game theory to highlight their respective constant-sum or variable-sum characters. His essential argument is that the rise of a new "trading world" offers the possibility of escaping major international conflicts and establishing new patterns of cooperation among states. The benefits of trade greatly exceed those of military competition and territorial aggrandizement as exemplified by such countries as Japan.

Territorial acquisition may harm the ability of a state to increase its national wealth. Rosecrance does not deny that traditional military competition will continue but rather suggests states will calculate out of self-interest that an open international trading system will allow them to find a productive niche in the structure of world commerce. Part of the reason for such an opportunity is that since 1945 the threat of an all-out nuclear war has made major wars less likely to occur if not obsolete.

Following this logic, the prevalence of the trading option since 1945 increases peaceful possibilities among states that were lacking in the late nineteenth century and in the 1930s when competitive economic policies helped to drive the world into depression. As economic interdependence spreads, economic development through trade and foreign investment becomes a self-reinforcing process and an integral part of state strategy. Rosecrance thus expands our theoretical focus by including trade and commerce in strategic understandings, not just confining strategy to the military sector.

Realists have been skeptical if not outright hostile to the peace-through-economic interdependence proposition. Kenneth N. Waltz and John J. Mearsheimer, for example, have noted that the late nineteenth-century Western trading system had extremely high levels of interdependence, but this did not prevent the disaster of World War I; national security concerns trumped economic interests. If states feel threatened, they will take whatever military action is required despite the costs of breaking economic ties. This is even more the case if an aggressive great power attempts to upset the territorial status quo and embarks on a series of cumulative military conquests.

The question of how shifts in the international economy can affect international security relations has been examined under the popular rubric of *globalization*. One work in this genre is by Stephen Brooks.[16] His focus is not on the traditional debate concerning the hypothesized pacification of interstate rela-

---

[15] Richard Rosecrance, *The Rise of the Trading State: Commerce and Conquest in the Modern World* (New York: Basic Books, 1986). For a more recent assessment of this argument, see Jong-Wha Lee and Ju Hyun Pyun, "Does Trade Integration Contribute to Peace?" *Review of Developmental Economics* 20, no. 1 (2016): 327–44. See also Dale C. Copeland, *Economic Interdependence and War* (Princeton, NJ: Princeton University Press, 2014).

[16] Stephen G. Brooks, *Producing Security: Multinational Corporations, Globalization, and the Changing Calculus of Conflict* (Princeton, NJ: Princeton University Press, 2005, 2007).

tions through international trade, but rather on the impact of the globalization of production on great power security relations and security relations among states in general. Brooks argues that a historically unprecedented development has been left out of the debate: the geographic dispersion of production by multinational corporations (MNCs). Where and how these MNCs organize their international production activities are now the key integrating force of global commerce, not trade per se.

Unlike the work on MNCs in the 1970s that focused on the extraction of raw materials from exploited Global South states, Brooks's study on the globalization of production examines broader international security implications. Rather than focusing on a dependent variable and seeking to explain a particular case (such as the outbreak of World War I) or a general class of events (such as interstate wars), Brooks uses his independent variable—the globalization of production—and examines how it could influence security calculations. He does not assume that such production is a force for peace but wishes to leave this an open question.

Brooks examines three major means by which the international economy can influence security: changing capabilities, incentives, and the nature of the actors. The capabilities issue addresses whether the globalization of production has changed the parameters of weapons production. Is self-sufficiency still possible? He concludes that autarkic, go-it-alone arms production is in decline. To remain on the cutting edge of military technology requires engagement in the production of weaponry beyond one's borders. In terms of incentives, has the geographic dispersion of MNC production reduced the benefits of the physical conquest of other states? He concludes while there are exceptions, the economic benefits of military conquest have been greatly reduced, at least among the advanced industrial states. Finally, with regard to actors, has dispersed MNC production positively influenced the prospects for regional integration? He states it has, even where traditional security rivalries have existed. While perhaps not the primary cause of such integration, it can help deepen it. These three mechanisms are the primary focus of his book, although he examines others as well.

He concludes that the influence of the globalization of production is most evident in terms of great powers relations. While cognizant of other explanations such as democratic peace theory, Brooks believes his evidence strengthens the argument that international commerce indeed acts as a force for peace among great powers. As for the rest of the world, there is a differential impact. The security implications of the globalization of production are a mixed bag between the great powers and developing countries and are actually negative among countries of the Global South.

THE DEMOCRATIC PEACE

As noted earlier, for liberals the likelihood of war is reduced not only through the expansion of free trade but also democracy. Particularly ever since the end of the Cold War in 1991, scholars have attempted to answer empirically this question: "Are democracies more peaceful in their foreign relations?" The collapse of communism and the rise of an increasing number of fledgling democracies to replace authoritarian regimes provided a good test bed for *democratic peace theory*, at least until democratic backsliding began in the 2010s. Following in the tradition of Immanuel Kant, scholars such as Michael Doyle, Rudolph Rummel, and Bruce Russett have argued that liberal democracies are unique in that they can establish peaceful relations among themselves based on their shared values and a common approach to establishing legitimate domestic political orders.

Democracies tend not to go to war with each other.[17] Doyle brought renewed attention to this Kantian idea of democratic peace, reexamining the traditional liberal claim that governments founded on respect for individual liberty exercise restraint and peaceful intentions in their foreign policies. Despite the contradictions between liberal pacifism and liberal imperialism (both found in democratic practice), liberalism nevertheless does leave us with a coherent legacy on foreign affairs. Liberal states are different and indeed more peaceful, yet they also are prone to use force when they see it as in their interest to do so, albeit *not in wars with each other.*

Democracies certainly fight authoritarian regimes—sometimes representing themselves as "arsenals of democracy" as the United States did in its military campaign against fascism in World War II. As with authoritarian regimes, democracies have engaged historically in violent imperial expansions that also have provided opportunities to spread their own liberal, democratic ideologies. Furthermore, empirical work suggests that newly emerging democratic states may even be more prone to start wars than either long-established democracies or authoritarian regimes.[18] The key adjective or qualifier here is emerging.

The democratic peace literature's claims have spawned a substantial research program in liberal international relations that seeks to identify and explain patterns of behavior exhibited by democracies throughout the world. Indeed, some years ago, one scholar commented that "the absence of war between democracies comes as close as anything to an empirical law in international relations." Another observed that the democratic peace proposition is "one of the strongest nontrivial or non-tautological generalizations that can be made about international relations."[19]

The excitement generated, particularly during the 1990s, fueled an increasingly robust research program. While the proposition dates back at least to Kant, it was the collapse of the Soviet Union and breakup of the Warsaw Pact that produced a wave of new democracies and promised new empirical possibilities to test the theory. For liberals, here was a proposition that seemed to

---

[17] Michael W. Doyle, "Liberalism and World Politics," *American Political Science Review* 80, no. 4 (1986): 1151–69. For a survey of the literature, see Larry Diamond, *The Spirit of Democracy: The Struggle to Build Free Societies throughout the World* (New York: Times Books-Henry Holt, 2008).

[18] Edward D. Mansfield and Jack Snyder, *Electing to Fight: Why Emerging Democracies Go to War* (Boston: MIT Press, 2005).

[19] Jack Levy, "The Causes of War: A Review of Theories and Evidence," in *Behavior, Society, and Nuclear War*, vol. 1, ed. Phillip E. Tetlock et al. (New York: Oxford University Press, 1989), 270.

undermine the neorealist argument that it is the structure of the international system (not the nature of governments or societies) that explains a state's policies. To democratic peace theorists, state and society do matter as do the people who compose them.

The theory has even been used (many would say "misused") by politicians since the end of the Cold War to make optimistic predictions concerning the future of international politics. Much to the dismay of many liberal scholars, the virtues of the theory were invoked by neoconservatives who added democratization to the list of reasons used to justify the American invasion of Iraq in 2003. A democratic Iraq would not only bring benefit to the Iraqi people but also would provide a model for all Araby—a positive domino effect on the rest of this troubled region. A liberal theory embraced in this way by policy elites for their own purposes is hardly a blessing.

As in most new research programs, scholarship has taken different directions on both complementary and contradictory research paths. Key concepts are defined in different ways, and different variables are utilized. Consider, for example, the basic question of how one defines democracy. Critics complain that democratic peace theorists are all over the lot in defining their independent variable. Democracy (or states with democratic regimes) purportedly explain the propensity for peaceful relations with other democracies, but what constitutes a democracy is not entirely clear.

To begin with, Kant argued that republics made for more peaceful international relations, not democracies per se. Republicanism as we now understand it is representative democracy supported by the rule of law and respect for basic freedoms or rights in civil society. It is not direct democracy in which the popular will (or the majority) necessarily prevails. People may not even choose to be active participants in day-to-day politics, effectively leaving such matters to their representatives with varying degrees of accountability to the electorate.

If we are not clear or lack consensus on what constitutes a democracy (or liberal republic), testing democratic peace hypotheses becomes problematic. Highly inclusive definitions compete with those excluding a large number of cases. After all, it takes more than just having elections to make a democracy. It is not the forms of democratic practice (even dictatorships can use elections to mask their authoritarian designs) that count, it is the substance that matters. Fully developed, enduring democracies are buttressed by social structures, economies, and cultures of shared values conducive to democratic practice that are often lacking in emerging regimes we loosely refer to as democracies.

Even when we agree on what counts as a democracy, how are we to define the dependent variable, whether war or peace? How is it to be operationalized—measured or counted? If "war," does that include armed interventions with marines landing on the beach, or only major and long, drawn-out conflicts involving widespread death and destruction such as occurred in World Wars I and II? Similarly, if one wishes to utilize "peace" as the dependent variable, how is that defined? Is peace simply the absence of war? If so, are we left with a Hobbesian view that international anarchy is inherently a state of war and that the only remedy, then, is to eliminate anarchy, perhaps by establishing an all-powerful Leviathan or world government as the means to maintaining peace? How far must global governance go? Or can we rely more simply on peace-oriented norms of behavior—values shared by democracies?

Beyond such questions, what is the time we need to examine to test democratic peace hypotheses? Different historical periods result in different findings as in some periods certain cases are included and others not. Finally, is the attribute of democracy the only explanatory factor as to why democratic states do not fight one another? Is democracy not only necessary but also sufficient to provide an explanation of peace? Or are other factors of equal or even greater importance?

Take, for example, the fact that states in western Europe have not engaged in war or exhibited warlike behaviors among themselves since 1945. Is that due to the logic of the democratic peace? Or because the Soviet threat from 1945–1991 bound these states together under a US security umbrella that provided a comfortable deterrent effect against would-be invaders? Or perhaps historical memories of the devastation caused by two world wars on the continent are enough to discourage war? Or, as suggested earlier, are the pacifying effects of economic interdependence and the integration process the key to peace in the European context?

DECISION-MAKING

Perhaps the most important liberal insight on international relations is the centrality of state-society relations. This is most evident in the democratic peace literature. Instead of viewing the state as a rational, unified actor, the state is composed of diverse societal actors. Ideas, group interests, institutions, and individuals shape state preferences; they are not a given. When combined with the reality of the impact of interdependence and globalization, the liberal IR theorist has a catalog of independent variables that helps to account for state behavior in any particular issue area.

Pathbreaking work in the early 1960s on *Foreign Policy Decision-Making* by Richard Snyder, H. W. Bruck, and Burton Sapin set the stage for substantial work in this genre that looked inside the state and society, disaggregating the neorealist rational, unified actor. It reflects and parallels the perspectives of the authors summarized under the heading on Interest Group Liberalism discussed earlier. Included in the Snyder, Bruck, and Sapin (SBS) taxonomy are bureaucracies, interest groups, and both psychological and social-psychological factors that influence decision makers. Valerie Hudson led a reexamination of work by SBS, tracing its impact over the decades and on more recent work that would follow in this genre.[20]

SBS were well aware of the agent-structure issue. The debate is not really new. The state-as-actor has meaning only when we look within the state to the

---

[20] See Valerie M. Hudson, Derek H. Chollet, and James M. Goldgeier, *Foreign Policy Decision-Making* (Revisited) including the original text by Richard C. Snyder, H. W. Bruck, and Burton Sapin (New York: Palgrave, 2002).

decision makers themselves and examine how they are influenced by domestic factors and how they relate to their decision-making counterparts in other states. Material and ideational factors intersect not at the abstract level of the state, but rather at the decision-making level. Real people make decisions. Both situational and biographical factors influence foreign policy choices.

Agency is important in this classic understanding. The state-as-actor has meaning only when we look within the state to the decision makers themselves and examine how they are influenced by domestic factors and how they relate to their decision-making counterparts in other states.

Work in psychology and social psychology has contributed substantially to our knowledge of how and why decision makers act. The cognitive orientations and ontologies decision makers have directly influenced their perceptions and the meanings they ascribe to or infer from what they observe. Under what conditions are decision makers blinded from realities that contradict their prior expectations? Are our perceptions affected by what is called cognitive dissonance since we tend not to see what we do not expect to see?[21] If so, this can lead to intelligence failures and adversely affect decision-making whether in crisis or noncrisis conditions.

Perceptions thus clearly play a particularly important role in times of crisis as argued by Robert Jervis in his classic *Perception and Misperception in International Politics*. Individuals relate the images they have to the facts or at least to the information they have before them. Richard Ned Lebow tested similar ideas in his *Between Peace and War*. Content analysis of documents has been utilized to explore the pattern of decisions, mindsets, and assumptions that led to the outbreak, for example, of World War I. Work on crisis decision-making built upon this foundation, identifying how stress during crises compounded by the short time to receive and assess a large quantity of information can reduce the span of attention, results in cognitive rigidity, and causes dysfunctions that adversely affect decision-making tasks.[22]

Group dynamics can also result in dysfunctions with adverse effects on decision-making. In *Victims of Groupthink*, Irving Janis noted how consensus building and team play within a group—normally considered a plus—can lead the group to screen out information at odds with the consensus view. Any naysayers that challenge the common wisdom are likely to be ostracized or pay some high price for taking a contrary position.[23]

In *Essence of Decision*, Graham Allison challenged the rational-actor approach to explaining foreign policy choices.[24] The book expanded upon an earlier journal article on conceptual models and the Cuban Missile Crisis. The crisis almost led to war between the United States and the Soviet Union in Octo-

---

[21] Leon Festinger, *Theory of Cognitive Dissonance* (Stanford, CA: Stanford University Press, 1957).

[22] Robert Jervis, *Perception and Misperception in International Politics* (Princeton, NJ: Princeton University Press, 1976); Richard Ned Lebow, *Between Peace and War: The Nature of International Crisis* (Baltimore: Johns Hopkins University Press, 1984).

[23] Irving Janis, *Victims of Groupthink* (Boston: Houghton Mifflin, 1972).

[24] Graham Allison, *Essence of Decision: Explaining the Cuban Missile Crisis*, 2nd ed. (New York: Longman, 1971, 1999).

ber 1962. He and his colleagues questioned the conventional, realist assumption of rationality (referred to as Model I), in which states specify their objectives consistent with national interests, identify alternatives, and choose the options most likely to achieve these purposes.

By contrast, in Model II he asked whether organizational processes affect decisions—that is, the routines or standard operating procedures organizations employ and the ethos or perspectives that define their organizational essence and ways of doing the business of government. Allison has acknowledged that this insight owes much to Max Weber's perspective on bureaucratic rationality defined as routinizing recurrent functions in efforts to achieve efficiencies. Finally, in Allison's Model III, bureaucratic politics were added to the mix—coalition and countercoalition formation and the pulling-and-hauling of day-to-day struggles within and among bureaucracies.

By the 1980s, there was an evident decline in the amount of literature devoted to decision-making. Nevertheless, cognitive factors remained part of the discourse with attention given to the role of ideas in foreign policy as reflected in work by Robert O. Keohane and Judith Goldstein. Goldstein argues that to understand US trade policies over the years, reliance on international structural or domestic economic interests is insufficient. Rather, one must also take into account actors' causal beliefs as to which economic policies can best achieve preferred interests. For his part, Ernst Haas also underscored the importance of cognitive factors and ideas in his book *When Knowledge Is Power*.[25] As discussed in chapter 9, the role of ideas is also critical in constructivist theorizing about international relations and foreign policy.

Recent years have seen a revival of interest in the perception literature as applied to international relations. Dominic Johnson, for example, in his *Overconfidence and War* revisits the perennial question of why states are susceptible to exaggerated ideas of their ability to control events and foresee future outcomes, particularly when differences in power would seem to suggest it is foolish to go to war.[26] He examines the power of "positive illusions" and overconfidence in case studies of World War I, the Munich Crisis of 1939, Vietnam, and Iraq. He draws on a diverse body of theoretical and empirical work to include not only psychology but also evolutionary biology and international conflict.

Another good example is Johnson's teaming with Dominic Tierney in *Failing to Win: Perceptions of Victory and Defeat in International Politics*.[27] The decision-making literature has invariably focused on the decision to go to war or factors influencing decisions during a crisis. Johnson and Tierney, however, are interested in evaluations of success or failure once the shooting has stopped or the crisis is resolved. The question they pose is this: "What are the psychologi-

---

[25] Judith Goldstein, *Ideas, Interests, and American Trade Policy* (Ithaca, NY: Cornell University Press, 1994); Ernst B. Haas, *When Knowledge Is Power: Three Modes of Change in International Politics* (Berkeley: University of California Press, 1990).

[26] Dominic Johnson, *Overconfidence and War* (Cambridge MA: Harvard University Press, 2004).

[27] Dominic Johnson and Dominic Tierney, *Failing to Win: Perceptions of Victory and Defeat in International Politics* (Cambridge, MA: Harvard University Press, 2006).

cal, political, and cultural factors that predispose observers (whether leaders, the public, or the media) to perceive outcomes of international disputes as victories or defeats?" They argue that there is often a huge gap between perceptions (observers' personal interpretations) and reality. Sometimes perceptions and reality of events on the battlefield match, as in the case of the Fall of Berlin to the Soviet Union in April 1945. But other times they do not, or different observers judge similar events very differently.

Johnson and Tierney devise a conceptual framework to explain the dependent variable: people's perceptions of victory and defeat. First, they examine the conventional wisdom hypothesis that people's judgments of victory and defeat simply reflect the material outcome. They refer to this as score-keeping and provide five possible definitions of "victory" that can serve as empirically verifiable metrics. Second, the authors attempt to explain why the observed gains and losses made by each side often fail to explain people's perceptions of victory in wars or crises, arguing that the score-keeping approach fails to answer this question adequately. The explanatory concept they develop is termed "match-fixing" and relies on the vast body of literature on informational and psychological biases to include cognitive processes, affective processes, learning theory, and cultural influences.

In recent years there has also been substantive work done on individual leaders during crises that are meant as a corrective to the focus on system-wide variables.[28] Sarah Croco's *Peace at What Price*, for example, argues that leader culpability is a critical explanation for the decision to prolong wars, even wars that are obvious quagmires and seem destined to fail. Through a combination of rigorous theorizing and empirical research, she explicates the relationship among leaders, domestic politics, and war and why some leaders are held accountable for wars they initiate but not others.[29]

In terms of rigorous theorizing as opposed to developing models or taxonomies of factors to consider with regard to decision-making, groundbreaking work was done in the 1990s by the psychologists Daniel Kahneman and Amos Tversky. What they termed *prospect theory* was developed as an alternative to *expected utility theory* (rational choice) to provide insights into decision-making under conditions of risk and uncertainty. As with expected utility theory, the focus is on how individuals evaluate and choose between available options. But Kahneman and Tversky were intrigued by why individuals consistently deviated from predictions made by rational choice. They noted that most individuals were risk-averse when it came to securing gains, but risk-acceptant when it came to avoiding losses. In other words, loss aversion was a prime motivating factor; most people value items they already possess more than items they want to acquire.

---

[28] See, for example, Michael C. Horowitz and Mathew Fuhrmann, "Studying Leaders and Military Conflict: Conceptual Framework and Research Agenda," *Journal of Conflict Resolution* 62, no. 10 (2018).
[29] Sarah E. Croco, *Peace at What Price? Leader Culpability and the Domestic Politics of War Termination* (Cambridge: Cambridge University Press, 2015). See also H. E. Goemans, *War and Punishment: The Causes of War Termination and the First World War* (Princeton, NJ: Princeton University Press, 2000).

As scholars applied their work to international relations, the primary question was how to explain obvious anomalous choices made by leaders. Concepts from prospect theory were integrated with experimental literature on group risk-taking in the realm of foreign policy decision-making to include coercive diplomacy, bargaining, and deterrence.[30]

No one would deny that the study of ideas, perceptions, and organizations is important if we wish to improve our understanding of foreign policy or national security decision-making. Two important questions, however, are (1) How much emphasis should be placed on the domestic level of analysis as opposed to the international level when attempting to explain international outcomes and patterns? and (2) How can theorists link the two levels to provide a complete accounting of the phenomena under consideration? The perennial challenge for IR scholars is to develop theories that account simultaneously for the interaction of domestic and international factors, tasks more easily said than done.

CHANGE AND GLOBALIZATION

Liberals note that while a great deal of international relations involves continuity, change is also a constant. The Soviet Union collapsed. American domination of the international economy has eroded. Radical Islam, the power of religion in general, and international terrorism did not loom large on the radar screen of IR scholars even twenty years ago. China is rising. Russia is resurgent. To explain such changes by reference to shifts in the global distribution of power begs the question of how to explain those shifts in the first place. It is safe to say that all the images discussed in this book, liberalism is the most open (and expectant) of change. This is in part due to its emphasis on the voluntarism end of the determinism-voluntarism spectrum.

But liberalism, due to its emphasis on political economy as evident by the literature on integration and interdependence, would also seem to be well prepared to deal with the impact of globalization. Indeed, while interdependence was the buzzword of the 1970s, globalization attained a similar status in the 1990s and continues to have currency. The temptation to simply substitute one concept for the other has been resisted by liberal scholars. Globalization is not simply about linkages between societies and states but concerns the way aspects of social life have been reorganized due to the velocity and intensity of transnational flows encouraged by the liberalization of trade and deregulation of financial markets. As John Ruggie has stated, globalization is to interdependence as Federal Express is to the exchange of letters between separate post offices.[31]

Except for economic structuralism, compared to all the other images and understandings discussed in this book, the liberal perspective on world politics has the most affinity with globalization. Indeed, the concepts of transnationalism

---

[30] Jeffrey W. Taliaferro, "Prospect Theory and Foreign Policy Analysis," *International Studies*, December 22, 2017, https://doi.org/10.1093/acrefore/9780190846626.013.281.

[31] As cited by Robert O. Keohane, *Power and Governance in a Partially Globalized World* (New York: Routledge, 2002).

and interdependence are often component elements of definitions of globalization. This is not surprising. Liberal thinkers have long been concerned with meeting human desires for material well-being and the achievement of civil and political rights. Technological advances have helped spur the international transportation of goods and the spread of ideas, key aspects of globalization. Integration, regime, and neoliberal institutionalists have all studied how collaborative efforts (IMF, World Bank) can support global markets and upgrade the common interest in other areas as well such as human rights. This requires the establishment of legal and institutional arrangements to stabilize markets and assist the spread of liberal democracy across the globe.[32]

In the wake of the global financial crisis that began in 2008, two important practical and theoretical questions arise. First, to what extent does globalization threaten democratic peace? Realists have long noted that interdependence did not keep the major states from launching World War I. Particularly since the 1970s, the flow of trade and finance has changed the operation of the world's economy, increasingly creating one large market with a single division of labor. There have been winners and losers, and resultant political tensions within and between states. Could globalization, far from creating harmony among states, exacerbate political tensions and result in a scenario more in tune with realist expectations?

Second, will global governance continue to expand or retract in an age of contested globalization, at times expressed in the resurgence of nationalism? To what extent are the norms, institutions, and processes designed to enhance international collaboration sufficient to manage the challenge of globalization and the collective action problem it poses for states? Liberals are concerned over possible answers to these questions. There is an awareness that current levels of efficiency and even effectiveness of international institutions are not enough to sustain their viability. What is lacking is sufficient degrees of legitimacy that are required to sustain any institution over time.

A LIBERAL-INSTITUTIONALIST WORLDVIEW

The ascendency of the liberal image of world politics was quite evident beginning in the 1970s but reached its pinnacle in the decade of the 1990s. With the collapse of the Soviet Union in 1991 and its Eastern Europe empire, liberal application of such concepts as interdependence, regime theory, and democratic peace theory was popular. This is not surprising as a number of these approaches to IR theory were developed as a result of events in Europe, just as the literature on regional integration in the 1960s and 1970s owed their inspiration to early developments in the post–World War II period. Liberal perspectives were quite evident among key members of the Clinton administration and the Washington, DC, foreign policy elite who favored NATO expansion. They assumed that the end of the Cold War had transformed international politics and realist logic no longer dominated what was taking place on the European

---

[32] Jan Aart Scholte, *Globalisation: A Critical Introduction*, 2nd ed. (New York: Palgrave Macmillan, 2005), 124.

continent, with the obvious troubling exception being the Balkan wars during the end of the 1990s. The American unipolar moment allowed the United States to push for a zone of peace from the Atlantic to the Urals, the assumption being that it was self-evident the United States was a benign hegemon and there was no reason for a beaten-down Russia to view it as a threat.

Economic interdependence would help bind together Western Europe and the former East bloc. The EU that emerged in 2000 incorporated the earlier European Communities (EC) founded in the 1950s. Its economic policies would (and did) expand at the same time that a wave of democratic revolutions occurred. The logic of democratic peace theory provided hope that, over time, war would become unthinkable on the continent. A constant theme among foreign policy and national security analysts was the question of what was even the purpose of NATO given this seemingly inexorable expanding zone of peace?

Liberalism and the Russian Invasion of Ukraine

Much has changed since those years of optimism in the 1990s. Freedom House keeps track of the number of democracies worldwide. Over the past decade, there has been backsliding even among European states. The invasion of Ukraine in February 2022 came as a shock to many Western elites who assumed reliance on Russian oil and gas would have economic benefits for their countries, but would also make it highly unlikely that Moscow would be willing to pursue policies that threatened this lucrative trade. It seems, however, that the realist take on interdependence—seen as a source of vulnerability and a means to exert political pressure—was more accurate than the liberal vision of trade, investment, and other forms of commerce having a mutually pacifying effect on all parties; the case of a rising China seems to prove the same point. Equally troubling is the fact that over the years even some members of the EU have lost enthusiasm for the European project, Great Britain and Brexit (the UK's withdrawal from the EU) the most notable. Nationalism has not been pacified by the supposed ameliorating effects of economic gains and interdependence among states. Democracy made early post–Cold War gains, but authoritarian regimes have since emerged in Russia, Belarus, Hungary, Turkey, and elsewhere.

When it comes to explaining the Russia-Ukraine war, realists have focused primarily on the shifts in the balance of power since 1991 that, from Moscow's perspective, threatened Russia. Some assert that any Russian leader would have been insistent that the expansion of NATO eastward was a threat to Russia's core security interests. From their perspective, liberal explanations of world politics seemed to fare poorly compared to realist understandings. Liberal advocacy that greater interdependence and interconnectedness in an increasingly globalized world would expand a zone of peace—a liberal, rule-based order—ultimately had not worked.

On the other hand, critics of the realist position who see Russia's invasion due to NATO expansionism and alterations in the balance of power miss a decisive psychological factor—President Putin's extreme narcissism. Narcissistic personalities exhibit "a pervasive pattern of grandiosity (in fantasy or behavior), need for admiration, and lack of empathy."[33]

From a liberal perspective that focuses on the importance of individual and their agency, the key factor was Vladimir Putin himself. No doubt Putin and many other Russians resented NATO enlargement in a time of Russian weakness, but Putin's mission-driven purpose in life became the restoration of Russian greatness in the spirit of the historic icons he has invoked—Josef Stalin, Czar Nicholas I, and even Peter the Great. Grandiose indeed! In sum, it was Putin's personal obsessions, distortions of historical events, and enduring antagonism toward the West that are critical in explaining the road to war.

After all, it is not a coincidence that it has been termed "Putin's War" and "Putin's regime."[34] How might history have been different if someone else held power in the Kremlin? The literature on the individual level of analysis such as perception, motivated bias, and the tendency of leaders to be overconfident in deciding to go to war is applicable. Putin obviously miscalculated Ukrainian resolve, the Western response, and the ability of his military. The phenomenon of groupthink might be applicable as well with Putin excluding (or intimidating) any possible dissenting voices. Perhaps prospect theory has something to contribute as well, given Putin's apparent willingness to take risks to avoid the potential loss of Ukraine to the west. As we find in so many cases involving war and peace, we are again confronted with the agent-structure debate and problem—how much of the explanation is due to the structure of the international system and how much is due to human agency?

LIBERALS AND THEIR CRITICS

Anarchy

As noted, liberals argue that the role of anarchy and the security dilemma is overemphasized in explaining international relations, or they argue that its worst aspects can be overcome through purposeful collaborative behavior to include international organizations, institutions, and regimes. It has been argued

---

[33] The criteria for the narcissistic personality are found in American Psychiatric Association, *Desk Reference to the Diagnostic Criteria from DSM-5* (Washington, DC: American Psychiatric Publishing, 2013). According to this *DSM* and consistent with this profile, one finds "grandiose sense of self-importance" [witness Putin's *grand entrance* and standing at political events]; preoccupation "with fantasies of unlimited success, power [and] brilliance" [the invasion of Ukraine merely a "military operation," success allegedly to be achieved easily]; belief that one is "special" [self-tasked with restoring Russia's lost territories, power, and status]; need for "excessive admiration"; "a sense of entitlement" that requires "favorable treatment or automatic compliance with his or her expectations" [an authoritarian disposition that is both directive and dismissive of the views of others—surrounding oneself with "yes men" who will not contest the leader's views]; being "interpersonally exploitative"—"taking advantage of others to achieve his or her ends"; a person who "lacks empathy" and "is unwilling to recognize or identify with the feelings or needs of others" [most evident in bombing of civilian targets without any apparent concern with killing and otherwise harming human beings to achieve his ends]; one who is "often envious of others or believes that others are envious of him or her"; and one who "shows arrogant, haughty behaviors or attitudes."

[34] See, for example, the series of articles under the heading "Inside Putin's Head," *Foreign Policy*, March 27, 2022.

by realists, however, that any analysis of world politics must begin with the anarchical structure of the system being taken into account. How is it possible to assess realistically the possibilities for cooperation and peace between states unless the role of anarchy in creating suspicion and distrust is recognized? The realist would contend that if one ignores or reduces the importance of such considerations, thinking can quickly become utopian with little relation to reality. Furthermore, realists argue that states often have fundamentally different interests in which the drive for relative material gains makes conflict inevitable and part of the eternal landscape of international relations.

A liberal response is that placing so much emphasis on the security dilemma loads the dice against any change from the status quo. To see the world as nothing more than competition and conflict born of mistrust among states is itself a distortion of reality or even a self-fulfilling prophecy. One's acts, if born of suspicion and distrust, will tend to produce similar responses in others, thus confirming one's initial suspicions.

Furthermore, the history of world politics is a history not only of conflict but also of collaboration. Studying instances when the security dilemma has been overcome is just as important as studying instances when it has contributed to the onset of war. Liberals claim they have the conceptual tools to do so whether it is integration, interdependence, neoliberal institutionalism, regime theory, or democratic peace and the role of ideas in accounting for actor preferences.

Theory-Building

Realists have argued that much of the work in the liberal tradition is highly descriptive and lacking theoretical content, hence, the generally disparaging attitude toward a term such as *globalization* that is more of a popular buzzword than a theoretically useful concept. Realists claim that by describing the world in greater and greater detail, descriptive accuracy increases at the expense of developing parsimonious theories of international relations that can explain patterns of behavior. In other words, theories should be as simple as possible. Understanding increases by moving away from the real world, not by moving closer to it. At first, this statement might seem counterintuitive or different from what one might expect. But ambitious theories aim at producing valid generalizations by viewing the entire forest, not individual trees. By faithfully cataloging the complexity of the world, many liberals, according to critics, are in danger of remaining in the realm of merely describing things as opposed to explaining why things happen the way they do.

Scholars operating within the liberal image make several rebuttals. First, one only has to point to neoliberal institutionalism to rebut the charge of description at the expense of theoretical parsimony. The work of Keohane and his colleagues has often been characterized as a theoretical counterpoint to neorealist approaches to international relations, although both research agendas employ rational-actor assumptions and positivist standards of evidence.

Second, liberals note this obsession with parsimony is most attributable to structural or neorealists. Classical realists such as Hans J. Morgenthau and Arnold Wolfers examined the role of a multitude of factors at various levels of analysis, just as more recent scholars in the classical realist tradition seek to understand the reciprocal interactive effects of the state and the international system.

Finally, the liberal research agenda in recent years has perhaps offered more theories and testable hypotheses than any other image of international politics, contributing to the ultimate social science goal of cumulative knowledge. In particular, varying liberal research agendas tend to coalesce around the unifying theme of the pacifying effects of democracy, economic interdependence, and international institutions. Far from being unrelated research agendas, these three topics reinforce one another. Yes, it is admitted, the diversity of approaches under the liberal image is not as neat and streamlined as the realist image with its traditional focus on issues of conflict among states. The liberal image consists of many different actors operating within and across state boundaries which makes for complexity, but theories of international relations should aspire to deal with such complexity and not pretend that it does not exist. How adequate are theories that fail to deal with and explain many of the changes that have occurred in the nature of world politics over the past half-century? While realism is a useful "first cut" at understanding world politics, too much is left out: the role of individuals, institutions, transnational relations, domestic politics, and ideas.

The Democratic Peace

With the demise of the Soviet Union in the early 1990s, Francis Fukuyama in his *End of History* stated that liberal democracy had no serious ideological rival and hence it was "the end point of mankind's ideological evolution" and the "final form of human government."[35] Indeed, democracy seemed to be gaining adherents, not only in states of the former Soviet empire in Eastern Europe but also in areas of the Third World where nascent democratic transitions were occurring. Realists, to put it mildly, were skeptical, not only doubting how long the expanded zone of democratic peace would last in the new Europe, but also pointing to the conflict in the Balkans, conflict among some African states, India-Pakistan tensions, and the gradual rise of China as a global economic, political, and military power.

Liberals responded that the democratic zone of peace in Western Europe is no small achievement. Even if it is subject to debate how much the spread of democracy contributes to the explanation of this situation as opposed to the economic interdependence and enticements provided by membership in the EU, the fact remains that realist predictions of an incessant drive for domination and the supposed built-in systemic incentives for armed conflict have not threatened the Western European peace. The major threat has come from illiberal Russia. As for the Global South, few liberals have claimed this to be an appropriate test bed for democratic peace theory. Indeed, the Global South is more often

---

[35] Francis Fukuyama, *The End of History and the Last Man* (New York: Free Press, 1992), xi–xii. For a more recent, sobering assessment of the state of the world, see his *Identity: Contemporary Identity Politics and the Struggle for Recognition* (London: Profile Books, 2018).

characterized as a zone of conflict where internal conflicts and weak states now seem more the norm than interstate conflict.

Nevertheless, from a global perspective, there has been backsliding in terms of democracy. According to the V-Dem Institute: "The level of democracy enjoyed by the average global citizen in 2021 is down to 1989 levels. The last 30 years of democratic advances are now eradicated, Dictatorships are on the rise and harbor 70% of the world population—5.4 billion people." The democratic score of even the United States has dropped since 2015.[36] By the logic of democratic peace theory, such developments would not seem to bode well in terms of global conflict.

Voluntarism

If realists have been criticized for being excessively pessimistic concerning the human condition and the ability of individuals to control international events and forces, liberals can be criticized for their heavy reliance on the assumption of voluntarism, or effective free will. Their emphasis on agency over structure reflects voluntarism in much of liberal theory. Some liberal writings leave one with the impression that international harmony can be achieved if only leaders really wanted it—that it is a simple matter of human volition, a mere matter of desiring cooperation as opposed to competition. Hence, the transformation of the nature of world politics is seen to be desirable as well as attainable. Either "bad and ignorant leaders" or "bad governments" stand in the way; if they could be educated or removed, the world would be a better place. Once again, the influence of liberal philosophy is evident. And, once again, the realist evaluation would be that this view of international change and how it can be achieved ignores constraints placed on all leaders and states by the anarchical nature of the international system, the drive for relative gains, and the balance of power. Moreover, some realists would argue that people are indeed aggressive with a proclivity toward warlike behavior; it is part of human nature to behave so.

The emphasis on voluntarism is not always acknowledged in liberal writings. Nor is it necessarily a function of a philosophical commitment to a belief in free will that can influence outcomes. It could also derive from the fact that the focus of analysis for many liberals happens to be factors operating at the domestic level of analysis, which involves the study of actual institutions, individual actors, and collective belief systems held by flesh and blood policy makers. When one studies real individuals within real institutions, it is obvious that agency matters. World politics takes on a human face, understandably resulting in a reliance on the assumption of voluntarism.

REFERENCES

Allison, Graham. *Essence of Decision: Explaining the Cuban Missile Crisis*, 2nd ed. New York: Longman, 1971, 1999.

---

[36] V-Dem Institute, Democracy 2022, p. 6.

American Psychiatric Association. *Desk Reference to the Diagnostic Criteria from DSM-5*. Washington, DC: American Psychiatric Publishing, 2013.

Diamond, Larry. *The Spirit of Democracy: The Struggle to Build Free Societies throughout the World*. New York: Times Books-Henry Holt, 2008.

Haas, Ernst B. *When Knowledge Is Power: Three Modes of Change in International Politics*. Berkeley: University of California Press, 1990.

Haas, Peter M., ed. "Knowledge, Power, and International Policy Coordination." *International Organization* 46, no. 1 (1992).

Keohane, Robert O. *After Hegemony: Cooperation and Discord in the World Political Economy*. Princeton, NJ: Princeton University Press, 1984.

———. *Power and Governance in a Partially Globalized World*. New York: Routledge, 2002.

Keohane, Robert O., and Joseph S. Nye Jr. *Power and Interdependence: World Politics in Transition*. Boston: Little Brown, 1977.

———, eds. *Transnational Relations and World Politics*. Cambridge, MA: Harvard University Press, 1971.

Rosecrance, Richard. *The Rise of the Trading State: Commerce and Conquest in the Modern World*. New York: Basic Books, 1986.

Rosenau, James N. *Turbulence in World Politics*. Princeton, NJ: Princeton University Press, 1990.

7

Economic Structuralism: Global Capitalism and Postcolonialism

★ ★ ★

MAJOR ACTORS AND ASSUMPTIONS

We have seen how many realists organize their work around the basic question: How can stability or order be maintained in an anarchic world? Many liberals or neoliberal institutionalists ask how international collaboration and peaceful change can be promoted in a world that is increasingly interdependent politically, militarily, socially, and economically. Economic structuralism concentrates on the broad question of why so many countries in Latin America, Africa, and Asia (the Global South) have been unable to develop or have suffered from economic booms, busts, and financial instability. For some economic structuralists, this question is part of a larger effort to develop a theory of world-capitalist development. Hence, for them, globalization is not a new phenomenon but can be traced back several centuries. Given this context, we include commentary here on a growing literature on postcolonialism—a term that captures not only the period since the formal end of colonialism following World War II but one that also takes us back to the historical imperial and colonial experiences that have so many implications for the present day. We have avoided the label Marxism because there are both Marxists (and neo-Marxists) as well as non-Marxists who work within what we have chosen to call an economic-structuralist image. Indeed, some economic structuralists decidedly avoid Marxian modes of analysis.

Since the end of the Cold War, there have been decidedly fewer theoretical and empirical challenges levied against economic-structuralist approaches to IR theory. Indeed, they tend to be ignored in mainstream literature including IR journals. This may be due in part to the demise of the Soviet Union and other Leninist regimes in Eastern Europe, which dampened scholarly interest in this mode of scholarly analysis, particularly in the United States. This is ironic, however, for one could argue that at least the capitalist world-system perspective was quite prescient, anticipating the continual unfolding of the

275

logic of capitalism and its inexorable spread to virtually every nook and cranny around the globe. Hence, we note that economic structuralism as an image of international relations or world politics—especially the capitalist world-system approach—remains highly relevant. Particularly at times of global economic hardship, one witnesses a revival in interest in approaches we place under the economic-structuralist umbrella.

As an intellectual image informing the development of theory, economic structuralism has always been independent of the rise and fall of those regimes occurring within a capitalist mode of production. Indeed, from this perspective, the still-surviving self-professed communist regimes (China, North Korea, Vietnam, and Cuba) are best understood by their different adaptations to domination within a capitalist world-system. Finally, in recent years, much of the scholarly literature and debate dealing with economic, political, and social crises in the developing world are cast in the wider net of *postcolonialism* theorizing. As we will see, while this literature accommodates economic-structuralist approaches, it has had relatively little impact on the debates occurring within mainstream IR journals.

Economic structuralists are guided by four key assumptions. First, it is necessary to understand the global context within which states and other entities interact. Economic structuralists argue that to explain behavior at all levels of analysis (the individual; group, *class*, bureaucratic, or institutional units; state and society as a whole; and between or among states or societies), one must first understand the overall structure of the global system within which such behavior takes place. As with structural or neorealists discussed in chapter 5, most economic structuralists believe that the starting point of analysis should be the international or, for them, the *capitalist world-system*. To a large extent, the behavior of individual actors is explained by a system that provides both opportunities and constraints. The essential difference between structural realists and economic structuralists, of course, is focus by the former on structure as the distribution of power among states, the latter on global economic structures—whether expressed as North versus South, First versus Third Worlds, core versus *periphery*, or capital-owning bourgeois versus toiling (working or peasant) classes.

Second, economic structuralists stress the importance of historical analysis in comprehending the international system. It is this historical focus that postcolonial studies also bring to economic-structuralist understandings. Only by tracing the historical evolution of the system is it possible to understand its current structure. The key historical factor and defining characteristic of the system as a whole is capitalism. This particular economic system or mode of production works to the benefit of some individuals, states, and societies but at the expense of others. Even the few remaining self-professed socialist states must operate within a capitalist world-economy that significantly constrains their options. Hence, for economic structuralists, the East-West division during the height of the Cold War is not nearly as important as the North-South divide and competition among such advanced capitalist states as Germany, Japan, the United States, and, it could be argued, China.

Third, economic structuralists assume that particular mechanisms of domination exist that keep states comprising the Global South from developing, contributing to worldwide *uneven development*. Understanding these mechanisms requires an examination of dependency relations between the "northern" industrialized, capital-rich states (principally those in Europe and North America, Japan, Australia, and New Zealand) and their capital-poorer neighbors in the southern hemisphere (Africa, Latin America, Asia, and the Pacific island states). Although most capital-poor countries are located south of Europe, North America, and Japan, the North-South designation is more figurative than geographic since much of Asia lies in the Northern Hemisphere as do Central America, the Caribbean, and the northern part of South America—not to mention that Australia and New Zealand are in the Southern Hemisphere.

In economic-structuralist discourse, which we take up later in this chapter, the First World or northern, capital-rich countries are often referred to as constituting the *core* of global capitalism. The Third World or southern, capital-poor countries are set at the *periphery* of this capitalist world-system. The *semiperiphery* is a residual category reserved for those states somewhere in between core and periphery. What is most important in economic-structural analyses, however, is the capital position that describes the level of economic development or productive capacity a country has achieved regardless of its geographic location.

For this reason some prefer still to refer to the capital-rich countries as First World and capital-poor ones as Third World. The reference to "third" has its origins in French-socialist discourse in the early 1960s which saw the term Third World as capturing the aspirations for a better life where most people live. The concept can be traced back to the term "third estate," which broadly referred to the downtrodden classes of prerevolutionary eighteenth-century French society. The other two estates were the upper rungs of French society—the nobility or aristocracy and the clergy. Calling these poor countries Third World, then, was not intended to be a put-down as if they somehow were third rate. To the contrary, that ultimately the people will triumph was the hopeful implication of this "Third World" label.

Changes in the global economy since the end of the Cold War have had an impact on economic-structuralist analyses, requiring adaptation of concepts and terms more readily used in a Cold War world. The demise of Soviet and other Leninist regimes and their command economies in Eastern Europe at the end of the Cold War, coupled with the embrace of capitalist modes of economic development by regimes in China and Vietnam, have made the "Second World" designation as obsolete as "East versus West"—both terms now artifacts of the past and thus rarely in discussions about the present-day world order. The term Second World (sometimes called socialist or communist) once captured a large number of countries—a category generally separate from those linked within the dependency mechanism in which the capital-poor, Third World countries, and classes in the south are dominated by the capital-rich, First World countries and classes in the north.

Finally, and as should be apparent from the discussion thus far, economic structuralists assume that economic factors are absolutely critical in explaining the evolution and functioning of the international or capitalist world-system and the relegation of Global South states to a subordinate position. These factors have an important impact on political, social, cultural, ethnic, and gender issues, which also are captured in the more recent postcolonialism literature.

The economic-structuralist approach does share some commonalities with the other three images, although differences clearly outweigh any similarities. As noted, both economic structuralists and structural realists (neorealists) place greater emphasis on the importance of the systems level, or world as a whole, in affecting actors' behavior than do liberals and scholars in the English School. But they differ in terms of ontology as to how they characterize systems-level components. Thus, economic structuralists tend to focus on economic structure (e.g., classes or blocs, core versus periphery, North versus South) within a capitalist mode of production while for neorealists structure is to be found in the distribution of aggregate power among states (e.g., unipolar, bipolar, and multipolar labels for structure). Furthermore, economic structuralists are much more likely than realists to emphasize the intimate connection between the international or capitalist world-system and domestic politics. State and society are never viewed as being encapsulated by a metaphorical hard shell. Class structure, for example, transcends the boundaries of states and their component societies.

Economic structuralists and liberals share at least three commonalities that can be viewed as criticisms of the realist perspective. First, both stress an approach to international relations grounded in political economy. The distinction between high politics and low politics (the relative importance of political-military as compared to economic factors) is rejected—if not totally reversed for certain economic structuralists. For the economic structuralist, various manifestations of political and military power generally reflect the driving force of underlying economic factors. Politics depends on economics; it is not an autonomous realm.

Second, both economic structuralists and liberals are much more attuned to events, processes, institutions, and actors operating both within and between states; the impermeable billiard ball (the unitary, rational actor common in many realist understandings) is broken down into its parts. Both approaches tend to range up and down the levels of analysis and focus on a greater variety of actors, but economic structuralists place a much greater emphasis on the context (i.e., the capitalist nature of the international system) within which these actors operate than do liberals. Agency matters to both economic structuralists and liberals. But on the whole, there is decidedly more voluntarism in liberal understandings, more determinism in economic-structuralist theorizing.

Third, both the economic structuralists and those liberals who write in the transnationalist tradition emphasize socioeconomic or welfare issues. Some liberals have a normative commitment to peaceful change. International relations do not have to be viewed and played as a zero-sum game with winners and losers but can be seen as a positive-sum game in which the restructuring of interstate relations is achieved through bargaining and compromise, allowing all parties to gain. Although economic structuralists are also concerned with the welfare of least developed countries (LDCs), they are not so optimistic about the possibility of peaceful change. The hierarchical nature of world politics with South subordinated to North and the economic dictates of the capitalist world-system make it unlikely that the northern industrialized states will make any meaningful concessions to the Third World. Change, peaceful or revolutionary, is problematic until the capitalist world-system reaches a point of systemic crisis. In sum, there are indeed major differences between economic structuralists and liberals. There is also little in common between economic structuralism and the English School—the latter more of a middle path between realism on the one hand, liberalism and idealism on the other.

Although the economic structuralists are primarily concerned with the question of why the euphemistically termed "developing world" or "emerging economies" cannot develop, answering such a query is difficult. How and why did capitalism develop in Europe? How did it expand outward to other continents? As an international phenomenon, how has capitalism changed over the centuries? What are the specific mechanisms of dependency that allow for the maintenance of exploitative relations? What are the relations between the elites of the wealthy, capital-rich center countries (the First World) and the elites of the poorer periphery? Is it possible for an LDC to break out of a dependent situation? Economic-structuralist answers to such questions are addressed in the subsequent pages of this chapter.

INTELLECTUAL PRECURSORS AND INFLUENCES

In chapter 4 we discussed writers from the nineteenth- and early twentieth centuries who have influenced work on international political economy in general. Here we will simply provide brief introductions to the most influential voices that have had a particular impact on the economic-structuralist image.

All economic structuralists have been influenced either directly or indirectly by the works of Karl Marx (1818–1883). This is certainly not to suggest that all economic structuralists are Marxists (any more than alleging that all Marxists accept without qualification the sum total of Marx's efforts). It is simply to acknowledge that they all owe an intellectual debt to him in terms of their methods of analysis and certain critical insights into the functioning, development, and expansion of the capitalist *mode of production*. Marx focused attention on unequal and exploitative relations and thus set an important backdrop or context for scholarship by economic structuralists, whether they be Marxist, neo-Marxist, or non-Marxist in orientation. To appreciate Marx as a scholar, one does not have to ascribe to the views of Marx as a revolutionary.

Marx's discussion and analysis of capitalism have influenced economic structuralists in at least three ways. First, Marx was concerned with exploitation of the many by the few, in particular the patterns and mechanisms of exploitation in different modes of economic production. He no doubt recognized the historically progressive role played by capitalists (the proletarian revolution would not be possible until after the establishment of a capitalist system), but his personal sympathies were with the downtrodden who were alienated from the means of production.

Second, according to Marx, capitalism exhibits certain lawlike qualities in terms of its development and expansion. He views capitalism as part of a world-historical process unfolding *dialectically*, an economic system riddled with clashing contradictions or internal tensions that could be resolved only by a revolutionary transformation into a socialist mode of production. While recognizing the important role of human agency in moving history forward, he feels that historical economic and social realities are paramount in explaining outcomes. As we noted earlier in the context of the *agent-structure* debate, Marx argues, "Men make their own history, but they do not make it just as they please; they do not make it under circumstances chosen by themselves, but under circumstances directly found, given, and transmitted from the past. The tradition of all dead generations weighs heavily like a nightmare on the brain of the living."[1] Not unlike many present-day IR theorists, Marx was interested in the interplay or dialectic between agents and structures, in particular the processes by which the latter was historically constructed.

Finally, Marx insists that a society must be studied in its totality, not piecemeal. An analyst must be aware of how various parts of society were interrelated, including those aspects not so apparent to the casual observer. As Robert L. Heilbroner states, "The entire contribution of Marxism to social thought rests ultimately on its effort to penetrate the veil of appearances to discover the hidden essence of things, the web of relations that is the real ground of reality and not the surface manifestations that are its facade."[2] Put another way, Marx is an intellectual precursor of present-day critical theorists.

This perspective has deeply influenced the economic structuralists, some of whom earlier in their careers had little use for history and were preoccupied almost exclusively with such units of analysis as states or individuals. As two leading economic structuralists have argued: "If there is one thing which distinguishes a world-system perspective from any other, it is its insistence that the unit of analysis is a world-system defined in terms of economic processes and links, and not any units defined in terms of juridical, political, cultural, geographical, or other criteria."[3] Although such units of analysis are not ignored by the economic structuralists, they take on connotations different from those of the realist, liberal, or English School theorist. The state, for example, is not viewed in terms of its being a sovereign entity preoccupied with security concerns. Rather, it derives its significance from the role it plays in actively aiding

[1] Karl Marx, "The Eighteenth Brumaire of Louis Bonaparte," in *The Marx-Engels Reader*, ed. Robert C. Tucker (New York: Norton, 1972), 436.

[2] Robert Heilbroner, *Marxism: For and Against* (New York: Norton, 1980), 49. See also Andrew Gamble, David Marsh, and Tony Tant, eds., *Marxism and Social Science* (Champaign: University of Illinois Press, 1999).

[3] Terence K. Hopkins, Immanuel Wallerstein, and Associates, "Patterns of Development of the Modern World-System," in *World-System Analysis: Theory and Methodology*, ed. Hopkins, Wallerstein, and Associates (Beverly Hills, CA: Sage Publications, 1982), 72.

or hindering the capitalist accumulation process. Any one state is not viewed in isolation but in terms of how it fits into the overall global capitalist system.

In sum, Marx has influenced contemporary scholars working within the economic-structuralist image by his emphasis on exploitation, discernible historical patterns of capitalist development and expansion, the methodology of *historical materialism*, how change occurs, and the importance of understanding the "big picture" and then asking how individual parts fit into the whole.

Marx sees capitalism as a worldwide mode of production. His observations on capitalism in the nineteenth century were applied subsequently in various theories of imperialism. *Imperialism* assumes an international, hierarchical division of labor between rich and poor regions of the world, but the relation is not one of mutually beneficial *comparative advantage*. Rather, it is one of exploitation.

Ironically, perhaps one of the most significant theories of imperialism was devised by a non-Marxist, the English economist John A. Hobson (1858–1940). Near the turn of the century, Hobson notes that capitalist societies are faced with three basic interrelated problems: overproduction of goods, underconsumption of these goods by workers and other classes, and oversavings on the part of capitalists. As the capitalist owners of industry continued to exploit workers and pay the lowest possible wages, profits mounted and goods began to pile up. What could capitalists have done with excess goods and profits, and how could they have resolved the problem of underconsumption? Redistribute wealth? Highly unlikely. Because capitalist European and North American powers were experiencing overproduction and domestic underconsumption, investment opportunities in other developed countries remained limited.

The solution reached by capitalists was to invest in what came to be known during the Cold War as Third World countries. The result was imperialism: "the endeavor of the great controllers of industry to broaden the channel for the flow of their surplus wealth by seeking foreign markets and foreign investments to take off the goods and capital they cannot sell or use at home." Hobson argues against "the supposed inevitability of imperial expansion." He states that it is "not inherent in the nature of things that we should spend our natural resources on militarism, war, and risky, unscrupulous diplomacy, in order to find markets for our goods and surplus capital."[4] Hobson hence rejects the determinism so often found in the work of Marxist scholars who write on imperialism.

V. I. Lenin's *Imperialism: The Highest Stage of Capitalism* is his most important theoretical work of interest to economic structuralists. Writing in the middle of World War I (1916), Lenin (1870–1924) develops a theory that claimed to explain the necessity for capitalist exploitation of lesser-developed countries and the causes of war among advanced capitalist states. He draws heavily upon the works of Hobson and the German Social Democrat, Rudolf Hilferding (1877–1941).

From Hobson, Lenin accepts the key argument that underconsumption and overproduction caused capitalists to scramble for foreign markets beyond

---

[4] John A. Hobson, *Imperialism: A Study* (Ann Arbor: University of Michigan Press, 1965), 85–86.

Europe and to engage in colonialism. From Hilferding, Lenin takes the notion that imperialist policies reflect the existence of monopoly and finance capital, or the highest stage of capitalism. In other words, capitalism had developed such that oligopolies and monopolies controlled the key sectors of the economy, squeezing out or taking over smaller firms and milking domestic markets dry. The result was a need to look elsewhere for investment opportunities. This logically entailed the creation of overseas markets. As markets expanded, they required more economic inputs such as raw materials, which encouraged the further spread of imperialism to secure such resources.

By buying off the European working class in the short term through higher wages, imperialism delayed the inevitable domestic revolutions. But an important trade-off was involved. Domestic stability was achieved at the cost of wars among the capitalist powers that resulted from the continual struggle for overseas markets. Once the globe had been effectively divided up, further expansion could come about only at the expense of a capitalist rival.

Strictly as a theorist, Lenin has particularly influenced the economic-structuralist literature with his emphasis on the global nature of capitalism and its inherent exploitation that primarily benefits the bourgeoisie in advanced capitalist states at the expense of poorer countries. Although there is arguably a good deal of determinism in his theory of imperialism, his work as a revolutionary (like that of Marx) reflects considerable voluntarism in practice. Agency matters to Lenin as apparent in his call for a "vanguard of the proletariat" led by a communist party to push history down its revolutionary path. This is an idea he developed not only in theory but in practice as well. The actions of revolutionaries are at the very least to serve as catalysts to the worldwide proletarian revolution whenever the objective conditions of working-class exploitation are ripe or have reached their revolutionary stage.[5]

Others who would later write in this tradition would argue that revolutionaries play more of a role than mere catalysts. They can actually create the conditions for revolution; the "subjective" can create the "objective"; agency matters. This is most explicit in the writings, for example, of practitioners such as Che Guevara (1928–1967) and Mao Zedong (1893–1976).

DEPENDENCY THEORISTS

ECLA and UNCTAD Arguments

Some of the more provocative work in the economic-structuralist tradition was pioneered by Latin American scholars in the 1960s and 1970s. Representing various branches of the social sciences, they came to be known collectively as *dependency* theorists. Several of these writers were associated in the 1960s with the Economic Commission on Latin America (ECLA) and the United Nations Conference on Trade and Development (UNCTAD). They were concerned with the important problem of explaining why Latin America and other Third World

---

[5] For example, see Lenin's "What Is to Be Done?" in *The Lenin Anthology*, ed. Robert C. Tucker (New York: Norton, 1975), 12–114.

regions were not developing as anticipated. North American social science models had predicted an economic takeoff for *LDCs*. What had gone wrong? What explained economic stagnation, balance of payments difficulties, and deteriorating terms of trade? Why was the North American–Western European experience not being repeated?

One response came from mainstream modernization writers. This modernization literature attempts to answer these questions by exploring the difficulties of LDCs in moving from "traditional" to "modern" societies. The tradition-modernity dichotomy has been used in one form or another by social scientists as a tool of analysis since the nineteenth century. The ethos and organization of a traditional society, it is argued, are both a cause and an expression of underdevelopment. The cultural values of a traditional society are postulated to be a hindrance to modernization. The LDCs are wedded to their pasts, reflecting a lack of entrepreneurial spirit that was found in European society during the rise of capitalism in the sixteenth century.[6]

This view of development and underdevelopment as the outcomes of internal processes has been criticized on many grounds. Two important criticisms are, first, that the modernization writers assume that the tradition-modernity dichotomy is universally applicable. But is the Latin American experience so similar to the European experience? Are there no significant historical differences between the African and European (or American) experiences? Of course, there are and they are substantial, such as colonialism. Second, the modernization literature usually neglects a state's or a society's external environment, particularly international political and economic factors. Instead, modernization writers have tended to focus internally or within particular states or societies, generally ignoring that state's or society's place in the world-capitalist order. Is there any society, even in the European historical experience, that is immune to outside influences? Very unlikely, respond the dependency theorists, who place particular emphasis on Latin America's colonial heritage and a historical legacy of exploitation also experienced in Africa.

The focus of the ECLA and UNCTAD economists was initially quite narrow. They examined the unequal terms of trade between LDCs that exported raw materials and northern industrialized countries that exported finished manufactured goods. They questioned the supposed benefits of free trade. The ECLA at one point favored the diversification of exports, advising that LDCs produce goods instead of importing them. This policy did not result in the anticipated amount of success and in fact increased the influence of foreign multinational corporations brought in to facilitate domestic production.

Did all countries fail to experience economic growth? No, some economies did grow, but growth tended to occur in an LDC only when the developed countries needed a particular raw material or agricultural product. Because many LDCs are dependent on only a few of these commodities for their foreign exchange earnings, a drastic decline in the demand for one of them (perhaps

---

[6] The classic statement in terms of Europe is found in Max Weber, *The Protestant Ethic and the Spirit of Capitalism* (New York: Scribner's, 1958).

caused by a global recession such as in 2008) would have a calamitous impact on an LDC's economy. Or, alternatively, a bumper crop in several LDCs heavily dependent on one particular export (such as coffee or sugar) would also cause prices to fall.

The volatility of prices for minerals and agricultural products and the general downward tendency of those prices contrast sharply with more stable and gradually increasing prices for manufactured items produced by industrial countries. Thus, the terms of trade are thought to be stacked against those Third World states that export farm products or natural resources.

Radical Critiques

Writers in ECLA and UNCTAD (e.g., Argentine economist Raúl Prebisch, 1901–1986), although critical of the more conservative views of development, nevertheless tended to restrict their analyses to economic dimensions and to cast their arguments in terms of nationalism and the need for state-guided capitalism.[7] Other writers, however, more boldly emphasize political and social factors within the context of a capitalist economic system that bind Latin America to North America. Development, it was argued, is not autonomous. If it occurs at all, it is reflexive—subject to the vagaries and ups and downs of the world's advanced economies. Choices for Latin American countries are restricted or constrained not only as a result of the dictates of capitalism, but also due to supporting political, social, and cultural relations. The result is a structure of domination. This multifaceted web of dependency reinforces unequal exchange between the northern and southern parts of the hemisphere. Opportunities for LDCs are few and far between because LDCs are allocated a subordinate role in world capitalism.

That various states and societies produce those things of which they are relatively the most efficient producers or sell those items in which they have a comparative advantage is seen by dependency theorists as a "one-way advantage." Economic exploitation of LDCs by industrialized states is not an accident or simply an additional means by which these states enrich themselves. Rather, economic exploitation is an integral part of the capitalist system and is required to keep it functioning.

The result is a condition of dependency, succinctly defined as a "situation in which a certain number of countries have their economy conditioned by the development and expansion of another . . . placing the dependent countries in a backward position exploited by the dominant countries."[8] The modernization experience of a particular society should not be seen in isolation, "but as part of the development of an internationalist capitalist system, whose dynamic has a determining influence on the local processes." As a result, underdevelopment

---

[7] Raúl Prebisch, *Towards a Dynamic Development Policy for Latin America* (New York: United Nations, 1963).

[8] Theotonio dos Santos, as cited in J. Samuel Valenzuela and Arturo Valenzuela, "Modernization and Dependency: Alternative Perspectives in the Study of Latin American Underdevelopment," *Comparative Politics* 10, no. 4 (July 1978): 544.

is not "a moment in the evolution of a society which has been economically, politically and culturally autonomous and isolated."[9] Instead, Latin America and other Third World countries are attempting to develop under historical conditions quite different from those of the northern industrialized states.

Some economic structuralists use Marxist terminology and Gramscian insights to explain this situation of dependency. More important than relations between states are transnational class coalitions linking elites in industrially developed countries (the center or core) with their counterparts in the South (or periphery). This version of class analysis emphasizes how transnational ties within the global bourgeois or capitalist class work to the disadvantage of workers and peasants in the periphery.

Multinational corporations and international banks, therefore, are viewed from a much different perspective than that found in other IR images. To the liberal or English School scholar, multinational corporations and international banks appear merely as other, potentially benign, actors in world politics or global society. To the realist, they tend to be of secondary importance because of the emphasis on the state-as-actor. To the economic structuralist, however, they are central players in establishing and maintaining dependency relations. To economic structuralists of Marxist persuasion, multinational corporations and banks are agents par excellence of the international bourgeoisie. They represent two of the critical means by which states in the Global South are maintained in their subordinate position within the world-capitalist economy.

Domestic Forces

Dependency theorists dealt not only with external factors (such as foreign states, multinational corporations, international banks, multilateral lending institutions, foreign control of technology, and an international bourgeoisie). They also examined internal constraints on development (such as patterns of land tenure, social structures, class alliances, and the role of the state). These internal factors tend to reinforce instruments of foreign domination. It is argued, for example, that the inability to break out of a dependent situation is often strengthened by citizens of a Latin American country who accrue selfish benefits at the expense of the country as a whole. This so-called comprador class, or national bourgeoisie, aids in the exploitation of its society. Allied with foreign capitalists, this class and its self-serving policies encourage the expansion of social and economic inequality, which may take the form of an ever-widening rural-urban gap. Although limited development may occur in a few urban centers, the countryside stagnates and is viewed only as a provider of cheap labor and raw materials. These exploiters, therefore, have more in common with the elites of the center countries than they do with their fellow citizens of the periphery.

---

[9] Osvaldo Sunkel, "Big Business and Dependencia: A Latin American View," *Foreign Affairs* 50, no. 3 (1972): 519–20. Sunkel's later work can be found in several volumes coedited by Bjorn Hettne, Andras Inotai, and Osvaldo Sunkel to include *Globalism and the New Regionalism* (New York: Palgrave Macmillan, 1999).

Such arguments are rather sweeping in scope. The importance of internal dimensions, however, will vary depending on the particular country under examination. Class coalitions, for example, will differ and may relate to external actors in a variety of ways. As two dependency theorists have stated:

> We conceive the relationship between external and internal forces as forming a complex whole whose structural links are not based on mere external forms of exploitation and coercion, but are rooted in coincidence of interests between local dominant classes and international ones.[10]

In some cases, this "coincidence of interests" might even involve portions of the working class.

As a result of the interplay of external and internal factors, the nature of the development or underdevelopment of a society will vary. Changes in the international economy will affect LDCs in different ways. Dependency theorists, therefore, do not claim that economic stagnation in LDCs is always and inevitably the norm. They argue, however, that development benefits some at the expense of others, increases social inequalities, and leads to greater foreign control over Third World economies.

The dependency literature had its academic moment in the sun. But the concept virtually disappeared from the literature by the 1990s. This was not only a function of empirical and theoretical criticism (discussed at the end of this chapter), but many governments in Latin America were pursuing free market economic policies with at least some degree of initial success. One prominent scholar, Fernando Henrique Cardoso, even became president of Brazil for eight years—setting aside his earlier sociological work on dependency and pursuing in office conservative fiscal policies he saw as central to the country's economic development. In the field as a whole, dependency insights and arguments were subsumed under the broader concept of the capitalist world-system literature and the even broader postcolonialism research programs.

THE CAPITALIST WORLD-SYSTEM

The dependency theorists pointed out the way for scholars who write from what is known as the capitalist world-system perspective. This perspective is truly economic structuralist and differs from dependency in two ways.

First, advocates of the capitalist world-system perspective not only are concerned with the lack of Third World development, but also wish to understand the economic, political, and social development of regions throughout the entire world. Developed and underdeveloped states—winners and losers—are all examined in attempts to explain the global existence of *uneven development*.

Second, the goal is to understand the fate of various parts of the world at various times in history within the larger context of a developing world political

---

[10] Fernando Henrique Cardoso and Enzo Faletto, *Dependency and Development in Latin America* (Berkeley: University of California Press, 1979), xvi. See Cardoso's more recent *The Accidental President of Brazil: A Memoir* (New York: Public Affairs, 2007).

economy. Latin America, for example, is not unique. Its experience is an integral part of the capitalist world-system. Third World underdevelopment and exploitation are central to maintaining the present structure of dominance in the capitalist world-system. The priority, therefore, is to understand this global system from a historical perspective. Only then can the fates of particular societies or regions of the globe be understood.

The writings of Immanuel Wallerstein represent the most ambitious of economic-structuralist work and were the catalyst for an extensive amount of subsequent research. In attempting to understand the origins and dynamics of the modern world-economy and the existence of worldwide uneven development, he and his followers aspire to no less than a historically based theory of global development, which he terms *world-system theory*.[11]

Wallerstein begins by analyzing the emergence of capitalism in Europe, tracing its development into a capitalist world-system that contains a *core*, a *periphery*, and a *semiperiphery*—a decidedly different understanding of globalization from that offered by liberals. The core areas historically have engaged in the most advanced economic activities: banking, manufacturing, technologically advanced agriculture, and shipbuilding. The periphery has provided raw materials such as minerals and timber to fuel the core's economic expansion. Unskilled labor is repressed, and the peripheral countries are denied advanced technology in those areas that might make them more competitive with core states. The semiperiphery is involved in a mix of production activities, some associated with core areas and others with peripheral areas. The semiperiphery also serves some other functions such as being an outlet for investment when wages in core economies become too high. Over time, regions of the world may gravitate between core, peripheral, and semiperipheral status.

Class structure varies in each zone depending on how the dominant class relates to the world-economy. Contrary to the liberal economic notion of specialization based on comparative advantage, this division of labor requires increases in inequality between regions. States in the periphery are weak in that they are unable to control their fates, whereas states in the core are economically, politically, and militarily dominant. The basic function of the state is to ensure the continuation of the capitalist mode of production.

Wallerstein's explanatory goals are breathtaking in scope, and his debt to Marx and other economic-structuralist intellectual precursors is evident. He deals with such topics as the cause of war among states and factors leading to the rise and fall of core powers. These issues are discussed in the context of the creation and expansion of capitalism as a historical world-system. The focus is first and foremost on economic processes and how they in turn influence political and security considerations.

---

[11] Immanuel Wallerstein, *The Modern World-System I: Capitalist Agriculture and the Origins of the European World-Economy in the Sixteenth Century* (New York: Academic Press, 1974); *The Modern World-System II: Mercantilism and the Consolidation of the European World-Economy, 1600–1750* (New York: Academic Press, 1980).

System

Wallerstein and other economic structuralists insist that to understand the development of global economic, political, and social processes, we must keep our eyes on the development of capitalism. Capitalism is a systemwide or global phenomenon. We should not concentrate on individual states and national economies and then extrapolate from their experiences. Instead, we should examine capitalism as an integrated, historically expanding system that transcends any particular political or geographic boundaries. By first understanding capitalism as a truly integrated world-system, we then can better understand the fate of particular countries. This emphasis on the system as the key to understanding may sound familiar. It should—some realists also claim that to develop a true theory of international relations, one must give precedence to the system as opposed to focusing on individual states. Do economic structuralists operating from the world-system perspective in fact share the realist view as to what constitutes the international system? There are some interesting parallels, particularly if one closely examines Wallerstein's work.

First, some realists acknowledge that Wallerstein is attempting to develop a systems-level theory, although he emphasizes economic factors over political variables.[12]

Second, Wallerstein explicitly recognizes the importance of anarchy, a concept of critical importance to many realist writers. Recall that anarchy simply refers to the absence of a superordinate or central political authority. Wallerstein notes that "the absence of a single political authority makes it impossible for anyone to legislate the general will of the world-system and hence to curtail the capitalist mode of production."[13] Anarchy, therefore, is defined in political terms for both Wallerstein and those realists who discuss the importance of the absence of any central authority in the world.

The implications of anarchy for the realist and economic structuralist are quite different, however, as evidenced by the latter part of the quotation: "to curtail the capitalist mode of production." For the realist, anarchy leads one to examine international political stability, war, and balance-of-power politics involving major states. For the economic structuralist, the economic ramifications of political anarchy are paramount. The political anarchy of the interstate system facilitates the development and expansion of world capitalism because no single state can control the entire world-economy. The result is an economic division of labor involving a core, a periphery, and a semiperiphery that is the focal point of economic-structuralist analysis. Political anarchy becomes a backdrop for an extensive analysis of capitalist dynamics.

Finally, Wallerstein addresses the issue of the international distribution of capabilities or power. Once again, it would appear that Wallerstein has much in common with realists. The following quotation is illustrative:

> Of course, we shall find on closer inspection that there are periods where one state is relatively quite powerful and other periods where power is more diffuse

---

[12] Kenneth N. Waltz, *Theory of International Politics* (Reading, MA: Addison-Wesley, 1979), 38.

[13] Immanuel Wallerstein, *The Capitalist World-Economy* (Cambridge, UK: Cambridge University Press, 1979), 69.

and contested, permitting weaker states broader ranges of action. We can talk then of the relative tightness or looseness of the world-system as an important variable and seek to analyze why this dimension tends to be cyclical in nature, as it seems to have been for several hundred years.[14]

There is, however, a major difference in how realists and Wallerstein use this notion of distribution of capabilities.

For Wallerstein, the very existence of a distribution of power or capability cannot be explained without reference to the underlying economic order. In other words, he would argue that realists spend a great deal of time talking about the balance of power but that they fail to appreciate that there are important economic processes at work that are critical in accounting for the particular distribution of capabilities or balance of power in the first place.

In sum, despite sharing a similar systems vocabulary, the use and relative importance of these concepts are quite different. For an economic structuralist such as Wallerstein, merely focusing on the distribution of capabilities among states is insufficient if one wishes to comprehend fully the nature of the world-system. The international system has always been composed of weak and strong political units. Differential power alone is not the defining characteristic of the system. Once again, what is critical for the Wallersteinian economic structuralist is the fact that the key aspects of the system are its capitalist nature, the existence of global class relations, and the various functions states and societies perform in the world-economy.

Capitalism has been the defining attribute of the international system since the sixteenth century. It is capitalism that helps to account for a core, a periphery, and a semiperiphery. It is capitalism that provides the critical environment in which states and classes operate by constraining, shaping, and channeling behavior. Some states and classes are rewarded. Others are doomed to play subordinate roles in a worldwide division of labor determined by the dictates of capitalism. So, although states and politics are certainly important to the economic structuralist, they must be analyzed in the context of the capitalist world-system. To Wallerstein and his followers, material structure clearly matters more than agency.

In a post–Cold War volume, Wallerstein puts the events of 1989 and since in historical perspective, taking a long, multicentury view of global capitalism. Liberalism—an ideology he identifies as associated with the capitalist world-system—has served as a "legitimating geoculture." On North-South relations, he depicts the North's wealth as largely the result of a transfer of surplus value from the South. Vulnerability in a capitalist world-economy comes from a ceaseless accumulation of capital that approaches its limit "to the point where none of the mechanisms for restoring the normal functioning of the system can work effectively any longer." Grossly unequal distribution of material gains contributes to multiple strains on the system and undermines state structures, notably "their ability to maintain order in a world of widespread civil warfare, both global and [at the] state level."[15]

---

[14] Wallerstein, *Capitalist World-Economy*, 25.
[15] Immanuel Wallerstein, *After Liberalism* (New York: New Press, 1995).

Political, Economic, and Social Factors

As stated in earlier chapters, realists understand the importance of economic factors, but they focus on power, the balance of power, and political explanations of international relations. Liberals interested in transnationalism emphasize political, economic, and social factors, depending on the issue. The English School tends to subordinate economic factors to their concern with elaborating the concept of "international society." As noted, economic structuralists tend to stress economic factors as underlying or driving politics in a capitalist world-economy or system.

These are generalizations, and as with all generalizations, they are subject to qualification. All economic structuralists emphasize economic factors in their conceptions of the world-system, but the degree of their emphasis varies. There even has been debate as to whether the capitalist mode of production has been overemphasized. At one extreme, there is Wallerstein, who is claimed by critics to have reduced the derivation and operation of the state system (or system of states) to economics. Other economic structuralists, although accepting the logic of the capitalist world-system approach, stress the interdependence of political and economic variables.

Christopher Chase-Dunn, for example, argues that "the capitalist mode of production exhibits a single logic in which both political-military power" and exploitative economic processes play an integrated role. Political processes, however, are still basically derivative of the world-capitalist mode of production, or they are placed in the context of economic structures and processes. He states that "both the attempts and the failures of imperium can be understood as responses to the pressures of uneven development in the world-economy. . . . The interstate system is dependent on the institutions and opportunities presented by the world market for its survival."[16]

Johan Galtung goes one step further in his perspective on imperialism, which had a major impact on economic structuralists.[17] In examining the mechanisms of imperialism that cause and perpetuate the tremendous inequality within and among nations, Galtung parts company with Marx and Lenin in that for him imperialism is not simply an economic relation arising out of capitalism. Imperialism is a structural relation of dominance defined in political, economic, military, cultural, and communications terms. These types of imperialism have to be seen in their totality. It is not enough for IR scholars to be preoccupied with only political and military factors, or for economists to restrict their focus to economic factors. The entire structure of dominance has to be comprehended. The parallels to Antonio Gramsci's perspective are apparent, although Galtung does not cite him.

Equally important, Galtung argues that one must look inside societies to understand the effects of interactions among them. Imperialism means, for example, that elites in center (or core) nations dominate and collaborate with

---

[16] Christopher Chase-Dunn, "Interstate System and Capitalist World-Economy," in *World System Structure: Continuity and Change*, ed. W. Ladd Hollist and James N. Rosenau (Beverly Hills, CA: Sage Publications, 1981), 31, 50–51.

[17] Johan Galtung, "A Structural Theory of Imperialism," *Journal of Peace Research* 2 (1971): 81–98.

elites in periphery nations to the disadvantage of the majority of people in the latter. This would be a political effect of imperialism. Economic effects would include the production of only a few commodities by a periphery state, trade being concentrated with a particular center state. Equal emphasis, however, is given to other forms of imperialism.

GRAMSCI AND HEGEMONY

The Italian Marxist Antonio Gramsci (1891–1937) departs from more hardline, Marxist-Leninist formulations and offers a volitional approach to both theory and practice that has proven appealing to some economic structuralists. Written in prison during the fascist period in Italy under Benito Mussolini, his *Prison Notebooks* are a rich source of his views. Gramsci's emphasis on political voluntarism—the subjective—clearly has roots in his study of Machiavelli, who understood the importance of practical action. A key concept in his work that influences some present-day economic-structuralist scholarship is the historical and ideological bloc, which may well be a "block" or obstacle to social change, thus maintaining a pattern of dominance in society or even on a global scale.[18] We note that such blocs are social constructions that serve dominant class interests. The historic bloc (*blocco storico*) is an instrument of hegemony. To Gramsci, it is decisive, composed as it is of both structures and superstructures, the objective and the subjective, respectively.

Of particular importance is his argument that this hegemonic position relies mainly on consent rather than mere coercion. Dominant classes provide a social vision that supposedly is in the interests of all. This vision can be articulated and reflected in popular culture, education, literature, and political parties. If subordinate social groups buy into this vision, then the ruling classes will not have to rely on coercion to stay in power. Gramsci hopes that this dominant ideology or social vision can be challenged by elements of civil society by articulating a counterhegemonic vision that would open the way for a postcapitalist future.

Gramsci's influence is apparent in Robert Cox's work on social forces and hegemony, relating as he does ideas to global economic and political structures to avoid the limitations of state-centric IR theory. For Cox, realism and liberalism underestimate the powerful and expansive nature of what he terms world hegemony. At the international or systems level, hegemony is not merely an order among states. It is rather an order within a world-economy with a dominant mode of production that penetrates all countries. Hegemony is also evident in the complex social and political relations that connect the social classes of these different countries. World hegemony, therefore, is a combination of social structure, economic structure, and political structure. This world hegemony is expressed in universal norms, institutions, and other mechanisms that constitute

---

[18] See Quintin Hoare and Geoffrey Nowell Smith, eds., *Selections from the Prison Notebooks* (New York: International Publishers, 1971), especially Part II, Chapter 1 on the Modern Prince, Machiavelli, Marx, Voluntarism, and Social Masses, 123–205. On Gramsci, see the three-volume set of his *Prison Notebooks*, trans. and ed. Joseph A. Buttigieg (New York: Columbia University Press, published serially in 1991, 1996, and 2007).

general rules of behavior for states as well as transnational, civil society actors. Ultimately these rules support the dominant capitalist mode of production. In contrast to the liberal view, international organizations are a mechanism through which universal norms of world hegemony are expressed.

Similarly, Craig Murphy sees a Gramsci-style, North-South historical bloc composed of an "Atlantic" or "Trilateral" ruling class, some of the subordinate classes within advanced industrial states, and a rising governing class in dependent Global South states that maintain a collective position of dominance over those that are subordinate to them. The bloc has many interrelated or interconnected reinforcing faces—economic, political, and cultural—that facilitate maintenance of this dominance. As with Cox, he sees the ideas and values institutionalized in international organizations as designed to serve identifiable interests in a capitalist, global economy.[19]

CHANGE AND GLOBALIZATION

Many international relations scholars are interested in understanding system change. A common distinction is between changes of the system and lesser changes within an existing system that retains its basic characteristics. For economic structuralists, changes within the world-system appear to fall into three categories. First, there are changes in the actors' positions within the capitalist world-economy. As Wallerstein states: "There is constant and patterned movement between groups of economic actors as to who shall occupy various positions in the hierarchy of production, profit, and consumption."[20] The Dutch empire of the seventeenth century, for example, gave way to British domination, and eventually the United States rose to prominence in the twentieth century. Despite different core powers, however, the hierarchical nature of the system remains the same.

Second, some scholars identify phases or cycles of capitalist growth and contraction that affect all societies. A period of relative social stability and economic stagnation precedes twenty or thirty years of rapid economic growth. This is then followed by another two or three decades of economic decline, followed again by expansion. Overproduction, a key factor discussed by Hobson, is central to the interplay of economic, social, and political forces.[21]

Third, there is what has been termed a *structural transformation* of the system. This term refers to the historical and geographical expansion of the capitalist world-system, incorporating new areas of the globe and nonintegrated sectors of the world-economy.[22] Although the term *transformation* is

---

[19] Robert W. Cox, "Gramsci, Hegemony, and International Relations," in *Approaches to World Order,* ed. Robert W. Cox and Timothy J. Sinclair (Cambridge, UK: Cambridge University Press, 1996); Craig Murphy, *International Organization and Industrial Change: Global Governance since 1850* (Oxford, UK: Oxford University Press, 1994).

[20] Wallerstein, *Capitalist World-Economy,* 67.

[21] Terrence Hopkins and Immanuel Wallerstein, *World-System Analysis: Theory and Methodology* (Beverly Hills, CA: Sage Publications, 1982), 121–22.

[22] Hopkins and Wallerstein, *World-System Analysis,* 123.

used, these changes could still be viewed as changes within the system because the capitalist mode of production, while perhaps changing its character, is still capitalist. In sum, the economic-structuralist view of the capitalist world-system is hardly static. The world-system is dynamic, reflecting a myriad of activities and changes.

But what about changes *of* the capitalist system? Is globalization a new transforming force, or is it the mere continuation of long-established capitalist trends? World-system theorists point to one major historical transformation occurrence: the movement from feudalism into capitalism in sixteenth-century Europe. World-system theorists, therefore, claim that they have been talking about globalization long before the word was even coined and became popularized. Indeed, the process of globalization goes back to the aforementioned sixteenth century and the rise of capitalism. Globalization is not just a twentieth- and twenty-first-century phenomenon.

What are the chances of going beyond capitalism? Economic structuralists are ambivalent on this point. Wallerstein may title one article "The Rise and Future Demise of the World Capitalist System," but he also refers to "The Limited Possibilities of Transformation within the Capitalist World Order." Similarly, in the early 1980s, several theorists discussed how Eastern European and socialist states might succumb to the powerful forces of the capitalist world-system. Their analysis proved accurate.[23]

Other economic structuralists point to possible transformational processes that might make significant system change possible. Such non-Marxist scholars as Hayward Alker and Johan Galtung, for example, downplay the notion of constraints that supposedly limit the evolution of alternative world orders. Alker sees change occurring through the dialectical clash of world forces and different visions of world futures. These contradictory world order contenders (capitalist power balancing, socialism, collective self-reliance, and corporatist authoritarianism) make system transformation possible. For his part, Galtung sees the international system as open and subject to change. He even speculates on the decline not only of the nation-state but also of multinational corporations and even any world government that may be constructed in the distant future.[24] Although neither used the term *globalization*, much of what they discussed would fall under the common contemporary conceptions of globalization.

What role does human volition play in system change? We once again come to the agent-structure question. At one extreme, some scholars see large-scale historical processes as relatively immune from the actions of human beings. A strong dose of determinism seems to be reflected in their work. They are

---

[23] Immanuel Wallerstein, "The Rise and Future Demise of the World Capitalist System," *Comparative Studies in Society and History* 16, no. 4 (September 1974): 387–415, and his "Dependence in an Interdependent World: The Limited Possibilities of Transformation within the Capitalist World Economy," *African Studies Review* 18, no. 1 (April 1974): 1–26. Christopher Chase-Dunn, ed., *Socialist States in the World-System* (Beverly Hills, CA: Sage Publications, 1982).

[24] Hayward R. Alker Jr., "Dialectical Foundations of Global Disparities," in *World System Structure*, ed. Hollist and Rosenau, 80–109; Johan Galtung, "Global Processes and the World in the 1980s," in *World System Structure*, ed. Hollist and Rosenau, 110–38.

challenged by critics who downplay constraints. Some of these critics call for revolutions to end capitalist exploitation. They argue that despite the "particularity" of Latin America or other Third World regions that is emphasized by dependency theorists, these areas remain consistent with the patterns of capitalist development discussed by Marx. The "subordinated classes," they claim, have been neglected by some economic structuralists in favor of a focus on exchange relations among societies. Such critics state that class contradictions and the intensification of class conflict still make possible the type of worker revolution discussed by Marx. Hence, these authors have taken the more voluntarist position in a long-standing Marxist debate on the potential for revolution in the Third World—that revolutionaries can help produce world-system change.[25] Do agents merely have to wait for objective conditions to be ripe, perhaps serving as catalysts when they are, or can they do something subjectively to effect these conditions? With the collapse of the Soviet Union and China's embrace of capitalism, however, little has been heard from these writers in recent years.

Some world-system theorists have taken an intermediate position. Powerful "structures of domination" are acknowledged, but so also is the permanent struggle among classes. As Cardoso states of dependency theory: "Instead of accepting the existence of a determined course in history, there is a return to conceiving of it as an open-ended process. Thus, if structures delimit the range of oscillation, the actions of humans, as well as their imagination, revive and transfigure these structures and may even replace them with others that are not predetermined." Similarly, Terence Hopkins and Immanuel Wallerstein have argued that the study of the capitalist world-economy is the "theoretical side of the practical work of transforming the modern world-system into the socialist world order that modern social change has made at once politically necessary and historically possible."[26] In this formulation, there is room for human political will to effect transformation. Thus, if one accepts economic structuralists at their word (and some critics do not), economic-structuralist theory is not determinist. It allows for (and even requires) political action.

A good deal of interesting work has been done under the heading of *neostructuralism*. This work was a response to the so-called Washington Consensus in the 1990s with its emphasis on austerity and free market–oriented policies as the way for countries to solve their development problems. In keeping with the economic-structuralist emphasis, these authors are critical of the realist reliance on the unitary, rational state-as-actor. While they recognize the importance of earlier dependency and world-system work, their influences also include Fernand Braudel, Karl Polanyi, and Antonio Gramsci.

Neostructuralism is interested in understanding how global processes interact with other processes of state and social transformation occurring at many other levels of analysis of the world-system. The study of international relations,

---

[25] For example, Augustin Cueva, "A Summary of Problems and Perspectives of Dependency Theory," *Latin American Perspectives* 3, no. 4 (Fall 1976): 12–16.

[26] Fernando Henrique Cardoso, "The Consumption of Dependency Theory in the United States," *Latin American Research Review* 12, no. 3 (1977): 10–11; Hopkins and Wallerstein, *World-System Analysis*, 8.

therefore, is not limited to foreign policy or patterns of distributions of capabilities, nor confined to reducing international relations to economic variables. Given the fact that the focus of analysis is on transformative processes, states as well as economic and social forces have to be taken into account. A web of relations and forces are intricately linked, transcending all levels of analysis. Nevertheless, neostructuralists are consistent with the economic-structuralist tradition in that governments play a secondary role in socioeconomic structures and forces when it comes to explaining world politics.[27]

POSTCOLONIALISM

There is a vast, diverse, and ever-expanding literature that falls under the heading of *postcolonialism* and effectively subsumes the approaches discussed earlier. The literature began to emerge in universities in the 1980s in the United States and Great Britain and is indebted to earlier anticolonial writings from the Global South. As with realism and liberalism, there are divergences in terms of focus and assumptions, leading to lively debates. Nevertheless, to generalize, postcolonialism emphasizes an interdisciplinary perspective that encompasses economic, political, social, and cultural aspects of colonialism and decolonization. It highlights the importance of race, gender, and ethnicity in understanding anticolonial struggles and the lingering effects of the colonial experience after the end of formal imperial rule. Furthermore, a good deal of the work is interested in examining the impact of decolonization on both the metropolitan (usually Western) and colonized societies. Hence, under the conceptual umbrella of postcolonialism, one finds not only Wallerstein's capitalist world-system, but also the influence of both critical theory and postmodern critiques with the latter's focus on discourse (see chapter 10). With this caution in mind concerning the breadth and diversity of the literature, what follows is an attempt to give the reader at least a flavor of the postcolonial perspective and its internal debates that encompass academic disciplines ranging from history, political science, and economics to sociology, cultural anthropology, and linguistics.

In terms of historical background, Third World countries at the Bandung Conference in Indonesia in 1958 established the nonaligned movement. This was followed a decade later in 1966 by the Tricontinental Conference in Havana that identified the movement as spanning Latin America, Africa, and Asia. These activities provided a foundation for the call for a new international economic order in the 1970s and later a "postcolonial politics" or "grass roots movement to fight a system of injustice and gross material inequality that is sustained by powerful local interests and international power structures of banks, businesses and investment funds."[28]

---

[27] See, for example, Alicia Bárcena and Antonio Prado, eds., *Neo-Structuralism and Heterodox Currents in Latin America and the Caribbean at the Beginning of the XXI Century* (CEPAL 2015) in Spanish, available in pdf.

[28] Robert J. C. Young, *Postcolonialism: An Historical Introduction* (Oxford, UK: Blackwell, 2001), 17, 18. See also Barbara Bush, *Imperialism and Postcolonialism* (Harlow, UK: Longman, 2006); Leela Gandhi, *Postcolonial Theory: A Critical Introduction* (Edinburgh, UK: Edinburgh University Press, 1998).

One ongoing debate within the literature involves the basic question of the definition of key concepts. This is true of all the theories and images we examine in this book. Such concepts as imperialism, colonialism, and certainly postcolonialism are hotly contested and reflect differing theoretical positions and political values. Can there be, for example, only "formal" imperialism, meaning a country forfeits its sovereignty and is incorporated into an empire? Or can there be "informal" imperialism? If so, is that the same as "neocolonialism"? What about cases where an indigenous elite work with the foreign imperial power to exploit their own people? Would this be an example of "internal colonialism"? Can one speak of a postcolonial "hegemonic" power?

This latter issue brings in the matter of how to characterize the United States. Can and should the United States be viewed as an imperial power? The answer depends on how a particular author defines imperialism and associated terms. Conventional historians have tended to reinforce the narrative that the United States is not an imperial power due to its own historical struggle for independence from British colonialism and the supposed resultant anti-imperialist culture. Only in the late nineteenth century as in the Spanish-American War (1898) would we find a brief imperial turn in American policy, albeit one that would continue in the early twentieth century.

Not surprisingly, many postcolonialist writers view this story merely as myth, part of the "American exceptionalism" tale, augmented as well by President Woodrow Wilson's championing of national self-determination for oppressed peoples after World War I. If anything, American imperialism dates at least from the time of the Monroe Doctrine (1823) when hegemony was proclaimed over Latin America. The Vietnam War only reinforced this perspective in the minds of many postcolonial historians and theorists. Other postcolonial works take a different view, simply assigning the United States as an imperial power as part of the West in general. US continental expansion and the dealings with indigenous Native Americans are often considered a separate phenomenon that may not be captured by concepts such as colonialism devised to explain the European experience in Africa, Asia, and the Middle East, but are still part of the imperial project engaged in by the United States in its own sphere.

While colonialism in terms of the physical occupation of a state is no longer the hallmark of the international system, empire and imperialism, postcolonialists argue, are alive and well. Hence, while the term *postcolonial* presumes going beyond the era of colonialism, it is not clear what constitutes the temporal dividing line. Some postcolonial theorists question the utility of even trying to pinpoint the divide between the colonial and postcolonial eras, instead viewing the period from at least the fifteenth century to today as a seamless web of relations between the West and what has variously been termed the "non-West," Third World, developing world, or the Global South.

In other words, while formal empires may have disintegrated, strategies were developed to retain Western power and influence before and during the decolonization process and are still in existence today in the postcolonial world. Earlier approaches designed to maintain power during direct colonial rule (exploiting ethnic and racial divisions among subject people, co-opting activists into colonial administrations, and extending judicious concessions in trade) have been supplemented by more subtle mechanisms of domination ranging from the use of the International Monetary Fund and World Bank to the manipulation of language designed to encourage "mental colonialism."[29]

Put another way, as it is by some, the postcolonial world still exhibits neocolonial forms of cultural, economic, and even political-military dominance over these former colonies. Independence has not really brought liberation when former colonies are still so linked to the metropole—the seat of power in the former colonial country. Thus, to understand politics in any African country, it remains important to identify the "former" colonial power, whether Britain, France, Belgium, the Netherlands, Spain, or Portugal. Neocolonial patterns of dominance remain important in the postcolonial period. One can see this even in trade and other economic arrangements the European Union has with former colonies in Africa, the Caribbean, and the Pacific (the so-called ACP countries) that keep these states in relations that still work to the net advantage of the metropole.

An interesting aspect of the postcolonial literature concerns an increased focus on the recipients of colonial policies. Early work on imperialism and colonialism had a distinct Western focus. Great Britain, in particular, tended to be the favorite object of analysis. Much of the historical work emphasized the motives and mechanisms of British imperialism and colonialism and delved deeply into archival material. The French experience, particularly in Africa and southeast Asia, has also been a wellspring of academic study. It is not surprising that a large number of postcolonial theorists and historians are also from British and French universities. One of the major contributions they have made is to draw attention to the perspectives and experiences of those people who were on the receiving end of British, French, or other colonial and imperial policies. By giving voice to them (often in creative ways), scholars have highlighted what has been obscured in more mainstream work on colonialism: the attempts to resist military, political, economic, and cultural repression and oppression. As one writer who acknowledges the voices and experiences of the downtrodden puts it: "Postcolonialism claims the right of all people on this earth to the same material and cultural well-being." It is the "politics of 'the subaltern,' that is, subordinated classes and peoples."[30]

As noted earlier, the concepts and arguments of Marx, Lenin, and Hobson informed much of the post–World War II work on imperialism such as dependency theory. Interest in the impact of capitalism on the Third World, however, was not limited to Marxists. Some authors pursued detailed case studies of colonial policies and relations between Great Britain and a single colonized people. Others took a more global approach, tracing capitalist development and its global expansion over the centuries. Wallerstein's work is a good example, and the emphasis on economic drivers continues to be a primary concern of many postcolonialist theorists.

---

[29] Jurgen Osterhammel, *Colonialism* (Princeton, NJ: Marcus Weiner/Ian Randle, 1997), 119.

[30] Young, *Postcolonialism*, 2, 6.

Some theorists within the postcolonial perspective, however, have argued that capitalism should not be conflated with imperialism. Older, precapitalist empires have existed throughout recorded history, certainly well before the rise of capitalism as a mode of production. Whatever the era under investigation, the hallmark of all empires is the subjugation of weaker people. This is true whether the empire was Roman, Ottoman, British, or French. Why privilege the capitalism-imperialism nexus as opposed to placing it under a broader perspective on imperialism?

But scholars who emphasize the critical role of capitalism in terms of the development of the modern world offer the rebuttal that while ancient empires came and went, those empires that emerged in conjunction with the rise of capitalism exhibited unique characteristics linked to particular intellectual, technological, and scientific innovations. These characteristics, often placed under the heading of modernity, were most evident in what has been termed the New Imperialism that emerged in the nineteenth century and is associated with Western Europe and eventually the United States. Certainly, weapons technology and firepower were critical factors to explain the success of imperialist policies, but so, too, were intellectual and ideological claims ("white man's burden," social Darwinism, and virulent racism[31]) that accompanied, were used to justify, and perhaps even motivate imperial policies.

Aside from equating capitalist expansion with imperialism, a second point made is that a "Eurocentric" analytical perspective tends to restrict capitalism as an economic mode of production to Europe. Far from being some sort of European miracle, it has been argued that African-Asian market and capitalist practices existed before developments in Europe. India, China, and Japan were as advanced as Europe before the eighteenth century. As one postcolonialist scholar has written:

> There is something puzzling about the excitement with which European historians hail the arrival of cities, trade, regular taxation, standing armies, legal codes, bureaucracies . . . and other common appurtenances of civilized societies as if they were unique and self-evident stepping stones to modernity: to the non-European they simply indicated that Europe had finally joined the club.[32]

Many cities in Asia were larger than any eighteenth-century European city. There is agreement, however, that with the development of long-distance trading networks in the late fifteenth century and the beginning of overseas colonization, the advantage turned to Europe. This was not a function, it has been argued, of European superiority, but rather the coalescing of political, economic, environmental, cultural, and population changes that enabled capitalism and modernity to emerge. This facilitated, as it does today, the dominance of the global political economy.[33] The most advanced European empires such as

---

[31] It has been argued that racism is a significant but inadequately addressed aspect of imperialism. Furthermore, it is a concept that the IR field has failed to address as a motivating factor of state behavior and diplomacy. See Ko Unoki, *Racism, Diplomacy, and International Relations* (Routledge, 2022).

[32] Patricia Crone, *Pre-Industrial Societies: Anatomy of the Pre-Modern World* (Oxford, UK: Blackwell, 1989), 148, as cited by Bush, *Imperialism and Postcolonialism*, 80.

[33] Kenneth Pomerantz, *The Great Divergence: Europe, China and the Making of the Modern World Economy* (Princeton, NJ: Princeton University Press, 2000), 17–19.

France, Holland, and Great Britain were either the most economically advanced or most influenced by modernity as stimulated by the ideas of the Enlightenment. Spain stagnated in semifeudalism and Russia declined to second-tier imperial status.[34]

A final point of contention within the postcolonial literature in recent years involves the concept of globalization and its relation to imperialism and the postcolonial era, however, defined. For some, globalization is simply a new stage in Western imperialism and has deepened racial, class, and gender hierarchies and inequalities. There is total rejection of the idea that globalization could be of benefit to any people except those in dominant positions of power. Others argue that while there might be an increase in economic interdependence, politically the world is breaking into blocs characterized by different forms and mutations of capitalism. World-system theorists wonder what all the fuss is about. For them, globalization is not new but can be traced back to the origins of capitalism. This global world-system was essentially completed in the twentieth century but has moved into a prolonged period of crisis that in time will bring the system to its end.

ECONOMIC STRUCTURALISTS AND THEIR CRITICS

The economic-structuralist literature has been either subject to a great deal of criticism by specialists in international relations and comparative politics or simply ignored. In particular, postcolonial literature is rarely even referenced in mainstream IR journals. Much of the criticism is harsh, particularly of dependency theorists and Wallerstein's ambitious work. While some of this criticism undoubtedly reflects divergent ontological and epistemological issues as reflected in the positivist-postmodern divide, there is perhaps also an element of ideological preference. We first discuss some of the more telling critiques and then present rebuttals from economic structuralists.[35]

The Question of Causality

Some critics question whether dependency creates and sustains underdevelopment (as economic structuralists claim) or whether it is this lesser level of development that leads to a situation of dependency. In short, there is no agreement on causality—whether dependency is the *cause* of underdevelopment or whether it is the *effect* of this condition.

Reliance on Economics

Critics have argued that some economic structuralists have reduced the operation of the international system down to the process of capital accumulation

---

[34] Bush, *Imperialism and Postcolonialism*, 80.

[35] See, for example, Robert A. Packenham, *The Dependency Movement: Scholarship in Development Studies* (Cambridge, MA: Harvard University Press, 1992); Andreas Velasco, "The Dustbin of History: Dependency Theory," *Foreign Affairs* (November–December 2002): 44–45; Daniel Garst, "Wallerstein and His Critics," *Theory and Society* 14, no. 4 (July 1985): 469–95.

and related dynamics. What of other, noneconomic explanations of imperialism and relations among states? Are not political and strategic motives equally or even more important? For example, how can one account for nineteenth-century European states scrambling for economically low-value pieces of terrain such as present-day Chad or lifeless Pacific atolls? What was the economic motive? If the competitive interstate system is derived from the capitalist mode of production, how does one explain similar competitive behavior among political units in precapitalist eras before the fifteenth century? For example, recall Thucydides's discussion of the Peloponnesian War that lends support to the validity of such notions as anarchy and the security dilemma. This suggests the autonomy of the political realm and a distinctly political dynamic involving competition among sovereign units well before the emergence of a capitalist world-system.

The economic variable, critics claim, cannot carry the very great explanatory weight assigned to it. Insights generated from the contemplation of international relations over the centuries should not be ignored. Structural realists, for example, would argue that, if anything, it is the international political-security system that largely determines the international economic system, not the other way around.

System Dominance

Despite economic-structuralist references to internal factors, it is fair to ask if there is an excessive reliance on international economic factors in explaining poverty and dependence in the periphery and that domestic variables at the societal level of analysis are downplayed. The cruder dependency work, it is argued, is too sweeping in its claims, blaming virtually every southern hemispheric political, economic, and social problem on the northern industrialized states. Lack of economic growth, social unrest, and repressive governments are all laid at the doorstep of the richer capitalist countries. Critics see structure as occupying too central a role, effectively marginalizing agency in what is essentially a system-dominant, if not system-determined, theoretical enterprise.

Theoretical Rigidity

The criticism of economics and system dominance as bases for causality logically leads to the following: Individual cases are examined solely in terms of general theoretical constructs such as the capitalist world-system. A society's experiences are reduced to (or explained in terms of) one or two concepts. Major political, economic, and social changes all supposedly fall under the general explanatory logic of a term such as *dependency*. Furthermore, rather than modifying the theories or concepts in light of empirical evidence (often supposedly lacking) or questions raised by case studies, it is claimed that case studies are used by economic structuralists only when they appear to provide evidence to support the line of argument. There is no tension between theory and findings, little questioning of the framework, and an unwillingness to consider alternative hypotheses. Such criticisms, of course, are also often leveled at work associated with realists and liberals.

Accounting for Anomalies

Economic structuralists have trouble accounting for non-Western countries that have been relatively successful economically despite their ups and downs: Taiwan, Brazil, Singapore, and South Korea. In addition, there are the greatest success stories of any non-European, non-North American country: Japan and now China. What is it about these countries that have allowed them either to escape abject poverty or, at least in the case of China, make such amazing strides forward? Neither are examples of autonomous development. They seem to have benefited greatly from being enmeshed in the global capitalist system.

In response, it should be noted that no theory or approach can be expected to explain everything. The virtue of good theorizing is that it points out and accounts for commonalities, and what particular cases have in common. Anomalies are expected and do not detract from the utility of the theory if it can be adequately explained why a unique case does not fit the general pattern.

Critics comment, however, that economic structuralists such as Wallerstein simply group all anomalies under the concept of the semiperiphery, a theoretically and empirically poorly defined concept. Furthermore, what of the insights of authors who argue that there are certain advantages to backwardness when a state is trying to catch up economically with more advanced states? What of the work by scholars who emphasize the importance of different types of state structures, political and social coalitions, and shifting alliances in accounting for the differential modernization success of various countries?[36] Such literature is ignored, it is argued, because the economic-structuralist perspective refuses to give due consideration to domestic factors that are not the result of capitalist dynamics.

Defining Alternatives and Science as Ideology

It is argued that some economic structuralists have done a poor job in defining reasonable alternative world futures, let alone strategies, for states in the Global South to pursue. What is meant, for example, by the call for autonomous development? Is such a goal feasible? How is it to be achieved? Would redistributive policies of government be combined with political repression and the abuse of power?

Critics also charge that value preferences infuse economic-structuralist work. Economic structuralists, however, are not apologetic for their normative commitment to fundamental changes in the relations between the North and the South. As one noted writer has stated, in analyses of dependency relations: "There is no presumption of scientific neutrality." Such works are considered to be "more true because they assume that, by discerning which are the historical agents capable of propelling a process of transformation . . . these analyses thus grasp the meaning of historical movement and help to negate a given order of domination."[37]

---

[36] See, for example, Alexander Gerschenkron, *Economic Backwardness in Historical Perspective* (New York: Praeger, 1965); Barrington Moore, *Social Origins of Dictatorship and Democracy* (Boston: Beacon Press, 1966); Theda Skocpol, *States and Social Revolutions* (New York: Cambridge University Press, 1979).

[37] Cardoso, "Consumption of Dependency Theory," 16.

Responses

Why has the economic-structuralist literature—when it has not been totally ignored—received such a great deal of criticism? Is it simply because it is deserving of such critical scrutiny? Three comments are in order.

First, it is not surprising that most of the criticism comes from scholars working within mainstream North American social science. The vocabulary of the economic-structuralist literature is alien to many of these scholars. Analyses based on Marxian insights and categories are generally viewed with distrust in North American universities and are often dismissed out of hand. And although some of the economic-structuralist work is characterized as being ideological, economic structuralists have similarly surmised that the attacks on them are based less on dispassionate critiques and more on the value preferences of the reviewer. Ideological biases are wrapped in the cloak of supposedly objective criticisms.

Second, it was pointed out that many critics charge that the dependency literature in particular has been insufficiently empirical, failing to marshal evidence based on the canons of positivist science. Where are the data, they ask? In fact, it is claimed that the empirical testing of selective hypotheses from the dependency literature indicates that these hypotheses simply do not hold up.[38]

Dependency theorists respond that such a charge is based on the assumption that the rationalist or positivist methods are the only means to comprehend reality. As noted in chapter 1, there are alternative epistemological premises or assumptions from which one can start that question the value of formal hypothesis testing with its often-exclusive focus on what can be measured, counted, and added. As one theorist notes:

> The divergence is not merely methodological-formal. It is, rather, at the very heart of studies of dependency. If these studies do in fact have any power of attraction at all, it is not merely because they propose a methodology to substitute for a previously existing paradigm or because they open up a new set of themes. It is principally because they do this from a *radically critical* viewpoint.[39]

Even from the perspective of a positivist approach to knowledge, however, a hallmark of much of the world-system literature is its conspicuously empirical, cross-national focus. And while much of the broader postcolonial literature does not engage in statistical analysis, it does rely heavily on detailed case studies drawing on in-depth archival research.

To conclude, judging by the IR textbooks currently on the market in the United States, it is apparent that the economic-structuralist perspective is not considered mainstream. Realist, liberal, and constructivist perspectives dominate the literature, but this certainly does not mean that the economic-structuralist image of international relations is unimportant or undeserving of attention. Its

---

[38] Velasco, "Dustbin of History," 45.
[39] Cardoso, "Consumption of Dependency Theory," 16.

contribution to increased understanding of the world around us should not be seen only as a function of its degree of popularity at a particular point in time. By providing a very different, challenging, and provocative perspective on world politics, it remains in our view worthy of attention.

After all, dominant scientific paradigms or research programs of one particular period tend to decay. What is at one time considered to be heretical or at the fringes of normal science may one day become the prevailing orthodoxy.[40] At a minimum, the economic-structuralist perspective should encourage the student of international relations to analyze critically the realist, liberal, and English School rationalist images and the assumptions on which they are based. At the maximum, economic-structuralist writers have provided challenging hypotheses and insights concerning the dynamics and development of international relations and world politics that still constitute an important, if less prominent, image.

REFERENCES

Cardoso, Fernando Henrique, and Enzo Faletto. *Dependency and Development in Latin America*. Berkeley: University of California Press, 1979.

Hettne, Bjorn, Andras Inotai, and Osvaldo Sunkel. *Globalism and the New Regionalism*. New York: Palgrave Macmillan, 1999.

Hollist, W. Ladd, and James N. Rosenau, eds. *World System Structure: Continuity and Change*. Beverly Hills, CA: Sage Publications, 1981.

Huggan, Graham, ed. *Oxford Handbook of Postcolonial Studies*. Oxford: Oxford University Press, 2013.

Loomba, Ania. *Colonialism/Postcolonialism*. London: Routledge, 2005.

Unoki, Ko. *Racism, Diplomacy, and International Relations*. London: Routledge, 2022.

Wallerstein, Immanuel. *The Capitalist World-Economy*. Cambridge, UK: Cambridge University Press, 1979.

Young, Robert J. C. *Postcolonialism: An Historical Introduction*. Oxford, UK: Blackwell, 2016.

---

[40] Thomas S. Kuhn, *The Structure of Scientific Revolutions* (Chicago: University of Chicago Press, 1970).

8

The English School: International Society and Grotian Rationalism

The primary research task of the English School has been to trace the history and development of international society and to uncover its nature and functioning. The English School is an interesting blend of realist understandings of power and balance of power and the liberal perspective on the ways international law, rules, norms, and institutions operate internationally. It can be viewed, therefore, as a middle path or *via media* between the two traditions. Hence, perspectives on international politics associated with Niccolò Machiavelli or Thomas Hobbes, Hugo Grotius, and Immanuel Kant have all influenced the development of the English School. In terms of methodology, it emphasizes a historical-sociological approach and, most recently, interpretive understandings that reflect deep skepticism about the scientific and causal approach to IR theorizing.

Although formal origins as a "school" were in the 1950s, with the end of the Cold War, the English School's nuanced conceptual eclecticism seemed well suited to an era of change and globalization. As one scholar observes, the English School is an "underutilized research resource. The time is ripe to develop and apply its historicist, constructivist, and methodologically pluralist approach to IR."[1]

MAJOR ACTORS AND ASSUMPTIONS

The first assumption underlying the English School image is that the world can be understood as an international or anarchical society in which both states and nonstate actors operate. The emphasis is on the concept of society, which realists would tend not to pair with anarchical. An anthology of papers published in 1968 indicates quite clearly that the frame of reference from the outset was

---

[1] Barry Buzan, "The English School: An Underexploited Resource in IR," *Review of International Studies* 27 (2001): 472.

international society.[2] As later succinctly stated by Adam Watson and Hedley Bull, an *international society* is

> [A] group of states (or, more generally, a group of independent political communities) which not merely form a system, in the sense that the behavior of each is a necessary factor in the calculations of the others, but also have established by dialogue and consent common rules and institutions for the conduct of their relations, and recognize their common interest in maintaining these arrangements.[3]

Although recognizing the importance of the historical existence of an "international system of states" (as realists frequently use the term), it is the overarching term international society that captures the essence of English School thinking. English School scholars are skeptical of the view that because the international system lacks a common power to keep citizens in awe, we cannot speak of an international society but rather only a system of states.

Second, for the English School the concept of *order* in the anarchical society plays an important theoretical role. Order, however, results not simply from power and the balance of power, but also from the acceptance of rules and institutional arrangements that are in the enlightened, rational self-interest of states and other actors. Like classical realists, those in the English School understand the importance in international affairs of power—the material component—and ideas, values, and norms.

The reliance on the tradition of international law is particularly evident. As noted in chapters 5 and 6, realists, liberals, and neoliberal institutionalists often use the concept of rationality as an underlying or simplifying assumption that contributes to the development of parsimonious theories. *Rationalism* in the English School, however, has a different meaning. Invoking a tradition associated with Grotius—the "father of international law"—English School rationalism refers to the rules, laws, and institutional arrangements states have established to provide some degree of order to an anarchic international society. Hence, as opposed to the realist emphasis on defining structure in terms of polarity or the distribution of capabilities, structure is more closely associated with this broadly conceived rule-based institutional framework.

Finally, the English School recognizes the importance of Immanuel Kant's ethical and moral understandings, but this is balanced by a pragmatic view of the anarchical society as one in which considerations of power and interest remain important. The concept of *world society* in English School usage is reserved for this Kantian or revolutionist (some would say utopian) strain of thought—realizing a universal cosmopolitanism and thus transforming the world as we know it into a society based on norms with broad moral acceptance.

---

[2] See Herbert Butterfield and Martin Wight, eds., *Diplomatic Investigations: Essays in the Theory of International Politics* (Cambridge, MA: Harvard University Press, 1968).
[3] Hedley Bull and Adam Watson, eds., *The Expansion of International Society* (Oxford, UK: Clarendon Press, 1984), p. 1.

This English School usage of world society is decidedly different from the liberal view of world or global society. For liberals, world society goes beyond international or interstate relations to encompass a complex array of state, nonstate, and transnational actors that engage with each other globally. Put another way, the concept of international society reflects the Grotian rationalist influence so central to the English School while world society is reserved in the English School for the revolutionist usage influenced by Kant.

In sum, the English School has avoided a parochial perspective on world politics. As noted by Martin Wight (1913–1972), who was a founder of the English School, all three perspectives—realist (international system), rationalist (international society), and revolutionist (world society)—are important to understanding world politics. The traditions are not like "railroad tracks running into infinity." Rather, "they are streams, with eddies and cross-currents, sometimes interlacing and never for long confined to their own river bed."[4] The idea that international system, international society, and world society perspectives can all exist simultaneously as understandings of reality and be subject to analysis is core to the English School.

INTELLECTUAL PRECURSORS AND INFLUENCES

Hugo Grotius (Huig de Groot, 1583–1645) is the generally recognized "father of international law" and as such he looked beyond the power and balance-of-power politics we read in the Florentine Niccolò Machiavelli (1469–1527) or the Englishman Thomas Hobbes (1588–1679). States observe the norms or rules (many of which have standing as international law and form the "rational" bases of international or world politics) because they produce some degree of *order* or security that is in their enlightened self-interest. It is this interest-driven, rule-following dimension that leads Martin Wight to adopt the term "rationalism," which his follower Hedley Bull (1932–1985) later places in the context of a still anarchic, international society of states.

Grotius does not ignore power and power politics among states. Indeed, conflict among states including the use of force is central to his discussion on the *Law of War and Peace* (*De jure belli ac pacis*). Similarly, his treatment in other works of economic activities including freedom of navigation on the high seas provides the intellectual basis for what would become international commercial law. Notwithstanding the independence of *sovereign* states, it is in their (rational) interest to follow rules that set the parameters of international relations in peacetime and even provided criteria for resorting to (and conduct of) war. The result, he hopes, is perhaps to make the use of force somewhat less barbarous than it otherwise would be.

Both a scholar and a very practical man living in the Dutch commercial town of Delft, Grotius turned his attention to these concerns—commercial issues and matters of war and peace—of governments, trading companies, and businesses

---

[4] Martin Wight, *International Theory: Three Traditions*, ed. Gabriele Wight and Brian Porter (London: Leicester University Press, 1991), 260.

of newly formed states in his day. Writing with the horrors of the Thirty Years' War in mind, Grotius offers formulations of law drawn from several sources. One can see, for example, the influence on Grotius of the philosophical and historical legacy of a Roman imperial *jus gentium* (a law to govern relations among diverse peoples in the ancient Roman empire) as well as natural law thinking.

Natural law is a philosophical view that claims there are laws inherent in nature that transcend any laws made by mere mortals. Such thinking is closely tied to the writings of Augustine, Thomas Aquinas, and other Christian writers of the late Roman Empire and Middle Ages we discuss in chapter 3. Grotius also knew how to make general principles and customary practice central to his constructions of legal rules-of-the-road for states in a newly emerging, state-based European society. Later colonial and imperial extension of European states in the eighteenth, nineteenth, and twentieth centuries resulted in Grotian understandings of international law becoming global in the scope of their application, particularly as the European construct of the sovereign state spread worldwide.

Aided by new transportation and communications technologies, territorial states became the principal actors in this new international societal order. Following Grotius and other writers, international law developed rapidly in diplomacy. For example, the territorial sea came to be defined by a three-mile limit from the shoreline of the coastal state. The reason three miles was chosen was a practical one—artillery technology of the time limited the range of a cannonball to about three miles, the practical distance that any country could expect to defend from the shore without actually going to sea. Principles of just war (limits on, resort to, and conduct in warfare) developed by Cicero, Augustine, Aquinas, Alberico Gentili, Francisco Vitoria, Francisco Suarez, and other philosophers over more than 1,500 years of Western civilization now have become matters of international law, not just moral preachings. Ideas concerning mutual respect for the welfare of foreign diplomats and their embassies and consulates also have become legal obligations based on the customary practice of states.

In contrast to Grotius, with some exceptions, founders of the English School clearly are not as persuaded by the writings of the East Prussian, Immanuel Kant (1724–1804). Martin Wight, for example, makes no secret of his characterization of Kantians as revolutionists who try to substitute moral principles for the realities of politics. For his part, E. H. Carr (1892–1982) rejects any Kantian invocation of morality as attempts to transform international relations as if they were (or would become) independent of power and interest.

Kant's major influence is most evident in concerns about justice in international society. This is particularly true with those in the follow-on generation of English School scholars interested in establishing global, cosmopolitan norms in a transformed international or, more precisely, world society.[5]

Although not a formal member of the "British Committee" that was established in the 1950s, Carr (usually categorized as a classical realist) is now widely acknowledged as an intellectual precursor to the emergence of the English

---

[5] See, for example, Andrew Linklater and Hidemi Suganami, *The English School of International Relations* (Cambridge, UK: Cambridge University Press, 2006), especially chaps. 5, 7.

School. For Carr, "the inner meaning of the modern international crises" experienced in the interwar period (1919–1939) is "the collapse of the whole structure of utopianism based on the concept of the harmony of interests."[6] International politics involves a continuing tension between power and interest on the one hand and moral considerations on the other. Thus, Carr rejects as utopian the pure idealism of focusing only on moral values and trying to exclude power and interest. Similarly, he finds unrealistic any so-called realism that pretends values somehow can be dropped from the political equation. Carr's observation of the inherent tension in international relations between interest and power on the one hand and moral considerations on the other sets the intellectual stage for development within the English School for a rationalist middle path. This can be traced back to Grotius who falls between the realism of Machiavelli or Hobbes and the idealism (or revolutionism) in Kant.

THE DIVERGENCE OF BRITISH AND AMERICAN SCHOLARSHIP

How did the English School emerge as having a distinct, societal-based, rationalist image of international relations? We begin to find an answer to this question in the divergence that took place in the decades following World War II between British and American scholarship on politics in general and international politics in particular. Still wedded to the strengths to be found in classical understandings and more traditional methods of analysis, British scholars did not embrace the *behavioralism* movement that in the 1950s and 1960s was gradually overtaking American political science, albeit somewhat more slowly in the IR field.

Classical scholarship in both American and British studies of diplomacy and international politics—influenced by historically based understandings and drawing as well from philosophy, law, and institutional studies—had indeed been challenged by the behavioral movement that emerged in American social sciences by the 1930s. This movement gained steam in the years after World War II and began establishing a prominent position in the IR field by the 1960s when realism still occupied center stage.

Debate in the interwar period (1919–1939) and after had occurred between realists who preferred to focus on the realities of power and interest and those who, given the devastation of world war, wished to change this business-as-usual approach by turning to greater reliance on international law and institutions as a substitute for the brutality of realpolitik, or power politics. More troubling for many classically trained scholars, however, was the attempt within the behavioral movement in the United States to make the social "sciences" more scientific, emulating the natural sciences and adopting (or at least trying to adapt) their methodologies to include formal hypothesis testing and quantitative methods of analysis.

---

[6] E. H. Carr, *The Twenty Years' Crisis* (London: Macmillan, 1939), 80, as cited by Tim Dunne, *Inventing International Society: A History of the English School* (New York: Palgrave, 1998), 29.

The divergence within Anglo-American scholarship in international relations is clearly identified in Hedley Bull's critique in the late 1960s of the direction American scholarship was taking. Indeed, he argues the case for a "classical approach" and opposed "the scientific approach [that] has contributed and is likely to contribute very little to the theory of international relations." Moreover, he observes that "in so far as it is intended to encroach upon and ultimately displace the classical approach, it is positively harmful."[7]

In a call for continued reliance on judgment that scholars should bring to the theory of international relations, Bull takes exception to "confining [our] selves to what can be logically or mathematically proved or verified according to strict procedures." He is skeptical about scientific claims made by Americans wedded to these methods: "The practitioners of the scientific approach are unlikely to make progress of the sort to which they aspire." He hastens to add that "where practitioners of the scientific approach have succeeded in casting light upon the subject, it has been by stepping beyond the bounds of that approach and employing the classical method."

In this critique Bull rejects the "construction and manipulation of so-called 'models'" entertained by the "scientific school" and warned against the dogmatism that can be found among modelers—"attributing to the model a connection with reality it does not have," sometimes "distorting the model itself by importing additional assumptions about the world in the guise of logical axioms." Similarly, he also objects to the work of the scientific school that in some cases he found to be "distorted and impoverished by a fetish for measurement."

Still calling for rigor and precision in the theory of international politics, Bull found these accommodated readily enough within the classical approach, which "should undoubtedly attempt to be scientific in the sense of being a coherent, precise, and orderly body of knowledge, and in the sense of being consistent with the philosophical foundations of modern science." Offensive to Bull was the arrogance of practitioners of the scientific approach who, "by cutting themselves off from history and philosophy, have deprived themselves of the means of self-criticism." He observes that the consequence is that they "have a view of their subject that is callow and brash."

Bull is representing in this discourse not only his views, but also those shared by many of his colleagues in the yet unnamed, still-emerging English School. His comments are pointedly directed to American scholars and reflective of the divergence then well underway between British and American methodological and epistemological approaches in the IR field. The earlier convergence in Anglo-American approaches around history, law, and institutional studies was clearly giving way in the United States to positivist, quantitative approaches to which Bull was objecting.

British scholarship would retain traditional approaches in the field even as their own "school" substantially developed a societal focus in studying

---

[7] Hedley Bull, "International Theory: The Case for a Classical Approach," in *Contending Approaches to International Politics*, ed. Klaus Knorr and James N. Rosenau (Princeton, NJ: Princeton University Press, 1969), 26. Subsequent quotes are also from this article.

international relations and world politics—one that not only found a middle path between realism and idealism as well as between realism and liberalism but also opened itself to both historical sociology and constructivist understandings.

GENESIS OF THE ENGLISH SCHOOL

To find the genesis of what would become the English School, our journey ironically starts in the United States. In 1954 with sponsorship of the Rockefeller Foundation, Dean Rusk (1909–1994, later to be secretary of state in the Kennedy and Johnson administrations), and Kenneth Thompson (1921–2013), a student and then colleague of Hans J. Morgenthau, established an American Committee of academic and policy-oriented realists.[8] Other members included William T. R. Fox (1912–1988), Hans Morgenthau (1904–1980), Reinhold Niebuhr (1892–1971), Paul Nitze (1907–2004), Arnold Wolfers (1892–1968)—the senior generation—and Kenneth N. Waltz (1924–2013), then about thirty (and one of Fox's students while at Columbia). Institutionally located in New York at Columbia University, the focus of this American Committee was to develop a theory to comprehend, explain, and guide the study of international relations and the formulation of foreign policy. Given deep divisions among these realists on theory and policy, however, the American Committee did not last long.

It was Thompson who reached out across the Atlantic in 1954 to his friend and colleague, historian Herbert Butterfield (1900–1979) at Cambridge University, to see about forming a parallel group. After considerable discussion, Butterfield turns initially to diplomatic historian Desmond Williams (1921–1987). In 1958 IR scholar Martin Wight, then in his mid-forties and at the London School of Economics (LSE), was invited to join them in forming what became the British Committee, locating it at Cambridge. Bringing academics and policy-oriented scholars together, other members included Adam Watson (1914–2007) from the British Foreign Office, William Armstrong (1915–1980) from the Treasury, military historian Michael Howard (1922–2019) from the University of London (later at Oxford), Donald Mackinnon (1913–1994) of Aberdeen University, and Wight's protégé at the LSE, the Australian Hedley Bull, then just twenty-six years of age.

Two prominent scholars not invited to join were E. H. Carr, apparently because, given his stature, it was thought his presence would become too dominant a force in the group, and F. H. Hinsley (1918–1998), whom Watson later portrayed as seeing "Europe, and the world, as more of an anarchy and less of a society than Bull or myself." This quote is quite telling, given the direction that the British Committee would take in the decades to follow under the successor-generation leadership of Watson and Bull as well as Bull's mentee and follower, R. J. Vincent (1943–1990). As Tim Dunne comments: "Both [Bull and Vincent] had an interest in strategic studies. . . . Both deployed Wight's three traditions [the realism of Machiavelli or Hobbes, the rationalism of Grotius, and the

---

[8] This section draws on Tim Dunne, *Inventing International Society: A History of the English School* (London: Macmillan, 1998).

revolutionism of Kant] as a means to engage with classical theorists, and most significantly of all, they shared a theoretical investigation into the nature of order and justice in international society."[9]

Viewing international relations and world politics primarily as a society rather than a system (the latter characterization then prominent among American scholars to include Waltz) became a central understanding within the English School. Of course, one can speak in English School parlance of a system of states, but any such system lacks the bonds, common norms, or cohesion one finds usually in international society. The interesting question for English School theorists is how a system of states can be transformed into an international society and how the latter can slip back into a system of states.

Bull followed Wight's lead in his now classic *The Anarchical Society: A Study of Order in World Politics*.[10] A central question in Bull's work is where order comes from in such an anarchical international society. Is it from the operation of power and the balance of power as Hobbesian realists would have it? Or does it spring at least as much from the rules or laws that have been constructed in international society as Grotian rationalists would be prone to claim? Finally, is order to be found as Kantian understandings of moral principle that come to be accepted in a progressive improvement not only of states themselves but also in their relations with other states?

For his part, Bull takes us beyond the realism inherent in Hobbes to find in Grotian internationalism the rules or norms that are a source of order in international society. Bull thus exemplifies in his rule-oriented construction the *via media* between the Hobbesian realism of power and balance of power and the Kantian idealism of universal moral principle.

LEVELS OF ANALYSIS AND THEORY

Given the three key concepts (international system, international society, world society), it is not surprising that the primary *level of analysis* is the global or systems level. States are the major actors in the international society, even in an era of globalization. This is perhaps not surprising as the historical-sociological approach emphasized the rise of the European state and societal systems. This development led to the spread of Western conceptions such as *sovereignty* to the rest of the world. As we will see next, the expansion of the concept of world society has in recent years opened up other units and levels of analysis to include individuals, groups, and transnational organizations.

Ontological primacy is given to the English School's conception of international society. The impact of constructivism with its emphasis on social relations and the agent-structure debate has lent substance and nuance to this scholarly orientation (see chapter 9). In terms of methodology, the English School generally prefers the more traditional approaches defended by Bull. These entail developing a set of interrelated concepts and categories to guide research and

---

[9] Dunne, *Inventing International Society*, 161.

[10] Hedley Bull, *The Anarchical Society: A Study of Order in World Politics* (London: Macmillan, 1977).

help structure questions that guide scholarly inquiry. The emphasis on historical sociology is also important and can be seen as a rebuttal to the apparent historicism of some neorealist conceptions of international relations.

Causal theorizing based on positivism, associated with realism and liberalism in particular, found few advocates among the early English School theorists. Yet younger scholars have avoided the positivist explanatory versus interpretive understanding dichotomy and offered a synthesis of different perspectives and concepts. Hence, this chapter is appropriately placed between IR images that, for the most part, have spawned positivist theories and the interpretive understandings that also guide much of contemporary IR theorizing.

CHANGE

From System to International Society

Realists emphasize the continuity of international relations throughout history; the insights of Thucydides are as relevant today as in the fifth century BCE. Liberals have faith that change is possible, with much of their work focused on the role of institutions, regimes, and norms particularly since the end of World War II. Economic structuralists have a normative commitment to change yet are cognizant of the restraints resulting from the capitalist world-system. The fact that English School theorists situate their work in the context of the realist, rationalist, and revolutionist frameworks shows a sensitivity and recognition of both the possibilities and limitations of change in international relations and world politics.

The interest in applying a historical-sociological approach to the development of international society is another indicator of English School interest in understanding change. Adam Watson took up the mantle of Martin Wight in conducting in-depth studies of the historical development of systems of states. From Hedley Bull, Watson adopted the distinction between a system of states (an impersonal network of pressures and interests that binds states together and operates essentially outside the will of the members) and a society of states (a set of common rules, institutions, codes of conduct, and values to which states agree to be bound).

While realist writings on systems of states tend to revolve around the issue of power and the struggle for power among states, the English School is particularly interested in the societal aspects of systems, which include an emphasis on how authority is developed and how practitioners have contributed to the development and monitoring of rules of the game. How can we understand the current international system and the extent to which it represents an international society unless we understand how it came into being? Furthermore, such a historical assessment might also provide insight into how the current system may change in the future.

Such an investigation requires casting one's net beyond Europe, which is exactly what Watson does in his *The Evolution of International Society*.[11]

---

[11] Adam Watson, *The Evolution of International Society: A Comparative Historical Analysis* (London: Routledge, 1992). See also Barry Buzan and Richard Little, *International Systems in World History: Remaking the Study of International Relations* (Oxford, UK: Oxford University Press, 2000).

He investigates ancient state systems such as Sumer, Assyria, Persia, Classical Greece, Macedonia, India, China, Rome, and the Byzantine and Islamic systems as well as the development of the European international society through case studies of medieval Europe, Renaissance Italy, the Hapsburg empire, the rise of the modern Westphalian commonwealth of states, and the Napoleonic empire. Each system varies along a continuum of hegemony or dominance by one political entity as opposed to a system characterized by relative autonomy or decentralization of power and authority.

Such case studies provide insight on the English School's concern with the conditions for international order—how did these systems regulate their political entities? How did the societal aspects of the system develop over time? Can we learn from their trial and error? Watson's analysis therefore takes issue with the realist conception of international relations being characterized by a repetitive condition of anarchy through recorded history, and instead he claims that relations among states can be viewed through the lens of international societies regulated by rules and practices. These are not based on some idealist conception of what the world should be, but rather the result of actual experience. By placing the current international system in a historical context, he raises the question of how permanent it is and how it might change in the future.

The English School's interest in continuity and change in international relations can also be stated as an interest in the relation between international order and the aspiration for human justice. This concern is particularly evident among younger scholars associated with the English School who have responded to changes in international relations since the end of the Cold War. While Watson examined the expansion of international society, others have studied the phenomenon of failed states and the resultant human cost.

Contrasting if not clashing views of what constitutes international society from the point of view of non-Westerners have also been investigated. Similarly, some scholars have joined liberals and constructivists in examining the changing relations among state sovereignty, human rights, and the norms of humanitarian intervention. Other research topics that initially received less attention in the English School such as European integration, international political economy, and global environmental politics have been investigated.[12]

From International Society to World Society

This renaissance of the English School is remarkable in that its obituary and even a call for its disbandment were suggested in the early 1980s.[13] One scholar who is responsible for the resurrection and reformulation of the English School approach to international relations is Barry Buzan. Buzan engages in one of the most extensive critiques of the English School as exemplified by Wight, Bull, and Herbert Butterfield. He notes internal debates, inconsistencies, and conceptual and empirical voids. For Buzan, the rise of constructivism deserves credit for

---

[12] Linklater and Suganami, *The English School of International Relations*, 2.

[13] Roy Jones, "The English School of International Relations: A Case for Closure?" *Review of International Studies* 7, no. 1 (1981): 1–13.

reinvigorating the English School's important yet underdeveloped emphasis on the social or societal dimension of international relations.[14]

Buzan notes that the English School actually consists of several complementary elements that are not always made explicit in the first generation of theorizing: the School as a set of ideas to be found in the minds of statesmen, a set of ideas in the minds of political theorists, and a set of externally imposed concepts that define material and social structures of the international system. It is the latter that is his main concern, particularly the key goal of addressing the conceptually weak concept of world society, the third element of the English School triad.

The traditional discussion within the English School was generally limited to a debate between a pluralist versus a *solidarist* conception of international society, a topic of concern to Hedley Bull in particular. The debate centered on the actual and potential extent of shared norms, rules, institutions, and international law within international society. The *pluralist* view finds that states have relatively little in common other than the calculations of interest. This is a thin morality in which states can agree to a framework of international order that allows for mutually advantageous cooperation. At best, it is a world of enlightened self-interest in which states are most concerned with security and maintaining order under anarchy. Practical policies emphasize mutual recognition of sovereignty, diplomacy, and maintaining the nonintervention principle in terms of the domestic affairs of states. This reflects more of a realist influence.

The opposing *solidarist* view sees the world in cosmopolitan terms, arguing international society has a relatively high degree of shared norms, rules, and institutions among states. This is a thick morality with the capacity even to enforce universalist ethics. As a result, ideas of individual rights and the extent to which a community of humankind exists inevitably enter into consideration. This reflects a Kantian influence. Whether viewed as a dichotomy or a spectrum, the traditional debate among English School theorists was essentially conducted *within* the international society framework, the flagship concept, as opposed to a realist international system or a Kantian-style world society.

Buzan's contribution to reformulating the English School is to argue that the world society concept is more accurately composed of a set of *normative* goals for theorists, but conceptually and analytically it has remained at the margins. He aims to correct this by examining world society from the perspective of norms and ideas as forms of social structure (hence, the interest in constructivism). In other words, his interest is in a theory about norms as opposed to normative theory. Such an approach closes the gap, discussed earlier, between the English School view of theory as simply a way to organize and structure questions, concepts, and categories systematically and the positivist emphasis on causal explanations.

Buzan argues that a conceptually robust concept of world society could become the best approach to coming to grips with the phenomenon of

---

[14] Barry Buzan, *From International to World Society? English School Theory and the Social Structure of Globalisation* (Cambridge, UK: Cambridge University Press, 2004).

globalization, a challenge for IR theory in general. The relation between international society and world society is not only the biggest weakness of existing English School theory, but also where the biggest theoretical if not practical gains can be made. Working out the relation between order and a more cosmopolitan culture in "international" society is one of the unfinished legacies of Bull's work. A revised English School theory, therefore, has potential to improve how globalization is conceptualized, but only if world society can be developed as a coherent theoretical concept.[15]

Buzan argues that the English School's triad of concepts captures key aspects of globalization to include the simultaneous existence of state and nonstate systems to include transnational actors such as nongovernmental organizations. Just as Watson examined the historical relation and transition between systems of states and international societies (Hobbes and Grotius, realism and rationalism), the development of the world society concept can help us understand the potential and obstacles for transitioning to post-Westphalian world politics. Unless the weakness of world society as a pillar of English School thought is overcome, further progress within the English School is constrained. Constructivist insights and its approach to social relations can provide a useful tool.

In the process of his ambitious effort to rethink the English School in an era of globalization, therefore, Buzan (a) retools the international system, international society, and world society triad; (b) reconstructs the pluralist-solidarist debate; (c) thinks through the analytical and normative implications of the world society concept; and (d) examines the concept of institutions that is the underpinning of order in international relations. In terms of the final task, he compares and contrasts the English School approach to institutions to the ways realists, liberal institutionalists, and regime theorists deal with the concept.

THE ENGLISH SCHOOL, LIBERALS, AND SOCIAL CONSTRUCTIVISTS

Given the English School emphasis on an anarchical, international society, it is important to note similarities with liberalism discussed in chapter 6 and social constructivism in chapter 9. Norms that become established in the form of either tacitly accepted understandings or explicitly agreed-upon rules (some of which have the binding quality of international law) lie at the foundation of international regimes. For liberals, such regimes consist of voluntarily agreed sets of principles, norms, rules, and procedures concerning diverse issues—human rights, war and peace, commercial transactions, and the like—and their servicing institutions, both governmental and nongovernmental organizations.

These regimes and institutions are the outcomes of human design efforts over centuries intended to provide an authoritative basis for regulating or at least influencing the behavior of both state and nonstate actors. So understood, the development of international society can be viewed as a constructivist enterprise. As noted in chapter 9, social constructivists portray self-help, power

---

[15] Buzan, *International to World Society?* 2.

politics, sovereignty, and similar concepts as having been socially constructed or having evolved under the anarchy of international relations and world politics. They are not inevitable or essential attributes of international politics, but rather have been socially constructed. The key point is that international relations and world politics do not have an independent existence; they are what people make (or have made) of them. Ideas, culture, and norms matter and can influence behavior, including the creation of multilateral institutions.

Among English School theorists, scholars sympathetic to the solidarist perspective are more prone to examine human rights and humanitarian intervention. Similar interest has been expressed about the global environment. Such concerns reflect normative aspirations within the English School.

THE ENGLISH SCHOOL AND ITS CRITICS

Methodological Muddle

The affinity between aspects of liberalism, constructivism, and the English School is reflected in the fact that friendly criticism of the English School has come from both liberals and constructivists. Martha Finnemore, for example, has written widely on humanitarian intervention from a constructivist perspective. She argues that improving the visibility of the English School among American IR academics would enrich the latter's scholarship due to the English School's historical and normative orientation. Unfortunately, "the School's lack of clarity about both method and theoretical claims has made it difficult for American scholars to incorporate it into their research. . . . For many American scholars, simply figuring out what its methods are is a challenge" as "English School authors . . . almost never provide systematic discussion about rules of evidence."[16]

Historical Knowledge

As noted, the historical-sociological approach is a hallmark of the English School. It is one thing to claim, as do Bull and Watson, that historical knowledge is important. But the question is why is this so? Is it because the present and the future are part of a historical narrative or story slowly unfolding from time past? Is what we observe today in international society grounded in historical developments over centuries in time? Or is historical knowledge important because the present and the future are similar to the past, all subject to similar types of forces? Or is the past a guide to predicting the future? Or an indispensable tool for speculating about future options?

Political Economy, the Environment, and Gender

The economy and the global environment as integral to international and world society is a topic conspicuously absent from the work of early English School authors. On the one hand, perhaps they were more concerned with the high

---

[16] Martha Finnemore, "Exporting the English School?" *Review of International Studies* 27, no. 3 (2001): 509.

politics of diplomacy, collective security, and alliance politics, discounting the salience of political-economic and environmental issues. As Buzan has stated: "The English [S]chool's founding fathers . . . were too much in thrall to universalist principles of order and justice derived from debates in political theory and were too disinterested in international political economy."[17] Although the founders may have given less attention to the international economy, the environment, and human rights, successor generations in the English School are examining the possibilities and limitations of integrating such concerns into the English School's triad and its understanding of international society.

The English School shares with other images presented in this book almost a complete lack of knowledge or interest in the feminist gender perspective on international relations. As Jacqui True argues: "This neglect of gender reveals the concept of international society to be neither open nor sufficiently dynamic enough to capture or explain the social sources and dimensions of interstate behavior, and world politics more broadly." To do so requires a serious examination of the question, "Where are women in international society?"[18]

Conceptual and Philosophical Eclecticism

As noted, the English School image of international relations has been influenced by works ranging from Hobbes and Machiavelli to Grotius and (to a lesser extent) Kant. As such, scholars operating from alternative perspectives of international relations can find much with which to identify. Realists can applaud the English School recognition of anarchy, just as realists as well as liberals can agree on the importance of Grotius to our understanding of international relations. Social constructivists find English School discussions of the evolution of international society and the development of norms to be quite compatible with their worldview. Alexander Wendt's description of Lockean culture, discussed in chapter 9, comes close to the Grotian rationalist perspective in the English School. Hence, recognition of diverse traditions of thought can be appealing as there is a bit of something for everyone.

But such an eclectic intellectual heritage can also lead to criticism. This is particularly the case for those positivists who aspire to develop parsimonious, deductively based theories. If one is a structural or neorealist, for example, then the English School smorgasbord is unappealing. While they may agree with Hedley Bull's critique of behavioralism, they question to what extent a truly "classical" and historical-sociological approach to understanding international relations can help in developing new explanatory theories. Even neoliberal institutionalists who rely on the rationality assumption in attempting to account for the conditions under which institutions can aid international cooperation might find the English School and its assumptions too diverse.

The fact of the matter, however, is that the English School is attempting to do something that is at odds with the warring conceptual camps of IR theory

---

[17] Buzan, *International to World Society?* 11.

[18] Jacqui True, "Feminism," in *International Society and Its Critics*, ed. Alex J. Bellamy (Oxford, UK: Oxford University Press, 2005), 8.

from the 1960s onward: integration of the field. Positivist and interpretive understandings compete. Images clash based on diverse underlying assumptions.

One could argue that this is not a burning issue, and in fact, a multiplicity of interests, methods, paradigms, images, concepts, and value preferences is beneficial and should be applauded. Greater unity, it is feared, could result in uniformity and the intellectual tyranny of a dominant paradigm or school of thought. Hence, from this point of view, eclecticism is to be encouraged, and any signs of uniformity regarded with suspicion. No one would argue against diversity per se—it is the lifeblood of scholarly inquiry. Seemingly unrelated research someday may come together to help explain a significant aspect of international relations.

The concern, however, is whether diversity amounts to no more than multiple parochialisms—closing off and effectively encapsulating work in separate domains within the field, treating them as if they were mutually exclusive. Scholars at times engage in narrowly focused research programs that ignore alternative conceptual approaches, develop specialized jargon that unintentionally serves to confuse and mystify the uninitiated, and unduly restrict their course syllabi to literature that reinforces their own value and theoretical preferences. For this reason alone, the English School is a useful antidote to such closure.

REFERENCES

Bellamy, Alex J., ed. *International Society and Its Critics*. Oxford, UK: Oxford University Press, 2005.

Bull, Hedley. *The Anarchical Society: A Study of Order in World Politics*. London: Macmillan, 1977.

Buzan, Barry. *An Introduction to the English School of International Relations: The Societal Approach*. Cambridge, UK: Polity Press, 2014.

———. *From International to World Society? English School Theory and the Social Structure of Globalisation*. Cambridge, UK: Cambridge University Press, 2004.

Buzan, Barry, and Laust Schouenborg. *Global International Society: A New Framework for Analysis*. Cambridge, UK: Cambridge University Press, 2018.

Buzan, Barry, and Richard Little. *International Systems in World History: Remaking the Study of International Relations*. Oxford, UK: Oxford University Press, 2000.

Dunne, Tim. *Inventing International Society: A History of the English School*. New York: Palgrave, 1998.

Linklater, Andrew, and Hidemi Suganami. *The English School of International Relations*. Cambridge, UK: Cambridge University Press, 2006.

Watson, Adam. *The Evolution of International Society: A Comparative Historical Analysis*. London: Routledge, 1992.

PART III

INTERPRETIVE UNDERSTANDINGS AND NORMATIVE CONSIDERATIONS

9

Constructivist Understandings

★ ★ ★

In recent decades constructivism (or, more precisely, social constructivism) has provided a provocative, intriguing, and fruitful approach to our understanding of international politics. It is fair to say that it ranks among the top three perspectives on international politics, joining realism and liberalism. Constructivism does not claim to offer a global or worldwide vision of international relations as do the images we have identified in the previous chapters. What it offers instead is an approach to interpretive understanding that already has had an enormous impact on theorizing throughout the IR field.

As we will see, constructivism has several important intellectual precursors and influences. But its gradual rise in importance in international relations was also due to unforeseen events in the 1980s and 1990s. The Cold War (roughly 1946–1991) involving the Soviet Union, the United States, and their respective allies and ideological partners seemed destined to go on forever. Who was a friend and who was an enemy in a world divided between liberal and communist (or socialist) states was particularly clear-cut. IR theorists simply failed to anticipate the peaceful end of the Soviet Union and the collapse of its empire.

Realist power-transition theory might have expected an eventual clash between the superpowers, but not the internal collapse of one of the rivals. Within a few years, the traditional enemy of the West was gone. While theory does not aim at making specific point predictions, surely there should have been greater theoretical anticipation of this momentous process. At the same time, there was a noticeable decline in state sovereignty as military intervention and normative justification on humanitarian grounds became evident. Globalization—the intensification of economic, political, social, and cultural relations across borders—also tended to raise doubts about the explanatory power of existing theories and approaches. Economic-structuralist theories that relied on Marxist concepts also suffered in academe at a time when liberal democracy and capitalist precepts seemed increasingly to hold sway around the world.

What began in the early 1980s as a constructivist critique of realism and liberalism has dramatically expanded into a robust research program and significant force in empirical research pursued via a diversity of approaches. Yet what they all have in common is an interpretive understanding of observed phenomena, opening us to the subjective dimensions of not only knowing but also creating the world of which we are so integral a part. At its core, social constructivism, as the term implies, relates to the irreducibly *intersubjective* dimension of human action to include what we consider to be knowledge and reality, with the assumption that the objects of our knowledge are not independent of our interpretations. Constructivists are particularly interested in the key concepts of norms, rules, and identities and how they affect the conception of ourselves and how we relate to the world.

Constructivism can be seen as a middle ground or bridge between other conceptual approaches to international relations discussed in this book. On one end of the spectrum are the positivist, often material-based images in realist and liberal theories that emphasize explanations based on natural science criteria. To explain the actions of actors, it is assumed that rational choices are made among alternatives by evaluating their likely consequences in terms of objectives being sought. Ideas may matter, but in many of these theories they are secondary to (or reflections of) materially oriented interests. Although many constructivists utilize empirical data and some embrace positivist scientific standards for testing hypotheses, their conception of what constitutes explanation very often differs. The English School has the closest affinity to constructivism, which is apparent in the School's emphasis on norms and the importance of history as well as its application of the concept of society to international relations.

At the other end of the spectrum are the more radical postmodern, poststructuralist, and some feminist interpretivists whose sociology of knowledge comes close to arguing that only ideas matter, science is merely power disguised as knowledge, and explanation in the realist and liberal sense is an impossibility. Yet, as we will see, one can make the case that they are close cousins of constructivism due to the emphasis on the power of ideas and the importance of interpretive understandings of "the world out there." Given the assertion that there are fundamental differences between causal and interpretive understandings of the world, however, it makes sense to emphasize constructivism's key ontological and epistemological assumptions.

MAJOR ACTORS AND ASSUMPTIONS

First, constructivism seeks to problematize the identities and interests of states. This is in contrast to neorealists and neoliberals who come close to believing identities and interests are givens. Constructivists are not only interested in the state as an *agent* or actor, but also transnational organizations and international organizations. They emphasize the importance of subjective and intersubjective exchanges and actions taken by human beings as agents of these state and non-state organizational entities.

Second, constructivists view international *structure* in terms of a social structure infused with ideational factors to include norms, rules, and law. This structure can influence the identities and interests of agents, as well as international outcomes in such areas as humanitarian interventions and taboos on the use of weapons of mass destruction. This emphasis on the social dimension of structure is in contrast to the neorealist and neoliberal, which are, by contrast, heavily materialist.

Third, constructivism, as the term implies, views the world as a project always under construction, a case of becoming as opposed to being. This is in contrast to the much more restricted view of change on the part of realists and even many liberals and economic structuralists.

Finally, constructivists have done hard thinking on ontological and epistemological issues. Such debate and discussion are a far cry from most causal theorizing where positivist premises lead theorists confidently to seek as objective an explanation of reality as possible, somehow minimizing the subjective part of our understanding. Given the subjectivity of human beings, constructivists underscore the impossibility of pure objectivity.

Constructivists do not reject the scientific method nor deny that explanation in international relations is possible. But, as noted in chapter 1, instead of adopting only the causal-explanation approach that tends to be dominated by covering law accounts grounded in theories that presume instrumentally rational behavior on the part of actors, many constructivists also look to models of value-rational behavior. This involves focusing on the ontological orientations and epistemological preferences they bring to their research as well as the normative concerns and principled beliefs of actors or agents. Doing so often results in rich historical and empirical analysis, explaining an event or outcome by detailing the impact of such factors and how they influence the construction and changes of interests and identities over time.

INTELLECTUAL PRECURSORS AND INFLUENCES

The philosophical and sociological foundations of constructivism are deep, consisting of centuries of intellectual development. For our purposes we will limit the discussion to those aspects of the work of several key scholars who have directly influenced current constructivist understandings. The importance of these scholars is evident in that other approaches to international relations also draw from the wellspring of their insights.

We discuss in several chapters the varied and important intellectual contributions by German philosopher Immanuel Kant (1724–1804). Here and in chapter 10, we note his impact on the development of phenomenology—how human consciousness affects our understandings of what we observe or what appears to us. The objects we observe are *phenomena*, which Kant distinguishes from what he calls *noumena*—the unknowable essence of objects as things in themselves, quite apart from how we may see them or how they may appear.

His followers, the neo-Kantians of the late nineteenth and early twentieth centuries, transferred this perspective from nature to culture and social relations. The net effect was to set the social sciences apart from the natural sciences. Our knowledge—what we think we "know"—flows from our subjectivity, imposing our mental frameworks not just on nature, but also on the social world of which we are so integral a part. It is one thing to observe phenomena in nature around us. It is quite another, as human beings, to be very much a part of—not separate from—the social world we are observing.

Constructivists and others who follow this line of thinking not surprisingly are highly skeptical of the idea that the epistemological and methodological standards of the natural sciences can be directly applied to international relations or another social science inquiry. We take in what appears to us, but then probe to discover what we can about the underlying essence of what we observe. Knowing is indeed a highly subjective endeavor. We also establish shared knowledge or understandings of nature or the world "out there" with others when we engage intersubjectively with them. Hence, constructivists see individuals (and states) as essentially social beings enmeshed in an interactive normative context, which influences who they are and how they see others.

Although Kant does not take the argument to these lengths, much less to the social sciences, his original insights on the subjectivity of knowledge—his distinction between the phenomena we observe and the inner essence of these objects—have had a profound impact on phenomenologists and on those who extend his claims to the social sciences—a set of intellectual understandings from which constructivists also draw.

The English theorist John Locke (1632–1704) influenced constructivist views on the nature of anarchy. He argues that before society is formed one may be at peace in a state of nature or move from it to a state of war and back again; a state of nature is not necessarily a state of war. It bears repeating: Locke does not see the anarchic state of nature—"want of a common judge," government, or central authority—as necessarily warlike. In this Locke clearly opposes the view taken earlier by Thomas Hobbes (1588–1679) who portrays the state of nature as perpetually in a state of war—either actively engaging in fighting or always on guard, preparing for the fight.

Locke posits that a social contract among individuals establishes domestic society. This coming together by contract or agreement and his argument that a state of nature is not necessarily warlike are what capture the interest of some social constructivists. What Locke applied to the domestic level of analysis, Alexander Wendt and other social constructivists have applied to international relations. States and the relations established among them are constituted by a *Lockean*, social-contract, or rule-oriented culture—not a Hobbesian, dog-eat-dog, jungle-like one as many realists assume. Hence, to constructivists the realist view of anarchy is not the only way to conceptualize a world without legitimate centralized authority; there can be multiple types of anarchy. It is not a state of nature without rules.

The Lockean culture, then, is one of rivalry, not enmity as Hobbists would have it. The concept of sovereignty, for example, involves a shared expectation concerning the rules of the game in the relations among states. These shared expectations are the result of interactions, a socialization and internalization of norms or agreed rules that mitigate the danger of international relations becoming nothing more than a Hobbesian "war of all against all." States, therefore, may reach agreements with one another to maintain peace, whether they remain in a Lockean state of nature or leave it by forming a more peaceful international community as envisioned by Kant or those following his lead.

Emile Durkheim (1858–1917) has been cited by neorealists as an inspiration for the idea that structure (in this case, the international system) shapes and constrains relations among the units. But Durkheim also engages in a series of empirical studies to explain how various social outcomes—such as individual feelings of social estrangement and suicide rates—are influenced by different bonds within social orders. He claims, for example, that the lower incidence of suicide rates in rural areas of France during the Industrial Revolution was due to the strong moral and social bonds of their more traditional communities in the French countryside. The important point in terms of constructivism is that forms of sociality—the nature of relations and interactions among actors—have causal impact. Durkheim believed these relations cannot be reduced just to material factors. Of equal importance, Durkheim states that like material reality, ideational factors can be studied scientifically. Thus, constructivist scholars are prone to argue that the tenets of positivism are not inherently antithetical to their interpretive approach to understanding international relations.

As noted in chapter 1 and discussed in the subsequent chapters as well, the German sociologist Max Weber (1864–1920) has influenced both causal and interpretive understanding approaches to international relations. Writing in the late nineteenth and early twentieth centuries, Weber raised serious questions about objectivity in the social sciences—that what we know is based on interpretations of what we think we see. That knowledge in the social sciences depends upon interpretive understanding of the phenomena we observe—an insight that some apply to the natural sciences as well—is central to the discussion of theory in general, particularly to constructivism, feminism, postmodernism, and critical theory. All these lenses emphasize interpretive understanding we find in Weber's writing. For their part, realism, liberalism, economic structuralism, and the English School are themselves framed by the images, standpoints, or perspectives that inform the way they approach international relations theory. We also find in Weber reference to the state as collective actor and the contexts within which human behavior takes place—insights that anticipate the levels of analysis that figure so prominently in present-day international relations theory.[1]

Causal models often assume that behavior is instrumentally rational and designed to achieve specific goals that may conflict with other actors' goals. This is a starting point for many realists and liberals interested in developing explanatory theory. But Weber also develops the idea that human actions can be value driven—a value rationality in which choices follow from beliefs or commitments often rooted in moral, ethical, or religious understandings. This is not any less "rational" than behavior that follows an instrumental approach of maximizing gains or minimizing losses. As Weber argues: "We are *cultural* beings endowed with the capacity and the will to take a deliberate attitude toward the world

---

[1] See Max Weber, *The Theory of Social and Economic Organizations*, trans. A. M. Henderson and Talcott Parsons (Glencoe, IL: Free Press, 1947).

and to lend it *significance*."[2] This ability of actors to interpret the meaning and significance of their social actions differentiates the social from the natural sciences. Furthermore, Weber states that ideas also can play a normative role that goes beyond the narrow end of maximizing utility. Both Durkheim and Weber argue that the critical ties that bind individuals to groups are ideational, and such ideas are subject to investigation by social-scientific methods.

We now examine key building blocks or concepts of the constructivist approach to understanding international relations. The intellectual debt to foundational work by Kant, Locke, Durkheim, and Weber will become apparent.

INTERSUBJECTIVITY

Central to constructivism is the understanding that international politics is guided by intersubjectively shared and *institutionalized* norms, rules, ideas, beliefs, and values held by actors (or agents). *Intersubjective* by definition means shared by people—defined by their person-to-person, self-other exchanges—the ideational component of international relations not simply being the total of the beliefs of individuals. Institutionalized means these collective ideas are established or constituted in the social world as structures or institutions, practices, and identities. These shared norms and rules set expectations about how the world works and what constitutes legitimate behavior. Although there are differences of opinion among them, all constructivists at a minimum hold that normative or ideational factors or structures are at least as (and likely more) important than material structures composed of such elements as population size, weapons systems, manufacturing output, and geographic factors that are themselves subject to interpretation.

To neorealists, economic structuralists, and many liberals, the material constitutes the baseline, and ideas tend to be derivative. Neorealist explanations in particular argue that material objects—power defined as material capabilities—have a decisive impact on outcomes unmediated by the ideas people have concerning these objects. Classical realists incorporate international norms or rules in their analyses as do scholars in the English School. Such ideational factors, however, are discounted by neorealists who see them as variables dependent on the preferences of powerful states rather than having an impact independent of the international distribution of power among states.

As noted in chapter 5, for example, neorealists such as Kenneth N. Waltz and John J. Mearsheimer see the distribution of material capabilities or power as key to understanding the conduct of states in international relations. In chapter 6, we discuss neoliberalism and its focus on institutions as exemplified in work by Robert O. Keohane and also Judith Goldstein. While they understand the importance of ideas, material interests remain an important part of explaining outcomes driven by actors who make cost-benefit calculations either within or outside of institutional settings. In sum, constructivists would claim that

---

[2] Max Weber, *Methodology of the Social Sciences*, trans. Edward Shils and H. A. Finch (Glencoe, IL: Free Press, 1949), 81.

commitment to materially based understandings found in much realist, liberal, and economic-structuralist theorizing does not grant ideas the important standing they warrant as an independent variable or factor that shapes IR patterns and outcomes.

To make these complex ideas easier to grasp, let's provide three examples to clarify the constructivist emphasis on intersubjectively shared and institutionalized norms and rules. First, we take up the social construction of the concept of sovereignty, which consists of a set of rules or standards of behavior guiding states interacting with one another. Specifically, sovereign states come to claim under international law a right to complete jurisdiction over their territories (the internal or domestic dimension), hence, the development of the international norm prescribing noninterference in the internal affairs of other states. Second, states claim a right to be independent or autonomous in the conduct of their foreign relations (the external or international dimension). Sovereignty is therefore not simply a property of individual states but can be viewed as an intersubjectively shared and socially constructed institution or normative structure among states.

The Peace of Augsburg (1555) and the Peace of Westphalia (1648) marked the emergence of sovereignty among the Germans and other states as a convenient norm that effectively placed authority in ruling princes, dukes, and kings of the day. Even though practice among them preceded the formalization of sovereignty—respecting the prerogatives of other sovereign states—the new norm in time became globalized in both its internal and external dimensions. Sovereignty came to be expressed through rules of behavior as exemplified by diplomatic practices. These practices reflected mutual understandings about providing order in the international system, stabilizing actors' expectations, and managing power relations. Similarly, the development of the norm of territorial integrity helped reinforce the norm of sovereignty by acknowledging the socially constructed sanctity of state boundaries.

Of course, the internal dimension of sovereignty—noninterference in a state's internal affairs—has been violated many times over the centuries as when one country has invaded another or otherwise intervened in its domestic politics or other matters. But the claim to being sovereign in both its internal and external dimensions has remained. Violations of sovereignty when recognized as such do not extinguish the norm, its legitimacy is often underscored by the victims of its violation. Estonia, Latvia, and Lithuania were incorporated by force within the Soviet Union in 1940, but the idea that they were still sovereign states was kept alive. This contributed directly to these Baltic states reemerging at the end of the Cold War. The Russian invasion of Ukraine in February 2022 led to a virtual global consensus that Ukraine's sovereignty had been violated.

This intersubjective consensus on the sovereign rights of states, however, has been partially weakened as another consensus has gradually emerged: growing international support for human rights and a sense that there is a collective responsibility to do something about human rights violations. This idea of universal human rights and attendant responsibilities has encouraged and justified military intervention for humanitarian purposes to include cases in which states violate the human rights of minority groups or even their citizens. Prohibitions against genocide—the slaughter of people because of their racial, ethnic, or other identities—and the inhumane treatment or torture of captive human beings are vivid examples of widely accepted, intersubjective, socially constructed norms that have also eroded claims to state sovereignty. If states decide that acts of genocide or other inhumane acts demand international diplomatic or armed intervention in the domestic affairs of states, such actions run counter to rights claimed by sovereign states to exercise complete internal jurisdiction over their territories.

Where the states in question have no particular strategic or economic value to the great powers, it is hard for realists to explain efforts by these great powers to curb human rights violations when no apparent material interests are at stake. But from a constructivist perspective, the normative context has shifted over the decades since 1945 as human rights have been accepted gradually as a widely held norm. Indeed, concern for human rights has had a broad pattern of effect in shaping many states' conceptions of interest. Put another way, commitment to human rights as an idea matters.

A second example is also drawn from human rights. Consider how slavery and the slave trade were once accepted practices in international relations. From the standpoint of the United States and many European countries, slavery was considered an economic imperative—an institution of critical importance to the economic interests of the slave-trading states (and their slave owners) as late as the eighteenth and well into the nineteenth centuries. This intersubjective consensus gradually broke down. Domestic and internationally accepted norms against such exploitation of fellow human beings were slow in development, but by the late nineteenth century they finally became part of the fabric of rules prohibiting such violations of human rights. Various forms of human bondage persist to the present day, but social constructivists note that global and national norms now make such practices not only morally illegitimate but also illegal. As social constructions, intersubjective norms and the laws or rules associated with them can (and do) change, however slowly.

A third example relates to norms concerning the legitimacy of warfare. Consider that in the first half of the twentieth century, European states were engaged in two major world wars, supposedly in defense of their respective national interests. But now at least Western Europe has created what amounts to a zone of peace in which it is hard to imagine that for centuries Germany and France had been bitter rivals resorting to the use of force against each other in major wars. How could a realist explain these developments? From a constructivist perspective, an intersubjective consensus has emerged among elites, citizens, governments, and nongovernmental organizations that force is no longer the appropriate way to resolve differences. Peace as a value and a normative commitment to maintaining it multilaterally has an impact on how states define their interests.[3]

The reference to Western Europe is an appropriate segue to the constructivist recognition that intersubjective understandings can vary across regions and also

---

[3] See Emanuel Adler and Michael Barnett, *Security Communities* (New York: Cambridge University Press, 2002).

over time. Hence, constructivist research programs often attempt to understand how these shifts in collective meanings occur through detailed empirical research and rich description. How have actors viewed existing normative structures and rules of behavior? How have alternative understandings been devised and propagated through not only state bureaucracies but also international organizations, transnational nongovernmental organizations, and advocacy networks?

For example, the post–Cold War decline of communist ideology left intact the current globalized market system and its associated liberal financial institutions, norms, and rules by which state and nonstate actors operated. The global financial crisis that began in 2008 alerted constructivists to the possible weakening of this intersubjective, capitalist consensus, thus opening the door for states and nonstate actors to begin modifying, adapting, or constructing alternatives to the status quo. To reiterate, these and other ideas about international relations in global society do not exist somehow in nature. Instead they are of human origin or, in the language of social constructivists, they are constituted or socially constructed.

STRUCTURE, RULES, AND NORMS

Constructivists define *structure* in terms of social relationships and shared meanings, differing on the component elements and their relative importance. These elements may include clusters of rules, norms, principled beliefs, shared knowledge, practices, and even material elements. Material resources, however, acquire meaning for human action only through the structure of shared knowledge in which they are embedded. International politics may be seen as anarchic, but the structure is essentially defined in cultural rather than in realist, essentially material, terms. A security dilemma may exist among states, but this dilemma is viewed as itself an ideational social structure composed of intersubjective understandings in which states are prone to make worst-case assumptions about one another's intentions.

Beyond self-help, states may seek allies or coalition partners. The Cold War can be understood as a social structure of intersubjectively shared knowledge and meanings that governed the relations among the United States, the Soviet Union, and their allies. As tentative steps toward reassurance were made by the Soviet Union in the mid-1980s and were reciprocated by the United States, the structure of shared knowledge or meanings began to change. In the immediate aftermath of the Cold War, they stopped acting based on a structure of shared knowledge that emphasized egoistic identities and self-help, shifting for a time from zero-sum (one side's gain, the other's loss) to more positive-sum understandings (seeking mutual gains). Constructivists, therefore, can agree with realists that the world can be a nasty and violent place, but they take issue with the realist explanation and offer an alternative perspective that emphasizes the importance of subjective and intersubjective understandings.

If anarchy is socially constructed and given meaning by actors, international relations is not doomed to take place in a Hobbesian world of constant strife. By examining in detail the historical context within which such structures arise, constructivists attempt to explain how and why particular practices become relatively fixed in some cases, but fluid and subject to change or decay in others.

Rules and meanings of expected behavior that reflect mutual, intersubjective understandings provide order to international politics, stabilize actors' expectations, and help to manage relations among actors.

Generally accepted diplomatic practices are one example. When such ideational structures persist and become institutionalized or routinized over time, they gain causal and normative force, leading to patterns of behavior that can be empirically analyzed. These structures can either facilitate or serve as obstacles to courses of action that states choose to follow. To recognize that structures can and have changed over time, however, is no guarantee that these social constructions necessarily will be changed in the future. Changing structures affecting states, for example, involves altering an existing set of mutually reinforcing expectations.

This conception of structure has come to be applied by constructivists in several ways at different levels of analysis from the global to regional or issue-specific international regimes. These ideational structures can impact the behavior of both state and nonstate actors at least as much as the materially based power or class structures one finds respectively in realist and economic-structuralist thought.

Rules

Let's delve more deeply into one characterization or component of structure: rules. Constructivists make a distinction between *constitutive* and *regulative rules* and in so doing contrast their approach to international relations with that of neorealists and neoliberals. An illustration might be useful. The act of driving cars or other vehicles existed before establishing the socially accepted rule in the United States and most other countries that one should drive on the right-hand side of the road and as you enter a traffic circle keep to the right.[4] Or in Britain, Japan, and several other countries, a left-hand rule applies. Such rules, whether right- or left-oriented, were instituted due to increased traffic and the possibility of accidents. As examples of regulative rules, they are formulated to regulate an existing activity—driving cars. Other regulative rules are soon added to include issuing licenses, setting speed limits, and yielding at intersections.

Contrast this illustration with that of chess. It was not a matter of people pushing bits of wood around the board and bumping into one another that created the need for regulative rules. Rather, the rules of chess create the very possibility of playing chess in the first place: "The rules are constitutive of chess in the sense that playing chess is constituted in part by acting according to the rules." Regulative rules are designed to have a causal effect, such as getting people to drive on the right- or left-hand side of the road. "In contrast constitutive rules define the set of practices that make up any particular consciously organized social activity—that is to say, they specify *what counts* as that activity."[5]

These two illustrations make the constructivist point that the epistemology or ways of knowing present in neorealism, for example, lack this concept of

---

[4] John Gerard Ruggie, *Constructing the World Polity* (London: Routledge, 1998).

[5] Ruggie, *Constructing the World Polity*, 22. For more on the causal-constitutive distinction made by constructivists, see David Dessler and John Owen, "Constructivism and the Problem of Explanation: A Review Article," *Perspectives on Politics* 3, no. 3 (September 2005): 597–610.

constitutive rules. For them, it is a world of antecedent or preexisting actors and their relations in an anarchic world. The role of theory is basically to explain their conduct or behavior within a system essentially not of their making. Stated another way, constructivists claim that neorealists tend to focus on things as they are or have come to be, thus failing to explain the origins of states or the system of states that figure so prominently in their analyses.

John Ruggie, for example, has argued that the very concept of the modern state was only possible when a new rule for differentiating the components of the emerging European system replaced the medieval system of overlapping jurisdictions and authorities claimed by popes, kings, feudal lords, and trading associations. He examines not only material but also ideational factors that produced the concept of exclusive territoriality that serves as the constitutive rule defining the modern state system.[6] Constitutive rules are logically prior to what is the focus of most realist and liberal theorists who tend to take as a given the existence of the state and nonstate actors engaged in international politics.

Norms

Norms are generally accepted values that define standards of appropriate behavior for agents (actors) with a given identity. Following from the earlier discussion, in situations where norms operate like rules that define the identity of an actor, they are said to have "constitutive effects" that "specify what actions will cause relevant others to recognize a particular identity." In other situations, norms operate as standards "that specify the proper enactment of an already defined identity. In such instances norms have 'regulative' effects that specify standards of proper behavior." Norms, therefore, either define (constitute) identities or prescribe (regulate) behavior, or they do both.[7]

How norms are developed is an important research interest of constructivists. They can be international or domestic in their origin. When norms take the form of principled beliefs (such as support for decolonization, end of apartheid, human rights, emergence of taboos on certain types of weapons, prohibiting bribery of government officials as the means to secure contracts, etc.), they can lead in certain circumstances to states redefining their interests and even sense of self (identity) as well as influence international outcomes. The impact of these beliefs can be facilitated by transnational networks of nonstate actors. Ongoing empirical research also has examined norms governing the conduct of interstate war and humanitarian intervention and the situations under which norms are violated. While repeated violations of international norms on the part of states can erode or eventually invalidate norms, occasional violations usually do not.[8]

---

[6] John Ruggie, "Continuity and Transformation in the World Polity: Toward a Neorealist Synthesis," in *Neorealism and Its Critics*, ed. Robert O. Keohane (New York: Columbia University Press, 1986), 131–57.

[7] Peter Katzenstein, ed., *The Culture of National Security: Norms and Identity in International Politics* (New York: Columbia University Press, 1996), 5.

[8] V. P. Shannon, "Norms Are What States Make of Them: The Political Psychology of Norm Violation," *International Studies Quarterly* 44 (2000): 293–316.

AGENTS

The constitutive logic is played out in the important constructivist ontological assumption concerning the relations between structures and agents. Constructivists do not privilege any particular agent, actor, or unit of analysis. The agents may be states, but also nonstate actors to include individuals or groups as well as social movements, corporations, international organizations, nongovernmental advocacy groups, or classes.[9] All such nonstate agents have the potential to influence the creation of international norms, identities, and the behavior of states, just as states can similarly impact nonstate agents.

As noted earlier, structure (social relations and shared meanings) can have a constitutive—not just a regulative—effect on actors. Structure can encourage actors or agents to redefine their interests and identities in an ongoing socialization process. Thus, unlike neorealism and neoliberalism which tend to hold interest and identities constant to isolate the causal factors related respectively to power among states and the dynamics within and between international institutions, constructivism is interested in how ideational structures shape the way actors define themselves and relate to other actors.

Of equal importance, these actors or agents have an impact on structures and how they are altered and produced. Hence—and this is the key point—agents (actors) and structures mutually constitute one another. Structures are not objects that simply influence actors in a unidirectional manner. As difficult as it may be, agents can change structures and escape from situations that encourage and replicate, for example, conflictual practices such as war. There is a reciprocal relation between agency and structure. The Hobbesian international system of perpetual war of all against all or the pessimistic Thucydidean view of interstate war is not necessarily an inevitable state of affairs endlessly replicated through the ages, but rather a socially constructed structure developed over time. Due to the logic of *mutual constitution*, states may change the rules of the game and escape into a more Lockean (or even Kantian) culture of agreed rules or accepted norms to guide the conduct of international politics. Conversely, a community of peaceful states can degenerate into a more Hobbesian world marked by conflict; change is not necessarily always positive.

IDENTITY

Identities are relatively stable, role-specific understandings and expectations about one's self. They are acquired by interacting with or defining the self in relation to a structure composed of social relationships, shared meanings, rules, norms, and practices. Due to this conception of interaction, identity breaks down the realist and liberal dichotomy between the systemic and state levels of analysis and provides a broader perspective on the mutual constitution of state and system or agent and structure, respectively.

---

[9] For a constructivist argument that international organizations, for example, can be treated as autonomous actors, see Michael N. Barnett and Martha Finnemore, "The Politics, Power and Pathologies of International Organizations," *International Organizations* 53, no. 4 (Autumn 1999): 699–732.

At the level of the individual, human consciousness is important—the "self" that interprets (and thus constitutes the "other" outside of oneself), much as the other outside of the self gives meaning or identity to the self. For example, the respective identities of professor and student make sense within the context and interaction of a classroom setting; the identities are mutually constituted. But over time these identities can change. For example, the student goes to graduate school and eventually becomes a professor herself and rejoins her alma mater as a faculty member. The student-professor identities evolve into one of colleagues.

In terms of international relations, the dominant intersubjective understanding and social relationship between the Soviet Union and the United States during the Cold War was that of enemies. Being anti-Soviet and anticommunist was a critical element of how Americans tended to identify themselves and their role in the world. It also provided the framework through which Americans viewed with suspicion and interpreted all Soviet actions. As this social relationship changed in the late 1980s and early 1990s when communist regimes collapsed, the part of American identity associated with anticommunism began to change. As a result, the US definition of international threats and national interests started to shift as well. Similarly, the Russian invasion of Ukraine in 2022 has led to speculation of a new Cold War and a return to an antagonistic relationship between the United States and Russia.

How can one recognize the existence of a particular identity? First, one would look for habitual actions consistent with this identity and interpretations such as US attempts during the Cold War to block the expansion of Soviet influence in the Third World and Western Europe. Such actions are often referred to as practices. Second, one would monitor the discourse or combination of language and techniques employed to maintain these practices (such as diplomatic language emphasizing constructive engagement, balance of power, the use of force, and deterrence).

Identities can change over time and across contexts. Hence, identities are not immutable characteristics of individuals, groups, states, or whatever agent one is examining. Identities are produced and are not givens, any more than a state's interests are. The empirical research task for constructivists, therefore, is to explore how interaction and context influence the development of the meaning of self—whether self is at the level of individual decision maker, decision makers as a group, a nongovernmental organization, or conceptualized as an aggregate applying to the state, nation, or society as a whole. Interactions, such as those during the Cold War, may bolster, undermine, or even change these identities resulting in either positive or negative outcomes.

Influences on identities can stem from any number of sources. Domestic or endogenous sources may include broad cultural aspects of a society or military doctrine resulting from the internal distribution of political power. Identity could also be influenced by race, gender, nationality, religion, or ideology. External or exogenous sources can include such international norms as multilateralism that may contribute to defining a country's identity and the role it assumes in relations with other countries. Principled beliefs such as the moral illegitimacy of slavery and commitment to human rights are additional examples. Empirical studies have examined the development of a collective identity during the Cold War among members of the western North Atlantic Treaty Organization (NATO), which was created in 1949 to counter the perceived Soviet threat. Other studies have examined identity creation and transformation in the case of alliances in the Middle East and shifts in identity in Japan, Germany, and the Soviet Union.[10]

The construction of identity, therefore, is not limited to perceptions of another actor being friend or foe. Note that the idea of mutual constitution of states and structures goes beyond simply recognizing that there is interaction between them. All images and approaches to international relations discuss the impact of interactions. The point is that while the interactions of states contribute to the construction of the norms, shared meanings, and institutions of international relations, they in turn also influence the identity and behavior of states (and, of course, human agents who represent them). Through this reciprocal process, both can be redefined.

LOGIC OF APPROPRIATENESS

Identities, rules, and norms come together in the constructivist concept of the *logic of appropriateness*. In the IR literature, a distinction is made between consequence-based and rule-based actions. The former sees actions as driven by actors rationally rank-ordering their preferences or interests while being aware that other actors are doing the same. In other words, the actions of actors (individuals, organizations, or states) are driven by the calculation of consequences measured against prior preferences. Neorealists and neoliberals exemplify this approach.

What is missing in the logic of consequences is an appreciation of how norms, rules, and shared understandings of legitimate behavior can also shape actors' behaviors. The logic of appropriateness assumes human actors follow norms and rules that associate particular identities with particular situations. Stated another way, action is associated more with identities informed by norms and rules than just with narrow understandings of self-interest. As noted by James G. March and Johan P. Olsen: "As a cognitive matter, appropriate action is action that is essential to a particular conception of self. As an ethical matter, appropriate action is action that is virtuous. We 'explain' foreign policy as the application of rules associated with particular identities to particular situations."[11]

In terms of international relations, the identity perspective sees actors as acting in accordance with legitimated rules and norms that are socially constructed. International relations is portrayed at least potentially as a community of rule followers tied to one another through intersubjective understandings, sociocultural ties, and a sense of belonging.

---

[10] See the articles in Katzenstein, *The Culture of National Security*.
[11] James G. March and Johan P. Olsen, "The Institutional Dynamics of International Political Orders," *International Organization* 52, no. 4 (Autumn 1998): 951.

If identities are associated with and influenced by current standards of "appropriateness," then how does change in terms of international norms come about? One way is when norm "entrepreneurs" emerge who can create alternative norms or frames of reference. The challenge is that when promoting a new norm, it is done within the current standards of appropriateness defined by existing norms. To overcome the constraint imposed by an existing normative framework, norm entrepreneurs and activists may have to act explicitly inappropriately. For example, suffragettes positing alternative norms as to what constituted women's interests chained themselves to fences, engaged in hunger strikes, damaged property, and refused to pay taxes. In the case of international relations, norm entrepreneurs such as Greenpeace, Amnesty International, Transparency International, and other transnational advocacy networks as well as those operating within UN or other international organizations have made advocacy arguments often with strong moral content concerning the environment, human rights, illicit business practices, and other topical concerns.

INTERESTS

Constructivists claim that the interests of actors (what realists and liberals have tended to take for granted as givens) are constructed and subject to change by the actors themselves as they interact with others. The constructivist takes on interests is best understood in contrast to other approaches.

The concept of national interest has long been a central focus in the study of international relations. Particularly for realists, the specific goals of states vary, but all states have an interest in survival, wealth, security, and enough power to secure those interests. The origins of these interests are exogenous (external) to any state as a result of the condition of international anarchy and the security dilemma states face. While a realist may agree that these are indeed ideas about basic needs, they are still materially grounded primary interests that drive state behavior, influenced as well by relative circumstances—that is, the situation a state is in compared to other states.

Constructivists would argue, however, that interests and understandings of opportunities and threats are highly subjective. Consider, for example, a popular constructivist example: How can some 260 nuclear weapons of the United Kingdom be less threatening (or even nonthreatening) to the interests of the United States than a small number of North Korean or Iranian nuclear weapons would be? Obviously, North Korean and Iranian words and deeds have led the United States to view North Korea and Iran as hostile and thus threats to its interests. Here is where a constructivist would argue that American leaders are responding to the social dimension of relations between the United States and other countries, rather than merely to the material nuclear hardware they may possess or seek to acquire.

These social relations are not fixed in stone for all time, but the American national interest cannot be ascertained without considering them. Yes, the United States has an interest in deterring or containing North Korea and Iran because of perceived hostility (the same holds true for North Korean and

Iranian perceptions of the United States). By contrast, the United States has no apparent interest in containing the United Kingdom, given the more positive, nonthreatening pattern of relations between the two countries. The importance of this bilateral, essentially social relationship is augmented by international norms and how a state conceives its identity. All such factors influence a state's definition of its particular national interests.

The historical construction of national interests is a primary research interest of such constructivists as Martha Finnemore and Jutta Weldes.[12] Finnemore has documented successive waves in the diffusion of cultural norms among states. While these states may be very different in terms of their circumstances and role in the international system, they still tend to express identical preferences for national policies and the creation of similar bureaucratic structures. Constructivists also see the concept of security to be historically conditioned by social interaction rather than an objective calculation determined by the distribution of military capabilities. Canada, for example, does not fear invasion or feel its security threatened by the United States despite geographic proximity and the overwhelming superiority of American military capabilities. Subjectivity matters in the understanding Canadians have of their interests and the threats or opportunities facing them.

THE DIVERSITY OF SOCIAL CONSTRUCTIVIST THOUGHT

There is substantial diversity in constructivist thought that has made providing an overview of key concepts and assumptions related to constructivism particularly challenging. Definitions and their application to research questions and case studies can vary from scholar to scholar. Indeed, as we will see, much of the criticism of constructivism comes from within the constructivist camp itself. Although Alexander Wendt's work on constructivism warrants the attention we will be giving to it, we note important (and early) contributions by others who also have pursued this line of inquiry.

In the 1970s well before the constructivist label came into use, Ernst B. Haas, John Ruggie, and others were working in this vineyard. Although their work then and since has been identified for the most part as being based on the assumptions of the liberal image, Ruggie has observed that "in those days [the 1970s] we were all constructivists, but didn't know it!"[13] Reflecting "on the role of ideas in the heads of actors," Haas came to see not just ideas as such, but ideas grounded in interests as motive forces in international politics: "Ideas have very often acted as the switches and channeled the dynamics of the interests."[14] Indeed, while many scholars brought such interpretive understandings to their

---

[12] Martha Finnemore, *National Interests in International Society* (Ithaca, NY: Cornell University Press, 1996); Jutta Weldes, *Constructing National Interests: The United States and the Cuban Missile Crisis* (Minneapolis: University of Minnesota Press, 1999).

[13] Annual Meeting, American Political Science Association, Philadelphia, August–September 2003. See also Ruggie, *Constructing the World Polity*, 19, 35.

[14] Ernst B. Haas, *Nationalism, Liberalism, and Progress*, vol. 1 (Ithaca, NY: Cornell University Press, 1997), 2–3.

work in earlier decades, the language and label of social constructivism have only come into common use in international relations since the late 1980s.

Schools of Thought

Influences on the role of ideas drawn from both Durkheim and Weber inform what Ruggie refers to as "neoclassical" constructivism still within explanatory social science. He has subscribed to this perspective along with Nicholas Onuf, Friedrich Kratochwil, Emanuel Adler, Martha Finnemore, Peter Katzenstein, the late Ernst B. Haas, and feminist scholars like Jean Elshtain. While their theorizing incorporates values, norms, and other ideational factors, they do not reject the canons of science, standards, and methodologies for testing hypotheses or propositions.

Nicholas Onuf's pathbreaking *World of Our Making* (1989) in particular set the stage for the important role constructivism has continued to play in IR theory. Onuf's observation that "people make society and society makes people"[15] is core to constructivist understanding precisely because humans are social beings—we would not be human but for our social relations. Thus, human agency matters, and our theories should address the choices agents make. The structure or social arrangement of society within which they operate is given by its rules and institutions. Just as these rules and institutions are made by human agency, they also provide the basis and context for agents to act. To Onuf, the use of the term institutions is not restricted to brick-and-mortar organizations but rather may refer to such concepts as balance of power, spheres of influence, treaties, and international regimes. As with domestic societies, international society is itself "a complex institution within which many other related institutions are to be found."

Friedrich Kratochwil and Emanuel Adler also underscore the importance of rules and norms in constructivist understandings. Kratochwil comments: "Norms not only establish certain games and enable the players to pursue their goals within them, they also establish inter-subjective meanings that allow the actors to direct their actions towards each other, communicate with each other, appraise the quality of their actions, criticize claims and justify choices."[16] Emphasis is placed on the shared understandings that provide the context for political interactions.

Adler focuses on "the role of identities, norms and causal understandings in the constitution of national interests." Taking the broad view, he identifies constructivism as "a social theory about the role of knowledge and knowledgeable agents in the constitution of social reality." The goal is to advance understandings of "the role of inter-subjectivity and social context, the co-constitution of agent and structure, and the rule-governed nature of society." Adler comments

---

[15] This quote and subsequent citations in this paragraph are taken from Nicholas Onuf, "Constructivism: A User's Manual," in *International Relations in a Constructed World*, ed. Vendulka Kubálková, Nicholas Onuf, and Paul Kowert (London: M. E. Sharpe, 1998), 58–78.

[16] Friedrich Kratochwil, "The Embarrassment of Changes: Neo-Realism as the Science of Realpolitik without Politics," *Review of International Studies* 19 (1993): 75–76.

that "constructivism sees the world as a project under construction, as *becoming* rather than *being* [emphasis added]."[17]

"Postmodernist" constructivism is a second category or school of constructivist thought. Ruggie identifies this with the works of David Campbell, James Der Derian, R. B. J. Walker, and such feminist scholars as Spike Peterson. Postmodernist constructivism, in contrast to neoclassical constructivism, rejects the conventional epistemology of social science. It emphasizes instead the linguistic construction of subjects, resulting in "discursive practices" constituting the ontological or foundational units of reality and analysis. (We discuss postmodernism in chapter 10 as a different category of interpretive understanding, but one which also has had influence within the constructivist camp.)

Finally, Ruggie places Alexander Wendt along with Roy Bhashkar and David Dessler in a "naturalistic" constructivism category between the other two. As with the neoclassical approach, it approaches international relations as part of the social sciences and emphasizes the intersubjective aspects or structures of social life. These ideational structures usually exist independently of human thought and interaction and can, therefore, be treated as nonobservables, much like physical nonobservables (e.g., subatomic particles) that underlie what we observe in nature. Following Wendt, we probe deeply into the human psyche to find the ideational core underlying the subjectivity and intersubjectivity that define understanding.

Levels of Analysis

Aside from categorizing constructivism by schools of thought, another way to cut into the literature is by levels of analysis. While committed to the basics of constructivism (agents, structures, identities, norms, etc.), research designs vary in their emphasis. One scholar has characterized these as systemic, unit-level, and holistic constructivisms.[18] The systemic focus is on the interaction of unitary state actors with domestic politics being ignored. It is the interaction and relation of actors to one another that matter. Much of Alexander Wendt's work exemplifies a similar systemic form of constructivism that focuses on the interactions of states and the cultures of rules and norms that have been constructed to guide them.

Unit-level constructivism takes the opposite approach, emphasizing the relation between domestic legal and social norms on the one hand and the identities and interests of states on the other. Peter Katzenstein's work on the national security policies of Germany and Japan is an example.[19] The puzzle he hopes to solve is why two states that both experienced military defeat in World War

---

[17] See Emanuel Adler, "Constructivism and International Relations," in *Handbook of International Relations*, ed. Walter Carlsnaes, Thomas Risse, and Beth A. Simmons (London: Routledge, 2002), 95–114.

[18] We refer here to insights offered in Christian Reus-Smit, "Constructivism," in *Theories of International Relations*, 3rd ed., ed. Scott Burchill et al. (New York: Palgrave Macmillan, 2005), 199–201.

[19] Peter Katzenstein, *Tamed Power: Germany in Europe* (Ithaca, NY: Cornell University Press, 1999); *Cultural Norms and National Security: Police and Military in Postwar Japan* (Ithaca, NY: Cornell University Press, 1996).

II, foreign occupation, and economic and democratic development, ended up adopting different domestic and external national security policies. Constitutive national, social, and legal norms are critical to understanding this outcome.

Finally, as the name suggests, holistic constructivists aim to bridge the classic international-domestic divide. Factors at these two levels of analysis are two faces of a single social and political order. The primary concern tends to be on the dynamics of global change such as Ruggie's work on the rise of sovereign states out of European feudalism and Kratochwil's theorizing on the end of the Cold War.

WENDT'S "NATURALIST" CONSTRUCTIVISM

It was in Alexander Wendt's now-classic essay "Anarchy Is What States Make of It" that he claimed that self-help and power politics are socially constructed under anarchy.[20] Over the years he has continued to elaborate, refine, and defend his arguments. During a period when many IR scholars attempted to apply constructivist concepts to empirically based case studies, Wendt exhibited a distinct philosophic turn in his writings.

His most complete statement on social constructivism is to be found in his book *Social Theory of International Politics*. Wendt's interpretive approach to international relations is quite clear. For him, the challenge we have as subjective creatures is finding a correct understanding of the world around us in which we are so integral a part. We use science as far as it will take us, fully knowing that we may not get it right. We assume an objective world is out there but are always constrained in our search for reality by our own subjectivities as human beings—a problem identified by Wendt as affected by the ontologies we have and the epistemologies we are prone to adopt. Nevertheless, Wendt is not a pessimist: While we may not have unmediated access to the world, we can still make great strides in understanding how it works, yet be humble about the truth claims we assert.

For Wendt the two basic tenets of constructivism are: "(1) that the structures of human association are determined primarily by shared ideas rather than material forces, and (2) that the identities and interests of purposive actors are constructed by these shared ideas rather than given by nature."[21] His ontology of international relations therefore is social—"that it is through ideas that states ultimately relate to one another" and it is "these ideas [that] help define who and what states are."[22] It is not a coincidence that the title of his book parallels that of Kenneth N. Waltz's *Theory of International Politics*.

Wendt sees the identity of the self as a function of the other, so it is that agency and structure are mutually constituted—in effect shaping one another.

---

[20] Alexander Wendt, "Anarchy Is What States Make of It: The Social Construction of Power Politics," *International Organization* 46, no. 2 (Spring 1992): 391–425.

[21] Alexander Wendt, *Social Theory of International Politics* (Cambridge, UK: Cambridge University Press, 1999), 1.

[22] Wendt, *Social Theory of International Politics*, 372.

Put another way, states (more precisely, people acting for states) over time have constituted the international or global culture of generally accepted norms and concepts that have legitimacy as part of international relations. This ideational structure, in turn, constitutes and sustains the states in the system or society of states they have constructed. States continue to reinforce or support existing norms, adapting them or constituting new ones that reflect changing circumstances or new points of consensus (such as the norm against slavery). And so, this reciprocal process continues.

It should be noted, however, that as opposed to postmodern constructivists, Wendt does not completely reject the materially based structure used in neorealist theorizing (the distribution of capabilities or power among states), but rather incorporates it and redefines it in his conception of social structure. Wendt sees the ideational—a culture of generally accepted norms and other values that have been constructed under anarchy—as the fabric of system structure. It is, however, not that material power and interests are unimportant to Wendt, "but rather that their meaning and effects depend upon the social structure of the system, and specifically on which of the three 'cultures' of anarchy is dominant"—Hobbesian, Lockean, or Kantian.[23]

In other words, instead of a single anarchy and a singular logic, there are different understandings of anarchy. Going beyond the Hobbesian anarchy as "state of war" of all against all, for Wendt a Lockean culture is one of rivalry but guided by mutually agreed rules, and a Kantian culture is one of a community of accepted norms. The amount of war and conflict is conditioned by the type of anarchy in existence. All these social structures have three elements: material resources and, more importantly, shared knowledge (ideas), and human practices.

States (and other actors) as agents can shape the world within which they are immersed and not just be prisoners of the status quo. Anarchy need not be the dog-eat-dog, jungle-like Hobbesian world as portrayed by many realists in which, drawing from Thucydides, the strong do what they will and the weak do what they must. Wendt sees agreed rules and institutions as giving the systemic culture of international relations today a Lockean character. Although Wendt rejects any claims of inevitability, he is optimistic that the international culture can grow beyond current common understandings of the rules that states and other agents follow in their relations with each other.

Wendt addresses the important interrelations among ideas, material factors, and social interaction. He agonizes over the essence of the mind-body relation and the issue of consciousness. His interest is in how ideational and material factors interact in nature as a whole, human beings and social relationships in particular. Is the material before the ideational as realists and other "physicalists" claim? After all, isn't the source of ideas the human brain—a material entity? Wendt objects to contemporary thinking about the mind that is dominated by the materialist worldview of classical physics and the assumption that ultimately reality is purely material.

---

[23] Wendt, *Social Theory of International Politics*, 20. The three cultures are discussed in detail in chapter 6 of *Social Theory of International Politics*.

He raises what he terms a heretical thought: Why do we have to assume that contemporary social science and its conceptualization of the relation of mind (ideas) to body (the material world) must be compatible with classical physics? What if consciousness is instead viewed as a quantum mechanical phenomenon, the domain of the subatomic physics of particles and waves? From this perspective, human beings are in effect walking wave particles, not classical material objects.[24] Just as physicists have pondered over the question of whether the character of light is particle (and thus material) or waves of energy (analogous to the ideational in the social sciences), Wendt asks if we can assume there is an ideational-material composite in the social sciences similar to the wave-particle relation posited in the natural sciences. These two interactive factors in physics are encapsulated by the term quantum.

Consciousness—to Wendt "the basis of social life"[25]—is the core concept in much theorizing about interpretive understanding. And, as noted, it is understood by him as "a macroscopic quantum mechanical phenomenon." It is incorrect to view matter as purely material or inanimate; it is both "material and phenomenal, outside and inside." As Wendt summarizes his ontological position: "Matter . . . is an active, 'minded' phenomenon, not the inert, mindless substance of materialism." To him "the mind-body problem is a fundamental problem of *social* science, not just neuroscience."

The material and the ideational, then, are bound together in human consciousness. It is not as if consciousness is external to or separate from human actions, but is integrally a part of them. To rational-choice theorists and others who discount subjective experiences and other aspects of consciousness, "human beings are nothing but sophisticated information-processing machines." He laments this purging of subjectivity from social science, observing that in this "rationalist" position there is "an implicit materialism telling us that consciousness is epiphenomenal"—that it is secondary and thus not causal. Put another way, in physicalist understandings the material determines the ideational, not the other way around.

Wendt explicitly rejects this physicalist understanding that all materialists share—"a belief that in the end it is 'matter all the way down.'"[26] Because human consciousness effectively drops out of this materialist equation, Wendt finds the physicalist approach unacceptable. Indeed, Wendt finds many similarities between the social lives of human beings and the unpredictability or uncertainty one finds in the subatomic or quantum world. He refers to a "quantum consciousness" and a "participatory epistemology" as defining the social context in which human beings act.[27]

---

[24] Alexander Wendt, "Social Theory as Cartesian Science," in *Constructivism and International Relations: Alexander Wendt and His Critics*, ed. Stefano Guzzini and Anna Leander (London: Routledge, 2006), 183. For Wendt's more recent views, see *Quantum Mind and Social Science: Unifying Physical and Social Ontology* (Cambridge, UK: Cambridge University Press, 2015). See also his article, "Forum: Social Theory Going Quantum-Theoretic? Questions, Alternatives and Challenges," *Millennium* 47, no. 1 (September 2018): 67–73.

[25] Wendt, "Social Theory as Cartesian Science," 184. Subsequent quotes are from, respectively, pages 183, 195, and 185.

[26] Wendt, "Social Theory as Cartesian Science," 185.

[27] Wendt, "Social Theory as Cartesian Science," 205.

We have come a long way from the initial formulations of social constructivism. Wendt does not resolve the dialectic between the ideational and material, any more than physicists have found a new particle-wave synthesis. For Wendt it may be enough merely to posit the material-ideational dualism in the form of a quantum found naturally in human beings. His critics will be quick to note the *reductionism* inherent in Wendt's mind-body formulation—trying to go ever deeper within the human psyche (effectively, they will say, to brain waves or the synapses between nerve endings) to depict the relation between the ideational and the material.

Some of a positivist bent also object to Wendt's *metaphysics*—his characterization of the ideational metaphorically as a "wave" lacking the materiality of particles, thus coming close to identifying a life force or spirit. In such matters conventional or positivist science is silent, leaving such speculations to theologians. Finally, others will find fault with Wendt's metaphorical use of quantum, borrowed from subatomic physics as if it were analogous to a similar structure in human beings (and presumably other forms of life, although Wendt does not so extend his argument).

Aside from his earlier analysis of the agent-structure issue and the investigation of the relations among mind, body, and consciousness, Wendt also grapples with other dualisms or dialectics that challenge theoretical work in the entire IR field. Is there a synthesis to be found (or should we learn to live with the tensions) between (1) positivism and interpretivism—objective science and human self-understanding; (2) rationalism and constructivism; and (3) idealism and realism—ideas and the material world?

What is interesting is that Wendt does not see a necessary contradiction between science or positivism and interpretive understanding, rejecting the either/or position. In so doing he draws criticism from causal and interpretive theorists alike. Wendt believes one can be informed by (and thus compatible with) the other unless we build them as straw men—constructing them as if they were mutually exclusive. Wendt's positivism is a broad "commitment to *science*, understood as a method for gaining knowledge about the world out there." He therefore sees positivism with a lowercase or "small *p*." What he rejects is a certain kind of positivism (capitalized *P*) when it is treated as "a particular *philosophy* of science" that "privileges Humean [David Hume] causation, lawlike generalizations, deductive theory" and the like.[28]

What Wendt tries to do, then, is to combine a positivist epistemology with an interpretivist ontology. To him, there is a complementarity between positivism and interpretivism. We need not be forced to choose "between a positivism in which consciousness makes no difference and an interpretivism in which it has no naturalistic basis."[29]

---

[28] Wendt, "Social Theory as Cartesian Science," 214. David Hume (1711–1776) was a Scottish philosopher and essayist known for his empiricist approach to philosophy.

[29] Wendt, "Social Theory as Cartesian Science," 188, 190, 214.

CONSTRUCTIVIST AFFINITIES IN THE BROADER IR FIELD

In sum, constructivism shares at least one characteristic with realism and liberalism: All are rather broad tents within which numerous perspectives and theories can be found. One finds constructivist understandings not only in some critical theory and postmodernist interpretations, but they also are present in feminist scholarship. We also can see constructivist currents in the English School's "Grotian" focus on rules and law in international society to include an emphasis on historical sociology (how these ideational factors emerged over time, which also dovetails nicely with constructivist understandings of how structures come to be).

Constructivism also shares affinities with some liberals who emphasize the role of ideas, learning, and shared expectations in the construction of regime theory. We would even argue that some classical realists have a constructivist flavor in their work when they have a more voluntarist (rather than determinist) take on such matters as the historical development of balance of power. As realist Hans J. Morgenthau states: "The confidence in the stability of the modern state system . . . derives . . . not from the balance of power, but [rather] from a number of elements, intellectual and moral in nature, upon which both the balance of power and the stability of the modern state repose." The balance of power in the nineteenth century was embedded in this moral and intellectual climate [read "structure"] that resulted in "temperate and undecisive contests."[30] One could even argue that given Thucydides's emphasis on the power of rhetoric to shift Athenian conceptions of interest, he also has some affinities with constructivism. Yet the realist and liberal emphasis on asocial actors primarily concerned with material interests ultimately separates them from constructivist understandings.

Constructivist interpretations are not as prevalent or as well developed in economic-structuralist work and the associated literature. That said, Antonio Gramsci developed the concept of the historical and ideological bloc, an obstacle to social change that maintains a pattern of dominance in society or even on a global scale. We note that such blocs are social constructions that economic structuralists see as serving dominant class interests that go well beyond the boundaries of particular states and their societies.

CONSTRUCTIVISTS AND THEIR CRITICS

Liberal and Realist Critiques

Given the fact that early constructivist work consisted of a critique of the epistemological and ontological assumptions of neorealism and neoliberalism, it is not surprising that there was a response. An initial sympathetic take on interpretive understandings came from Robert O. Keohane. In contrasting his neoliberal institutionalism approach to that of what he terms the "reflective school," he states that a research program is lacking in the latter. Until that is achieved, and it can be shown via empirical studies that it can "illuminate important issues in

---

[30] Hans J. Morgenthau, *Politics among Nations: The Struggle for Power and Peace*, 4th ed. (New York: Knopf, 1967), 211, 213.

world politics, they will remain on the margins of the field, largely invisible to the preponderance of empirical researchers." These reflective approaches (what we call interpretive understandings), he argues, had been adept at pointing out the limitations of rational actor and game-theoretic approaches to international institutions, rather than developing theories of their own.[31]

Five years later, the neorealist John J. Mearsheimer took on not only constructivism but also other interpretive understandings of international relations as they gained prominence.[32] Mearsheimer argues it is one thing to criticize hegemonic research programs like realism with its pessimistic view on the possibility of peaceful change. But the problem with social constructivism, critical theory, and postmodernism is that they have little to say on the feasibility of the international system evolving into a more peaceful world, the mechanisms as to how this would even occur, little empirical support for their assertions, and even an inability to explain why particular discourses rise and fall. Supposed examples of more communitarian systems such as the feudal era are subject to dispute as are claims that the end of the Cold War illustrated the eroding explanatory power of anarchy and the self-help nature of the international system.

A great deal has changed in recent years regarding the application of constructivist concepts to IR issues, which has reduced the saliency of the Keohane and Mearsheimer critiques. Numerous empirical case studies have been based upon, for example, constructivist concepts while remaining cognizant of the contribution of causal theorizing generally associated with positivism.[33] But the bottom line is that interpretive understandings and realist and liberal approaches to international relations still stand in contrast to each other due to basic underlying epistemological and ontological differences. This was particularly evident around 2000 when constructivists pointedly noted the weaknesses of neoliberal and neorealist theorizing on international organizations based upon assumptions of instrumental rationality at odds with subjective or social insights generated by sociological approaches favored by constructivists.[34]

---

[31] Robert O. Keohane, "International Institutions: Two Approaches," *International Institutions and State Power* (Boulder, CO: Westview Press, 1989), 173.

[32] John J. Mearsheimer, "The False Promise of International Institutions," *International Security* 19, no. 3 (Winter 1994/95): 5–49. See also the 2000 article by Dale Copeland, "The Constructivist Challenge to Structural Realism: A Review Essay," in *Constructivism and International Relations*, ed. Stefano Guzzini and Anna Leander (London: Routledge, 2006), 1–20.

[33] See, for example, Michael Struett, *The Politics of Constructing the International Criminal Court: NGOs, Discourse, and Agency* (New York: Palgrave Macmillan, 2008); Edward Keene, "A Case Study of the Construction of International Hierarchy: British Treaty-Making against the Slave Trade in the Early Nineteenth Century," *International Organization* 61 (Spring 2007): 311–39; Judith Kelley, "Assessing the Complex Evolution of Norms: The Rise of International Election Monitoring," *International Organization* 62 (Spring 2008): 221–55; Emanuel Adler, "The Spread of Security Communities: Communities of Practice, Self-Restraint, and NATO's Post–Cold War Transformation," *European Journal of International Relations* 14, no. 2 (2008): 195–230; Neta Crawford, *Argument and Change in World Politics: Ethics, Decolonization, and Humanitarian Intervention* (Cambridge, UK: Cambridge University Press, 2002).

[34] Martha Finnemore and Stephen J. Trope, "Alternatives to 'Legalization': Richer Views of Law and Politics," *International Organization* 55, no. 3 (Summer 2001): 743–58; Alexander Wendt, "Driving

Debates within Constructivism and Postmodern Challenges
The most fruitful debates concerning the promise and limitations of constructivism as an approach to international relations have really come from within the constructivist camp itself. It is difficult, for example, to get a handle on exactly who is a constructivist and what they have in common beyond the assumptions outlined at the beginning of the chapter. Is constructivism a middle path between causal theory and postmodernism? Or does it also include postmodernism? If so, there is a great difference between Alexander Wendt who accepts a positivist epistemology (in the broad sense of a commitment to science as a way to gain knowledge of the world out there) and treats states as actors or people with intentions and a postmodernist such as Andreas Behnke who claims Wendt is not really that far removed from Kenneth N. Waltz's neorealism.[35]

Such "family" disagreements stem from several sources. For example, for analytic purposes should the state as agent be a given? Should scientific methods be used? A positivist epistemology would maintain that a socially constructed international system contains patterns that are subject to generalization and falsifiable hypotheses. Wendt, Martha Finnemore, and Michael Barnett fall into this camp. A postmodernist, by contrast, might ask if such work is really all that different from the methodological and epistemological conventions of realism and liberalism. What about the role of ethics? Can the "is" be distinguished from the "ought"? Postmodern constructivists are decidedly skeptical about such distinctions. Is anarchy a fundamental organizing principle of the international system? Or does enough authority (or legitimated power) exist in international organizations, international law, and even firms and institutions that it is questionable whether the world is really as anarchic as it is usually portrayed?

The debate on the relation between agency and structure as sources of change in international politics—an ongoing discourse conducted throughout the 1990s that continues to the present—remains unresolved. How important is agency—whether states or nonstate actors including human beings acting for them or in their own right? How important is structure—the external or exogenous factors that facilitate or constrain agents? What impact do agents have on these structures that, after all, are of human construction or subject to interpretation by human beings?

The agent-structure debate has moved on from a clash between neorealists and neoliberals on the one hand and constructivists on the other. Others have joined in the fight from postmodern or poststructuralist critical ranks. As noted by Emanuel Adler, the latter argues that "what matters is neither structures nor agents, but the role of discursive practices." Social "realities" are a function of linguistic construction, our understanding of cultural meanings found in language interactions, and the verbal and nonverbal communications we employ.[36]

---

with the Rearview Mirror: On the Rational Science of Institutional Design," *International Organization* 55, no. 4 (Autumn 2001): 1019–49.

[35] Andreas Behnke, "Grand Theory in the Age of Its Impossibility," in *Constructivism and International Relations*, ed. Stefano Guzzini and Anna Leander, 49.

[36] Emanuel Adler, "Constructivism and International Relations," in *Handbook of International Relations*, ed. Walter Carlsnaes, Thomas Risse, and Beth A. Simmons (London: Routledge, 2002), 104. Adler's references are to Roxanne L. Doty, "Aporia: A Critical Exploration of the Agent-Structure

As a result, Adler doubts whether the agent-structure debate will ever be fully resolved. He states, however, that we are nevertheless left with a much better understanding of how agents and structures relate in the theoretical formulations offered by constructivists.

In sum, constructivism continues to be a leading perspective on international relations. It has evolved from a critique of realism and liberalism to a research program that has provided important insights into world politics. In the process, it has caused other perspectives or approaches to take into account constructivist concepts and arguments.

REFERENCES

Adler, Emanuel, and Michael Barnett. *Security Communities*. New York: Cambridge University Press, 2002.

Finnemore, Martha. *National Interests in International Society*. Ithaca, NY: Cornell University Press, 1996.

Gergen, Kenneth J. *An Invitation to Social Construction*, 3rd ed. London: Sage Publications, 2015.

Guzzini, Stefano, and Anna Leander, eds. *Constructivism and International Relations: Alexander Wendt and His Critics*. London: Routledge, 2006.

Katzenstein, Peter, ed. *The Culture of National Security: Norms and Identity in International Politics*. New York: Columbia University Press, 1996.

Kubálková, Vendulka, Nicholas Onuf, and Paul Kowert, eds. *International Relations in a Constructed World*. London: M. E. Sharpe, 1998.

Ruggie, John Gerard. *Constructing the World Polity*. London: Routledge, 1998.

Weber, Max. *The Theory of Social and Economic Organizations*. Trans. A. M. Henderson and Talcott Parsons. Glencoe, IL: Free Press, 1947.

———. *Methodology of the Social Sciences*. Translated by Edward Shils and H. A. Finch. Glencoe, IL: Free Press, 1949.

Wendt, Alexander. "Anarchy Is What States Make of It: The Social Construction of Power Politics." *International Organization* 46, no. 2 (Spring 1992): 391–425.

———. *Social Theory of International Politics*. Cambridge, UK: Cambridge University Press, 1999.

Problematique in International Relations Theory," *European Journal of International Relations* 3, no. 3 (1997): 365–92; and to Hidemi Suganimi, "Agents, Structures, Narratives," *European Journal of International Relations* 5, no. 3 (1999): 365–86.

10

Positivism, Critical Theory, and Postmodern Understandings

★ ★ ★

We undertake in this chapter a discussion of the vigorous critiques of mainstream positivist IR theorizing by critical theorists and postmodernists (or poststructuralists). As in the previous chapter on constructivism, a similar critique that relies on interpretive understanding made by feminists is presented in chapter 11. Scholars associated with critical theory and postmodernism have been referred to generically as postpositivists or poststructuralists. Such terminology, however, can be misleading. Although their critiques underscore the subjectivity of human inquiry and reject notions of pure objectivity or value-free science they associate with positivism, many critical theorists (as with constructivists and feminists) have not bolted completely from science per se as is evident by their use of empirical evidence in case studies.

For its part, science is open to scholarship that incorporates interpretive understandings along with the canons of logic and evidence that are central to positivism. Furthermore, the line between critical theory and postmodernism is a thin one, with some scholars crossing over from one side to the other. Linguistic analysis in postmodern studies, for example, has a clear place in critical theory that scrutinizes "cover stories" and unpacks or deconstructs the language used and the roles played by those in positions of power. We represent this boundary, then, as a permeable or dotted line between critical theorists who have not made as radical a departure from the positivist mainstream as most postmodern (or poststructural) scholars have.

What we observe in international relations and the other social (as in the natural) sciences is heavily influenced by the interpretive understandings we have of the concepts we employ. Many (though not all) of these critiques or interpretive understandings are informed by *phenomenology*—a subjective or interpretive understanding in human consciousness of what we observe or think we see in the world around us. Before addressing these critiques of mainstream IR scholarship, however, we need first to specify further what we mean by positivist, scientific, or "modern" approaches to theory building in international relations that go beyond the summary in chapter 1. This also entails a summary of intellectual precursors. Without such background, it is difficult to understand the arguments of critical theorists and postmodernists. In essence, these approaches are primarily concerned with critiquing the mainstream literature discussed in chapters 5 and 6 of this book.

POSITIVISM

Positivism involves a commitment to a unified view of science, a belief that it is possible to adapt the *epistemologies* and *methodologies* of the natural sciences to explain the social world, which includes international relations. Positivists believe that objective knowledge of the world is possible and, hence, have faith and commitment to the eighteenth-century Enlightenment's rationalist tradition.

We find in the writings of the Frenchman René Descartes (1596–1650) a key contribution to mathematics and the rational bases of modern science. Quarrels between rationalists like Descartes who emphasized the logic to be found in the canons of *deduction* and *empiricists* who made *inductive* inferences from what they observed ultimately was resolved in a new rational-empirical synthesis that remains at the core of positivism—a "scientific" approach to knowing.

It was the Scottish writer David Hume (1711–1776) who objected to causal inferences being drawn too readily. A skeptic at heart, Hume recognized that causality is itself not directly observable but merely a construct used by human beings to make what they observe around them understandable or even predictable. To Hume, causality is no more than an inference human beings draw from the conjunction of impressions about the things we observe. For example, when we perceive that some factor or event (X) precedes another (Y), our minds may be prone to think that X is the cause of Y.

Consistent with Hume and also influenced by the positivism of the French philosopher Auguste Comte (1798–1857), John Stuart Mill (1806–1873) developed formal canons of induction that allow both natural and social scientists to arrive at causal truth claims by applying systematically one or another of a series of specified tests or methods to observed phenomena.

MILL'S CANONS OF CAUSALITY

John Stuart Mill's understandings of causality underlie the application of the "scientific" method to the testing of *hypotheses* in the social sciences in general, international relations in particular. Using one or another of these canons of induction leads us to infer a causal relation between an *independent variable* (X) and the *dependent variable* (Y) it purportedly explains:

Inductive Canon No. 1: The method of agreement—X is always present whenever Y is also present. Hypothetical example: When in our research we always see an arms race (X) having begun before the outbreak of war (Y).

Inductive Canon No. 2: The method of difference—X is always absent whenever Y is also absent. Hypothetical example: When in our research we observe no arms races in prolonged periods of peace marked by the absence of war.

Inductive Canon No. 3: The joint method of agreement and difference—when X and Y are both present in one set but not in another, as in controlled experiments when X is put in one experiment to see if Y appears, but X is omitted from the other experiment in the expectation that Y will not appear. Hypothetical example: When in two separately controlled experimental simulations, an arms race is introduced in one simulation, but not in the other, the former results in the outbreak of war, but the latter simulation remains without war.

Inductive Canon No. 4: The method of concomitant variation—when X and Y both vary in relation to one another either in the same or opposite directions. In other words, a positive or direct relation: As X increases (or decreases), Y also increases (or decreases). Or a negative or inverse relation: As X increases, Y decreases, or as X decreases, Y increases. Hypothetical example: When in our research we assemble all the cases we identify of arms races and all the cases of the outbreak of war, we find a direct correlation between the two; the more arms racing occurs, the more wars tend to break out. If, by contrast, we were to find an inverse correlation (rather unlikely in this example), then we would observe that the more arms racing occurs, the lesser the frequency of war breaking out.

Inductive Canon No. 5: The method of residues—as when, in a statistical analysis of the percentage of explained and unexplained variance, a certain independent variable (X) or certain independent variables (X1, X2, etc.) have been identified as accounting for some of the variations in Y, the remaining variation can be accounted for as due to other independent variables present even if they have not been identified as such. Hypothetical example: When in our research arms races account for much, but not all of the cases in which wars break out, we conclude that other factors we may or may not be able to identify and account for the rest of the explanation.

Positivists identify one or another of these causal sequences in the hypotheses or causal models they test empirically. For example, if X is present, then (one tends to find) Y directly or inversely follows variations in X. We find different combinations of cause-effect sequences in the often complex causal models constructed by positivist theorists. Some factors that must be present to effect a certain outcome are referred to as necessary, but they may not be sufficient to have this effect. Theorists wedded to a positivist epistemology try to identify conditions or factors—variables or constants—that are necessary or sufficient to produce expected effects or outcomes.[1]

CAUSE-EFFECT RELATIONS

We also can identify five different patterns of cause-effect relations employed in positivist theorizing:

---

[1] Adapted from A. James Gregor, *Metapolitics: A Brief Inquiry into the Conceptual Language of Political Science* (New York: Free Press, 1971), 146–50.

1. *There can be, as we have discussed, a single causal or independent variable X that can be used to explain or predict an effect on another variable Y that depends causally upon or reacts to variations in X:*
   X → Y
   Hypothetical example: When our hypothesis holds that international tensions (X) are causally related to the outbreak of war (Y).
2. *Sometimes an intervening variable Z comes between the independent variable X and the dependent variable Y, moderating or altering the effect X otherwise would have had on Y:*
   X → Z → Y
   Hypothetical example: When our hypothesis holds that international tensions (X) that can lead to war are exacerbated when policy elites (Z) with a militant orientation come to power or, conversely, reduced when peace-prone policy elites oriented toward conflict resolution take office, the former are more likely to go to war (Y) than the latter. The intervening variable—whether war- or peace-oriented policy elites come to power—matters causally.
3. *In other cases, the independent variable X is itself the result of (or caused by) some third variable Z in what effectively is a "developmental sequence":*
   Z → X → Y
   Hypothetical example: In this case, our hypothesis holds that whether war or peace-oriented elites (Z) come to power has a causal effect on the level of international tensions causally related to the outbreak of war (war-oriented policy elites tending to increase tensions leading to war and peace-oriented elites tending to reduce tensions or create a climate more propitious to peace).
4. *Sometimes we see dual or double causes as when X and Z are both causally related to Y, still the dependent variable:*

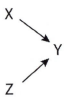

Hypothetical example: In this case our hypothesis holds that international tensions (X) and orientations of policy elites in power (Z) separately are causally related to war (Y)—thus international tensions can cause war or policy elites on their own to choose to go to war quite apart from whether the climate of relations (X) is one of high or reduced tensions. An extension of double cause is the case of multiple causation involving three or more independent variables identified in this case as causally related to the outbreak of war.

5. *Looking to the outcome side,* dual *or* double *effect occurs when X is causal to both Y and Z:*

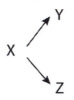

Hypothetical example: In this case our hypothesis holds that the climate of relations or level of international tensions (X) may produce a greater or lesser likelihood of going to war (Y) and, at the same time, influence whether war-like or peace-oriented policy elites (Z) come to power. As with multiple causation, we also can extend this reasoning to cases of multiple effects involving three or more dependent variables. Dual or multiple effect is also the "spurious correlation" case in which the apparent association or correlation between Y and Z is due only to the fact both are affected caus- ally by the same variable X; variations in Y (likelihood of the outbreak of war) and Z (orientations of policy elites toward war or peace) are each due to variations in X (international tensions).[2]

Given such causal understandings in models and associated hypotheses, positivists then turn to operationalizing their variables, putting them in mea- surable form or constructing data-based indicators that allow the researcher to test these cause-effect propositions empirically. Evidentiary tests— whether quantitative or nonquantitative—are used to confirm hypotheses with some degree of confidence, refute them, or consider the empirical tests inconclusive, thus calling for more data gathering and further tests. This approach to testing truth claims captures the essence of what is commonly referred to as scientific method.

The epistemological empiricism adopted by scholars in the "Vienna circle" of the 1930s took a somewhat extreme rationalist, scientific form called *logical positivism*—the pursuit of a pure science that was supposed to separate fact from value and achieve the precision of mathematics. Among members of the Vienna circle were such luminaries as Moritz Schlick (1882–1936), Otto Neur- ath (1882–1945), and Rudolf Carnap (1891–1970). They were also influenced by the earlier work of their contemporary, Ludwig Wittgenstein (1889–1951), whose *Tractatus Logico-Philosophicus* (1921) relates the thought and ideas we have to the words we use, focusing on the necessary logic and precision of language applied to observations about the world. Following Wittgenstein, the Vienna circle and its followers sought both logical precision and clarity in scientific language.

---

[2] We draw these cause-effect relations from Hayward R. Alker Jr., *Mathematics and Politics* (New York: Macmillan, 1965) as presented in Ted Robert Gurr, *Politimetrics* (Englewood Cliffs, NJ: Prentice Hall, 1972), 167.

In the mid-1930s, Karl Popper (1902–1994) addressed empirical tests of hypotheses drawn from theories. To "prove" empirically that a certain hypothesis or universal proposition is true is virtually impossible since to do so in an absolute sense would mean submitting it to an infinite number of tests in space and time. Popper argues that to be scientific, claims or propositions have to be stated in falsifiable form. *Falsifiability* means simply that if a proposition is false, it must be possible empirically to show that it is false. With varying degrees of confidence based on logical consistency and available evidence, one can accept a falsifiable proposition as possibly true at least until, by experiment or other scientific means, one actually shows it to be false.

In the post–World War II period, a broad, somewhat watered-down application of positivist premises to the social sciences—an approach that also included incorporation of statistical methodologies and the use of mathematical equations to specify causal relations among variables—reflected a critical reaction to this "modernist" epistemology. Taking various critiques into account, refinement of positivist epistemology continued during the 1950s and 1960s. Carl Hempel (1905–1997), for example, sets forth a *deductive-nomological* schema for scientific explanation. Hempel applies this formalized deductive approach in the formulation of both universal and probabilistic lawlike statements. This *covering-law* approach to theory is still the preferred choice of many scholars working within the positivist framework (see chapter 1).

Thomas S. Kuhn's (1922–1996) effort in his identification of "scientific revolutions" focused on the natural sciences, but it has perhaps had an even greater impact on understanding in the social sciences.[3] Arguing that *paradigms*, or frameworks of understanding, influence the way we observe and make sense of the world around us, Kuhn is criticized for his alleged *relativism*—a direct challenge to the positivist school. To some of his opponents, knowledge is understood to be empirically grounded and not so arbitrary as to be based on such pre-existing or newly discovered frameworks of understanding.

To be fair, Kuhn does not reject empirically based claims as such. He argues only that when theories and component concepts associated with a particular paradigm are challenged empirically or theoretically, holders of this paradigm may be forced through some modification to accommodate the new finding or insight or give way to a new paradigm. Thus, the Ptolemaic idea of the Earth as center of the universe—an understanding also closely tied to and reinforcing certain underlying religious beliefs—was toppled by the Copernican revolution in human understanding of the heavens, a paradigm shift developed further from the empirical observations of Galileo. A highly complex, Earth-centric, Ptolemaic astronomy—still used in celestial navigation (Ptolemy a Roman residing in Egypt, c. 100–170 CE)—was replaced by a vision offered in 1512 by Copernicus (1473–1543) and later by Galileo (1554–1642) that portrayed the Earth as merely one among many planets revolving around the Sun—the solar system.

---

[3] Thomas S. Kuhn, *The Structure of Scientific Revolutions*, 2nd ed. (Chicago: University of Chicago Press, 1962, 1970).

Similarly, it was Albert Einstein's (1879–1955) theory of relativity that challenged Isaac Newton's (1642–1727) understanding of gravity and the laws of motion, effectively reducing the Newtonian mechanics paradigm to Earth-based, observable laws. These laws were not as directly applicable either to the macro-universal domain of astrophysics or to the micro-domain concerning motion of subatomic particles in quantum mechanics. Of course, even these new paradigms have remained subject to challenge in an eternally skeptical, scientific approach to knowledge.

There is substantial debate within the social sciences generally, and in particular fields such as international relations, as to whether these fields are developed sufficiently to justify the identification of paradigms. Setting this issue aside, the important point in Kuhn's thesis is that knowledge, even in the natural sciences, is grounded in human understanding in the form of paradigms that influence observation and the construction of concepts and theories. At least as much or even more so, such interpretive understanding or agreed meaning would seem to apply to the social sciences that deal with human behavior in all its forms.

Although Kuhn's work receives criticism from positivists, by no means does he abandon scientific premises. That is why we represent his argument as coming from within the scientific or positivist community. There is no rejection of science per se, but his work on paradigms has influenced or is similar to much of the thinking we place under the umbrella of interpretive understanding.

The same is the case with Stephen Toulmin (1922–2009) who argues the lenses or "spectacles" one wears affect science and scientific progress in the continuing quest to make the world around us more intelligible.[4] Accordingly, we need to scrutinize closely and critically the principal images that currently inform much IR theory. Although Toulmin's critique occurs within the positivist, natural science discourse, he takes a stand against any claim to the idea that work in the sciences can ever be value-free. Instead, we need to be more humble in developing our understandings, taking explicitly into account as best we can the subjective dimensions that influence our inquiries. Critical scrutiny of our work by others not wedded to our projects is a safety valve institutionalized in scientific discourse. This discourse helps to keep us from errors to be found in the logic of the arguments we make or the evidence we use to buttress our truth claims.

For his part, Imre Lakatos (1922–1974) prefers to see the pursuit of science not as a series of paradigmatic revolutions, but rather in more positive terms as in the spawning of multiple research programs and the ensuing competition among them.[5] Progress in international relations from this perspective is facilitated by the development of research programs comparable in durability to those in the natural sciences. Changes in research programs occur only in the

---

[4] See Stephen Toulmin, *Foresight and Understanding: An Enquiry into the Aims of Science* (Bloomington: Indiana University Press, 1961), especially 99–102, 108–9, 114–15.

[5] Imre Lakatos, *The Methodology of Scientific Research Programmes: Philosophical Papers*, vol. 1, ed. John Worrall and Gregory Currie (Cambridge, UK: Cambridge University Press, 1978), 8–10, 47–52, 70–72, 85–93.

fullness of time, often many years after initial challenges to theories within its scope. One falsification is not enough. The bases for such a research program change do not become established overnight, but rather as part of a progressive process over time.

INTELLECTUAL PRECURSORS: PHENOMENOLOGY AND HERMENEUTICS

Contemporary critiques of mainstream theorizing in international relations and the other social sciences reflect to a greater or lesser degree the influence of *phenomenology*. It is, as noted earlier, a philosophical understanding that leads one to reject claims to knowing any "objective" reality independent of the human consciousness that, after all, gives meaning to the world around us. Interpretation is central to what we see—a reflective, intuitive process by which we gain understanding. We find the influence of phenomenology not just in critical theory and postmodernism, but also in the interpretive understandings of constructivism discussed in chapter 9, feminist scholarship we take up in chapter 11, and aspects of green theory in chapter 12.

Phenomenology responds to what is a very old philosophical question. It was, after all, Plato (c. 427–347 BCE) who raised the problem of distinguishing between appearances and underlying realities—the ideal forms, essence, or spirit that lies beyond our senses or world of appearances. In the Platonic understanding, "knowledge has for its natural object the real—to know the truth about reality."[6] There is a unity to be found in knowledge between an object we observe and its underlying essence or form. Something may appear to be beautiful, for example, but it is the underlying idea or "essential form of beauty" that makes it appear to us as such. Realizing an underlying form of justice in Plato's ideal republic is an aim or challenge not just within state and domestic society, but also by extension to international relations. This concern for justice continues to resonate today, particularly among critical theorists.

In his *Critique of Pure Reason*, published in 1781, Immanuel Kant (1724–1804) takes up this question or distinction between appearance and reality. Kant calls the objects we observe "phenomena," which he distinguishes from the abstract "noumena"—the unknowable essence of objects as things in themselves, quite apart from how we may see them or how they may appear.[7]

Georg W. F. Hegel (1770–1831) in his *Phenomenology of Spirit* (1807) accepts Kant's claim that we cannot know the "in-itself"—this inner essence of what we observe. Hegel explores the ways and means by which we can unify the objective (the "in-itself" or "what something actually is") with the subjective (the "for-itself" or "what we understand it to be") in our consciousness of ourselves and the world around us that we experience. How are we to unify what actually *is* (the objective—the "in-itself") with what we observe or experience in our

---

[6] Plato, *The Republic*, trans. Francis MacDonald Cornford (New York: Oxford University Press, 1941), chap. XIX, v. 477, 185.

[7] Immanuel Kant, *Critique of Pure Reason*, Book II, chap. 3.

consciousness (the subjective—the "for-itself")? How can we know "what truth is . . . if consciousness [is] still filled and weighed down with . . . so-called natural representations, thoughts, and opinions?" We seek to get beyond these prior perspectives or illusions and focus instead on the phenomena themselves—what Hegel called following the phenomenological path. To him, we try to grasp or understand the essence or "spirit" underlying appearances: "Through an exhaustive experience [in the subjective or conscious] 'of itself'" (the phenomenological path we follow), we can in principle attain "the knowledge of what it [the phenomenon] is in itself."[8]

More easily said than done! As with Kant, phenomenologists following the leads of Edmund Husserl (1859–1938) and his student Martin Heidegger (1889–1976) dispute Hegel's claim that such reality can be uncovered so decisively. Phenomenologists following Husserl have engaged in reflective study of phenomena to approach knowledge of underlying realities in developing what we in this volume, following Weber, prefer to call interpretive understandings. In our reflections about what we observe, we try to identify the meanings or essence of what we experience. For his part, Heidegger focuses not only on the objects we experience but also on the sense of our own being and what we understand to be the essence of things in general—our ontology in relation to the world we experience. Although Heidegger denies being an existentialist, Husserl's influence is reflected in the *existentialism* found particularly in French literary and philosophical circles; among others, Jean-Paul Sartre (1905–1980) was directly influenced by Husserl.

In sum, phenomenology leads one not to take things as they may at first appear (or have been made to appear). We probe for what underlies or stands behind appearances. We take "a close look at certain phenomena specifically considered in isolation from current or dominant theories of explanation" that may cloud or bias our vision. More to the point, we include "all phenomena of experience" and exclude all "metaphysical and reality judgments."[9]

The language scientists use is a major research concern of postmodernists in particular. *Hermeneutics* directly challenges positivism, arguing that social facts are constituted and given meaning by the structures of language and that consciousness can be studied only as mediated by language. Language is what gives material conditions meaning for humans. Hermeneutic approaches seek to understand or recover the meanings common to actors by interpreting the self-understanding of actors. This is in contrast to the positivist explanation of independent causal processes. Luminaries include Heidegger and Wittgenstein in his later work. Indeed, Wittgenstein's *Philosophical Investigations* (1953) paints a picture more prone to coping with ambiguities that come from the context of language use.

We will withhold until later in the chapter discussion of German and French continental European perspectives that have also had an impact on the IR field:

---

[8] George W. F. Hegel, *Hegel's Phenomenology of Spirit*, trans. Howard P. Kainz (University Park: Pennsylvania State University Press, 1994), 8, 9–10, 10–11, 96–97.
[9] Don Ihde, *Experimental Phenomenology* (Albany: State University of New York, 1986), 14–15, 36.

(a) Jürgen Habermas (b. 1929) and his associates in what is commonly referred to as the Frankfurt School of critical theory and (b) influences on postmodernism such as Friedrich Nietzsche (1844–1900) and an updating of his ideas by postmodernist French scholars Michel Foucault (1926–1984), Jacques Derrida (1930–2004), and Jean-François Lyotard (1924–1998).

To summarize the postmodern and critical theory critique, positivism has been under assault for its attempts to separate facts from values, to define and operationalize value-neutral concepts into precisely and accurately measurable variables, and to test truth claims in the form of hypotheses drawn from or integral to theories. Whether using quantitative or statistical methods or such nonquantitative (or "qualitative") methods as case and comparative case studies, those who have tried to be scientific have been criticized for ignoring or taking insufficient account of the personal or human dimension of scholarship.

Human consciousness and the inherent subjectivity of human beings matter. As essentially subjective creatures, we are not really able to separate ourselves from the world we are observing. We are part of it. Even if human agency does not impact the "laws" that govern the natural world, what we say and do has effects in the social world. Thus, we are hampered by an inability to be completely independent of the phenomena we are observing, however hard we may try to be objective. Our inherent subjectivity just gets in the way.

This happens even in the natural sciences when the concepts we develop and use often have their origins as metaphors drawn from human experiences. Thus, physicists speak of "particles" or "waves" of light, references that evoke seashore imagery. That there are "black holes" in outer space is yet another example of the human side grappling with meaning in the natural sciences, describing extraterrestrial phenomena with Earth-bound vocabularies. We leave it to others to determine whether such metaphors are apt or whether they mislead us. What interests us here is simply to recognize that positivist science—whether dealing with natural or social phenomena—cannot escape human subjectivity. Put another way, complete value-free science is just not possible.

Of the two, postmodernists are the more skeptical of "scientific" truth claims that are so dependent on the meanings we assign to the concepts we employ. In the extreme, some postmodernists see knowledge in entirely relativist terms. Critical theorists, by contrast, tend not to abandon science but try merely to expose ideological claims often masquerading as theories with scientific bases of support—false pretenses used to legitimate self-serving practices. Indeed, critical theorists search for the ways and means by which the powerful attempt to legitimate their often exploitative positions of dominance; their self-serving manipulation of ideas or meanings in theories others are led to believe have scientific underpinnings.

CRITICAL THEORY: MAJOR ASSUMPTIONS

While IR scholars who are self-proclaimed critical theorists may have their differences, they would agree on the following assumptions. First, the study of international relations should be about emancipatory politics. Whatever knowledge critical theory may generate, it is geared toward social and political transformation. To achieve this transformation, the first step is the critical scrutiny of the current understanding of international politics to understand and explain the existing realities of international relations and how they develop over time. To avoid mere idealism—"this is what the world should be"—IR scholars must explain and criticize the current political order in terms of the principles embedded in political institutions and cultural practices. Work done on the comparative historical sociology of states illustrates the use of empirical evidence.[10]

The concept of emancipation is particularly important and can be traced back to the Enlightenment and particularly the work of Kant. He was interested in, among other things, how competitive power relations among states could be transformed into a more cosmopolitan order of perpetual peace.

Emancipation consists of an essentially negative conception of freedom that emphasizes removing repressive constraints or relations of domination. Simply put, critical theorists are interested in the relation between power and freedom. Influenced intellectually by Karl Marx (1818–1883), many critical theorists draw from his analysis of human inequality and his normative goal of eliminating exploitation.

The theme of emancipation is a primary concern among those who identify with the Frankfurt School, which is in some respects an outgrowth of the critical work of an earlier generation within this school of thought that included Theodor Adorno (1903–1969), Max Horkheimer (1895–1973), and Herbert Marcuse (1898–1979). The Frankfurt School essentially turned a Marxist critique of political economy into a critique of ideology.

The development of critical theory has included rather diverse philosophical influences: escaping from ideological constraints, as in the revolutionary spirit of Jean-Jacques Rousseau; searching for universal moral principles with the universality of application found in Kant; identifying the oppression of class or other socioeconomic structures observed by Marx; understanding the role of human psychologies in relationships of dominance drawn from the work of Sigmund Freud (1856–1939); and rejecting determinism in favor of a more Gramsci-style Marxism that adopts a normative, but practical approach to challenging and overthrowing structures of domination.

From the beginning, the Frankfurt School and its best-known theoretician, Jürgen Habermas, have taken seriously Marx's assertion that heretofore philosophers had only interpreted the world, but the point was to change it. Normative and ethical concerns cannot or should not be separated from our theories of international relations but should be embedded in them. Instead of using our reason for technical, instrumental means to maintain the stability of society, the larger questions that animated ancient Greek scholars such as Plato need to be seriously addressed: What is the good and just society?

---

[10] Paul Keal, *European Conquest and the Rights of Indigenous Peoples* (Cambridge, UK: Cambridge University Press, 2003); Heather Rae, *State Identities and the Homogenisation of Peoples* (New York: Cambridge University Press, 2002).

Systematic investigation of the existing order includes criticism, which, in turn, supports practical political theory that can map routes to societal and political transformation. For critical IR theorists, the good society is a just and democratic order that should be extended beyond the state to the international domain in the creation of a cosmopolitan community. Simply put, critical theorists are on the voluntarist extreme end of the voluntarism-determinism continuum, seeing great transformative potential residing in those able to see through ideological and other ideational masks that disguise or obscure unjust, exploitative realities.

Andrew Linklater, for example, analyzes what he terms a "triple transformation" required to undermine the relations among sovereignty, territory, and national conceptions of citizenship. These transformations involve widespread recognition (1) that certain moral, political, and legal principles need to be universalized; (2) that material inequality must be reduced; and (3) that there is need for respect for ethnic, cultural, and gender differences.[11]

Second, critical theorists have investigated the relation between knowledge and interest. Knowledge-seeking is inherently political. Detached theorizing is an impossibility and a sham. As Robert Cox succinctly stated: "Theory is always for someone and for some purpose."[12] With theories being embedded in social and political life, critical theory examines the purposes served by particular theories. Some critical theorists argue that beliefs held by many positivist scholars necessarily bias their truth claims and may well be part of global ideological schemes to legitimate particular world orders. In supporting an alleged agenda of domination, it may be convenient to advance ideologies often masquerading as scientifically based theories. One of the tasks of critical theorists is to unmask such deceptions, probe for deeper understandings or meanings, and expose the class or elite interests these ideologies or alleged theories are designed to serve. As for themselves, critical theorists believe in putting their cards on the table by being self-reflective.

Third, and following from earlier, critical IR theorists have scrutinized the work of realists and liberals in particular. This even applies to the supposed founding fathers of realism. It has been argued, for example, that Thucydides's concern with language and practices (as evident in the numerous dialogues he reconstructs in his *History of the Peloponnesian War*) can be viewed as the beginning of critical theory. Far from being driven by events outside their control (anarchy, distribution of capabilities, or balance of power), individuals are the conscious initiators of the events described. Similarly, it has been suggested that Machiavelli is really an interpretive theorist due to his sensitivity to the historical context of political action. At the time he was writing, the modern nation-state was just emerging as a new form of political community in the shadow of Christian universalism. With the political world in flux, Machiavelli

---

[11] See, for example, Andrew Linklater, *The Transformation of Political Community: Ethical Foundations of the Post-Westphalian Era* (Cambridge, UK: Polity Press, 1998).

[12] See Robert Cox, "Social Forces, States, and World Orders," in *Neorealism and Its Critics*, ed. Robert O. Keohane (New York: Columbia University Press, 1986), 207.

did not immediately reject the established Christian temporal understanding for a new form of realist universalism.[13]

According to critical theorists, both realism and liberalism claim to be problem-solving technical approaches to international relations. As a result, there is a built-in bias toward stability and maintaining the status quo of international politics. Their work essentially provides answers on how to manage international relations and keep the international system within stable bounds and avoid disruption. They are not revolutionaries. Transforming international relations for the betterment of the vast majority of humanity is supposedly not the goal of these realists and liberal rationalists.

In the IR theories they examine, critical theorists' major goal is to uncover underlying power and other motives these theories allegedly advance. Not surprisingly, much of their critique about the IR mainstream has been directed particularly toward realists and neorealists whose theories knowingly or unknowingly give legitimacy to states and relations among them. To some critical theorists, these are not really theories. They are instead cover stories—ideologies serving state, class, or elite interests merely masquerading as if they were theories.

One example of criticism applied to a positivist understanding of international relations is Richard Ashley's comment on Kenneth N. Waltz's system-level structural explanation for the behaviors we observe among states. The influence of Habermas's critical theory is apparent in the following passage. Referring to Waltz and the "poverty of neorealism," Ashley asserts:

> What emerges is a positivist structuralism that treats the given order as the natural order, limits rather than expands political discourse, negates or trivializes the significance of variety across time and place, subordinates all practice to an interest in control, bows to the ideal of a social power beyond responsibility, and thereby deprives political interaction of those practical capacities which make social learning and creative change possible. What emerges is an ideology that anticipates, legitimizes, and orients a totalitarian project of global proportions: the rationalization of global politics.[14]

Neoliberal institutionalism hardly fares much better, given its emphasis on maintaining international stability at times of international economic unrest. As Cox has noted, neoliberalism is situated between the system of states and the capitalist world-economy, providing insight into how the two can coexist. Theory can provide insight into how to resolve crises between them.[15]

Critical theory may be viewed separately from postmodernism since most critical theorists retain strict methodological criteria to guide their work. Theirs

---

[13] See, for example, Daniel Garst, "Thucydides and Neorealism," *International Studies Quarterly* 33 (1989): 3–27; R. B. J. Walker, "The Prince and the Pauper: Tradition, Modernity, and Practice in the Theory of International Relations," in *International/Intertextual Relations: Postmodern Readings of World Politics*, ed. James Der Derian and Michael J. Shapiro (Lexington, MA: Lexington Books, 1989).

[14] See Richard K. Ashley, "The Poverty of Neorealism," in *Neorealism and Its Critics*, ed. Robert O. Keohane (New York: Columbia University Press, 1986), 258.

[15] Robert Cox, "Multilateralism and World Order," *Review of International Studies* 18 (1992): 173.

is not a complete rejection of science or of positivism. Nevertheless, in terms of intellectual precursors and key assumptions, aspects of critical theory overlap with or can be understood more broadly as related to, a postmodernist understanding of international relations.

QUEER THEORY—THINKING CRITICALLY ABOUT IR

Although feminism has had a substantial impact on IR (see chapter 11), queer theory has had decidedly less. This is due, at least in part, to the fact that queer theory in relation to IR is relatively new to the field. Feminists have been more open than others to discussing sexuality. Feminists like Cynthia Weber have been among those in the lead.[16]

Lesbians, gay men, bisexuals, and transgender persons (*LGBTQ*) have a long history in humankind across cultures. These "labels" are themselves social constructions that are present-day understandings of the fluidity of sexuality and gender identities—other categories including nonbinary pansexual, intersex (I), and asexual (A). The term *queer* is itself an integral concept that, for many, includes all of these categories—everyone except completely heterosexual women and men. Queer studies, then, have had a human security focus on discrimination, marginalization, and violence toward queer individuals and communities throughout the world. A global problem, it is decidedly worse in some regions and countries than others. The intersection of cultural biases and religious teachings against LGBTQ constitute a toxic environment extraordinarily dangerous to queer persons. It is a human rights, human security, and global challenge.

On the other hand, "queer" theory goes beyond these issues, probing how sexual orientation and gender identity relate to understandings in the IR field. As such, queer theory is a subset of critical theory that owes much to the earlier writings of Michel Foucault in his *History of Sexuality*. Much as one examines and finds wanting the binaries in gender and sexuality (male/female, gay/straight, masculine/feminine, etc.) in favor of terms that allow for greater fluidity (pansexual, spectrum of orientations and gender identities), queer theory in IR challenges the war/peace, powerful/weak, just/unjust, developed/undeveloped, democratic/authoritarian, and other binaries. Indeed, international relations are far more complex than being reduced to such either-or binaries.

Sovereignty becomes sexualized as a form of male dominance. Given its masculinist orientation, Melanie Richter-Montpetit notes Richard Ashley's observation that identifies *statecraft* under the claim of sovereignty as a form of *mancraft*. The Westphalia system of sovereign states is really one of sovereign man. In her review of several books in the queer theory IR genre, Richter-Montpetit observes that

> the emerging "queer turn" in IR extends and reworks critical IR epistemologies, ontologies and methodologies. Engaging with queer scholarship will further expand and refine the notion of the political in IR, and help produce more

---

[16] Cynthia Weber, *Queer International Relations: Sexuality, Sovereignty and the Will to Knowledge* (Oxford, UK: Oxford University Press, 2016).

complex and robust understandings of the operations of contemporary formations of international power, including beyond unhelpful binaries of power and resistance.[17]

Richter-Montpetit notes how Cynthia Weber goes beyond Foucault: "Weber explores how Man is fundamentally constructed in relationship to sexuality . . . and how 'sexualized sovereign man' then intersects with race and gives rise to particular racialized figures ('the Al Qaeda terrorist')."

Exactly where queer theorizing will take us in relation to IR is unclear. How much does sexuality matter as an explanatory variable? Will queer theory take us past where feminist work on masculinist orientations has brought us? On such questions, the jury is still out.

POSTMODERNISM: MAJOR ASSUMPTIONS

For postmodernists, what we see, what we choose to see or measure, and the mechanisms or methods we employ are all of human construction that essentially rely on perception and cognitive processes influenced particularly by prior understandings and meanings. Even the language we use reflects an embedded set of values that are an integral part of any culture and found in the narratives or stories people commonly employ to depict understandings of their observations and experiences in the world around them. As means to understand international relations, postmodernists engage in linguistic deconstruction of what has been said or written, employing discursive practices that emphasize reasoned argument.

First, as with critical theorists and feminists, postmodernists assume an intimate connection between power and knowledge in the analysis of international relations. Following the arguments of Michel Foucault, the production of knowledge is a political process that has a mutually supportive relation to power. This is true not only in international relations but also in all aspects of political life where power is exercised. This is not a realist emphasis on the material basis of power, but rather a focus on how actors and commentators (such as during the Cold War or after the September 11, 2001, attacks on the World Trade Center and Pentagon) attempt to impose authoritative interpretations on events. Hence, reality is structured by language, and the development of linguistic discourses results in a structure or system consisting of knowledge, subjects, and objects. For example, the development of the concept of *sovereignty* and associated terms and assumptions—state, anarchy, borders, security, and such human identities—is at the heart of much postmodern work in international relations.

Second, in terms of methodology, some postmodernists follow Friedrich Nietzsche's lead in tracing over time the genealogy and significance of power-knowledge relations and such dominant discourses in international relations

---

[17] Melanie Richter-Montpetit, "Everything You Always Wanted to Know about Sex (in IR) but Were Afraid to Ask: The 'Queer Turn' in International Relations," in *Millennium* 46, no. 2 (January 2018): 93–248.

as sovereignty and anarchy.[18] Knowledge is always conditioned by a particular time and place. Understanding how particular interpretations of the past continue to guide current thinking and behavior also involves highlighting what has been excluded in historical narratives. Hence, as Foucault argued, history is not about the uncovering of facts and building up a composite picture of the past, but rather exposing "the endlessly repeated play of dominations."[19] In his studies of sanity, sexuality, and punishment, Foucault explored how concepts we use commonly developed or were socially constructed over time, challenging the generally accepted meanings these concepts purport to convey and the power-based human relations they sustain.

In engaging in this genealogical excavation, many postmodernists follow the approach of Jacques Derrida, who sought both text and subtexts to deconstruct—unpack and take apart—the meanings embedded in what we say or write and even in the ways we act. By the term text he did not simply mean what is written, but rather text as a metaphor for the need to understand the world as a whole and how different interpretations not only represent but also constitute the world—an ontological position.[20]

Derrida led us to a poststructural turn, going beyond or not being bound by the accepted symbols or established structures that effectively channel our understandings—a reaction by him and other poststructuralists of similar mind to the universal claims we find in the structuralism of both French philosophical thought and the branch of anthropology called semiotics. Particularly objectionable to them is any attempt to unify the social sciences with a single structuralist methodology based on identifying linguistic or cultural signs and differences. For their part, Jean-François Lyotard and his followers reject grand metanarratives employed purportedly to explain all of the world in scientific terms. Scholars arguing in this genre raise similar objections to balance of power and other metanarratives in international relations they see masquerading as if they were scientifically based theoretical explanations.

Third, in the process of engaging in genealogical excavations of dominant discourses and power-knowledge relations, postmodernists highlight competing historical perspectives, narratives, or trajectories. Following Nietzsche, there is no single historical truth, but rather multiple ones—there being no standard to judge them as no objective standard for truth exists.

This view is different from that of Kuhn's and Toulmin's use of paradigms or lenses that influence scientific work. They assume a real, discoverable objective reality out there, but we adopt different lenses that highlight and interpret "facts" in different ways. For postmodernists, these perspectives actually constitute the "real world." A basic ontological assumption, the identification of a

---

[18] Note that the work of Richard Ashley predates Alexander Wendt's constructivist critique of anarchy. Ashley, "Untying the Sovereign State: A Double Reading of the Anarchy Problematique," *Millennium: Journal of International Studies* 17 (1988): 227–62.

[19] Michel Foucault, *Discipline and Punish: The Birth of the Prison* (Harmondsworth, UK: Penguin, 1977), 228.

[20] Jacques Derrida, *Limited Inc.* (Evanston, IL: Northwestern University Press, 1988).

historical narrative, is not simply the interpretation of a series of actions, but rather how "reality" is conferred upon events.

Just as postmodernists reject the idea that there is a knowable, single truth to be discovered, so, too, do they reject the idea that the only way to gain knowledge is through a positivist methodology whose application is restricted to conventional approaches favored by realists and liberals. For example, postmodernists have taken the lead not only in textual analysis but also in the interpretation of art and theater. Christine Sylvester, for example, shows how international relations influences the mission of museums and, in turn, how visitors experience and interpret the art that is displayed.[21]

Finally, many postmodernists have a normative commitment to the idea that the sovereign state is not the only means by which to organize political and social life. The language of international relations that emphasizes states in a condition of anarchy reinforces the current exclusionary paradigm that effectively precludes alternative forms of political and social organization. Furthermore, the territorialization of political identity justifies a political discourse and policies that affirm the right of state officials to brutalize their subjects and restrict the possibility of expanding democratic values. Hence, postmodernists take issue with the ontological perspective of realists and liberals that privileges the state as the unit of analysis and makes it an ontological given for IR theorizing. In some postmodernist understandings, states do not simply use force in an instrumental, means-ends calculation to achieve certain objectives. Rather, the role of violence is important even in the origins and constitution of the state itself.[22]

In sum, postmodernists dive beneath the surface—they deconstruct the words and phrases or text we use—and look for underlying meanings or subtexts in our communications or the narratives we adopt to depict our understandings. As subjective creatures, we human beings are the source of knowledge we have about the world around us. Even our own identities are formed by the way we come to understand the world around us; the self is defined subjectively by each of us in relation to (an)other.

CRITICAL THEORISTS, POSTMODERNISTS, AND THEIR CRITICS

Mainstream international relations has consistently ignored critical theory and postmodernism. When it has addressed these interpretive understandings, there have been two major lines of argument.

First, similar to charges leveled against economic structuralists, critical theorists and postmodernists substitute ideology for explanation and engage in wishful thinking unconstrained by reality. A realist would no doubt suggest

---

[21] See Christine Sylvester, *Art/Museums: International Relations Where You Least Expect It* (Boulder, CO: Paradigm, 2008).

[22] One of the initial analyses remains the best. See R. B. J. Walker, *Inside/Outside: International Relations as Political Theory* (Cambridge, UK: Cambridge University Press, 1993). For an excellent case study of all of these arguments coming into play, see David Campbell's *National Deconstruction: Violence, Identity, and Justice in Bosnia* (Minneapolis: University of Minnesota Press, 1998).

this literature belongs in this volume's chapter 13 on normative theory where the *ought* compared to the *is* holds sway. One realist, Randall Schweller, has commented that Andrew Linklater in his *The Transformation of Political Community* "argues by fiat rather than by the weight of hard evidence, which is in scant supply here." Radical propositions are "supported by nothing more than references to some other critical theorist who shares Linklater's vision or tendency to rely on slippery, undefined, and unmeasured concepts." With Linklater not taking seriously the obstacles to his triple transformation of the international system (increased moral and economic equality while remaining sensitive to cultural differences), Linklater's work "will appear as little more than an intellectual exercise in historical speculation and theoretical wishful thinking."[23]

Second, and following from earlier, is the charge that critical theorists, particularly postmodernists, simply do not follow the canons of positivism and causal theorizing. The editors of one of the major IR journals, for example, justified the exclusion of critical theory and postmodernist articles and associated critiques of positivism in the following manner:

> Little of this debate was published in IO [*International Organization*], since IO has been committed to an enterprise that postmodernism denies: the use of evidence to adjudicate between truth claims. In contrast to conventional and critical constructivism, postmodernism falls clearly outside the social science enterprise, and in international relations research risks becoming self-referential and disengaged from the world, protests to the contrary notwithstanding.[24]

As one postmodernist responded: "There is a brazen acknowledgment of censorship and suppression in the statement about the publication history of arguably the discipline's most influential journal." For their part, critical theorists reject as a false claim that their enterprise stands apart from scientific methods of analysis. On the contrary, they uncover the ways and means by which "science" has been used to mask power-driven or exploitative agendas.

It is true that for many postmodernists, claims made to empirically based, objective truth are necessarily hollow. Our understandings and meanings are, after all, humanly constructed. In the extreme, no knowledge or truth is possible apart from the motivations and purposes people put into their construction. From this extreme perspective (not all postmodernists go so far), truth is entirely relative. It is this highly relative approach to human understanding that leads some postmodernists to deny even the possibility of any empirically based truth claims, thus underscoring their total rejection of positivism.

These are, to say the least, examples of significant challenges to "modernist" science or positivism more generally and to IR theory in particular. It is difficult,

---

[23] Randall L. Schweller, "Fantasy Theory," *Review of International Studies* 25 (1999): 147, 148.

[24] Peter J. Katzenstein, Robert O. Keohane, and Stephen D. Krasner, "*International Organization* and the Study of World Politics," *International Organization* 52 (1998): 678. The rebuttal quotation in the subsequent paragraph is found in Anthony Burke, "Postmodernism," in *The Oxford Handbook of International Relations*, ed. Christian Reus-Smit and Duncan Snidal (Oxford, UK: Oxford University Press, 2008), 370.

however, to deny or dismiss scientific methodologies that have produced so much accumulated knowledge in so many diverse fields of human inquiry. Defenders of positivism see critical and postmodernist thinkers as misrepresenting the positivist scientific enterprise which, after all, retains an inherently skeptical orientation to truth claims and demands continued and unending empirical tests of such propositions.

On the other hand, postmodern critiques make us skeptical of truth claims made by mainstream journals inducing us to exercise critical scrutiny of the assumptions made about causality, the categories we adopt, the factors we select, how we define these variables or constants, and the way we relate them to each other in the explanatory or predictive theories positivists generate. The cover stories identified by critical theorists and the narratives and particular uses of language that inform postmodernists already have influenced substantially how concepts are developed and research is conducted across the IR field. Taking the human or subjective into account has encouraged IR theorists—no matter what image or interpretive understanding influences their work—to be more theoretically self-consciousness.

SUMMATION

Positivism—modernist science and the scientific method that combine the logic of rational theorizing with empirical testing—has occupied the mainstream of IR theory. In recent decades, however, the Weberian concept of *Verstehen* and phenomenology—a focus on human consciousness as essential to our coming to know the world of which we are a part—is at the root of interpretive understandings in both critical theory and postmodern thought.

If the central question of epistemology is how we know what we think we know, critical theorists and postmodernists set aside many of the abstract universalist claims of logical positivists, focusing instead on the human perception and understandings that give diverse meanings to the concepts and theories we formulate and the behavior we observe. Although some in the extreme entirely reject the scientific or modernist project and the truth claims associated with it, others seek merely to temper blanket claims of objectivity with interpretive understanding—subjectivity and intersubjectivity that necessarily are a part of what human beings observe, think, and do. As such, the scholar or researcher still wedded to science and its canons is at the same time encouraged or cajoled to be humble about truth claims, knowing how much they remain a function of human subjectivity. Just as it historically has accommodated empirical, theoretical, and philosophical critiques by modifying its methods and understandings, science remains open to critical, postmodernist, and other challenges.

REFERENCES

Ashley, Richard K. "The Poverty of Neorealism." In *Neorealism and Its Critics*. Edited by Robert O. Keohane. New York: Columbia University Press, 1986.

Booth, Kenneth, ed. *Critical Security Studies and World Politics*. Boulder, CO: Lynne Rienner, 2005.

Der Derian, James, and Michael J. Shapiro, eds. *International/Intertextual Relations: Postmodern Readings of World Politics*. Lexington, MA: Lexington Books, 1989.

Ihde, Don. *Experimental Phenomenology*. Albany: State University of New York, 1986.

Jones, Richard Wyn, ed. *Critical Theory and World Politics*. Boulder, CO: Lynne Rienner, 2001.

Kuhn, Thomas S. *The Structure of Scientific Revolutions*, 2nd ed. Chicago: University of Chicago Press, 1962, 1970.

Linklater, Andrew. *The Transformation of Political Community: Ethical Foundations of the Post-Westphalian Era*. Cambridge, UK: Polity Press, 1998.

Toulmin, Stephen. *Foresight and Understanding: An Enquiry into the Aims of Science*. Bloomington: Indiana University Press, 1961.

Walker, R. B. J. *Inside/Outside: International Relations as Political Theory*. Cambridge, UK: Cambridge University Press, 1993.

Weber, Cynthia. *Queer International Relations: Sexuality, Sovereignty and the Will to Knowledge*. Oxford: Oxford University Press, 2016.

11

Feminist Understandings
in IR Theory

★ ★ ★

Feminism as interpretive understanding or lens includes diverse perspectives to include liberal, radical, and postmodern versions as applied to the subject matter of IR. As a result, methodologies may vary. Feminist IR perspectives cannot be divorced from broader historical concerns of the feminist movement whether postcolonial struggles or civil and political rights in the West. Accordingly, we place feminism as a separate critique or interpretive understanding of conventional IR theory that offers an alternative perspective and starting point for both theory and practice.

Feminist approaches are important for highlighting major blind spots in mainstream international relations, providing an alternative lens—gender—through which to view world politics and offering new insights on the often-overlooked political, social, and economic roles that women play in international relations. Feminists argue that the IR discipline falls into the trap of believing that the masculine experience is the human experience. Feminism in all its forms has a strong normative commitment to enhancing the prospects of peace and reducing violence and conflict, the latter effects all too often suffered by women.

INTELLECTUAL PRECURSORS AND INFLUENCES

Although feminist approaches to international relations began to appear in the 1980s, feminism has deep intellectual and policy-oriented roots. Certainly Plato (c. 427–347 BCE) elevated the role of women alongside men in the idealized republic he constructed even if Aristotle (384–322 BCE) subsequently did not afford women the same equal standing. For his part, the ancient playwright Aristophanes (c. 446–386 BCE) portrayed women in *Lysistrata* not only as more oriented toward peace and less prone to resort to warlike activities than men but also as powerful, often decisive actors in their own right. In his *Assembly-women* we see women assuming control of politics and establishing in Athens a society in which communal, egalitarian values become prominent. That the oracle of Delphi was always a woman—not to mention belief in goddesses who could impose themselves on world events—is also indicative of feminine power in the ancient Greek world.

This theme—that women matter and can be decisive, trumping the decisions and actions of men—also can be found in the modern political theory of Niccolò Machiavelli (1469–1527). Indeed, Machiavelli portrays *Fortuna* metaphorically as a powerful woman who not only challenges but also can reverse even the most powerful of men.[1] The chances of beating *Fortuna* are at best fifty-fifty.

This is not the place to elaborate in detail on the very rich, multicentury social history of modern liberal movements to emancipate women and legitimate feminine understandings. We select here only a few representative samples from extensive literature and history of feminist movements. For example, we note the ideas advanced by an early feminist writer, Mary Astell (1666–1731), who articulated what has become a "core liberal feminist belief that men and women are equally capable of reason, and that therefore they should be equally educated in its use." Moreover, one even can find in Astell, albeit in embryonic form, some of the core ideas of recent radical feminism: the idea that "man (whether as sexual predator or tyrannous husband) is the natural enemy of woman" as well as "the idea that women must be liberated from the need to please men."[2]

Better known among the early modern feminist writers but still reflecting Astell's insights, Mary Wollstonecraft (1759–1797) in her persuasive *Vindication of the Rights of Women* (1792) refutes the claim "that women were less capable of reason than men" and argues (as Astell had) that since "men and women are equally possessed of reason, they must be equally educated in its use."[3] Critical of the lesser place afforded women in French revolutionary thought and actions, Wollstonecraft argued that the education of women would enable them not only to exercise their reason but also to realize their inner virtues as fellow human beings. Consistent with this logic, women are (and should be treated as) the equals of men in the rights they possess.

One finds similar views expressed in both socialist and liberal writings of the nineteenth and early twentieth centuries. In his *Subjection of Women* (1861), the utilitarian John Stuart Mill (1806–1873) built upon these earlier, foundational writings, railing against the subordinate and often abusive condition women had to endure. The remedy could be found in legislation that equalized the position of women, assuring access to education and employment as well as full protection of the law and political rights as fellow citizens and full participants in society.

Karl Marx (1818–1883) did not address feminist issues as directly as his revolutionary and intellectual partner, Friedrich Engels (1820–1895), did in two key works—*The Origin of the Family, Private Property and the State* and *The*

---

[1] Hanna F. Pitkin, *Fortune Is a Woman* (Chicago: University of Chicago, 1984, 1999).
[2] For eighteenth- and nineteenth-century thought, we draw on Valerie Bryson, *Feminist Political Theory*, 2nd ed. (New York: Palgrave Macmillan, 1992, 2003), 9–10.
[3] Bryson, *Feminist Political Theory*, 16.

Condition of the Working Class in England. Engels referred to "the world historical defeat of the female sex" as "the man took command in the home also; the woman was degraded and reduced to servitude; she became the slave of his lust and a mere instrument for the production of children."[4] Liberation of women will come with the revolution that frees them from the bondage of being treated as private property controlled by men: "The supremacy of the man in marriage is the simple consequence of his economic supremacy, and with the abolition of the latter [economic supremacy based on private property] will [male supremacy over women] disappear of itself." Engels also observed the abuse of women and men in the workplace in early industrial capitalism: "Women made unfit for childbearing, children deformed, men enfeebled, limbs crushed, whole generations wrecked, afflicted with disease and infirmity, purely to fill the purses of the bourgeoisie."

Building upon nineteenth-century challenges posed by Maria Stewart (1803–1879), a free black woman, and Elizabeth Cady Stanton (1815–1902), Susan B. Anthony (1820–1906), and others, the stage was set for the twentieth-century suffrage movement. American women finally received the right to vote in 1919. Parallel efforts were also underway in Europe and much later in Latin America and elsewhere. It was after the Second World War, however, that feminist writings and associated movements put in place the intellectual foundation not just for feminist scholarship in our own times, but also for important efforts to transform the conditions experienced and roles played by women in what has become a truly global project.

In popular literature, feminist writers challenged exclusionary policies toward women, unequal treatment, and other patterns of male dominance.[5] Feminist understandings have had and likely will continue to have substantial impact on a global scale concerning human rights with regard to equal treatment and the empowerment of women, allowing them the same opportunities that traditionally and historically have been reserved in most cultures for men. Some feminists note that empowering women will also give them the means to limit family size voluntarily, thus reducing population growth rates to economically sustainable levels. Countering what they see as predominantly male misogynism that restricts legally a woman's choice on reproductive health, feminists (joined by others) argue that women have the right to make their own decisions about their bodies, as in whether to carry a fetus to term. This is particularly so in cases of rape, incest, and the mother's health. Finally, women are also seen by many feminists as more prone to approaching issues of peace and conflict resolution from a broader, often social and cultural perspective.

MAJOR ASSUMPTIONS

First, feminist approaches in international relations use *gender* as the major category of analysis to highlight women's perspectives on social issues and

---

[4] Friedrich Engels, *The Origin of the Family, Private Property and the State* (Peking, China: Foreign Languages Press, 1978), 65 as cited by Bryson, *Feminist Political Theory*, 59. Subsequent quotes same page.

[5] For example, see Betty Friedan's now classic *Feminine Mystique* (New York: Dell, 1964).

research. Gender is a set of socially and culturally constructed characteristics that are (often stereotypically) associated with what it means in any culture to be masculine or feminine. Masculinity is associated with power and forceful activity, a rationality often cold to human concerns, self-empowered autonomy, and assumption of leadership in public roles. Conversely, feminine characteristics supposedly include less assertive or less aggressive behavior, willful dependence on—or interdependence in—nurturing relationships with others, sensitivity to emotional aspects of issues, and a focus on the private realm.

The two gender categories are dependent upon one another for their meaning and permeate all aspects of public and private life. One's gendered identity or self comes to be defined in relation to (an)other—relationships, for example, between mother, father, and child or male and female peers. For its part, society reinforces the idea that to be a "real man" means not to display "feminine" characteristics. Hence, the emphasis on gender is not just about women, but men and masculinity as well. In terms of *epistemology*, many feminists, as we will see, pursue empirical research. Yet the strict *positivist* dichotomies such as the separation of fact and value are rejected by many feminists who adopt a constructivist approach to their work, emphasizing how knowledge is shaped by culture, history, and context. Although some feminists can be found among realists and even more among liberals, they are more likely to be critics of scholars within any of the IR images who marginalize gender as an interpretive lens.

In sum, feminist scholars claim that as gender permeates social life, it has profound and largely unnoticed effects on the actions of states, international organizations, and transnational actors. Feminist scholarship seeks to develop a research agenda and associated concepts to trace and explain these effects. Feminist approaches to international relations first began to appear frequently in the IR literature in the 1980s.

Second, from the feminist perspective gender is particularly important as a primary way to signify relationships of power not only in the home but also in the world of foreign policy and international relations. When we privilege masculinity, women socially but also legally can be cast into a subordinate status. Gender hierarchies perpetuate unequal role expectations, contributing to inequalities between men and women in international relations. Feminists emphasize social relations as the key *unit of analysis*, obviously interested in the causes and consequences of unequal power relationships between men and women. Unequal power relations exist through time, across cultures, and at all *levels of analysis*. This perspective on power is obviously quite different from that of scholars associated with the images earlier outlined in this book in which power is usually viewed in terms of states, international organizations, multinational corporations, other nongovernmental organizations, or classes. The realist rational, unitary, power-maximizing state—which many feminists have noted interestingly is associated with male characteristics—leaves no room for gender as an analytical category.

More conventional IR theories are therefore riven with unexamined assumptions about the international system to include the belief that its concepts are gender-neutral. Feminists would take issue with this, and even argue that virtually the entire Western philosophical tradition ignores feminine perspectives or even exalts a masculine bias. This is why, it has been argued, an important task for feminist theory is to make strange what has heretofore appeared familiar or natural. The basic assumptions and concepts of international relations have been taken as unproblematic by mainstream theorists.[6] Not surprisingly, there are critical theory and postmodern strains of thought within the broader feminist approach to IR.

Third, many contemporary IR theory feminists are dedicated to the emancipatory goal of achieving equality for women via the elimination of unequal gender relations. Rather than basing their analysis on abstract speculation of how anarchy may influence the behavior of rational, unitary states (as many realists are prone to do), the emphasis is on how, for example, military conflict among and within states directly affects the lives of the dispossessed, women in particular.[7] Far from states being viewed as a security provider, they are just as likely to threaten the security of women if one empirically examines not only the system level of analysis but also the state, societal, or local levels. Hence, many feminists find highly suspect the view that the levels of analysis demarcate a clear division between the international system and state-society, with the former being characterized as one of anarchy and the latter one of community. When gender is introduced as a category of analysis, old assumptions about security as well as new assumptions about who benefits from globalization can be examined in a new, more humane light.

STRANDS OF FEMINISM IN INTERNATIONAL RELATIONS

Feminist interpretive understandings can be found within a number of the images and approaches discussed in this book.[8] Liberal feminists emphasize the exclusion of women from important public spheres of social, political, and economic life. There are two strands of research. The first seeks to expose the many areas of international relations where women are underrepresented and to identify ways to overcome barriers to expanded participation. Such studies look at the underrepresentation of women in security and arms control policy-making circles or international organizations. Liberal feminism of this strand, therefore, tends to accept the position of mainstream international relations that the important subject of research is the so-called high politics of military security beloved by realists. As gender stereotyping historically has consigned women to the private sphere, success for women in international relations becomes

---

[6] Sandra Harding, *Whose Science? Whose Knowledge? Thinking from Women's Lives* (Ithaca, NY: Cornell University Press, 1991), 123. See also Eric M. Blanchard, "Why Is There No Gender in the English School?" *Review of International Studies* 37, no. 2 (April 2011): 855–79.

[7] See, for example, Sara Meger, *Rape Loot Pillage: The Political Economy of Sexual Violence in Armed Conflict* (Oxford: Oxford University Press, 2016).

[8] This section draws on Sandra Whitworth, *Feminism and International Relations: Towards a Political Economy of Gender in Interstate and Non-Governmental Institutions* (New York: St. Martin's Press, 1994), 12–25.

a practical matter of upping their numbers in diplomatic and security policy-making positions.

The second strand of research looks to uncover ways in which women have actually been there—participants in and witnesses of major events, but their presence is not reported. If women were not in international organizations or on the battlefield, where were they? Behind the scenes in organizational settings, factories, hospitals, peace campaigns, and even battlefields? Unsung heroes ferrying planes across oceans for use in war zones?[9]

One important example of this work is Cynthia Enloe's *Bananas, Beaches, and Bases*[10] in which she finds some women (spouses, mothers, daughters, girlfriends, and the like) "protected" while other categories (non-Americans, racial minorities, prostitutes—so-called camp followers or those cultivated in communities outside military bases at home and abroad) are exploited. Often denigrated as "common whores," camp followers provide necessary support services such as securing supplies, doing laundry, and nursing. Protection (a form of subordination) and exploitation are, then, two manifestations of male dominance associated historically with militaries at home and abroad.

Masculinist behaviors associated with militarization of social life thus have adverse effects on women the larger society has tended to ignore. Moreover, such conduct is by no means unique to the American experience. It is indeed a global phenomenon. Other studies look at the role of women on the home front and their role in filling positions in factories vacated by conscripted men. Liberal feminist accounts have also examined the important but usually unreported role of women in the economic development of the Global South.

Some feminists take issue with the liberal feminist approach. The argument is that there is an underlying assumption that including more women in positions previously denied them will eliminate gender inequalities. But feminists approaching the issue from the perspective of class or patriarchy claim that inequalities define the very structures in which women might participate. Participation alone will not alter this fundamental fact.

Some feminists argue that subordination and domination of women by men is the most basic form of oppression. Much of society is structured to reinforce and maintain patriarchy. Masculine perspectives emphasizing conflict dominate the social sciences and IR theorizing, focusing on such key ideas as defining security in terms of aggregating power. A feminist perspective would expand the concept of security to include the empowerment of women, economic development, human rights, and concern for the global ecological commons. Some feminists also take the perspective of women as nurturers and, hence, they are more likely to be peace-oriented than men. Some say this is the genetic code in men who are aggressive and territorial. Others reject biological determinism,

---

[9] The centennial of World War I led to an outpouring of work on this issue. See, for example, Lynn Dumenil, *The Second Line of Defense: American Women and World War I* (Chapel Hill: University of North Carolina Press, 2017).

[10] Cynthia Enloe, *Bananas, Beaches, and Bases: Making Feminist Sense of International Politics* (London: Pandora, 1989).

pointing to young men raised in societies that educate them in martial values (e.g., competitive "contact" or combative sports) and devalue by comparison the work of women to include their running households and raising children.

One of the contributions of feminists is to reject the idea that international relations is limited to high politics, a position logically following the rejection of the distinction between public and private realms. The danger, say some, is that the supposedly more peace-loving and nurturing female also plays to stereotypes of those who would prefer to confine them to subordinate status and caution against the role of women in national security policy-making positions.

Finally, postmodern feminism aims to displace realist and liberal positivist discourse and epistemology with a commitment to skepticism concerning truth claims about international relations. The emergence of *postcolonial theory*—assessing the historical legacy of colonial and imperial experiences that Global South societies and cultures still have to confront—also has an important feminist component relating in particular to these development and human rights challenges. Much of this work has focused on developing countries and the roles women have played and continue to play in tribal and other settings. Postmodernists are therefore allied with postcolonial critics of liberal and radical feminism by rejecting the implicit assumption that women are essentially a homogeneous group unaffected by race, class, culture, sexuality, and history. What connects all of them is a concern for the nature of power relationships up and down the levels of analysis.

Postmodernists tend to reject the idea that there is some ultimate core or essential identity to women that would have the effect of constraining them. The category of women is a socially constructed fiction and postmodernists engage in the task of deconstructing that fiction composed as it is of particular social or cultural understandings. Feminist critics of postmodernism, however, are concerned that if the category of women is essentially indeterminate, then how can an alternative world order with a different role for women be suggested? If critical discourse has the subversive effect of undermining concepts and creating conceptual disarray, what will be the replacement? Despite differences and often pointed criticisms of each other, there is consensus among these feminists on the paucity of both women in international relations and the perspectives they represent in what is still a male-dominant field replete with masculinist understandings taken uncritically as givens.

GENDER, WAR, AND SECURITY STUDIES

Scholars with a feminist perspective have been critical of masculinist approaches to conflict that tend to emphasize power and balance-of-power politics, coercive diplomacy, unilateralism, and the use of force. From this perspective, conduct in international relations seems similar to schoolyard conflicts, particularly among boys in which the strong do what they will and the weak do what they must. As such, arms races and the use of force in warfare are masculinist constructs. It is not surprising that with some exceptions the perpetrators of guerrilla, terrorist, and other examples of politically motivated violence in international relations tend to be men or boys, rarely women or girls. Women are not usually found on the battlefront but rather consigned to the home front. Those engaged in supporting the war effort through work such as in munitions factories are expected to relinquish these roles once the male heroes return from the war.

One of the first feminist works to examine war from conventional and unconventional perspectives was Jean Bethke Elshtain's *Women and War* (1987). She was not interested in contemporary IR research on war but cast her net much more broadly. Her starting point is Georg W. F. Hegel's (1770–1831) Just Warriors/Beautiful Souls dichotomy—Western men are seen fit to plan, conduct, and narrate wars while women are viewed as too soft and motherly to do much more than be the receivers of warrior tales. Her testimony is followed by historical perspectives on war, peace, and armed civic virtue dating back to ancient Greece. Women are absent from historical accounts, and part of her mission is to show how women have made sense of war and have not merely stood by to suffer it or stand by their warrior men out of duty.[11]

A major effort to summarize empirical studies ranging up and down all levels of analysis is Joshua Goldstein's *War and Gender*.[12] The puzzle he is interested in is the fact that despite political, economic, and cultural differences, gender roles in war are consistent across all known human societies (although this is changing). Historically, when faced with the prospect of war, the response has been in a gender-based way to assemble fighters who were usually exclusively male. War is a diverse, multifaceted enterprise, just as gender norms outside war show similar diversity. Yet such diversity vanishes when it comes to the connection between war and gender. Goldstein applies the three strands of feminist thought outlined earlier to provide possible answers to this puzzle.

On sexual orientation, homophobic prejudices drawn from the larger society become particularly acute in an all-male military setting, given an institutional culture emphasizing the masculine and discounting the feminine. Only in more recent decades are women allowed to assume combat roles in US military units—the masculinist orientation that historically or traditionally warfare is essentially a male enterprise. In the United States, women are allowed to serve in combat-related tasks at sea and as fighter, bomber, and helicopter pilots, but even now their full integration with men in ground-combat units remains a work in progress.

The roles women and men play in society intersect with sexuality. In military settings, for example, lesbians, gay men, bisexuals, and *transgender* members of the armed services have struggled with deeply held homophobic and gender prejudices. Although legally accepted now in the United States and many Western-oriented states, "coming out" as gay or transgender may expose oneself to various forms of discrimination including reduced chances for promotion and other career opportunities. Even worse, *LGBTQ* members may become victims of assault.

---

[11] Christine Sylvester, *Feminist International Relations: An Unfinished Journey* (Cambridge, UK: Cambridge University Press, 2002), 8–14. In chapter 2 the author provides excellent overviews of the life and work of not only Jean Bethke Elshtain but also Cynthia Enloe and J. Ann Tickner.

[12] Joshua Goldstein, *War and Gender: How Gender Shapes the War System and Vice Versa* (Cambridge, UK: Cambridge University Press, 2001).

Transgender persons, in particular, have been marginalized or discriminated against not only in society as a whole, but also among lesbians, gays, and bisexuals who differentiate themselves on sexual orientation, not the genders with which they identify. Feminist scholarship has been particularly sensitive to such matters as it also has been to discrimination against women, religious, and racial or ethnic minorities in the military or in societies as a whole. Discrimination on such grounds is indeed a human security problem global in scope.

The concept of security itself has come under scrutiny and become a contested concept. The question asked by feminists is "Security for whom?" Does it make sense to continue to view the patriarchal state as the mainstay of security? Is the security of individuals or groups adequately understood in terms of being members of a given national community? Is achieving security to be found in the traditional realist conception?

An even more basic question is "What is meant by security?" Is it limited to deterring or preventing an outside power from attacking the state of which one is a citizen? Perhaps the denial of basic human rights, widespread poverty, environmental degradation, and gender inequality could also be viewed as human security issues that are applicable to men, women, and children. Challenging the entire discourse of security is in line with the concerns of critical theorists and postmodernists and an expansive notion of security attune to many liberal conceptions.[13] This struggle over meaning—what is meant by security and peace in relation to masculinity or femininity—is a constant concern of feminists.

GENDER, THE STATE, AND CIVIL SOCIETY

J. Ann Tickner takes on what she sees as misrepresentations of feminism and the feminist standpoint. She provides feminist understandings about how and why gender matters not only to theorizing about IR but also about the challenges women face globally. "IR feminists" want to rid the field of "idealistic associations of women with peace, idealism, and impracticality," particularly since such characterizations effectively "disempower women and keep them in their place, which is out of the 'real world' of international politics." What feminists want is for "women and men [to] participate in reducing damaging and unequal hierarchical structures, such as gender and race." Indeed, "constructed gender hierarchies" not only "result in the devaluation of women's lives and their economic and social contributions to society," but also "contribute to conflict, inequality and oppression."[14]

Gender clearly matters in understanding the construction of what Iris Marion Young calls the security state, which directly reflects masculinist understandings.[15] She observes how the "protection" role assumed by males—

---

[13] For examples of feminist thought on security, see Jill Steans, "Security and Peacekeeping," in *Gender and International Relations*, 3rd ed. (Cambridge, UK: Polity Press, 2013).

[14] J. Ann Tickner, "Why Women Can't Rule the World: International Politics According to Francis Fukuyama," *International Studies Review* 1, no. 3 (1999).

[15] Iris Marion Young, "The Logic of Masculinist Protection: Reflections on the Current Security State," *Signs: Journal of Women in Culture and Society* 29, no. 1 (2003). Subsequent quotations in this and the next paragraph are from this source.

frequently characterized by them as "loving self-sacrifice"—effectively subordinates "those in the protected position." So it is with the "security state" that assumes the male-protective role and uses this responsibility to impose its will on the citizenry, particularly when faced with threats or dangers: "The logic of masculinist protection positions leaders, along with other officials such as soldiers and firefighters, as protectors and the rest of us in the subordinate position of dependent protected people."

The security state thus has two faces—"one facing outward to defend against enemies and the other facing inward to keep those under protection under necessary control." As a practical matter, of course, the world is full of risks, and "no state can make any of us completely safe." Following the ideal of "democratic citizenship," Young rejects "the hierarchy of protector and protected," opting instead for the "defender" role that both women and men customarily perform. Generalized at a global level, democratic citizenship avoids the authoritarian, masculinist orientation of the security state in favor of "respect and political equality among the world's peoples where none of us think that we stand in the position of paternal authority who knows what is good for the still developing others."

In *War, Women and Power*, Marie Berry compares Rwanda and Bosnia. On sexualized violence, in both countries "perpetrators employed rape as a deliberate strategy of violence with ethnic, class and gender dimensions." In Rwanda, the aim was "to emasculate and humiliate Tutsi men by abusing their" women—considered their "property" in this "patrilineal society." In addition to adverse physical and psychological effects on rape victims in Bosnia, they "faced stigma from their communities." In short, rape was "a political act designed to carry out an officially orchestrated policy."[16]

Notwithstanding these abuses, the displacement of persons and consequent fragmentation of social networks and "destruction of previous patterns of life" ironically opened doors for women in postconflict years: "Displaced women in both countries developed new social networks." They sought help from others and "engage[d] in forms of everyday politics, which led to the formation of self-help organizations." Berry finds that "war can serve as a period of rapid social change that reconfigures gendered power relations by precipitating interrelated demographic, economic, and cultural shifts."[17]

That women are not only victims but also important agents in their own right is a conclusion Hilary Matfess draws in her study of the Boko Haram insurgency in Nigeria. She finds that notwithstanding their victimization in sexual violence and other forms of discrimination against them in a very masculinist space, "women throughout the region have organized and advanced their own interests."[18] Not all women were abducted and coerced into Boko Haram.

---

[16] Marie E. Berry, *War, Women and Power: From Violence to Mobilization in Rwanda and Bosnia Herzogovina* (Cambridge, UK: Cambridge University Press, 2018), xxv, 52–53.

[17] Berry, *War, Women and Power*, 213–14.

[18] Hilary Matfess, *Women and the War on Boko Haram: Wives, Weapons, Witnesses* (London: Zed Books, 2017), 63.

Some joined willingly and found ways to exercise their agency. As such, Matfess also sees women as key players in post–conflict reconstruction and peacebuilding efforts.

For their part, Erica Chenoweth and Maria J. Stephan explore nonviolent civil resistance, which they find far more effective than armed resistance in overthrowing regimes and achieving other social objectives.[19] In her follow-on volume, Chenoweth defines civil resistance as "a form of collective action that seeks to affect the political, social, or economic status quo without using violence or the threat of violence against people to do so." She gives Mohandas Gandhi credit for developing the concept of civil resistance in his campaign against British colonialism in India. Among the tactics that constitute civil resistance are "strikes, protests, demonstrations, boycotts, [and] alternative institution building."[20]

GENDER AND INTERNATIONAL ORGANIZATIONS

Feminist critiques are not limited to the state, mainstream theories of international relations, and conceptions of security. International organizations and nongovernmental organizations, so often seemingly beloved by liberal scholars, have also come under scrutiny. The purpose of such work is to ask questions that have gone unasked and view such organizations from the perspective of gender.

One of the best-known IR feminist scholars working on these topics for many years is Sandra Whitworth. A recurrent theme of her work is how international organizations are part of complex political and social processes that aid in the construction of assumptions about the proper roles of women and men in the workforce. Early case studies involved the International Planned Parenthood Federation (IPPF) and the International Labour Organization (ILO).[21] The case studies examine how such organizations over time understood and organized their programs around shifting views of gender. How these understandings came to exist and how activists managed to influence their construction and redefinition is the main theme of the book. The underlying assumption is that such institutions are a reflection of the interests, norms, and ideas of hegemonic groups.

Whitworth's *Men, Militarism, and UN Peacekeeping*[22] brings gendered understanding to national participation in international organizations. As a professor at a Canadian university, she is all too well aware of the positive global image of UN peacekeepers in general and Canadian forces in particular. Widespread faith and a belief in the necessity of peacekeeping were reinforced

---

[19] Erica Chenoweth and Maria J. Stephan, *Why Civil Resistance Works* (New York: Columbia University Press, 2012).

[20] Erica Chenoweth, *Civil Resistance: What Everyone Needs to Know* (Oxford, UK: Oxford University Press, 2021), 1–2.

[21] Sandra Whitworth, *Feminism and International Relations: Towards a Political Economy of Gender in Interstate and Non-Governmental Institutions* (New York: St. Martin's Press, 1994).

[22] Sandra Whitworth, *Men, Militarism and UN Peacekeeping: A Gendered Analysis* (Boulder, CO: Lynne Rienner, 2004).

with the end of the Cold War and the dramatic expansion in the number of peacekeeping missions. Not only did the number increase, but the scope of the missions did as well. Mandates went beyond military and peacekeeping responsibilities to include also monitoring human rights, conducting elections, delivering aid, helping to repatriate refugees, and rebuilding state bureaucracies.

At a peacekeeping workshop sponsored by Canada's Department of National Defence, Whitworth was given three minutes to comment on the workshop proceedings. Her remarks were not about what had been discussed, but what had been ignored: Who benefits from peacekeeping operations? Who is excluded? What is the effect of peacekeeping operations on the local people? Audience reaction was silence. Problematizing the impact of peacekeeping operations on those most affected from Whitworth's feminist perspective was encouraged by disturbing press reporting that challenged blanket assertions that UN peacekeepers were in all cases selfless, benign soldiers. It is one thing to point to the actions of men in combat, but rather a unique approach to examine militarized masculinity from the perspective of peacekeeping missions. For soldiers involved in the latter operations, there is the seeming contradiction between what is generally regarded as appropriate masculine behavior inculcated from basic training onward to the demands of restricted weapons use and the ability to engage skillfully in community relations.

As Whitworth notes, in some cases states and even the UN tends to dismiss any information that contradicts the image of UN peacekeepers as altruistic and benign, preferring to view negative reports as merely isolated examples of "a few bad apples." But over time the United Nations and national governments have confronted the charges of sexual exploitation and physical violence against those who are supposed to be protected. Whitworth, however, argues that while attention to gender has made such concerns more visible within the UN, such critiques have had minimal impact on the actual UN way of doing business. In other words, by incorporating the language of gender into official UN policy, it ironically has had the effect of silencing criticism by ensuring that broader issues such as militarized masculinity do not end up on formal UN agendas.

Whitworth and other feminist scholars have addressed the empirical neglect of women and gender relations. In no small way they have contributed to the growth of transnational women's networks that have worked with sympathetic actors in states and international organization bureaucracies to effect policy changes. Amnesty International in 1990, for example, added gender to its list of forms of political persecution. As a result of media coverage of the Yugoslavian civil war in the 1990s and political pressure, rape is now considered a war crime under the Geneva Conventions Against War Crimes and, hence, can be prosecuted by the International Criminal Court.

GENDERED UNDERSTANDINGS AND IR THEORY

Feminists utilize gender as an interpretive lens through which to view international relations in general and IR theory in particular. With such a perspective, we become more aware of inequality and patterns of dominance, making us more sensitive to the discourse and concepts used to analyze international relations. As such, feminist scholarship offers a counterweight to masculinist understandings that are more prevalent in IR theories that emphasize power, balance of power, and instrumental rationality in the conduct of state and nonstate institutions and their agents.

It is not as if men are incapable of producing gendered analysis such as that done by Whitworth and her feminist colleagues any more than women cannot be hard-headed realists. Perhaps to be taken seriously in a still male-dominated world that extends as well to academic communities, it may be that many women seeking positions in public or university life have been forced to adopt what some feminist theorists have labeled masculinist understandings.

Our principal focus here, however, is on the interpretive understandings associated with gender. Gendered understandings lead us to be critical of theoretical work in international relations that masks the masculine or overlooks the feminine. Such a task can be done from a diverse series of perspectives although feminists tend to be more associated with liberal, postcolonial, constructivist, postmodern, or critical theory than with realism. Many liberal feminist theorists are also likely to see themselves comfortably within the positivist or scientific camp, merely introducing gender as an important albeit frequently overlooked or neglected explanatory factor in IR or other social-scientific work.

FEMINISTS AND THEIR CRITICS

What Critics?

Given the vigorous feminist critique of mainstream IR theorizing over the past several decades, one would expect a robust response. This has not been the case. Silence, not spirited rebuttal, more often has been the result. Perhaps the best way to interpret this lack of response is to note the lack of feminist work in the leading IR journals. One exception has been the British publication, *Review of International Studies.* Approaches compatible with feminism such as constructivism and even critical theory and postmodernism have received critiques, but feminist perspectives on international relations are usually an afterthought in such reviews. It is always possible that mainstream scholars often find feminist IR understandings, at least in terms of their own work, to be irrelevant, interesting but tangential, or dangerous to address for fear of being cast as an ignorant male "who just doesn't get it."

Research Program and Cumulative Knowledge

One early sympathetic observer of feminist literature is Robert O. Keohane, who called for dialogue across paradigms.[23] He claims that aspects of feminist understanding could fit comfortably under the neoliberal institutionalism research program. Indeed, what is missing is a feminist research program that could produce cumulative knowledge about international relations.

---

[23] Robert O. Keohane, "International Relations Theory: Contributions of a Feminist Standpoint," *Millennium* 18 (1989): 245–53.

What still stands today as the best rejoinder, not only to Keohane but also to mainstream theorists in general, is J. Ann Tickner's "You Just Don't Understand: Troubled Engagements between Feminist and IR Theorists."[24] It is all the more interesting as it was published in one of the major IR journals, *International Studies Quarterly*. Tickner notes that very often IR-trained feminists frequently encounter awkward silences when presenting academic papers at conferences. She raises the key question of whether the difficulty in cross-cultural conversations is essentially due to the very different realities, epistemologies, and research interests of feminists and mainstream IR scholars. Furthermore, she argues that these differences themselves are gendered, making communication all the more difficult.

In particular, conventional IR scholars (realists, neorealists, neoliberals, peace researchers, behavioralists, and empiricists committed to data-driven methods) misunderstand the feminist meaning of gender that emphasizes the socially constructed nature of gender and the fact that it embodies relationships of power inequality. Second, feminists and nonfeminists ontologically see different realities when they look at international politics. Feminists look at unequal social-power relations across the levels of analysis as opposed to a realist ontology in which supposedly rational, unified states are the most important players.

Finally, there is an epistemological divide for those feminists questioning the positivist approach to knowledge. Although committed to epistemological pluralism, many feminists are skeptical of methodologies that claim facts are neutral and prefer more historically based, interpretive understandings that raise the question of the extent to which gender roles and patriarchy are variable across time and space. The problem-solving framework of mainstream international relations implicitly accepts the given order in international relations, and feminists join with constructivists, critical theorists, and postmodernists to question this assumption.

REFERENCES[25]

Berry, Marie E. *War, Women and Power: From Violence to Mobilization in Rwanda and Bosnia Herzogovina.* Cambridge, UK: Cambridge University Press, 2018.

Chenoweth, Erica. *Civil Resistance: What Everyone Needs to Know.* Oxford, UK: Oxford University Press, 2021.

Chenoweth, Erica, and Maria J. Stephan. *Why Civil Resistance Works.* New York: Columbia University Press, 2012.

Chenoweth, Erica, and Zoe Marks. "Why Autocrats Fear Women." *Foreign Affairs* (March/April 2022): 103–16.

Elshtain, Jean Bethke. *Women and War.* New York: Basic Books, 1987.

Enloe, Cynthia. *Bananas, Beaches, and Bases: Making Feminist Sense of International Politics.* London: Pandora, 1989.

---

[24] J. Ann Tickner, "You Just Don't Understand: Troubled Engagements between Feminist and IR Theorists," *International Studies Quarterly* 41 (1997): 611–32.

[25] Oxford University Press has published dozens of books under the heading of "Oxford Studies in Gender and International Relations."

Goldstein, Joshua. *War and Gender: How Gender Shapes the War System and Vice Versa.* Cambridge, UK: Cambridge University Press, 2001.

Grant, Rebecca. "The Sources of Gender Bias in International Relations Theory." In *Gender and International Relations*, edited by Rebecca Grant and Kathleen Newland, 8–26. Bloomington: Indiana University Press, 1991.

Kaufman, Joyce P., and Kristen P. Williams. *Women at War, Women Building Peace: Challenging Gender Norms.* Boulder, CO: Kumarian Press, 2013.

Matfess, Hilary. *Women and the War on Boko Haram: Wives, Weapons, Witnesses.* London: Zed Books, 2017.

Parashar, Swati, J. Ann Tickner, and Jacqui True, eds. *Revisiting Gendered States: Feminist Imaginings of the State in International Relations.* Oxford, UK: Oxford University Press, 2018.

Peterson, V. Spike. *Global Gender Issues in the New Millennium.* 3rd ed. Boulder, CO: Westview Press, 2011.

Sjoberg, Laura. *Gendering Global Politics: Toward a Feminist Theory of War.* New York: Columbia University Press, 2013.

Stearns, Jill. *Gender and International Relations*, 3rd ed. Cambridge, UK: Polity Press, 2013.

Sylvester, Christine. *Feminist International Relations: An Unfinished Journey.* Cambridge, UK: Cambridge University Press, 2002.

Sylvester, Christine, and Laura Sjoberg, eds. *Feminism and International Relations: Conversations about the Past, Present, and Future.* New York: Routledge, 2011.

Tickner, J. Ann. *A Feminist Voyage through International Relations.* Oxford, UK: Oxford University Press, 2014.

———. "Why Women Can't Rule the World: International Politics According to Francis Fukuyama," *International Studies Review* 1, no. 3 (1999): 380–88.

True, Jacqui. *Gender, Globalization and Postsocialism: The Czech Republic after Communism.* New York: Columbia University Press, 2003.

Whitworth, Sandra. *Feminism and International Relations: Towards a Political Economy of Gender in Interstate and Non-Governmental Institutions.* New York: St. Martin's Press, 1994.

12

Green Theory and Environmental Understandings

★ ★ ★

"Green Theory" is an environmental lens through which we can view international relations and world politics. As such, it is not a *theory* in the way realists, liberals, economic structuralists, the English School (or we) use the term. It is an interpretive understanding of how the global environment impacts all human beings—not to mention plants, animals, and the physical world in which we live. The litany of concerns is well known: Extinction of species and collapsing fishing stocks as warming oceans accelerate with global climate change. A warming planet melts the polar ice caps and causes sea levels to rise, particularly problematic for islands and sea coasts. Extremes in weather patterns include increased number and intensity of tornadoes, hurricanes, cyclones, and typhoons. As parts of the planet warm and become drier, plants suffer, which poses a food security challenge. Droughts are indirectly the cause of wildfires. The speed by which climate change is occurring leaves precious little time to adapt to altered circumstances.

Atmospheric scientists tell us that ongoing carbon emissions (carbon dioxide, carbon monoxide, and methane) are the major (but not the only) cause of global climate change. Industrial production that depends on carbon fuels, burning or cutting forests that take in carbon dioxide from the atmosphere, melting tundra that has contained much carbon, massive agricultural use of fertilizers, the flatulence of cattle and other animals raised for food, and rotting food and other organic materials in garbage dumps are among the many sources of carbon emissions that create a "greenhouse" or heat-containing effect. Put another way, heat from the sun enters the atmosphere by day but is trapped by carbon dioxide and methane in the upper atmosphere, thus reducing the cooling that nighttime normally would affect.

There is a vast literature on the global environment dating back at least to the 1960s when the focus on economic development at any cost was subject to

385

much criticism. Rachel Carson's book *Silent Spring*[1] was a wake-up call on the loss of species and the adverse impact on human beings due to the widespread use of pesticides. Insensitivity to the environmental impact of economic development (pollution of land, air, waterways, and oceans) was the focus. In the mindset of policy makers, concern about the environment was more a domestic than a global matter calling for collective action. Only in the past few decades has the environment entered the international relations discourse.

Many consider global climate change as the number one international security concern. Global warming and its various consequences over time are an existential threat to life on the planet. This is quite apart from the concerns of environmental movements in the 1960s that raised the alarm about chemicals on land and in waterways and pollutants in the air over major cities. Environmental concerns are now truly seen as global, not simply restricted to discrete states or even regions. As a global collective-action problem, however, the challenges to achieving globally effective policies are truly daunting.

A major problem in terms of policy is that there is a fundamental asymmetry between those states who have contributed most to the problem of global warming (the capital-rich countries or "Global North") and those that have suffered the most (the capital-poor countries or *Global South*). The impact on Africa, for example, is particularly severe as global warming has contributed to food and nutrition insecurity with more than double the number of hungry persons than any other region of the world. As one study predicts:

> Life-threatening temperatures above 40°C are projected to increase by 10 to 140 days a year, depending on the scenario and region. The continent will see drier conditions in most regions, with more droughts but also more flooding. With the rise in sea level (as much as 0.9 meters by 2100 under high-warming scenarios) and more frequent flooding, a current 1-in-100-year flood event will become 1-in-10 or -20 years by 2050, and 1-in-5 years to annually by 2100, even under moderate warming.[2]

For their part, countries in the Global South—the extreme victims of global climate change—have been seeking financial compensation from Global North countries that, since the nineteenth-century industrial revolution, have been the principal cause of present-day global climate change.

For researchers and scholars interested in global politics, climate change was originally viewed by many as an international security issue as it may compound existing political and socioeconomic challenges. Migration induced by drought or typhoons can cause political instability and states may become involved in wars over such scarce resources as water. Fragile states intersect with environmental vulnerability as climate change and environmental degradation serve as threat multipliers that increase domestic and transnational security risks.

---

[1] Rachel Carson, *Silent Spring* (New York: Houghton Mifflin, 1962). See also Douglas Brinkley, *Silent Spring Revolution: John F. Kennedy, Rachel Carson, Lyndon Johnson, Richard Nixon, and the Great Environmental Awakening* (New York: Harper, 2022).
[2] Brookings, *Foresight Africa 2022*, https://www.brookings.edu/research/foresight-africa-2022/, chap. 4.

The International Committee of the Red Cross links climate change and environmental degradation to conflict and violence in the Global South. The UN Secretary-General adds that competition over scarce resources is responsible for some 40 percent of civil wars and conflicts over the last six decades.[3] Indeed, in the late eighteenth century, Thomas Malthus warned that population growth eventually would outstrip natural resources.[4] This pessimistic view was also central to thinking that there are limits to growth.[5]

Even the US Department of Defense has declared that climate change is a threat to US national security.[6] Melting in the Arctic Ocean opens the region to international competition for fishing, oil, gas, and other mineral resources with both allies (Canada) and adversaries (Russia). As a matter of policy, primary responsibility for the twelve-mile territorial waters off of Alaska rests with the US Coast Guard, and deep-sea waters beyond that limit with the US Navy. While traditional military threats and actions—such as Russia's invasion of Ukraine in 2022—are deliberate actions that can be pinpointed down to a specific date and specific actors, environmental challenges are often long term and slow to develop, with actual impacts subject to a debate involving a wide range of state and nonstate actors.

In this chapter are overviews of how the various perspectives on IR theory have viewed (or ignored) environmental issues. We begin with realism, liberalism, and the English School, which essentially seek to incorporate environmental issues into their respective worldviews. We then briefly address economic structuralism and then the interpretive understandings discussed in the preceding three chapters. As will become evident, so-called green theory has a strong affinity if not a basis in constructivist, critical theory, and feminist understandings.

UNDERSTANDING ENVIRONMENTAL CHALLENGES

Rationalist approaches one finds in realist, liberal, and English School accounts look scientifically for causes of undesirable outcomes and, using this knowledge, seek remedies that will reduce, if not eliminate, these adverse effects. In one form or another, carbon emissions into the atmosphere are causally related to acid rain, ozone layer depletion in the upper atmosphere, and global climate change: (a) exhausts from automobiles, trucks, buses, ships, aircraft, smokestacks, power plants burning fossil fuels and other sources combine with water in the atmosphere to form carbonic and other acids, raining upon forests and contributing to the death of trees—the greater acidity in lakes and streams adversely affecting fish and other wildlife; (b) chlorofluorocarbons (CFCs) from

---

[3] See "Special Report: Environment, Fragility and Conflict," https://foreignpolicy.com/2022/01/12/environment-fragility-and-conflict/?.

[4] See Thomas Robert Malthus, *An Essay on the Principle of Population and Other Writings*, ed. Robert Mayhew (London: Penguin Classics, 2015).

[5] See Denis L. Meadows, Jorgen Randers, and William W. Behrens, *The Limits to Growth* (London: Universe Books, 1972).

[6] "Climate change is reshaping the geostrategic, operational, and tactical environments with significant implications for U.S. national security and defense." *DoD Climate Risk Analysis*, October 2021.

spray cans, refrigerants, and other sources rise to the upper atmosphere and, through chemical reactions, deplete the stratospheric ozone layer that protects humans and other wildlife from skin cancer-causing exposure to direct sunlight; and (c) carbon dioxide, methane, and other "greenhouse" gases trap heat from the sun and cause global warming or, more broadly, climate change.

In his study of organizations, J. D. Thompson noted how uncertainties can make decision-making difficult for practitioners.[7] If we apply his insights to environmental problems like global warming, we find increasing certainty about devastating outcomes if we fail to reduce carbon emissions or do not find productive ways to remove carbon from the atmosphere. Emissions from industrial smokestacks, automobiles and trucks, aircraft, ships, livestock raised for slaughter, melting tundra, and forest and other fires are among the culprits. Clearing forests as in the Brazilian rain forest and other locations removes the recycling effect of trees and other plant life that take in and store carbon from the atmosphere and emit oxygen as part of their photosynthesis processes. Even though these causes are well known, there is still some uncertainty among atmospheric scientists about both the relative importance of different causes and the effectiveness of diverse remedies such as cutting emissions from one or another of the different sources or engaging in activities like massive tree-planting. Is developing technologies that directly remove carbon from the atmosphere an answer? To maximize the reduction of overall emissions, where should our emphasis be?

Quite apart from adverse economic impacts, uncertainty about possible remedies adds to the difficulty in forming a global political consensus on what is to be done, particularly because many of the proposed remedies are very costly. Although there have been numerous international conferences on climate change, progress has been very slow—some might say progress at a glacial pace. The asymmetry in levels of development among states party to any agreements adds to the difficulties of achieving consensus. Least developed, capital-poor countries are less inclined to submit to constraints on carbon emissions, particularly since they see global climate change as caused by earlier industrialization by capital-rich countries, not to mention their ongoing economic production and enormous amounts of carbon emissions that continue.

By contrast to global climate change, the scientific understanding of ozone-layer depletion caused by CFC emissions one finds in spray cans, refrigerators, air conditioners, and other sources has been far clearer, making a political consensus in the late 1980s on remedies much easier to achieve in what became the Montreal Protocol and the Vienna Convention, which aim to eliminate or substantially reduce CFC emissions. Somewhere in between global warming and ozone-layer depletion in terms of the degree of uncertainty is the case of increased acidification of precipitation. Carbon emissions have been blamed for increased amounts of acidification in the lower atmosphere—the cause of acid rain. Replacing fossil fuels with electricity ideally produced by such renewable sources as solar, wind, and geothermal is a remedy, but one that takes decades to implement.

---

[7] James D. Thompson, *Organizations in Action: Social Science Bases of Administrative Theory* (New York: McGraw-Hill, 1967).

Preferences Regarding Possible Outcomes

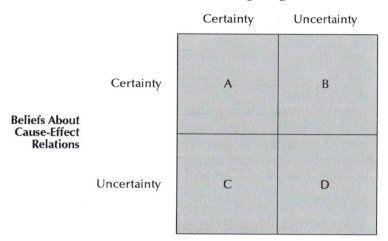

Figure 12.1 Decision-Making Matrix *Source:* J. D. Thompson, *Organizations in Action* (New York: McGraw-Hill, 1967), 134–35.

Thompson's matrix (figure 12.1) sheds light on these atmospheric environmental problems analytically on degrees of uncertainty as we explore building political consensus nationally and globally on appropriate remedies for global warming, ozone-layer depletion, and acid rain.

The primary problem in dealing with many global environmental global challenges, however, is not just the issue of a need for scientific consensus to achieve a plan of action. The problem is that many countries understandably have made economic development their primary goal. In countries with a large youth population with few prospects, creating jobs is a concern. Owners and managers of capital (OMC) also have a financial interest in economic growth. While the long-term effects of global environmental degradation are recognized, the challenges of the here and now are of immediate and often greater concern to policy makers.

IR THEORY PERSPECTIVES ON THE ENVIRONMENT

IR theory, as we have demonstrated, overwhelmingly focuses on conflict in general, and wars in particular. States are preeminent actors from the perspective of the four major images discussed. Climate change, however, does not always discriminate among states and state borders as the effects are felt across the globe, albeit unevenly. Sovereign political borders are a mismatch with the global ecological system. Due to differential impact, dealing with climate change is an example of a collective action, a global governance problem.

This was highlighted in 1968 by the ecologist Garrett Hardin's discussion of the "Tragedy of the Commons."[8] In this scenario individuals (herdsmen) have

---

[8] Garrett Hardin, "The Tragedy of the Commons," *Science* 13 (December 1968): 1243–48.

access to a shared resource such as pasture land in a village ("the commons"). It is rational from the perspective of short-term self-interest to allow one's sheep to graze on the commons. But if everyone does the same thing at the same time, overgrazing occurs, ultimately depleting the resource. Everyone loses in the long term.

It is analogous to Rousseau's stag hunt fable discussed in chapter 5 on realism in which by following one's narrow self-interest, everyone eventually suffers. To put it in economic and IR theory terms, the solution to a collective-action problem is to design a policy that leads people (or states) to agree to upgrade the common interest to the benefit of all over the long haul. For most realists and liberals, states (or the international organizations of which they are a part) remain the starting point for finding answers and solutions while others see states as a major stumbling block and indeed a cause of ecological problems.

Realist theorists have tended not to focus their attention on climate change. This is perhaps not surprising as threats traditionally emanate from states, not from nature. Even resource scarcity is viewed from the prism of state competition and becomes important when it subtracts from or adds to a state's material power. In a world in which relative gains matter, for example, it is rational for a state to secure as much energy as possible even when it comes from oil, gas, and coal pollutants. Striving for independent energy security, in other words, trumps concern for the global environment. As many European states learned after the Russian invasion of Ukraine in 2022, energy dependence on Russia was a source of security vulnerability. Similarly, as harsh as it may sound, if a state rival suffers from devastating drought or some other form of catastrophic climate event, this might enhance the relative power of a competitor state—a matter of concern to realists.

It is not hard to figure out what the realist position would be on climate change. If it is to be slowed, if not halted, states will have to take the lead, typically in the international organizations in which they play a major role. As such, states ultimately will have to find a way to upgrade their common interest and solve the collective-action problem, whether framed as the tragedy of the commons or as players in the stag hunt analogy. International organizations, as realists note, are ultimately controlled by member states and hence will reflect state interests, particularly those of more powerful states. So much the better if nongovernmental organizations also lobby for green policies and private-sector companies contribute to technological breakthroughs that reduce a state's dependence on foreign sources of energy.

What about realist power-based regime theory discussed in chapter 6? One of the best-known realist regime theories is hegemonic stability. Regimes (for example, agreed rules that constitute a global climate regime) are established and maintained when a single state holds a preponderance of power resources. But once a dominant state's hegemonic power declines in relative power as other states rise, it may not have the same capacity to lead and, consequently, the regimes in which it has played a dominant role may decline and, with it, the collective efforts on the part of states.

As some realists argued, the post–Cold War unipolar "moment" of the United States was destined to devolve into a multipolar world, the lack of such leadership (or hegemony) undermining prospects for a strong global climate regime. As one might expect, liberals—particularly liberal institutionalists—are more optimistic about the prospects of international efforts and collaboration when it comes to tackling such global environmental problems as climate change. The liberalism literature on global civil society, transnationalism, interdependence, international regimes, neoliberal institutionalism, and global governance (chapter 6) provides a plethora of potentially useful concepts and hypotheses to analyze the collective-action problem. Liberals assume that states, while the major actors in world politics, are not the only ones. Nonstate, transnational actors are important as well including international organizations, transnational organizations, influential individuals, and norms that have emerged over the decades to address such global problems as climate change.[9]

In the late 1980s a conceptual framework for dealing with the environment was developed under the concept of "sustainable development," which essentially resulted from a series of compromises between the capital-rich Global North and those in the capital-poorer Global South. For years the Global South claimed the north, after having polluted and exploited the environment, now wanted the south to forgo economic policies that harmed the global environment. The idea behind sustainable development was to legitimate economic development in the south in the context of environmental protection; both could be achieved and not at the expense of one or the other. Given liberal interest in both economic and environmental regimes, sustainable development was a popular concept for these scholars.

Even a brief perusal of the contents of the journal *International Organization* over the past thirty years will reveal the interest of liberal scholars of different generations trying to understand the challenge of achieving cooperation in the global commons and the complex interactions among various international regimes.[10] Neoliberal institutionalists in particular utilize rigorous methodologies to address basic research questions concerning the environment to include under what conditions do states tend to support international regimes and why do some states defect?

As noted earlier, whatever differences might exist between realists and liberals, they share a basic rationalist approach to understanding international relations. The same can be said for most of the work by the English School, given its straddling the lines between realism and liberalism. The English School was a latecomer to the topic of environmentalism, but in recent years has incorporated

---

[9] See, for example, Ronnie D. Lipschutz, *Global Civil Society and Global Environmental Governance* (Albany: State University of New York Press, 1996). For overviews of various transnational actors and regimes, see Robert Falkner, *The Handbook of Global Climate and Environment Policy* (New York: Wiley, 2013).

[10] For example, the seminal 1992 collection of articles exploring the concept of epistemic communities contained several essays on climate change: *International Organization* 46, no. 1 (1992). See also Robert O. Keohane and David G. Victor, "The Regime Complex for Climate Change," *Perspectives on Politics* 9, no. 1 (March 2011): 7–23. And more recently, see Amanda Kennard, "The Enemy of My Enemy: When Firms Support Climate Change Regulation," *International Organization* 74, no. 2 (2020): 187–221.

the topic into its framework of international or world society. The key questions are what impact has global environmentalism had on world society? How can one reconcile the tension between global environmental responsibility and justice on the one hand with sovereignty, international law, and the global market on the other?

The rise of environmental ethics and values within the society of states promoted by environmentalists has influenced the development of what could be called a guardianship norm in international society. The idea has been implanted in the minds of state leaders that they are responsible (or should feel guilty if they are not) stewards of the planet. At a minimum, states have come to accept environmental multilateralism as a procedural norm within international organizations, but barriers to deep-seated change continue to exist.[11] After years of pressure by states in the Global South, capital-rich countries finally have agreed to establish a fund to compensate them for some of the costs or losses sustained due to global climate change. Advocates applaud the creation of the fund, but important details on the size of the fund, the amounts to be contributed by particular states, and how the money will be distributed remain undecided.

Economic structuralists not surprisingly see the environment as yet another example of capitalist exploitation—the environment is a source of material power and wealth, not a concern for the welfare of human beings.[12] During European global expansion, not only was economic development uneven, but so, too, was environmental degradation. The postcolonialism literature in particular (chapter 7), which also reflects the influence of critical theory and postmodern critiques (chapter 10), has developed the concept of *postcolonial ecocriticism*. This concept is an umbrella term for several topics including gender, justice, and the differential impact of globalization.[13]

As for social constructivism, its focus on the development of norms understandably has had a major impact on many scholars working on global environmental issues, particularly liberals and economic structuralists. With its challenge to positivism and the argument that scientific knowledge is constructed, the prospects for cooperation among states are not simply defined by material power but also by ideational elements and intersubjective agreement among actors (state as well nonstate). If state interests and identity are not merely givens, but rather are constructed due to the assumption of human agency, then it is logically possible that policies can be designed to enhance the

---

[11] Robert Jackson, *The Global Covenant: Human Conduct in a World of States* (Oxford: Oxford University Press, 2003). And see also Robert Falkner, "English School Theory and Global Environmental Politics," *Environmentalism and Global International Society*, ed. Robert Falkner (Cambridge: Cambridge University Press, 2021), 15–34.

[12] Mary Lyn Stoll, "Environmental Colonialism," in *The SAGE Encyclopedia of Business Ethics and Society*, ed. Robert Kolb (Thousand Oaks, CA: SAGE, 2018). Guillaume Blanc argues that conservation organizations have little regard for the welfare of the people of Africa, preferring to focus on the need to protect a supposedly pristine natural world. Guillaume Blanc, *The Invention of Green Colonialism* (Cambridge, UK: Polity, 2022).

[13] Dana Mount and Susie O'Brien, "Postcolonialism and the Environment," *Oxford Handbook of Postcolonial Studies*, ed. Graham Huggan (Oxford: Oxford University Press, 2013), 521–59.

global public good in the environmental realm, expanding global governance on such matters.

The problem, however, is that while there might be a growing consensus among scientists and policy experts concerning the threat of climate change, domestic politics can be a barrier to significant change both at home and internationally. In many countries, like the United States, one's position on climate change is strongly associated with one's political affiliation. Scientific evidence and policy expertise have a difficult job overcoming anti-environmental political ideology, given the allegiance to one's political affiliation.

The modern feminist movement in the West emerged in the 1970s and 1980s, roughly the same time as the environmental movement. The concept of "ecofeminism" brings these two movements together and adds the assumption of capitalist exploitation, particularly involving the Global South. The hierarchical economic order under capitalism is combined with a patriarchal understanding of the world resulting in a series of binaries—man/women, humans/nature, exploiters/exploited. The white, male, "human" subject dominates and is in opposition to the rest who are categorized as the "other/s."

As one author argues:

> The climate crisis is not gender neutral. Climate change is a powerful "threat multiplier," making existing vulnerabilities and injustices worse. Especially under conditions of poverty, women and girls face greater risk of displacement or death from extreme weather disasters. . . . There is growing proof of the link between climate change and gender-based violence, including sexual assault, domestic abuse, and forced prostitution. Tasks core to survival, such as collecting water and wood or growing food, fall on female shoulders in many cultures. These are already challenging and time-consuming activities; climate change can deepen the burden, and with it struggles for health, education, and financial security.[14]

Empirically documenting these impacts and disparities is required and a vast literature has been produced over the years. Moral clarity, empathy, and action, however, are also required. So as with the case of environmentalism, for ecofeminists there is also a strong normative, policy-oriented focus and agenda.

GREEN THEORY

As with the other approaches to IR theory discussed in this book, in practice "green theory" covers a multitude of diverse approaches. Some fall within the social science canon and seek to derive empirically testable hypotheses—"green theory" from a positivist or rationalist perspective. Extensive work has been done, for example, on the diffusion of innovative environmental policy among states and the role of domestic actors. It is fair to generalize, however, that most of the green literature that is labeled "green theory" can be more appropriately

---

[14] Ayana Elizabeth Johnson and Katharine K. Wilkinson, eds., *All We Can Save: Truth, Courage, and Solutions for the Climate Crisis* (New York: One World, 2020), xviii.

categorized as interpretive understandings, drawing on critical theory and constructivism and hence in opposition to the more rationalist realist and liberal approaches. To greater or lesser extent, all such authors embrace a normative concern and seek to provide some degree of policy guidance, and could, therefore, also fit comfortably in the following chapter on normative IR theory.[15]

At the highest level of abstraction, some green theorists suggest a radical change in mindset is required to deal with the environment broadly conceived. Anthropogenic climate change—meaning caused by humans—does not simply have an impact on human societies, although this is the primary concern. A truly ecological perspective would take into account the interests of nature itself—not just humans, but also the plant and animal kingdoms and the physical world in which they live and thrive. This is more than the traditional theologically tinged view that humanity has to take seriously its "stewardship" of Nature (with a capital N) as Nature is God's creation. It requires us to go beyond the traditional human/nature dichotomy and instead take seriously the idea of a symbiosis between the two. Some green theorists would go a step further and adopt an ecocentrist perspective that prioritizes the environment as without a healthy global ecosystem, human well-being is increasingly problematical, if not impossible.

Hence it would be fair to say that green theory, for the most part, belongs to the critical theory and constructivist traditions. Environmental concerns, if not impending ecological disaster, raise a host of questions, not the least of which is how do we think about or conceptualize international relations? From a green perspective, for example, the concept of an anarchic system of states should be viewed within a broader context of the Earth's biosphere—an additional, if not higher level of analysis encompassing not only states but the English School's focus on world society. From this systems perspective, the impact of climate change on the natural world requires a critical examination of the constructed norm of state sovereignty. Can states continue to claim the sovereign right to pollute within their borders when the effects transcend borders; that is, when effects are imposed on others, the problem of negative *externalities*? What does sovereignty mean in a world where small, low-lying islands such as the Maldives are threatened with physical extinction? How might shifting shorelines impact agreements under the United Nations Law of the Sea concerning territorial waters and maritime claims? If coastlines change, won't maritime boundaries have to change as well? What would this mean for international law?[16]

Given green theory's critical perspective on state sovereignty, it logically follows that many scholars also embrace the idea of an expanded notion of political community that transcends state borders. One possible consequence of this broader perspective is to question the relentless production and consumption of goods that meet immediate needs and desires but is at the cost

---

[15] On varieties of green political thinking, see Andrew Dobson and Robyn Eckersley, eds., *Political Theory and the Ecological Challenge* (Cambridge: Cambridge University Press, 2006).

[16] Maxine Burkitt, "The Nation Ex-Situ: On Climate Change, Deterritorialized Nationhood and the Post-Climate Era," *Climate Law* 2, no. 3 (2008): 345–74.

of the environment and long-term ecological sustainability required for life on earth. As such, continuing material consumption and exploitation of the earth's resources gives rise not only to instrumental questions concerning politics and economics but also from a broader communitarian or global perspective moral or normative questions. For example, shouldn't we consider placing greater limits on individual choice due to long-term concerns for the global environment and, in turn, humanity? Such a view would be at odds with the prevailing liberal assumption that emphasizes the autonomy of the individual. Similarly, what about global environmental justice? Green theorists readily express normative concerns for those individuals, particularly in the Global South, whose voices are unheard or ignored in the corridors of power whether local, national, or international.

GREEN THEORY AND THEIR CRITICS

As we noted in chapter 11, critics of feminist thought are hard to find; silence tends to be the norm. It is similar in the case of green theory. Who would wish to make the case that concerns over the environment and the future of the planet are overblown? Even the conservative British news magazine *The Economist* has been covering climate change for years and produces a newsletter on climate-related issues. One does not have to read, however, the Intergovernmental Panel on Climate Change (IPCC) reports or specialized newsletters but only has to peruse the daily news for discussion of extreme weather patterns, wildfires, droughts, crop failures, floods, typhoons, and tornadoes. What was termed earlier an "inconvenient truth"[17] about environmental degradation is now a concrete threat to life as we know it.

As noted earlier, one can at least infer a critique of green theory from the basic tenets of more mainstream perspectives on IR theory such as realism and liberalism. To reiterate: concerns over the climate and the environment are certainly recognized. But to address these challenges, even if they are viewed as existential challenges, will be achieved through the existing state system—not just states, but also the international organizations to which they belong. Dealing with the environment as a collective action problem certainly also involves nongovernmental actors and the role of scientific *epistemic communities* as epitomized by the experts who comprise the IPCC.

Insisting on the desperate need for some sort of global shift in consciousness to an ecocentric, green perspective due to the dangers to the global environment is a hard sell to those focused on short-term economic and other gains—the here and now. That leaves us with an incremental approach, however halting and dissatisfying that might be. States remain the preeminent actors and will continue to address collective action challenges through the prism of calculations of self-interest. Perhaps it will take some catastrophic climate event to change such calculations. But for many green theorists and environmentalists in general, at that point, the planet may be beyond recovery.

---

[17] Al Gore, *An Inconvenient Truth: The Crisis of Global Warming* (Emmaus, PA: Rodale Press, 2006).

REFERENCES

Brinkley, Douglas. *Silent Spring Revolution: John F. Kennedy, Rachel Carson, Lyndon Johnson, Richard Nixon, and the Great Environmental Awakening*. New York: Harper, 2022.

Carson, Rachel. *Silent Spring*. New York: Houghton Mifflin, 1962.

Christoff, Peter, and Robyn Eckersley. *Globalization and the Environment*. Lanham, MD: Rowman & Littlefield, 2013.

Clapp, Jennifer, and Peter Dauvergne. *Paths to a Green World*. Cambridge, MA: MIT Press, 2011.

Dobson, Andrew, and Robyn Eckersley, eds. *Political Theory and the Ecological Challenge*. Cambridge, UK: Cambridge University Press, 2006.

Eckersley, Robyn. *The Green State: Rethinking Democracy and Sovereignty*. Cambridge MA: MIT Press, 2004.

Falkner, Robert. *Environmentalism and Global International Society*. Cambridge, UK: Cambridge University Press, 2021.

———. *The Handbook of Global Climate and Environment Policy*. New York: Wiley, 2013.

Goodin, Robert E. *Green Political Theory*. Cambridge, UK: Polity Press, 1992.

Gore, Al. *An Inconvenient Truth: The Crisis of Global Warming*. Emmaus, PA: Rodale Press, 2006.

Huggan, Andrew, and Helen Tiffin. *Postcolonial Ecocriticism: Literature, Animals, Environment*. 2nd ed. London: Routledge, 2015.

Jackson, Robert. *The Global Covenant: Human Conduct in a World of States*. Oxford, UK: Oxford University Press, 2003.

Johnson, Ayana Elizabeth, and Katharine K. Wilkinson, eds. *All We Can Save: Truth, Courage, and Solutions for the Climate Crisis*. New York: One World, 2020.

Lipschutz, Ronnie D. *Global Civil Society and Global Environmental Governance*. Albany: State University of New York Press, 1996.

Malthus, Thomas Robert. *An Essay on the Principle of Population and Other Writings*. Edited by Robert Mayhew. London: Penguin Classics, 2015.

McDonald, Matt. *Security, the Environment, and Emancipation*. London: Routledge, 2011.

Meadows, Denis L., Jorgen Randers, and William W. Behrens. *The Limits to Growth*. London: Universe Books, 1972.

Napikoski, Linda. "Top 10 Books about Ecofeminism." ThoughtCo, February 16, 2021, thoughtco.com/10-books-about-ecofeminism-3528842.

Newell, Peter. *Globalization and the Environment: Capitalism, Ecology and Power*. Cambridge, UK: Polity Press, 2012.

Newell, Peter, and Matthew Paterson. *Climate Capitalism: Global Warming and the Transformation of the Global Economy*. Cambridge: Cambridge University Press, 2010.

Okereke, Chukwumerige. *Global Justice and Neoliberal Environmental Governance*. London: Routledge, 2008.

Schlosberg, David. *Defining Environmental Justice*. Oxford: Oxford University Press, 2007.

Thompson, James D. *Organizations in Action: Social Science Bases of Administrative Theory*. New York: McGraw-Hill, 1967.

Wapner, Paul. *Environmental Activism and World Civic Politics*. Albany: State University of New York Press, 1996.

13

Normative IR Theory: Ethics and Morality

Normative theory has deep roots in the works discussed in parts II and III. In this chapter we discuss the role of normative theory in international relations, important contributors to this literature, and the challenge of applying normative concerns to actual foreign policy choices. The intellectual traditions underlying the IR field as a whole are a blend of normative (what *should* be the case?) and empirical questions (what *is* the case?). For writers as divergent as Niccolò Machiavelli, Hugo Grotius, Immanuel Kant, E. H. Carr, or Karl Marx, it was inconceivable to discuss politics without at least some attention to the relation between facts and values. The two were thought by them to be inseparable, although they differed on the relative importance of each. Constructivists, critical theorists, postmodernists, feminists, and green theorists necessarily incorporate normative considerations within the subjectivities and intersubjectivities that define their interpretive understandings. The examination of socially constructed norms or rules that have guided actual conduct in international relations often rests on or is buttressed by normative theories that contribute to their legitimacy or acceptance over time. The law of war, intervention, norms on distributive justice, human rights, and humanitarian law all relate to the domain of normative theory.

NORMS, ETHICS, AND MORALITY

Philosophers differ on what is meant by norms, morality, and ethics.[1] For our purposes in the context of IR theory, what they have in common is that they

---

[1] We use the terms *normative, moral, ethics,* and *value* interchangeably. Morality in other contexts is sometimes viewed narrowly as the religious principle of a particular tradition, group, or individual. Ethics can be viewed as either the philosophical study of moral questions or merely a decidedly secular word for morality. Some normative considerations are nonmoral values, as when an artist uses the terms *ought* and *right* in an aesthetic context that does not have the moral content usually associated with these words.

all prescribe what the world should be and what ought to be right conduct. Explicit in this conception is the idea that norms might require people, states, or international and transnational actors to act in ways that may not promote the actor's narrow understanding of its self-interest.

Issues central to an understanding of normative international relations theory are profound. When, if ever, is war just, and what is just conduct in war? Are there universally understood *human rights*? On what grounds are armed or other forms of intervention legitimate? On what moral bases should those in authority make foreign policy choices? Over the centuries, many IR theorists have grappled with such normative questions. We want here only to alert the readers to some of the most critical of these.

We also want to recognize normative IR theory building as a legitimate enterprise worthy of more scholarly efforts. As discussed in chapter 1, normative theory differs fundamentally from empirical theory. Propositions in normative theory that deal with what ought to be are not subject to the formal empirical tests of hypotheses about what is, which is the realm of empirical theory. Normative theory is informed by human experience of war, peace, human rights, and other questions. Arguments made on such matters in normative theory are, of course, still subject to the same canons of logic that also apply in empirical theory. Critical thinking about any truth claim involves an assessment of whether the argument is logical and whether the facts brought to bear by the theorist hold up under scrutiny.

Values are at the core of normative theory, but value orientations are also present among empirical theorists in all four IR images we identify in chapters 5–8. What is studied and how it is studied are preferences that vary from theorist to theorist. Although empirical theorists as *positivists* (see chapter 10) try to minimize the effect of individual value bias through objective testing of hypotheses, personal values cannot be filtered out completely. Values are somewhat less problematic in social constructivism, critical theory, postmodernism, feminism, and green theory (chapters 9–12) as they are central to interpretive understandings.

Finally, normative IR theory is important, if not inescapable, in the realm of foreign or international policy. Policy-making is all about making choices. Choices among competing alternatives made by policy makers are informed not just by knowledge of what is or could be the possible outcome of a decision, but also by a rationale for what ought to be. Developing the bases for such choices is the domain of normative theory.

NORMATIVE THEORY: ALTERNATIVE PERSPECTIVES

The Levels of Analysis

There are differing perspectives on how to approach a discussion of normative theory and international relations. One way of looking at this is in terms of the *levels of analysis*—the individual, the community, state and society, regions or cultural areas, and the world as a whole. In terms of the individual, the simple yet important question is this: Do we have duties beyond borders? Particularly in an era of globalization, how might we live in a world threatened by not only weapons of mass destruction but also water and food shortages, pandemics, global climate change, and other challenges within and outside of the borders of states?

The national or community position on norms holds that obligations to fellow citizens take priority over those of strangers living in other nations, states, or cultures. The attempt to develop and justify normative universal criteria is questionable from this perspective. This does not mean, however, that states are unable to come to common agreement in certain areas. In fact, international law provides bases for states to respect one another's autonomy. Furthermore, the idea that there is a pluralism of values among societies or groups does not mean there is no basis for criticizing, for example, the abuse of human rights.

A third perspective—and our major focus in this chapter—concerns universal or cosmopolitan normative theorizing. This dates back to the Stoics and natural law thinking, Kantian moral imperatives, utilitarian principles, and social-contract bases for moral choice.

Moral Relativism

Universal or cosmopolitan perspectives are in direct conflict with the idea of *moral relativism*, which holds that no universal standard exists by which to assess an ethical proposition's truth. If we believe, however, in a strict moral relativism—that values and rights can have no independent standing of their own—then we are saying in effect that there is no such thing as morality or ethics.

One significant problem with moral relativism is that it gives us no universal basis for condemning atrocities and such human tragedies as the Holocaust and other acts of genocide. Just because eliminating the Jews as a people may have been considered legitimate within a Nazi political subculture, this belief did not make it right. Even if we have difficulty agreeing on many other values, genocide is so offensive to the human spirit that it is condemned as mass murder on universal, not just on particular cultural grounds. Any rational human being, regardless of cultural origin, should understand the immorality of such atrocities.

What about a religious basis for universal human rights? Islam, Christianity, Judaism, Hinduism, Buddhism, and other religions typically do not just limit themselves to their followers, but frequently also make universally applicable moral claims. As a practical matter, rejection of religion by some and the absence of theological consensus even among the followers of various religious groups prevent us from using particular religions as the solitary bases for common, worldwide acceptance of human rights and other moral claims. Instead, many writers have tried to identify secular or nonreligious bases for their universalist positions to which we now turn.

Secular Bases for Moral or Ethical Choice

Stoics

As discussed in chapter 2, the Stoics argue that we are all part of a larger community of humankind, regardless of our different political communities and cultures. The ability to reason is a quality shared by all humans, and this makes it possible for us to determine the laws of nature that apply to all regardless of the community in which one lives. Stoic ideas were very influential in republican and imperial Rome. For example, the Roman orator Cicero (106–43 BCE) states that "true law is right reason in agreement with nature; it is of universal application, unchanging and everlasting." He asserts: "Justice is one; it binds all society, and is based on one law." Indeed, he claims: "Justice does not exist at all if it does not exist in Nature."[2]

This universalism was the basis for the idea of law common to the nations of the Roman empire—a law of the peoples or, in Latin, a *jus gentium*. That values transcend a single community or state was also central to the thought of St. Augustine, Thomas Aquinas, and other religious writers of the Middle Ages. As discussed in previous chapters, Grotius and others would contribute to a secular basis for international law—whether based on general principles consistent with reasoned understanding of *natural law*, customary international practice, the writings of jurists (as in decisions rendered by judges or justices), or commitments in treaties or conventions voluntarily undertaken by states. These are the four generally accepted sources of international law. Similarly, natural law thinking played an important role in the social-contract theories of Thomas Hobbes and John Locke.

Kant

Immanuel Kant (1724–1804), whose work has already been mentioned in earlier chapters, has us use our rational faculty to look inward. The moral element is captured by the oft-quoted phrase of one standing alone at night and looking upward reflectively at "the starry sky above me and the moral law within me." This vision of the universal transcends space and time and yet can be discovered within oneself. Because this inherent sense of right and wrong stems from one's *ontology*—the worldview a person has or how one internally sees or understands the essence of things—the Kantian approach to ethics is often referred to as deontological. The term is derived from the Greek *deont* (being necessary). One can know through reason what is right and she or he is, following Kant, duty bound to follow that imperative.

Kant is best known for his writings on reason with direct application to discovering universal maxims or ethical imperatives we are duty bound to follow not just in our private lives, but also in the positions we may hold in our public lives. For Kant, a fundamental principle is to act always so that you respect every human being as a rational, thinking agent capable of choice. According to Kant, the individual has free will to choose the correct moral course, clearly a *voluntarist* position. Individual behavior is not predetermined, but the individual is obligated, nevertheless, to follow the moral law that is discoverable through the proper exercise of reason.

Kant believed one should exercise free will and act according to the *categorical imperative*—independent of contingencies—whereby one acts "according to

---

[2] See, for example, Cicero, "'The Republic' and 'The Laws,'" in *Great Political Thinkers*, 4th ed., ed. William Ebenstein (New York: Holt, Rinehart and Winston, 1969), 136–38.

the maxim which you can at the same time will to be a universal law." Moreover, one should "treat humanity, in your own person, and in the person of everyone else as an end as well as a means, never merely as a means." Put another way, we are to treat other human beings as ends worthy in themselves, not just as means. Finally, the correct prescription for a moral conduct is knowable by the individual and amounts to those precepts that have universally binding character.[3]

It is this universal dimension in Kantian ethics that is also the basis for his thinking on international relations. Kant addresses war and peace in *international society*, looking toward an improvement in state behaviors among liberal republics that would make them decidedly less prone to use force against other states—in effect, a *democratic peace* (see the discussion in chapter 6). The Kantian ideal is indeed a future, cosmopolitan international society of individuals, states, or other actors following ethical principles and aiming toward perfection. In other words, right reason is to be used to discern obligations stemming from universal law that transcends the laws made by individual states. This was to be the path toward "perpetual peace"—a world free of war. A federation of peaceful states could (but would not necessarily) come to be established as a response to the very real security needs of states.

Utilitarians

In contrast to Kantian ethics, the writings of Jeremy Bentham (1748–1832), John Stuart Mill (1806–1873), and others focus on attaining the greatest good for the greatest number as the principal criterion of *utilitarian* thought. We should be concerned with assessing outcomes or the consequences of our actions. A society is rightly ordered, according to utilitarians, if "its major institutions are arranged so as to achieve the greatest net balance of satisfaction."[4] Utilitarians take this abstract principle and apply it to a wide range of human circumstances, including a defense of liberty and other human rights as representing the greatest good for the greatest number. The main application of utilitarian principles is to be within domestic societies. In principle, however, utilitarian and Kantian criteria provide a philosophical basis for international law because the application of these criteria transcends the boundaries of any given state or society. In practice, of course, we face enormous obstacles trying to apply either Kantian or utilitarian ethics as the basis for constructing some radically new and just world order, given the present division of the world into separate, sovereign states with very different perspectives on global issues.

Social-Contract Theorists

The question of the scope of justice is an issue dating back to the beginning of philosophy. Should conceptions of justice have boundaries, limiting it to

---

[3] Immanuel Kant, *Foundations of the Metaphysics of Morals*, trans. Lewis White Beck (Indianapolis, IN: Bobbs-Merrill, 1959), 66–67. The literature on Kant is vast, and no attempt is made to summarize it here. We are particularly drawn, however, to the late Hannah Arendt's *Lectures on Kant's Political Philosophy* (Chicago: University of Chicago Press, 1982).

[4] See John Rawls, *A Theory of Justice* (Cambridge, MA: Harvard University Press, 1971), 22.

particular societies or cultures? Or is justice by nature universal and cosmopolitan? *Social-contract* theorists are of interest to normative IR theory as they begin with the domestic question of justice and have provided insight into the expansion of such normative concerns to international politics.

The social-contract approach as a guide to right behavior assumes that individuals may voluntarily agree to bind or obligate themselves to some set of principles. The challenge is explaining how this might come about. In Jean-Jacques Rousseau's stag hunt analogy discussed in chapters 5 and 6, the hunters in a state of nature can be understood as maximizing individual, short-term self-interest by going for the hare. In a world with no sovereign authority to compel collaboration or to force the honoring of contracts, no other outcome can be expected. For Thomas Hobbes, escaping the state of nature can only be achieved by the people elevating a sovereign—whether a monarch or legislature—to provide the order and security that comes from governance.

Although Hobbes finds a way out of a figurative state of nature for domestic politics, he sees no such social-contract remedy to resolve the problems of cooperation among states existing in an anarchic international system. As noted by English School theorists and some constructivists, however, different assumptions about the state of nature result in different prospects for international collaboration.

The seventeenth-century English writer John Locke reasoned that human beings have certain *natural rights* to life, liberty, and property, which they surrender only as part of a social contract. The notion among social-contract theorists that, quite apart from the cultural context, human beings have rights as part of their nature obviously provides another secular ground for making universalistic moral claims. To Locke (and to Thomas Jefferson who followed Locke's lead), human rights are thus part of human nature. The citizenry or people who empower governments in the first place must therefore strictly limit the authority of governments to abridge them. Governments are created in part to guarantee certain civil rights, which are those rights that individuals have as members of the societies to which they belong. This conception can be applied to the domestic as well as the international levels of analysis.

Building on this social-contract approach as a means to finding justice within a society, John Rawls (1921–2002) asks what would be considered fair if individuals were in a state of nature and none knew in advance what one's place in society, class position, wealth, or social status would be. Behind this common "veil of ignorance" about outcomes, what principles of distributive justice would these hypothetically free agents choose?

One principle taken from Rawls's analysis is that "all social values—liberty and opportunity, income and wealth, and the bases of self-respect—are to be distributed equally unless an unequal distribution of any, or all, of these values is to everyone's advantage." Beyond that, socioeconomic inequality is admissible only if it benefits everyone in society and if there is an equal opportunity for everyone to acquire those positions associated with unequal rewards.

Whether one extends such propositions as the basis for global justice for individuals or for states as if they are individuals is not altogether clear in Rawls's now classic *A Theory of Justice.* In that volume he formulates a "conception of justice for the basic structure of society," observing that "the conditions for the law of nations may require different principles arrived at in a somewhat different way."[5]

In his later work, however, Rawls takes up this challenge by exploring the ways and means of extending a "law of peoples" that transcends the borders of states and their respective societies. The idea of constructing an international or global society logically calls for the application of universal norms. Similar to the intended universal applicability of the Roman law of peoples (or, in Latin, the *jus gentium*), he finds that behind a veil of ignorance "a well ordered non-liberal society" or authoritarian regime in our times "will accept the same law of peoples that well ordered liberal societies accept."[6] Not surprisingly, he finds the fabric of this law in the liberal understandings of human rights, freedom, independence, and nonintervention.

If one allows social-contract theory to be applied to states as if they were individual persons, it becomes a basis for a positivist (in the legal, not epistemological sense) interpretation of international law. Among positivists, international law and the obligation to follow other international rules or norms stem not from natural law or natural rights, but rather from affirmative actions taken by states. Kantian, utilitarian, or other principles may be part of the calculus of deciding which rules are to be made binding, but it is the voluntary contract, or choice, made by states in the form of a treaty, convention, or customary practice (so routine in performance as to amount to an implicit contract) that creates the obligation.

Norms, morality, and ethics, therefore, are not new to the study of international relations. They may be addressed in terms of right reason to discern obligations stemming from some aspect of natural law or provide the greatest good for the greatest number under utilitarian reasoning. Alternatively, they may conform more closely to a positivist approach to constructing international law—that treaties, for example, are binding and that such obligations ought to be kept. The Kantian perspective in particular contrasts sharply with the views of Machiavelli and Hobbes. Although concerns for moral choices certainly are present in classical realism, power and the balance of power have clearly been the more important considerations in this tradition. It is, however, incorrect to view power and values as if they were mutually exclusive approaches to international politics. As E. H. Carr, an intellectual precursor in the realist tradition and of the English School, has observed:

> The utopian who dreams that it is possible to eliminate self-assertion from politics and to base a political system on morality alone is just as wide of the mark as the realist who believes that altruism is an illusion and that all political action is self-seeking.[7]

---

[5] Rawls, *Theory of Justice*, 62, 8, respectively.

[6] See John Rawls's lecture on "The Law of Peoples," in *On Human Rights*, ed. Stephen Shute and Susan Hurley (New York: Basic Books, 1993), 41–82. The quote is on page 43. See also his later *The Law of Peoples* (Cambridge, MA: Harvard University Press, 2001). See also his *Justice as Fairness: A Restatement* (Cambridge, MA: Belknap Press of Harvard University Press, 2001).

[7] E. H. Carr, *The Twenty Years' Crisis, 1919–1939* (New York: Harper & Row, 1964), 97.

In short, international politics involves a blend of values and power, utopianism and realism. Such a perspective can be found in virtually all the intellectual precursors discussed throughout this book. There is disagreement, however, as to the relative importance of values and power, and which values should be pursued.

JUSTICE AND WAR

One fairly well-developed area that stands as an exception to our general observation of the paucity of normative IR theory is that which deals with the morality of war itself (*jus ad bellum*) and the ethical or moral constraints within any given war (*jus in bello*). Scholars of all perspectives have examined this issue,[8] and it is therefore an appropriate place to start our overview of normative theory and the challenges of its application.

Informed speculation on this subject builds on a tradition in Western thought extending back to the ancient Greeks. Contrary to the absolute pacifism of many early Christians, the writings of St. Augustine (354–430 CE) drew from the work of Cicero (and Plato before him), addressing war as something that was to be avoided but that was sometimes necessary: "It is the wrong-doing of the opposing party that compels the wise man to wage wars."[9] The corpus of just war theory grew with additions made by Aquinas, Francisco Suárez, Francisco de Vitoria, and other religious and political philosophers of the medieval period.

That we can develop a theory of just war through the exercise of right reason and right conduct are philosophical assumptions underlying normative theory on armed conflict. Perhaps not surprisingly, given their preoccupation with national security issues, much contemporary thinking on just war has occurred primarily among realists, particularly classical realists. The subject has also been of substantial interest in the English School, steeped as it is in the history of international relations and the Grotian and other philosophical understandings that go with it. Not all realists would accept the Machiavellian characterization of war as something useful for acquiring or maintaining rule and that, if postponed, might work only to the advantage of the enemy. A Machiavellian principle underscored by Carl von Clausewitz, as noted in chapter 5, is that war is decidedly not a legitimate end in itself, but is merely a means used to achieve essentially political purposes. That war should not be waged without legitimate purpose—that it should at least be subordinate to the political objective or serve some national interest—can be understood as a limited but nevertheless moral statement in itself.

Defense against provoked aggression is generally conceded (except by absolute pacifists) to be a legitimate political objective justifying war. Nevertheless, in just war thinking, war is a last resort to be undertaken only if there appears to be some chance of success. The death and destruction wrought by war are to be

---

[8] Recent works on the subject include Jens Bartelson, *War in International Thought* (Cambridge, UK: Cambridge University Press, 2017); Daniel R. Brunstetter and Cian O'Driscoll, eds., *The Just War Thinkers: From Cicero to the 21st Century* (London: Routledge, 2017); and Tamar Meisels, *Contemporary Just War* (London: Routledge, 2017).

[9] St. Augustine, "The City of God," in *Great Political Thinkers*, Ebenstein, 181–84.

minimized, consistent with achieving legitimate military purposes. Indeed, there can be no positive moral content in war unless legitimate political objectives and military purposes are served. Following conventional military logic found in Clausewitz, the purpose of any war is to destroy or substantially weaken an enemy's war-making capability. Military necessity, so defined, however, does not justify the use of means disproportionate to the ends sought or the use of weapons that are indiscriminate or that cause needless human suffering. Moreover, the lives of noncombatants are to be spared to the maximum extent possible.

Just war theory does not confine itself merely to whether one has a right to use armed force or resort to war in international relations. It goes beyond the *jus ad bellum* to raise questions of right conduct in war once armed conflict breaks out—the *jus in bello*. Very real limits are set to confine the death and destruction of warfare to what is militarily necessary, thus reducing war's barbarity. These principles that specify the bases for moral legitimacy of going to war and the conduct or use of force in war are summarized in table 13.1. As with any set of moral or ethical principles, their application depends upon right intention, which critics observe cannot always be assumed when it comes to the conduct of states still sovereign in an anarchic world lacking in viable enforcement authority.

Scholars in the English School, liberals, and classical realists of Grotian persuasion identify rules or laws that constrain states, statesmen, and soldiers in the exercise of their war powers. Treaties or conventions based largely on earlier just war thinking have come into force beginning with the Hague Conventions in the late nineteenth and early twentieth centuries. These were followed by the twentieth-century Geneva Conventions and other agreements that collectively provide the basis for the contemporary law of war. Defining aggression and dealing with insurgencies in which the very legitimacy of the parties is in question remain on the agenda of important moral and legal challenges.

Just war thinking is rooted in the pre-Christian, non-Judaic Greco-Roman world of Cicero, writing as he did in the Platonic tradition. To use a modern word, it was a secular thesis that did not rest on religious premises. Christian writers (notably St. Augustine and Aquinas) took up and developed the argument further, which became part of church doctrine. These ideas also made their way into Islamic thought which had to deal with the practical challenges related to the use of force.

Table 13.1 Just War Principles

Jus Ad Bellum	***Jus In Bello***
1. Just cause	1. Military necessity
2. Legitimate authority	2. Spare noncombatants and other defenseless persons
3. Proportionality of war	
4. Chance of success	3. Proportional means
5. War as last resort; exhaust peaceful means to resolve dispute	4. Means not immoral per se: not indiscriminate or causing needless suffering

Note: Application of all principles assumes right intention.

The term jihad, for example, has often been misinterpreted (as well as misused by some) to justify mass murder perpetrated upon the innocent in much the same way as the just war doctrine has been manipulated over the centuries by those who seek to legitimate untoward decisions and actions taken by those in authority. The fault lies not with doctrines that seek to constrain the use of force, but rather with the perpetrators who intentionally misconstrue the meanings of moral criteria in efforts to justify their conduct.

From the perspective of doctrine, jihad is an acknowledgment of a moral struggle that may call for the use of force. One writer defines the term succinctly as "struggle"—"a Muslim's striving to fulfill his Islamic responsibility, both in outward actions and in inward correction of his own mistakes." At the same time, it is "working or fighting in the cause of Allah" that may require the use of force. It is this point, however, that is open to multiple interpretations: "Jihad does not necessarily involve waging war (offensive or defensive). Different [Islamic] jurists have taken different positions in interpreting it."[10]

As with other religions, Islamic understandings vary from country or region in relation to culture and historical experience. Given the rather benign Arabic translation of jihad—"to strive for some objective," it is "combative jihad," of course, that is at the center of controversy: the declaration of war against belligerent and aggressive non-Muslim powers or against fellow Muslim transgressors. Conditions justifying combative jihad include "aggressive designs against Islam; . . . concerted efforts to eject Muslims from their legally acquired property; and, that military campaigns are being launched to eradicate them." The Imam or religious leader has authority to declare combative jihad that the ruler carries out.[11] Thus, as with the just war doctrine, combative jihad requires just cause and legitimate authority. Peaceful means ought to be employed, if possible, and the aim remains to reestablish peace.

Applying Just War Theory in the Twenty-First Century

Quite apart from such concerns, however, the focus on limits in just war theory and international law could be seen as impractical in an age dominated by weapons of mass destruction. Furthermore, can just war theory be used to legitimate deterrence doctrines arguing that to maintain peace one must threaten devastation even on a global scale? The continuing proliferation of nuclear weapons capabilities has made countries in some regions—the Middle East and South and East Asia—particularly vulnerable. Nevertheless, just war theory, imperfect as it may be, ought not to be set aside. Indeed, in a time of increasing global insecurity, the effort in just war theory to put practical limits on the use of force and thus to reduce, if not completely eliminate, the barbarity of warfare remains salient in what is at best a still emergent, global civil society.

---

[10] See AbdulHamid AbuSulayman, *Towards an Islamic Theory of International Relations* (Herndon, VA: International Institute of Islamic Thought, 1993), 19, 167.

[11] Shaykh Muhammad Hisham Kabbani (Chairman Islamic Supreme Council of America) and Shaykh Seraj Hendricks (Head Mufti, Cape Town, South Africa), "Jihad, A Misunderstood Concept from Islam," accessed September 3, 2018.

Just war theory did not prevent the obliteration bombing of cities or other population centers in World War II. At the time, many defenders of this strategy saw these raids as undermining societal morale in enemy countries, thus weakening an enemy's will to resist. But postwar evaluation of strategic bombing and other uses of air power raised a serious challenge to this rationale. Rage among survivors contributed in many cases to an increased will to resist rather than submit. If so, then obliteration bombing proved to be counterproductive or dysfunctional, even militarily speaking. With the benefit of hindsight, obliteration bombing of population centers has been discredited both militarily and morally in the years since World War II. Put another way, there can be no moral justification under just war doctrine for such mass death and destruction, particularly because these military actions did not serve legitimate military purposes. Just because military purposes are served, of course, is not enough to justify any conduct in war. Additional conditions need to be met to satisfy *jus in bello* obligations.

Although the principle of military necessity can be construed so broadly in the interest of national security as to allow almost any conduct in war, we expect political authorities or military commanders to approach the use of force with a spirit consistent with the human cost-reduction purpose of just war theory. Indeed, it is a narrow construction of military necessity that is prescribed by just war theory. Destroying an enemy's war-making capability focuses destructive efforts on an adversary's armed forces and *only* those parts of the society's infrastructure that directly contribute to its war-making effort. It is not a call to destroy an entire society, its population, or anything else of material or cultural value. People will still be killed and property destroyed, but probably far less damage will be sustained when the principle of military necessity is narrowly interpreted to limit the destructiveness of war to what is absolutely necessary for military purposes.

A distinction is therefore often drawn between counterforce and countervalue targets. Counterforce targets include military headquarters, troop or tank formations, combat aircraft, ships, maintenance facilities, and other military installations the destruction of which would directly weaken an enemy's war-making capability. Countervalue targets are factories, rail junctions, airports, and power plants in or near cities that contribute to an enemy's war-making capability or overall war effort. Even if people are not the intended victims, the bombing of countervalue targets usually produces more civilian, noncombatant casualties than counterforce targeting.

Moreover, compatible with the *jus in bello*, the means used to accomplish military purposes need to be proportional to the goal. If a three-hundred-pound bomb can be used to destroy a particular military target, a ten-thousand-pound bomb ought not to be used, particularly if doing so increases the collateral destruction of lives and property. In the same spirit, navy warships may choose to avoid sinking an enemy merchant ship by disabling the propeller. If feasible, they can then board and search the cargo. Again, just war theory aims to reduce unnecessary death or other damage.

One possible way to achieve this is to invoke the dual- or double-effect principle in dealing with the moral problem of killing noncombatants and producing collateral damage in warfare. Any action may have two or more effects or consequences. If the intent is to destroy a legitimate target that contributes to an enemy's war-making capability or overall war effort, then every reasonable effort must be made to avoid unnecessary casualties or other destruction. The "good effect" is destroying the legitimate military target. Dropping bombs, sending missiles by drones, landing artillery shells, or firing on such a target may also have unintended human and material consequences—the "bad effect."

Following double-effect logic and assuming proportionality—that the target is worth destroying in light of its military value when weighed against the expected consequences—just war theory would seem to support the idea that killing noncombatants or destroying civilian property may be morally justifiable when both effects occur simultaneously or the good effect precedes the bad. For example, in targeting an armaments factory at night when most workers were expected to be at home, it is accepted that a few workers may still be killed when the factory is destroyed. Or a bomb may go astray and kill some people in a residential area next to the factory, even though efforts were made to avoid this unfortunate outcome. That is the misfortune of war. Bad things happen in war, which is why just war theory puts so much emphasis on avoiding war in the first place.

If warriors intend the bad effect or if it precedes the good, such conduct does not satisfy the double-effect principle and is understood, therefore, to be morally wrong. Bombing workers at their homes next to the armaments factory (the bad effect) will likely reduce or eliminate the production capacity of the factory (the good effect, militarily speaking). The problem is that this good effect depends upon achieving the bad effect first. However good one's objectives or purposes may be, just war theorists argue that good ends cannot justify evil means: The ends do not justify the means. It would be morally wrong to bomb the village. If factory production must be halted, then the factory itself should be targeted, preferably at a time when as many workers as possible can be spared.

Morality and Weaponry

Any weapon can be used immorally, but some could not be used morally even if one intended to do so. Immoral weapons are those that are indiscriminate or cause needless suffering. A rifle is not immoral in itself; if used properly, it can be used with discrimination, sparing noncombatants. If used improperly to murder noncombatants, for example, it is the action and not the immoral weapon.

The same is true for most conventional bombs delivered accurately by airplanes or missiles. They can be used morally or immorally, depending for the most part on the target selected and how it is to be destroyed. The more accurate, the better is true from both a military and a moral position. Indeed, destruction of a legitimate military target is more likely, and collateral or unnecessary death and destruction, if not eliminated, can at least be minimized if accurate weapons are employed.

By contrast, wildly inaccurate weapons—including chemical or biological agents as in gas or germ warfare—by their very nature eliminate the distinction between combatant and noncombatant. Such weapons usually are not useful militarily, as winds disperse chemical agents indiscriminately, and diseases can spread to both sides of the battlefield and more generally across societies. Such weapons are immoral in themselves and have been declared illegal. Treaties prohibit the use of chemical and biological weapons.

The international consensus that led to these chemical and biological conventions rests on this moral argument. Not only are these weapons indiscriminate, but also they fail another moral test by causing needless suffering. Rifle bullets or other antipersonnel weapons designed to prolong or otherwise increase agony also fail this moral test. Killing in war is supposed to be as humane as possible. Most categories of weapons that are intended to enhance rather than reduce human suffering have also been defined in treaties as illegal. In 1997, for example, 122 governments signed a treaty banning antipersonnel landmines that cause the death and disfigurement of thousands of civilians every year.

Nuclear weapons are a more controversial case. The two atomic bombs that the United States dropped on the Japanese cities of Hiroshima and Nagasaki in 1945 were justified at the time by many on the utilitarian grounds that the bombings would shorten the war and thus reduce casualties on both sides. Those who made this argument saw the loss of life at Hiroshima and Nagasaki as precluding an even greater loss of life that would have resulted from an Allied invasion of the Japanese home islands. The Japanese had fought tenaciously to defend islands in the Pacific such as Iwo Jima and Guam; it was believed they would fight with even greater determination to defend their homeland. Others questioned the morality of bombing people even for this purpose, suggesting that if the bombs were to be used at all, they should have been directed toward strictly military targets, not population centers interspersed with military targets. Decision makers responded that the Japanese leaders should take the blame, as they decided to locate military-related plants where they did.[12]

Each of the weapons dropped on Japan was less than twenty kilotons (twenty thousand tons) in yield. Many nuclear weapons today have a much larger multimegaton (multimillion tons) yield, with such heat, blast, and radiation effects that they cannot be used with discrimination, so these weapons fail on grounds of human suffering as well. On the other hand, some have argued that lower-yield, tactical nuclear weapons (perhaps as small as one kiloton or less, with reduced-radiation effects) can be used with discrimination and need not cause unnecessary suffering. Critics are skeptical of any such claim. They also counter that using any nuclear weapons at all "opens Pandora's box," legitimating this category of weaponry and increasing the likelihood that even larger nuclear weapons will be employed by one or another of the parties. Indicative of the lack of consensus on these issues, and unlike chemical and biological agents, nuclear weapons have not yet been declared illegal, however ill-advised or immoral their use might be.

---

[12] For an argument questioning whether the atomic bombs actually explain the Japanese surrender, see Ward Wilson, "The Winning Weapon: Rethinking Nuclear Weapons in Light of Hiroshima," *International Security* 31, no. 4 (Spring 2007): 162–79.

JUSTICE AND HUMAN RIGHTS

The quest for universal understanding of socioeconomic, political, and legal rights belonging to individuals, groups, classes, societies, and humanity as a whole has proven to be an evolutionary and still-ongoing process.[13] Particularly challenging is the unequal, adverse treatment human beings suffer based on such factors as race or ethnicity, national origin, social or economic class, age, gender, and sexual identity or orientation. Gross violations of labor, safety, and health standards for adults as well as children, illegal trafficking of persons for prostitution or slave labor, torture, and genocide are among the more extreme forms of human exploitation on the global human rights agenda.

The Enlightenment

Although the concept of rights in Western thought has roots in ancient Greek, Roman, and religious writings, it was the Enlightenment and the social-contract theorists that collectively provided stronger philosophical ground for specifying human aspirations for liberty and equality coupled with communitarian concerns and human obligations in society. The liberal spirit of the Enlightenment would be developed further in work by Kantians and utilitarians.

Hobbes, Locke, Rousseau, and other classic social-contract theorists differ on the relative emphasis or importance each place on liberty, equality, community, and order, but a common theme is that human beings—the people—are the ultimate source of legitimate political authority in society. This democratic understanding is explicit in Locke and Rousseau. Even for Hobbes, the monarch (or "assembly" acting as legislature) rested legitimately not on divine right, but rather on the people who vested the sovereign with authority and power to maintain societal order in the interest of their own security.

The thirteenth-century English *Magna Carta* and the late eighteenth-century US Bill of Rights and French Declaration of the Rights of Man are documentary statements of aspirations for rights taking a political or legal form. Content analysis of these documents, however, reveals a greater focus on individual political and legal rights in the English and American documents. The French declaration, by contrast, extends itself to the socioeconomic realm with applications not just to individuals, but also to larger aggregations at both communal and societal levels. In short, people may have rights as a class, group, or society as a whole.

In the present-day global society, these differences in understandings across societies and cultures remain. Culture obviously matters in how we interpret or understand rights in different social contexts. There are differences in relative importance, for example, of liberty, equality, and order, and whether rights or obligations are to be applied primarily at the individual level of analysis or at larger human aggregations. Thus, the United States tends to focus on human rights as individual political and legal rights and liberties, whereas many other

---

[13] For an overview, see Jack Donnelly and Daniel J. Whelan, *International Human Rights*, 5th ed. (London: Routledge, 2017).

states and societies accept these civil rights and liberties as part of a much larger package that also puts a higher premium on socioeconomic rights and communitarian understandings.

Though advocacy of human rights has been grounded predominantly in Western political thought, the philosophical bases for human rights are also found in other non-Western traditions. William Theodor de Bary (1919–2017) spent much of his professional life translating and interpreting classic works in both the Chinese and Japanese traditions. Particularly relevant to human rights are the Confucian communitarian understandings he identified. In Islamic writings one also finds philosophical and legal bases for human rights.[14] The primary Islamic sources are the *Qur'an* and the *Sunnah*—the sayings and actions of the Prophet Muhammed, which give a basis for "human dignity and human rights."[15] That human rights understandings are found in such diverse cultural settings underscores the universality of such core values as respect for life, human dignity, and justice as fairness.

Current Application

Notwithstanding different cultural understandings or interpretations of how human rights should be defined and implemented, human rights advocates adopt a universalist rather than a relativist view. Whether using a methodology of social contract, utilitarian, Kantian, Aristotelian, virtue-based, or of religious origin, advocates search for universal, underlying values that inform our understandings of human rights in practice. Thus, respect for life, human dignity, and justice or fairness broadly are understood and accepted even as there is disagreement on how these values are to be applied in particular human rights contexts. Even so, because there is an understanding of such underlying, universal values as respect for life and human dignity, there is at least a basis for discourse aimed in the interest of justice and fairness at resolving differences in how these values are applied across societies.

Although politics clearly plays a role in these determinations (giving a relatively louder voice to the preferences of some states over others), at a more fundamental level is the continuing discourse that develops consensus across cultures and societies on the realization of these values in common practice.

---

[14] See William Theodore de Bary, *Asian Values and Human Rights: A Confucian Communitarian Perspective* (Cambridge, MA: Harvard University Press, 1998) and his *East Asian Civilizations: A Dialogue in Five Stages* (Cambridge, MA: Harvard University Press, 1988). For documentary sources, see de Bary, Wing-tsit Chan, and Burton Watson, *Sources of Chinese Tradition* (New York: Columbia University Press, 1960); Ryusaku Tsunoda, de Bary, and Donald Keene, *Sources of Japanese Tradition* (New York: Columbia University Press, 1958), and de Bary, *Sources of Indian Tradition* (New York: Columbia University Press, 1958). On the Islamic tradition, see Maher Hathout, *In Pursuit of Justice: The Jurisprudence of Human Rights in Islam* (Los Angeles: Muslim Public Affairs Council, 2006).

[15] AbuSulayman, *Towards an Islamic Theory of International Relations*, 160. For other discussions of Islamic thought as it relates to international relations theory, see Shahrbanou Tadjbakhsh, "International Relations Theory and the Islamic World View," in *Non-Western International Relations Theory*, ed. Amitav Acharya and Barry Buzan (London: Routledge, 2010), 174–96; and Kamran Matin, "Decoding Political Islam," in *International Relations and Non-Western Thought*, ed. Robbie Shilliam (London: Routledge, 2011), 108–24.

Thus, the Universal Declaration of Human Rights adopted by the UN General Assembly in 1948 emphasizes the political and legal, individual preferences of its sponsors. Nevertheless, six of the thirty articles—20 percent of the declaration—do address socioeconomic and cultural rights, albeit in individual, rather than collective terms. Importantly, this 20 percent would serve as a foundation for later expansion in UN treaties or agreements not just on civil and political rights, but also on such matters as economic, social, and cultural rights, the elimination of discrimination based on race and against women, and the creation of a children's bill of rights.

Humanitarian Treatment and the Sovereign State

Claims for human rights and demands for humanitarian treatment grounded in treaty commitments often collide with the prerogatives of a sovereign state. States claim a right under international law to exclusive jurisdiction over all persons within their territory. Many human rights advocates, however, see both moral and legal bases for action (including armed intervention in such severe cases as genocide) when decisions or policies of governments violate human rights. This is particularly so when states have legally bound themselves in treaties specifying commitment to these same rights. When national security considerations conflict with these obligations, compliance by states cannot be taken for granted.

There are difficulties, of course, beyond the question of when armed intervention in the domestic affairs of a sovereign state legally can be legitimate, which we discuss below. For example, the jurisdiction of the International Court of Justice (ICJ) as a legal remedy or alternative to using force is limited to ruling on disputes or cases states voluntarily bring to the court for judicial decision. Even when the court has rendered a decision, compliance still depends on the will of states to carry out their obligations specified in these rulings. Beyond states as parties to legal disputes on human rights or other matters, an International Criminal Court (ICC) has been established to hold individuals accountable for genocide, crimes against humanity, war crimes, and the crime of aggression. The kinds of cases the ICC may take are important, but remain limited, as its jurisdiction is also severely constrained by the fact that not all states have yet authorized this tribunal. Although it was part of its drafting, the United States has been among the most prominent nonsubscribers to the Rome Statute of the ICC (agreed in 1998, entering into force in 2002).

The Convention on the Prevention and Punishment of the Crime of Genocide (1948, entering into force in 1951) defined genocide as "any of the following acts committed with intent to destroy, in whole or in part, a national, ethnical [*sic*], racial or religious group": "(a) killing members of the group; (b) causing serious bodily or mental harm to members of the group; (c) deliberately inflicting on the group conditions of life calculated to bring about its physical destruction in whole or in part; (d) imposing measures intended to prevent births within the group; [and] (e) forcibly transferring children of the group to another group."

Although the convention does not provide armed intervention as an explicit remedy to stop genocide, when such severe human rights violations threaten international peace and security, there is a legal basis for humanitarian intervention under UN auspices (namely under Articles 34, 41, and 42). Beyond using threats to international peace and security to legitimate armed intervention, some see emerging in customary international law the occurrence of genocide as a legitimate basis in itself for armed intervention. By contrast, opponents of this view (particularly governments complicit in genocidal actions) politically oppose what they see as an expansion of the UN agenda. They claim such efforts are meddling in the internal affairs of sovereign states, which amounts to a violation of international law.

In just war theory and the law of war discussed previously, an effort must be made to spare noncombatants and other defenseless persons. Guilty or not, noncombatants—civilian populations—are not the proper object of warfare. Even captured enemy soldiers are now defenseless persons who may be taken prisoner but may not be executed just because they are prisoners. Prisoners of war (sometimes called PWs or POWs) have rights, and under the Geneva Conventions, these guarantees of humanitarian treatment have been made part of international law.

This is why the establishment by the United States of the prison at Guantánamo Bay, Cuba, has been so controversial. The prison was established following the overthrow of the Taliban regime in Afghanistan in the fall of 2001 to hold suspected terrorists (as were prisons also established at Bagram Air Base in Afghanistan and other locations, some secret). The US government, relying on laws dating back to the Civil War and World War II, declared that these individuals were not prisoners of war, but rather "enemy combatants" held as "detainees." As a result, they allegedly could not invoke the international legal rights associated with prisoners of war—a perspective hotly disputed by critics of American prison policies in Cuba and elsewhere.

For its part, the US Supreme Court in *Hamdan* v. *Rumsfeld* (2006) ruled that Common Article 3 of the Geneva Conventions that provides safeguards to those held in such prisons does apply. In this regard, the article holds that they are to be treated "humanely" with the following prohibitions: "(a) violence to life and person, in particular murder of all kinds, mutilation, cruel treatment and torture; (b) taking of hostages; (c) outrages upon personal dignity, in particular, humiliating and degrading treatment; and (d) the passing of sentences and the carrying out of executions without previous judgment pronounced by a regularly constituted court affording all the judicial guarantees which are recognized as indispensable by civilized peoples." Moreover, those who are "wounded and sick shall be collected and cared for."

Practical concern for finding information deemed vital to national security frequently conflicts with the moral and legal obligations to afford humane treatment in the interrogations of those taken captive. The Convention against Torture and Other Cruel, Inhuman or Degrading Treatment or Punishment (1984, entering into force in 1987) defines torture as any act by which severe pain or suffering, whether physical or mental, is intentionally inflicted on a person for such purposes as obtaining from him or a third person information or a confession, punishing him for an act he or a third person has committed or is suspected of having committed, or intimidating or coercing him or a third person, or for any reason based on discrimination of any kind, when such pain or suffering is inflicted by or at the instigation of or with the consent or acquiescence of a public official or other person acting in an official capacity. It does not include pain or suffering arising only from, inherent in or incidental to lawful sanctions.

Those who argue that torture is legitimate—or who stretch the operational definitions of what constitutes torture—are in effect saying that the *end* (national security) *justifies the means* to that end. By no means, of course, is the claim that moral purposes justify immoral means a legitimate basis for actions taken.

ARMED INTERVENTION AND STATE SOVEREIGNTY

The issue of armed intervention is a good example of where traditional concerns with the laws of war blend with concerns over human rights. The 1928 Pact of Paris (or Kellogg-Briand Pact) was an unsuccessful attempt to eliminate the use of force in international relations. It was supposed to help outlaw "recourse to war for the solution of international controversies." Hope was placed in world peace through law in a system of collective security under the League of Nations. As such, collective security is different from collective defense—alliances or coalitions that rely ultimately on armed defense or military power rather than international law enforcement against aggressor states.

The League of Nations tried to substitute law-abiding behavior for individual and collective-*defense* relations based on power, balance of power, and military might. Law-abiding states under collective-*security* arrangements enforce international law against law-breaking states. But the League of Nations seemed powerless to counter such aggressive actions as French intervention in Germany and the Italian capture of the Mediterranean island of Corfu (1923), the outbreak of the China-Japan war (1931), the Bolivia-Paraguay Chaco war (1932–1935), Italy's invasion of Ethiopia (1935), Germany's annexation of Austria and part of Czechoslovakia (1938), and finally the outbreak of World War II in 1939.

In an attempt to put the lessons of the interwar period to practical effect, the UN Charter (1945) does specify conditions under which force may legally be used: (1) unilaterally in self-defense; (2) multilaterally when authorized by the UN Security Council "to maintain or restore international peace and security"; and (3) in multilateral, often regional, collective-defense action as, for example, in NATO.

Armed interventions still occur frequently enough, sometimes justified by the participants as serving humanitarian purposes or as a measure to maintain or restore international peace and security—a broad grant of legal authority for UN-sponsored actions. In a world of sovereign states, diplomatic and other forms of intervention in the domestic affairs of another state, especially armed intervention, are normally prohibited under international law. Article 2 of the UN Charter establishes the United Nations "on the principle of sovereign equality of all its Members." Members pledge themselves to "settle their international disputes by peaceful means" and to "refrain in their international relations from the threat or use of force against the territorial integrity or political independence of any state."

States that have suffered violation of their legal rights may choose arbitration, mediation, or a judicial remedy as offered by the ICJ or an appropriate regional or national court. As noted, a critical weakness is that these tribunals do not have enforcement powers. As a practical matter, then, states often resort to self-help to include the use of force, which obviously remains very much a part of international relations. As we have observed, in an anarchic world that lacks a central government or other governing authority with the power to enforce international law, sovereign states do not always comply with such legal authorizations and restrictions. States sometimes choose to violate or ignore their obligations under international law. At other times, political leaders and diplomats have proven to be quite capable of interpreting or manipulating legal principles to justify what they already have done or plan to do in any event.

Intervention and Civil Wars

If applying international law is difficult in the case of interstate wars, it is even more complicated when the conflict is internal to a particular state and society— a civil war. Given the crises of authority faced by so many states today, it is not surprising that internal wars, not interstate wars, are the most likely threat to international peace and security. It is often difficult to contain civil wars within the borders of the affected state. Quite apart from outside interference, civil wars can spill beyond their borders and become interstate wars.

Even when motives are legitimate and not contrived, interventions in the domestic affairs of sovereign states conflict with a long-established principle of international law that prohibits them. Consider the American Civil War (1861–1865) and the debate in Great Britain as to whether or not Britain should support the South. The southern states claimed sovereignty as the Confederate States of America and sought outside assistance in their struggle against the United States of America, from which they claimed to be separate.

The Lincoln administration in Washington, DC, denied the South's claim, arguing that the southern states had no right to secede from the Union in the first place. Thus, to Lincoln it was not a war between sovereign states, but rather a civil war fought between loyal US armed forces and those loyal to the rebellious states. Through careful diplomacy, Washington made its interpretation of events clear to the British, stressing that outside intervention was illegal. Whether they accepted the Lincoln administration's rationale or not, London chose not to intervene either diplomatically or militarily even as it continued to trade with the South.

Determining the difference between an interstate war and a civil war is often difficult. American armed intervention in Vietnam in the early 1960s, for example, was justified by the United States as coming to the defense of South

Vietnam (the Republic of Vietnam) against aggression from North Vietnam (the Democratic Republic of Vietnam). If this were factually correct, then going to the aid of a victim of aggression was legitimate under international law. On the other hand, if the situation in Vietnam were understood as a civil war, with a single state torn between two rival governments and an insurgent movement tied to one of the parties, then outside intervention in such an internal matter would not have been legitimate under international law.

The war in Vietnam was fought not only by the regular forces of North and South Vietnam, the United States, the Republic of Korea, and Australia; it also involved guerrilla warfare supported by North Vietnam. This capitalized on North Vietnam's ties with the people in the countryside. By using anti-government and ideological appeals, knowledge of the terrain, and the protective cover of the jungle canopy, both regular army forces and non-uniformed irregulars (or guerrillas) conducted a very successful campaign against the South Vietnamese government and its allies. Guerrilla warfare included terrorism, ambushes, rocket attacks, and sometimes even firefights with regular forces. Guerrillas that were part of an anti-government insurgent movement, coupled with the efforts of North Vietnamese regulars, eventually succeeded in winning the war against the United States in 1975 and soon thereafter the South Vietnamese government.

The former Yugoslavia provides another example of the important distinction between civil war and interstate war. Serbs opposed both the secession of "breakaway republics" and their recognition in the early 1990s by outside states as independent, sovereign states. From the Serbian perspective, the ensuing war among competing parties was really a civil war precluding any legal right to intervention by outside parties. Having been recognized as separate, independent, and sovereign states by UN members, however, Croatia, Slovenia, and Bosnia-Herzegovina were seen by other observers as engaging in a war among states against Serbia. As an interstate war, then, outside intervention or other activities by the UN, NATO, the Organization of Security and Cooperation in Europe, or other legitimate authorities acting in compliance with the UN Charter was presented as legitimate.

Criteria for Humanitarian Intervention

In the absence of an invitation from the legitimate government of a state, even humanitarian intervention—such as using force to stop the fighting among competing groups, providing the necessary security to feed starving people, halting genocide or ethnic cleansing, or performing actions for similar humanitarian purposes—legally conflicts with the principle of nonintervention in the domestic affairs of a state. As noted, a basis under customary international law may be emerging to give legal legitimacy to intervention intended to stop genocide or other human rights abuses. For its part, the UN Charter does not give the Security Council authority to use force for humanitarian purposes per se. Armed intervention under UN auspices in the internal affairs of a state, however justifiable the humanitarian purpose might seem, is legitimate in this strict interpretation only if the problem cannot likely be contained to the state in which it is occurring, thus posing a threat to international peace and security.

The case of Kosovo in 1999 illustrates this point. No one denied that Kosovo was a province of Yugoslavia. The Serbs stated that whatever actions they took in the province were, therefore, an internal matter and outside intervention was a violation of Yugoslavian sovereignty. The Serbian policy of systematic ethnic cleansing (forcing the ethnic separation, movement, or murder of peoples), however, led to NATO military action on the grounds of humanitarian intervention and the claim that Serbian actions were a threat to regional peace and security.

Humanitarian motives may genuinely accompany actions taken primarily for national interest reasons. In other cases, however, humanitarian motives are presented as a pretext used by political leaders and diplomats to justify armed interventions done exclusively (or almost entirely) for national interest reasons. Propagandists like to present humanitarian purposes as a cover for armed interventions conducted for national interest purposes, thus making the behavior seem less self-serving. Such thinking has been leveled against Russia following its February 2022 invasion of Ukraine.

Events in 1989 brought an end to the Cold War, but not to armed intervention. Subsequent years have been marked by a continuation of armed interventions by outside states and multilateral coalitions of states in response to Iraq's armed intervention and takeover of Kuwait, civil strife in Somalia and Haiti, and genocide in the Balkan states and central Africa. Following terrorist attacks engineered by *al-Qaeda* on the United States, regimes were overturned by interventions under NATO auspices in Afghanistan in 2001 and in Iraq in 2003 by the United States, United Kingdom, and a coalition of other states. The latter invasion was justified, among other reasons, on the presumption that Iraq possessed (and likely would use) weapons of mass destruction.

Policy makers face decisions about whether or not to intervene with armed force to respond to aggression, prevent or stop genocide, restore order, or maintain the peace. Bombing and other abuses of populations in Syria and Yemen produced outcries of condemnation against the perpetrators, but not the kind of massive armed intervention that would have been necessary to cease these human rights violations. Political factors—Russian involvement in Syria and Saudi Arabia in Yemen—kept the United States and other countries from intervening militarily. The Russian and American veto power kept the Security Council from taking significant action: the Russians were protective of the Assad regime in Syria and the United States was reluctant to take action against Saudi Arabia, which it was supporting militarily.

Both economic and military capabilities as well as domestic political support (or opposition) typically are part of the decision-making calculus. We can also identify at least five additional and often-competing criteria or factors typically weighed by policy makers considering armed intervention. Moreover political support for (or opposition to) armed intervention is often expressed in terms of one or more of the several criteria we now take up in turn:

1. *Sovereignty.* Under international law, states are normally prohibited from intervention in the domestic affairs of other sovereign states unless requested by the legitimate government of the state subject to such intervention.

However, as noted earlier, use of force (including armed intervention) is allowed under the UN Charter for collective security as when the Security Council authorizes using force in response to a contingency endangering international peace and security (Chapter VII, particularly Article 42). Similarly, self-defense or collective defense by alliances or coalitions of states is justified in responding to aggression against a sovereign state (Chapter VII, Article 51).

2. *National Interest.* Armed intervention is an option often weighed against considerations of national interest and related national security objectives. Some argue that armed intervention should be pursued only if there is a vital national interest to be served. Even if one considers this criterion to be decisive, as many realists do, there is no escaping the practical difficulty in trying to define precisely what the national interest (much less vital national interest) might be in a particular case. The national interest is subject to multiple interpretations, but even with this ambiguity, it remains part of the decision-making calculus. Thus, when states act in self-defense or come to the aid of other states to repel aggression, they claim legal legitimacy for acting in the national interest. Indeed, the UN Charter in Article 51 recognizes "the inherent right of individual or collective self-defense." Of course, not all interventions taken to advance national interest meet this self-defense criterion and instead they amount to acts of aggression.

3. *Human Rights.* A consensus has been forming, mainly in the last half of the twentieth century that continues to the present, that holds that human beings have rights that may supersede those claimed by sovereign states. The groundwork was laid by the Universal Declaration of Human Rights, passed by the UN General Assembly in 1948. This human rights consensus rests on increasing understanding and acceptance of respect for life, human dignity, and justice or fairness as universal ethical or moral principles that have global application to individuals, groups, and other categories or classes of human beings.[16] Both unilateral and multilateral voluntary assistance for relief in natural disasters are manifestations of these principles in action. The enormous human and material cost suffered by the victims of mass destruction and atrocities throughout the twentieth century resulted in substantial growth in international law, which has come to (1) define certain civil or political, social, and economic rights and (2) prohibit certain acts defined as war crimes, genocide, and other crimes against peace and humanity. When such human rights violations are also understood to endanger international peace and security, there is clearer legal ground for humanitarian, armed intervention under UN Security Council auspices. This follows Chapter VII of the UN Charter or is based on an emerging consensus in customary international law of a human rights rationale for intervention at least in such extreme cases as stopping genocide.

---

[16] Other conventions address Racial Discrimination (1966), Discrimination against Women (1979), Torture and Other Cruel, Inhuman or Degrading Treatment or Punishment (1984), and the Rights of a Child (1989).

4. *Expected Net Effect on the Human Condition.* Armed intervention has very real costs not just to people and property in states and societies subject to intervention, but also to the armed forces conducting such interventions. The extent of these costs usually cannot be known with certainty, but policy makers nevertheless try to estimate what they are likely to be. It is extraordinarily difficult, if not impossible, to quantify with precision the net effect (benefits minus costs) on the human condition even after an armed intervention has occurred. Deaths and other casualties can be counted and property losses estimated, but some human costs (e.g., psychological damage) may not be known for many years, if then. The problem is compounded when one tries to estimate what these costs might be in advance of an armed intervention. Nevertheless, this criterion typically plays on the minds of policy makers who contemplate whether armed intervention will improve or worsen the human condition. At the very least, the expected net effect on the human condition can influence how an armed intervention is implemented. Using this criterion, policy makers may select options expected to minimize or reduce adverse consequences to both armed forces and the people subject to their actions.

5. *Degree of Multilateralism.* As unilateral armed intervention, regardless of motivation or justification, has come increasingly into disfavor, policy makers have been more prone to look for multilateral support and cooperation in conducting armed interventions. UN Security Council mandates, for example, provide political and legal ground for proceeding. In the absence of such Security Council action, proceeding multilaterally under Article 51 as a collective-defense response is still viewed by most policy makers as politically preferable to unilateral action. This helps explain why the George W. Bush administration, despite a generally dismissive attitude toward the United Nations, sought a UN Security Council resolution in the fall of 2002 requiring Iraq to readmit weapons inspectors. This effort ultimately included an elaborate oral and visual presentation by Colin Powell, then secretary of state, to the UN Security Council on alleged Iraqi weapons of mass destruction.

These five criteria often compete with each other, and choices concerning how much weight to give to one over the other have to be made sooner or later. That said, we are left with an analytical framework that specifies factors that typically are part of decisions to engage in armed intervention. Because states usually intervene to serve their interests does not mean that they always do so for only self-serving purposes. They may wish to intervene quite genuinely for humanitarian reasons or, consistent with their broad interests, to contribute to restoration of international peace and security. This seems to have been the case in NATO's intervention in Kosovo in 1999. In such cases, states may weigh the costs and benefits of armed intervention or in terms of how well they serve the human condition.

In some cases, the use of force for humanitarian purposes may cause even more bloodshed than if no intervention had taken place. In other cases the reverse is true: Armed intervention at relatively low cost may succeed in providing greater security and meeting human needs. The difficulty, of course, is that expected net costs or benefits to human beings are not always easy to estimate accurately.

ALTERNATIVE IMAGES AND FOREIGN POLICY CHOICE

The relative emphasis placed on order, justice, freedom, and change—values that are part of foreign policy-making and that have a direct bearing on international politics—varies widely among realists, liberals, economic structuralists, and adherents to the English School that are the subject of chapters 5–8. Realist concern with power and the balance of power is closely related to value commitments of those in authority who see order as essential to national security. If they are committed further to the avoidance of war, they may see their tasks as one of managing conflict and seeking to maximize accomplishment of state objectives, however constrained by states comprising the balance. Following Machiavelli, the realist sees national security or the national interest—at a minimum, survival in an anarchic world—as the *raison d'état* justifying state policy. The first generation of English School scholars such as Hedley Bull also emphasized the importance of international order. Bull's major question was in fact where order comes from in what he termed an anarchical society.

To some extent, the value bias among liberals is also conservative, if not to the same degree. To liberals and more recent work in the English School, change should be (and usually is) evolutionary and incremental. If change is to be willed, then reformist, not revolutionary, measures typically are the appropriate ones. Liberal theories, given the fragmentation of states and proliferation of actors that are their starting point, focus on the formation of coalitions and counter-coalitions, whether within a state or across national borders. This is hardly the environment for radical changes that would require greater societal unity or at least strong and unitary leadership. Faction against faction, governmental department against governmental department—the Madisonian model underlying the American Constitution—is not the means to sweeping change. There are simply too many obstacles (or potential obstacles in the form of opposing groups or factions) to make change easy to come by.

Many liberals, however, place greater emphasis on democratic notions of human rights and justice for individuals, groups, and societies than they do on order within and among states. Richard Falk (b. 1930), for example, identifies four values to be maximized as part of his World Order Models Project: (1) minimization of collective violence, (2) maximization of economic well-being, (3) maximization of social and political justice, and (4) maximization of ecological quality. To minimize collective violence, order remains important to Falk, but his focus quickly shifts to social and welfare issues that need to be addressed as part of the world order. The liberalism in Falk's approach is evident in his characterization of it as "a transnational social movement dedicated to global reform."[17]

---

[17] See Richard A. Falk, *A Study of Future Worlds* (New York: Free Press, 1975), 11–30; and *The End of World Order: Essays on Normative International Relations* (New York: Holmes and Meier, 1983), 53. See also his *Human Rights Horizons* (London: Routledge, 2000) and *Achieving Human Rights* (London: Routledge, 2008).

Justice, especially distributive justice, is a central concern not only to many liberals but also to many economic structuralists. As noted, John Rawls presents a non-Marxist formulation that supports the normative preferences of both liberals like Falk and those economic structuralists who focus on patterns of human exploitation and inequalities in the distribution of wealth between the industrial countries of the North and the least developed countries of the South. Economic structuralists of Marxist persuasion and many postcolonial theorists and historians do not need Rawls, of course, given their own long-standing moral concern with exploitative class relations and associated prescriptions for overturning what they see as the existing, unjust world order.

To many economic structuralists, reformism and incremental change are merely prescriptions for maintaining the status quo dominance by the owners and managers of capital (OMC). If justice is to be served, what may be needed is revolutionary change that sweeps out an unjust world order and replaces it with one that allows for an equitable distribution of wealth and resources. Whether understood as exploitation of peasants and workers by an international *bourgeoisie* (in non-Marxist terms the OMC) or as domination by highly industrial core states and societies over poor, industrially underdeveloped peripheral states, the answer is always the same: Justice requires change. Order, peace, and individual freedom will only be established after fundamental (or revolutionary) change of the existing order has been effected.

RATIONALITY AND FOREIGN POLICY CHOICE

Foreign policy choice is the domain in which moral and ethical values apply directly. Based on some set of criteria, decision makers ultimately choose authoritatively among competing alternatives. Can the rational choice model allow us to avoid or side-step normative issues?

The rational model, often a critical element in realist thinking, amounts to policy makers' ordering of alternatives, making decisions, and taking actions to achieve the most efficient outcome in terms of the ends sought. This process is, however, not value-free. First, determining the objective or ends to be sought obviously involves value choices. Second, the idea that the means chosen to achieve these goals should be the most efficient, the best, or even just "good enough" is itself a value underlying the decision-making calculus. Finally, even if statesmen can reach a consensus on what general values should be pursued internationally, there may be honest disagreement as to how these values are to be defined and implemented. A good example of this problem involves human rights, which we already have mentioned previously.

Notwithstanding the Universal Declaration of Human Rights in 1948 and many human rights conventions since then, it often has been difficult to forge a consensus among governments on which criteria should apply in approaching questions of human rights: Which rights are to be protected, the relative importance or weight of different values when they conflict, and whose rights—individuals, groups, classes, states—take precedence?

In sum, contrary to what one might first presume, the rational model of foreign policy decision-making is by no means a value-free approach, particularly given the wide range of values pursued by statesmen and different views as to how a particular value should be defined and implemented. As has been discussed in chapter 6, some liberals challenge whether foreign policy decision-making can ever conform to a rational model when the actors involved are various organizations and small groups of individuals and when decisions are typically the outcome of bargaining, compromising, "end-running," or related tactics. Each separate actor may act rationally to achieve its own goals and values, but this is not the same thing as assuming that those in authority act rationally to achieve the goals or interests of the entire state and society. Similarly, some economic structuralists may question the rationality of a decision-making or foreign policy process that, from their point of view, is dominated by narrow class interests. Whatever may be the rationality of individuals, institutions, or classes in maximizing or serving their own values or interests, the outcome for the whole may be suboptimal or less than the best.

VALUES, CHOICES, AND THEORY

The case for normative theory is not subject to debate by critical theorists, postmodernists, feminists, and green theorists. Normative theory has a place in many English School and classical realist formulations. The same is probably true for most constructivists. The idea of divorcing norms from inquiry is at a minimum difficult to achieve, if not impossible. The traditional debate has been over the role of normative theory in the four images. For realists and liberals of positivist bent, explanatory theory and normative theory occupy separate realms.

We conclude, however, that normative theory is indeed relevant to each of the images, lenses, and associated theories we discuss in this book to the extent that one finds allowance for the exercise of human will. How much can political leaders, heads of international organizations, or directors of transnational or nongovernmental organizations affect the course of events? If decision makers are driven internally, consistent with some psychological theories, or if they are severely constrained by their external environment, then normative theory plays a reduced, if any, role in their decision-making. On the other hand, if human beings do have some degree of control over their affairs, including international relations, and if causal theories take this effect of the will into account and exclude determinist inevitabilities, then why has the normative part often been neglected in IR theory?

A central argument we make in this book is that the image, set of assumptions, and interpretive understandings one holds concerning international relations do affect the sense one makes of "facts" and the types of explanations or predictions one offers. Although it is important to come to an understanding of biases or perspectives associated with any particular image or interpretive understanding of international relations and world politics, we are by no means making the argument that such knowledge is a function only of prior assumptions, preferences, or values. When what we see as facts contradicts the image or understanding we hold, then it is the image or understanding that should be altered or even overturned to accommodate new information.

Our knowledge of international relations is imperfect and various biases color our vision, but the world has a way of breaking down our preconceptions when these preconceptions are fallacious. Scientific skepticism about claims to truth forces testing of various propositions or hypotheses with historical, interpretive, or other empirical data. Whether in the natural or social realms, scientific progress that enhances our knowledge of the world is painfully slow, but it is persistent.

REFERENCES

AbuSulayman, AbdulHamid. *Towards an Islamic Theory of International Relations.* Herndon, VA: International Institute of Islamic Thought, 1993.

Acharya, Amitav, and Barry Buzan, eds. *Non-Western International Relations Theory.* London: Routledge, 2010.

Bartelson, Jens. *War in International Thought.* Cambridge, UK: Cambridge University Press, 2017.

Brunstetter, Daniel R., and Cian O'Driscoll, eds. *The Just War Thinkers: From Cicero to the 21st Century.* London: Routledge, 2017.

Donnelly, Jack, and Daniel J. Whelan. *International Human Rights*, 5th ed. London: Routledge, 2017.

Falk, Richard A. *Achieving Human Rights.* London: Routledge, 2008.

Meisels, Tamar. *Contemporary Just War.* London: Routledge, 2017.

Rawls, John. *A Theory of Justice.* Cambridge, MA: Harvard University Press, 1971.

Shilliam, Robbie, ed. *International Relations and Non-Western Thought.* London: Routledge, 2011.

Glossary

★ ★ ★

absolute gains *See* **relative and absolute gains**.

agent-structure An ontological question raised by social constructivists in particular. To what extent can states (and other actors) as agents shape the world within which they are immersed and not just be prisoners of the structure of the international system? How much of structure is a given, and how much is created by human agency?

anarchy The absence of legitimate political authority. International politics or the international system is said to be anarchic in that there is no central or superordinate authority over states.

assumption A premise or statement taken to be true without empirical or factual proof. The theorist typically makes assumptions as the starting point in developing a given theory. For example, some balance-of-power theorists make assumptions about the state as principal, unitary, and rational or purposive actor.

autarky An independent posture of self-sufficiency without dependence on other actors. Autarky occurs when a state attempts as a matter of policy to exist in economic isolation from other states.

authority A legitimate right to direct or command and to make, decide, and enforce rules. The term authority has a moral or legal quality and, as such, can be distinguished from control by brute force or by coercion.

autonomous development *See* **development**.

balance of power A key concept among realists that refers to a condition of equilibrium among states. Realists differ on whether the equilibrium or balance among states (a) is created by policy makers or (b) occurs quite apart from their will as an inherent characteristic of international politics. Balance-of-power considerations may be used by decision makers as justification for a given foreign policy. Some critics have noted that the multiple definitions or meanings of balance of power diminish its utility as a concept in IR theory.

behavioralism One of the dominant approaches to research particularly in the decades after World War II is the view that the subject matter of political science should be limited to phenomena that are independently observable and quantifiable.

bipolar, bipolarity The condition of having two poles is when the distribution of power or capabilities in international politics is said to be bipolar. Some theorists consider the Cold War international political system to have had a bipolar structure—the United States and the former Soviet Union. Others consider it today to be unipolar, multipolar, or to conform to some other characterization. *See* **structure, unipolar, multipolar**.

bourgeoisie The capitalist (and, at the time of its emergence, the "middle") class. The class is defined in Marxian terms by its relation to the means of production—its ownership of capital, including factories and other machinery of production in a capitalist economic mode as well as means of finance. A member of this class is sometimes referred to as a bourgeois. Alternatively, in non-Marxist terms one can refer simply to the owners and managers of capital (OMC).

bureaucratic politics The formulation of policy is a function of the competition among opposing individuals who represent diverse governmental institutions. Coalitions and counter-coalitions typically form as a part of the process of bureaucratic politics.

capitalism An economic system or, in Marxist terms, mode of production that emphasizes private ownership of the means of production and a free market. When the state is the primary owner of capital—its government making important investment, production, and other economic decisions—we can refer to the economic system as a form of state capitalism. One who owns the means of production is a capitalist, or bourgeois. *See also* **bourgeoisie.**

capitalist world-system An economic-structuralist or Marxist approach to international relations that emphasizes the impact of the worldwide spread of capitalism; a focus on class and economic relations and the division of the world into a core, periphery, and semiperiphery. *See also* **core, periphery, semiperiphery, class.**

categorical imperative Concept associated with the work of Immanuel Kant—that one ought to act "according to the maxim that you can at the same time will [such conduct] to be a universal law" and that one should treat others "as an end [worthy in themselves] as well as a means, never merely as a means."

causal modeling The depiction, such as by a computer simulation or diagram, of sequential relations among two or more variables and how they result in a particular event, action, or outcome, including the relative importance or "weight" of each variable in producing a particular outcome. Causal models depict cause-effect relations, as in a model of an arms race that hypothesizes a causal connection between the decision of country A to increase the level of its military expenditure and an increase in the later military expenditure of country B as in an action-reaction sequence or arms-race spiral.

civil society Term associated with the rule of law that includes networks of relationships among people and the groups or organizations to which they belong. *See also* **international (global) civil society.**

class An analytical component of society with an identifiable characteristic or set of characteristics that differentiate it from other components. In Marxian usage, the term is defined by relations to the means of production. Under capitalism the bourgeoisie is defined by its ownership of capital (not only money but, significantly, the factories and machinery that are the means of production), and the proletariat, or working class, is defined by its labor. Under feudalism, the aristocracy is defined by its ownership of land, and the serfs, or peasants, by their labor. As such, class is different from a stratum of society defined, for example, as a socioeconomic category based on income, wealth, or level of living.

classical realists These scholars include such twentieth-century figures as E. H. Carr, Hans J. Morgenthau, and Arnold Wolfers. While appreciating the importance of conceptualization, they were skeptical of quantitative approaches to understanding international relations. Heavily influenced by reading history and the works by the likes of Thucydides, Niccolò Machiavelli, and Thomas Hobbes, they also differ from modern-day neorealists by emphasizing norms or values that also play a part in international politics, not just balance of power as an abstract structure.

coercive diplomacy Term developed by Alexander George and his associates to describe how threats of force are used successfully or unsuccessfully as part of diplomacy to achieve national objectives. Both positive and negative measures (carrots and sticks) are part of the coercive-diplomacy kit. Thomas Schelling coined a similar term *compellence* in which one state, alliance, or coalition of states tries to force the opposition to take some action it would not otherwise take. *Compellence* as an active measure to get an opponent *to take some action* is thus differentiated from *deterrence* as a passive measure that tries to keep the opposition *from taking some action.*

cognition The process by which human beings come to know or acquire knowledge through perception, reasoning, and (some would say) intuition. The term *cognitive* refers to this process.

cognitive dissonance A concept developed by Leon Festinger wherein human beings tend not to perceive what is contrary to their preconceived or previously held perspectives. To avoid cognitive dissonance, individuals either (a) unconsciously screen out information or evidence that contradicts what they already believe to be true, or (b) interpret such discordant information in such a way as to support their preconceptions.

collective goods theory Relates to the allocation of, and payment for, goods that, once provided, cannot easily be denied to others and whose use does not deny their use to others. Providing national security or international security through alliances has been described by some theorists as collective goods. Collective goods are referred to by some as public goods. *See also* **public choice theory.**

collective security The idea that if one state behaved aggressively, other states have a legal right to enforce international law by taking collective (group) action.

comparative advantage The concept holds that countries specialize in the production of those goods and services which they produce more efficiently. In a free trade environment there would be, according to theory, a global specialization or division of labor with aggregate productivity maximized. As critics point out, however, free trade theory does not address such matters as equity in the distribution of wealth. Some dependency theorists see free trade theory as the vehicle by which Global South countries are kept in a status of dependency and precluded from development.

compellence *See* **coercive diplomacy.**

complex interdependence A term developed by Robert Keohane and Joseph Nye that refers to the multiple transnational channels that connect societies, including interstate, transgovernmental, and transnational relations. The resulting relations are extremely complex, with economic interests assuming far greater importance than in classical realism. *See also* **interdependence, globalization.**

constant A factor that does not vary. *See also* **variable.**

constitutive From the constructivist perspective, defines the set of practices or means by which any particular consciously organized social activity or institution comes to be. *See also* **regulative rules.**

core A term sometimes used synonymously with center, a reference to the industrialized countries in the global political economy. The term is also sometimes used to refer to the elites or dominant classes. *See also* **periphery.**

correlation An association between two, or among more than two, variables of such a nature that a change in one seems to be tied or related to a change in another. A correlation among variables, however, does not necessarily mean that they are causally linked. *See also* **variable.**

covering laws *See* **deductive-nomological.**

customary international law Established practice by states over time gives a customary basis for international law. For example, centuries of practice had established immunities and other diplomatic rights long before they were codified formally in a treaty.

decision-making IR literature that examines the structure and processes of how individuals, groups, or other units of analysis make foreign policy and national security decisions.

deduction Conclusions drawn logically and necessarily from specified premises; reasoning from general rules to particular cases. *See also* **induction**.

deductive-nomological Formal approach to scientific explanation often associated with work by Carl Hempel and others who focus on covering laws that relate the explanans (explanatory sentences) to the explanandum (what is to be explained).

defensive realists Maintain that states seek to maximize security, preserve the existing distribution of power, and hence are not inherently aggressive.

democratic peace That democracy or republican forms of governance are propitious to peace is central to Kantian thought. This hypothesis has generated a great deal of research. The Wilsonian idea of making the world safe for democracy as the principal remedy for ending warfare is often referred to by critics of democratic-peace theory (in other words, President Woodrow Wilson's representation of World War I as the "war to end all wars" and thus "make the world safe for democracy" to flourish). For his part, Michael Doyle's claim is not that democracies are inherently less prone to war, but rather that they tend not to go to war with other democracies.

dependency A situation in which the low-income, capital poorer economies of the Global South are conditioned by, and subordinate to, the economic development, expansion, and contraction of the higher-income, capital-rich economies of the Global North. It is a situation of exploitation by Global North countries and is examined in a historical context. Domestic constraints and structures (such as land tenure patterns) are also critical in inhibiting balanced economic development. In its earlier formulations, it was the dependency of the Third World (now referred to as Global South) upon the First World (now referred to as the Global North). *See also* **Global North**.

dependent variable The thing that is to be explained or accounted for. Some theorists, for example, have tried to explain, or find the causes of, war, which is their dependent variable.

description A verbal statement that provides an understanding or meaning. Description is often differentiated from explanation or prediction, which are understood to be theoretical tasks. Thus, theory is considered to be different from mere description. From this perspective, description is a necessary, but pre-theoretical task.

determinism, deterministic A philosophical view that what we observe inevitably occurs as the consequence of factors over which human beings have no volition or control. Most social theorists who accept the characterization or who can be labeled as determinists do not reject totally the role of human will, as the strict definition of determinism would imply, but they do allow much less freedom of action for individuals to affect outcomes than those theorists labeled as voluntarists. A variant is the agency-structure issue raised in constructivist and other thinking: how much of a role does human agency play in establishing or changing structures or are they largely constrained by them? The determinism-voluntarism issue among social science theorists has its analog in theological disputes over determinism or predestination on the one hand and free will on the other. Critics consider structural realists and Marxist class analysts and other economic structuralists to be overly deterministic, but this claim is often rejected by these theorists. *See also* **voluntarism**.

development The process associated with the industrialization of societies. Modernization is a term sometimes used synonymously with development, but some theorists differentiate between the two. For some, modernization refers to societal values and processes that undergo major changes from pre-industrial traditional society, including the effects of industrialization, whereas development refers to the building of societal or governmental administrative infrastructure more capable of coping with increasing demands brought on by the modernization process. Autonomous development occurs in isolation, or independent of what is going on outside of a given country, a circumstance more difficult to achieve in the present period than may have been true in the nineteenth century. Reflexive development, when and if it occurs, is responsive to external economic conditions and may well be dependent on them. *See also* **uneven development.**

diachronic Refers to a study over a period of time; sometimes referred to as a longitudinal study, as in a study of the causes of war between 1815 and 1945. *See also* **synchronic.**

dialectic, dialectical materialism A form of reasoning or argument that juxtaposes contradictory ideas with the goal of resolving the contradiction and thus moving closer to the truth. The term is associated with the ancient Greek philosophers, the German philosopher Georg W. F. Hegel, and Karl Marx. Marx substitutes materially based class conflict and the contradictions between relations and modes of production for the Hegelian clash of ideas—dialectical materialism. Whereas Hegel argues that the dialectical clash of ideas moved history forward, Marx focuses on the importance of material forces as when technology and the emergence of markets drives a shift from feudal to capitalist modes of production. Class conflict occurs when shifts in these modes of production occur—the increasingly obsolete land-based aristocracy of feudalism forced to give way through revolution or other means to the capital-owning bourgeoisie that is dominant in capitalism.

distributive justice The question of the rightness of (or moral criteria associated with) the allocation of scarce resources, particularly material or economic resources. The rightness of a particular distribution of wealth or profit could be subject to normative standards of distributive justice. *See also* **normative.**

dyad, dyadic As between two units. *See also* **interdependence.**

ecocentrism Putting a priority on the environment upon which human well-being depends, a concern that extends to plant and animal life.

ecofeminism A perspective that environmental degradation results from male dominance in society.

econometrics Quantitative techniques used in economic analysis.

embedded liberalism A theory that suggests that the global economy, particularly from 1945 to 1980, is shaped by a combination of state power and international institutions, and that these institutions serve to "embed" the international economic system within a framework of rules and norms that promote cooperation.

empirical, empirically Factual or known through observation. Propositions or hypotheses may be subject to empirical or factual tests to determine whether observed "facts" are consistent with what is predicted.

empiricism, empiricist The epistemological position that the only grounds for making truth claims is through direct observation of the world using our senses. Consistent with the philosophical view that knowledge is rooted in experience, empiricists adopt a scientific focus on observation of facts and hypothesis testing as the virtually exclusive source of knowledge.

endogenous factor *See* **system.**

epistemic community Term used by Peter Haas, Emanuel Adler, and others to refer to expert elites that operate transnationally or globally often affecting policy outcomes on issues in which their particular knowledge makes them relevant. Scientists and other technical elites (though not referred to as epistemic communities) were also the subject of earlier policy-related studies by the late Ernst B. Haas. *See also* **functionalism** and the reference there to *neofunctionalism.*

epistemology The study of how one knows or how one acquires knowledge. Put another way, how do we know what we think we know?

equilibrium When various elements of a system are in balance. When disturbed, some systems are said to have an inherent tendency to restore this balance or equilibrium. For example, when a state or group of states upsets the balance of power, other states respond in opposition, restoring the balance.

existentialism An approach that believes philosophical thinking begins with the human subject who is free willfully to chart her or his own course; much of academic philosophy, in both style and content, is viewed as too abstract, superficial, and remote from actual human experience.

exogenous factor *See* **system.**

expected utility, expected utility theory (model) Rational choice concept in which actors compare the relative attractiveness of options and choose the alternative that maximizes expected gains or minimizes expected losses. Concept used by Bruce Bueno de Mesquita and others concerning conflict situations that may lead to war. The expected utility model also addresses how policy positions emerge in the presence of competing interests, leading to predictions and strategic opportunities for altering them. *See also* **rational choice theory.**

externality When an international actor takes an action that has an intended or unintended impact (positive or negative) on another actor.

factor analysis A quantitative technique by which the analyst tries to identify underlying and related elements or factors (usually as part of a causal explanation of some observed phenomenon or phenomena).

falsifiability Associated with Karl Popper's thought, "scientific" propositions or hypotheses have to be stated in a form that, if they are false, they can be shown to be false through empirical tests. When empirical tests fail to show a proposition or hypothesis is false, we gain greater confidence that it may be true.

First World *See* **Global North.**

functionalism, neofunctionalism A focus on purposes or tasks, particularly those performed by organizations. Some theorists have explained the growth of organizations, particularly international organizations, as a response to an increase in the number of purposes or tasks demanding attention. *Neofunctionalism* as a theory of regional integration emphasizes the political calculation and payoff by or to elites who agree to collaborate in the performance of certain tasks. *See also* **integration.**

fungibility The condition that exists when one element or unit has no unique identity and can easily be exchanged or replaced by another of like nature. Money is said to be fungible (for example, funds in a national budget can easily be shifted from one account to another when cuts are made in one area of the budget to fund increases in another). Whether the power of states, like money, is fungible and can readily be transferred from one issue area to another is a point of some dispute among IR theorists.

game theory A decision-making approach based on the assumption of actor rationality. Each actor tries to maximize gains or minimize losses often under conditions of uncertainty and incomplete information, which requires each actor to rank order preferences, estimate probabilities, and try to discern what the other actor is going to do. In a competitive, two-person zero-sum game, what one actor wins, the other loses; if A wins 5, B loses 5, and the sum is zero. In a two-person, non-zero-sum or variable-sum game, gains and losses are not necessarily equal; it is possible that both sides may gain. This is sometimes referred to as a positive-sum game in which the parties effectively cooperate. In some games, both parties can lose, and by different amounts or to a different degree. So-called *n*-person games include more than two actors or sides. Game theory has contributed to the development of models of deterrence and arms race spirals, but it is also the basis for work concerning the question of how collaboration among competitive states in an anarchic world can be achieved: The central problem is that the rational decision for an individual actor such as a state may be to "defect" and go it alone as opposed to taking a chance on collaboration with another state actor. Dealing with this problem is a central concern of much of the literature on international regimes, regional integration, and conflict resolution.

gender Refers to masculine, feminine, or transgender identities people have. As such, gender can be differentiated from sex as a biological category and sexual orientation as another form of identity. Gender is the core factor contributing to feminist interpretive understandings. Nonbinary persons do not identify as either exclusively masculine or feminine. *See* **sexual orientation, LGBTQ, transgender.**

global civil society *See* **international (global) civil society.**

globalization The continued increase in transnational and worldwide economic, social, and cultural interactions that transcend the boundaries of states, aided by advances in technology.

global governance *See* **governance.**

Global North Reference generally to high-income, capital-rich countries that has replaced, for the most part, in common usage the term *First World*. By contrast the term *Global South* that refers generally to lower-income, capital-poorer countries previously referred to commonly as *Third World*. The latter term came to be understood as pejorative—as if these countries were third-rate when, in fact, French socialists who originally coined the term in the early 1960s saw it as referring to the mass of the world's people who ultimately would triumph much as the French people in the "third estate" defeated the aristocracy and clergy (the first and second "estates") in the French revolution that began in 1789. *See also* **Second World.**

Global South *See* **Global North, Second World.**

governance As defined by Robert O. Keohane, governance involves the processes and institutions, both formal and informal, that guide and restrain the collective activities of groups. Globally, the question of governance (or "partial global governance") is one of how the various institutions and processes of global society could have meshed more effectively in a way that would be regarded as legitimate by attentive publics around the world.

Grotian Refers to the influence of Hugo Grotius, a seventeenth-century Dutch scholar usually identified as the father of international law. The Grotian view is that international relations, although lacking central authority, can be subject to rules or norms, some of which have the binding character of law, that are expressly or tacitly agreed to by states. Thus, a global society can be a rule-based order.

groupthink According to Irving Janis, a "mode of thinking that people engage in when they are deeply involved in a cohesive in-group, when the members' strivings for unanimity override their motivation to realistically appraise alternative courses of action." Indicators of groupthink include social pressure to enforce conformity, limiting discussion to a few alternatives, failing to reexamine initial decisions, and making little attempt to seek information from outside experts who may challenge a preferred policy. As a counter to becoming "victims" of groupthink, some groups designate a person or persons to play "devil's advocate" by offering alternatives to the mainstream of the group's thinking.

hard power *See* **power.**

hegemonic stability The view that stability in international relations stems from the presence of hegemony or dominance. The absence of hegemony or hegemons would imply a lack of order in the relations among states whether in commercial activities (trade, the exchange of money, and investment), social issues, or security concerns. *See also* **hegemony.**

hegemony, hegemon Relations of dominance as when a major power exercises hegemony over countries within its sphere of influence. A state exercising hegemony is sometimes referred to as a hegemon. An alternative characterization reflecting preeminent position of a state, but not necessarily implying dominance, is to refer to it as a state exercising leadership of other states within its sphere. The difference between hegemony and leadership is often a subtle distinction and perhaps more a matter of nuance or connotation intended by the user of the terms. *See also* **hegemonic stability.**

hermeneutics Subordinates explanation and description to interpretation and understanding of meaning. As a field of study, it owes much to Ludwig Wittgenstein's work on how human beings interpret or draw meanings as is reflected in the language they construct and use. Social facts are constituted by the structures of language.

heuristic Refers to the illustrative value of some device or schematic presentation. Such a presentation is not intended as an actual or precise, empirically verified representation of relations among variables in a model, but it is useful for gaining a better understanding of some concept or set of concepts under investigation.

high politics Refers to matters of security, particularly the strategic interests of states. Realists have tended traditionally to distinguish between such high political concerns and those dealing with socioeconomic or welfare issues supposedly of lesser interest to government leaders or diplomats—the so-called low politics.

historical materialism Economically oriented methodological approach to the study of society and history that was first articulated by Karl Marx. Historical materialism looks for the causes of developments and changes in the means by which people in societies live and are organized. The starting point is the economic base, with everything else (social classes, political structures, ideologies) influenced by this material base.

human rights Regardless of culture, national, state, or other identity, human beings possess certain rights by virtue of being human. Many of these rights have been codified in treaties and conventions. Intellectual foundations of human rights may be found in normative theories associated with Kantian, utilitarian, and social contract as well as Aristotelian virtue-based modes of thought.

hypothesis, hypotheses A proposition usually relating two or more variables (such as "Arms races cause wars") but subject to empirical or factual tests. In one view, hypotheses may be verified or confirmed to the extent that tests do not show the hypotheses to be false. Repeated tests, including replication of earlier work, increase confidence in the correctness of the original hypothesis, although it is always subject to being shown to be false in subsequent tests and thus can never be confirmed with 100 percent certainty. A null hypothesis, the starting point, is a proposition in which no relation between or among variables is specified (as in "there is no relation between arms races and the onset of war") in contrast to a working hypothesis in which such a relation is specified. If one's empirical tests show no relation, then the null hypothesis is retained and the working hypothesis is rejected.

idealist, idealism One who sees such values or human preferences as justice or a desire for world peace as potentially decisive and capable of overcoming obstacles to their realization. Critics sometimes refer to idealists as utopian since, in their view, the idealist does not understand or take account of the political or other realities that constrain human choice. An idealist considers ideas alone as having important causal effects as opposed to others who see power or material factors as being the determinants of political outcomes. A classic debate within international relations pits idealism against realism. Accused by realists of being an idealist (he referred to himself as a "rational optimist"), the late Ernst Haas observed that ideas grounded in the interests of the relevant players were the motive forces of politics.

ideal (pure) type A concept developed by the German sociologist Max Weber to describe an extreme, or pure, case that is not found in this form anywhere but that serves as an analytical benchmark useful in comparing real-world cases. Strictly defined, ideal types for democracy or modern and traditional societies are constructed by theorists even though the actual cases they examine are, at best, only approximations of the conditions they specify.

idiographic A detailed study of a particular case or event. *See also* **nomothetic.**

imperialism In its classic meaning, a position or policy of preeminence or dominance with respect to foreign elements, as in the Roman, Ottoman, or British empires. Imperialism in earlier centuries involved the establishment of colonies, which led to so-called colonialism. Although most of these colonies have become formally independent states, the relations of economic, social, cultural, and even political dominance by the former colonial power remain—so-called neocolonialism. Some theorists also contend that contemporary imperialism involves economic and other forms of exploitation or dominance by multinational corporations in least developed countries. Marxist theories of imperialism tend to emphasize the economic dynamics of capitalism and associated class relations.

independent variable A factor used to explain some outcome. *See also* **variable, dependent variable, intervening variable.**

induction, inductive Logical and inferential process by which we posit general statements based on observation of only a part or sample of a class of facts; as the late James Rosenau frequently observed, the general statement is an answer to the question: "Of what is this an instance?" *See also* **deduction.**

institutionalized As used by constructivists, collective ideas are expressed in actual social orders (termed *structures* or *institutions*) and in established practices and identities.

integration The coming together of separate states or other political units under a common authority. Integration may occur as an international or regional phenomenon with varying degrees of authority given to institutions established to deal with common issues or problems facing member states. Integration can be viewed either as process or as outcome that reflects and encourages cooperation among states operating under conditions of international anarchy (i.e., lack of common government). Research on integration has tended to focus on the assignment of economic and social tasks to regional or international authorities. Earlier theories of regional integration saw political union as a possible outcome of collaboration in economic or social issues. *See also* **functionalism.**

interdependence, interdependent A relation or relations between two (a dyadic relation) or among more than two units in which one is sensitive or vulnerable to the decisions or actions of the other or others. The flow of capital or money to or from one country may respond to (or be sensitive to) changes in the interest rates in other countries—so-called *sensitivity* interdependence. To the extent that one unit may be adversely affected by decisions or actions of another, it is said to be vulnerable to the other unit or units, as when State A depends on State B as the principal source of its oil or gas supply and thus is vulnerable or would be adversely affected by its cutoff. To many theorists, particularly realists, such vulnerability interdependence is to be minimized or avoided altogether. Interdependence may be symmetric (affecting both or all sides equally), but it is more likely to be asymmetric or uneven (with effects varying from actor to actor). State A may be more or less dependent on a supply of oil or gas from State B than State B is on the security of its investments in State A. *See also* **complex interdependence, balance of power.**

interest group liberalism An approach to politics that emphasizes competing groups or institutions. Not only is interest group liberalism thought to be an accurate description of democratic politics, particularly in the United States, but it is also thought by many to be the way politics should be conducted.

international (global) civil society Just as the rule of law is central to domestic understandings of civil society, so it is with international law and norms in what some see as an increasingly global, rules-based civil society beyond the borders of particular states. This society includes networks of relationships among people around the world that are not necessarily associated with the state *per se* as well as organizations that aggregate individual interests below the level of the state but operate across the border of any single state. Nongovernmental organizations are an example. The role of institutions and norms are associated with the English School and liberal images of international relations. For the English School, the concept of international society is heavily associated with Hugo Grotius. *See also* **civil society.**

international regimes *See* **regime.**

international society Term used within the English School that sees relations among states and other actors subject to rules or law, a perspective that owes much to insights drawn from Dutch legal writer Hugo Grotius. This Grotian position is sometimes referred to as "rationalist"—seeing order and justice in international politics as a function of rules that both facilitate and constrain decisions and actions.

international system An aggregation of similar or diverse entities united by regular interaction that sets them apart from other systems; for example, the interstate or international system of states or world politics understood as a system composed of both state and nonstate actors. *See also* **system.**

intersubjective, intersubjectivity Interpretations or understandings one derives from reflecting on exchanges or interactions with others. The idea that shared knowledge results from the exchange of ideas, depicting the social world in terms of collectively meaningful understandings or identical structures—itself an ontological assumption.

intervening variable A variable that may come between the cause(s) or independent variable(s) and the effect or dependent variable, thus affecting the outcome. *See also* **variable, dependent variable, independent variable.**

jus gentium The idea that certain laws are applicable to all of humanity, nations, and individuals. Dates at least from the time of the Roman Empire and is to be found in Stoic thought.

LDCs Least developed countries. Synonym for Global South and Third World.

level of analysis Individuals, groups, state and society, international system or international society are separate points of focus. Such levels help scholars to be systematic in their approach to understanding international relations. In explaining a phenomenon such as war, for example, the theorist may identify possible causes as having some characteristic or characteristics of the international system, states and their societies, groups, or individuals. In accounting for or explaining such a phenomenon, one may look both within a unit such as a state as well as how the unit relates to its external environment, which are different levels of analysis. In current usage, "unit level" factors such as state, society, interest groups, bureaucracies, and individuals are contrasted to structural factors operating at the system level. This levels-of-analysis approach was central to the late Kenneth Waltz's explanation in *Man, the State and War* (the three images or levels being individuals, the state, and system of states).

LGBTQ Abbreviation referring to lesbian, gay, bisexual, transgender, queer (or questioning). The term LGBTQIA also includes intersex, and asexual persons. *See* **gender, sexual orientation, transgender.**

liberal institutionalism *See* **neoliberal institutionalism.**

Lockean Constructivists such as Alexander Wendt use this term as a shorthand to refer to John Locke's understanding of people in society coming together by contract or agreement. Unlike Thomas Hobbes, Locke does not see the anarchic state of nature—"want of a common judge," government, or central authority—as necessarily warlike. In applying Locke's insight to international relations, we need not see states as necessarily in a state of war with one another. Moreover, states (as if they were persons in a state of nature) may reach agreements with one another to maintain peace, whether they remain in a state of nature or leave it by forming a community.

logical positivism Pursuit of a pure science that would separate fact from value and achieve the precision of mathematics, a perspective identified with scholars in the "Vienna circle" of the 1930s.

logic of appropriateness A concept associated with social constructivism in which it is assumed human actors follow norms and rules with which they identify, not just narrow understandings of self-interest. These norms become embedded in organizations and institutional settings. Changes in these "rules of the road" may require norm "entrepreneurs" willing to take actions that may be seen as inappropriate by defenders of existing, generally accepted norms.

longitudinal *See* **diachronic.**

low politics *See* **high politics.**

metaphysics The study of the fundamental nature of reality and being which is outside of objective experience—an often abstract understanding of non-observables that constitute or influence the "reality" we do observe empirically.

methodology The approach one takes to an academic study; modes of research and analysis, as in the use of historical case and comparative case studies, or the use of statistics as in formal hypothesis testing or causal modeling of variables. *See also* **causal modeling.**

modes of production The organization of the economy for the production of goods, as in such historical epochs identified by Karl Marx as slavery, feudalism, and capitalism. According to Marx, as technology advances, the mode of production also changes—feudalism being a more productive mode than slavery and capitalism being more productive than feudalism.

moral relativism An approach to normative debates which holds that no universal standard exists by which to assess an ethical proposition's truth and that values and rights can have no independent standing of their own.

multilateralism Refers to an effort to cooperate or collaborate with other states rather than trying to go it alone. *See* **unilateralism.**

multipolar, multipolarity A distribution of power in the international system with more than two centers or "poles," such as a world in which there are three, four, five, or more principal or major powers. *See* **unipolar, bipolar.**

mutual constitution For constructivists, there is a reciprocal relation between agency (actors) and structure. Structures are not objects that simply influence actors in a unidirectional manner. Rather, agents can change socially constructed structures and escape from situations that encourage and replicate, for example, conflictual practices such as war.

natural law, universal law A philosophical view dating back at least to the time of the ancient Greeks and developed further by the Romans that posits there are laws inherent in nature that transcend any laws made by mere mortals. All leaders and all forms of government, it is argued, are bound by these laws, and they should not be violated. Some scholars have dealt with natural law as a means to develop a body of international law to govern the relations among states.

natural rights Reference is to a theory that finds human rights in nature that can be discovered through reason. Social contract theorists such as John Locke and Jean-Jacques Rousseau see rights in this naturalist understanding; however, utilitarians such as Jeremy Bentham and John Stuart Mill argue that human rights rest on other grounds also discoverable through reason—the greatest good or happiness for the greatest number. *See also* **utilitarian.**

neoclassical realists These scholars, while perhaps appreciating the insights of neorealism and the importance of systemic structure, have attempted to incorporate international institutions and explanatory factors at the state-society level of analysis to explain war. They tend to take their cue from classical realists. *See* **classical realists.**

neocolonialism *See* **imperialism.**

neofunctionalism *See* **functionalism.**

neoliberal institutionalism Like realism, neoliberal institutionalism is utilitarian and rational in orientation. States are treated as rational egoists and interstate cooperation occurs when states have significant interests in common. The goal is to discover how, and under what conditions, institutions matter. As such, neoliberal institutionalism addresses both security and nonsecurity or welfare issues. In this regard, institutions provide information, reduce transaction costs, make commitments more credible, establish focal points for coordination, and aid in the operation of reciprocity and multilateralism among states. The term institution may also refer not just to organizations, but also to such accepted patterns of such recurrent or institutionalized relations as multilateralism—a meaning advanced by the late John Ruggie and others. The concept is particularly associated with Robert O. Keohane, although he rejects the "neoliberal" adjective.

neoliberalism, neoliberal Critical of liberal theories that discount the relative importance of states, the neoliberal position is that states also matter alongside a wide array of nonstate actors. *See also* **neoliberal institutionalism.**

neorealism A label applied to structural realists or those realists who are interested in explaining state behavior under conditions of anarchy and who emphasize the importance of the structure of the international system (the distribution of power among states) and how this influences and constrains state behavior. The term may also have negative connotations in the eyes of some critics who claim that the neorealists have neglected the importance of values and norms as stressed by earlier realists such as Hans J. Morgenthau and E. H. Carr. Neorealists deny the validity of such charges, and some even reject the neorealist label.

neostructuralism Associated with economic structuralism, neostructuralism is interested in understanding how global processes interact with other processes of state and social transformation occurring at multiple levels of the world-system. The study of international relations, therefore, is not limited to foreign policy or patterns of distributions of capabilities, nor confined to reducing international relations to economic variables. Influencers include Fernand Braudel, Karl Polanyi, and Antonio Gramsci.

nomology Study relating to discoverable scientific laws that contribute to human understanding. *See also* **deductive-nomological.**

nomothetic Related to finding general or universal laws that cover numerous, different cases over time. *See also* **idiographic.**

non-zero-sum *See* **game theory.**

nonbinary *See* **gender, sexual orientation.**

normative, norm A principle of right action; a standard to guide behavior, as in norms or obligations governing the conduct of war, transit on the high seas, diplomacy, trade, and commerce. Normative judgments are often equated to value judgments and the idea of what ought to be; some norms may have the binding character of international law. For constructivists and many liberals, norms define generally accepted standards of appropriate behavior. For constructivists they are part of international structure.

normative theory Value-oriented or philosophical theory that focuses on what ought to be. As such it is usually differentiated from empirical theories that try to explain the way things are or predict what they will be.

n-**person game** *See* **game theory.**

offense-defense balance The realist argument that at any point in time military power can favor the offense or the defense. If defense dominates over offense, then conquest is difficult and states have little incentive to use force to gain territory. If, however, offense has the advantage, then the temptation is for states to attempt to conquer one another.

offensive realists Argue that states seek power and influence to achieve security through domination. States strive for maximum power relative to other states as this is the only way to guarantee survival.

ontology Consists of our assumptions (often unstated) of what the world ultimately consists of—how we see or understand the essence of things around us. A philosophical term referring to the study of existence or being or, in Immanuel Kant's terms, "the more general properties of things." Are there, for example, actual "structures" out there that influence the behavior of actors? If so, are they essentially materially based (a view associated with structural realism) or ideationally based (a view associated with constructivism)? Dialectical materialism as universal law or a set of laws with historical implications for humanity is an example of a materialist ontology central to Marxist thought.

order As used by the English School, international order results not simply from power and the balance of power, but also from the acceptance of rules and institutional arrangements that are in the enlightened, rational self-interest of states and other actors.

paradigm A pattern, model, or perspective that helps one organize and guide research. A paradigm may include key assumptions about the world and the best way to go about understanding it. The concept was central in Thomas Kuhn's influential *The Structure of Scientific Revolutions* (1962) and has since been applied to the social sciences. According to Kuhn, a scientific era is characterized by a dominant paradigm that represents "normal science"; the majority of scholars work within this paradigm, often accepting the assumptions of the paradigm in an unquestioning manner. These assumptions have an impact on how research is conducted and the resultant scholarly work. *See also* **research program.**

periphery The least developed countries or areas of Asia, Latin America, and Africa. In the dependency literature, the periphery is dominated by the center or core, which consists of the economically and politically dominant countries of the world (usually viewed as those in North America, Europe, and Japan). The literature on the capitalist world-system has applied the concept of periphery back to the origins of capitalism in Europe. The periphery plays a subordinate but important role in a worldwide capitalist division of labor by providing raw materials and cheap labor. As capitalism expanded, some countries that at one time were part of the center slipped into peripheral or semiperipheral status. *See also* **core, semiperiphery.**

phenomenology A philosophical term referring to a subjective or interpretive understanding in human consciousness of what we observe or think we see—*phenomena*—in the world around us. Classification and description of phenomena, including identifying their formal structures, have been part of an attempt to establish their scientific foundations. Following Edmund Husserl and others, the focus is on carefully describing the phenomena we experience—an interpretive approach to human understanding and the categories of understanding we construct. For our purposes in this volume, we see phenomenology contributing to constructivism, critical theory, postmodernism, and other interpretive understandings.

pluralist *See* **solidarism.**

political economy There are at least two major ways in which this term is used in international relations research: (1) the view that politics and economies are inextricably linked, leading one to study the interrelations of political and economic variables, and (2) the use of economic models of rationality to explain political actions. For example, some theorists use economic models of rationality to determine under what conditions international collaboration can be achieved among states.

positive-sum game *See* **game theory.**

positivism A view of scientific inquiry that assumes (1) the unity of the natural and social sciences—we can study society as we study the natural world; (2) we can draw a distinction between facts and values; (3) regularities exist in the social as well as the natural world and they can be identified; and (4) empirical validation or falsification is the hallmark of "real" inquiry. Hence knowledge comes from empirical testing of propositions or hypotheses against evidence or facts. In terms of international law, the view that laws stem only from the actions of those having the political authority to make them rather than being the derivation of divine or natural law.

postcolonialism An interdisciplinary perspective that encompasses economic, political, social, and cultural aspects of decolonization and afterward, highlighting the importance of race, gender, and ethnicity in understanding anticolonial struggles. Postcolonialism would include the literature on dependency and the capitalist world-system as well as long-lasting adverse effects of dominance by former colonial masters—*postcolonial ecocriticism* relating to the negative legacy of colonialism on justice, gender, and the differential impact of globalization.

power Capabilities, or the relative capabilities, of actors such as states. The ability to control or influence outcomes. Hard power refers to military and economic capabilities. Soft power refers to values and culture that define a country and the image it projects abroad, potentially leading other states to wish to emulate it.

power transition theory A realist perspective arguing that when the distribution of power among states is in transition, war is more likely to occur. The international system is hierarchically ordered, with the most powerful state dominating the rest, which are classified as satisfied or dissatisfied with the ordering of the system. When one state is in the process of overtaking the power position of another, the likelihood of war increases markedly.

prospect theory An alternative to expected utility theory (rational choice) to provide insights into decision-making under conditions of risk and uncertainty. The key question is why individuals consistently deviate from predictions made by rational choice. It is claimed that most individuals are actually risk-averse when it came to securing gains, but risk-acceptant when it came to avoiding losses. In other words, loss aversion is a prime motivating factor; most people value items they already possess more than items they want to acquire.

public choice theory The use of economic methods to analyze what are essentially political problems (issues involving choices or decisions by political authorities). *See also* **collective goods theory, rational choice theory.**

pure type *See* **ideal (pure) type.**

qualitative Data that is descriptive, referring to things that can be observed but not measured. Examples include in-depth case and comparative case studies.

quantitative Data represented numerically, anything that can be counted, measured, or given a numerical value.

rational, rationalism, rationalist To act rationally requires a rank ordering of preferred goals, consideration of all feasible alternatives to attain those goals in the light of existing capabilities, and consideration of the costs and benefits associated with using particular methods to attain particular goals. The assumption is often made in IR research that actors do indeed act rationally in this way. The assumption is made to develop hypotheses and to produce insights on world politics. On the other hand, one can, as Max Weber did, refer to *value rationality*—subscription to values like duty, loyalty or commitment, courage or bravery, trust, and the like. Thus, following value rationality, risks are taken and losses suffered that would not have been willfully taken were instrumental rationality the driving criterion. Institutional or bureaucratic rationality is yet another form of rational action identified by Weber in the procedures and routines that enhance organizational or bureaucratic efficiency in the way decisions are made, recurrent tasks are pursued, and follow-up actions are taken. Finally, we take note of rationalism or the rationalist position in the English School that refers to rules or laws that are mechanisms for providing order and justice in international society.

rational choice theory Assumes actor rationality in economics and politics, focusing on the instrumentally rational dimension—maximizing interest or utility—in the development of explanatory and predictive theories. *See also* **collective goods theory, expected utility, game theory, rational.**

reductionism An analytic approach leading to oversimplification and incompleteness of explanation. In some usages (as developed by the late Kenneth Waltz), the term refers to explanations that look only within a unit, such as state or individual, ignoring the environment within which the unit is immersed and the interaction of that unit with elements in its environment. Reducing the explanation of some phenomenon such as war among states to something deep within the human psyche (as being, for example, at the level of synapses between nerve endings) is an extreme example of *reductio ad absurdum*—explanation reduced to an absurd degree of oversimplification and incompleteness—as if one could explain the recurrence of war among states purely in neurological terms. Similarly, theorists who have tried to explain revolution solely in social or social-psychological terms, ignoring economic, political, and other factors, have been criticized for reductionism.

reflectivism, reflectivist As opposed to a purely rationalist view as in abstract cost-benefit calculations, reflectivists take into account the ideas, understandings, or consciousness in relation to interests that influence the decisions we make and the actions we take. *See also* **cognition.**

regime, international regime In its domestic context, an existing governmental or constitutional order defined in terms of sets of rules and institutions established to govern relations among individuals, groups, or classes within a state. In its international context, the term is defined as voluntarily agreed-upon sets of principles, norms, rules, and procedures around which actor expectations converge in a given area of international relations. The literature on international regimes blossomed in the 1970s. Scholars argue that international collaboration is obviously not restricted to formal international organizations such as the United Nations—cooperation is necessary in monetary and trade areas, telecommunications, maritime and air traffic control, and a whole host of areas of greater and lesser importance.

regulative rules For constructivists, formal or informal practices that influence behavior. *See* **constitutive.**

reified, reification Giving a concrete reality to what is in fact an abstract concept of analysis. For example, some critics claim that realists have reified the state, attributing to it human characteristics such as rationality, or treating the state as if it operates in the international arena like an actual human being. The concept of system, used by some realist, liberal, English School rationalist, and economic-structuralist theorists, has also been criticized on similar grounds.

relative and absolute gains This distinction is important as it can be viewed as a key assumption underlying much of IR theorizing. If, for example, one believes the international system is composed of states that are satisfied as long as everyone receives some positive payoff (absolute gains), then stability or peace seems more likely. If, however, states are driven by relative gains and both gain but one more than the other (thus changing their overall positions relative to each other) then conflict may be more likely.

relativism Humans can understand and evaluate beliefs and behaviors only in terms of their historical or cultural context; truth is always relative to some particular frame of reference.

research program A term developed by Imre Lakatos to identify work within a particular school of thought or understanding.

satisficing A less-than-optimal choice that does not completely maximize the values or goals one is pursuing but is good enough; work by Herbert Simon and others on decision-making shows that people often choose the first viable option that is at least minimally acceptable.

scientific method An approach to explaining and understanding the natural and social world. To accept the scientific method is to adopt positivist assumptions that assume (1) the unity of the natural and social sciences—we can study society as we also study the natural world; (2) we can draw a distinction between facts and values; (3) regularities exist in the social as well as the natural world and they can be identified; and (4) empirical validation or falsification is the hallmark of "real" inquiry. Hence knowledge comes from empirical testing of propositions or hypotheses against evidence or facts.

Second World Post–World War II Cold War term referring to the Soviet Union, People's Republic of China, and other communist countries not part of either the high-income, capital-rich "First World" countries group or the lower-income, capital-poorer "Third World" countries group. *See* **Global North.**

security dilemma A term coined by John Herz: In an anarchic international system, State A may sincerely increase its level of defense spending only for defensive purposes and self-preservation, but it is rational for other states to assume the worst and impute aggressive intentions to State A. They therefore also increase their level of arms, leading State A to feel insecure and contemplate a further increase in military spending.

Hence, by initially trying to enhance its own security, State A sets in motion a process that results ironically in its feeling less secure. In another usage, the term merely refers to the security problem faced by all states in a world without central authority or lack of common government among states. *See also* **anarchy, self-help.**

self-help In the international arena, there is no superordinate authority, world government, or "leviathan" to ensure order or to see that all parties to an agreement keep their end of the bargain. Each state must look after its own security and not assume the help of other states. *See also* **anarchy.**

semiperiphery As used by capitalist world-system theorists, the term refers to those countries or regions that occupy an intermediate position between core and peripheral areas. The semiperiphery is engaged in a mix of activities, some associated with the core and some with the periphery. It serves as an outlet for investment when wages, and thus the cost of production, in core areas become too high. The semiperiphery may at one time have been a core or peripheral area, or it may be moving into either status. *See* **core, periphery.**

sensitivity interdependence *See* **interdependence.**

sexual orientation An identity in which a person is drawn to the opposite or same sex—for many, one is somewhere on a spectrum between completely heterosexual (zero on the Kinsey scale) and completely homosexual (six on the Kinsey scale). Some reject this binary categorization. *See also* **gender, transgender.**

social contract The idea that human beings, acting in their own enlightened self-interest, would agree to bind themselves to one political or governing arrangement or another. Associated with Jean-Jacques Rousseau, Thomas Hobbes, John Locke, and John Rawls.

soft power *See* **power.**

solidarism Term used in the English School to describe a cosmopolitan "thick morality" among states in international society that goes well beyond a "pluralist" conception of ephemeral calculations of mutual advantage by states. Shared norms, rules, and institutions among states define this solidarist understanding of international society.

sovereign, sovereignty The supreme, independent, and final authority. The attribute of a state that refers "internally" to its right to exercise complete jurisdiction over its own territory. In international relations, states as sovereign units have a right "externally" to be independent or autonomous with respect to other states. States may differ in their power, but as sovereign entities all are legal equals.

state of nature A philosophical construct referring to a time before the creation of civil society—a world without governmental authority. An analogy to the anarchic structure of the international system. An important concept, particularly for realists who follow the thinking of Thomas Hobbes, as it raises the issue of how order and stability can be achieved in an international system of states competing for power and prestige.

structural determinist One who believes that the structure of the international system largely determines the behavior of individual states and that there is very little effective choice for leaders of states. The term is usually used in a negative or critical sense against realists, neorealists, and some Marxists. Few, if any, theorists would admit to complete structural determinism in their theories, but some do assign greater weight to structure as a determinant of the behavior of states and other actors.

structural realism, structural realist A term preferred by Kenneth N. Waltz and other neorealists because in their view it more accurately describes neorealism's focus on structure (the distribution of power) as a principal determinant of the behavior of states, the principal units in the international system. *See also* **neorealism.**

structural transformation As used by economic structuralists, the historical and geographical expansion of the capitalist world-system, incorporating new areas of the globe and nonintegrated sectors of the world economy.

structure The arrangement of parts of a whole, as in the structure of the international system being defined by *structural realists* in terms of the distribution of capabilities or power among states. The international system structure, following this usage, may be bipolar, multipolar, or unipolar. Some theorists look for underlying structure associated with the anarchy of the system—the lack of central authority. For others, structure refers to observed patterns of behavior as among states, although still others contend that such a definition confuses underlying structure with behavior, or the interactions of states—concepts that are, and should be, kept analytically separate. Some *economic structuralists* use the term structure to describe relations or mechanisms of dominance, dependence, and exploitation as in the Global North dominating the Global South or, in Marxist terms, the worldwide capital-owning bourgeoisie dominating worker and peasant classes. From the perspective of the *English School*, structure is defined in terms of rules, laws, and institutional arrangements states have established to provide some degree of order to an anarchic international society. For *social constructivists*, structure is made up of shared meanings, practices, rules, and norms. Structures thus may be ideational or cultural, not just material. Finally, structure may be defined as exogenous or external to agents, whether these agents be units like states or individuals.

synchronic A study at a particular point in time. By contrast, a diachronic or longitudinal study is over some period. *See* **diachronic**.

system A set of interrelated parts or an arrangement of units connected in such a way as to form a unity or whole; an abstract concept used by many theorists to bring order to their work. The use of the term varies. For example, some theorists see the international system as being composed of states and, perhaps, other nonstate actors, whereas some authors see world capitalism as a system composed of classes with conflicting interests. Some systems are said to be open to external influences, whereas others are closed systems. Factors external to a system that may affect it are exogenous, whereas those internal to the system are often referred to as endogenous factors. Some systems are said to have certain inherent qualities or attributes, such as a tendency toward balance or equilibrium, although not all systems theorists assign such automaticity to systems. Some theorists use systems merely as taxonomies, or frameworks, for organizing research and analysis.

system transformation *See* **transformation**.

taxonomy, taxonomies A classification as in a categorization of states as democratic, autocratic, socialist, or fascist.

Third World *See* **Global North** for mention of First and Third Worlds. *See also* **Second World**.

transformation A fundamental change in the system, as in a shift from a multipolar to a bipolar world or vice versa. The creation of a world government to replace an anarchic system of sovereign states would be such a system transformation. In a Marxist context, the overthrow of the bourgeoisie by the proletariat (working class) would be or lead to a transformation of the political, social, and economic order.

transgender An identity with male or female gender when one's sexual organs are those of the opposite sex. Put another way, gender identity is different conceptually from sexual orientation. It is also different from *intersex* in which one may have both male and female sexual organs. The LGBT abbreviation combines sexual orientation (lesbian, gay, and bisexual) with transgender identity—transgender persons sometimes feeling marginalized even by others in the LGBT communities, not to mention society as a whole. *See* **LGBTQ, sexual orientation.**

transgovernmental *See* **transnational.**

transnational, transnationalism Interactions and coalitions across state boundaries that involve such diverse nongovernmental actors as multinational corporations and banks, church groups, and terrorist networks. In some usages, transnationalism includes both nongovernmental as well as transgovernmental links (as when ministries of defense, foreign affairs, police, and other governmental units establish cross-national relationships separate and sometimes independent of state-to-state relations). The term transnational is used both to label the actor (for example, a transnational actor) or a pattern of behavior (for example, an international organization that acts transnationally—operates across state borders). Theorists focusing on transnationalism often deemphasize the state as if it were the only important or primary and unitary actor.

uneven development A concept used by Marxists and other theorists that emphasizes capitalism's unequal spread of global economic benefits. *See also* **development.**

unilateralism A tendency to go it alone, serving a particular state's interest with its own resources. *See* **multilateralism.**

unipolar A distribution of power in the international system with one dominant state or "pole."

unit of analysis That which is being studied, such as a state.

universalism A Kantian, cosmopolitan view consistent with Greco-Roman Stoicism portraying a world in which principles or values have applicability everywhere—a perspective that also influences Liberal and English School scholars in particular.

utilitarian, utilitarianism An ethical doctrine developed in the nineteenth century that postulates that the greatest happiness or greatest good for the greatest number should be the aim of all action. Thus, for example, respect for life can be viewed as a universal principle that benefits all, thus a rejection of murder or other unnecessary harm imposed on others. The term can also mean a belief that the value of anything is determined solely by its utility. Utilitarian thinking as applied to theory building tends to emphasize a rational decision-making process in which actors seek to maximize benefit or minimize cost.

variable A characteristic of an object or class of objects that may take on different values. The variable may be quantitative (such as height) or qualitative (such as marital status). In international relations research, for example, the class of objects may be states and the variable military power. Researchers wish to operationalize a variable, which means finding a way to measure the variable. Military power may be operationalized, for example, by using such indicators as the number of nuclear weapons, the amount of the gross national product devoted to military expenditures, or the number of persons under arms. A dependent variable is simply what one is trying to explain, such as the frequency and intensity of war since 1800. Independent variables are factors that may help to explain or predict the dependent variable.

variable-sum game *See* **game theory.**

voluntarism, voluntarist A philosophical position that reality is created by human will; that humans as agents can affect, if not control, their destinies. In international relations, it generally means that decision makers have effective choice and can influence outcomes. As used in this volume, voluntarism is in opposition to the philosophical idea of determinism. *Social constructivism*, for example, is a voluntarist formulation. One also finds theories premised on voluntarism among most liberals and English School rationalists and many classical realists. *See* **agent-structure.**

vulnerability interdependence *See* **interdependence.**

world society A concept associated with Immanuel Kant and the English School in which the goal is the realization of a universal cosmopolitanism that transforms the world as we know it into an international society based on norms with broad moral acceptance. For liberals, world society goes beyond international or interstate relations to encompass a complex array of state, nonstate, and transnational actors that engage with each other globally.

zero-sum game *See* **game theory.**

Index

Page numbers in *italics* refer to figures and tables.

About the Authors

★ ★ ★

Mark V. Kauppi has been an adjunct professor at Georgetown University's School of Foreign Service for the past twenty-three years where he has taught courses on strategic thinking, the causes of war, and Machiavelli and the Italian wars (the latter as resident faculty member at Georgetown's Villa Le Balze in Fiesole, Italy). For thirty years he was employed at the Defense Intelligence Agency where, among other duties, he was in charge of counterterrorism analytical training, arranging and conducting conferences for intelligence community analysts, and teaching graduate courses at what is now the National Intelligence University. In all his courses a recurrent theme is how conceptualization and theory can be applied to understanding real-world national security challenges. He has published articles on several topics including intelligence analysis and Thucydides's relevance to contemporary IR theory. Kauppi received academic degrees from the University of Southern California, UC Berkeley, and the University of Colorado, Boulder.

Paul R. Viotti is professor of international studies at the University of Denver. A classmate of coauthor Mark Kauppi at the University of California at Berkeley, the two have sought via seven editions of this volume to provide an overview of approaches to international relations theory that includes respect for intellectual precursors and influences on contemporary IR thinking. In addition to this collaboration, Viotti has published *The Dollar and National Security, U.S. Foreign Policy*, and *U.S. National Security Policy* as well as other books and articles. Born and reared in New York, Viotti has spent most of his professional life in Colorado with twenty years on the Air Force Academy faculty and thirty years at the University of Denver. A retired Air Force colonel, Viotti received his PhD at the University of California, Berkeley in 1978. He also has degrees from the Air Force Academy, Georgetown University, and George Washington University. On sabbatical, he spent two years as deputy political adviser in the US European Command in Stuttgart, Germany—experiences that sharpened his understanding of the policy world that began more than a decade earlier with three years at the Defense Intelligence Agency in Washington, D.C., after military service in Vietnam.